HERALD 1200, 12/50, 13/60
VITESSE 6
and
SPITFIRE Mk.1, 2, & 3
WORKSHOP MANUAL

PART NUMBER 511243

ISBN 0 946 489 99 8

Issued by the

SERVICE DIVISION

STANDARD-TRIUMPH SALES LIMITED

A member of the Leyland Motor Corporation

COVENTRY ENGLAND

TRIUMPH
HERALD, VITESSE 6
and
SPITFIRE
WORKSHOP MANUAL

Comprising:

GROUP 0

General Specification

GROUP 1

Engine—Cooling—Fuel and Exhaust Systems

GROUP 2

Clutch—Gearbox—Overdrive—Propellor Shaft

GROUP 3

Rear Axle—Brakes—Wheels and Tyres

GROUP 4

Suspension—Steering

GROUP 5

Underframe and Body

GROUP 6

Electrical

INTRODUCTION

This Workshop Manual, which is in loose-leaf form for easy amendment, has been compiled to assist Standard-Triumph Distributors and Dealers throughout the world in the efficient repair and maintenance of the Triumph Herald 1200, 12/50, 13/60, Vitesse 6 and Spitfire models.

Whilst retaining the same grouping system as is used for Service Information Sheets and previous Workshop Manuals, this book includes an additional group having the designation "0". The contents of each group is listed on the first page following its "tabbed" marker card.

Special Tools

The use of special tools mentioned in the text contributes to an efficient and profitable repair. Some operations are, in fact, impracticable without their use, particularly those, for example, which deal with the assembly of the differential unit. Distributors are therefore urged to check their tools against the list provided and order those necessary.

Numbering Pages and Section

The running headline, at the top of the page, names each section within a group. For example, group 1 contains four sections, namely: Engine, Cooling, Fuel, and Exhaust Systems, these being numbered 1 to 4 respectively.

The group number is shown at the top outer edge of each page and is followed by a decimal point.

Each section number is placed after the decimal point following the group number.

Two numerals placed after the section number are used to identify the pages which comprise a particular section, thus page 5 of the cooling section would appear 1·205.

***Service Information and Amendment Procedure**

Design modifications, changes in procedure and notice of amendment subsequent to the preparation of this manual are given in Service Information Sheets which are issued regularly to all authorised dealers. Should existing instructions be affected or additional information be warranted, new pages will be included with each consecutively numbered notice of amendment. This will also give details of the pages and groups affected. See page 4.

To ensure that this manual is kept up-to-date, write the amendment number, the page number and the group number in the space provided on the following page as the amended pages of text are inserted. Any gaps in the sequence of amendment numbers will then be readily apparent and immediate action can be taken to obtain the missing sheets.

Schedule of Repair Operations

The operations listed in the "Schedule of Repair Operation Times" refer to those described in this manual. The time set against each operation in the schedule is evolved by performing the actual operations on a standard vehicle using special tools where stated. The "Schedule of Repair Operation Times", for use with this manual, is issued as a separate publication and may be obtained from the Spares Division under part number 545022 (English); 545024 (German) and 545023 (French).

**NOTE: Service information and amendment sheets are issued to the motor trade only and are not for general publication.*

TRIUMPH
HERALD, VITESSE 6
AND
SPITFIRE
WORKSHOP MANUAL

GROUP 0

TRIUMPH
HERALD, VITESSE 6
and
SPITFIRE MODELS

GROUP 0

CONTENTS

Engine type	Engine Nos. from	Engine Nos. to	Comp. ratio	CAMSHAFT TIMING Inlet opens BTDC	Inlet closes ABDC	Exhaust opens BBDC	Exhaust closes ATDC	PERFORMANCE DATA Max. BHP	at r.p.m.	Max. torque lb/in.	Max. torque kg.m.	at r.p.m.	Equiv. BMEP lb/in.^{2}	Equiv. BMEP kg/cm.^{2}
HERALD 1200 (High compression)	GA.1HE GA.177,973HE GB.1HE	GA.164,889HE GA.178,000HE GB.2,700HE	8·0 : 1	12°	52°	52°	12°	39	4500	730	8·316	2250	131	9·19
	GA.164,890HE GA.178,001HE GA.190,301HE	GA.177,972HE GA.190,223HE GA.190,340HE	8·0 : 1	18°	58°	58°	18°							
	GA.190,224HE GA.190,341HE GD.110,001HE	GA.190,300HE GA.235,664HE and future	8·5 : 1	18°	58°	58°	18°	48	5200	740	8·517	2500	133	9·33
(Low compression)	GA.1LE	and future	6·8 : 1	18°	58°	58°	18°	43	4750	675	7·763	2250	121	8·50
HERALD 12/50 (High compression)	GD.1HE	GD.103,470HE	8·5 : 1	18°	58°	58°	18°	51	5200	756	8·710	2600	136	9·54
HERALD 13/60 (High compression)	GE.1HE	and future	8·5 : 1	18°	58°	58°	18°	61	5000	875	10·32	3000	139	9·75
(Low compression)	GE.1LE	and future	7·5 : 1	18°	58°	58°	18°	54	5200	800	8·4	3000	127	8·92
SPITFIRE 4 (High compression)	FC.1HE	FC.50,000HE	9·0 : 1	18°	58°	58°	18°	63	5720	804	8·47	3500	144	10·10
(Low compression)	FC.1LE	FC.50,000LE	7·0 : 1	18°	58°	58°	18°	53	5600	720	8·3	3500	130	9·12
SPITFIRE Mk. 2 (High compression)	FC.50,001HE	and future	9·0 : 1	25°	65°	65°	25°	67	6000	804	8·47	3760	144	10·10
Mk. 2 (Low compression)	FC.50,001LE	and future	7·0 : 1	25°	65°	65°	25°	57	5800	720	8·3	3760	130	9·12
Mk. 3 (High compression)	FD.1HE	and future	9·0 : 1	25°	65°	65°	25°	75	6000	900	10·37	4000	144	10·10
Mk. 3 (Low compression)	FD.1LE	and future	7·5 : 1	25°	65°	65°	25°	65	5800	820	9·4	4000	130	9·12
Mk. 3 (High comp) Emission controlled	FE.1HE	and future	8·5 : 1	10°	50°	50°	10°	68	5500	880	10·13	3000	140	9·82
VITESSE 6 (1600 cc) (High compression)	HB.1HE	and future	8·75 : 1	18°	58°	58°	18°	70	5000	1110	12·78	2800	143	10·03
(1600 cc) (Low compression)	HB.1LE	and future	7·0 : 1	18°	58°	58°	18°	64	4800	1000	11·52	2800	129	9·06

	HERALD 1200, 12/50	HERALD 13/60	SPITFIRE 4 & Mk. 2	SPITFIRE Mk. 3	VITESSE 6
ENGINE					
Number of cylinders	4	4	4	4	6
Bore of cylinders	2·728 in. 69·3 mm.	2·900 in. 73·7 mm.	2·728 in. 69·3 mm.	2·900 in. 73·7 mm.	2·628 in. 66·75 mm.
Stroke of crankshaft	2·992 in. 76·0 mm.	2·992 in. 76·0 mm.	2·992 in. 76·0 mm.	2·992 in. 76·0 mm.	2·992 in. 76·0 mm.
Piston area	23·45 in.^{2} 151 cm.^{2}	26·5 in.^{2} 171 cm.^{2}	23·45 in.^{2} 151 cm.^{2}	26·5 in.^{2} 171 cm.^{2}	32·55 in.^{2} 210 cm.^{2}
Swept volume	70 in.^{3} 1147 cm.^{3}	79·2 in.^{3} 1296 cm.^{3}	70 in.^{3} 1147 cm.^{3}	79·2 in.^{3} 1296 cm.^{3}	97·39 in.^{3} 1596 cm.^{3}
Compression ratio	Refer to performance data on page 0·102				
Valve timing	Inlet and exhaust valves to be equally open at T.D.C. Refer to camshaft timing data, page 0·102.				
Valve clearances (cold)	0·010 in. 0·25 mm.	As 1200	As 1200	As 1200	As 1200
LUBRICATION					
Oil pressure at 2,000 r.p.m.	40-60 lb/in.^{2} 2·8-4·2 kg/cm.^{2}	As 1200	As 1200	As 1200	As 1200
IGNITION SYSTEM					
Contact breaker gap	0·015 in. 0·4 mm.	As 1200	As 1200	As 1200	As 1200
Spark plug — type	Lodge CLNY fitted up to engine numbers GA.185794E and GD.65575E, future fitment of Champion L87Y	Champion N-9Y	Lodge CLNY fitted up to engine number FC.64762E, future fitment of Champion L87Y	As 13/60	Lodge CLNY fitted up to engine number HB.28207E, future fitment of Champion L87Y
— gap	0·025 in. 0·64 mm.	As 1200	As 1200	As 1200	As 1200
Firing order	1, 3, 4, 2	As 1200	As 1200	As 1200	1, 5, 3, 6, 2, 4
Ignition timing — static	15° B.T.D.C.	9° B.T.D.C.	13° B.T.D.C.	6° B.T.D.C.	10° B.T.D.C.
COOLING SYSTEM					
Radiator	A.C. pressurized to 7 lb/in.^{2}, introduction of 13 lb/in.^{2} at engine number GA.240782E	A.C. pressurized to 7 lb/in.^{2}, introduction of 13 lb/in.^{2} at engine number GE.22521E	A.C. pressurized to 7 lb/in.^{2}	A.C. pressurized to 7 lb/in.^{2}	A.C. pressurized to 7 lb/in.^{2}
FUEL SYSTEM					
Carburettor	Single Solex B.30 PSEI new jet sizes introduced at engine number GA.34986. See group 1	Single sidedraught 150 CD Stromberg	Twin sidedraught S.U. H.S.2	As Spitfire 4 Fitment of emission controlled S.U. H.S.2 carburettors for U.S.A. market (N.A.D.A. Specification A.U.D.285)	Twin semi-downdraught Solex 32 PIH Introduction of twin Stromberg 150 CD at engine number HB.27986E
Air cleaners	A.C. replaceable air cleaner element. Introduction of pancake type at engine number GA.34986E	Replaceable element A.C. pancake type	Twin A.C. replaceable air cleaner elements	As Spitfire 4	Single paper element fitted up to engine number HB.27985E. Future fitment of twin A.C. replaceable element type and silencer box assembly

	HERALD 1200, 12/50	HERALD 13/60	SPITFIRE 4 & Mk. 2	SPITFIRE Mk. 3	VITESSE 6
FUEL SYSTEM—continued					
Fuel pump	A.C. mechanically operated diaphragm	As 1200	As 1200	As 1200	As 1200
Pressure	1·5 to 2·5 lb/in.² 0·1 to 0·18 kg/cm.²	As 1200	As 1200	As 1200	As 1200
CLUTCH					
Type	Borg & Beck coiled spring—6¼ in. 15·87 cm. diameter. At engine number GA.204020E and GD.44446E, introduction of 6½ in. 16·51 cm. diameter diaphragm spring type	Borg & Beck diaphragm spring—6½ in. 16·51 cm. diameter	Borg & Beck coiled spring—6¼ in. 15·87 cm. diameter. At engine number FC.17136E, introduction of 6½ in. 16·51 cm. diameter spring type	Borg & Beck diaphragm spring—6½ in. 16·51 cm. diameter	Borg & Beck coiled spring—8 in. 20·32 cm. diameter
GEARBOX					
Type	Four forward speeds and one reverse. Synchromesh on 2nd, 3rd and top gears	As 1200	As 1200	As 1200	As 1200
Gear ratios	Gearbox / Overall				Gearbox / Overall
— Top	1·00 / 4·11				1·00 / 4·11
— 3rd	1·40 / 5·74	As 1200	As 1200	As 1200	1·25 / 5·16
— 2nd	2·16 / 8·88				1·78 / 7·31
— 1st & reverse ..	3·75 / 15·42				2·93 / 12·06
— Overdrive (optional extra)			Laycock de Normanville		Laycock de Normanville
— acting on — Top			0·80 / 3·30	As Spitfire 4	0·80 / 3·30
— 3rd			1·12 / 4·60		1·00 / 4·14
REAR AXLE					
Type	Hypoid bevel gears	As 1200	As 1200	As 1200	As 1200
Ratio	4·11 : 1	As 1200	As 1200	As 1200	As 1200
BRAKES					
Type	Girling hydraulic system	As 1200	As 1200	As 1200 Fitment of tandem braking systems for appropriate markets	As 1200
Front	8 in. × 1¼ in. 20·32 cm. × 3·17 cm. drum—1200 9 in. 22·86 cm. diameter disc—12/50	As 12/50	As 12/50	As 12/50	9 in. 22·86 cm. diameter disc
Rear	7 in. × 1¼ in. 17·78 × 3·17 cm. drum				8 in. × 1¼ in. 20·32 × 3·17 cm. drum
SUSPENSION					
Type — front	Independent. Coil springs controlled by telescopic dampers and anti-roll bar. (Anti-roll bar not fitted on courier)	As 1200	As 1200	As 1200	As 1200
— rear	Swing axle independent. Transverse leaf spring controlled by telescopic dampers	As 1200	As 1200	As 1200	As 1200

	HERALD 1200, 12/50	HERALD 13/60	SPITFIRE 4 & Mk. 2	SPITFIRE Mk. 3	VITESSE 6
STEERING					
Type	Rack and pinion unit Telescopic steering column	As 1200	As 1200	As 1200	As 1200
WEIGHT					
Dry — Saloon	15¾ cwt. 800 kg,	16 cwt. 815 kg.			17¼ cwt. 885 kg.
— Coupé	15¼ cwt. 770 kg.				
— Convertible	14⅞ cwt. 725 kg.	15½ cwt. 785 kg.	13¼ cwt. 675 kg.	14 cwt. 712 kg.	17¼ cwt. 885 kg.
— Estate	16⅛ cwt. 820 kg.	17 cwt. 865 kg.			
— Courier	15⅝ cwt. 794 kg.				
Complete (inc. fuel, oil, water and tools)					
— Saloon	16 cwt. 810 kg.	16¾ cwt. 850 kg.			
— Coupé	15¾ cwt. 787 kg.				
— Convertible	16⅝ cwt. 790 kg.	16¼ cwt. 826 kg.	14 cwt. 710 kg.	14¾ cwt. 748 kg.	18¼ cwt. 927 kg.
— Estate	16⅞ cwt. 860 kg.	17¾ cwt. 900 kg.			
— Courier	16¼ cwt. 825 kg.				
Gross vehicle weight					
— Saloon	23 cwt. 1169 kg.	23 cwt. 1169 kg.			24¾ cwt. 1252 kg.
— Coupé	20¾ cwt. 1049 kg.				
— Convertible	23 cwt. 1169 kg.	23 cwt. 1169 kg.	17¾ cwt. 900 kg.	17¾ cwt. 900 kg.	24¾ cwt. 1252 kg.
— Estate	24 cwt. 1229 kg.	24 cwt. 1229 kg.			
— Courier	24 cwt. 1229 kg.				

	HERALD RANGE			SPITFIRE RANGE			VITESSE 6		
CAPACITIES	**Imperial**	**U.S.**	**Metric**	**Imperial**	**U.S.**	**Metric**	**Imperial**	**U.S.**	**Metric**
Engine — from dry	8 pts.	9·6 pts.	4·6 litres	8 pts.	9·6 pts.	4·6 litres	8 pts.	9·6 pts.	4·6 litres
Drain and refill	7 pts.	8·4 pts.	4·0 litres	7 pts.	8·4 pts.	4·0 litres	7 pts.	8·4 pts.	4·0 litres
Gearbox	1·5 pts.	1·8 pts.	0·85 litres	1·5 pts.	1·8 pts.	0·85 litres	1·5 pts.	1·8 pts.	0·85 litres
— with overdrive				2·38 pts.	2·85 pts.	1·35 litres	2·4 pts.	2·9 pts.	1·64 litres
Rear axle	1·0 pt.	1·2 pts.	0·7 litres	1·0 pt.	1·2 pts.	0·57 litres	1·0 pt.	1·2 pts.	0·57 litres
Cooling system — with heater and water bottle ..	8·5 pts.	10·2 pts.	4·8 litres	9 5 pts. (Spitfire Mk. 3 8 pts.	11·4 pts. 9·6 pts.	7·4 litres 4·5 litres)	14·0 pts.	15·6 pts.	7·4 litres
Fuel tank	6·5 galls.	7·3 galls.	32·0 litres	8·25 galls.	10 galls.	37·0 litres	8·75 galls.	5 galls.	10·0·04 litres
Estate and Courier — fuel tank ..	9·0 galls.	10·8 galls.	41·0 litres						

	HERALD 1200 and 13/60 ESTATE CAR					
PAYLOAD CAPACITY	**Area**		**Weight**		**Volume**	
with rear seat folded flat —— 4 up ..	10·5 ft.²	81·3 m.²	1 cwt.	50·8 kg.	19 ft.²	540·7 m.³
— 2 up ..	20 ft.²	1·85 m.²	5 cwt.	254 kg.	45 ft.³	1·275 m.³
— Courier	19 ft.²	1·76 m.²	5 cwt.	254 kg.	45 ft.³	1·275 m.³

UNIT SERIAL NUMBERS AND DESIGNATION

The following list of serial numbers apply to all vehicles contained in this manual and serve to assist exact identification of a vehicle or unit being serviced.

Identification of Prefix and Suffix letters is as follows:—

Commission Numbers

GA	Denotes the model range.
L	Denotes Left Hand Steering (No letter is used to denote Right Hand Steering).
DL	Denotes the body type, e.g., De-luxe saloon.
O	Denotes Overdrive is fitted.

Engine Numbers

GA	Denotes model range.
H	Denotes High Compression.
L	Denotes Low Compression.
E	Denotes Engine Unit.

Gearbox and Rear Axle Number

GA	Denotes model range (No Suffix letters added to these numbers).

Body Numbers

GA	Denotes model range.
C	Denotes Convertible body.

HERALD MK. I 1200

Commission Numbers	GA1 — Built from February 1961 to June 1962.
Engine Numbers	GA1 .... HE or LE.
Gearbox Numbers	GA1.
Rear Axle Numbers	GA1.
Body Numbers — Saloon	1 .... GAT.
Coupe	1 .... YAT.
Convertible	1 .... RAT.
Estate Car	1 .... EAT.

HERALD MK. II 1200

Commission Numbers	GA 80,001 and future — built from July 1962.
*Engine Numbers	GA 80,001 HE or LE and future; GD 110,001 HE or LE and future — built from February 1968.
Gearbox Numbers	GA 80,001 and future.
Rear Axle Numbers	GA 80,001 and future; GE and future.
	*From October 1965, spares condition of stripped engine units with 8·5 : 1 compression ratio, were identified with Prefix and Suffix letters as follows:— GD .... HESK.
Body Numbers — Saloon	80,001 GAT and future.
Coupe	80,001 YAT and future.
Convertible	80,001 RAT and future.
Estate Car	80,001 EAT and future.

NOTE. A quantity of cars were built with letters GB, this was to suit inter-factory identification.

HERALD MK. II 1200 — EXPORT

Commission Numbers	GB 10,001 LDL and future — built from July 1963.
Engine Numbers	GD .... HE or LE, GD 110,001 HE or LE and future — built from February 1968.
Gearbox Numbers	GA ....
Rear Axle Numbers	GA and GE.
Body Numbers	As Herald Mk. II Saloon.

HERALD MK. II — COURIER

Commission Numbers	GA 80,001V and future — built from July 1962 up to December 1964.
Engine Numbers	GA 80,001 HE or LE and future.
Gearbox Numbers	GA 80,001 and future.
Rear Axle Numbers	GA 80,001 and future.
Body Numbers	80,001 GVB and future.

NOTE. A quantity of cars were built with letters GB, this was to suit inter-factory identification.

HERALD 12/50

Commission Numbers	GD .... RS — Built from December 1962 up to September 1967.
*Engine Numbers	GD1 .... HE or LE
Gearbox Numbers	GA ....
Rear Axle Numbers	GA ....
	*From October 1965, spares condition of stripped engine units, were identified with Prefix and Suffix letters as follows:— GD .... HESK.
Body Numbers	1 GDT and GATR.

HERALD 13/60

Commission Numbers	GE1 and future — built from August 1967.
Engine Numbers	GE1 .... HE or LE.
Gearbox Numbers	GA ....
Rear Axle Numbers	GE ....
Body Numbers — Saloon	1 GET.
Convertible	1 RET.
Estate Car	1 EET.

VITESSE 6

Commission Numbers	HB1 — Built from April 1962 up to June 1963; HB 15001 — built from July 1963 up to August 1966.
Engine Numbers	HB1 .... HE or LE and HB 15001 HE or LE.
Gearbox Numbers	HB1 ....
Rear Axle Numbers	HB ....
Body Numbers — Saloon	1 .... HBD.
Convertible	1 .... HBC.

SPITFIRE 4

Commission Numbers	FC1 — built from October 1962 up to November 1964.
Engine Numbers	FC1 .... HE or LE.
Gearbox Numbers	FC1 ....
Rear Axle Numbers	FC1 ....
Body Numbers	1 .... FC.

SPITFIRE MK. 2

Commission Numbers	FC 50,001 and future — built from December 1964 up to December 1966.
Engine Numbers	FC 50,001 HE or LE and future.
Gearbox Numbers	FC 50,001 and future.
Rear Axle Numbers	FC 50,001 and future.
Body Numbers	50,001 FC.

SPITFIRE MK. 3

Commission Numbers	FD1 and future — built from January 1967.
Engine Numbers	FD1 .... HE or LE.
Gearbox Numbers	FD1 ....
Rear Axle Numbers	FC .... (As Spitfire Mk. 2).
Body Numbers	81311FC to 81732FC; 422FD and future.

LOCATION OF COMMISSION AND UNIT NUMBERS

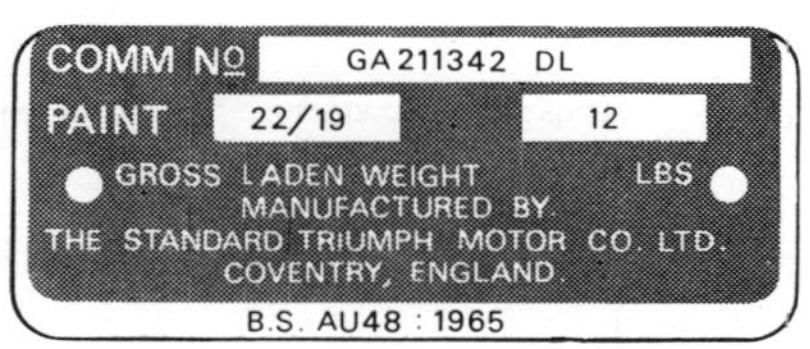

J192

In all communications relating to service or spares, please quote the vehicle Commission Number, the paint and trim code, if relevant, and the Serial Number of the unit affected.

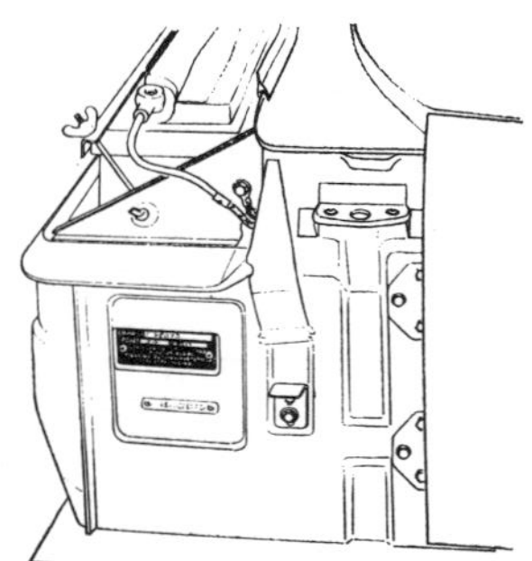
J191/1

The Commission Number (Chassis Number), paint and trim code numbers are stamped on the plate attached to the dash side panel. The Body Number is stamped on a separate plate mounted below the Commission Number plate (Spitfire).

LOCATION OF COMMISSION AND UNIT NUMBERS

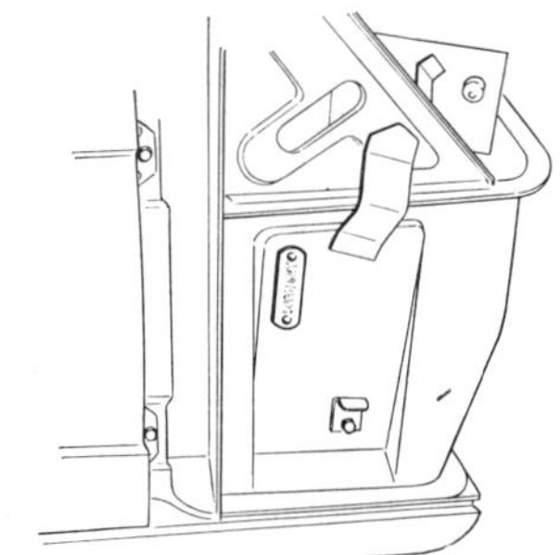
J191/2

The Body Number is on the right-hand side of dash and the Commission Number (Chassis Number) on the left-hand side of the dash (all models other than Spitfire).

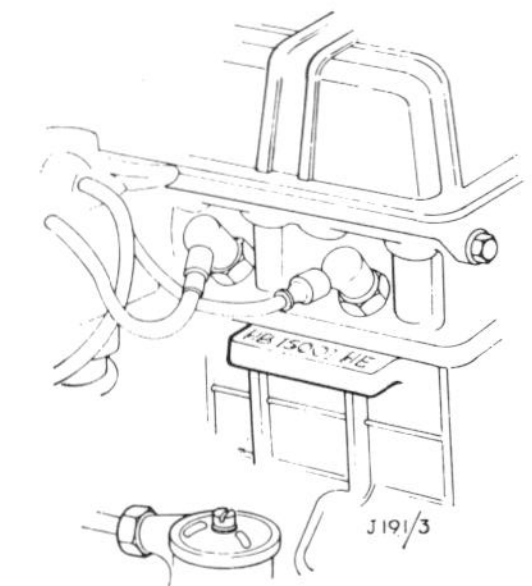
J191/3

The Engine Serial Number is stamped on the left-hand side of the cylinder block.

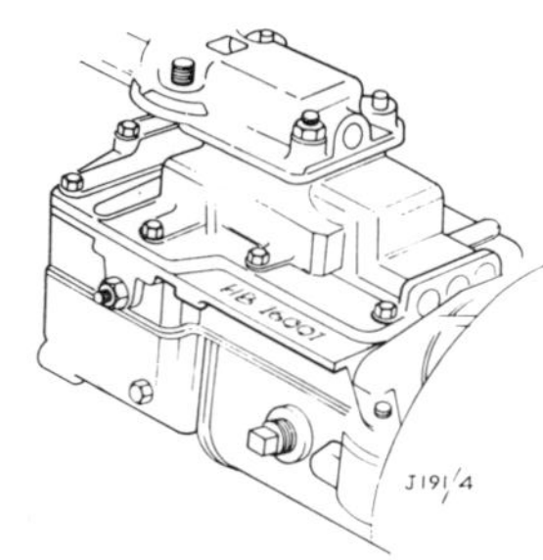
J191/4

The Gearbox Serial Number is stamped on the side of the gearbox casing flange.

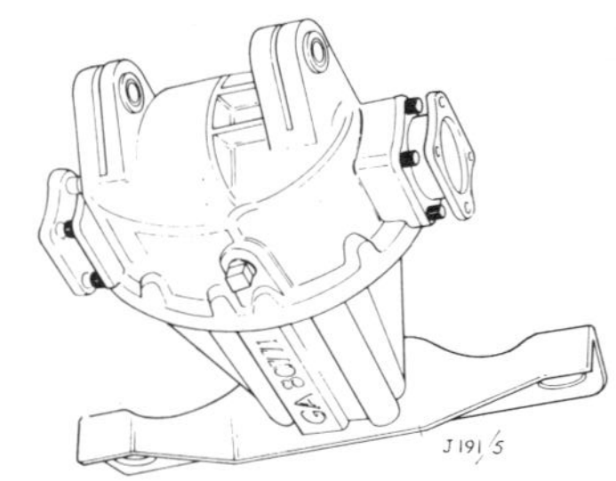
J191/5

The Rear Axle Serial Number is stamped on the underside of the hypoid housing flange.

PAINT AND TRIM CODING SYSTEM

The commission number plate affixed to the scuttle side panel bears code symbols for identification of the vehicle's exterior colour, trim material and trim colour.

Colour Code

Nine basic colours are allocated a number as shown in the table. Shades of these colours are classified as 1st shade, 2nd shade, 3rd shade, etc. The number of each shade change prefixes the basic colour to indicate the shade colour. Dual colours are identified by two code numbers separated by a stroke, e.g., 22/19 denotes "cherry" and "white", the predominant colour being cherry, this symbol being quoted first.

The main trim material is identified by prefixing the colour code number with a letter, e.g.:

Leathercloth — No prefix letter
Leather — Prefix letter H.
Cloth — Prefix letter C.

Basic colour	Basic colour number	1st shade	2nd shade	3rd shade	4th shade	5th shade	6th shade
Black	01	11					
Red	02	12 Matador	22 Cherry	32 Signal	42 Burgundy	52 Scarlet	
Brown	03	13 Light Tan					
Yellow	04	14 Jonquil	24 Wimpey Yellow	34 Jasmine Yellow			
Green	05	15 Cactus	25 Conifer	35 Olive	45 Lichfield		
Blue	06	16 Midnight	26 Wedgwood	36 Dark Blue	46 Renoir	56 Royal	66 Valencia
Purple	07	17 Damson	27 Shadow Blue				
Grey	08	18 Gunmetal	28 Dark Grey	38 Phantom	48 Dolphin		
White	09	19 White	29 Sebring White				

Thus: Paint 22/19   Trim 12

denotes that the vehicle is painted "cherry" and "white" and trimmed in leathercloth coloured Matador Red.
NOTE. Acrylic paints bear the suffix A.

The following Special Tools, recommended for the efficient servicing of the Triumph Herald 1200, 12/50, 13/60, Vitesse 6 and Spitfire, should be ordered from Messrs. V. L. Churchill & Company Limited, P.O. Box No. 3, London Road, Daventry, Northants.

TOOL No.	DESCRIPTION	Herald 1200 12/50 13/60	Vitesse 6	Spitfire 4 and Mk. 2	Spitfire Mk. 3
60A	Valve Guide Remover and Replacer	*	*	*	*
S.60A-2	Adaptor Set	*	*	*	*
S.60A-4	Adaptor Set	*			
S.60A-6	Adaptor Set	*	*	*	*
20.SM.90	Propeller Shaft Flange Holder	*	*	*	*
S.98A	Pre-Load Gauge	*	*	*	*
S.101	Differential Case Spreader	*	*	*	*
S.108	Pinion Bearing Setting Gauge	*	*	*	*
S.109C	Rear Hub Remover	*	*	*	*
S.123A	Pinion Bearing Outer Cup Remover	*	*	*	*
S.124	Pinion Bearing Outer Cup Replacer	*	*	*	
S.144	Gearbox Mainshaft Circlip Remover	*	*	*	*
S.145	Gearbox Mainshaft Circlip Replacer	*	*	*	*
S.160	Ball Joint Separator	*			*
S.300A	Rear Hub Needle Bearing Remover/Replacer	*	*	*	*
S.304	Rear Hub Bearing Replacer	*	*	*	*
S.306	Brake Adjusting Tool	*	*	*	*
S.309A	Engine Bracket	*		*	*
S.310	Engine Bracket		*		
S.334A	Gudgeon Pin Remover and Replacer	*		*	
S.335	Crankshaft Rear Oil Seal Centraliser	*	*	*	*
S.3600	Steering Wheel Remover	*	*	*	*
S.4221A	Multi-purpose Hand Press	*	*	*	*
S.4221A-4A	Pinion Bearing Cone Replacer and Remover	*	*	*	*
S.4221A-5	I.F.S. Coil Spring Remover and Replacer Adaptor	*	*	*	*
S.4221A-7B	Inner Axle Shaft Bearing Remover/Replacer Adaptor	*	*	*	*
S.4221A-8C	Differential Bearing Remover Adaptor	*	*	*	*
S.4221A-14	Rear Hub Bearing Remover Adaptor	*	*	*	*
S.4221A-19	Gearbox Mainshaft Ball Race Remover/Replacer Adaptor	*	*	*	*
4235A	Impact Remover	*	*	*	*
S.4235A-2	Constant Pinion Remover Adaptor	*	*	*	*
S.4235A-7	Constant Pinion Shaft Bearing Remover Adaptor	*	*	*	*
6118B	Valve Spring Compressor	*	*	*	*
S.6118-1	Valve Spring Compressor Adaptor	*	*	*	*
	OVERDRIVE TOOLS				
L.178	Freewheel Assembly Ring		*	*	*
L.183A	Pump Barrel Remover (Main Tool)		*	*	*
L.183A-2A	Adaptor		*	*	*
L.188	Hydraulic Test Equipment		*	*	*
L.201	Dummy Drive Shaft		*	*	*
L.202A	Tailshaft Ball Race Remover		*	*	*
L.206A	Oil Pump Body Replacer		*	*	*
L.213	Oil Pump Body Key		*	*	*
	CONNECTING ROD ARBOR ADAPTORS				
S.336-3	Adaptor	*		*	*
S.336-4	Adaptor		*		

Except where otherwise stated, the following torque figures relate to all vehicles described in this manual.

OPERATION	DESCRIPTION	SPECIFIED TORQUES lbs. ft.	kgms.
ENGINE			
Chain Wheel Attachment	5/16″ U.N.F. Setscrew	24 – 26	3·318 – 3·595
Clutch Attachment	5/16″ U.N.F. Setscrew	18 – 20	2·489 – 2·765
Connecting Rod Bolts	3/8″ U.N.F. Bolt	38 – 42	5·254 – 5·807
Cylinder Head	3/8″ U.N.F. Nut	42 – 46	5·807 – 6·36
Engine Mounting to Frame Brackets	5/16″ U.N.F. Setscrew	18 – 20	2·489 – 2·765
Fan to Pulley	1/4″ U.N.F. Bolt	6 – 8	0·820 – 1·106
„ „ „ (Vitesse only)	5/16″ U.N.F. Bolt	12 – 14	1·659 – 1·936
Flywheel Attachment	3/8″ U.N.F. Bolt	42 – 46	5·807 – 6·36
Front Engine Bracket and Front Engine Plate	5/16″ U.N.F. Bolt	18 – 20	2·489 – 2·765
Camshaft Locating Plate to Block	5/16″ U.N.F. Bolt	18 – 20	2·489 – 2·765
Fuel Pump	5/16″ U.N.F. Stud	12 – 14	1·659 – 1·936
Generator Bracket to Block	5/16″ U.N.F. Setscrew	16 – 18	2·212 – 2·489
„ „ „ „ (13/60 only)	5/16″ U.N.F. Setscrew	18 – 20	2·489 – 2·765
Generator Pulley Attachment	7/16″ U.N.F.	10 – 12	1·383 – 1·659
Generator to Engine Plate	5/16″ U.N.F. Bolt	16 – 18	2·212 – 2·489
Generator to Mounting Bracket	5/16″ U.N.F. Bolt	18 – 20	2·489 – 2·765
Gearbox and Rear Engine Plate Attachment	5/16″ U.N.F. Stud	12 – 14	1·659 – 1·936
„ „ „ „ „ „	5/16″ U.N.F. Setscrew	14 – 16	1·936 – 2·212
Header Tank Attachment (where fitted)	1/4″ U.N.F. Setscrew	6 – 8	0·830 – 1·106
Main Bearing Caps	7/16″ U.N.F. Bolt	50 – 55	6·913 – 7·604
Manifold Exhaust Outlet	5/16″ U.N.F. Stud	12 – 14	1·659 – 1·936
„ „ „ (Vitesse only)	5/16″ U.N.F. Stud	14 – 16	1·936 – 2·212
Manifold to Cylinder Head	3/8″ U.N.F. Stud	24 – 26	3·318 – 3·595
„ „ „ „ (Vitesse only)	3/8″ U.N.F. Bolt	20 – 22	2·489 – 3·042
Oil Filter to Crankcase		15 – 18	2·074 – 2·489
Oil Gallery Setscrews	5/16″ U.N.F. Setscrew	18 – 20	2·489 – 2·765
Oil Pump to Block	1/4″ U.N.F. Bolt	6 – 8	0·830 – 1·106
„ „ „ „ (13/60 only)	1/4″ U.N.F. Bolt	8 – 10	1·106 – 1·383
Rear Oil Seal Attachment	5/16″ U.N.F. Bolt	18 – 20	2·489 – 2·765
Rocker Cover Nuts	5/16″ U.N.F. Stud	1½	0·105
Rocker Pedestals	3/8″ U.N.F. Stud	24 – 26	3·318 – 3·595
Starter Motor Attachment	3/8″ U.N.F. Bolt	26 – 28	3·595 – 3·871
Sump Attachment	5/16″ U.N.F. Bolt	16 – 18	2·212 – 2·489
Sump to Front and Rear Seal	5/16″ U.N.F. Setscrew	10 – 12	1·383 – 1·659
Timing Cover Attachment	5/16″ U.N.F. Setscrew	14 – 16	1·936 – 2·212
„ „ „	5/16″ U.N.F. Setscrew (slotted)	8 – 10	1·106 – 1·383
Water Elbow to Water Body	5/16″ U.N.F. Setscrew	16 – 18	2·212 – 2·489
Water Pump to Cylinder Head	5/16″ U.N.F. Bolt	18 – 20	2·489 – 2·765
Water Pump Pulley Attachment	5/16″ U.N.F.	14 – 16	1·936 – 2·212
GEARBOX			
Clutch Housing to Gearbox	3/8″ U.N.F.	24 – 26	3·318 – 3·595
Countershaft Location	5/16″ U.N.F. Bolt	14 – 16	1·936 – 2·212
Coupling Operating Shaft Attachment	1/4″ U.N.F. Bolt	6 – 8	0·830 – 1·106
Extension to Gearbox	5/16″ U.N.F. Setscrew	14 – 16	1·936 – 2·212
Extension to Top Cover	5/16″ U.N.F. Stud	12 – 14	1·659 – 1·936
Flange to Mainshaft	9/16″ U.N.F. Nyloc Nut	70 – 80	9·678 – 11·060
Fulcrum—Reverse Operating Lever	3/8″ U.N.F.	14 – 16	1·936 – 2·212
Mounting Bracket to Frame	5/16″ U.N.F. Setscrew	18 – 20	2·489 – 2·765
Operating Shaft to Gear Lever	1/4″ U.N.F. Bolt	6 – 8	0·830 – 1·106
Reverse Idler Shaft	5/16″ U.N.F. Bolt	14 – 16	1·936 – 2·212
Selector Fork Attachment	5/16″ U.N.F. Taper Wdgelok	8 – 10	1·106 – 1·383
Slave Cylinder Attachment to Mounting Bracket	5/16″ U.N.F. Bolt	10 – 12	1·383 – 1·659
Speedo Sleeve Attachment	5/16″ U.N.F. Bolt	14 – 16	1·936 – 2·212
Top Cover Attachment	1/4″ U.N.F. Bolt	6 – 8	0·830 – 1·106

OPERATION	DESCRIPTION	SPECIFIED TORQUES lbs. ft.	kgms.
REAR AXLE AND SUSPENSION			
Back Plate Attachment (axle shaft and hub attachment)	5/16″ U.N.F. Bolt	16 – 18	2·212 – 2·489
Bearing Cap to Housing	3/8″ U.N.F. Bolt	32 – 34	4·424 – 4·701
Crown Wheel to Differential Casing	3/8″ U.N.F. Bolt	40 – 45	5·530 – 6·221
Hypoid Housing	5/16″ U.N.F. Setscrew	16 – 18	2·212 – 2·489
Hypoid Pinion Flange Attachment	9/16″ U.N.F.	70 – 85	9·678 – 11·752
Mounting Plate to Hypoid Housing	3/8″ U.N.F.	26 – 28	3·595 – 3·871
Radius Arm Brackets to Frame	3/8″ U.N.F. Bolt	24 – 26	3·318 – 3·595
Radius Arms to Brackets	3/8″ U.N.F. Bolt	24 – 26	3·318 – 3·595
Rear Axle Mounting Plate to Frame	3/8″ U.N.F.	26 – 28	3·595 – 3·871
Rear Axle to Frame	7/16″ U.N.F. Bolt	38 – 40	5·254 – 5·530
Rear Damper Lower Attachment	7/16″ U.N.F.	30 – 32	4·148 – 4·424
Rear Damper Upper Attachment	1/2″ U.N.F. Fulcrum Pin	42 – 46	5·807 – 6·36
Rear Hub to Axle Shaft	5/8″ U.N.F.	100 – 110	13·826 – 15·21
Road Spring to Axle Unit	3/8″ U.N.F. Stud	28 – 30	[illegible]·871 – 4·178
Shaft Joint to Inner Axle Shaft	5/16″ U.N.F. Bolt	24 – 28	[illegible]·318 – 3·595
„ „ „ „ „ „ (Vitesse only)	3/8″ U.N.F. Bolt	32 – 36	4·424 – 4·977
Spring Ends to Vertical Link Plate	7/16″ U.N.F. Bolt	42 – 46	5·807 – 6·36
Vertical Link Plates to Rear Hub Inner	7/16″ U.N.F. Bolt	42 – 46	5·807 – 6·36
FRONT SUSPENSION UNIT			
Anti-Roll Bar Link Assembly	7/16″ U.N.F.	38 – 42	5·254 5·807
Anti-roll Bar	3/8″ U.N.F. Stud	12 – 14	1·659 – 1·936
Anti-Roll Bar to Chassis	5/16″ U.N.F. "U" Bolts	3 – 4	0·415 – 0·281
Back Plates and Tie Rod Levers to Vertical Links	3/8″ U.N.F. Bolt	26 – 28	3·595 – 3·871
	5/16″ U.N.F. Bolt	16 – 18	2·212 – 2·489
Ball Assembly to Upper Wishbone	5/16″ U.N.F. Bolt	16 – 18	2·212 – 2·489
Ball Assembly to Vertical Link	7/16″ U.N.F.	38 – 42	5·254 – 5·807
Brake Disc to Hub	3/8″ U.N.F. Bolt	32 – 35	4·424 – 4·839
Caliper Mounting Plate to Vertical Link and Tie Rod Lever	5/16″ U.N.F. Setscrew	18 – 20	2·489 – 2·765
	3/8″ U.N.F. Bolt	32 – 35	4·424 – 4·839
Calipers to Mounting Plate	7/16″ U.N.F. Bolt	50 – 55	6·913 – 7·604
Front Damper—Bottom	7/16″ U.N.F. Bolt	42 – 46	5·807 – 6·360
Front Suspension and Engine Mounting Bracket to Frame	3/8″ U.N.F. Bolt	26 – 28	3·595 – 3·871
Fulcrum Brackets to Lower Wishbone	3/8″ U.N.F. Bolt	26 – 28	3·595 – 3·871
Stub Axle to Vertical Link	1/2″ U.N.F.	55 – 60	7·604 – 8·295
Tie Rod End Ball Joint Assembly	3/8″ U.N.F. Ball Pin	26 – 28	3·595 – 3·871
Top Wishbone Attachment	3/8″ U.N.F. Fulcrum Bolt	26 – 28	3·595 – 3·871
Trunnion to Wishbone	7/16″ U.N.F. Bolt	35 – 38	4·839 – 5·254
Wishbone Assembly to Frame	3/8″ U.N.F.	22 – 24	3·042 – 3·318
Vertical Link to Tie Rod Lever	3/8″ U.N.F. Bolt	32 – 35	4·424 – 4·839
STEERING UNIT			
Coupling Pinch Bolts	5/16″ U.N.F. Bolt	18 – 20	2·489 – 2·765
Lower to Upper Clamp	1/4″ U.N.F. Bolt	6 – 8	0·830 – 1·106
Safety Clamp Socket Setscrew	7/16″ U.N.F. Grub Screw	18 – 20	2·489 – 2·765
Steering Column Safety Clamp	1/4″ U.N.F. Bolt	6 – 8	0·830 – 1·106
Steering Unit to Frame	5/16″ U.N.F. "U" Bolt	14 – 16	1·936 – 2·212
MISCELLANEOUS			
Wheel Nuts	3/8″ U.N.F.	38 – 42	5·254 – 5·807

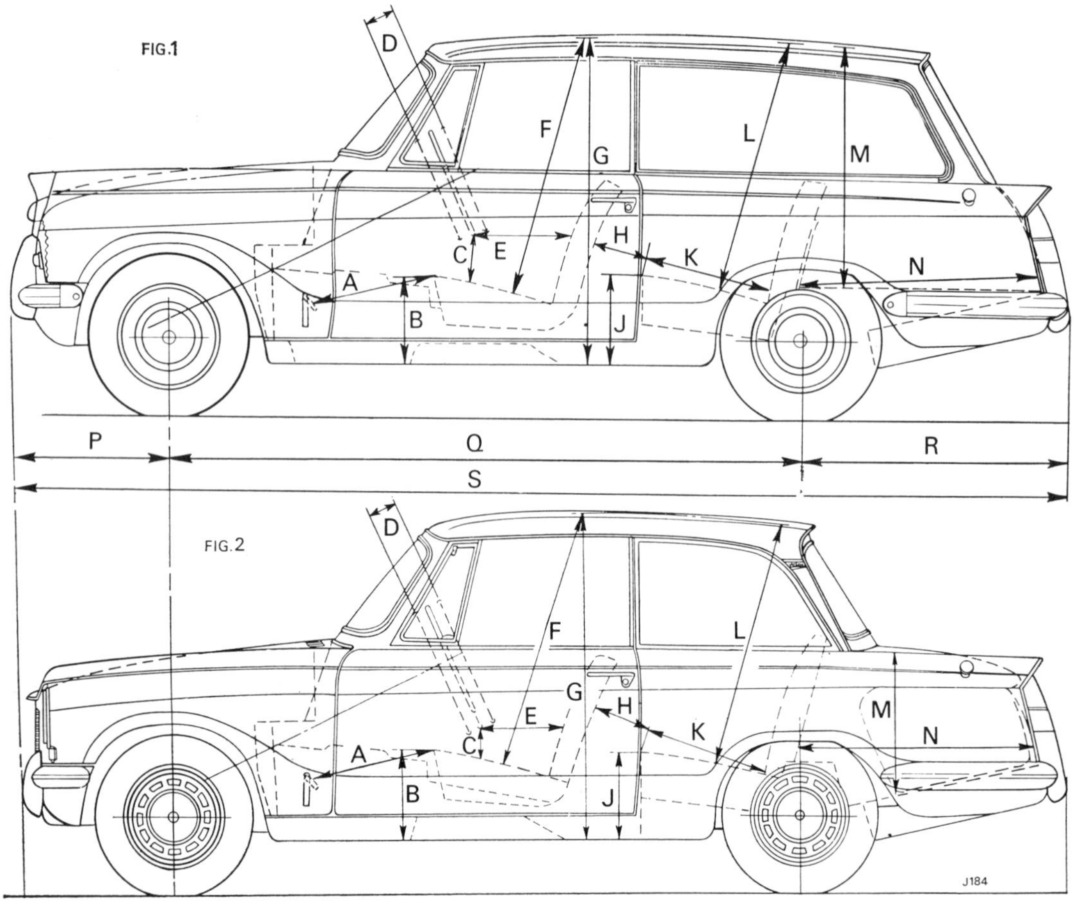

Fig. 1. Herald 1200 Estate Car **Fig. 2. Vitesse 6 Saloon**

VEHICLE DIMENSIONS

	.ESTATE CAR AND COURIER Fig. 1		13/60 ESTATE CAR Fig. 1		1200, 12/50 and VITESSE SALOON Fig. 2		13/60 SALOON Fig. 2	
A Max.	1′ 9¾″	55·29 cm.	1′ 8¾″	52·70 cm.	1′ 9¾″	55·25 cm.	1′ 8¾″	52·70 cm.
Min.	1′ 4″	40·64 cm.	1′ 1¼″	33·66 cm.	1′ 4″	40·64 cm.	1′ 1¼″	33·66 cm.
B	1′ 0″	30·48 cm.	1′ 0″	35·48 cm.	1′ 0″	35·48 cm.	1′ 0″	35·48 cm.
C	5½″	13·97 cm.	5½″	13·97 cm.	5½″	13·97 cm.	5½″	13·97 cm.
D	4″	10·16 cm.	4″	10·16 cm.	4″	10·16 cm.	4″	10·16 cm.
E Max.	1′ 4¼″	41·27 cm.	1′ 2½″	36·80 cm.	1′ 4¼″	41·27 cm.	1′ 2½″	36·80 cm.
Min.	10¼″	26·04 cm.	7″	17·80 cm.	10¼″	26·04 cm.	7″	17·80 cm.
F	3′ 0½″	92·71 cm.	3′ 0½″	92·71 cm.	3′ 0½″	92·71 cm.	3′ 0½″	92·71 cm.
G	3′ 9½″	1·156 m.	3′ 9½″	1·155 m.	3′ 9½″	1·156 m.	3″ 9½″	1·155 m.
H Max.	11¾″	29·84 cm.	1′ 1¾″	34·90 cm.	11¾″	29·84 cm.	1′ 1¾″	34·90 cm.
Min.	5¾″	14·60 cm.	6¼″	15·90 cm.	5¾″	14·60 cm.	6¼″	15·90 cm.
J	1′ 1″	33·02 cm.	1′ 1″	33·02 cm.	1′ 0″	30·48 cm.	1′ 0″	30·48 cm.
K	1′ 6″	45·72 cm.	1′ 6″	45·72 cm.	1′ 6″	45·72 cm.	1′ 6″	45·72 çm.
L	2′ 10″	86·36 cm.	2′ 10″	86·36 cm.	2′ 10″	86·36 cm.	2′ 10″	86·36 cm.
M	2′ 9″	83·82 cm.	2′ 9″	83·82 cm.	1′ 9″	53·53 cm.	1′ 9″	53·53 cm.
N	2′ 10″	86·36 cm.	2′ 10″	86·36 cm.	3′ 0″	91·44 cm.	3′ 0″	91·44 cm.
P	1′ 11″	58·42 cm.	1′ 11″	58·42 cm.	1′ 11″	58·42 cm.	1′ 11″	58·42 cm.
Q	7′ 7½″	2·324 m.	7′ 7½″	2·324 m.	7′ 7½″	2·324 m.	7′ 7½″	2·324 m.
R	3′ 2½″	97·79 cm.	3′ 2½″	97·79 cm.	3′ 2½″	97·79 cm.	3′ 2½″	97·79 cm.
S	12′ 9″	3·886 m.	12′ 9″	3·886 m.	12′ 9″	3·886 m.	12′ 9″	3·886 m.

FIG.3

FIG.4

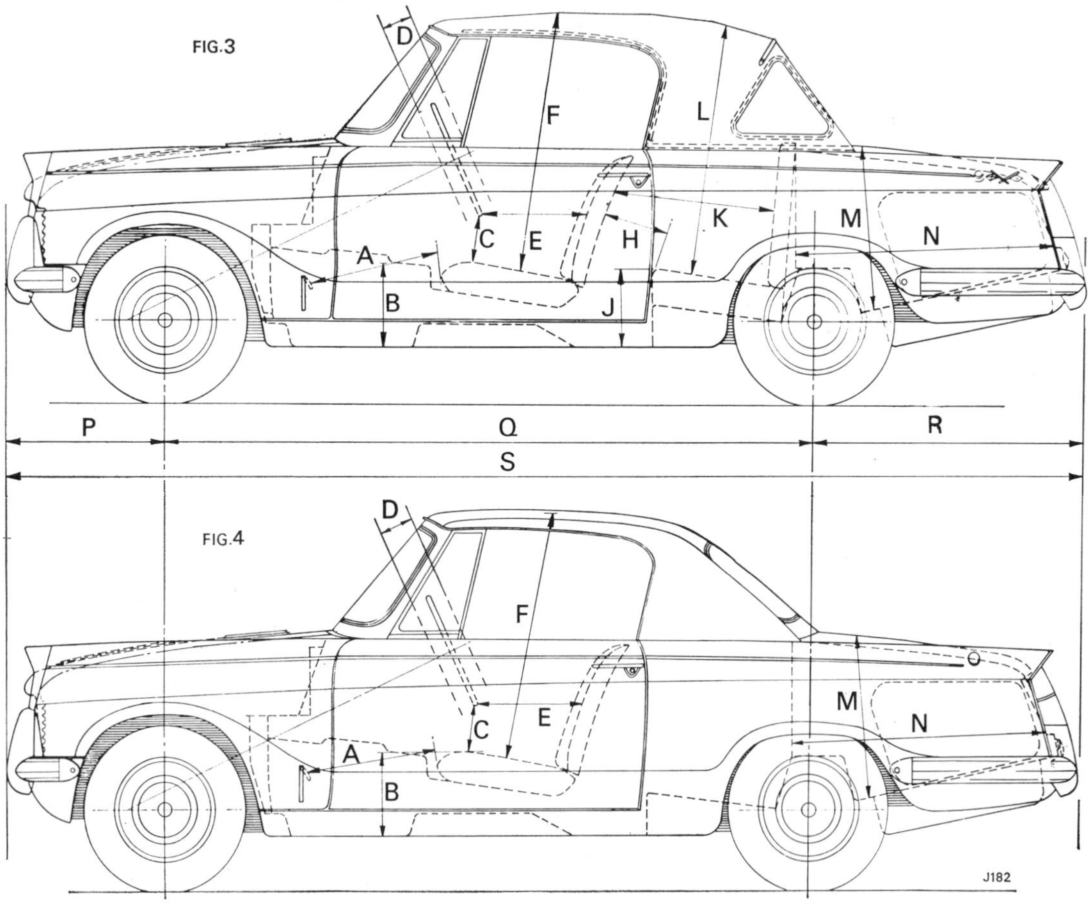

Fig. 3. Herald 1200 Convertible

Fig. 4. Herald 1200 Coupé

VEHICLE DIMENSIONS

		HERALD COUPE Fig. 4		HERALD 1200, 12/50 and VITESSE CONVERTIBLE Fig. 3		13/60 CONVERTIBLE Fig. 3	
A	Max.	1′ 9¾″	55·30 cm.	1′ 9¾″	55·30 cm.	1′ 8″	50·80 cm.
	Min.	1′ 4″	40·64 cm.	1′ 4″	40·64 cm.	1′ 1¼″	33·66 cm.
B		1′ 0″	30·50 cm.	1′ 0″	30·50 cm.	1′ 0″	30·50 cm.
C		5½″	14·00 cm.	5½″	14·00 cm.	5½″	14·00 cm.
D		4″	10·16 cm.	4″	10·16 cm.	4″	10·16 cm.
E	Max.	1′ 4″	41·27 cm.	1′ 4″	41·30 cm.	1′ 1¾″	34·90 cm.
	Min.	10¼″	26·04 cm.	10¼″	26·00 cm.	7″	17·80 cm.
F		2′ 11″	88·90 cm.	2′ 11″	88·90 cm.	2′ 11″	88·90 cm.
J				10″	25·40 cm.	11″	27·94 cm.
H	Max.			11¼″	29·80 cm.	1′ 2″	35·56 cm.
	Min.			5¼″	14·60 cm.	7¼″	18·42 cm.
K	Max.			2′ 3″	68·60 cm.	2′ 5″	63·50 cm.
	Min.			1′ 9″	53·30 cm.	1′ 10¼″	56·52 cm.
L				2′ 10″	86·36 cm.	2′ 10″	86·36 cm.
M		1′ 9″	53·30 cm.	1′ 9″	53·30 cm.	1′ 9″	53·30 cm.
N		3′ 0″	91·40 cm.	3′ 0″	91·40 cm.	3′ 0″	91·40 cm.
P		1′ 10⅜″	56·80 cm.	1′ 10⅜″	56·80 cm.	1′ 11″	58·42 cm.
Q		7′ 7½″	2·320 m.	7′ 7½″	2·320 m.	7′ 7½″	2·320 m.
R		3′ 2″	97·80 cm.	3′ 2″	97·80 cm.	3′ 2½″	97·80 cm.
S		12′ 8¾″	3·870 m.	12′ 8¾″	3·270 m.	12′ 9″	3·886 m.

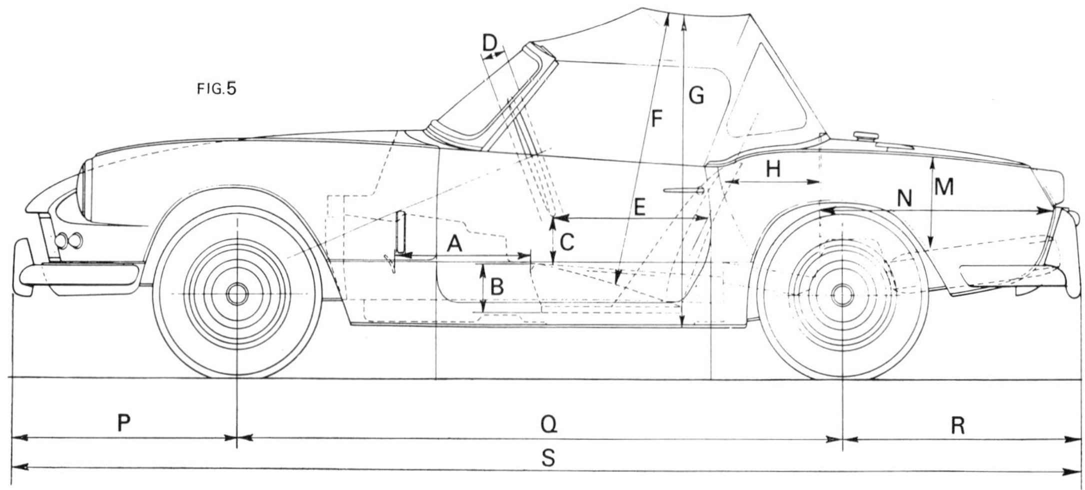

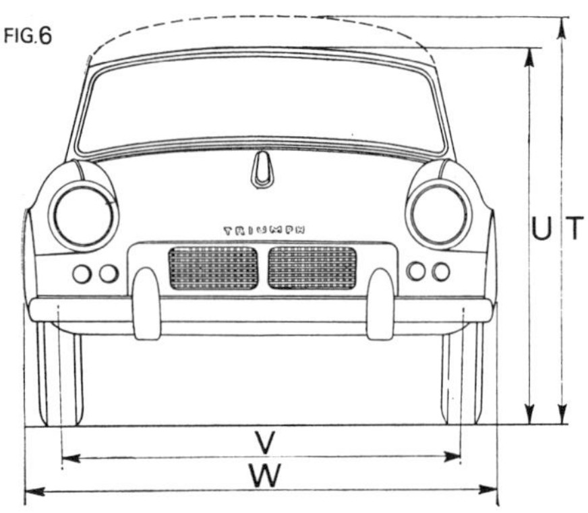

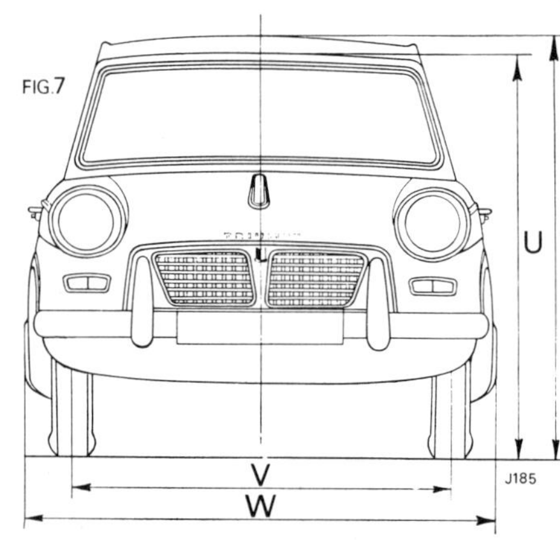

Fig. 5. Spitfire 4 and Mk. 2 **Fig. 6. Spitfire 4 and Mk. 2 End Elevation** **Fig. 7. Herald 1200 End Elevation**

VEHICLE DIMENSIONS

	SPITFIRE 4 and Mk. 2 Fig. 5	SPITFIRE Mk. 3 Fig. 5	SPITFIRE 4 Mk. 2 and Mk. 3 Fig. 6	HERALD AND VITESSE RANGE Fig. 7
A Max.	2′ 2½″ 67·00 cm.	2′ 2½″ 67·00 cm.		
Min.	1′ 7½″ 49·53 cm.	1′ 7½″ 49·53 cm.		
B	7″ 17·78 cm.	7″ 17·78 cm.		
C	7″ 17·78 cm.	7″ 17·78 cm.		
D	4″ 10·16 cm.	4″ 10·16 cm.		
E Max.	1′ 10″ 55·88 cm.	1′ 10″ 55·88 cm.		
Min.	1′ 2½″ 38·83 cm.	1′ 2½″ 38·83 cm.		
F	2′ 11″ 88·90 cm.	2′ 11″ 88·90 cm.		
G	3′ 8″ 111·76 cm.	3′ 8″ 111·76 cm.		
H Max.	1′ 4¾″ 42·54 cm.	1′ 4¾″ 42·54 cm.		
Min.	9½″ 24·15 cm.	9½″ 24·15 cm.		
N	2′ 11″ 88·90 cm.	2′ 11″ 88·90 cm.		
M	10″ 25·40 cm.	10″ 25·40 cm.		
P	2′ 7″ 78·74 cm.	2′ 7″ 78·74 cm.		
Q	6′ 11″ 210·82 cm.	6′ 11″ 210·82 cm.		
R	2′ 7½″ 80·01 cm.	2′ 7½″ 80·01 cm.		
S	12′ 1″ 368·30 cm.	12′ 2½″ 372·11 cm.		
T			3′ 11½″ 120·65 cm.	4′ 4″ 132·00 cm.
U			3′ 8¼″ 111·40 cm.	4′ 0½″ 123·19 cm.
V			4′ 1″ 124·46 cm. (Vitesse also)	4′ 0″ 121·90 cm.
Rear Track	4′ 0″ 121·90 cm.	4′ 0″ 121·90 cm.	4′ 0″ 121·90 cm.	4′ 0″ 121·90 cm.
W			4′ 9″ 144·78 cm.	5′ 0″ 152·40 cm.

TRIUMPH
HERALD, VITESSE 6
AND
SPITFIRE
WORKSHOP MANUAL

GROUP 1

Comprising :

TRIUMPH
HERALD, VITESSE 6
and
SPITFIRE

GROUP 1

CONTENTS

ENGINE — DIMENSIONS AND TOLERANCES

PARTS & DESCRIPTION	HERALD 1200, 12/50 & SPITFIRE 4				HERALD 13/60, SPITFIRE 4, & Mk. 3				VITESSE 1600 c.c.			
	DIMENSIONS		CLEARANCES		DIMENSIONS		CLEARANCES		DIMENSIONS		CLEARANCES	
	ins.	mm.	ins.	mm.	ins.	mm.	ins.	mm.	ins.	mm.	ins.	mm.
Crankshaft												
Main bearing journal dia.	2·0005 2·001	50·81 50·83			2·0005 2·001	50·81 50·83			2·0005 2·001	50·81 50·83		
Main bearing internal dia.	2·0015 2·0037	50·84 50·89			2·002 2·0025	50·85 50·86			2·002 2·0025	50·85 50·86		
Main bearing housing internal dia.	2·146 2·1465	54·51 54·52			2·146 2·1465	54·51 54·52			2·146 2·1465	54·51 54·52		
Rear journal width	1·2976 1·2995	32·95 33·01	0·006 to 0·014	0·15 to 0·35	1·2975 1·2995	32·95 33·01	0·006 to 0·014	0·15 to 0·35	1·3600 1·3620	34·54 34·59		
Thickness of thrust washers	0·091 0·093	2·31 2·36	0·006 to 0·014	0·15 to 0·35	0·091 0·093	2·31 2·36	0·006 to 0·014	0·15 to 0·35	0·091 0·093	2·31 2·36	0·006 to 0·014	0·15 to 0·35
Oversize thrust washers	0·096 0·098	2·44 2·49			0·096 0·098	2·44 2·49			0·096 0·098	2·44 2·49		
Crank pin dia.	1·6250 1·6255	41·27 44·28			1·6250 1·6255	41·27 41·28			1·875 1·8755	47·625 47·638		

Note. Crankshaft end-float 0·004″ to 0·008″. Undersize bearings available 0·010″, 0·020″, 0·030″, 0·040″ (0·254, 0·508, 0·762, 1·016 mm.)

PARTS & DESCRIPTION	HERALD 1200, 12/50 & SPITFIRE 4				HERALD 13/60, SPITFIRE 4, & Mk. 3				VITESSE 1600 c.c.			
Connecting Rods												
Big end bearing internal dia.	1·627 1·626	41·32 41·30			1·626 1·627	41·30 41·32					1·626 1·627	41·30 41·32
Con-rod end float on crank pin			0·0105 0·0126	0·266 0·320			0·0025 0·0086	0·063 0·218			0·0086 0·0125	0·218 0·317
I.D. small end bush dia.	0·8122 0·8126	20·63 20·64	Light push fit at 68°F		0·8110 0·8115	20·51 20·612	Interference fit		0·8122 0·8126	20·63 20·64	Light push fit at 68°F	
Gudgeon pin dia.	0·8125 0·8123	20·64 20·63			0·8125 0·8123	20·64 20·63			0·8125 0·8123	20·64 20·63		

Note. Undersize bearings available 0·010″, 0·020″, 0·030″ (0·254, 0·808, 0·762 mm.)
Con-rod bend and twist must not exceed ·0015″ in length of gudgeon pin. Max. weight variation not to exceed 4 drams.

ENGINE — DIMENSIONS AND TOLERANCES

PARTS & DESCRIPTION	HERALD 1200, 12/50 & SPITFIRE 4				HERALD 13/60, Spitfire 4 & Mk. 3				VITESSE 1600 c.c.			
	DIMENSIONS		CLEARANCES		DIMENSIONS		CLEARANCES		DIMENSIONS		CLEARANCES	
	ins.	mm.	ins.	mm.	ins.	mm.	ins.	mm.	ins.	mm.	ins.	mm.
Piston Rings (+0·010″, +0·020″, +0·030″ oversize rings available)												
Compression ring widths	0·077 0·078	1·97 1·99	0·015 to 0·0035	0·038 to 0·089	0·0625 0·0620	1·587 1·575	0·0015 to 0·0035	0·038 to 0·089	0·077 0·078	1·97 1·99	0·0019 to 0·0035	0·038 to 0·089
Oil control ring widths	0·1540 0·1560	3·90 3·96	0·001 0·004	0·025 0·100	0·1540 0·1560	3·90 3·96	0·0018 0·0048	0·038 0·089	0·1582 0·1563	3·94 3·97	0·0007 0·0027	0·02 0·07
Piston Ring Groove												
Compression rings	0·0812 0·0802	2·06 2·03			0·0650 0·0640	1·65 1·625			0·0797 0·0812	2·18 2·02		
Oil control rings	0·158 0·157	4·01 3·99			0·1588 0·1578	4·01 3·99			0·1552 0·1563	3·94 2·97		
Piston ring gaps in cylinders	0·008 0·013	0·20 0·33			0·012 0·022	0·30 0·85			0·008 0·013	0·20 0·33		

Note. Solid skirt piston introduced at Engine Nos. GA.137545, GD.21229, FC.24449 with compression ring groove of 0·0807/0·0797

PARTS & DESCRIPTION	HERALD 1200, 12/50 & SPITFIRE 4				HERALD 13/60, Spitfire 4 & Mk. 3				VITESSE 1600 c.c.			
Piston Pins												
Grade: High (colour, white)	0·81242 0·81250	20·63 20·64			0·81240 0·81250	20·637 20·64						
Medium (colour, green)	0·81234 0·81242	20·633 20·635			0·8123 0·8124	20·632 20·637			0·81234 0·81242	20·633 20·635		
Low (colour, yellow)	0·81226 0·81234	20·632 20·633							0·81226 0·81234	20·632 20·633		
Tappet dia.	0·6871 0·6867	17·45 17·46	0·002 to 0·0013	0·0508 to 0·033	0·8000 0·7996	20·320 20·294	0·002 to 0·0013	0·0508 to 0·033	0·6871 0·6867	17·45 17·46	0·002 to 0·0013	0·0508 to 0·033
Tappet bore in cylinder block	0·688 0·687	17·47 17·46			0·8002 0·8009	20·354 20·343			0·688 0·687	17·47 17·46		

Note. Larger diameter tappet introduced at Engine Nos. GA.177973, GD.59745, FC.61023, HB.28896.
Tappet diameter 0·8000/0·7996 (20·32/20·29 mm.).

ENGINE — DIMENSIONS AND TOLERANCES

PARTS & DESCRIPTION	HERALD 1200, 12/50 & SPITFIRE 4				HERALD 13/60 SPITFIRE 4 & Mk. 3				VITESSE 1600 c.c.			
	DIMENSIONS		CLEARANCES		DIMENSIONS		CLEARANCES		DIMENSIONS		CLEARANCES	
	ins.	mm.	ins.	mm.	ins.	mm.	ins.	mm.	ins.	mm.	ins.	mm.
Camshaft												
Journal dia.	1·8402 1·8407	46·75 46·74	0·0026 to 0·0046	0·07 to 0·12	1·9654 1·9649	49·92 49·91	0·0026 to 0·0046	0·07 to 0·12	1·8402 1·8407	46·75 46·74	0·0026 to 0·0046	0·07 to 0·12
Bore in block	1·8433 1·8448	46·82 46·86			1·9695 1·9680	50·025 49·98			1·8433 1·8448	46·82 46·86		
End float			0·008 0·004	0·20 0·10			0·0085 0·0042	0·216 0·11			0·008 0·004	0·20 0·11
Note. Camshaft bearings introduced at GA.177973, GD.59745, FC.61023. Size of bore in block identical to Herald 13/60 and Spitfire Mk. 3												
Oil pump												
Depth of rotor (inner)	0·9995 0·9985	25·37 25·36	0·0066 to 0·0017	0·015 to 0·043	0·9995 0·9985	25·36 25·37	0·0015 to 0·0035	0·038 to 0·0089	1·4985 1·4995	38·06 38·08	0·0006 to 0·0017	0·015 to 0·043
(outer)	0·9995 0·9985	25·37 25·36			0·9995 0·9985	25·37 25·36			1·4985 1·4995	38·06 38·08		
Max. permissible clearance between outer rotor & body			0·008	0·203			0·0075	0·190			0·008	0·203
Max. permissible clearance between outer and inner rotors			0·010	0·254			0·010	0·254			0·010	0·254
Distributor Drive Gear												
End float			0·003 0·007	0·08 0·18			0·003 0·007	0·08 0·18			0·003 0·007	0·08 0·18
Spindle diameter	0·499 0·498	12·67 12·65			0·4980 0·4985	12·65 12·67			0·499 0·498	12·67 12·65		
Bush bore	0·5005 0·501	12·71 12·73	0·0005 to 0·003	0·013 to 0·076	0·5005 0·501	12·71 12·73	0·0005 to 0·003	0·0127 to 0·076	0·5005 0·501	12·71 12·73	0·0005 to 0·003	0·0127 to 0·076

PAGES 1.105 AND 1.106 WILL BE FOUND ON THE LAST PAGE OF THE MANUAL

VALVE SEAT INSERT DIMENSIONS

	INSERT DIMENSIONS				BORE OUT				INSERT Part No.
	External dia.		Width		Diameter		Depth		
	Ins.	mm.	Ins.	mm.	Ins.	mm.	Ins.	mm.	
EXHAUST (Herald 1200, 12/50, 13/60, Spitfire 4, Mk. 2 and 3	1·2530 1·2520	38·83 31·80	0·250 0·248	6·35 6·15	1·250 1·2490	31·75 31·72	0·250 0·248	6·35 6·15	132242
INLET (Herald 1200, 12/50)	1·441 1·440	36·6 35·57	0·250 0·248	6·35 6·15	1·4280 1·4370	36·52 36·50	0·250 0·248	6·35 6·15	132241
INLET (Spitfire 4, Mk. 1, 2 & 3, and Herald 13/60)	1·3785 1·3795	35·014 35·039	0·250 0·248	6·35 6·15	1·3750 1·3760	34·92 34·95	0·250 0·248	6·35 6·15	130814
EXHAUST (Vitesse)	1·2535 1·2545	31·84 31·86	0·216 0·219	5·46 5·56	1·250 1·251	31·75 31·77	0·219 0·224	5·56 5·68	130813
INLET (Vitesse)	1·3785 1·3795	35·014 35·04	0·216 0·219	5·464 5·563	1·375 1·376	34·928 34·95	0·219 0·224	5·56 5·68	130814

ENGINE — DIMENSIONS AND TOLERANCES

HERALD 1200, 12/50 AND SPITFIRE

GRADE	F ins.	F mm.	G ins.	G mm.	H ins.	H mm.	Make
Cylinder Bore	2·7283 2·7280	69·3 69·29	2·7287 2·7284	69·31 69·30	2·7291 2·7288	69·32 69·31	
Piston Top Dia.	2·7254 2·7250	69·22 69·21	2·7258 2·7254	69·235 69·22	2·7262 2·7258	69·24 69·23	Automotive Engineering Co. Ltd.
Piston Bottom Dia.	2·7272 2·7268	69·27 69·26	2·7276 2·7272	69·28 69·27	2·7280 2·7276	69·3 69·28	
Piston Top Dia.	2·7120 2·7090	68·88 68·81	2·7120 2·7090	68·88 68·81	2·7120 2·7090	68·88 68·81	British Piston Ring Co. Ltd.
Piston Bottom Dia.	2·7271 2·7268	69·22 69·26	2·7275 2·7272	69·31 69·29	2·7279 2·7276	69·28 69·31	
Piston Top Dia.	2·7245 2·7242	69·30 69·20	2·7249 2·7246	69·21 69·27	2·7253 2·7250	69·22 69·21	Wellworthy
Piston Bottom Dia.	2·7271 2·7268	69·36 69·26	2·7275 2·7272	69·278 69·27	2·7279 2·7276	69·288 69·281	

HERALD 13/60 AND SPITFIRE 4 Mk. 3

GRADE	F ins.	F mm.	G ins.	G mm.	H ins.	H mm.	Make
Cylinder Bore	2·900 2·899	73·66 73·64	2·9005 2·9001	73·67 73·66			
Piston Top Dia.	2·880 2·875	73·15 73·03	2·880 2·875	73·15 73·03			Brico Co. Ltd.
Piston Bottom Dia.	2·8981 2·8976	73·61 73·59	2·8987 2·8982	73·62 73·617			
Piston Top Dia.	2·8799 2·8752	73·15 73·03	2·8799 2·8752	73·15 73·03			Hepworth Co. Ltd.
Piston Bottom Dia.	2·8981 2·8976	73·61 73·59	2·8987 2·8983	63·627 73·617			

VITESSE 1600 c.c.

GRADE	F ins.	F mm.	G ins.	G mm.	H ins.	H mm.	Make
Cylinder Bore	2·6279 2·6276	66·75 66·74	2·6283 2·6280	66·76 66·71	2·6287 2·6284	66·77 66·76	
Piston Top Dia.			2·6272 2·6250	66·685 66·675			Automotive Engineering Co. Ltd.
Piston Bottom Dia.			2·6272 2·6268	66·731 66·721			
Piston Top Dia.	2·6267 2·6264	66·56 66·55	2·6271 2·6268	66·73 66·72	2·6275 2·6272	66·74 66·73	British Piston Ring Co. Ltd.
Piston Bottom Dia.	2·6239 2·6236	66·65 66·64	2·6243 2·6240	66·657 66·650	2·6247 2·6244	66·667 66·660	

Note. +0·010″, +0·020″ and +0·030 oversize pistons available. When fitting liners, bore block out to: 2·625″ - 2·624″ (66·5 - 66·64 mm.) for Herald and Spitfire 4; 2·781″ - 2·780″ (69·6 - 69·61 mm.) for Vitesse 1600 c.c.; 3·031″ - 3·030″ (74·01 - 74·00 mm.) for Herald 13/60 and Spitfire 4 Mk. 3. Maximum weight variation on a set of pistons not to exceed 4 drams on Herald, Spitfire and Vitesse and 2 drams on Spitfire Mk. 3 and Herald 13/60.

INTRODUCTION

This section is devoted to the removal, overhaul and installation of Standard-Triumph engines in the Herald, Spitfire and Vitesse 1600 c.c. models. Basically the engines of these models are similar; such variations as exist, four cylinders or six, single or twin carburettors, open or closed crankcase ventilation systems, etc., are referred to and covered within their respective sub-sections.

Attention is drawn to the use within this section of the words *replace* and *renew*. *Replace* is used where a part previously removed is to be returned to its original location. *Renew* indicates that a part removed is *not* to be again used but a new item obtained and fitted.

LUBRICATION

Oil Circulation (Refer Fig. 1)

Oil is drawn from the engine sump by a rotor type pump which discharges via a non-adjustable relief valve to a full-flow filter. Spillage from the relief valve returns to the sump: the filtered oil passes to the engine main oil gallery from whence it is distributed to the camshaft and crankshaft journals. Drillings in the crankshaft webs permit oil flow to the crankpins. The cylinder bores, pistons and gudgeon pins are lubricated by splash thrown up by the crankshaft.

A reduced flow of oil to the hollow rocker shaft and the valve gear is supplied from, and metered by, a scroll and two flats on the camshaft rear journal. Oil from the valve gear spills to the cam-followers and cams before returning to the sump.

A restricted oil feed to the camshaft thrust plate and timing gear is obtained from drillings and oil grooves in the camshaft front journal. The timing gear is also lubricated by oil mist from the crankcase.

Crankcase oil retention is ensured by crankshaft lip type oil seals fitted front and rear.

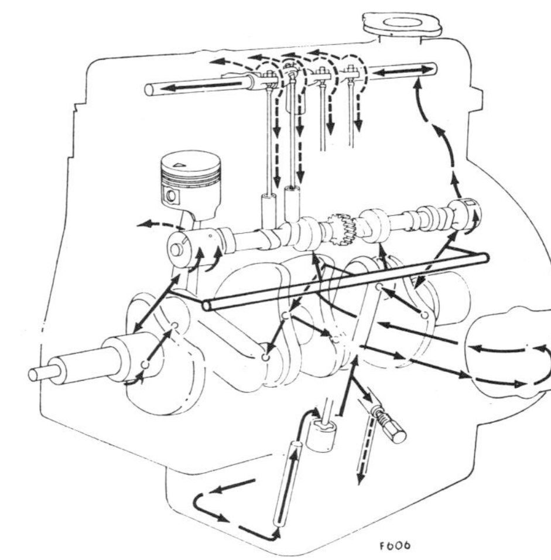

Fig. 1. Oil circulation (All engines)

Oil Filtration (HERALD and SPITFIRE)

Herald and Spitfire models employ a full-flow sealed filter unit screwed directly to the engine crankcase. Within the filter casing is a filter element and a by-pass valve assembly. Fig. 2 illustrates oil flow under normal conditions, and when the filter has become choked. Under the latter condition, where the filter unit has not been changed at recommended intervals, the by-pass valve ensures an adequate, albeit unfiltered supply of oil to the engine.

Renewing Oil Filter Unit (HERALD and SPITFIRE) (Fig. 2)

The screwed union (8) engages directly with the crankcase. To remove the filter unit grasp the body firmly and unscrew.

Before fitting new filter unit ensure that the sealing ring (7) is undamaged and is properly seated. Thoroughly clean filter and crankcase mating faces.

Smear sealing ring with clean oil and screw filter unit into crankcase.

Do not attempt to clean or reclaim used filter units.

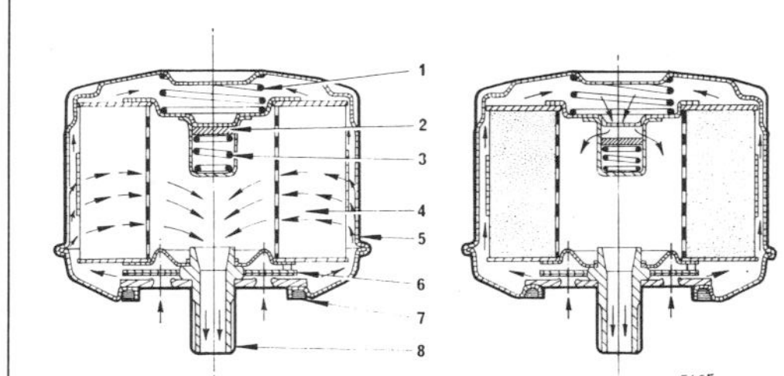

1 Spring
2 By-pass valve
3 By-pass valve spring
4 Element
5 Casing
6 Non-return valve
7 Seal
8 Union

Fig. 2. Oil filtration (Herald and Spitfire)

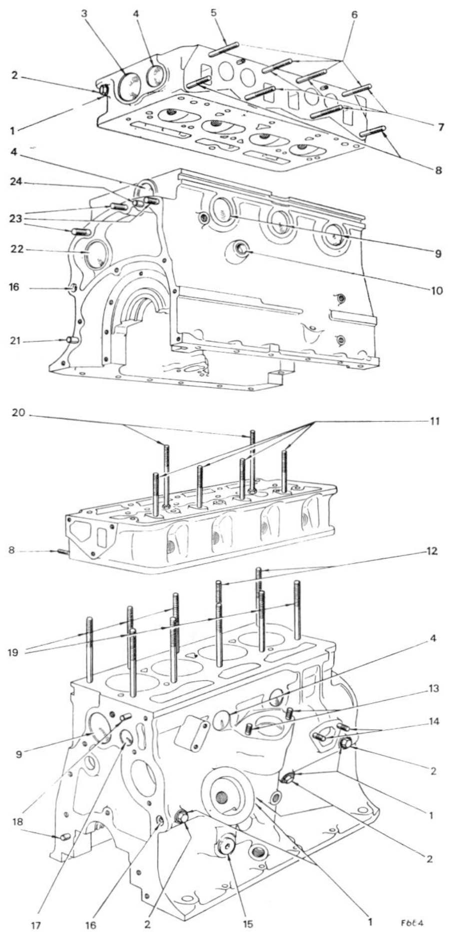

STUDS, PLUGS AND DOWELS
(1200, 12/50, 13/60 and SPITFIRE)

1	Washer—Copper ..	Rocker feed .. Oil gallery ..	(1) (4)
2	Setscrew, 5/16″ UNF × ·44″	Rocker feed .. Oil gallery ..	(1) (4)
3	Core plug, 1 5/8″	Rear of head ..	(1)
4	Core plug, 1 1/4″	Rear of head .. Block rear .. Block L.H. ..	(1) (1) (2)
5	Stud, 3/8″ UNF × 1·75″ ..	Manifold inner (13/60 and Spitfire 3)	(1)
6	Stud, 3/8″ UNF × 1·84″ ..	Manifold inner (13/60 and Spitfire 3)	(5)
7	Stud, 3/8″ UNF × 1·84″ ..	Manifold inner (1200, 12/50, Spit. 4 & 2)	(4)
8	Stud, 3/8″ UNF × 1·34″ ..	Manifold outer	(2)
9	Core plug, 1 1/2″	Block front .. Block R.H. ..	(1) (3)
10	Plug, 3/4″	Breather seal .. (13/60 and Spitfire)	(1)
11	Stud, 3/8″ UNF × 3·09″ ..	Rocker pedestal	(4)
12	Stud, 3/8″ UNF × 4·38″ ..	Lifting eye ..	(2)
13	Stud, 5/16″ UNF × 1·34″	Distributor ..	(2)
14	Stud, 5/16″ UNF × 1·16″	Petrol pump ..	(2)
15	Plug	Oil gallery ..	(1)
16	Plug	Oil gallery ..	(2)
17	Core plug, 1″	Block—front ..	(1)
18	Dowel, 5/16″ × 7/8″ ..	Front plate ..	(2)
19	Stud, 3/8″ UNF × 4·19″ ..	Cylinder head .. (1200, 12/50, Spitfire 4 and 2 only)	(9)
19	Stud, 3/8″ UNF × 4·19″ ..	Cylinder head .. (13/60 and Spit. 3 only)	(8)
20	Stud, 5/16″ UNF × 4·13″	Rocker cover ..	(2)
21	Dowel, 3/8″ × 5/8″	Rear plate ..	(1)
22	Core plug, 2″	Camshaft—rear	(1)
23	Stud, 5/16″ UNF × 1·131″	Rear plate ..	(3)
24	Dowel, 3/8″ × 1″	Rear plate ..	(1)

Fig. 7. Studs, plugs and dowels — Herald and Spitfire

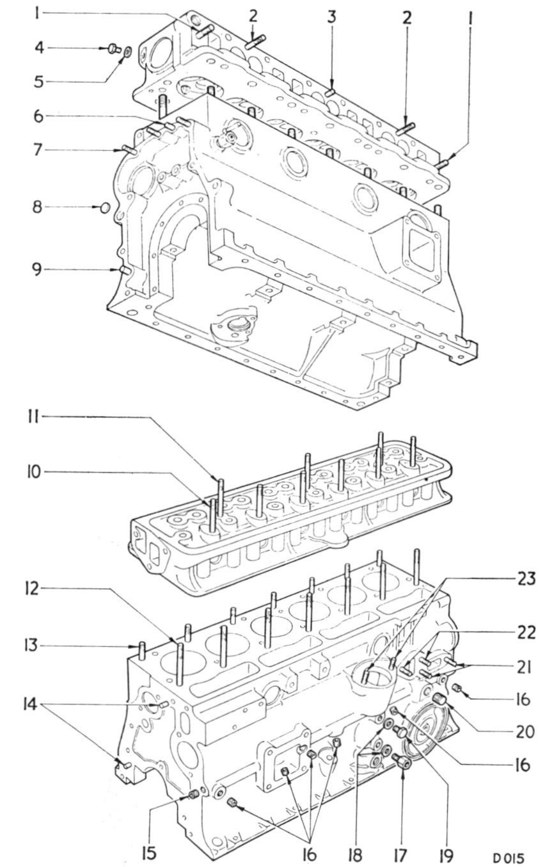

STUDS, PLUGS AND DOWELS
VITESSE

1	Stud, 3/8″ UNF × 1·34″	(2)
2	Stud, 5/16″ UNF × 1·38″	(2)
3	Dowel	(1)
4	Setscrew, 5/16″ UNF × 3/8″	(1)
5	Copper Washer, 5/16″ I/D	(1)
6	Dowel, 3/8″ × 1″	(1)
7	Stud, 5/16″ UNF × 1·31″	(3)
8	1/4″ NPSL Dry Seal Plug	(1)
9	Dowel, 3/8″ × 5/8″	(1)
10	Stud, 3/8″ UNF × 3·09″	(6)
11	Stud, 5/16″ UNF × 4·13″	(3)
12	Stud, 3/8″ UNF × 4·44″ HC .. .. 3/8″ UNF × 4·63″ LC	(7) (7)
13	Stud, 3/8″ UNF × 1·44″ HC .. .. 3/8″ UNF × 1·56″ LC	(7) (7)
14	Dowel, 5/16″ × 7/8″	(2)
15	Plug, 1/2″ NF × ·38″	(1)
16	1/8″ NP. Dry Seal Plug	(6)
17	Oil Pressure Switch Adaptor	(1)
18	Copper Washer, 7/16″ I/D	(2)
19	Setscrew, 7/16″ UNF × 1/2″	(1)
20	Plug, 3/4″ UNF × 1/2″	(1)
21	Stud, 5/16″ UNF × 1·16″	(2)
22	Stud, 5/16″ UNF × 1·16″	(2)
23	Stud, 5/16″ UNF × 1·31″	(2)

Fig. 7a. Studs, plugs and dowels — Vitesse

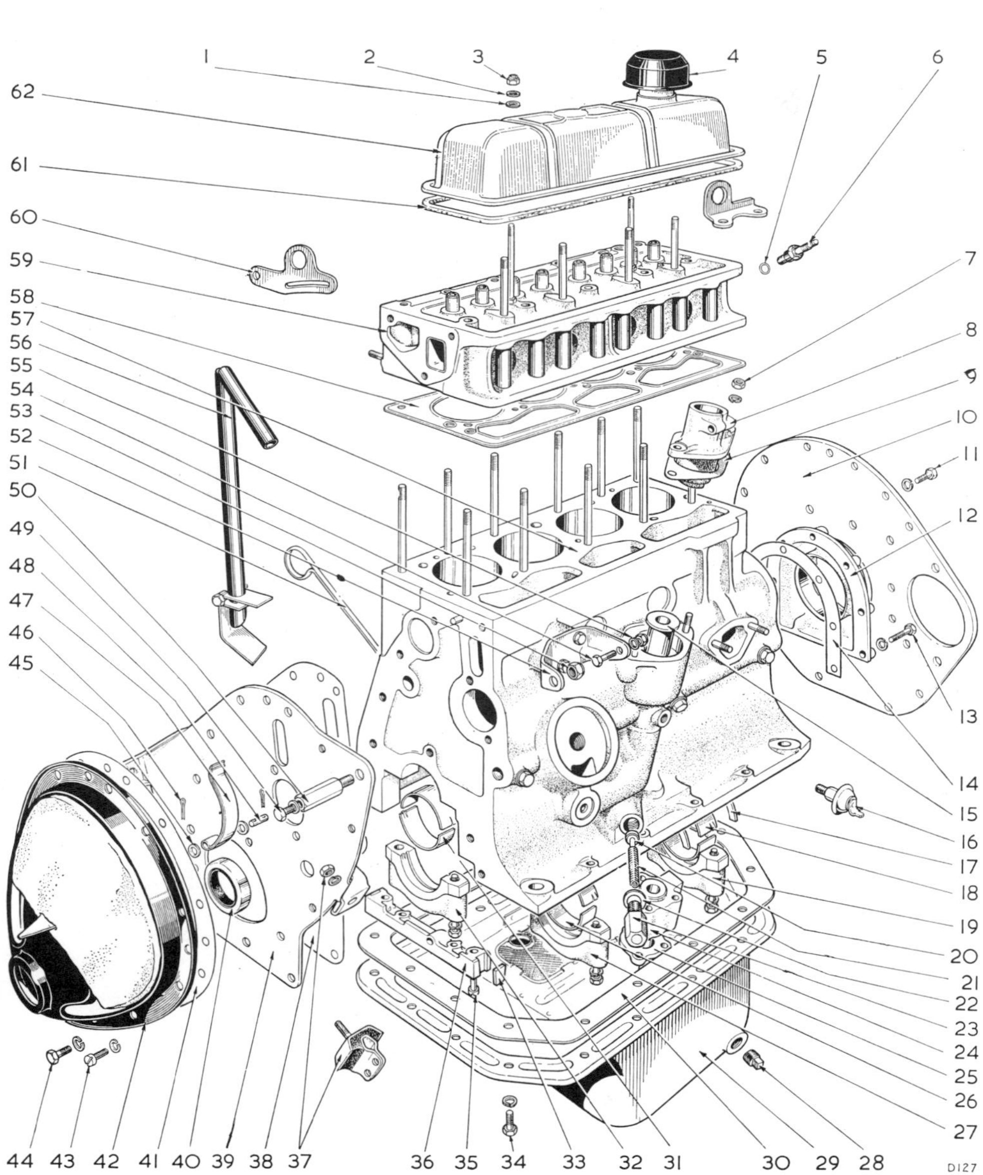

Fixed parts

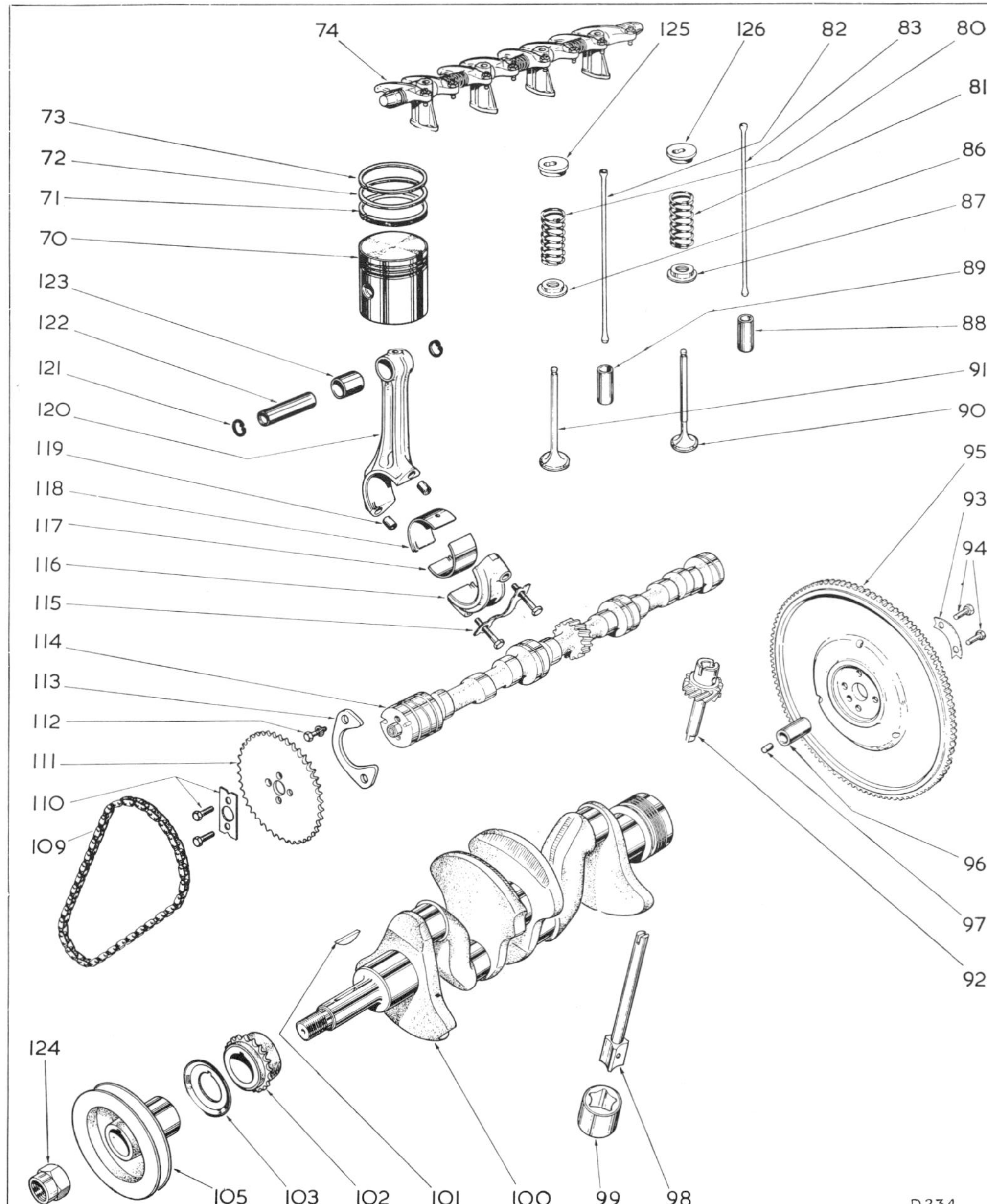

Moving parts

Fig. 8. Exploded views of Herald and Spitfire engine

Key to Fig. 8

Fixed Parts

1 Fibre washer
2 Plain washer
3 Nyloc nut
4 Filler cap
5 Copper/asbestos washer
6 Sparking plug
7 Nut
8 Adaptor
9 Gasket
10 Rear engine plate
11 Bolt
12 Rear oil seal
13 Bolt
14 Gasket
15 Oil pump drive shaft bush
16 Oil pressure switch
17 Crankshaft thrust washer
18 Rear bearing shell
19 Rear bearing cap
20 Relief valve
21 Spring
22 Copper washer
23 Cap nut
24 Oil pump body
25 Oil pump end plate
26 Centre bearing shell
27 Centre main bearing cap
28 Sump plug
29 Sump
30 Sump gasket
31 Front bearing shell
32 Front main bearing cap
33 Sealing wedges
34 Sump bolt
35 Slotted screw
36 Front sealing block
37 Front engine mounting
38 Gasket
39 Front engine plate
40 Oil seal
41 Gasket
42 Front timing cover
43 Slotted setscrew
44 Bolt
45 Plain washer
46 Split pin
47 Chain tensioner
48 Pivot pin
49 Bolt
50 Generator pedestal
51 Dipstick
52 Bracket
53 Nyloc nut
54 Bolt
55 Nyloc nut
56 Breather pipe
57 Cylinder block
58 Cylinder head gasket
59 Cylinder head
60 Generator adjusting link
61 Rocker cover gasket
62 Rocker cover

Moving Parts

70 Piston
71 Oil control ring
72 Taper compression ring
73 Plain compression ring
74 Rocker assembly
80 Spring—outer
81 Spring—outer
82 Push rod
83 Push rod
86 Lower collar
87 Lower collar
88 Tappet
89 Tappet
90 Exhaust valve
91 Inlet valve
92 Distributor and oil pump drive gear
93 Lock tab
94 Bolt
95 Flywheel
96 Bush
97 Dowel
98 Inner rotor and spindle
99 Outer rotor
100 Crankshaft
101 Key
102 Sprocket
103 Flinger
105 Crankshaft pulley
109 Timing chain
110 Bolts and lock tab
111 Camshaft sprocket
112 Bolt
113 Keeper plate
114 Camshaft
115 Bolt and locktab
116 Conn-rod cap
117 Conn-rod bearing shell—lower
118 Conn-rod bearing shell—upper
119 Dowels
120 Conn-rod
121 Circlip
122 Gudgeon pin
123 Gudgeon pin bush
124 Nut
125 Collet
126 Collet

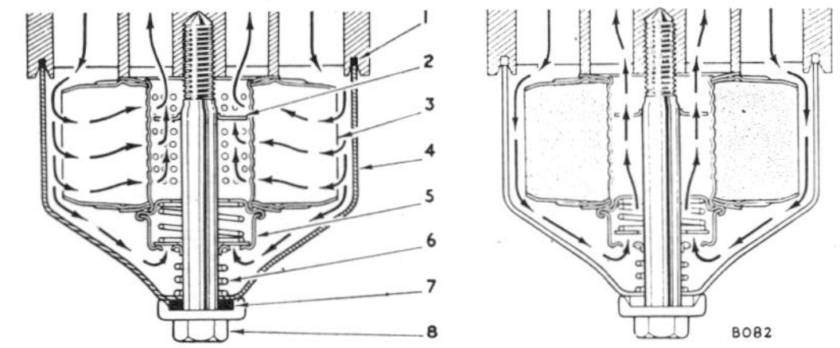

1 Seal 2 Locating washer 3 Element 4 Casing 5 By-pass valve 6 Spring 7 Seal 8 Securing bolt

Fig. 3. Oil filtration (Vitesse)

Fig. 4. Open ventilation system

Fig. 5. Closed ventilation system

Fig. 6. Emission control system

Oil Filtration (VITESSE 1600) (Fig. 3)

The cartridge type oil filter and oil flow are shown in Fig. 3.

Renewing Oil Filter Element (VITESSE 1600) (Fig. 3)

With a receptacle placed to catch escaping oil, unscrew securing bolt (8), withdraw bowl (4), filter element (3) and discard element.

Using non-fluffy material, thoroughly clean components. Examine for defective rubber seals and broken springs and renew as necessary. Remove the rubber sealing ring (1) and install the new ring provided with the replacement filter element.

Insert new element and re-assemble filter to crankcase. Check that lip of bowl is clean and undamaged and is properly seated in engine crankcase before finally tightening securing bolt. Do not overtighten.

CRANKCASE VENTILATION

Three types of crankcase ventilation systems occur in the engines with which this section is concerned.

Open Ventilation System (Fig. 4)

This method of crankcase ventilation provides for the relief of crankcase pressure by means of a simple, open pipe from the crankcase to atmosphere.

Closed Ventilation System (Fig. 5)

Engines fitted with closed ventilation dispense with the crankcase ventilation pipe and have the ventilation pipe aperture in the crankcase sealed. A breather pipe connects the rocker cover to the air cleaner. This pipe prevents the build-up of crankcase compression and also serves as a balance pipe to admit air to the crankcase, dependent upon air intake velocity and crankcase pressure.

Emission Control System (Fig. 6)

The emission control system is similar to the closed ventilation system but offers refined control in balancing crankcase ventilation and the escape of crankcase gases. This is achieved by using an oil filler cap which incorporates a non-return valve and an emission control valve through which the rocker cover is connected to the induction manifold.

The emission control valve responds to induction manifold depression, that is, when manifold depression is greatest during idling, over-run and light loading the emission valve restricts crankcase gas flow. The non-return valve in the rocker cover oil filler cap provides pressure balance between crankcase and atmosphere.

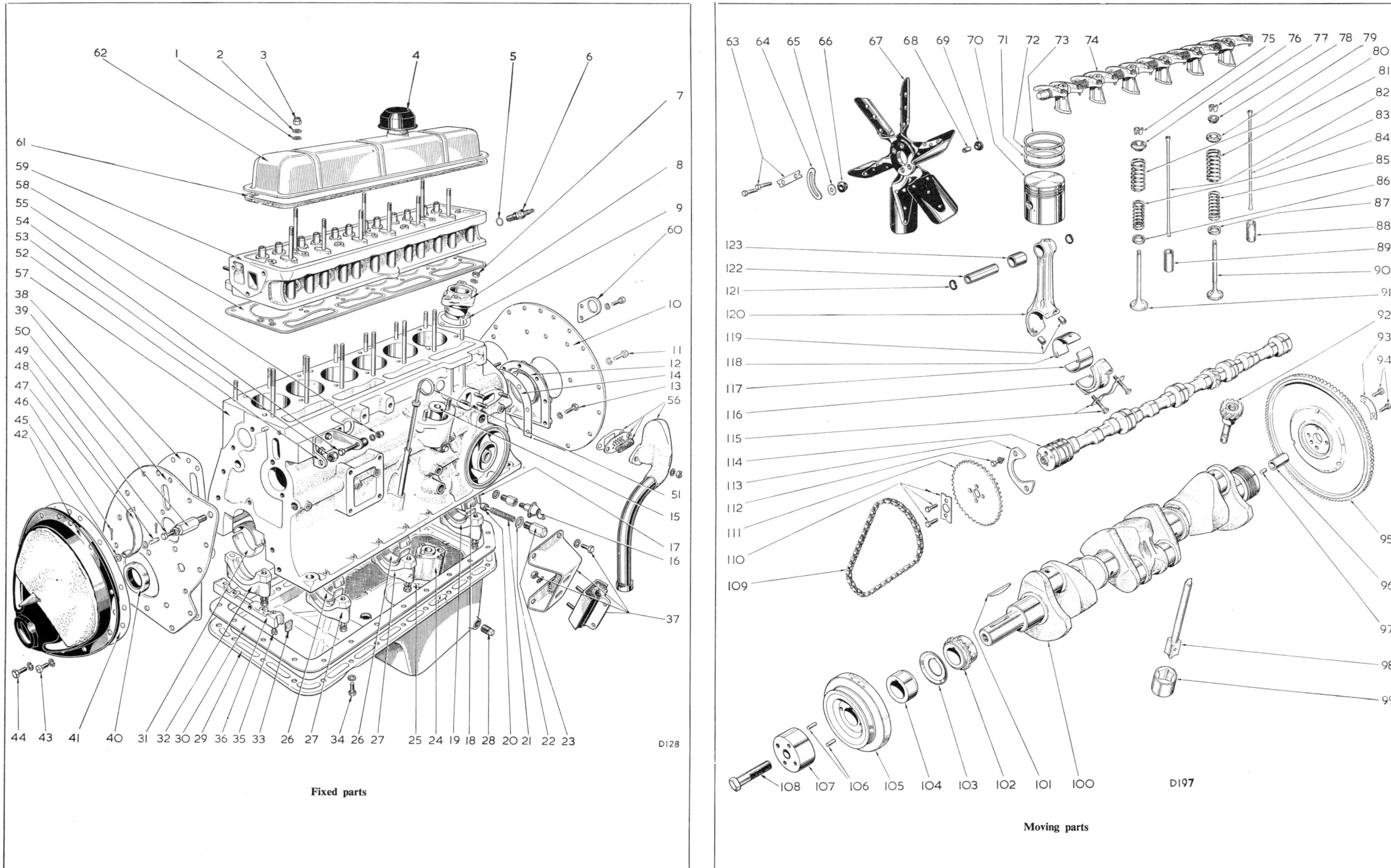

Fixed parts

Moving parts

Fig. 9. Exploded views of Vitesse engine

Key to Fig. 9

Fixed Parts

1 Fibre washer
2 Plain washer
3 Nyloc nut
4 Filler cap
5 Copper/asbestos washer
6 Sparking plug
7 Nut
8 Adaptor
9 Gasket
10 Rear engine plate
11 Bolt
12 Rear oil seal
13 Bolt
14 Gasket
15 Oil pump drive shaft bush
16 Oil pressure switch
17 Crankshaft thrust washer
18 Rear bearing shell
19 Rear bearing cap
20 Relief valve
21 Spring
22 Copper washer
23 Cap nut
24 Oil pump body
25 Oil pump end plate
26 Centre bearing shell
27 Centre main bearing cap
28 Sump plug
29 Sump
30 Sump gasket
31 Front bearing shell
32 Front main bearing cap
33 Sealing wedges
34 Sump bolt
35 Slotted screw
36 Front sealing block
37 Front engine mounting
38 Gasket
39 Front engine plate
40 Oil seal
41 Gasket
42 Front timing cover
43 Slotted setscrew
44 Bolt
45 Plain washer
46 Split pin
47 Chain tensioner
48 Pivot pin
49 Bolt
50 Generator pedestal
51 Dipstick
52 Bracket
53 Nyloc nut
54 Bolt
55 Nyloc nut
56 Breather pipe
57 Cylinder block
58 Cylinder head gasket
59 Cylinder head
60 Generator adjusting link
61 Rocker cover gasket
62 Rocker cover

Moving Parts

63 Bolts and lock tabs
64 Balancer
65 Washer
66 Rubber bush
67 Fan assembly
68 Steel bush
69 Rubber bush
70 Piston
71 Oil control ring
72 Taper compression ring
73 Plain compression ring
74 Rocker assembly
75 Split cotters
76 Collar
77 Split cotters
78 Inner collar (exhaust)
79 Outer collar (exhaust)
80 Spring—outer
81 Spring—outer
82 Push rod
83 Push rod
84 Spring—inner
85 Spring—inner
86 Lower collar
87 Lower collar
88 Tappet
89 Tappet
90 Exhaust valve
91 Inlet valve
92 Distributor and oil pump drive gear
93 Lock tab
94 Bolt
95 Flywheel
96 Bush
97 Dowel
98 Inner rotor and spindle
99 Outer rotor
100 Crankshaft
101 Key
102 Sprocket
103 Flinger
104 Distance piece
105 Crankshaft pulley
106 Dowels
107 Fan boss
108 Bolt
109 Timing chain
110 Bolts and lock tab
111 Camshaft sprocket
112 Bolt
113 Keeper plate
114 Camshaft
115 Bolt and lock tab
116 Conn-rod cap
117 Conn-rod bearing shell—lower
118 Conn-rod bearing shell—upper
119 Dowels
120 Conn-rod
121 Circlip
122 Gudgeon pin
123 Gudgeon pin bush

EXPLODED VIEWS OF VITESSE ENGINE

ENGINE AND GEARBOX REMOVAL

HERALD 1200, 12/50, 13/60 and SPITFIRE
(Figs. 10 and 11)

Fig. 10. R.H. view of engine

Fig. 11. L.H. view of engine

Disconnect the battery and drain the cooling system, engine and gearbox. Remove bonnet (Group 5).

To prevent fuel siphoning disconnect and plug the rubber fuel pipe, connecting the fuel pump to the tank in the engine compartment.

Refer to Fig. 10 and disconnect: (R.H.S.)

— Air cleaner/s (1).
— Carburettor, choke and throttle controls (2 and 3).
— Starter motor cable.
— Exhaust pipe flange (4) and bracket to clutch housing.
— Heater hoses (5 and 6).

Remove radiator and hoses.

Refer to Fig. 11 and disconnect: (L.H.S.)

— Coil cables (7 and 8).
— Oil pressure switch cable (9).
— Generator 'D' and 'F' cables (10 and 11).
— Earth strap.
— Fuel pipe to pump (12).
— Tachometer cable (Spitfire only).

Working inside the vehicle and referring to Figs. 12, 13 and 14, remove:

— Front seats and carpets.
— Cover attachments, facia support bracket (Spitfire) and gearbox cover.
— Speedometer cable.
— Clutch slave cylinder (7).
— Front end of propellor shaft (12 and 13).
— Overdrive solenoid cables (if fitted).

Remove the gearchange extension and fit a temporary cardboard cover to prevent the entry of foreign matter.

Attach a lifting cable to the engine lifting eyes and, supporting the engine on a hoist, release:

— Front engine mountings (14) Fig. 11.
— Rear engine mountings (10) Fig. 14.

Lift the engine and gearbox until the sump clears the chassis crossmember.

Continue to lift the unit and simultaneously move it forward until the gearbox is clear of the bulkhead aperture.

Manoeuvre the unit clear of the vehicle.

ENGINE AND GEARBOX INSTALLATION

HERALD and SPITFIRE
(Figs. 10, 11, 12, 13 and 14)

Refit the clutch unit and gearbox to the engine. Using a lifting cable and hoist, lift and manoeuvre the engine and gearbox unit into position.

Refit:

— Rear mountings (10) (Fig. 14).
— Front mounting (14) (Fig. 11).
— Gearbox extension.
— Propellor shaft.
— Clutch slave cylinder.
— Speedo cable.
— Overdrive solenoid cables (if fitted).
— Gearbox cover, facia support casting (Spitfire).
— Carpets and seats.
— Starter motor cable.
— Exhaust pipe flange (4) and bracket to clutch housing (Fig. 10).
— Heater hoses (5 and 6) (Fig. 10)
— Carburettor choke and throttle controls (2 and 3) (Fig. 10).
— Air cleaner (1) (Fig. 10).
— Radiator and hoses.
— Engine earthing strap.
— Fuel pipe to pump (12) (Fig. 11).
— Cables to coil (7) (8) and 'D' and 'F' cable to generator (10) (11) (Fig. 11).
— Oil pressure switch cable (9) (Fig. 11).

Refit the bonnet (see Group 5). Re-connect the battery, refill the cooling system, sump and gearbox to the correct levels.

Prime the carburettors, start the engine and tune the carburettors as described in Section 3.

Fig. 12. Facia support (Spitfire)

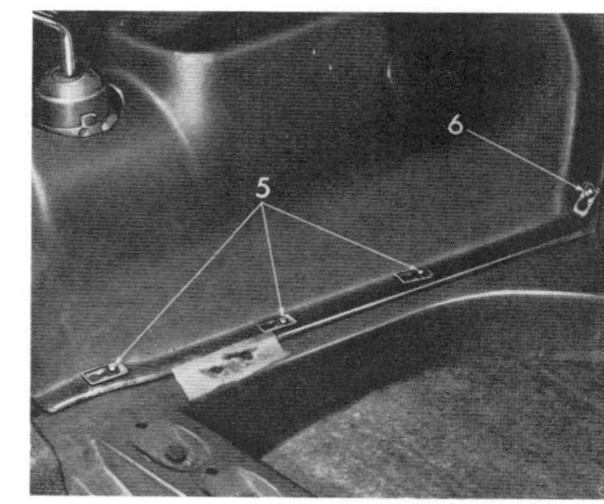

Fig. 13. Gearbox cover

Fig. 14. L.H. view of gearbox

ENGINE AND GEARBOX REMOVAL

VITESSE 1600 (Figs. 15 to 19)

Disconnect the battery and drain the cooling system, engine and gearbox. Remove bonnet (Group 5).

To prevent fuel siphoning disconnect and plug the rubber fuel pipe, connecting the fuel pump to tank in the engine compartment.

Refer to Fig. 15 and disconnect: (R.H.S.)
— Air cleaner/s (1).
— Carburettor, choke and throttle controls (2 and 3).
— Starter motor cable.
— Exhaust pipe flange and bracket to clutch housing.
— Heater hoses (5 and 6).

Remove radiator and hoses.

Refer to Fig. 16 and disconnect: (L.H.S.)
— Coil cables.
— Oil pressure switch cable (9).
— Generator 'D' and 'F' cables (10 and 11).
— Earth strap.
— Fuel pipe to pump (12).
— Fan assembly (13).

Working inside the vehicle and referring to Fig. 19 remove:
— Front seats and carpets.
— Cover attachments and gearbox cover.
— Speedometer cable (3).
— Clutch slave cylinder (5) and manoeuvre it through the aperture clear of gearbox.
— Front end of propellor shaft (1).
— Overdrive solenoid cables (if fitted).

Remove the gearchange extension and fit a temporary cardboard cover to prevent the entry of foreign matter.

Attach a lifting cable to the engine lifting eyes and, supporting the engine on a hoist, release:
— Front engine mountings (1), Fig. 18.
— Rear engine mountings (2), Fig. 19.

Lift the engine and gearbox until the sump clears the chassis crossmember.

Continue to lift the unit and simultaneously move it forward until the gearbox is clear of the bulkhead aperture.

Manoeuvre the unit clear of the vehicle.

Fig. 15. R.H. view of engine

Fig. 16. L.H. view of engine

ENGINE AND GEARBOX INSTALLATION

VITESSE 1600 (Figs. 15 to 19)

Refit the clutch unit and gearbox to the engine. Using a lifting cable and hoist, lift and manoeuvre the engine and gearbox unit into position.

Refit:
— Rear mountings (2), Fig. 19.
— Front mountings (1), Fig. 18.
— Gearchange extension.
— Propellor shaft.
— Clutch slave cylinder.
— Speedo cable.
— Overdrive solenoid cables (if fitted).
— Gearbox cover, Fig. 13.
— Carpets and seats.
— Starter motor cable.
— Exhaust pipe flange and bracket to clutch housing.
— Heater hoses.
— Carburettor choke and throttle controls.
— Air cleaner.
— Radiator and hoses.

Referring to Fig. 16, refit:
— Engine earthing strap.
— Fuel pipe to pump (12).
— Cable to coil (8) and 'D' and 'F' cable to generator (10 and 11).
— Oil pressure switch cable (9).

Fit the shouldered rubber bushes (66), Fig. 9, steel bushes (68), balancer (64) and fan (67), aligning the holes in the balancer, fan and boss (107) with the shank of a $\frac{1}{16}$ in. (1·6 mm.) dia. drill to maintain the original balance of the assembly.

Refit the bonnet. Re-connect the battery, refill the cooling system, sump and gearbox to the correct levels.

Prime the carburettors, start the engine and tune the carburettors as described in Section 3.

Fig. 17. Installing engine

Fig. 18. Front engine mountings

Fig. 19. Gearbox mountings

RECONDITIONED ENGINE UNITS

Engine reconditioning is a service function involving the use of special equipment. For this reason, and also to minimise the time a vehicle is withdrawn from service, an engine reconditioning scheme is operated by the Company.

Replacement engines are, in every respect, to Company standards and are comparable in finish, performance and longevity to new units. As such they are covered by the same terms of warranty as are applicable to new units. Figs. 20 and 21 show typical replacement units.

Engines withdrawn from service and returned for reconditioning should be drained, removed of the items listed below and have all apertures sealed.

Water pump.
Generator, generator bracket, and adjusting strap.
Fan belt.
Fan (Vitesse).
Fuel pump and fuel pipes.
Inlet and exhaust manifolds.
Distributor and vacuum pipe.
Oil filter body.
Breather pipe and gauze (when fitted).
Coil (Vitesse).
Oil filler cap.
Clutch unit.

Fig. 20. Herald and Spitfire reconditioned units

Fig. 21. Vitesse reconditioned unit

ENGINE DISMANTLING AND RECONDITIONING

Within the following pages will be found all information relating to engine dismantling, reconditioning and engine assembly procedures. The information given, together with the tolerances which precede this section, relate principally to complete restoration and new engine build. Where partial or temporary repair work is undertaken discretion is left to the experience of the repairer to extract and modify this information to suit individual requirements and circumstances.

For purposes of explanation it is assumed that the engine is drained of oil and is located on a bench or suitable engine stand. For operations performed with the engine 'in situ', refer to page 1·139.

Attention is drawn to the fact that maximum engine life can be obtained only if cleanliness in all aspects of engine tuning, repair and overhaul work is observed.

Auxiliary Equipment

Remove:

— Generator mounting bolts, fan belt and generator.
— Radiator fan (Heralds and Spitfire only: Vitesse fan is removed prior to engine removal).
— Auxiliary header tank (Early Vitesse and Spitfire 4 only).
— Water pump and thermostat housing.
— Fuel and vacuum pipes.
— Inlet and exhaust manifolds.
— Coil (Vitesse only), distributor, sparking plugs and fuel pump.
— Oil filter and dipstick.

Cylinder Head

Remove rocker cover nuts and lift off rocker cover and gasket.

Evenly slacken and remove rocker pedestal nuts. Lift off rocker gear, and withdraw push rods.

Remove cylinder head nuts in reverse sequence to that shown in Fig. 25, lift off cylinder head and gasket and withdraw cam followers.

Following the removal of the valves (described on page 1·123) remove carbon from combustion chambers and ports and run a plug tap through the sparking plug holes. Thoroughly clean cylinder head and examine for cracks and distortion. Renew core plugs.

Rocker Gear (1200, 12/50, VITESSE, SPITFIRE 4 and Mk. 2)

Drive out pins securing end caps to rocker shaft, withdraw end caps (2) and double spring washer. Slide off rockers, pedestals and springs, remove screw securing rear pedestal and withdraw rear pedestal from shaft.

Note locations and order of components (refer Fig. 24).

Renew all worn components and ensure oilways in rocker shaft are clear. The grinding of rocker tips is not recommended.

Renew end cap pins and assemble in reverse order ensuring that rear pedestal locating screw properly engages rocker shaft.

Fig. 22. Vitesse engine

Fig. 23. Spitfire engine

1 Rocker shaft
2 End cap
3 Mills pin
4 Locknut
5 Rocker, R.H.
6 Adjusting screw
7 Pedestal, rear
8 Shakeproof washer
9 Phillips head screw
10 Rocker, L.H.
11 Distance spring
12 Pedestal
13 Centre distance spring

NOTE: The Vitesse rocker assembly is similar but has 12 rockers, 6 pedestals and 5 distance springs.

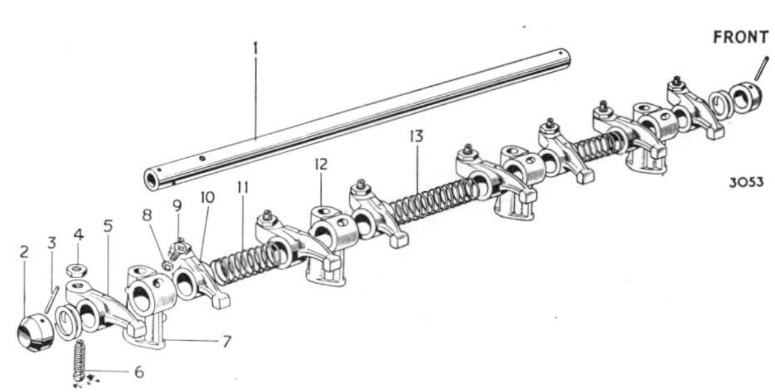

Fig. 24. Rocker gear (1200, 12/50, Vitesse, Spitfire 4 and Mk. 2)

Fig. 25. Cylinder head nut tightening sequence
(Refer also to Fig. 58)

Rocker Gear (13/60 and SPITFIRE Mk. 3)
Withdraw cotter pin at rocker shaft ends and slide off rockers, pedestals and springs from front end of shaft noting order and location of components (refer Fig. 26).

Remove screw locating rear pedestal to shaft and withdraw rear pedestal and rocker.

Renew all worn components and ensure oilways in rocker shaft are clear. The grinding of rocker tips is not recommended.

Renew cotter pins and assemble in reverse order ensuring that rear pedestal locating screw properly engages rocker shaft and that the double spring washers are correctly positioned in end pedestals.

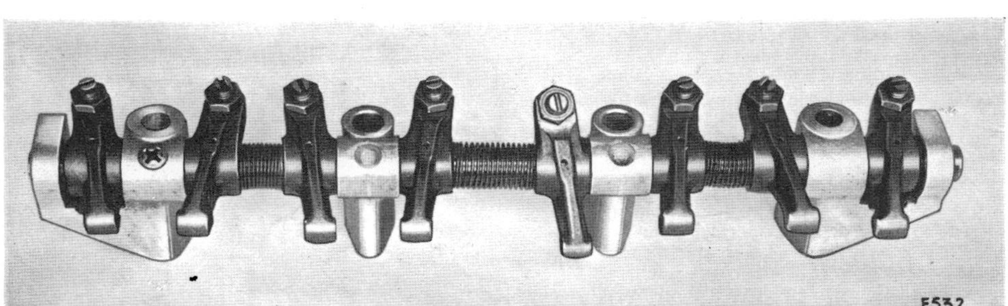

Fig. 26. Rocker gear (13/60 and Spitfire Mk. 3)

Valves
Using a suitable valve spring compressor remove valve split collets from all engines except the Herald 1200, 12/50 and 13/60, which employ special caps. These caps can be released by placing a block of wood under the valve, compressing the spring with the fingers and sliding the valve cap aside. Note the valve assembly details shown in Fig. 28.

Withdraw valves and springs and remove carbon from combustion chambers and ports.

Check valve stems for wear and straightness, replacing or renewing valves as required. A valve should be renewed if refacing has reduced its head thickness to less than $\frac{1}{32}$ in (0·8 mm.), Fig. 29.

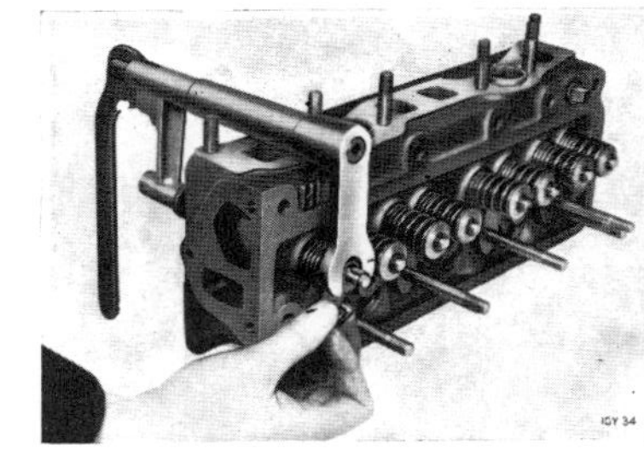

Fig. 27. Removing valves

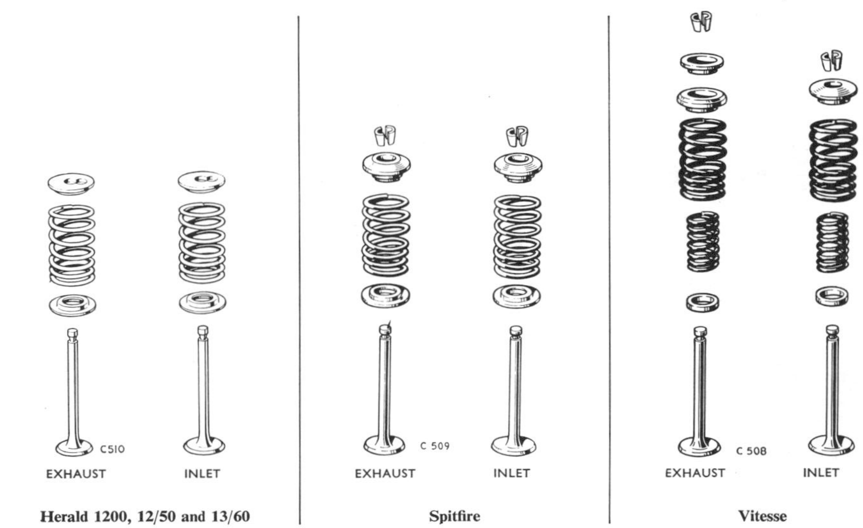

Fig. 28. Valve assembly details

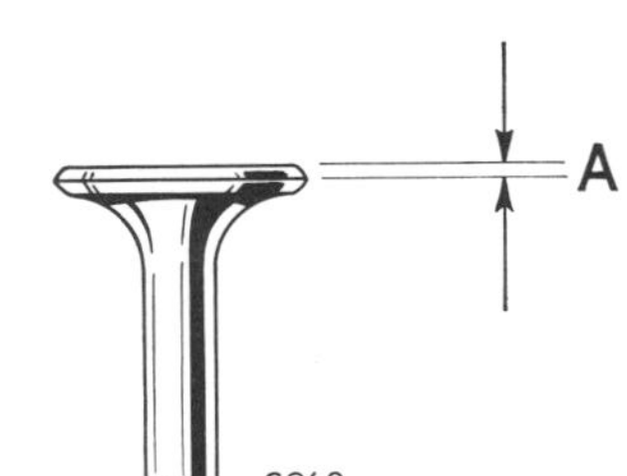

Fig. 29. Valve head thickness

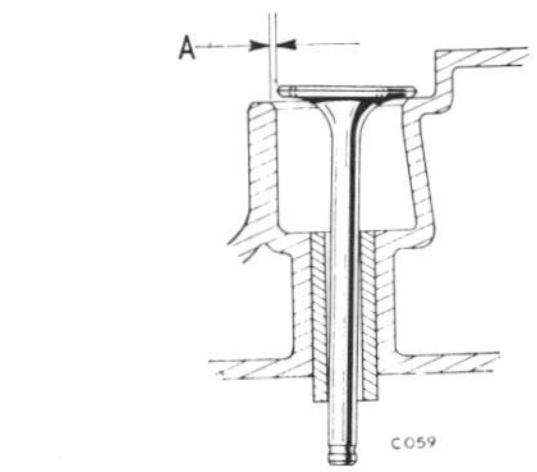

Fig. 30. Checking valve guide wear

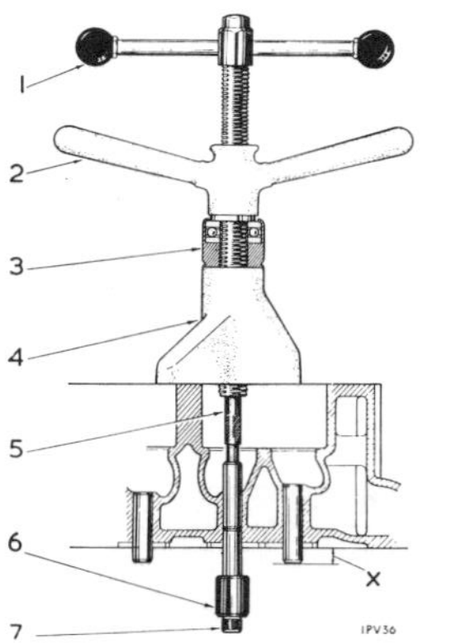

1 Handle
2 Threaded handle
3 Thrust race
4 Body
5 Adaptor
6 Distance collar
7 Knurled nut
X = 0·749″—0·751″

Fig. 31. Renewing valve guides

Valve Guides

Check the valve guide wear by inserting a new valve, lifting it ⅛ in. (3·2 mm.) from its seat and rocking it sideways (Fig. 30). Movement of the valve head across its seat must not exceed 0·020 in. (0·5 mm.). If required, renew the guide by using Churchill Tool No. S.60A-6 (Fig. 31).

Valve guide protrusion above the top face of the cylinder head must be:

0·749 in. to 0·751 in. (19·025 to 19·075 mm.).

With the chamfered edge leading, pull the new valve guide into the cylinder head from the valve spring side. Use of the correct limiting sleeves (item 6, Fig. 31) will ensure that the guide protrudes the correct distance of 0·75 in. (19·05 mm.) above the cylinder head when fitted. Always reface valve seat after renewing guide.

Valve Seats

Check valve seats for pitting and wear, and reface as necessary, removing the minimum of metal possible to obtain a gas tight seating. If a 15° cutter is used to reduce seat width and rectify pocketing the machined diameter must not exceed that given in Fig. 32.

Valve Seat Inserts

When valve seats cannot be rectified by refacing, the original condition can be restored by machining the cylinder head to the dimensions given on page 1·107 and fitting valve seat inserts.

Remove all swarf and press insert squarely into cylinder head. Secure by carefully peening the metal around the edge of the insert.

If both inlet and exhaust inserts are required, fit the inlet insert before machining the exhaust inset pocket. Cut or grind valve seat face.

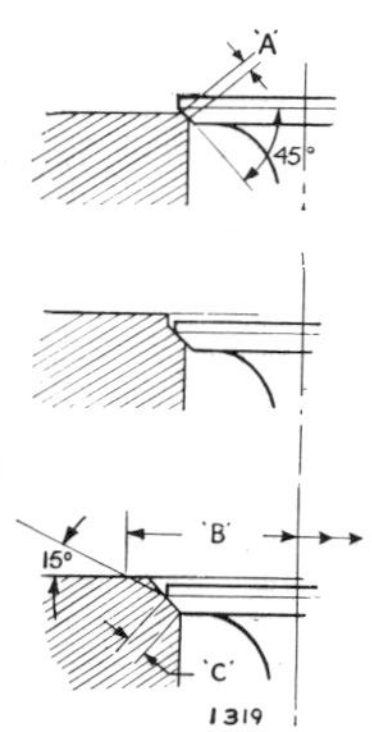

A = 0·060″ (1·52 mm.)

B	Inlet	Exhaust
Spitfire	1·378″ (35·0 mm.)	1·252″ (31·8 mm.)
Herald 1200, 12/50	1·440″ (36·5 mm.)	1·252″ (31·8 mm.)
Vitesse	1·378″ (35·0 mm.)	1·252″ (31·8 mm.)

C = 0·10″ (0·25 mm.) max.

Fig. 32. Correct and incorrect valve seat condition

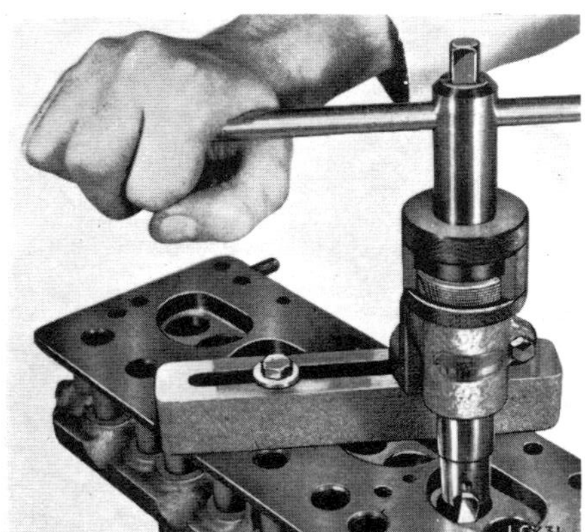

Fig. 33. Boring cylinder head for valve seat insert using tool No. MFS6056-1

Valve Springs

Check valve springs for cracks, distortion and load lengths. This data is included in page 1·106. When defective springs are evident fit a complete new set. Renew valve springs when top overhauls and complete reconditioning is carried out.

Grinding-in Valves

After valve seat refacing, grind-in the valves to their respective positions ensuring that all trace of grinding paste is removed. Do not intermix valves after grinding-in.

Cam Followers

Check cam followers for chips, scores, ridges and wear. Renew as necessary and ensure that cam followers are free to slide and rotate in their respective locations.

Flywheel and Backplate

Straighten lock plate tabs (if fitted), unscrew the flywheel bolts and withdraw the flywheel. Remove bolts securing backplate and withdraw backplate.

NOTE: The original bolts and lock plates used to secure the flywheel on early engines have been superseded by special bolts which can be used on all engines.

Flywheel Clutch Face

A scored flywheel clutch face can be rectified by refacing in a lathe provided that the original thickness of the flywheel is not reduced by more than 0·030 in. (0·762 mm.). Care must be taken to ensure that the run-out tolerance is observed and balance is maintained.

Renewing Flywheel Ring Gear

Support flywheel (clutch face, uppermost) on hardwood blocks evenly distributed and clear of ring gear. Evenly drive ring gear from flywheel in small movements. Thoroughly clean flywheel periphery and reverse flywheel on hardwood blocks (clutch face downwards). Clean and expand the new ring gear by evenly heating; uneven heat distribution will create ring distortion.

Remove starter ring from heat source and, with chamfered edge of ring teeth adjacent to clutch face of flywheel, evenly place ring gear in position on flywheel. Allow ring gear to cool before disturbing flywheel.

Rear Oil Seal and Housing (Fig. 39)

Oil sealing at the rear of crankshaft on early Heralds, Spitfires and all Vitesse 1600 engines, is effected by a close-fitting housing with an oil return scroll machined on its inner bore. A redesigned housing, fitted to all current engines, accommodates a renewable 'lipped' seal which can be ejected by driving a pin punch through the two holes provided in the housing. To remove the housing:

Take out the securing bolts and withdraw the housing and gasket from the cylinder block.

Fig. 34. Fitting valve seat inserts using Tool No. S56057. Inset shows combustion chamber peened over insert

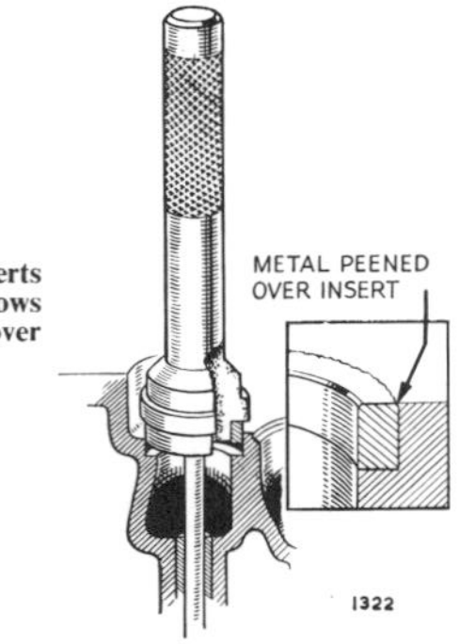

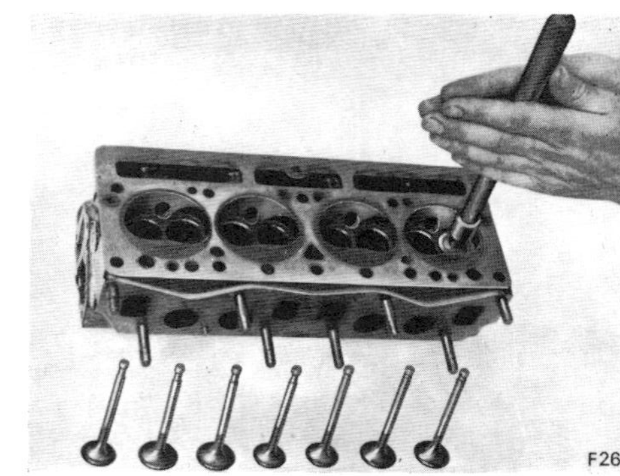

Fig. 35. Grinding-in valves

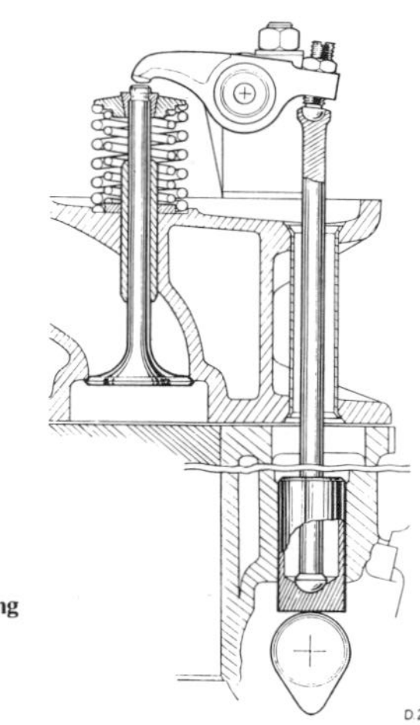

Fig. 36. Valve operating mechanism

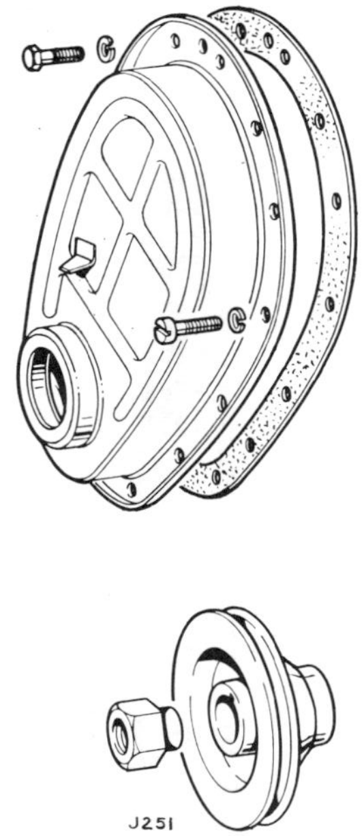

Fig. 37. Crankshaft pulley and timing case
Herald and Spitfire

Fig. 38. Crankshaft pulley and timing case
Vitesse

Crankshaft Pulley (1200, 12/50, 13/60 and SPITFIRE)

Straighten lock tabs, unscrew crankshaft pulley nut and withdraw the pulley.

Crankshaft Pulley (VITESSE)

Remove crankshaft pulley bolt and withdraw spacer, crankshaft pulley and damper assembly.

Timing Cover, Timing Gears and Front Plate

Remove bolts and screws securing timing cover to cylinder block and withdraw timing cover and gasket. Straighten locking tabs on camshaft sprocket bolts and remove bolts. Remove camshaft sprocket and timing chain. Withdraw oil thrower. Withdraw crankshaft sprocket and shims. Remove camshaft keeper bolts and keeper plate. Remove bolts securing front plate to cylinder block and withdraw front plate and gasket.

Camshaft

Camshaft withdrawal necessitates prior removal of the fuel pump, distributor pedestal and gear, cam followers, timing cover, timing chain and camshaft keeper plate. Withdraw camshaft taking care to avoid damaging cams and bearings.

Camshaft Bushes (SPITFIRE Mk. 2 and Mk. 3 only)

Pre-formed camshaft bushes fitted to cylinder blocks of Spitfire Mk. 2 and Mk. 3 engines should not be disturbed as special tools are not available. Where circumstances demand renewal, a suitable draw-bar and adaptor will be required and it will be necessary to remove the core plug at the rear of the camshaft. New bushes must not be line-bored or hand scraped and the oil holes must accurately register with corresponding drillings in the cylinder block.

Sump

Remove securing bolts and withdraw sump and gasket from crankcase. Sump strainers (where fitted) are retained by self-tapping screws. Renew damaged or choked strainers.

Oil Pump

Remove three securing bolts and withdraw oil pump from crankcase. With the oil pump assembled clean and dry, but minus the combined cover and intake pipe, check rotor clearances as illustrated (Fig. 40). Renew worn or unserviceable items as necessary.

Distributor Drive Shaft Bush

Insert the distributor drive shaft into its bush and rock the shaft to assess bearing wear. Use a stepped drift to eject a worn bush, extracting it via the distributor pedestal flange.

Enter a new bush from pedestal flange and drive carefully into position.

Connecting Rods and Pistons

Rotate crankshaft to bring each connecting rod in turn to the bottom of its stroke and straighten locking tabs (if fitted) on connecting rod bolts. Current engines are fitted with special bolts for which no locking device is required.

Remove connecting rod bolts, bearing caps and upper and lower shell bearing halves.

Withdraw connecting rods and piston from top of cylinder block: do not intermix bearings and caps.

Removing Pistons from Connecting Rods

Early and current engines are fitted with floating gudgeon pins. Some engines built between these periods are fitted with interference fit gudgeon pins. The latter type is held solely by the tightness of its fit in an unbushed connecting rod. Pistons employing this type of gudgeon pin are not fitted with circlips.

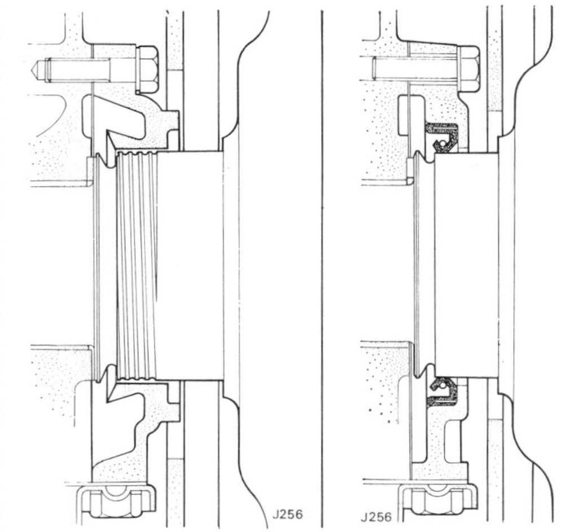

Scroll type Seal type

Fig. 39. Crankshaft rear seal

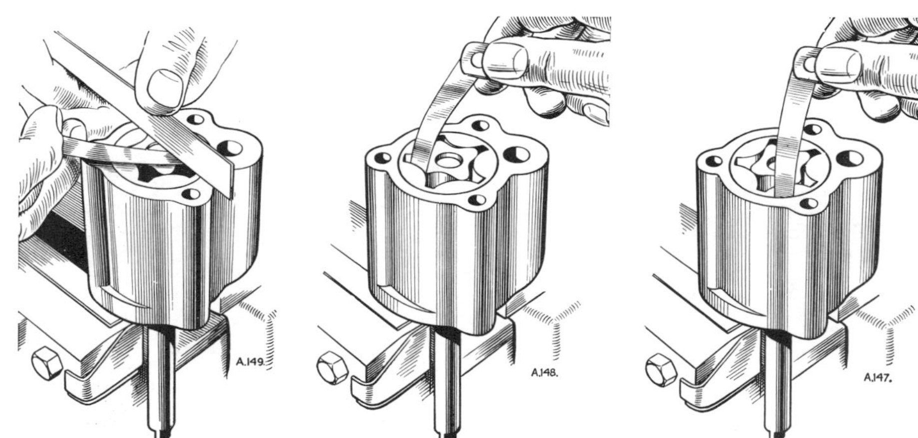

Fig. 40. Checking oil pump clearances

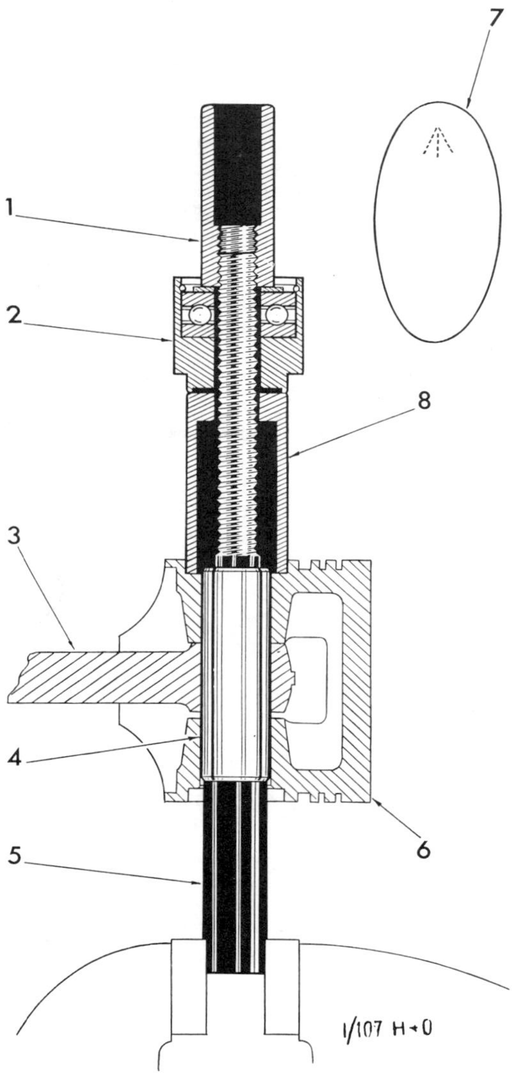

Fig. 41. Removing interference fit gudgeon pins

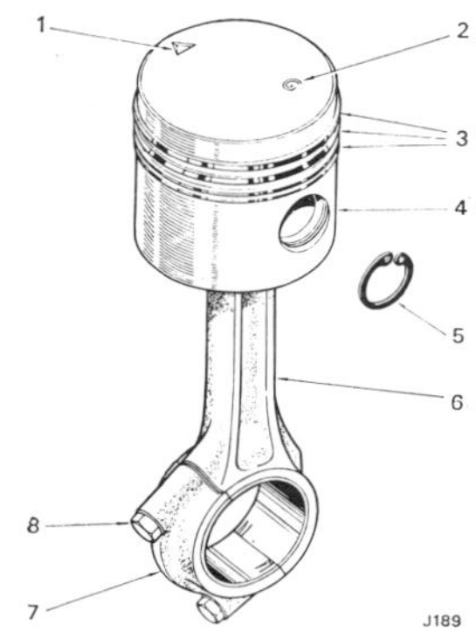

Fig. 42. Piston and connecting rod

Floating Gudgeon Pins. Remove circlips from pistons and withdraw gudgeon pins. Immerse piston in hot water to facilitate easy withdrawal of tight gudgeon pins.

Interference Fit Gudgeon Pins. Use tool S334 (Fig. 41) to remove and replace an interference fit gudgeon pin. Avoid repeated insertion and withdrawal as this will destroy the interference fit between pin and connecting rod. Lubricate threads of the special tool with normal lubricating oil as friction reducing oils or greases will give false torque readings. Assemble tool to piston (Fig. 41) noting that the sleeve (8) will locate only on one side of the piston. Tighten nut (1) and draw gudgeon pin (4) into sleeve (8).

Renewing Gudgeon Pin Bushes

Using a suitably stepped adaptor, eject worn bush from connecting rod and press new bush into position, ensuring that the oil hole is properly aligned. Fine bore or broach the new bush to the size determined by the gudgeon pin (refer page 1·102).

A correctly fitted gudgeon pin (dry) will pass through the bush with thumb pressure at 68°F room temperature. If a dry gudgeon pin passes through the bush under its own weight it is too slack.

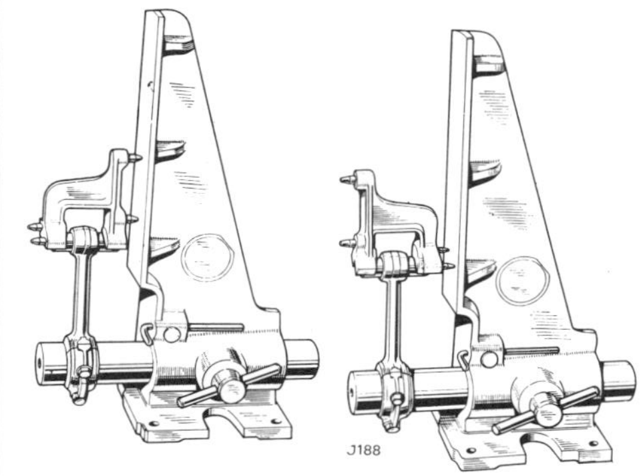

Fig. 43. Checking connecting rod alignment

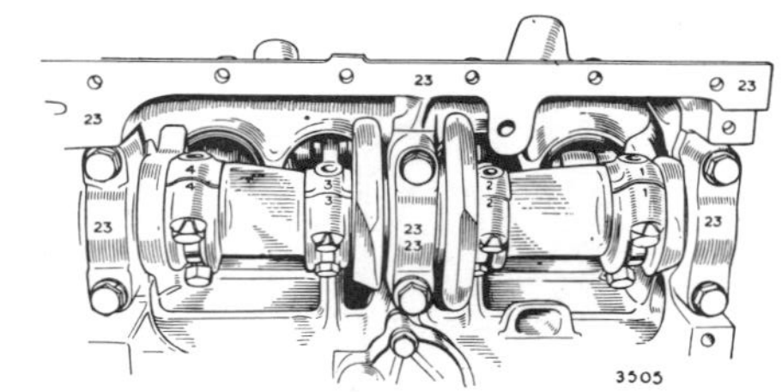

Fig. 44. Main and connecting rod bearing markings

Connecting Rod Alignment

Check connecting rods for alignment and twist. In both conditions the maximum tolerance over gudgeon pin length (see Dimensions and Tolerances) should not be exceeded. Rods found to exceed this tolerance should be renewed, or corrected with a suitable bending tool.

Crankshaft

Take out two securing screws and remove front sealing block from crankcase. Straighten locking tabs (if fitted to crankshaft main bearing cap bolts), unscrew the bolts and lift off bearing caps, lower shell bearing halves, thrust bearings, crankshaft and upper bearing halves. Do not intermix bearings or caps. Note that current engines are fitted with special bolts for which no locking device is required. Check crankshaft for scoring, taper and ovality and regrind as necessary to next undersize or to a limit of minus 0·040 in. (1·016 mm.).

Cylinder Block

Check cylinder bores and camshaft bearings for wear and damage and rebore cylinders as necessary. Refer to Page 1·108 for information relating to oversize bores and cylinder liners. When fitting new pistons and/or piston rings only, it is advisable to deglaze the bores by light honing or judicious use of medium grade carborundum paper. This will facilitate the bedding-in of piston rings. Ensure all traces of swarf and abrasive material are removed before commencing assembly.

Check that all oilways and water passages are clear, and joint faces are undamaged.

Check for satisfactory condition of studs and core plugs, renewing or rectifying as necessary.

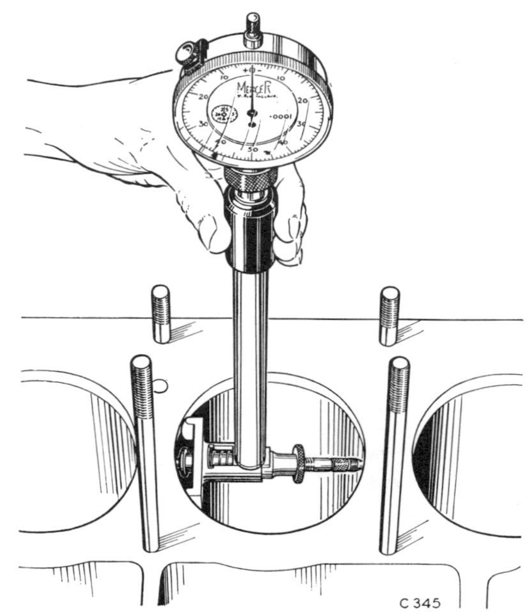

Fig. 45. Checking cylinder bore wear

ASSEMBLING THE ENGINE

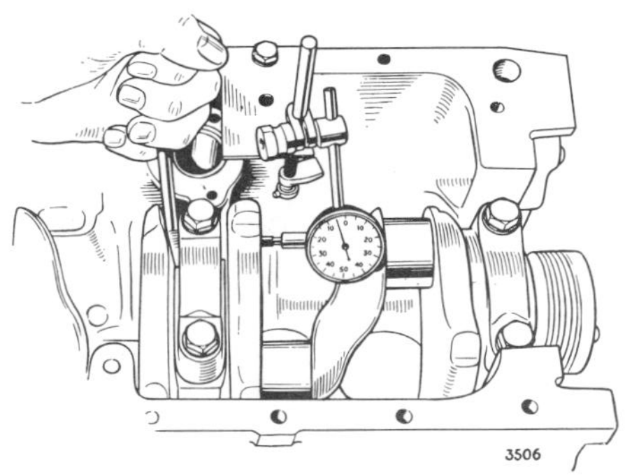

Fig. 46. Checking crankshaft end-float

Fig. 47. Fitting wedges to front sealing block

Fig. 48. Aligning front sealing block

Thoroughly clean cylinder block and all engine components. Ensure throughout assembly that all bolts and nuts are tightened to the recommended torque figures (Page 0·112).

Crankshaft and Bearings

During manufacture, the bearing caps are assembled to the cylinder block and machine bored as an assembly. The caps are, therefore, not interchangeable and must not be filed or altered in any manner. For identification, the cylinder block and its bearing caps are stamped with the same symbols. These may be found on one side of the engine sump face and on the corresponding side of each bearing cap (see Fig. 44).

Both standard and undersized bearings are pre-finished to precise limits and must not be filed, scraped or altered in any way.

The amount of undersize is stamped on the back of the bearings. If a reground crankshaft is fitted, the amount of undersize is stamped on the crankshaft webs. Ensure that the bearing sizes correspond with crankpin and journal sizes.

Fit main bearing shells to cylinder block and main bearing caps ensuring that bearing tags are properly located. Lubricate bearings and journals and place crankshaft in cylinder block.

Fit a thrust bearing to each side of rear main bearing, ensuring that thrust faces are adjacent to crankshaft, and assemble main bearing caps and shells.

Evenly tighten bearing cap bolts to recommended torque (Page 0·112). Bend over locking tabs—if fitted.

NOTE: A scroll is formed on the rear 'sealing' end of early crankshafts to facilitate oil return and must be fitted with a scrolled type rear seal housing. Current crankshafts have a plain end for use with lip type seal.

Crankshaft End-float

Using a dial gauge as shown in Fig. 46, or feeler gauge, check crankshaft end-float (see Dimensions and Tolerances). Reduce excessive end-float by fitting oversize thrust washers.

Front Sealing Block

Smear sealing block ends with jointing compound and assemble to cylinder block loosely tightening its two retaining screws. Smear the two wedge seals with jointing compound and drive them in the sealing block slots (Fig. 47).

Align faces of sealing block with front of engine, tighten sealing block retaining screws and trim wedges flush with crankcase. Do not undercut.

Crankshaft Rear Seal and Housing

Lip Type Seal. Current engines are fitted with a lip type seal which is pressed into the housing with the "lip" towards the crankshaft.

Coat both sides of a paper gasket with jointing compound and locate it on the cylinder block joint face.

Using engine oil, lubricate sealing lip, crankshaft and special centralising tool S335. To avoid damaging the seal, carefully slide the seal housing over the special tool, push this tool over the crankshaft and slide the housing into contact with the cylinder block.

Fit and evenly tighten the housing securing bolts and withdraw the centralising tool.

Scroll Type Seal. Coat a new gasket with jointing compound and secure this and the rear oil seal housing to the crankcase with bolts and spring washers, leaving the bolts semi-tight. Use a 0·003 in. (0·076 mm.) feeler strip and mallet to centralise the oil seal on the rear crankshaft journal before finally tightening the bolts.

From Commission Nos.: Spitfire FC.2794; Herald 1200 GA.115730; Herald 12/50 GD.8314, the original aluminium housing which has a clearance of 0·003 in. (0·076 mm.) was superseded by a cast iron housing having a clearance of 0·002 in. (0·508 mm.).

Engine Bearer Plates

Front. Locate a paper gasket and the front engine bearer plate on two dowels and secure the plate to the front face of the cylinder block, using one $\frac{5}{16}$ in. U.N.F. × $\frac{3}{4}$ in. (19 mm.) bolt in the centre hole, and two $\frac{5}{16}$ in. U.N.F. × $\frac{7}{8}$ in. (22 mm.) bolts in the lowest holes.

NOTE: The stud, which passes through the top centre hole of the bearer plate communicates with the water jacket. If this stud has been removed, coat the threads with jointing compound and screw it tightly home to prevent water seepage.

Rear. No gasket is fitted to the rear plate. Offer up rear plate to engine and fit and tighten securing bolts.

Flywheel

Ensure that the flywheel attachment flange on the crankshaft and the corresponding spigot and face on the flywheel are clean. Lightly smear crankshaft spigot bush with zinc oxide grease and insert bush in crankshaft. Fit the flywheel to the crankshaft flange, ensuring that the dowel and dowel hole correspond. Tighten the flywheel attachment bolts. Using a dial indicator gauge (Fig. 51) check the flywheel for run-out and concentricity.

When checking run-out ensure that false readings due to crankshaft end-float are not obtained. The crankshaft must be held against one or other of its thrust bearings when conducting this check.

Fig. 49. Fitting lip type seal

Fig. 50. Centralising Scroll type seal

Fig. 51. Checking flywheel run-out

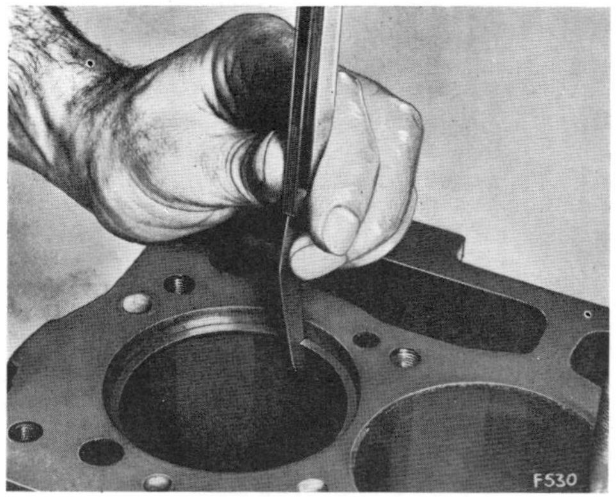

Fig. 52. Checking piston ring gaps

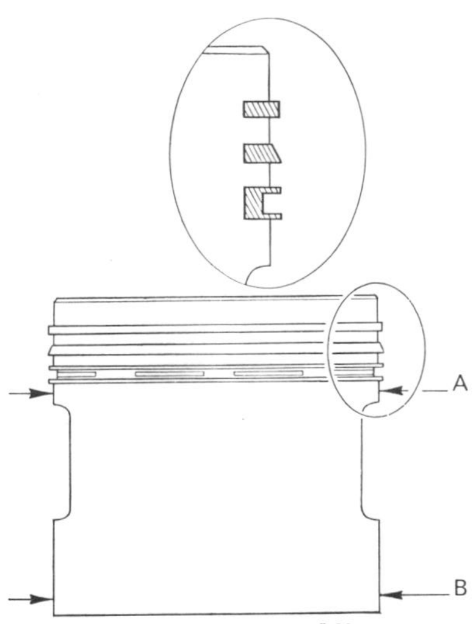

Fig. 53. Piston ring locations. Measure pistons at arrows (Refer page 1·108)

Pistons

Pistons and cylinder bores are graded and classified according to their diameter. This information is given on page 1·108. The appropriate identification letter is stamped on the piston crown and cylinder block face. This applies to standard bores only.

Piston Ring Gaps

Insert each piston ring into the cylinder bore in which it is to operate. Use a piston to locate the ring squarely in the bore. Measure the ring gap with feelers. Ring gap clearance should be as shown on Page 1·103.

Piston Balance

The weight variation in any set of pistons, lightest/heaviest, should be within the limits given on Page 1·108.

Fitting Piston Rings to Pistons

All engines employ pistons having two compression rings and one scraper ring fitted above the gudgeon pin. The top compression ring is chromium plated. On later engines the plain, second compression ring was discontinued and a taper-faced ring substituted. Spitfire Mk. 3 and 13/60 engines are fitted with a three-piece scraper ring.

Piston rings must not be stretched or twisted if breakages are to be avoided.

To fit the three-piece scraper ring take the spacer ring (corrugated member) and ease it over piston skirt into bottom piston ring groove. Ease a plain, flat ring over piston skirt and install between lower face of corrugated member and ring land. Ease remaining plain, flat ring over piston crown and install between upper face of corrugated member and ring land.

In the absence of a ring handling tool, ring removal and fitting may be facilitated using thin strips of plastic.

Piston rings are assembled as follows: scraper ring (gudgeon pin), second compression ring (middle), top compression ring (piston crown).

When fitting the taper-faced second compression ring, place the surface marked 'top' adjacent to the piston crown. Piston ring to groove clearances are given on Page 1·103.

Connecting Rod Balance

The weight variation in any set of connecting rods, lightest/heaviest, should be within the limits given on Page 1·102.

Fitting Pistons to Connecting Rods

Floating Gudgeon Pins. Note direction on piston crown indicating front of engine (timing case end).

Immerse piston in hot oil or water to expand piston and facilitate the movement of the gudgeon pin in piston bosses.

Lubricate connecting rod bush and gudgeon pin. Offer up connecting rod to piston ensuring that direction on piston crown is to timing case and that the connecting rod bearing cap bolts are to camshaft side of engine.

Align connecting rod bush with piston boss, slide gudgeon pin into position, and fit circlips ensuring they are properly seated.

Interference Fit Gudgeon Pins. Remove burrs, if present, from gudgeon pin and connecting rod bush. Lubricate gudgeon pin, connecting rod bush and piston bosses.

Offer up connecting rod to piston ensuring that direction on piston crown is to timing case and that the connecting rod bolts are to camshaft side of engine.

Assemble gudgeon pin tool as shown in Fig. 54 and align gudgeon pin with connecting rod.

Using a torque wrench, tighten nut (1) until the gudgeon pin contacts the limit stop.

If the torque required to draw the gudgeon pin into position is below 5 lbs/ft. or above 30 lb/ft. the interference fit is incorrect. In this circumstance a new connecting rod is required.

Remove the tool and check that the piston rocks evenly on the gudgeon pin. If uneven pressure is required to cause the piston to pivot on the gudgeon pin it indicates that the gudgeon pin has 'picked-up' due to misalignment when entering the connecting rod and transferred metal to the piston boss. Assembly to the engine in this condition can only result in rapid, premature wear of the piston bosses.

Fitting Pistons and Connecting Rods to Engine

Position numbers 1 and 4 or 1 and 6 crankpins at B.D.C. and smear cylinder bore and piston with clean engine oil.

Remove big-end bearing cap, stagger piston ring gaps, and fit piston ring sleeve or ring compressor to piston.

Enter connecting rod and piston in cylinder, ensuring that direction on piston crown is to front of engine and that big-end bearing cap positions are adjacent to camshaft.

Gently press piston into bore and remove ring tool. Lubricate crankpin and bearing shells.

Ensuring correct location of tabs, fit shells to connecting rod and cap, and assemble to crankpins, tightening cap bolts to recommended torque (Page 0·112).

Repeat above procedure for remaining pistons.

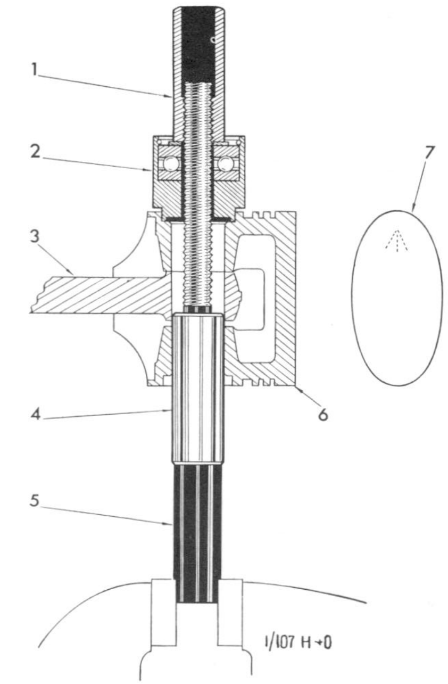

Fig. 54. Fitting interference fit gudgeon pins

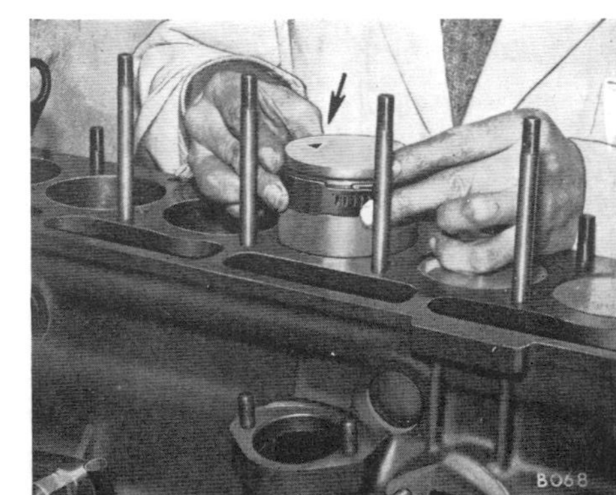

Fig. 55. Fitting pistons to engine. Note arrow to front of engine

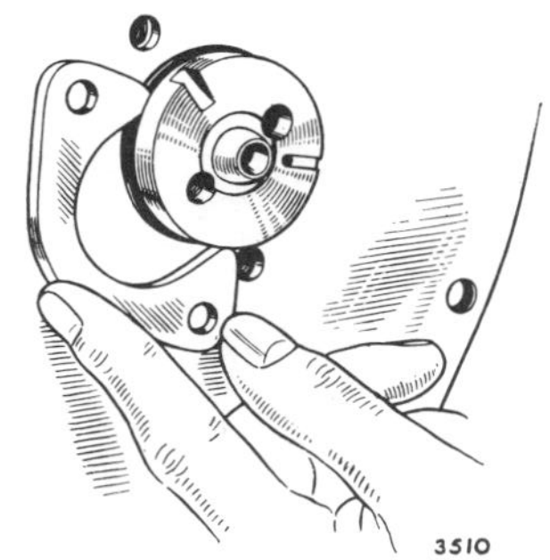

Fig. 56 Fitting camshaft keeper plate

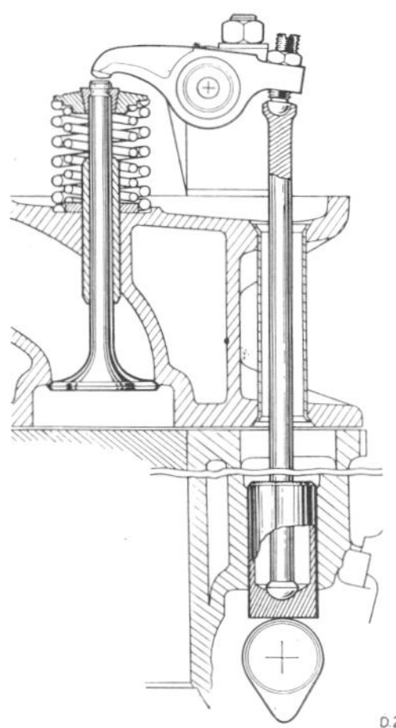

Fig. 57. Valve operating mechanism

Fig. 58. Cylinder head nut tightening sequence

Oil Pump

Lubricate rotors and assemble cover to body. Position pump in crankcase and evenly tighten the securing bolts.

Sump

Check sump flanges for distortion and rectify as necessary.

Fit gasket and sump to crankcase and secure with retaining bolts—do not overtighten. Ensure that the two short bolts are fitted to the front sealing block.

Relief Valve

Insert relief valve and spring into cap, fit sealing washer and screw the assembly into crankcase.

Camshaft

Lubricate camshaft journals and bearings, carefully thread camshaft into cylinder block and fit camshaft keeper plate.

Check camshaft end-float (refer page 1·104): excessive end-float may be reduced by fitting a new keeper plate.

Cam-followers

Lubricate cam-followers and install them in their respective locations checking that each is free to rotate and slide.

Cylinder Head

Thoroughly clean cylinder head and all components. Lubricate valve stems and guides.

Enter valves in guides and assemble valve spring seats, springs and collets as shown in Fig. 28, ensuring that closed spring coils are fitted next to cylinder head.

Position cylinder head gasket and cylinder on cylinder block and assemble engine lifting eye to rear cylinder head studs on right-hand side of head (Herald and Spitfire models). The rear lifting eye of the Vitesse is fitted to rear of cylinder block.

Fit and evenly tighten cylinder head nuts to recommended torque in appropriate sequence as shown in Figs. 25 and 58.

Rocker Gear

Assemble rocker gear as shown in Figs. 24 and 26 as appropriate: ensure star-headed screw on rear pedestal properly engages rocker shaft. Engage push rods in cam-followers, cupped end to rocker, and fit rocker gear assembly to cylinder head, taking care that adjusters are slackened off and that ball ends engage their respective push rod cups. Evenly tighten rocker gear in position.

Sprocket Alignment

Fit camshaft sprocket. Slide crankshaft sprocket (short hub boss outward) on to crankshaft and press fully home. The crankshaft key is not fitted at this stage.

Place a straight-edge across teeth of both sprockets and check alignment (Fig. 60): misalignment is corrected by placing shims of suitable thickness behind the crankshaft sprocket. Fit crankshaft key and press crankshaft sprocket into position.

Valve Timing (Marked Sprockets)

If the original, marked sprockets are being refitted assemble sprockets as shown in Fig. 61.

Valve Timing (Unmarked Sprockets)

Bring number 1 piston to T.D.C. (crankshaft key at twelve o'clock).

Rotate camshaft until number 1 push rod reaches the highest point of its travel (cam-follower on peak of cam).

Adjust clearance of number 8 valve (4 cylinder engines) or number 12 valve (6 cylinder engines) to 0·040 in. (1 mm.).

Rotate camshaft until number 2 push rod reaches the highest point of its travel.

Adjust clearance of number 7 valve (4 cylinders) or number 11 valve (6 cylinders) to 0·040 in. (1 mm.).

Turn camshaft in direction of rotation until the valves of number 4 or number 6 cylinder as appropriate are 'on the rock', i.e., the inlet valve about to open and the exhaust valve almost closed. This position may be checked using feeler gauges of equal thickness (Fig. 62).

Taking care not to disturb either camshaft or crankshaft, remove camshaft sprocket—if previously fitted.

Encircle both sprockets with the timing chain and offer up camshaft sprocket to camshaft. Manipulate the camshaft sprocket in relation to the chain to attain alignment of sprocket and camshaft holes.

The camshaft timing sprocket is provided with four holes which are equally spaced but offset from a tooth centre. Half tooth adjustment is obtained by rotating the sprocket 90 degrees from its original position. A quarter tooth adjustment may be obtained by turning the sprocket 'back to front'. By rotating it 90 degrees in this reversed position, three-quarters of a tooth variation is obtained.

The position of either crankshaft or camshaft **must not** be disturbed during this operation.

Fit camshaft sprocket lockplate and bolts, evenly tighten and bend over locking plate tabs. Adjust all valves to recommended clearances.

Fig. 59. Location of crankshaft shims

Fig. 60. Checking sprocket alignment

Fig. 61. Valve timing marks

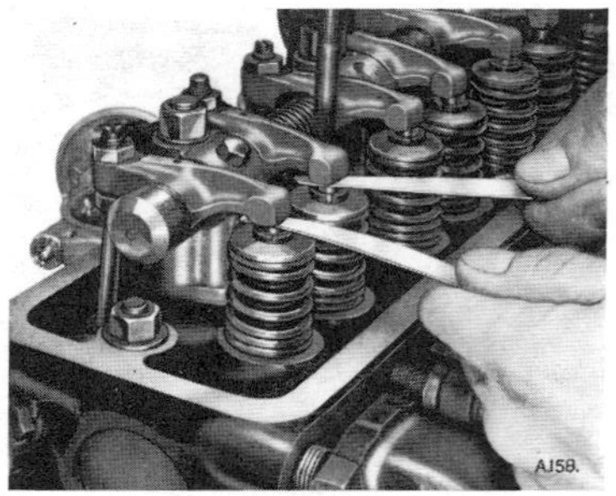

Fig. 62. Using feeler gauges of equal thickness to determine point of balance

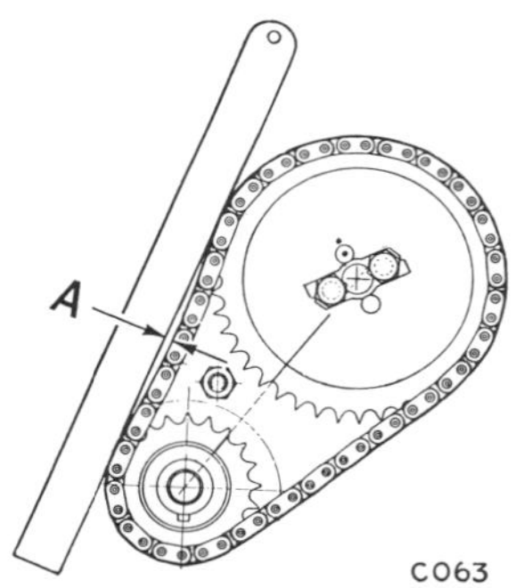

Fig. 63. Checking timing chain wear
[Dimension 'A' should not exceed 0·4″ (10 mm)]

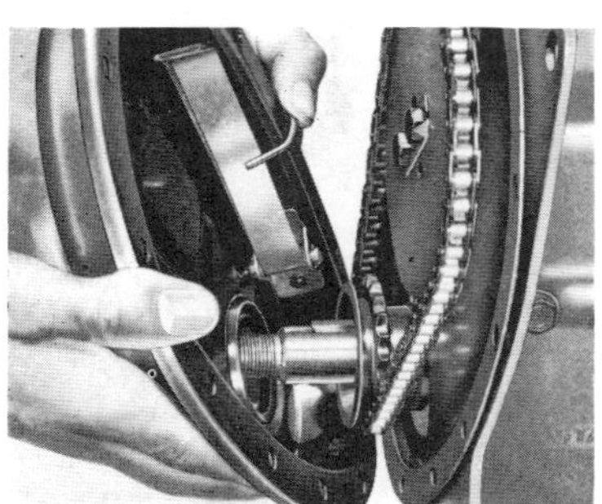

Fig. 64. Fitting timing cover

Timing Chain

Normal chain slack is shown in Fig. 63. Where play exceeds that recommended a new chain should be fitted. The continued use of sprockets with worn, hooked, or damaged teeth is not advised.

Timing Cover, Chain Tensioner and Crankshaft Pulley

Carefully remove timing cover oil seal taking care to avoid damage or distortion to the timing cover. Evenly press new seal into cover making sure that seal lip is fitted towards crankshaft sprocket. Using a straight-edge or a surface plate, check timing cover flanges for distortion and rectify as necessary.

Examine spring blades of tensioner and abutment point on inside of timing cover. The chain tensioner may be removed and replaced by simply opening the blade sufficiently to spring it over the pin.

Fit oil thrower to crankshaft (dished periphery towards timing cover). Lubricate lip of timing cover oil seal and its running surface on crankshaft pulley. Note that efficient seal operation cannot be obtained if the seal running face on the crankshaft pulley is worn or scored.

Fit timing cover gasket to engine front plate and offer up timing cover to engine.

A short length of welding rod bent and used as shown in Fig. 64 will enable the chain tensioner to be compressed sufficiently to facilitate fitting. Take care to avoid damaging the timing cover gasket when withdrawing welding rod.

Fit and tighten evenly timing cover bolts and screws.

Fit and tighten crankshaft pulley nut (Herald and Spitfire models).

Fit fan pulley adaptor and bolt and tighten bolts (Vitesse).

DISTRIBUTOR DRIVE GEAR AND PEDESTAL

Distributor Drive Gear End-float

Lubricate camshaft helical gear and distributor drive gear bush and enter distributor drive gear in cylinder block. In order for the distributor drive gear to seat correctly it is necessary to engage the camshaft gear and also the tongue of the oil pump spindle. To ensure engagement of the latter it may be required to rotate the engine until the slot of the drive gear aligns with the oil pump tongue when the drive gear will drop properly into position.

Place distributor pedestal in position on cylinder block. Using feeler gauges, check clearance between pedestal flange and cylinder block. It is important to ensure that with a gasket fitted to the pedestal flange, a nominal 0·002 in. to 0·007 in. (0·0508 to 1·78 mm.) end-float exists between the driving gear and the bottom of the pedestal boss. Gaskets must be fitted under the pedestal flange as necessary to obtain this clearance.

Drive gears assembled **without** end float will cause premature wear of crankshaft gear, distributor drive gear, spindle bush, and timing chain.

Distributor Drive Gear End-float (Fig. 65)

To determine the amount of packing required under the pedestal to produce 0·003″ to 0·007″ (0·076 to 0·178 mm.) drive gear end-float, adopt the following procedure:

1. Accurately measure the thickness of a plain washer, having an internal diameter of ·5″ (12·7 mm.), and place it over the distributor gear drive shaft.
2. Insert and lower the drive shaft assembly into the bush (5) until the gear and plain washer rest on the top of the bush. This may necessitate repeated removal of the gear shaft and turning the oil pump shaft until their driving dogs engage with each other.
3. Place the distributor pedestal in position and measure the gap between the pedestal and cylinder block as shown. Subtract this dimension from the washer thickness to determine the end-float of the gear.

Example

If the washer thickness is	0·062″	1·57 mm.
and the width of the gap is	0·060″	1·52 mm.
Then the gear float will be	+0·002″	0·05 mm.

The float of 0·002″ (0·0508 mm.) is insufficient and requires additional packing of 0·003″ (0·08 mm.) thickness to produce an end float of 0·005″ (0·12 mm.) (mean of tolerance).

Fitting Distributor Drive Gear and Pedestal

Set number 1 piston at T.D.C. on compression stroke. Mesh distributor gear with camshaft so that when fully home and engaged with tongue of oil pump spindle the offset slot is as shown in Figs. 67-70.

Fit pedestal gasket and pedestal, and tighten flange nuts.

Ignition Timing

Position number 1 piston at T.D.C.—compression stroke.

Clean or renew distributor contacts as necessary and set gaps to 0·015 in. (0·4 mm.). Fit distributor and clamp bracket to cylinder block and engage distributor dog with helical gear in pedestal.

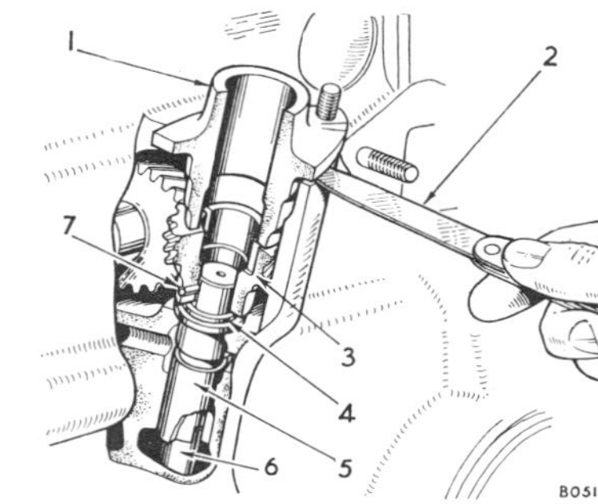

1 Adaptor
2 Feeler gauge
3 Driving gear
4 ½″ I/D washer
5 Bush
6 Oil pump shaft
7 Pin

Fig. 65. Determining the amount of packing required under the distributor adaptor

Fig. 66. Fitting pedestal and packing washers

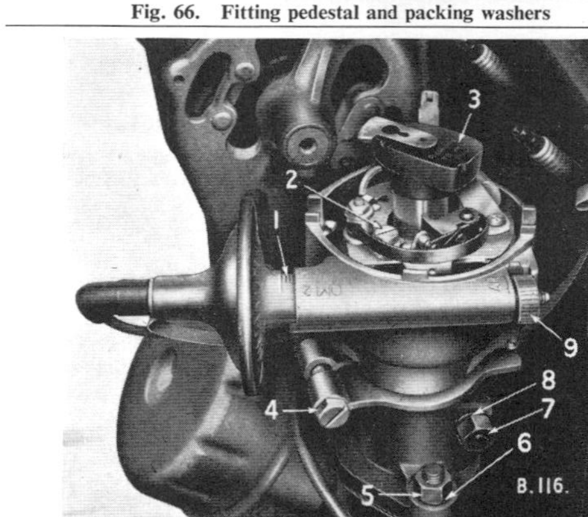

Fig. 67. Distributor rotor arm position at T.D.C. No. 1 compression (Herald 1200, 12/50)

Fig. 68. Distributor position (13/60)

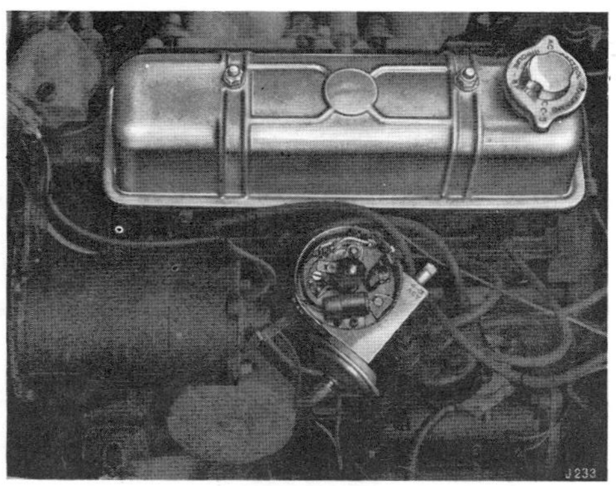

Fig. 69. Distributor position (Spitfire)

Fig. 70. Distributor position (Vitesse)

HERALD 1200, 12/50 and 13/60.

Set vernier adjuster to fully retard position. Rotate distributor body against rotation of rotor until the contact breaker points are about to open, and tighten pinch bolt (4).

Turn vernier screw (9) anti-clockwise until 2¼ divisions (6·8 : 1 compression ratio and 13/60) or 3¾ divisions (8 : 1 compression ratio) are visible at (1). One division on the vernier scale equals 4 crankshaft degrees.

Ignition settings are:

6·8 : 1 compression ratio	9° B.T.D.C.
13/60	9° B.T.D.C.
8 : 1 compression ratio ..	15° B.T.D.C.

Firing order: 1, 3, 4, 2.

SPITFIRE

Set vernier adjuster to fully retard position. Rotate distributor body against rotation of rotor until the contact breaker points are about to open.

Tighten pinch bolt on clamp plate and rotate vernier adjusting screw clockwise as necessary. (one click equals one crankshaft degree).

Ignition setting: 13° B.T.D.C.
17° B.T.D.C. (Spitfire Mk. 2).
6° B.T.D.C. (Spitfire Mk. 3).

Firing order: 1, 3, 4, 2.

SPITFIRE Mk. 3 (Emission Control only)

Position number 1 piston at T.D.C.—compression stroke. Renew or clean contact breaker points and set gap to 0·015 in. (0·4 mm.).

Engage distributor in pedestal and rotate distributor until contact breaker points are about to break.

Start engine and run at 800 to 850 r.p.m. Using stroboscope equipment, set distributor to 2° A.T.D.C. Tighten pinch bolt.

Firing order: 1, 3, 4, 2.

VITESSE (With Vernier Adjustment)

Position number 1 piston at T.D.C.—compression stroke. Renew or clean contact breaker points and set gap to 0·015 in. (0·4 mm.).

Engage distributor in pedestal and set vernier to fully retard position.

Turn distributor against direction of rotor rotation until points are about to break and tighten pinch bolt. Adjust vernier until 2½ divisions are visible on scale. One vernier division equals 4 crankshaft degrees.

Ignition timing: 10° B.T.D.C.

Firing order: 1, 5, 3, 6, 2, 4.

VITESSE (Without Vernier)

Set crankshaft at 10° mark on rim of damper with number 1 piston on compression stroke. Renew or clean contact breaker points and set gap to 0·015 in. (0·4 mm.).

Engage distributor in pedestal and turn distributor against direction of rotor rotation until points are about to break. Tighten pinch bolt.

OPERATIONS PERFORMED 'IN SITU'

Cylinder Head

Isolate battery. Remove radiator filler cap and drain cooling system.

Disconnect radiator top and bottom hoses at thermostat housing and water pump inlet respectively.

Disconnect header tank hose to radiator and remove header tank (Spitfire and Vitesse).

Disconnect heater inlet and outlet hoses at engine.

Remove air filter(s). Slacken generator bolts and remove fan belt.

Remove fuel pipe (pump to carburettor(s)) and disconnect throttle and choke controls at carburettor(s).

Remove water pump, thermostat elbow and thermostat.

Disconnect breather pipes from rocker cover and disconnect servo-vacuum pipe from inlet manifold (if fitted).

Disconnect exhaust pipe at exhaust manifold flange and remove inlet and exhaust manifolds.

Remove rocker cover, rocker gear and push rods and disconnect HT leads from sparking plugs.

Remove cylinder head nuts and lift off cylinder head and gasket. Do not remove carbon from piston crowns without first sealing off all oil and water passages.

Replace cylinder head in reverse sequence to above instructions ensuring that cylinder head nuts are tightened in proper order (Fig. 58).

Timing Cover, Oil Seal

Isolate battery, remove radiator filler cap and drain cooling system. Disconnect radiator top and bottom hoses at thermostat elbow and water pump respectively. Remove radiator.

Slacken generator bolts and remove fan belt.

Remove crankshaft pulley.

Remove bolts and screws securing timing cover to cylinder block and withdraw timing cover. Carefully extract oil seal avoiding damage to timing cover. Evenly press new seal into position making sure seal lip is fitted towards crankshaft sprocket. Lubricate lip of seal and also its running surface on crankshaft pulley. Efficient sealing cannot be obtained if the seal running face on the pulley is worn or scored.

Fit new gasket to cylinder block. Offer up timing cover to engine ensuring oil thrower is in position and its dished periphery is towards timing cover. Compress chain tensioner and slide timing cover into its locating dowels. Fit and evenly tighten timing cover bolts and screws.

Fit crankshaft pulley, fan belt, radiator and radiator hoses.

Renewing Timing Chain and Sprockets

Remove timing cover and straighten locking tabs on camshaft sprocket bolts.

Turn engine to T.D.C. (number one cylinder on compression) and slacken camshaft sprocket bolts (restoring sprocket to T.D.C. position if disturbed).

Withdraw camshaft sprocket, timing chain and crankshaft sprocket.

Offer up new sprockets, check alignment, and shim crankshaft sprocket as required.

Fit crankshaft sprocket and offer up new timing chain and sprocket to camshaft, rotating sprocket and chain as necessary to obtain alignment of camshaft sprocket holes **without** disturbing position of camshaft. Fit securing bolts and lockplate to camshaft sprocket, tighten bolts and bend over lock tabs.

Fit timing cover, crankshaft pulley, fan belt and radiator. Connect radiator hoses and refill cooling system. Connect battery.

Sump (HERALD and SPITFIRE)

Isolate battery, remove sump drain plug, run off oil and withdraw dipstick.

Remove sump bolts and withdraw sump. It may be found advantageous to remove the two lower bell housing bolts.

When replacing sump ensure that the two short sump bolts are fitted to the front sealing block. Do not overtighten sump bolts.

Sump (VITESSE)

Isolate battery and drain cooling system and engine sump.

Disconnect radiator top hoses from thermostat elbow and header tank. Remove dipstick.

Using lifting tackle take weight of engine.

Slacken right-hand engine mounting bolts and remove left-hand mounting bolts. Remove sump bolts.

Slightly raise engine and lever it towards rear of vehicle to enable sump to clear front crossmember and withdraw sump.

Replace in reverse order.

Oil Pump

Isolate battery and remove sump.

Remove the three oil pump securing bolts and withdraw oil pump. Assemble in reverse sequence.

Pistons and Connecting Rods

Isolate battery and remove cylinder head and engine sump.

Remove and replace pistons as detailed on pages 1·127 and 1·132.

Replace cylinder head and sump. Refill radiator and engine sump. Connect battery.

Camshaft

Isolate battery and remove cylinder head and timing cover. Withdraw camshaft sprocket and timing chain. Lift out cam-followers.

Remove distributor, distributor drive gear and fuel pump. Remove camshaft keeper plate bolts and keeper plate. Carefully extract camshaft taking care to avoid damage to cams and bushes.

When assembling engine after fitting camshaft refer to Page 1·135 for valve timing information and to Page 1·138 for ignition timing.

COOLING SYSTEM

Description

Circulation of water in the pressurised cooling system shown in Fig. 1 is assisted by a belt-driven, impeller type water pump and controlled by a thermostat.

Figs. 2 and 3 illustrate the water heated inlet manifolds of Spitfire and Herald 13/60 models.

Draining the Cooling System

Set heater control to "hot" position and remove radiator filler cap. Open drain cock on cylinder block and bottom of radiator. On engines not fitted with cylinder block drain cocks it will be necessary to remove the cylinder block drain plug.

NOTE: The radiator filler cap must not be removed whilst the engine is hot.

Filling the Cooling System

Set heater control to "hot" position and close drain cocks. Remove filler cap and fill cooling system with clean, soft water. Replace filler cap and warm up engine. Stop engine and top up cooling system. Half fill overflow reservoir.

Pressure Testing Cooling System (Fig. 5)

Warm up engine, remove filler cap and top up cooling system as necessary. Using an A.C. pressure tester or similar equipment install pressure tester in filler neck and pump up to the pressure marked on the filler cap. If no leaks are present the cooling system should maintain this pressure for at least ten seconds.

A more severe test is to apply the above procedure with the engine running. Pressure fluctuations combined with an absence of external leaks is generally indicative of a leaking cylinder head gasket.

Pressure Testing the Radiator Filler Cap (Fig. 4)

Rinse filler cap in water to remove sediment and, whilst still wet, fit pressure tester to cap and pump up pressure until gauge pointer ceases to rise. Reject the filler cap if it will not register and maintain a pressure of 1 p.s.i. (0·006 kg/cm²) below the figure stamped on the filler cap for a period of ten seconds without additional pumping.

Flushing the Cooling System

Periodically flush the cooling system using a proprietary flushing compound following the instructions supplied.

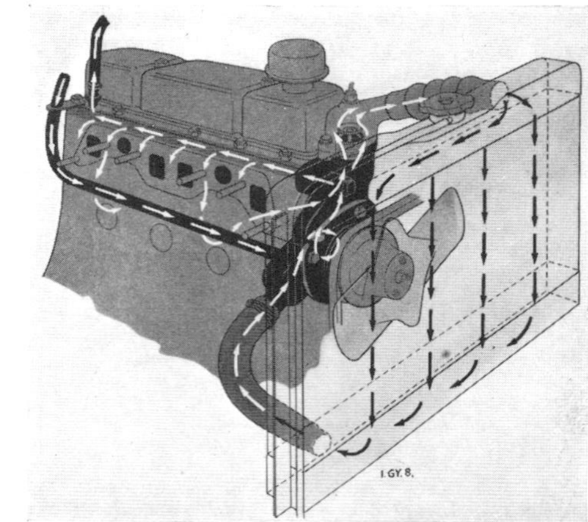

Fig. 1. Water circulation

Fig. 2. Spitfire heated inlet manifold

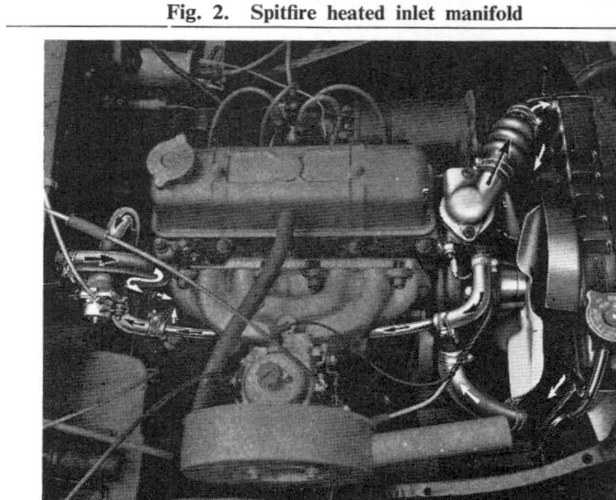

Fig. 3. Herald 13/60 heated inlet manifold

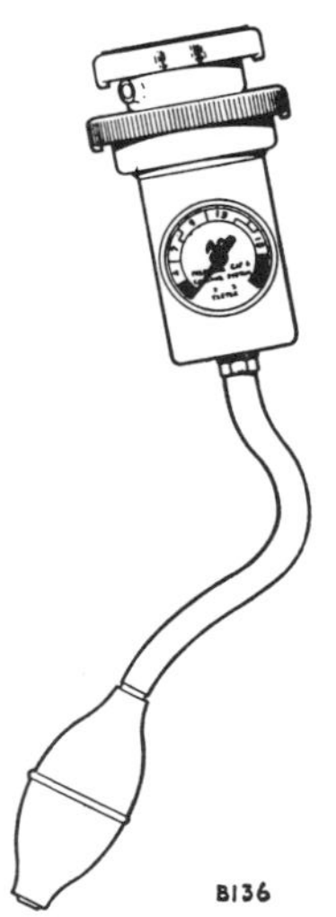

Fig. 4. Testing the radiator filler cap

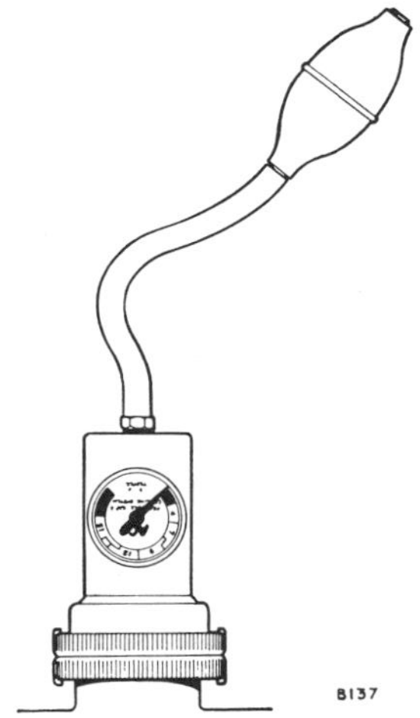

Fig. 5. Testing the cooling system

Fig. 6. Removing the thermostat

Anti-freeze

To protect the cooling system during frosty weather, use an inhibited Glycol base anti-freeze solution. Because of the searching effect of these solutions, check the system for leaks before adding the anti-freeze.

Approved brands of anti-freeze are given in the Owner's Handbook. For quantities of anti-freeze mixtures required to safeguard the system at specific temperatures, consult the manufacturers' recommendations.

It is recommended that fresh anti-freeze is used each year, since the inhibitor becomes exhausted and the components in contact with the cooling water may corrode. When topping up the coolant, use a mixture of anti-freeze and water.

Thermostat

Drain the cooling system, remove the outlet elbow of the thermostat housing and lift out the thermostat (Fig. 6). The opening temperature of the thermostat is fixed on manufacture; no servicing or adjustment is possible. A defective thermostat must be renewed.

A thermostat can be checked by immersing it in hot water of known temperature. The valve should commence to open at the temperature stamped on its flange.

Refit thermostat in reverse order to removal procedure and refill cooling system.

The Water Pump

Isolate the battery and drain cooling system. Slacken generator mounting bolts and remove fan belt. Disconnect water pump inlet and outlet hoses and the temperature transmitter cable, where fitted. Disconnect fuel pipe and vacuum pipe as necessary. Remove the three bolts securing water pump to cylinder head and withdraw water pump.

Replace in reverse order.

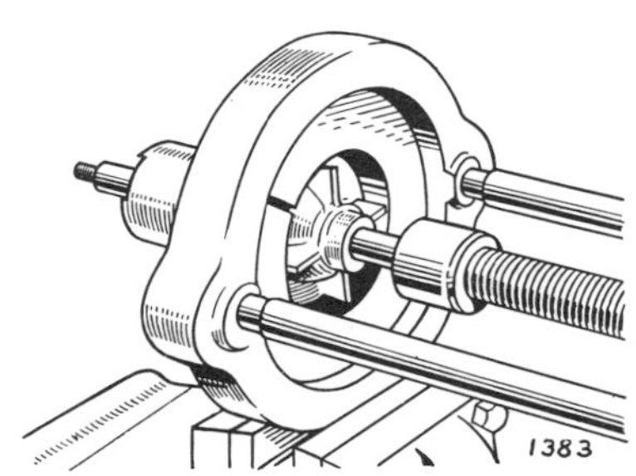

Fig. 7. Removing impeller from pump spindle

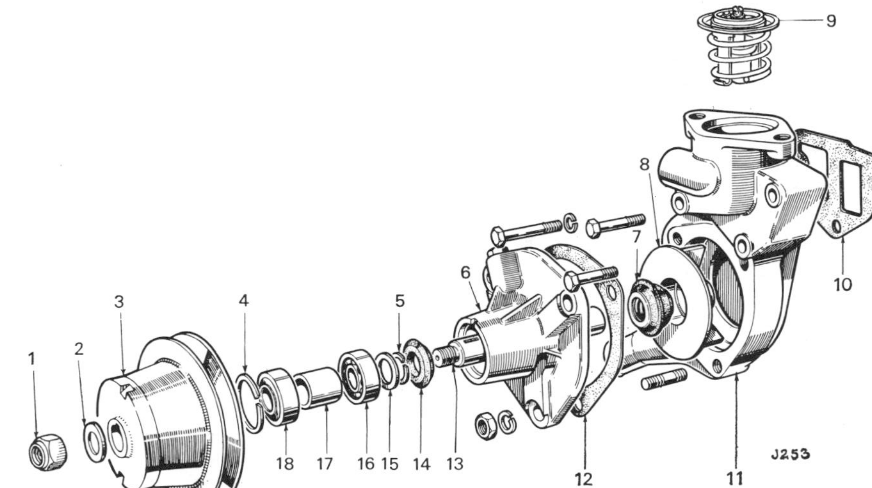

Fig. 8. Exploded view of water pump

KEY TO FIG. 8

1	Nut	10	Gasket
2	Washer	11	Body—water pump
3	Pulley	12	Gasket
4	Circlip	13	Spindle
5	Circlip	14	Spinner
6	Housing—bearings and spindle	15	Washer
7	Seal	16	Bearing—inner
8	Impeller	17	Spacer—bearings
9	Thermostat	18	Bearing—outer

Dismantling the Water Pump (Figs. 7 and 8)

Remove fan, pulley and Woodruff key. Remove the nuts securing bearing housing (13) to pump body and withdraw bearing housing. Using Tool No. FTS.127 with press S.4221A remove impeller (16) and seal assembly (14) (Fig. 8). Withdraw circlip (5) and drift out shaft and bearing assembly towards front of housing. Remove spinner (11), circlip (10) washer (9) and press off bearings (6 and 8) and distance piece (7).

Recutting Sealing Gland Face (Fig. 9)

Using tool No. S.126 insert pilot from gland side of bearing housing. Fit the bush (small diameter leading), tool bearing, and knurled nut to pilot. Gently tighten the knurled nut to bring cutter into contact with gland face. Rotate tommy bar, simultaneously maintaining light, even pressure on cutter. Remove only the minimum of metal necessary to obtain a smooth face. Periodically remove and clean the cutter. The depth of the gland face from the housing mounting face must not exceed 0·265 in. (6·7 mm.).

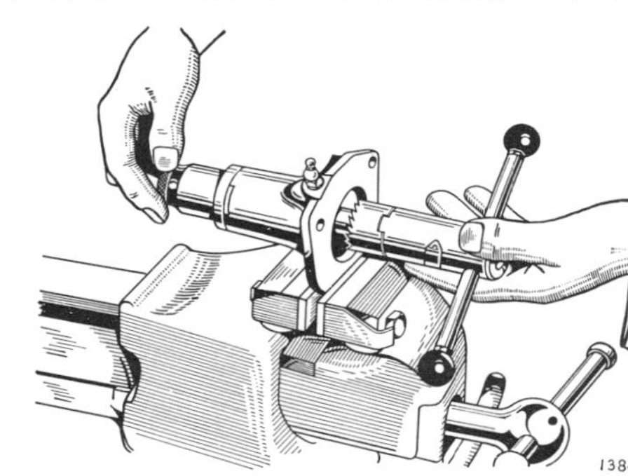

Fig. 9. Re-cutting sealing gland face

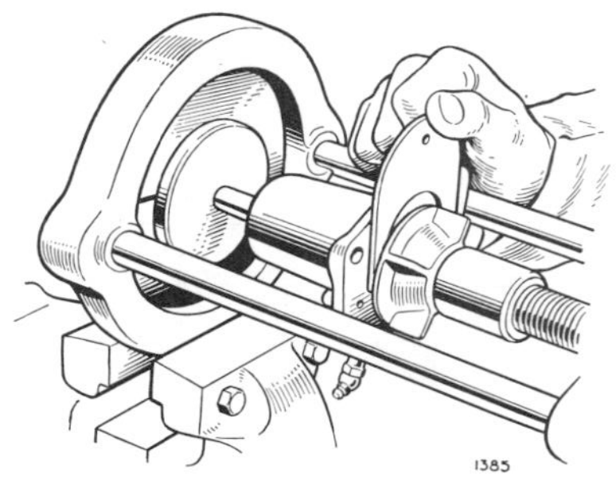

Fig. 10. Using gauge to obtain 0·030 in. (0·762 mm.) clearance between impeller and housing face

Assembling the Water Pump (Figs. 8 and 10)

Assemble spinner (11), circlip (10) and washer (9) to shaft (12). Fit bearings (8 and 6), separated by distance piece (7) to shaft (12).

NOTE: The unshielded sides of the bearings must be adjacent to the distance piece. Pack bearings with grease.

Using a tubular drift install shaft and bearings into housing (13) and secure with circlip (5). Press seal (14) into impeller (16). Using a 0·030 in. (0·762 mm.) spacer press impeller (16) on to shaft (12) as shown in Fig. 10. Solder end of impeller to shaft to prevent water seeping along shaft. Fit Woodruff key, pulley, and fan blades.

Radiator

The radiator, its associated components and attachment related to Herald, Spitfire, and Vitesse models are shown in Figs. 11 - 17.

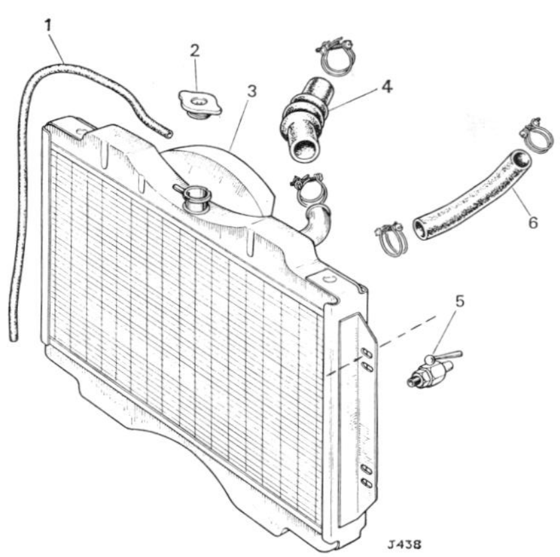

Fig. 11. Herald 1200 radiator (up to GA 80000)

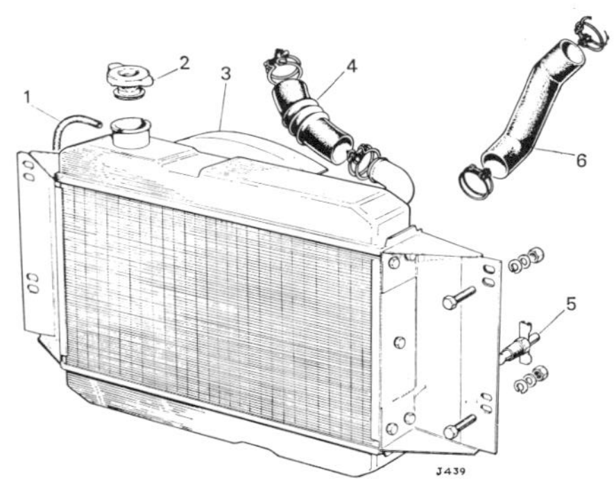

Fig. 12. Herald 1200 radiator (from GA 80001 and GB 1) and Herald 13/60 radiator

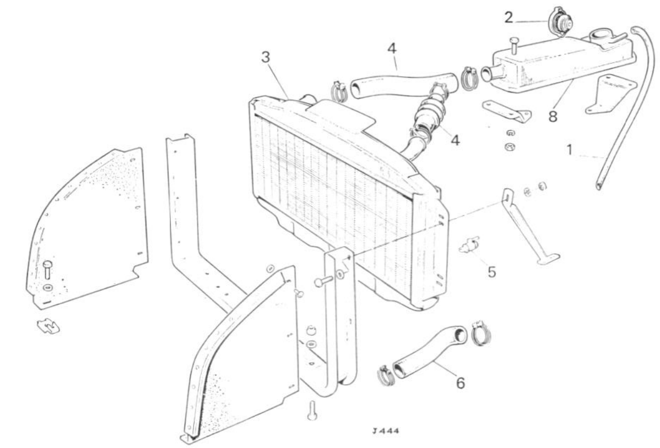

Fig. 13. Spitfire 4 radiator (up to FC 39925)

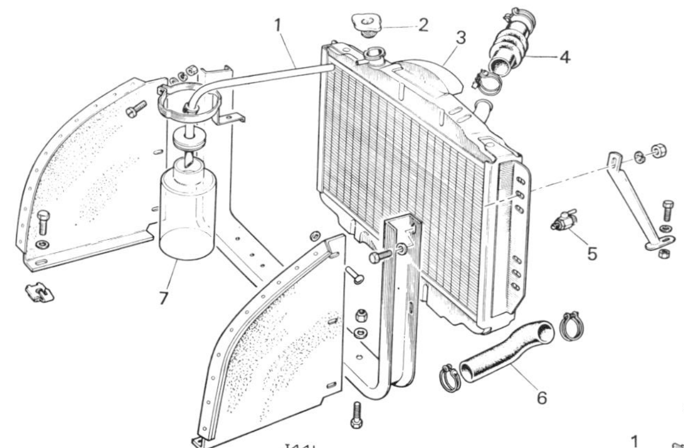

Fig. 14. Spitfire 4 radiator (from FC 39926) and Spitfire Mk. 2

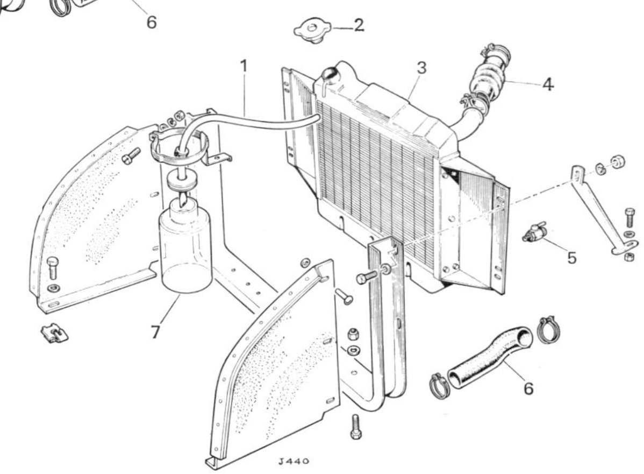

Fig. 15. Spitfire Mk. 3 radiator

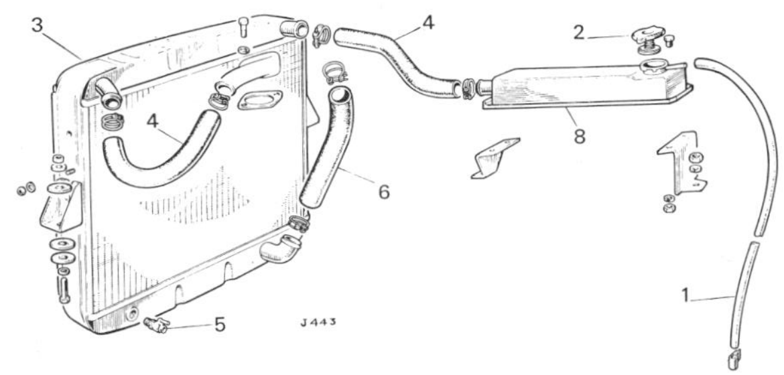

Fig. 16. Vitesse radiator (up to HB 26149)

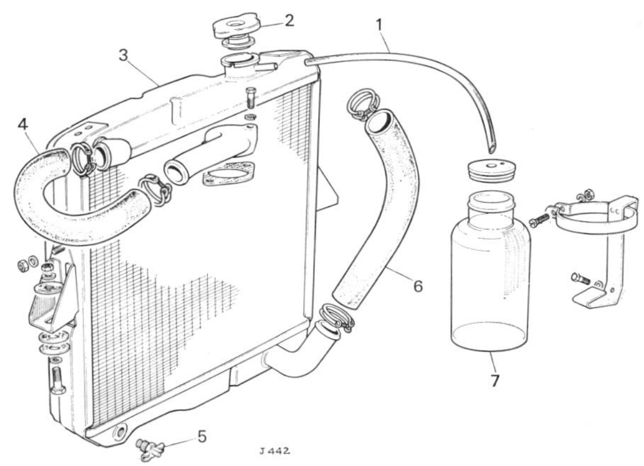

Fig. 17. Vitesse radiator (from HB 26149)

KEY TO FIGS. 11 to 17

1. Overflow pipe
2. Filler cap
3. Radiator
4. Top hose(s)
5. Drain cock
6. Bottom hose
7. Overflow reservoir
8. Header tank

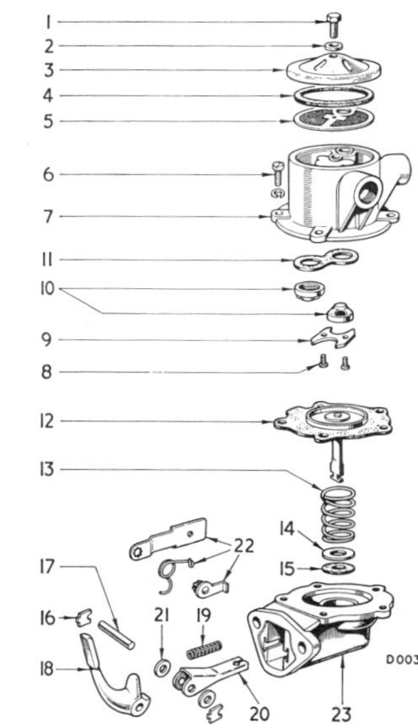

1	Retaining screw	12	Diaphragm assembly
2	Washer	13	Spring
3	Cover	14	Washer
4	Joint	15	Washer
5	Gauze	16	Retainer
6	Screw	17	Spindle
7	Body	18	Operating lever
8	Screws	19	Return spring
9	Retainer	20	Operating fork
10	Valves	21	Distance washer
11	Upper retainer	22	Priming lever assembly
		23	Lower body

Fig. 1. Exploded view of Spitfire and Herald 1200, 12/50 fuel pump

FUEL PUMP

To Dismantle Fuel Pump

(a) Clean the exterior of the pump and file a mark across both flanges to facilitate re-assembly.

(b) Dismantle in the sequence given on Figs. 1 and 2. Re-assemble by reversing the sequence.

(c) To remove the diaphragm assembly (12) first turn it through 90° in an anti-clockwise direction and lift it out of engagement with operating fork (20) (Fig. 1) or (21) (Fig. 2).

* The valves (10) are identical, but on fitting them to the upper body ensure that the inlet valve is pointing towards the diaphragm and the outlet valve points away from the diaphragm, as shown on the illustrations.

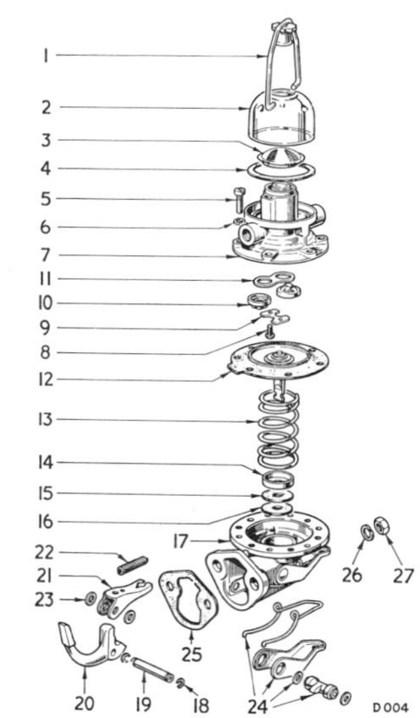

1	Stirrup	14	Cup
2	Sediment bowl	15	Washer
3	Filter gauze	16	Washer
4	Joint	17	Lower body
5	Screw	18	Circlip
6	Spring washer	19	Spindle
7	Body	20	Operating lever
8	Screw	21	Operating fork
9	Retainer	22	Return spring
10	Valves	23	Distance washer
11	Upper retainer	24	Priming lever assembly
12	Diaphragm assembly	25	Gasket
13	Spring	26	Spring washer
		27	Nut

Fig. 2. Exploded view of fuel pump—Vitesse

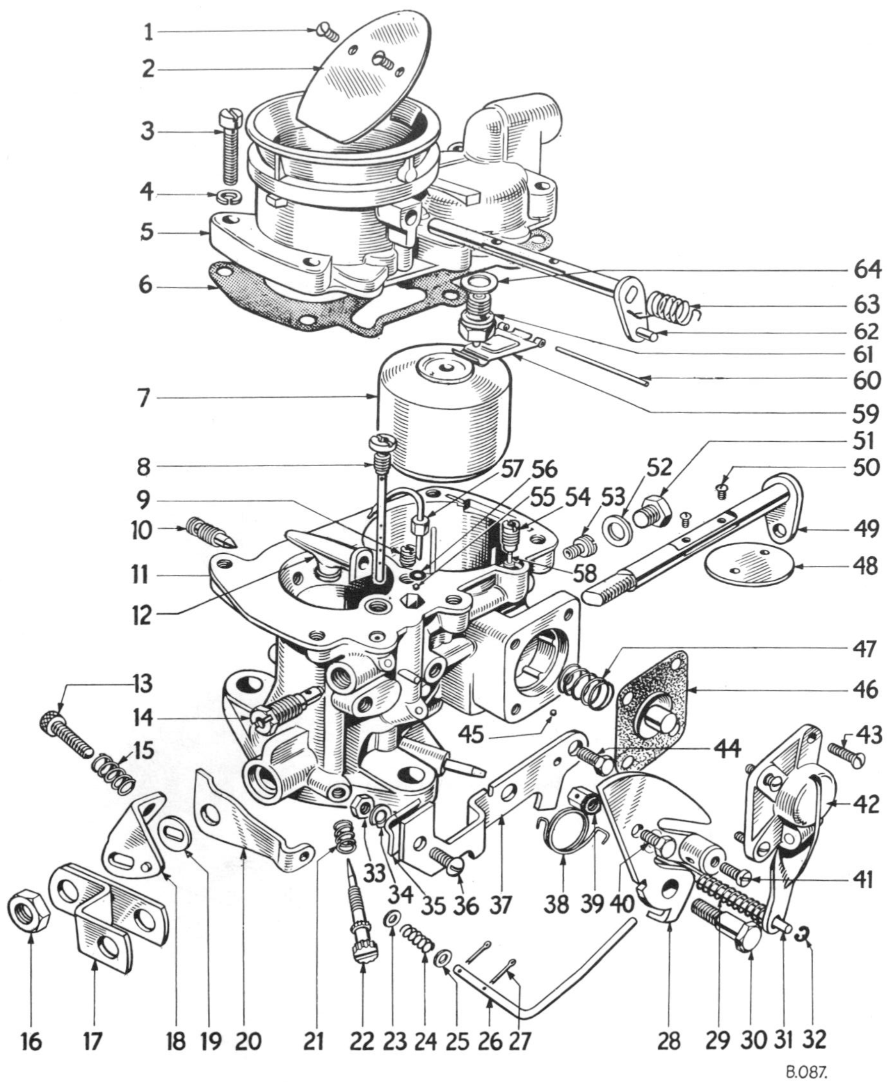

Fig. 3. Exploded B30 PSE1 carburettor

Key to Figs. 3 and 4

1 Screw
2 Strangler
3 Screw
4 Spring Washer
5 Top cover
6 Gasket
7 Float
8 Air correction jet
9 Econostat fuel jet
10 Spraying bridge retaining screw
11 Body
12 Spraying bridge
13 Slow running adjustment screw
14 Slow running fuel jet
15 Spring
16 Nut
17 Throttle lever
18 Stop lever
19 Slotted washer
20 Strangler—inter-connection lever
21 Spring
22 Volume control screw
23 Washer
24 Spring
25 Washer
26 Strangler inter-connection push rod
27 Split pin
28 Strangler operating cam
29 Spring
30 Pivot bolt
31 Accelerator pump push rod
32 Circlip
33 Nut
34 Spring washer
35 Cable clip
36 Screw
37 Abutment bracket
38 Spring
39 Solderless nipple
40 Pinch screw
41 Pinch screw
42 Pump cover and lever assembly
43 Screw
44 Setscrew
45 Non-return ball valve
46 Pump diaphragm
47 Diaphragm spring
48 Throttle butterfly
49 Throttle spindle
50 Screw
51 Main jet access plug
52 Fibre washer
53 Main jet
54 Pump chamber non-return valve body
55 Non-return ball valve
56 Fibre washer
57 Accelerator pump jet
58 Pump chamber non-return valve
59 Float lever
60 Float lever pivot
61 Needle valve
62 Strangler cam follower and spindle
63 Return spring
64 Fibre washer
65 Solderless nipple
66 Screw
67 Abutment bracket
68 Choke cable
69 Throttle cable
70 Nuts
71 Rubber sleeve
72 Fuel pipe

CARBURETTORS

HERALD 1200, 12/50 —
B.30 PSE1 CARBURETTOR

Idling Adjustment (Fig. 4)

1. Set the throttle (slow-running adjustment) screw (13) until the idling speed is approximately 500 r.p.m.
2. Unscrew the volume control screw (22) until the engine begins to hunt.
3. Screw in until the hunting disappears and the engine idles smoothly.
4. If the engine speed increases, re-adjust its speed to 500 r.p.m. by re-setting the slow running screw.
5. This may cause slight hunting, which may be corrected by further slight adjustment of the volume control screw. (Under no circumstances should this screw be fully tightened.)

Removal (Fig. 4)

1. Remove the air cleaner assembly, disconnect the fuel pipe (72) and withdraw the rubber sleeve (71) from the stub pipe on the carburettor.
2. Release the choke inner and outer cables (68) from the abutment bracket and cam plate screw (40).
3. Disconnect the throttle cable (69) from the throttle lever. Remove two nuts (70) and lift off the carburettor.

Re-fitting

Refit the carburettor by reversing the removal procedure. Fit a new flange gasket and adjust the length of the inner choke cable to ensure that the choke butterfly cam plate is against its stop on the abutment bracket when the choke knob is fully in.

Fig. 4. B30 PSE1 carburettor details

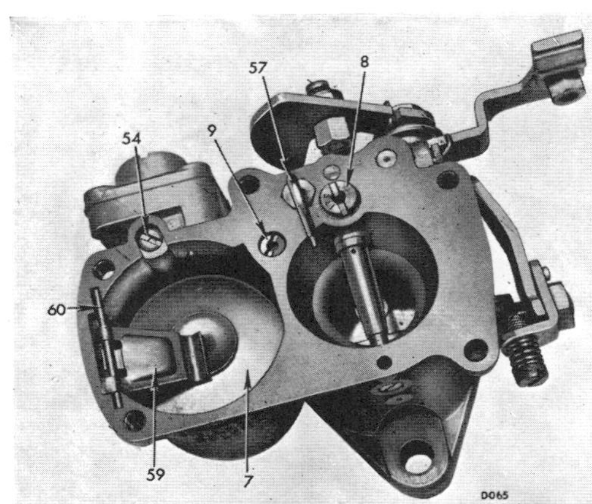

Fig. 5. B30 PSE1 carburettor, showing the top cover removed

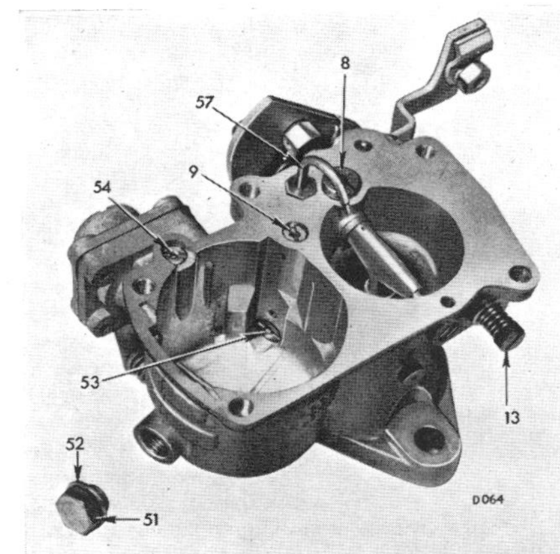

Fig. 6. Access to main jet (53) through plug orifice (51)

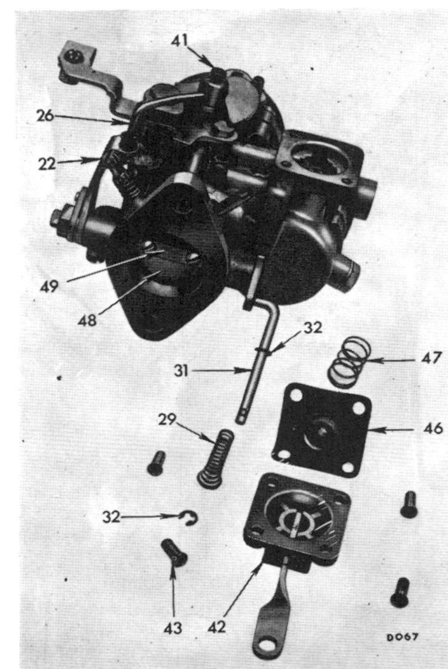

Fig. 7. Accelerator pump details

Dismantling (Fig. 3)

The following dismantling procedure is given in two stages. Stage one should be adopted only when it becomes necessary to clean out the float chamber, jet and passages. Stage two gives additional operations necessary for complete dismantling.

Stage 1

Disconnect the fuel pipe and remove: air cleaner, screws (3), spring washers (4), top cover (5) and gasket (6).

Lift out the spindle (60), float lever (59) and float (7).

Remove the plug (51), washer (52) and, using a long screwdriver, unscrew the main jet (53). Unscrew the pilot jet (14) and the air correction jet (8). Remove the valve body (54), valve (58) and take out the accelerator pump jet (57), taking care to catch the ball valve (55) from beneath it. Take out the screws (43) from the accelerator pump cover (42) and swing the cover to one side on the pump lever.

Remove the diaphragm (46) and spring (47), taking care not to lose the ball valve from its seating within the accelerator pump chamber.

Using clean fuel and an air line, clean out the float chamber, jets and fuel passage.

Re-assemble by reversing Stage 1 of the dismantling procedure.

Stage 2

TOP COVER

Unscrew the needle valve (61) and take off the fibre washer (64). Remove the screws (1), lift the strangler butterfly (2) from its slot in the spindle (62), withdraw the spindle from the top cover (5) and remove the spring (63).

MAIN BODY

Unscrew the nut (16) and remove the throttle lever (17), idling stop lever (18), washer (19) and strangler inter-connection lever (20).

Take out the screws (50), lift the throttle butterfly (48) from its slot in the spindle (49) and withdraw the spindle.

Release the push rod (31) and spring (29) by removing circlips (32) from both ends of the rod.

Slacken the screw (41), withdraw the push rod (26) from the strangler cam and release the lever (20), spring (24) and washers (23) (25) by extracting the split pins (27).

Remove the setscrews (44), pivot bolt (30) and take off the cam plate (28), spring (38) and bracket (37).

Remove the volume control screw (22) and spring (21). Unscrew the Econostat jet (9), take out the screw (10) and remove the spraying bridge (12).

Re-assembly

Fit the spraying bridge (12) to the body (11) and secure with the screw (10), secure the abutment bracket (37), return spring (38) and cam plate (28) to the carburettor body with screw (44) and pivot bolt.

Fit the volume control screw (22) with spring (21).

Assemble the throttle spindle (49) to the body (11) and fit the butterfly (48) retaining it with the screws (50). Position the washer (25) and spring (24) on the rod (26) and secure it to the lever (20) with the washer (23) and split pin (27). Secure the push rod (26) to the cam plate boss (28) with the screw (41). Assemble items (20), (19), (18) and (17) to the spindle (49), securing with the nut (16). Fit the push rod (31) to the spindle lever (49) and fit the spring (29), pump lever and circlip (32) positioning it in the first groove on the rod (31).

Assemble the ball valve (45), washer (52) and plug (51) the valve body (54) and valve (58), ball (55), washer (56) and pump jet (57), the Econostat fuel jet (9) and air correction jet (8), the float (7), lever (59) and pivot (60) to the body (11).

Assemble the spring (63) to the spindle (62) and fit the spindle to the top cover (5), fit the strangler (2) and secure with screws (1). Fit the needle valve (61) and washer (64), position the gasket (6) on the body (11), hold the strangler (2) open and fit the cover (5) to the body, securing with screws (3) and washer (4). Adjust the throttle/strangler inter-connecting rod (26) by inserting a length of 0·027″ (0·7 mm.) wire (A) between the throttle butterfly (48) and the bore of the carburettor body. With the strangler (2) held fully closed, tighten the screw (41) as shown on Fig. 9.

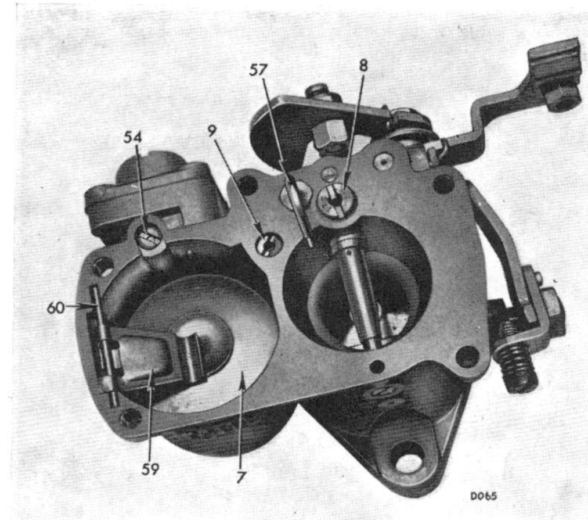

Fig. 8. Carburettor float and jet details

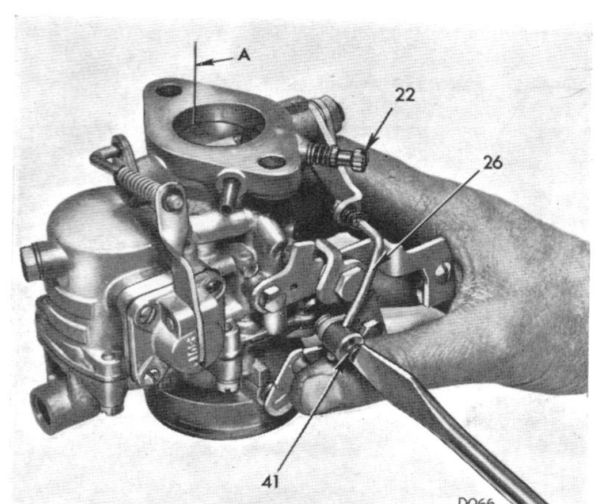

Fig. 9. Adjusting the throttle and choke inter-connection, using a piece of 0·027″ (0·7 mm.) wire "A" between the throttle butterfly and bore of carburettor body

SPITFIRE

CARBURETTORS

Replenishing Dampers (Fig. 11)

Remove the dampers and replenish the dashpots with thin engine oil, grade SAE 20 (but no thicker than SAE 30). The oil level is correct when the damper is approximately ¼″ (6 mm.) above the dashpots when resistance is felt.

Cleaning Suction Chamber and Piston

At approximate intervals of twelve months, detach the piston unit. Clean the piston and the inside bore of the suction chamber. Re-assemble dry except for a few spots of thin oil on the piston rod.

Replenish the damper reservoir.

Cleaning Float Chambers

Every 6,000 miles (10,000 km.) disconnect the fuel feed pipes and remove both float chamber lids and float assemblies. Remove any sediment from the float chambers, re-assemble the carburettors and re-connect the fuel pipes.

Jet Centralising (Fig. 12)

If the suction piston is lifted by hand and released, it should fall freely and hit the inside "jet bridge" with a soft metallic click when the jet adjusting nut (2) is screwed to its topmost position.

If a click is audible only when the jet is in the fully lowered position, the jet should be centralised as follows:—

Holding the jet (3) in its upper position, slacken the gland nut (1) and move the jet assembly laterally until the jet is concentric with the needle, then tighten the gland nut. The piston should now fall freely and hit the jet bridge with a soft metallic click.

Lower the jet and again lift and release the piston, noting any difference in the sound of impact. If a sharper impact sound results, repeat the centralising operation to achieve identical sounds with the jet raised and lowered.

Re-connect the jet lever (62) Fig. 10, replenish the dampers and tune the carburettors before replacing the air cleaners.

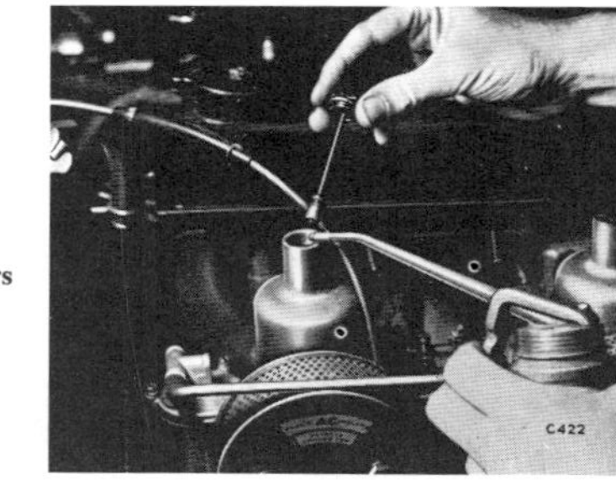

Fig. 11.
Replenishing damper chambers

1 Jet gland nut
2 Jet adjusting nut
3 Jet assembly
4 Nylon tube
8 Piston lifting pin
9 Oil well

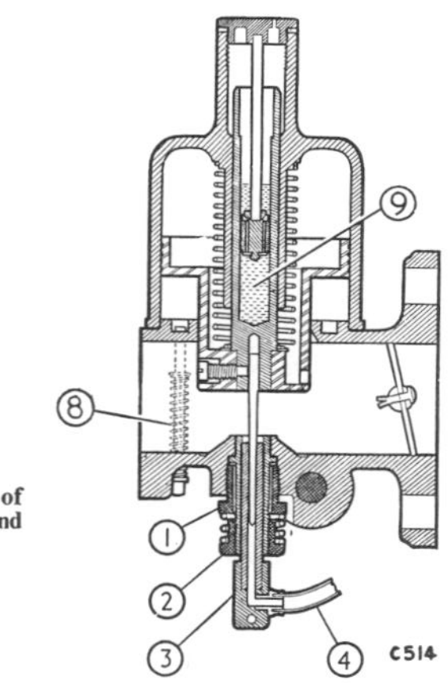

Fig. 12. Cross section of carburettor showing jet and piston assemblies

Fig. 13.
Method of lifting piston to check jet centralization

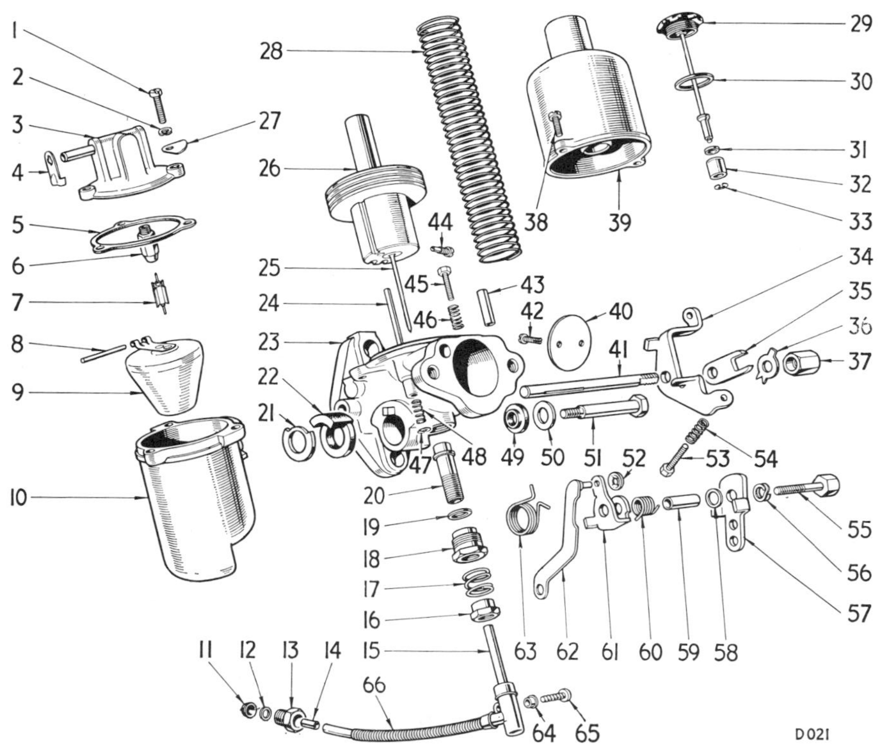

Fig. 10. Exploded S.U. carburettor

Key to Fig. 10

1 Screw
2 Spring washer
3 Float chamber lid
4 Breather hole shroud
5 Gasket
6 Needle valve body
7 Needle valve
8 Float spindle
9 Float
10 Float chamber
11 Cup
12 Washer
13 Union nut
14 Sleeve
15 Jet
16 Adjusting nut
17 Spring
18 Gland nut
19 Washer
20 Jet holder
21 Washer
22 Rubber seal
23 Main body
24 Lifting pin
25 Needle
26 Piston
27 Identification plate
28 Spring
29 Cap
30 Washer
31 Washer
32 Piston
33 Circlip
34 Throttle adjusting bracket
35 Throttle fork
36 Lock tab
37 Nut
38 Screw
39 Vacuum chamber
40 Throttle disc
41 Throttle spindle
42 Screw
43 Mixture enrichment cable abutment
44 Needle retaining screw
45 Throttle adjusting screw
46 Spring
47 Circlip
48 Spring
49 Rubber seal
50 Plain washer
51 Bolt
52 Circlip
53 Throttle adjusting screw
54 Spring
55 Bolt
56 Spring washer
57 Cam lever
58 Distance washer
59 Tube
60 Return spring
61 Pick-up lever
62 Jet lever
63 Return spring
64 Shouldered washer
65 Screw
66 Flexible pipe

Fig. 14. Using a 0·015″ (0·4 mm.) feeler gauge to obtain correct jet/throttle interconnection clearance

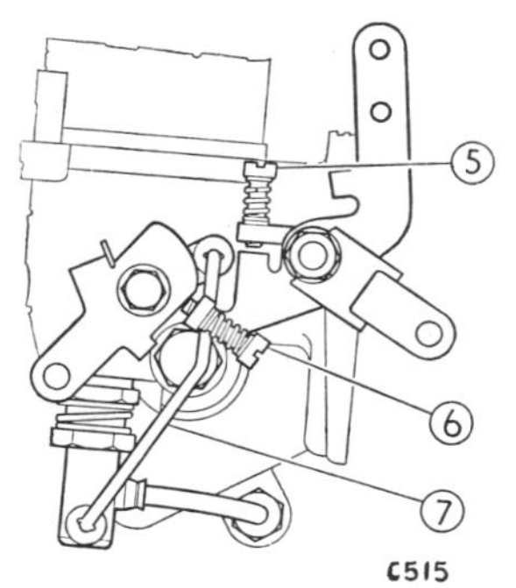

Fig. 15. Jet and throttle interconnection adjustment screws

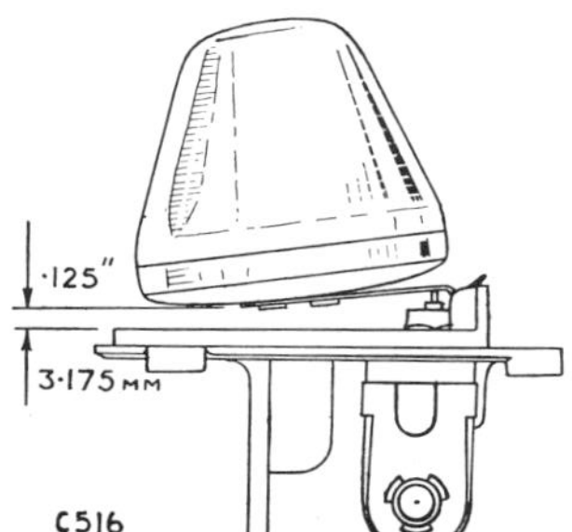

Fig. 16. Method of checking float level

Jet and Throttle Interconnection Adjustment (Figs. 14 and 15)

With the choke control fully "IN", the engine warm and idling on a closed throttle, adjust the screw (6) to give a clearance of 0·015″ (0·4 mm.) between the end of the screw and rocker lever.

Always check this adjustment when the throttle stop screw (5) is altered.

Float Chamber Fuel Level (Fig. 16)

The level of fuel in the float chamber is adjusted by setting the float lever on the float chamber lid, as follows:—

1. Disconnect the fuel feed pipe and remove the float chamber lid.

2. Invert the lid and, with the float lever resting on the needle valve, measure the gap between the lever and lower lid face as shown. This is easily measured by using a small piece of ⅛″ (10 SWG, 3·25 mm.) thick mild steel plate as a slip gauge.

3. If necessary, bend the float lever to obtain the correct setting.

4. Refit the float chamber lid, and re-connect the fuel pipe.

Carburettor Removal (Fig. 17)

1. Remove the air cleaners and disconnect the mixture enrichment cable (3), throttle control rod (7), throttle return springs (4), and fuel feed pipes (8) and (9).

2. Remove the flange nuts and lift off the carburettors complete with linkage.

Refitting

1. Using new gaskets, refit the carburettors, with the throttle and mixture enrichment spindles positioned between them.

2. Re-connect the throttle control rod (7), mixture enrichment control (3) and fuel feed pipes (8) and (9), and the return springs (4).

3. Ensure that the gaps between the spindle forks and pegs are correct by checking them as described in paragraph 7 on page 1·310 and shown on Fig. 23.

TUNING CARBURETTORS

Twin carburettor installations cannot be successfully tuned unless the general condition of the engine, ignition and the fuel system is satisfactory.

1. Remove the air cleaners and run the engine until it has attained its normal operating temperature. Slacken the clamping bolts on the throttle spindle connections. Close the throttles fully by unscrewing the idling adjustment screws and then open them by screwing down one and a half turns.

2. Remove the suction chambers and pistons. Rotate the jet adjusting nuts until each jet is flush with the bridge of its carburettor, or as near to this as possible. (Both jets being in the same relative position to the bridge of their respective carburettors.) Replace the pistons and suction chamber assemblies and check that the pistons fall freely onto the bridges of the carburettors. Turn down the jet adjusting nuts two complete turns (12 flats).

3. Start the engine and adjust the throttle adjusting screws (Fig. 20) to give the desired idling speed (approx. 550 r.p.m.) by moving each throttle adjusting screw an equal amount. Using a length of 0·3″ (3 mm.) approx. bore tubing, listen to the hiss in the intake (Fig. 21) and adjust the throttle adjusting screws until the intensity of the hiss is similar in both intakes. This will synchronize the throttles.

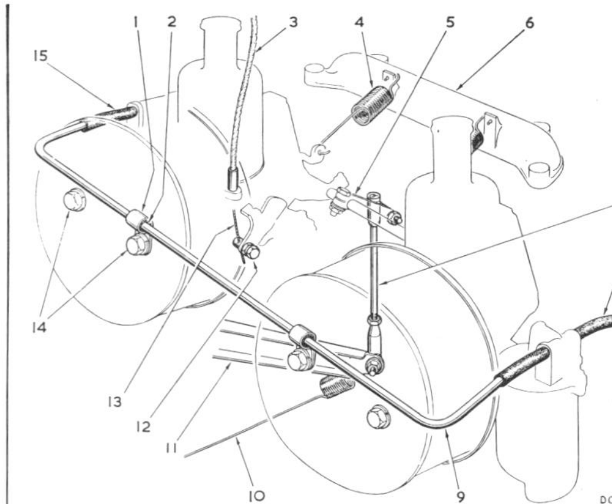

Fig. 17. Carburettor fuel pipe and control details

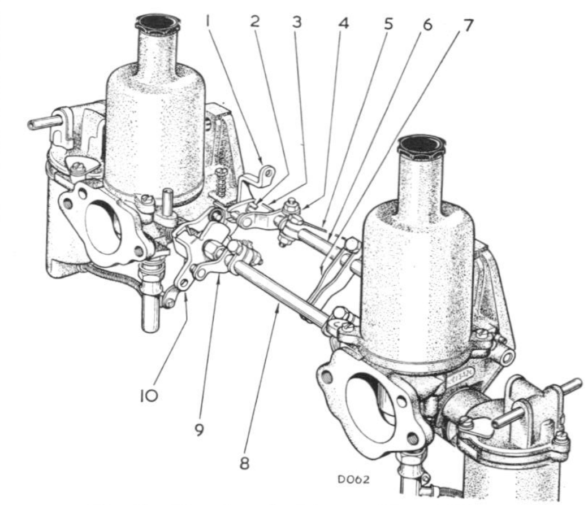

Fig. 18. Throttle and mixture enrichment linkages

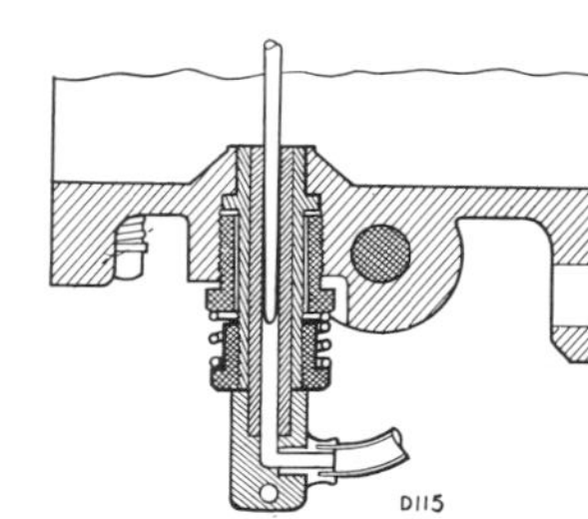

Fig. 19. Jet raised level with carburettor bridge

Fig. 20. Adjusting throttle stop screws

Fig. 21. Listening to volume of hiss at carburettor intakes

Fig. 22. Using piston lifting pin to check mixture strength

4. Adjust the mixture by screwing both the jet adjusting nuts up or down by the same amount until the fastest idling speed is obtained consistent with even firing. During the adjustment press the jets upwards and ensure that they are in contact with the adjusting nuts.

   As the jets are adjusted the engine will probably run faster, and it may be necessary to unscrew the throttle adjusting screws a little, each by the same amount, to reduce the speed.

5. Check the mixture strength by lifting the piston of the front carburettor by approximately $\frac{1}{32}''$ (·75 mm.) when:

   (a) If the engine speed increases, the mixture strength of the front carburettor is too rich ;

   (b) If the engine speed immediately decreases, the mixture strength of the front carburettor is too weak ;

   (c) If the engine speed momentarily increases very slightly, the mixture strength of the front carburettor is correct.

   Repeat the operation at the rear carburettor and, after adjustment, re-check the front carburettor, since the two carburettors are interdependent.

6. When the mixture is correct the exhaust note should be regular and even. If it is irregular with a splashy type of misfire and with a colourless exhaust, the mixture is too weak. If there is a rhythmical type of misfire in the exhaust beat together with a blackish exhaust the mixture is too rich.

7. The throttle on each carburettor is operated by a lever and pin with the pin working in a forked lever attached to the throttle spindle. A clearance exists between the pin and fork which must be maintained when the throttle is closed and the engine is idling to prevent any load from the accelerator linkage being transferred to the throttle butterfly and spindle.

   To set this clearance move each throttle shaft lever downwards in turn until the lever pin rests lightly on a ·015″ (·38 mm.) feeler inserted between the lever and the lower arm of the carburettor throttle lever fork (Fig. 23). Tighten the clamp bolt of the throttle shaft lever at this position. The pins on the throttle shafts should then have clearance in the forks.

8. Check that the jet control linkage has approximately $\frac{1}{16}''$ (1·5 mm.) free movement before it starts to pull on the jet levers.

   Set the mixture control knob on the dash panel to its maximum movement without moving the jets and adjust the fast-idling cam screws to give an engine speed of about 1,000 r.p.m. when hot.

   Make sure that the jet is hard up against the bottom face of the adjusting nut of each carburettor after any movement of the nut.

Before starting to tune the carburettors, check that each adjusting nut is unscrewed by the same amount. When slow running is satisfactory, one nut may be unscrewed more than the other. Such variation is normal on new carburettors and more pronounced on worn ones.

Effect of Altitude and Climatic Extremes on Standard Tuning

The jet needle used for normal tuning is suitable for temperate climates from sea level up to 6,000 ft. (1829 mm.). Above that altitude, depending upon climatic heat and humidity, the use of weaker tuning may be necessary. Because of the wide variations of such conditions, there is no arbitrary factory recommendation for a particular needle. The owner will need to experiment with weaker needles until a satisfactory one is determined. Occasionally, a weaker piston return spring may effect the necessary weakening.

Fig. 23. Adjusting throttle spindle clamps to give clearance of peg in fork

Fig. 24. Rotating the jet adjusting nuts with a spanner

B 32 P1H SEMI-DOWNDRAUGHT CARBURETTOR DETAILS

VITESSE

SOLEX B.32 P1H CARBURETTORS

(Fitted up to Engine No. HB 6798)

Early production Vitesse six cylinder engines are fitted with twin Solex B.32 P1H-32 mm. semi-downdraught carburettors, each having twin float chambers positioned astride the choke tube bore; a progressive Zero Starter with quick-drive away and fast-idle system, and an accelerator pump.

To improve hot starting, modifications were made, rendering both pumps inoperative, as described in Service Information Sheet 1/68. The pumps have since been completely discarded and blanking plates fitted in lieu.

The illustrations appearing in this section show the original carburettors with pumps attached. The pumps should be made inoperative as follows:

1. Remove the pump jets (68), Fig. 27, and fit blanking plugs, Part No. 512087.
2. Disconnect and remove the pump operating rods (63).
3. Remove the operating arms from the diaphragm covers (71), by drifting out the securing pins.

From engine number HB 858HE, the jet settings given on page 7 have been adopted and may be used to advantage on earlier carburettors.

Idling Adjustment

To facilitate correct carburettor tuning, ensure that the compressions on all cylinders are even. Check the following items and make the necessary adjustments.

1. **Ignition timing** — 10° B.T.D.C. static. Advance slightly on test if necessary.
2. **Valve clearances** (cold) — Inlet and exhaust, 0·010″.
3. **Choke control** — Ensure that both operating levers return to the fully closed position.
4. **Jets** — Ensure that all jets are perfectly clean.
5. **Carburettor floats** — Examine both floats for damage or punctures and renew if necessary.
6. **Needle valve height** — Remove each float chamber lid, invert it and place a straight edge across the machined face, directly over the needle valve. *The top of the needle valve should just touch the edge.*

   If the needle valve is more than 0·020″ (0·51 mm.) below the straight edge, fit an additional washer 0·020″ (0·51 mm.) thick (Solex Carb. Number 10593) between the needle valve and top cover.

Fig. 25. L.H. view of carburettors, showing flexible linkage clamping bolts (3) and throttle stop screws (1)

Fig. 26. R.H. view of carburettors, showing mixture control screws (2) and throttle stop screws (1)

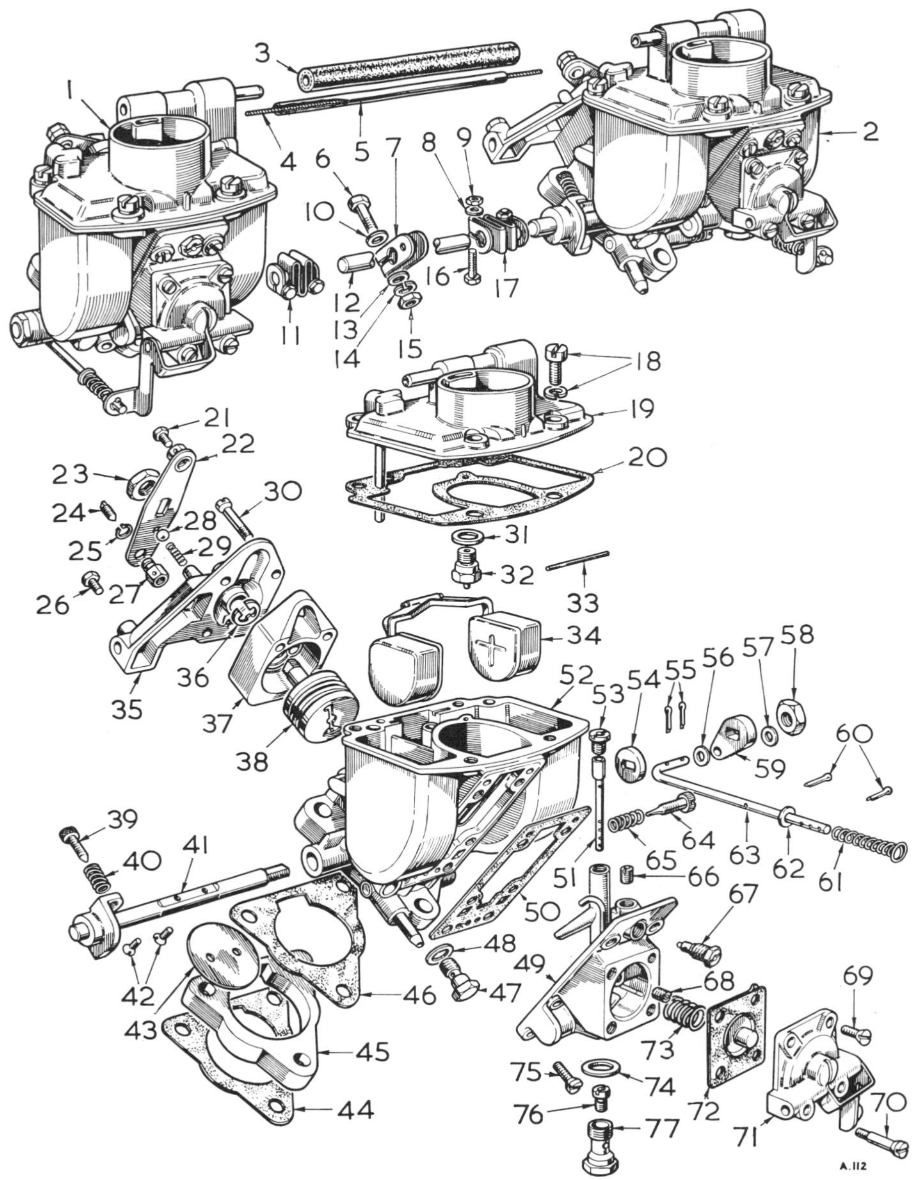

Fig. 27. Exploded B32 P1H semi-downdraught carburettor

Key to Fig. 27

1	Rear carburettor	27	Nipple	53	Air correction jet
2	Front carburettor	28	Ball	54	Distance piece
3	Fuel hose	29	Spring	55	Split pins
4	Choke cable—inner	30	Bolt	56	Plain washer
5	Choke cable—outer	31	Fibre washer	57	Plain washer
6	Pinch bolt	32	Needle valve	58	Nut
7	Accelerator lever	33	Pivot pin	59	Lever
8	Plain washer	34	Float assembly	60	Split pins
9	Nut	35	Starter cover	61	Spring
10	Plain washer	36	Circlip	62	Plain washer
11	Coupling assembly	37	Starter body	63	Push rod
12	Coupling rod	38	Disc valve	64	Idling mixture adjusting screw
13	Spring washer	39	Stop screw	65	Spring
14	Plain washer	40	Spring	66	Idling mixture air bleed jet
15	Nut	41	Throttle spindle	67	Idling mixture fuel jet
16	Pinch bolt	42	Screws	68	Pump jet
17	Spring coupling	43	Throttle disc	69	Screw
18	Screw and spring washer	44	Gasket	70	Screw
19	Top cover	45	Insulation gasket	71	Pump cover plate assembly
20	Gasket	46	Gasket	72	Pump diaphragm
21	Pinch screw	47	Starter jet	73	Spring
22	Lever	48	Washer	74	Fibre washer
23	Nut	49	Jet block assembly	75	Screw
24	Pinch screw	50	Gasket	76	Main jet
25	Circlip	51	Emulsion tube	77	Main jet carrier
26	Screw	52	Carburettor body		

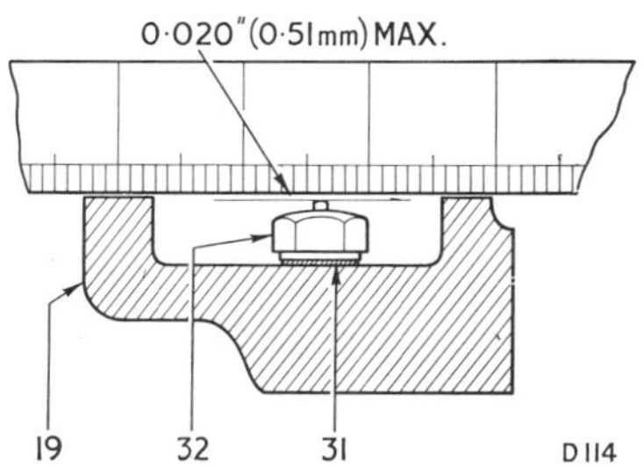

Fig. 28. Checking needle valve height

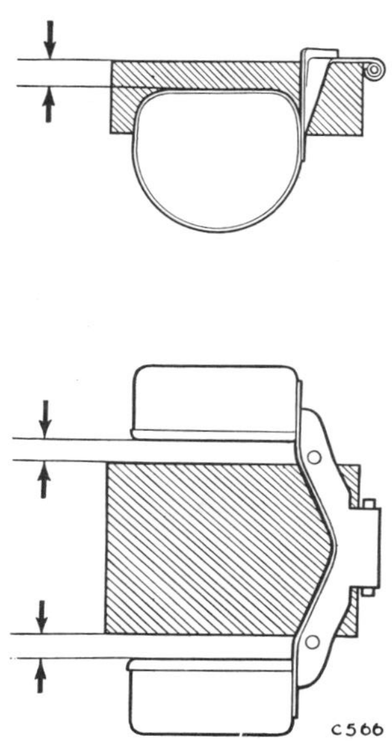

Fig. 29. Checking and adjusting float setting

7. **Float adjustment** — Using an oblong wood or metal block, 1½" × 2" × ½" (38·1 × 50·8 × 12·7 mm.), place the float on the block as indicated on Fig. 29.

   The pivot pin boss must lie squarely up to the edge of the block.

   Set each float individually to achieve symmetry between the tops and inner faces of the floats and the block as shown.

   Re-assemble the carburettors and ensure that the floats move freely in the float chambers.

8. **Tuning and synchronising the carburettors**—

   Slacken the clamping bolt (3) Fig. 25 on the flexible linkage between the carburettors and, whilst the engine is warm, adjust the carburettors as follows:

   (a) Unscrew both slow running screws (1) Fig. 25 and ensure that the throttles are closed by manual pressure on the screw heads. Open both throttles an equal amount by rotating the screws (1) one turn clockwise.

   (b) Gently screw the mixture control screws clockwise until **light contact** is made with the casting seat and then unscrew them approximately one full turn.

   (c) Start the engine and adjust the slow running control screws (2) Fig. 26 equally until the idling speed is approximately 500 r.p.m.

   (d) Screw out both mixture control screws a quarter of a turn at a time, until the engine begins to "hunt", indicating richness.

   (e) Screw the mixture screws in by equal amounts until the "hunting" disappears and the engine idles smoothly.

   (f) If the engine speed has now increased due to the mixture adjustment, reduce the speed to approximately 600-650 r.p.m. by adjusting the slow running screws by equal amounts.

   (g) If operation (f) causes irregular idling, re-adjust both mixture screws to maintain synchronisation.

   (h) Ensure that both throttles are against their stops and re-tighten the connecting linkage between the carburettors.

VITESSE

Removal (Fig. 27)

Dismantle and clean the carburettors as follows:—

1. Release the hose clips, detach the support strut and remove the air cleaner and air box assembly.

2. Disconnect the fuel pipes and vacuum advance pipe. Disconnect the connecting cables (4) and (5) and the choke control cable. Slacken the pinch bolts (16) and withdraw the spring couplings (11) and (17) from the throttle spindle.

3. Remove the flange nuts and lift off the carburettors.

Dismantling

1. Take out the screws (18) and lift off the top cover (19) and gasket (20). Unscrew the needle valve (32) with washer (31), and lift out floats (34) and pivot pin (33).

2. Take out the bolts (30) and detach the starter unit. Unscrew the nut (23) and remove the lever (22), ball (28) and spring (29). Remove the cover (35) circlip (36) and withdraw the disc assembly from the body (37).

3. Take out the screws (75) and remove the jet block assembly (49) and gasket (50). Remove the jets (66) and (67), main jet carrier (77), screw (64), emulsion tube (51) and air correction jet (53). Take out the screws (69) and (70) and remove the pump details (71), (72) and (73) and jet (68).

4. Remove the push rod (63), lever (59), screws (42), disc (43) and withdraw the spindle (41).

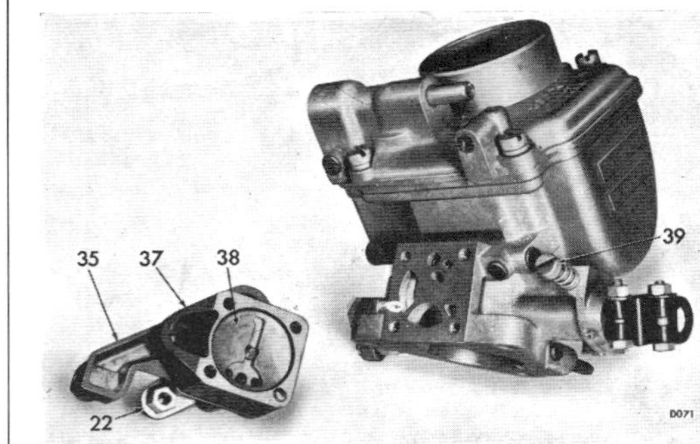

Fig. 30. Starter unit removed from carburettor

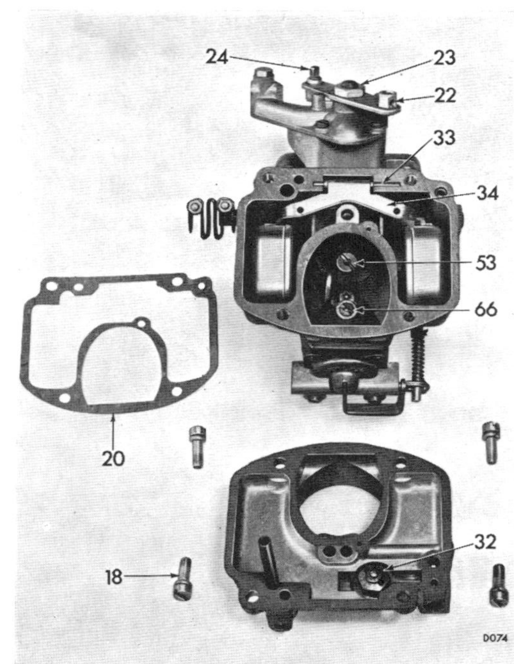

Fig. 31. Top cover details

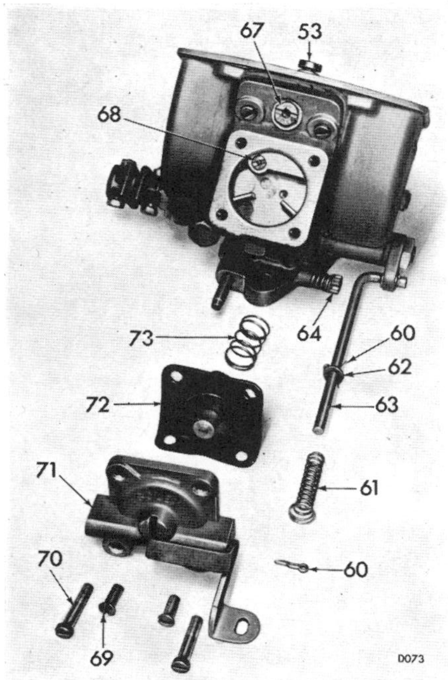

Fig. 32. Accelerator pump components

Re-assembly

Re-assemble the carburettor by reversing the dismantling procedure. Renew damaged gaskets and washers. Refit the accelerator pump push rod (63) with the outer split pin (60) in the centre hole.

Refitting

Refit the carburettors by reversing the removal sequence. Renew the gaskets (44) and (46) and the asbestos gasket (45). Ensure that throttle spindles and starting carburettor levers are synchronised and able to close fully.

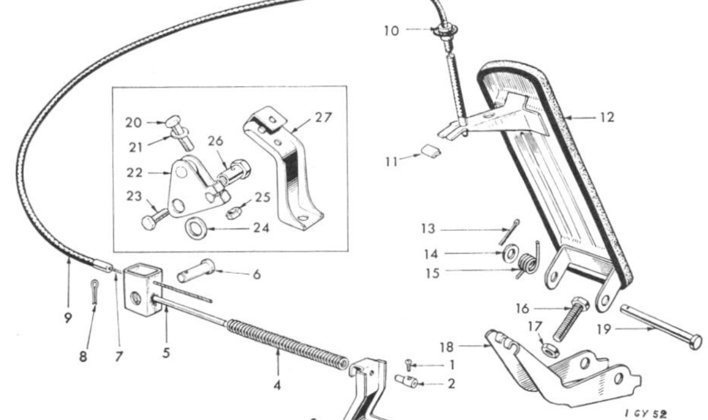

1 Screw
2 Nipple
3 Abutment bracket
4 Spring
5 Guide rod
6 Clevis pin
7 Inner cable
8 Split pin
9 Outer cable
10 Rubber washer
11 Clip
12 Accelerator pedal
13 Split pin
14 Washer
15 Return spring
16 Stop bolt
17 Lock nut
18 Bracket
19 Pivot pin
20 Pinch bolt
21 Plain washer
22 Lever
23 Setscrew
24 Washer
25 Nut
26 Nipple
27 Abutment bracket

NOTE : Items 20 to 27 in inset show Vitesse condition.

Fig. 33. Herald 1200 accelerator controls (inset showing Vitesse)

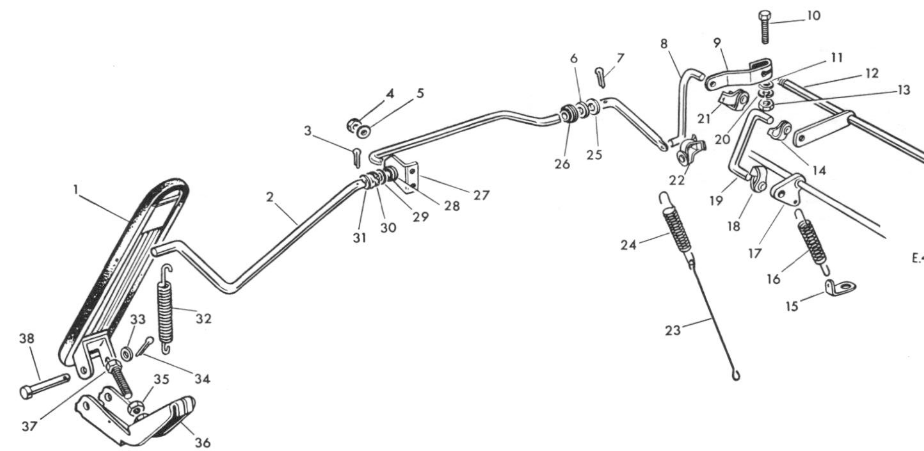

1	Pedal	14	Clip	*27	Bracket
2	Cross-shaft	15	Bracket	28	Bearing
*3	Split pin	16	Spring	*29	Plain washer
*4	Nut	17	Connecting rod assembly	*30	Double spring washer
*5	Plain washer	18	Clip	*31	Plain washer
6	Felt washer	19	Link	32	Spring
7	Split pin	20	Spring washer	33	Plain washer
8	Link	21	Clip	34	Split pin
9	Actuating lever	22	Clip	35	Locknut
10	Setscrew	23	Extension	36	Bracket assembly
11	Plain washer	24	Spring	37	Setscrew
12	Lever assembly	25	Plain washer	38	Pin
13	Nut	26	Bearing		

* R.H.S. only

Fig. 34. Vitesse accelerator controls (From Commission Nos. HC.7605 R.H.S. and HB.7556 L.H.S.)

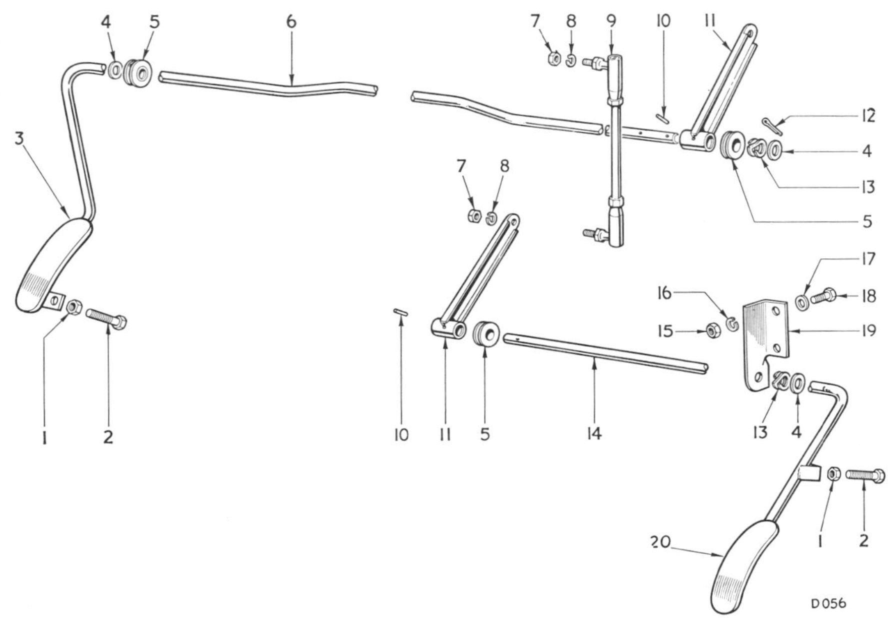

1	Nut	11	Lever
2	Stop bolt	12	Split pin
3	Accelerator pedal	13	Anti-rattle washer
4	Washer	14	Rod (R.H. drive)
5	Bearing	15	Nut
6	Rod	16	Spring washer
7	Nut	17	Plain washer
8	Spring washer	18	Bolt
9	Link	19	Bracket (R.H. drive)
10	Mills pin	20	Pedal

Fig. 35. Spitfire accelerator controls (L.H. and R.H. drive)

VITESSE

SOLEX B32.1H CARBURETTORS
(Fitted from Engine No. HB 6799 to HB 27985)

These carburettors are basically similar to those described on page 1·313 but differ in respect of the following:

1. The accelerator pump is discarded.
2. The jet block is of different form.

Jet settings are identical to those given on page 7.

To Check Needle Valve Height (Fig. 36)
Slacken the clips (2) and (3) (Fig. 40), securing air box (1) to carburettors and air cleaner hose (5) and remove the air box.

Remove the interconnecting fuel hose (3) from between the carburettors and disconnect the fuel line (60) to front carburettor.

Remove the screws (12), lift off and invert the float chamber cover.

Place a straight edge across the machined face (Fig. 28) and directly over the needle valve. The top of the needle valve should just touch the straight edge.

If the needle valve is more than 0·020″ (0·51 mm.) below the straight edge, fit an additional washer 0·020″ (0·51 mm.) thick (Solex Carb. Number 10593) between the needle valve and top cover.

Re-assemble the carburettor by reversing the part dismantling procedure above.

To Check Float Adjustment
Remove the float chamber lid as detailed above.

Remove the gasket (14) (Fig. 37), lift out the twin floats (19) and remove the pivot pin (18).

Using a wood or metal block, 1½″ × 2″ × ½″ (38·1 × 50·8 × 12·7 mm.) place the float assembly as shown in Fig. 29.

Set each float individually until the inner and top faces of the floats are symmetrical to the block.

Re-assemble the carburettors, ensuring that the floats move freely in the float chambers.

Jet Block — Removal (Fig. 36)
Remove the six screws (32) and withdraw the jet block (28).

Starter Block — Removal (Fig. 38)
Disconnect the choke cable (4) and (5) and interconnecting cable (62).

Remove the four screws (56), using a short or right-angle screwdriver, and lift off the starter block.

Fig. 36. R.H. view of carburettors

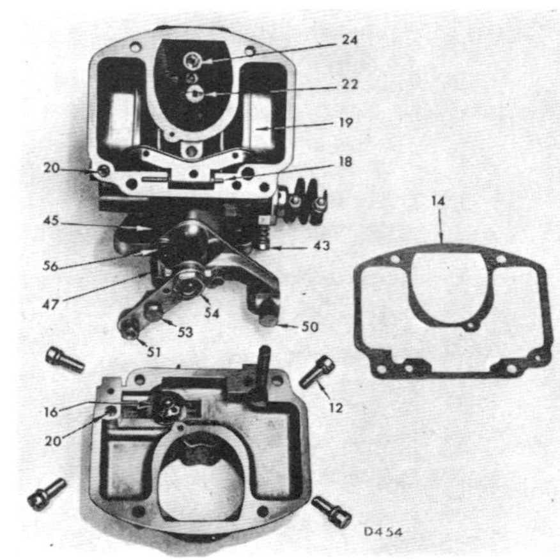

Fig. 37. Top cover and float chamber details

Fig. 38. L.H. view of carburettors

B32.1H SEMI-DOWNDRAUGHT CARBURETTOR DETAILS

Carburettor — Removal
Slacken the clips (2) and (3) (Fig. 43A) securing air box (1) to carburettors, and hose (5) to air cleaner. Remove the air box and hose.

Disconnect the fuel pipe (60) (Fig. 36) and advance vacuum pipe (61) from the front carburettor and remove the fuel hose (3) from between the carburettors.

Disconnect the choke control cable (4) (Fig. 38) and (5) and interconnecting cable (62).

Unhook the return spring from the throttle coupling rod (7) (Fig. 39). Slacken the clinch bolts (11) and withdraw the spring couplings (6) and (10) from the throttle spindles.

Remove the flange nuts and lift off the carburettors.

Dismantling (Fig. 39)
Remove the screws (12) and lift off the float chamber cover (13) and gasket (14). Unscrew the needle valve (16). Lift out the twin float assembly (19) and remove the pivot pin (18).

Remove the four screws (56) and lift off the starter unit. Unscrew the nut (54) and remove the lever (55), ball (57) and spring (58). Remove the cover (47), circlip (46) and withdraw the disc valve (44) from the body.

Remove the six screws (32) and withdraw the jet block assembly (28) and gasket (33). Remove idling mixture air bleed jet (24) and fuel jet (25), main jet carrier (31) and main jet (30), air correction jet (22) and emulsion tube (23). Remove the idling mixture adjusting screw (27) and spring (26) and the starter jet (34).

Remove the screws (40), withdraw the throttle disc (39) and spindle (41).

Re-assembly
Re-assemble the carburettor by reversing the dismantling procedure. Renew gaskets and washers as necessary.

Refitting
Refit the carburettors by reversing the removal sequence. Renew gaskets (36) and (38), and asbestos gasket (37). Ensure that the throttle spindles and starting levers are synchronised and able to close fully.

Tuning and Synchronising the Carburettors
The general condition of the engine, ignition and fuel system must be satisfactory to enable successful tuning of twin carburettor installation to be carried out.

1. With the engine at normal working temperature, slacken the throttle coupling pinch bolts. Unscrew the throttle stop screws (43) and ensure that the throttles are fully closed by manual pressure on the screw heads. Open both throttles an equal amount by rotating the screw (43) one turn clockwise.

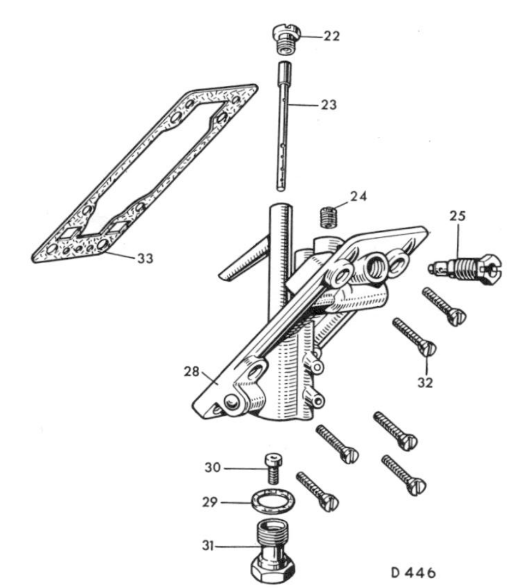

Fig. 40 Exploded view of jet block

Fig. 41. R.H. view of carburettors showing throttle stop screws (43) and mixture control screws (27)

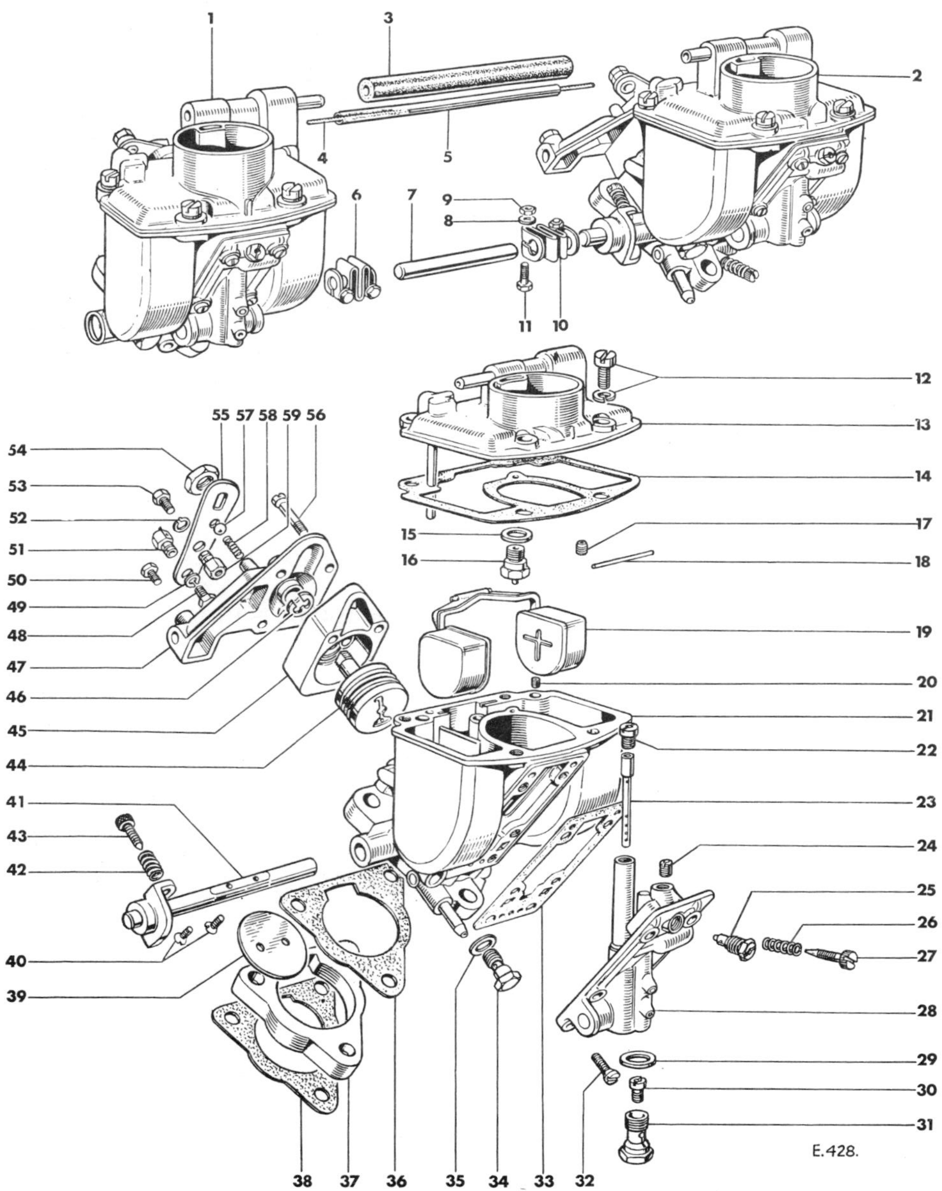

Fig. 39. Exploded B32.1H carburettor

Key to Fig. 39

1 Rear carburettor
2 Front carburettor
3 Fuel hose
4 Choke cable—inner
5 Choke cable—outer
6 Coupling assembly
7 Coupling rod
8 Plain washer
9 Nut
10 Spring coupling
11 Pinch bolt
12 Screw and spring washer
13 Top cover
14 Gasket
15 Fibre washer
16 Needle valve
17 Econostat air bleed
18 Pivot pin
19 Float assembly
20 Econostat jet
21 Carburettor body
22 Air correction jet
23 Emulsion tube
24 Idling mixture air bleed jet
25 Idling mixture fuel jet
26 Spring
27 Idling mixture adjusting screw
28 Jet block
29 Fibre washer
30 Main jet
31 Main jet carrier
32 Screw
33 Gasket
34 Starter jet
35 Fibre washer
36 Gasket
37 Insulation gasket
38 Gasket
39 Throttle disc
40 Screws
41 Throttle spindle
42 Spring
43 Throttle stop screw
44 Disc valve
45 Starter body
46 Circlip
47 Starter body cover
48 Inter-connecting cable locking screw
49 Circlip
50 Choke outer cable locking screw
51 Swivel
52 Circlip
53 Choke inner cable locking screw
54 Nut
55 Starter lever
56 Bolt
57 Ball
58 Spring
59 Swivel

2. Gently screw in the mixture control screws (27) until light contact is made with the casing seat and then unscrew them approximately one full turn.
3. Start the engine and adjust the throttle stop screws (43) equally until the idling speed is approximately 500 r.p.m.
4. Screw out both mixture control screws, a quarter of a turn at a time, until the engine begins to "hunt".
5. Screw in the mixture control screws until the "hunting" disappears and the engine idles smoothly.
6. If the engine speed has now increased due to the mixture adjustment, reduce the engine speed to approximately 600-650 r.p.m. by screwing out the throttle stop screws equal amounts.
7. If operation 6 causes irregular idling, re-adjust both mixture control screws.
8. Ensure that both throttles are against their stops and retighten the spring coupling pinch bolts.

Fig. 42A. 13/60 Air cleaner installed

Fig. 42B. Spitfire air cleaners

AIR CLEANERS

The correct maintenance of the air cleaner(s) is an important factor in combustion efficiency, a clogged filter will cause the mixture to become enriched and, ultimately all the symptoms associated with that fault will become apparent.

The illustrations in this section provide sufficient information for the removal and, where applicable, dismantling of the units.

Paper element air cleaners should be cleaned every 6,000 miles (10,000 km.) and the elements changed every 12,000 miles (20,000 km.). Use a soft brush or low pressure air line to clean between the folds of the paper element.

Wire gauze elements are fitted to certain market conditions and these should be cleaned in petrol, allowed to drain, dipped in clean engine oil, allowed to drain and refitted every 6,000 miles (10,000 km.).

Vehicle handbooks carry further details for specific models.

In dusty climates more frequent attention will be required.

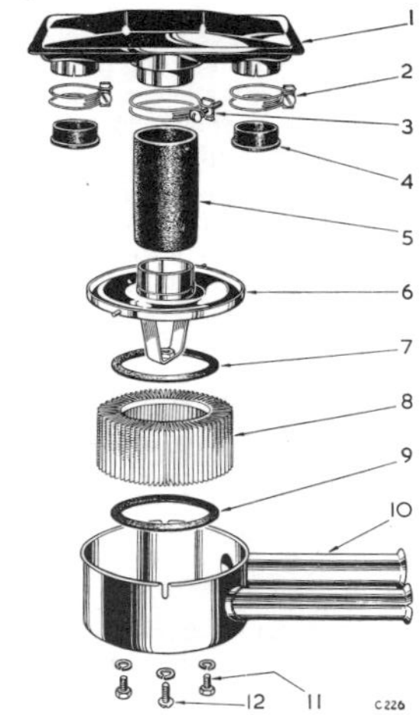

1 Air box
2 Clip
3 Clip
4 Rubber inserts
5 Hose—cleaner to air box
6 Closing plate
7 Gasket
8 Element
9 Gasket
10 Case
11 Screw—to support bracket
12 Screw—case to plate

Fig. 43A. Vitesse air cleaner (prior to Engine No. HB 27985)

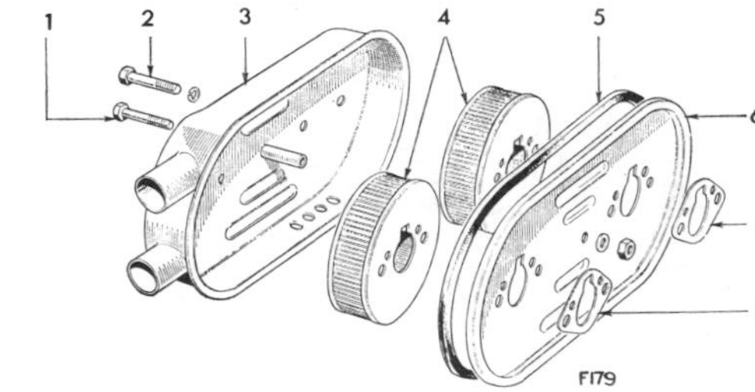

1 Securing bolt
2 Clamping bolt
3 Front cover
4 Element
5 Gasket
6 Closing plate
7 Gasket—to carburettor

Fig. 43B. Vitesse air cleaner (after Engine No. HB 27985)

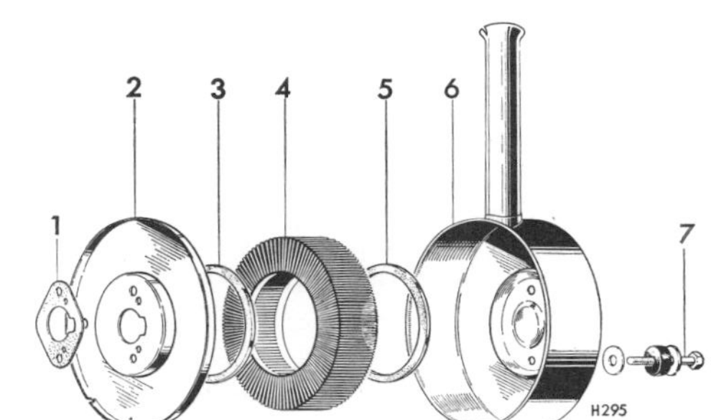

1 Gasket to carburettor
2 Closing plate
3 Gasket—element to plate
4 Element
5 Gasket—element to case
6 Case
7 Securing bolt

Fig. 43C. 13/60 air cleaner

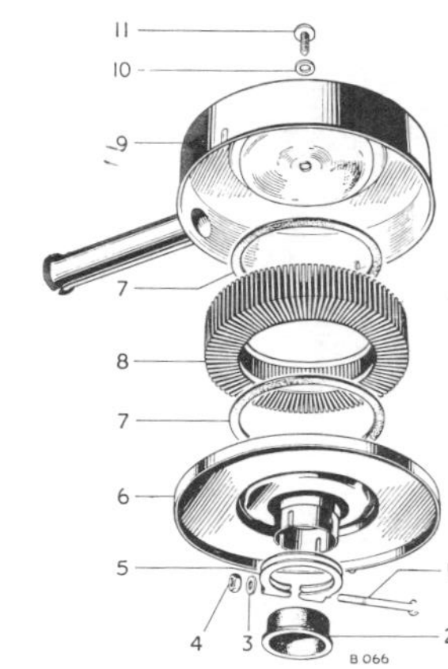

1 Clamping bolt
2 Rubber insert
3 Washer
4 Nut
5 Clamp
6 Closing plate
7 Gasket
8 Element
9 Case
10 Sealing washer
11 Retaining screw

Fig. 43D. 1200 and 12/50 air cleaner

ZENITH - STROMBERG (SERIES 150CD) CARBURETTOR DETAILS

ZENITH-STROMBERG CARBURETTORS
SERIES 150.CD

FITTED TO:

Vitesse 6 from ENGINE No. HB.27986 in twin carburettor arrangement. HERALD 13/60 All models in single carburettor arrangement.

NOTE:

When servicing 13/60 models disregard instructions which refer specifically to twin carburettor models.

Starting from Cold

The mixture is enriched for cold starting when the choke control is pulled. This operates a lever (71) which rotates the starter bar (28) to lift the air valve (9) and needle (11), thus increasing the area of the annulus between needle and jet orifice. Simultaneously, a cam on the lever (71) opens the throttle beyond its normal idle position to provide increased idling speed, according to the setting of the screw (69).

When the motor fires the increased depression will lift the air valve (9) to weaken the initial starting mixture and prevent the engine stalling through over richness.

While the choke remains in action the car may be driven away but the control knob should be released or pushed in gradually as the engine attains normal working temperature. This will progressively decrease the extent of enrichment and the degree of throttle opening for fast-idle to the point where the screw (69) is out of contact with the cam on the choke lever and the throttle is permitted to return to the normal idle position as determined by the setting of the throttle stop screw (29).

NOTE : The accelerator pedal should not be depressed when starting from cold.

Normal Running

With the opening of the butterfly throttle, manifold depression is transferred, via a drilling (78) in the air valve, to the chamber (77) which is sealed from the main body by the diaphragm (8).

The pressure difference between chamber (77) and that existing in the bore (79) causes the air valve to lift, thus any increase in engine speed or load will enlarge the effective choke area since the air valve lift is proportional to the weight of air passing the throttle (16). By this means air velocity and pressure drop across the jet orifice remain approximately constant at all speeds.

As the air valve (9) rises it withdraws a tapered metering needle (11), held in the base of the air valve by the screw (10), from the jet orifice (80) so that fuel flow is increased relative to the greater air flow.

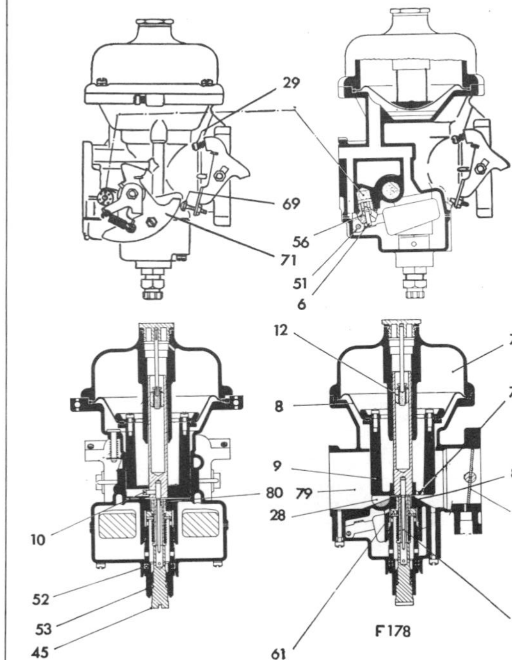

77 Chamber 78 Air valve drilling
79 Bore 80 Jet orifice 81 Bridge

Fig. 45. Functional diagram

Fig. 45a Stromberg CD.150 Single carburettor arrangement

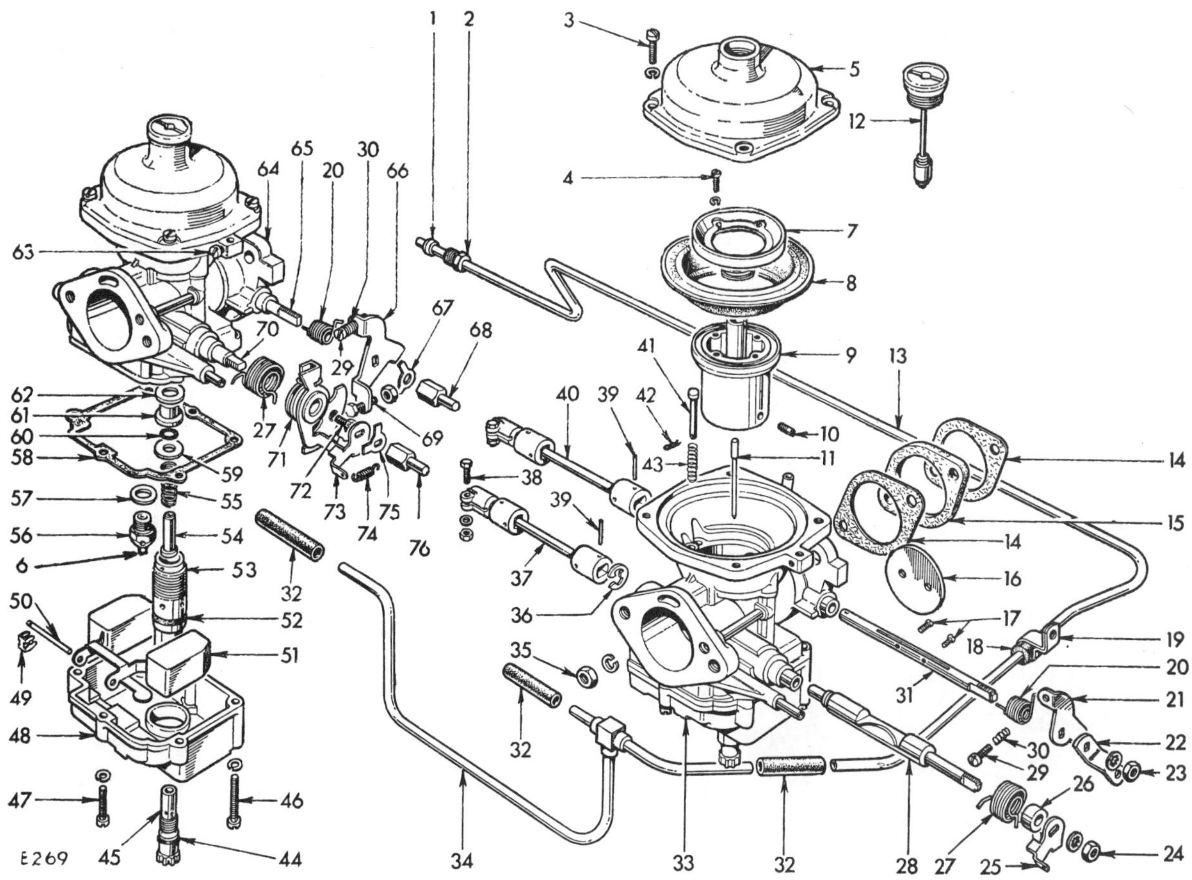

Fig. 44. Vitesse, Stromberg carburettor details

Key to Fig. 44

1 Sleeve
2 Nut
3 Screw
4 Screw
5 Cover
6 Needle
7 Retaining ring
8 Diaphragm
9 Air valve
10 Locking screw
11 Needle
12 Damper
13 Pipe
14 Gasket
15 Insulator
16 Throttle
17 Screw
18 Grommet
19 Bracket
20 Spring
21 Stop
22 Lever
23 Nut
24 Nut
25 Lever
26 Bush
27 Spring
28 Starter bar
29 Screw
30 Spring
31 Spindle
32 Connection
33 Float chamber
34 Pipe
35 Nut
36 Retaining ring
37 Coupling
38 Bolt
39 Pin
40 Coupling
41 Pin
42 Clip
43 Spring
44 "O" ring
45 Adjusting screw
46 Screw (long)
47 Screw (short)
48 Float chamber
49 Clip
50 Pin
51 Float assembly
52 "O" ring
53 Bushing screw
54 Jet
55 Spring
56 Needle seat
57 Washer
58 Gasket
59 Washer
60 "O" ring
61 Bushing
62 Washer
63 Screw
64 Body
65 Spindle
66 Stop
67 Washer
68 Nut
69 Screw
70 Starter bar
71 Lever
72 Screw
73 Lever
74 Spring
75 Washer
76 Nut

Fig. 46. Air box alignment

Fig. 47. Topping-up damper chambers

Fig. 48 Carburettor adjustment

Acceleration

At any point in the throttle range a temporarily richer mixture is needed at the moment of further throttle opening. To provide this, a dashpot or hydraulic damper is arranged inside the hollow guide rod of the air valve

The rod is filled with S.A.E. 20 oil to within a ¼″ of the end of the rod in which the damper (12) operates, when the throttle is opened, the immediate upward motion of the air valve is resisted by this plunger during which time the suction or depression at the jet orifice is increased to enrich the mixture.

Setting the Idling

Two adjustment screws are used to regulate the idle speed and mixture. The throttle stop screw (29) controls the speed and the jet adjusting screw (45) determines the ratio of air-fuel mixture entering the cylinders. Turn the jet adjusting screw **clockwise** to weaken the mixture strength; **anti-clockwise** to enrich it.

With the engine at normal working temperature, remove the air cleaner and hold the air valve (9) down on to the bridge (81) in the throttle bore. Screw up the jet adjustment screw (45)—a coin is ideal for this purpose—until the jet contacts the underside of the air valve. From this position turn down the jet adjusting screw three turns. This establishes an approximate jet position from which to work.

Run the engine until it is thoroughly warm and adjust the stop screw (29) to give an idle speed of 600/650 r.p.m.

The idling mixture is correct when the engine beat is smooth and regular and the air intake "hiss" is equal on both carburettors.

As a check, lift the air valve a very small amount ($\frac{1}{32}$″) using the piston-lifting pin (41) and listen to the effect on the engine. If the engine speed rises appreciably, the mixture is too rich, and if the engine stops, the mixture is too weak. Properly adjusted, the engine speed will either remain constant or fall slightly on lifting the air valve.

Adjusting and Synchronising Twin Carburettor Installation

Loosen the clamping bolts (38) on the throttle spindle couplings between the two carburettors. Unscrew the throttle stop screw (29) to permit the throttle in each carburettor to close completely, and re-tighten the clamping bolts (38).

Ensure that screw (69) is adjusted to give a gap of $\frac{1}{16}$″ (1·575 mm.) as shown arrowed Fig. 48.

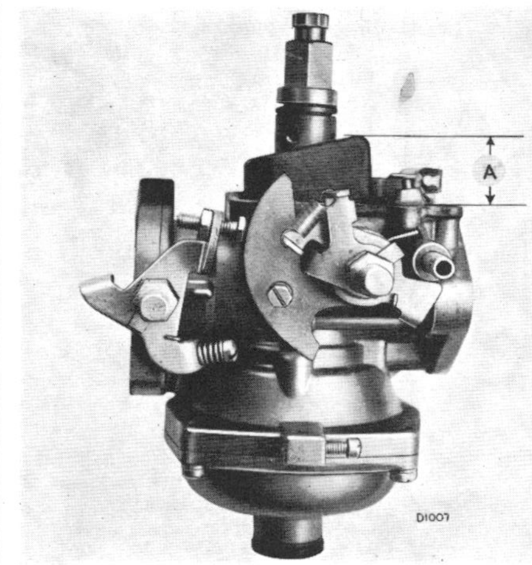

Fig. 49. Checking float chamber fuel level

Screw in the throttle stop screws (29) to the point where the end of the screw is just contacting the carburettor body. From this point rotate each stop screw one complete turn to open the throttles an equal amount to provide a basis from which final idling speed can be set.

Having reconnected the throttles and set each open an equal amount, regulate the jet adjusting screws (45) as detailed under the heading "Setting the Idling".

NOTE : Satisfactory idling depends upon the general engine condition and tappet adjustment, spark plugs, and ignition timing, which should be inspected if idling is not stable.

Float Chamber Fuel Level (Fig. 49)

To check the float level, remove the carburettor from the engine and remove the float chamber. Invert the carburettor. Check that the highest point of the float, when the needle is against its seating, is 18 mm. above the face of the main body. See "A". Reset the level by carefully bending the tag which contacts the end of the needle. The addition of a thin fibre washer under the needle valve seat will lower the fuel level.

Jet Centralisation

Efficient operation of the carburettor depends upon a freely moving air valve and a correctly centred needle in the jet orifice.

Check the air valve for free movement by lifting the valve. A valve failing to fall freely indicates a sticking valve or an off-centred jet, causing the needle (11) to foul the jet orifice.

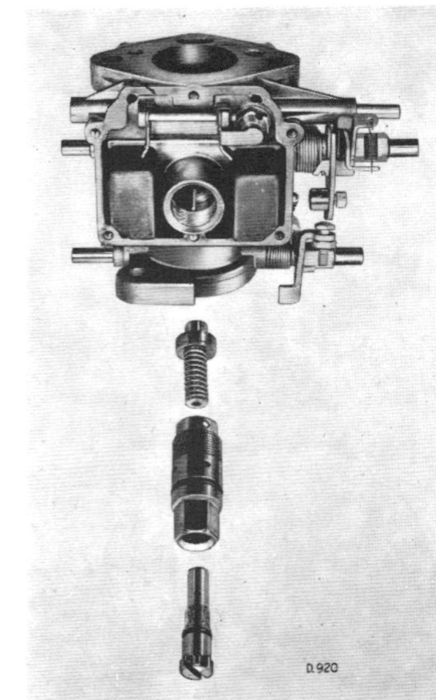

Fig. 50 Jet bushing screw and adjusting screw

Fig. 51 Float chamber details

Fig. 52. Diaphragm location

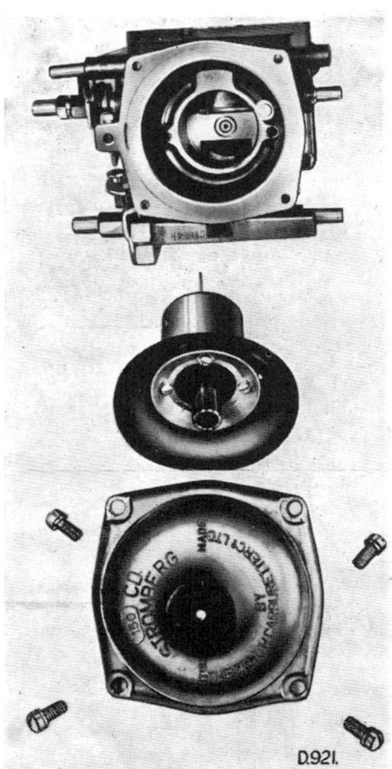

Fig. 53. Top view of carburettor with cover and air valve assembly removed

Rectify by removing and cleaning the valve and bore in paraffin, or by re-centralising the jet.

NOTE : When required, the jet needle must be renewed by one bearing the same code number. The shoulder of the needle must be fitted flush with the lower face of the air valve.

Procedure (Fig. 45)

1. Lift the air valve (9) and fully tighten the jet assembly (53).
2. Screw up the orifice adjuster until the top of the orifice (80) is just above the bridge (81).
3. Slacken off the jet assembly (53) to release the orifice bush (61).
4. Allow the air valve (9) to fall; the needle will then enter the orifice and thus centralise it.
5. Slowly tighten the assembly (53), checking frequently that the needle remains free in the orifice. Check by raising the air valve approximately ¼" and allowing it to fall freely. The piston should then stop firmly on the bridge.
6. Re-set the engine idling.

Carburettors—Emission Control System

The following information applies specifically to the emission control system of the Spitfire Mk. 3 which complies with Federal Regulations (31 C.F.R. Part 85) governing the emission of Hydrocarbons and Carbon Monoxide from vehicle exhaust systems.

S.U. Emission carburettors (N.A.D.A. Specification AUD 285) are produced to a special anti-pollution standard, and must not in any circumstances be interchanged with carburettors not to this specification.

Service requirements are restricted to those given in the owners handbook plus the reconditioning or fitting of reconditioned carburettors every 48,000 miles. This must be carried out by an authorised dealer carrying out the instruction detailed in this section.

Tuning

Tuning is dealt with in two parts, namely: Basic Tuning which will satisfy conditions where the carburettors are, due to normal processes, slightly out of attunement, and: Complete Tuning when the carburettors are required to be set up from a completely "out of attunement" condition as when fitting new carburettors or subsequent to reconditioning.

All tuning must be carried out by an authorised dealer using the methods described in this section.

Basic Tuning

1. Connect a tachometer as instructed by the instrument manufacturer.
2. Remove the air cleaner and gaskets.
3. Top up dampers.
4. Run the engine at approximately 1,000 r.p.m. until five minutes after normal operating temperature is reached then run the engine at 2,500 r.p.m. for half a minute.
5. Commence tuning at once and repeat the half minute of 2,500 r.p.m. every three minutes until the tuning is completed.
6. Use a balancing meter as shown in Fig. 54 to ascertain whether the carburettors are in balance.
7. If the carburettors are out of balance refer to "Complete Tuning" operations 12, 13 and 14.
8. If satisfactory idling cannot be achieved, after balancing, adjust the mixture as follows:
   (a) Turn the jet adjuster nut (28) Fig. 56 on both carburettors by the same amount within the limits of the restrictor to achieve the maximum speed consistent with smooth running.
   (b) Re-check the idling speed and adjust, if necessary, by altering both idling screws (5) Fig. 57 by the same amount. Re-check the balance.

Fig. 54. Using a balancing meter

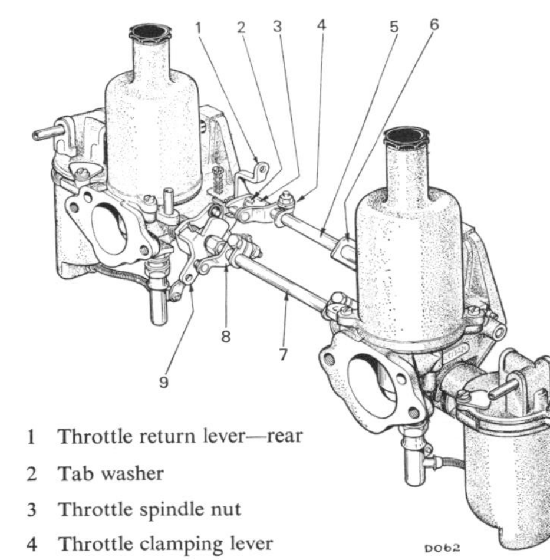

1 Throttle return lever—rear
2 Tab washer
3 Throttle spindle nut
4 Throttle clamping lever
5 Throttle connecting rod
6 Throttle actuating lever
7 Choke control connecting rod
8 Choke clamping lever
9 Choke actuating lever

Fig. 55. Carburettor linkages

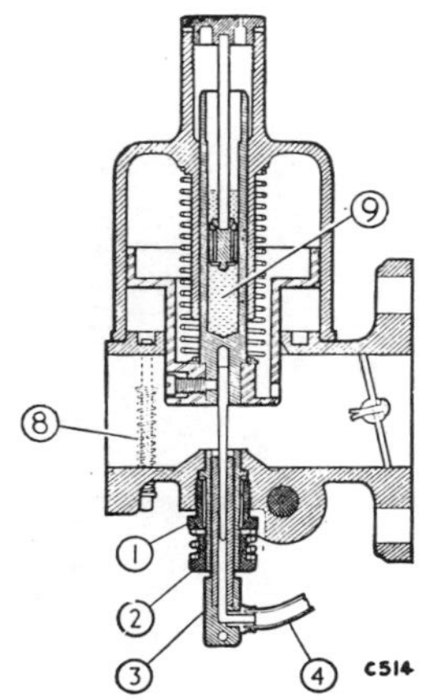

Fig. 56. Cross section of carburettor showing jet and piston assemblies

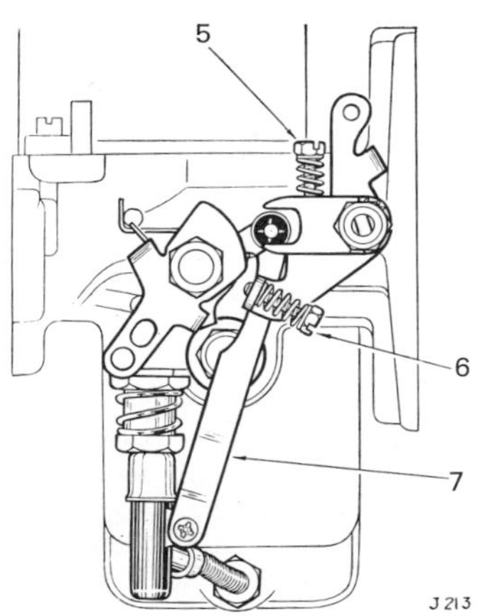

1 Jet gland nut
2 Jet adjusting nut
3 Jet assembly
4 Nylon tube
5 Throttle stop screw
6 Throttle adjusting screw
7 Jet/lever link
8 Piston lifting pin
9 Oil well

Fig. 57. Jet and throttle interconnection adjustment screw

9. With the carburettors in balance, idling at 800 to 850 r.p.m. and running smoothly, carry out the following checks.
   (a) Check the actuating pins of the interconnecting clamping levers are set 0·015″ (0·38 mm) from the lower edge of the fork (see Fig. 58) and that there is $\frac{1}{32}$″ (0·8 mm) end play between the interconnecting clamping levers and the throttle nuts.
   (b) Check that when the mixture control is operated both jets commence to move simultaneously.
   (c) Check that the carburettors are in balance at 1,500 r.p.m.
   (d) Ensure that there is $\frac{1}{16}$″ (1·6 mm) free movement of the choke control wire before it starts to actuate to jet levers.

If any of the above points require attention refer to "Final Adjustment", page 1·331.

Complete Tuning

Preparation

1. Slacken both clamping bolts on the throttle spindle interconnections (Fig. 55).
2. Unscrew the throttle-screw on each carburettor until both screws are well clear of their cams.
3. Disconnect the jet control interconnection by slackening the clamping bolts.
4. Disconnect the choke control cable.
5. Unscrew the throttle adjusting screws until they are just clear of their stops and the throttles are closed.
6. Set each throttle adjusting screw half a turn open.
7. Top up the dampers.
8. Connect the tachometer as directed by the instrument manufacturer.
9. Run the engine at approximately 1,100 r.p.m. for five minutes after normal working temperature is attained, then run the engine at 2,500 r.p.m. for half a minute.
10. Commence tuning at once and repeat the half minute of 2,500 r.p.m. every three minutes until tuning is complete.

Balancing

11. Adjust each throttle screw by the same amount to attain an idling speed of 800 to 850 r.p.m.
12. Use a balancing meter to measure the air intake of each carburettor and balance the carburettors in accordance with the instrument maker's instructions; maintain the idling speed by adjusting the throttle screws. NOTE: An inability to balance the carburettors may be due to leaks in the air intake (i.e., brake servo, inlet manifold, etc.). If no cause can be found refer to "Dismantling and Re-assembling", page 1·332.

Mixture Setting

13. Turn each jet adjusting nut by the same amount, up to weaken down to enrich, until the fastest speed is recorded on the tachometer. Turn both adjusting nuts very slowly up (weaken) until the engine speed just commences to drop, then turn each nut one half flat down (enrich).
    NOTE: Each time the adjusting nut is altered, gently tap the neck of the suction chamber with a non-metallic instrument, i.e., screwdriver handle.
14. Check that the idling speed and carburettor balance remain correct.
15. Using the exhaust gas analyser (either CO meter or air/fuel ratio meter), check the percentage CO reading or air/fuel ratio is within the limits (3·5 — 4·5% CO; air/fuel ratio approx. 13:1). If the reading falls outside these limits adjust both adjusting nuts by the minimum amount necessary to bring the reading just within the limits.
16. Hold the jet adjusting nut on each carburettor to prevent it from turning, and rotate the adjustment restrictor (A, Fig. 59) around the nut until the vertical tag contacts the carburettor body on the left-hand side when viewed from the air cleaner flange (see Fig. 59). In this position, bend down the small tag on the adjustment restrictor so that the restrictor locks to the nut and will follow its movement.

Final adjustments

17. Set the throttle interconnection clamping levers so that the actuating pins are 0·015″ (0·38 mm) away from the lower edge of the fork (Fig. 58). Ensure that there is $\frac{1}{32}$″ (0·8 mm) end play between the interconnecting clamping levers and the throttle nuts.
18. With both jet levers pressed down to their lowest points set the jet interconnection lever clamping bolts so that both jets commence to move simultaneously.
19. Run the engine at 1,500 r.p.m. and check carburettor balance.
20. Reconnect the mixture control cable allowing $\frac{1}{16}$″ (1·6 mm) free movement before it starts to actuate the jet levers.
21. Pull the choke knob on the dash panel to its maximum amount *without moving the jets* and adjust the fast idling cam screws to give an engine speed of 1,100 r.p.m. when hot.

Carburettors — Removing and Refitting

Remove the air cleaners.

Disconnect the fuel inlet pipe, choke cable, the accelerator cable and return springs.

Remove the four nuts and spring washers securing the carburettors to the inlet manifold.

Lift off the carburettors as a pair complete with interconnecting linkages.

Refitting is a reversal of removing but examine and, if necessary, replace the gaskets.

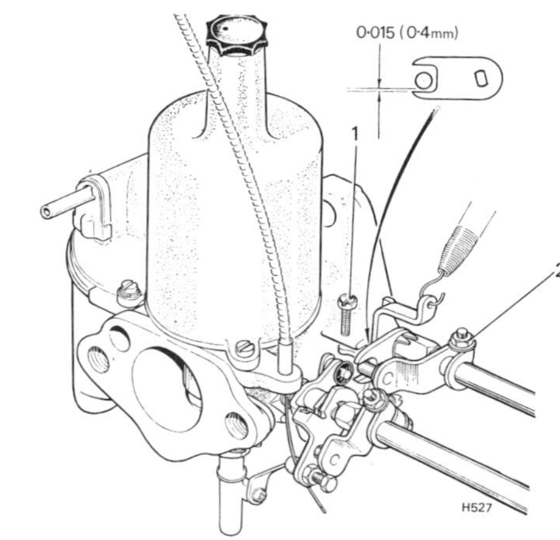

Fig. 58. Carburettor fork lever adjustment

A Restrictor B Jet adjusting nut

Fig. 59. Jet restrictor

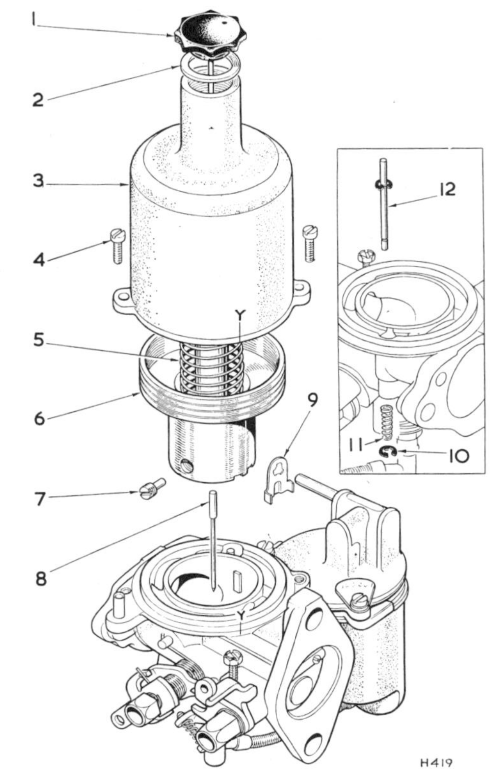

1	Damper	8	Needle
2	Damper washer	9	Baffle plate
3	Suction chamber	10	Circlip
4	Chamber retaining screws	11	Spring for lifting pin
5	Piston spring	12	Piston lifting pin
6	Piston assembly	YY	Marks for refitting
7	Needle locking screw		

Fig. 60. Suction chamber and piston assembly

DISMANTLING AND RE-ASSEMBLING

Dismantling

Suction Chamber (Fig. 60)

1. Unclip the baffle plate (9) from the inlet nozzle and thoroughly clean the outside of the carburettor.
2. Mark the relative positions of the suction chamber and the carburettor body to facilitate re-assembly.
3. Remove the damper (1) and its washer (2). Empty the damper oil from piston.
4. Unscrew retaining screws (4) and lift off the chamber (3) without tilting it.
5. Remove the piston spring (5) and carefully lift out the piston assembly (6).
6. Remove the needle locking screw (7) and withdraw the needle (8). If it cannot be easily removed, tap the needle inwards first and then pull outwards. Do not bend or scratch the needle.
7. Remove the retaining circlip (10) and spring (11), then push the lifting pin (12) upwards to remove it from its guide.

Jet Linkage and Assembly (Fig. 61)

8. Support the moulded base of the jet assembly (31) and slacken the screw (24) retaining the jet pick-up link (22).
9. Relieve the tension of the pick-up lever return spring (13) from the screw and remove screw (24) and brass bush (23), if fitted.
10. Unscrew the brass sleeve nut (34) retaining the flexible jet tube (32) to the float-chamber and withdraw the jet assembly from the carburettor body. Note the gland (36), washer (35) and ferrule (33) at the end of the jet tube.
11. Remove the jet adjusting nut (28), jet adjustment restrictor (27) and spring (26). Unscrew the jet locking nut (25) and detach the nut and jet bearing (29). Withdraw the bearing from the nut, noting the steel locking washer (30) under the shoulder of the bearing.
12. Noting the location points of the two ends of the pick-up lever return spring, unscrew the lever pivot bolt (18) together with its double coil spring washer (17). Detach the lever assembly (14) and return spring (13).
13. Noting the location of the two ends of the cam lever spring (16), push out the pivot bolt tube (19), taking care not to lose the spring. Lift off the cam lever (20) and take out the skid washer (21) from between the two levers.

Float Chamber Assembly (Fig. 62)

14. Slacken and remove the bolt (51) retaining the float-chamber to the carburettor body. Note the component sequence with flexible mounted chambers.
15. Mark the location of the float-chamber lid (37). Unscrew the lid retaining screws (39) and detach the lid (38) and its gasket (42), complete with float assembly.

16. Push out the float hinge pin (45) from the end opposite its serrations and detach the float (46).
17. Extract the float needle (44) from its seating and unscrew the seating (43) from the lid, using a box spanner ·338 in. (8·58 mm) across the flats. Do not distort the seating.

Throttle Disc Assembly (Fig. 63)

18. Close the throttle and mark the relative positions of the throttle disc (59) and the carburettor flange.
19. Unscrew the two disc retaining screws (58). Open the throttle and ease out the disc (57) from its slot in the throttle spindle (52). The disc is oval and will jam if care is not taken. Store the disc in a safe place until required for re-assembly.
20. Tap back the tab washer (55) securing the spindle nut. Note the location of the lever arm in relation to the spindle and carburettor body; remove the nut (56), detach the tab washer (55), fork lever (54), lever (53), and withdraw the spindle (52).

Re-assembling

Throttle Disc Assembly (Fig. 63)

1. Examine the throttle spindle (52) and its bearings in the carburettor body. Check for excessive play and renew parts as necessary.
2. Refit the spindle to the body. Assemble the operating levers (53) and (54) with tab washer (55) and spindle nut (56) to the spindle. Ensure that when the stop on the throttle lever is against the abutment on the carburettor body, i.e., throttle closed position, the countersunk ends of the holes in the spindle face outwards. Tighten the spindle and lock with the tab washer.
3. Re-insert the throttle disc (57) to its original position in the slot of the spindle as marked (59). Manoeuvre the disc in its slot until the throttle can be closed, taking care not to damage the throttle over-run valve. When assembled, the valve should be positioned below the throttle spindle and the head of the valve should face the engine. Fit two new retaining screws (58) but do not fully tighten. Check visually that the disc closes fully, and adjust its position as necessary. With the throttle closed there must be clearance between the throttle lever and the carburettor body. Tighten the screws fully and spread their split ends just enough to prevent turning.

Float Chamber Assembly (Fig. 62)

4. Examine the float needle (44) and seating (43) for damage. Check that the spring-loaded plunger in the end of the plastic-bodied needle operates freely.
5. Screw the sealing carefully into the float-chamber lid (38). Do not overtighten. Replace the needle in the seating, coned end first. Test the assembly for leakage with air pressure at 1½ to 2 p.s.i. (0·105 to 0·141 kg/cm²).

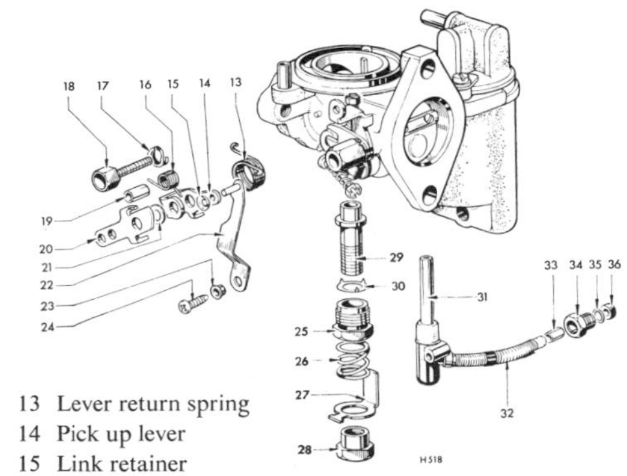

13	Lever return spring				
14	Pick up lever				
15	Link retainer				
16	Pick up lever spring				
17	Double spring washer				
18	Lever pivot bolt	25	Jet locking nut	31	Jet assembly
19	Pivot bolt tube	26	Spring	32	Flexible jet tube
20	Cam lever	27	Jet nut restrictor (U.S.A. only)	33	Ferrule
21	Washer	28	Jet adjusting nut	34	Sleeve nut
22	Lever/jet link	29	Jet bearing	35	Washer
23	Ferrule	30	Lock washer	36	Gland
24	Link retainer screw				

Fig. 61. Carburettor jet linkage

37	Marks for refitting
38	Float chamber lid
39	Lid retaining screws
40	Spring washers
41	Identification plate
42	Lid gasket
43	Needle seating
44	Float needle
45	Float hinge pin
46	Float assembly
47	Float chamber
48	Backing washer (steel)
49	Rubber mounting
50	Rubber washer
51	Retaining bolt

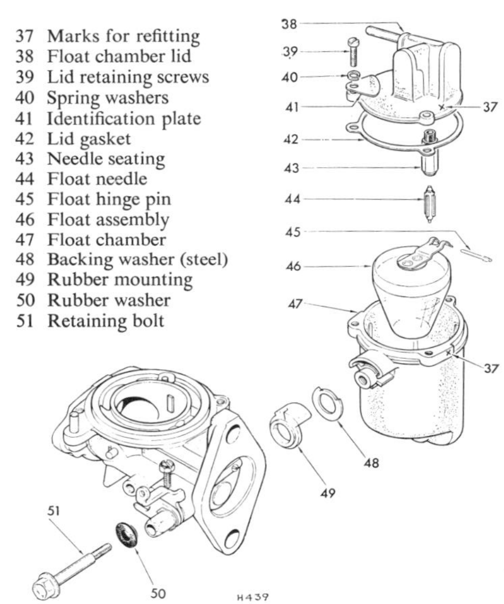

Fig. 62. Carburettor float chamber

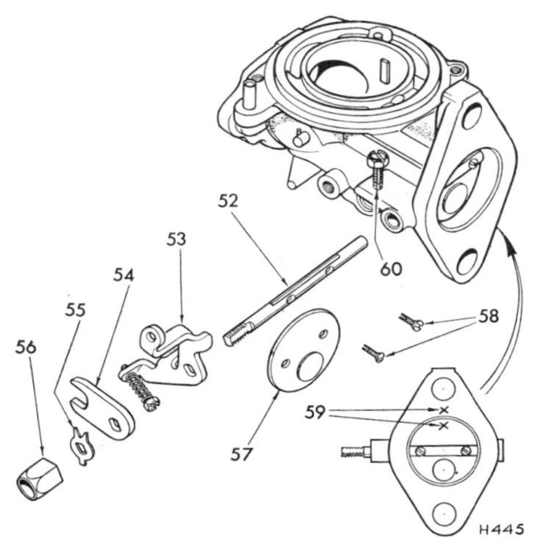

52 Throttle spindle
53 Throttle lever
54 Fork lever
55 Tab washer
56 Lever retaining nut
57 Throttle disc assembly
58 Throttle disc screws
59 Marks for re-assembly
60 Throttle adjusting screw

Fig. 63. Carburettor throttle disc and lever assembly

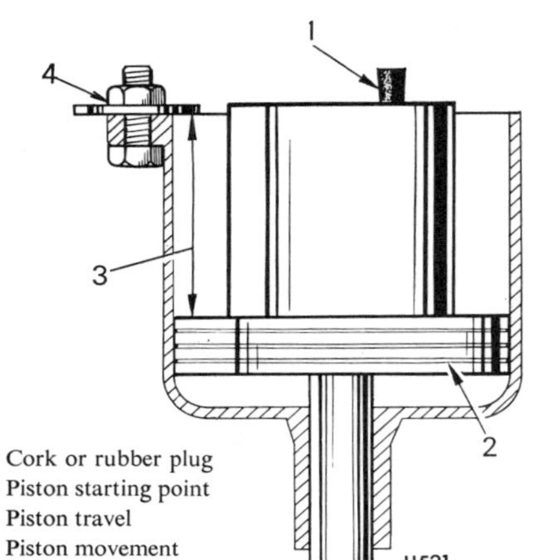

1 Cork or rubber plug
2 Piston starting point
3 Piston travel
4 Piston movement limiter

Fig. 64. Checking piston drop

6. Refit the float and lever (46) to the lid, insert the hinge pin (45) and invert the float-chamber lid. With the needle valve held in the shut off position, by the weight of the float only, there should be $\frac{3}{16}$" (4·8 mm) gap between the float lever and the rim of the float-chamber lid (see Fig. 66).
7. Examine the lid gasket (42) for re-use. If satisfactory, assemble the gasket to the lid and refit the lid to the float chamber in the position marked during dismantling. Tighten the securing screws evenly.
8. Refit the float chamber assembly to the carburettor body and fully tighten the retaining bolt (51), making sure that the rubber mounting details and backing washer, items (50), (49) and (48), are assembled in the correct order and engage with the register on the body. Do not intermix the rubbers of a pair of carburettors.

Suction Chamber (Fig. 60)

9. Refit the piston lifting pin (12), spring (11) and circlip (10).
10. Using gasolene or denatured alcohol as a cleaning agent, scrupulously clean and examine the surfaces of the piston and piston rod for damage. Wipe dry using a clean cloth. Do not use abrasives. Lightly oil the outside of the piston rod.
11. Similarly clean the inside of the suction chamber and piston rod guide. Refit the damper assembly (1) and washer (2). Seal the transfer holes in the piston assembly with rubber plugs or corks and fit the assembly to the suction chamber as shown on Fig. 64. This should take 3 to 5 seconds. If it takes longer, the cause is likely to be thick oil on the piston rod, or an oil film on the piston or inside the suction chamber. Remove the oil and re-check.
12. Refit the needle (8) to the piston assembly, ensuring that the lower edge of the needle shank is level with the bottom of the piston rod as shown on Fig. 65 (inset). Fit a new needle locking screw (7) and tighten. Invert the suction chamber and spin the piston assembly inside it to check for needle concentricity.
13. Check the piston key for security in the carburettor body. Refit the piston assembly to the body and replace the piston spring (5) over the piston rod. Fit the suction chamber (3) and retaining screws (4) taking care not to "wind-up" the piston spring during assembly. Tighten the screws evenly.

Jet Assembly (Fig. 61)

14. Refit the jet bearing (29), a new locking washer (30), and the locking nut (25). Do not tighten the nut. Ensure that the bore of the jet bearing is clean and dry.

Centralise the jet as follows:

15. Enter the end of the nylon feed tube (32) into the base of the float chamber, without the gland (36) or washer (35) fitted, and loosely secure with the retaining nut (34).
16. Feed the jet (31) into the jet bearing (29). Do not fit the spring (26), jet adjustment restrictor (27), or adjusting nut (28) at this stage.
17. With the carburettor positioned with its inlet flange downwards, and referring to Fig. 67, insert the piston loading tool into the damper tube at the top of the suction chamber and screw in until fully home. Screw the tool back until the arrow, on the tool, points towards the inlet flange of the carburettor.
The tool and carburettor must remain in this position throughout the centring operation.
18. With the piston at the bottom of its travel, that is resting on the bridge, and the jet hard up against the bearing, slowly tighten the jet locking nut. During the tightening process ensure that the jet does not bind within the bearing when the jet is drawn in and out. If tightness is detected, slacken the jet locking nut and repeat the process. Upon completion of this operation, check that the locking nut is fully tightened.
19. Remove the jet loading tool.
20. Withdraw the jet and tube, refit the spring (26), restrictor (27) and adjusting nut (28). Fit the gland (36) and washer (35) to the flexible tube (32), check that the internal ferrule (33) is positioned in the end of the tube. The end of the tube should project a minimum of $\frac{3}{16}$" (4·8 mm) beyond the gland. Refit the jet and tube. Tighten the sleeve nut (34) until the neoprene gland is compressed. Over-tightening can cause leakage.
21. Refit the damper (1) and washer (2).
22. Re-assemble the pick-up lever (14), lever jet link (22), cam lever (20), cam lever spring (16), skid washer(21) and pivot bolt tube (19) in the positions noted on dismantling.
23. Place the pick-up lever return spring (13) in position over its boss and secure the lever assembly to the carburettor body with the pivot bolt (18). Ensure that the double-coil spring washer (17) fits over the projecting end of the pivot bolt tube (19).
24. Register the angled end of the return spring in the groove in the pick-up lever, and hook the other end of the spring around the moulded peg of the carburettor body.
25. Fit the brass ferrule (23) to the hole in the end of the pick-up link (22). Relieve the tension of the return spring (13) and fit the link to the jet (31) with its retaining screws (24). When finally tightening the screw, support the moulded end of the jet.
26. Refit the baffle plate (9) to the float chamber lid nozzle.

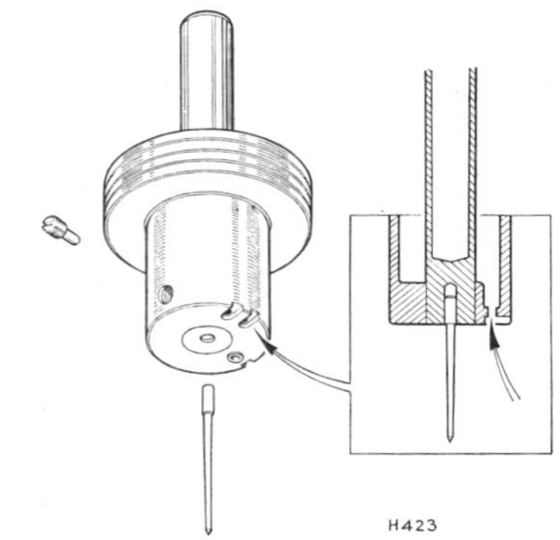

Fig. 65. Piston and needle assembly

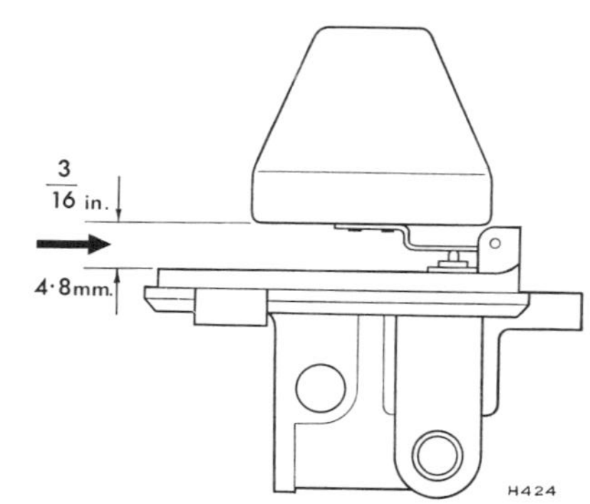

Fig. 66. Checking float height

Datum Settings

These settings should be carried out immediately upon completion of servicing procedure before carburettor is refitted to the engine.

NOTE: The following settings are merely a starting point with which to commence "Complete Tuning", see page 1·330. They must not be regarded as a final setting.

27. Without removing suction chamber, turn the jet adjusting nut up to its highest (i.e. weakest) position, and then turn the nut down until the jet is flush with the bridge (i.e., the platform on which the jet is positioned) of the carburettor. Turn down the jet nut by ten flats.
28. Refit the carburettors and linkage to the inlet manifold using new flange gaskets.
29. Tune the carburettors in accordance with the instructions given in "Complete Tuning" (see page 1·330).

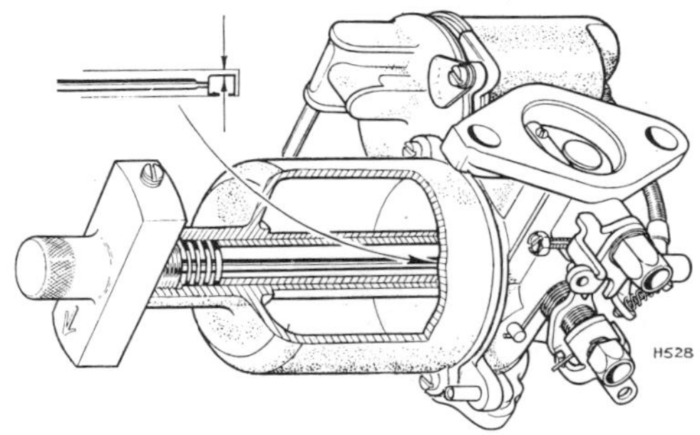

Fig. 67. Jet biasing

Crankcase Breather Valve (Fig. 68)

The crankcase breather valve enables the crankcase fumes to be fed into the inlet manifold and be burnt in the combustion chambers.

The valve is mounted on the inlet manifold and must be serviced every 6,000 miles (10,000 km.) as follows:

Disengage the clip (1) and lift off the cover and diaphragm (2), valve pin and spring (3). Clean the valve components in methylated spirits and ensure serviceability before re-assembling in the reverse order of dismantling.

1 Clip
2 Diaphragm
3 Spring
4 Body
5 Manifold

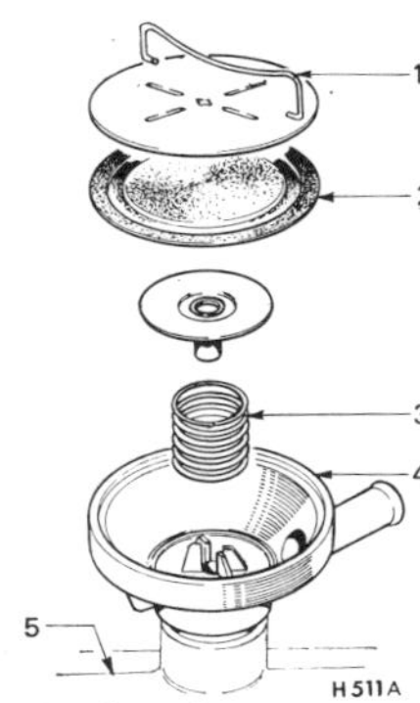

Fig. 68. Crankcase breather valve

Fuel Line Filter (Fig. 69)

A non-serviceable fuel filter is fitted on Spitfire 3 models for specified markets. The filter should be renewed every 12,000 miles (20,000 km.).

To remove: Slacken the bracket bolt and take out filter; clamp the lower (inlet) hose and remove hoses from filter.

To fit new filter: Ensuring correct direction of flow (marked on filter), place filter into bracket, fit hoses, remove hose clamp and tighten bracket bolt.

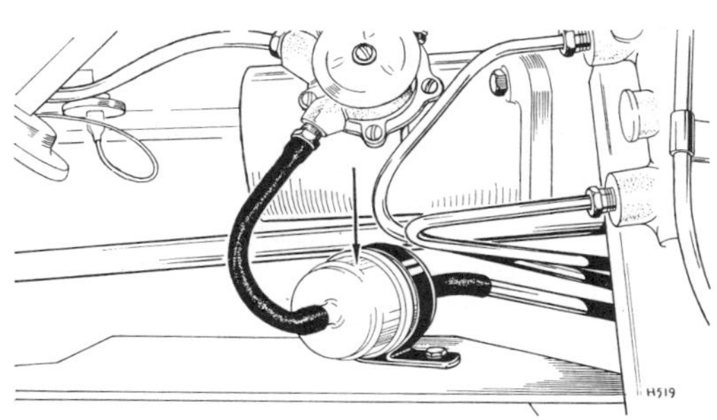

Fig. 69. Fuel line filter

STROMBERG SINGLE CARBURETTOR ARRANGEMENT

Spitfire III 1970 model year entering the American market use a single Stromberg CDSE 150 carburettor which is designed and built to stringent emission control standards.

The carburettor is an integral part of the emission and evaporation control systems which are dealt with in this section. For this reason it is desirable and, in many cases necessary, to include aspects of related systems (ignition timing, fuel tank, etc.) where their function is integral with the correct operation of the emission or evaporation control systems.

EMISSION CONTROL SYSTEM

Requirements

The Federal regulations governing the emission of Hydrocarbons and Carbon monoxide from the exhaust system and crankcase of 1970 model year vehicles is:

2·2 grammes per mile ..	Hydrocarbons
23 grammes per mile ..	Carbon monoxide

Test Data

Idle Speed r.p.m.	800–850
Ignition Timing	
Static (Approx.)	6° A.T.D.C.
Idle	2° A.T.D.C.
C.O. Level (Engine warm at Idle) ..	1% to 3½%
—Equivalent Air/Fuel Ratio ..	14·2:1 to 13·2:1

Description

Engine modifications

The following modifications to the engine assist in the control of emissions from the crankcase.

1. Exhaust valves are stellite faced to maintain effective sealing between intervals of servicing.
2. The Camshaft 10-10-50-50 timing gives greater control of emissions during idling and low speed cruising.
3. The Ignition Distributor has an extended range to permit a retarded static setting whilst maintaining the normal advance characteristics at higher engine speeds.
4. Crankcase depression to draw off blow by gases, is created by a connection from the rocker cover to the constant depression area of the carburettor.
5. Spark plugs Champion UN 12Y, are fitted to give improved combustion.
6. The Carburettor is a Stromberg 150 CDSE which operates on the principle of varying the effective choke and jet orifice areas in accordance with the degree of throttle opening, engine speed and load. The following emission control features are incorporated.

a. Fixed non-adjustable jet assembly and biased needle to achieve consistent air to fuel ratio.

b. Temperature compensator assembly, which progressively opens in line with the engine temperature, to correct the mixture and maintain even running.

c. Throttle by-pass valve which is set to open at a predetermined manifold depression to admit air during deceleration.

d. Wire-locked and sealed cover to discourage unauthorised tampering.

e. "Free movement", built into the accelerator linkage, permits fast idle without disturbing the otherwise closed position of the linkage.

Servicing

The importance of servicing at the correct intervals cannot be overstressed as improvements in design and manufacturing techniques count for nothing if the servicing standards are not upheld.

Because of the extreme improbability of analytical equipment being available generally, checks using "Sun" or similar equipment, will prove adequate for dealing with a stable system that has proper testing and monitoring when the vehicle is first built. Once the system has been correctly set it will remain so, and may well improve, until severe deterioration in performance or misfiring indicate the need for attention.

Routine servicing, carried out at the specific mileage intervals quoted in the publications provided with each new vehicle, will rectify deterioration in the system. In addition to normal lubrication and nut tightness checks, those items which should receive attention during routine servicing include distributor maintenance, carburettor dash-pot oil replenishment and slow running adjustment, spark plugs, valve rocker clearances, air cleaner and fuel filter.

The procedures listed below relate only to those items which affect emission control. This work must not be attempted by the owner but should be entrusted to an authorised Triumph Dealer.

Cylinder Compression

To maintain the quality of engine emission within the prescribed limits, given on this page, it is extremely important that the valve seatings and combustion chambers continue to remain gas-tight. The general condition of these items can be assessed by measuring and comparing the compression pressures of all cylinders, at 6,000 mile intervals, in the following manner:

(a) Immediately after a run, that is whilst the engine is at normal running temperature and the battery is fully charged, apply the handbrake, engage neutral and remove all sparking plugs.

(b) Assemble the correct adaptor to the compression tester and insert the adaptor into No. 1 plug hole in the cylinder head.

(c) Depress the accelerator pedal.

(d) Press the solenoid starter button and hold it for 2-3 seconds before reading and noting the pressure indicated on the gauge. Repeat the procedure with each of the remaining cylinders. The readings should be within 5 p.s.i. of each other.

As this service coincides with sparking plug servicing, clean, reset the gaps and test (at 6,000 miles) and renew the plugs (at 12,000 miles) before refitting them to the cylinder head.

Ignition Distributor

Full details of the ignition distributor are given in Group 6. To keep the distributor in the condition demanded by an efficient emission control system, ensure that the following servicing operations are carried out at the stated intervals.

At the first 1,000 miles

(a) Check the contact breaker gap and re-adjust if necessary to 0·014″ — 0·016″.
(b) Check the ignition timing at idling speed using a stroboscope.

At 6,000 miles

(a) Lubricate the distributor.
(b) Adjust or renew the contact breaker points as necessary.
(c) Ensure that the piping between distributor and carburettor are in perfect condition.

At 12,000 miles

(a) Carry out the 6,000 miles service.
(b) Check the ignition timing at idling speed using a stroboscope.

In addition to the above routine servicing the distributor should be given performance checks to ensure that it stays within the limits quoted in Group 6. These checks should be made subsequent to the fitting of new components, during overhaul of the distributor or if the distributor performance becomes suspect.

Ignition Timing

The ignition timing is as follows:

Ignition at idling speed (800 — 850 r.p.m.) — 2° A.T.D.C.

Ignition static (approx.) .. — 6° A.T.D.C.

A small hole drilled near the edge of the crankshaft pulley aligns with a pointer on the timing cover when pistons 1 and 4 are in the T.D.C. position: A line is scored on the pulley which is equivalent to 2° A.T.D.C. and is the idling timing mark. A static timing mark may be marked, if required, using a pair of dividers and scribing a line $\frac{3}{32}$″ in retard of the idling mark.

To set the ignition timing proceed as follows:

If the distributor has been removed from the engine, use the static timing procedure only for starting the engine. As this method cannot achieve the extreme accuracy required for the proper functioning of the emission control system, it is vitally important that the final ignition setting is made dynamically as follows:

(a) Prepare the timing marks as described above.

(b) Connect a stroboscopic timing lamp and tachometer to the engine in accordance with instructions provided by the manufacturer of the equipment in use.

(c) Start the engine and when normal running temperature is reached set the idling speed at 800-850 r.p.m. by turning the carburettor throttle stop screw to achieve this speed.

(d) Slacken the distributor clamping plate bolt and rotate the distributor body until the idling mark on the crankshaft pulley aligns with the timing pointer under the beam of the stroboscopic lamp. This may necessitate readjustment of throttle stop screw to maintain the correct idle speed.

(e) Re-tighten the distributor clamp bolt securely, re-check the timing and if satisfactory, remove the stroboscopic lamp and tachometer.

Carburettor Controls
Accelerator Linkage

The accelerator pedal is connected to the carburettor by rod linkage and no adjustment is required during normal operation.

When setting the vertical adjusting rod, after fitting replacement parts:

(a) Set the accelerator pedal just below the level of the brake pedal.

(b) Ensure the carburettor links allow full motion of the throttle (85° between stops).

(c) Adjust the vertical rod to suit, fit the rod and tighten lock nuts.

NOTE: A degree of "lost motion" (B, Fig. 70) incorporated in the linkage allows "fast idle" without disturbing the closed position of the throttle. This is not adjustable and must not be confused with wear. Occasionally apply a few drops of light oil to the linkage connections.

Choke Control

Carburettor choke control is by a bowden cable connected to the dash board, an abutment clip secures the outer cable to a bracket on the carburettor whilst the inner cable is clamped to the choke control lever.

Occasionally lubricate the cable with light oil.

CARBURETTOR
Adjustments

Because of the precise manufacturing limits and the assembly methods adopted to prevent unauthorised tampering, the only adjustments required and permitted are:

(a) Idling speed: Ensure that the fast idle screw (1, Fig. 70) is clear of the cam (2) and the choke lever is against its stop with the facia control pushed fully in. Unscrew the idling screw (3) until the throttle is just closed. Turn the screw in 1½ turns to provide a datum setting.

Start the engine and attain normal running temperature before final adjustment of the idling screw achieves a constant 800 to 850 r.p.m.

(b) Fast idling: Ensure that the choke lever is fully returned and the facia control knob pushed in. Set the gap 'A', between the fast idle screw and the cam, at ·030″. Start the engine and while it is still cold (68 to 86°F) pull the facia control fully out to check the fast idle speed and, if necessary, adjust to 1100 r.p.m. with the screw. Tighten the locknut and re-check the fast idling speed.

(c) Idle emission: An idle trimming screw is provided to give very fine adjustment to compensate for the difference between a new "stiff" engine and one that is "run in". THIS IS NOT AN ORDINARY MIXTURE ADJUSTING SCREW: it regulates a limited amount of air that can be introduced into the mixing chamber.

It is important to remember that the ear will not detect any difference between the fully "home" and fully "open" position of the screw. The setting should, therefore, be checked by means of a C.O. meter or an air/fuel ratio meter to the exhaust pipe. (The correct C.O. level and air/fuel ratio is given on page 1·337).

Carburettor Removing and Refitting

1. Remove the air cleaner.
2. Disconnect the fuel feed pipe.
   — choke control cable
   — accelerator linkage
   — constant depression tube
   — distributor vacuum tube
3. Remove the carburettor securing nuts.
4. Lift off the unit.

Refit the carburettor by reversing the above procedure, fit new gaskets and adjust controls as previously described.

Carburettor Servicing

To maintain the carburettors at peak efficiency, regular servicing at 6,000 mile intervals is essential. This also involves the use of coloured gaskets which give indication that the 24,000 mile service has been carried out. The appropriate servicing operations and the mileage intervals at which they should be performed are as follows:

Maintenance

1. **At the First 1,000 Miles (Free Service)**
   (a) Top up the air-valve damper reservoir (dashpot) with Zenith Lube-Pack or engine oil (see instruction book) within ¼″ of top of centre rod.
   (b) Check and, if required, adjust the slow-running.
   (c) Check and if necessary adjust the idle emission setting as described in "Carburettor Adjustments (C)".
2. **At 6,000 Mile Intervals**
   At these periods perform the operations listed under the 1,000 mile service.
3. **At 12,000 miles**
   Remove the piping connecting the rocker cover/evaporation canister and carburettor.
   Dismantle the piping and flame trap. Remove the rocker cover.
   Wash the above components in clean fuel, allow to dry and re-assemble.

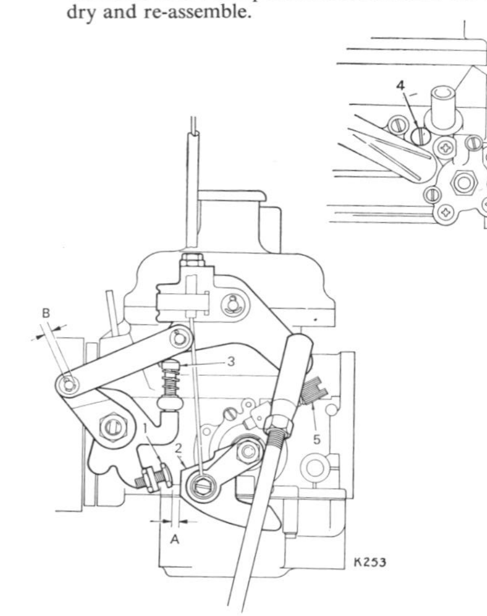

Fig. 70. Carburettor controls

1 Fast idle screw
2 Cam
3 Idling screw
4 Idle trimming screw
5 Winter/Summer setting

Fig. 71. Carburettor controls

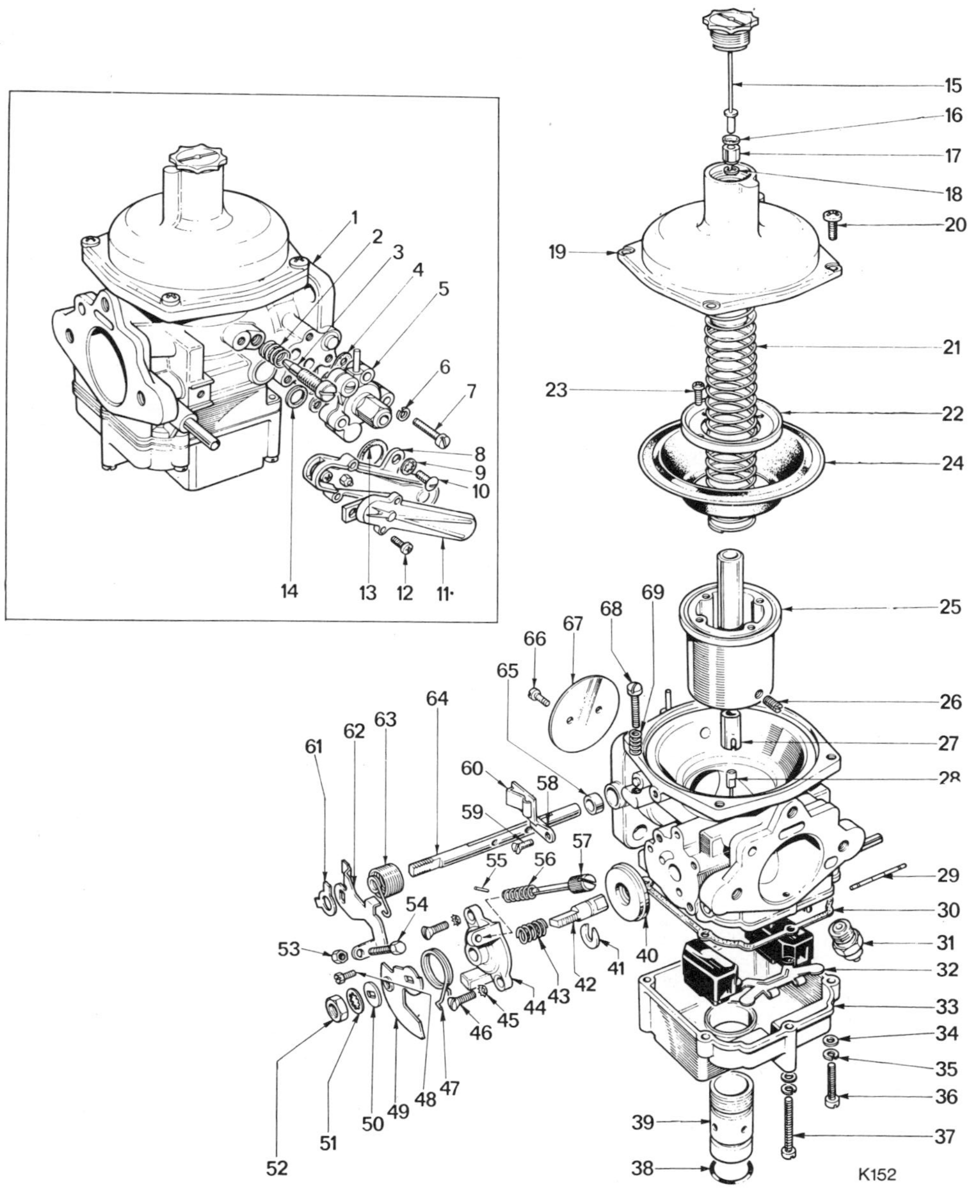

Fig. 72. CD SE 150 Carburettor

Key to Fig. 72

1	Carburettor	36	Screw—securing
2	Spring—idle trimming screw	37	Screw—securing
3	Idle trimming screw	38	Rubber "O" ring
4	Gasket—by pass valve	39	Plug
5	By pass valve	40	Valve plate
6	Lockwasher under (7)	41	Retainer
7	Screw—securing (5)	42	Spindle
8	Temperature compensator unit	43	Spring
9	Lockwasher under (10)	44	Starter box cover
10	Screw—securing (8)	45	Shakeproof washer
11	Cover—temperature compensator	46	Screw
12	Screw—securing (11)	47	Return spring
13	Seal—on compensator body	48	Screw cable attachment
14	Seal—inside carburettor	49	Lever
15	Damper rod } Damper Assembly	50	Washer
16	Washer } Damper Assembly	51	Shakeproof washer
17	Distance sleeve } Damper Assembly	52	Nut
18	Circlip	53	Locknut—securing
19	Cover—air valve	54	Screw—fast idle
20	Screws—securing (19)	55	Choke stop pin
21	Spring—air valve return	56	Stop spring
22	Ring—diaphragm attachment	57	Choke stop
23	Screw—securing (22) (24)	58	Cable abutment bracket
24	Diaphragm	59	Screw—securing
25	Air valve	60	Spring clip
26	Screw—securing (28)	61	Lockwasher—retaining
27	Needle holder assembly	62	Lever—throttle
28	Needle assembly	63	Spring—throttle return
29	Float pivot pin	64	Throttle spindle
30	Gasket—float chamber	65	Seal—throttle spindle
31	Needle valve	66	Screw—securing
32	Float assembly	67	Throttle disc
33	Float chamber cover	68	Idle adjusting screw
34	Washer	69	Spring—idle adjusting screw
35	Spring washer		

4. **At 24,000 Miles**

This service requires one Red Emission Pack "B" containing a float-chamber gasket (Red), an "O" ring, one needle valve, one diaphragm, two throttle spindle seals, two temperature compensator seals and one by-pass valve body gasket. Additionally, a "Pozidrive" screwdriver is required for removing special screws:

Float Chambers

Carry out the following operations using the new needle valves provided in the Red Emission Pack "B".

(a) Remove the carburettor from the manifold, place on a clean bench surface. Unscrew the centre brass plug (70) and drain the fuel from each carburettor into a suitable receptacle. Unscrew the damper (15) from the top of the carburettor and drain the oil from the dash-pot.

(b) Unscrew the float-chamber fixing screw (68) (69) and withdraw float-chamber (65) vertically from the body. Remove the float-chamber gaskets (62), unclip the float pivot pin (61) and take out the floats (64). Unscrew the needle valve (63) from the float-chamber cover and remove the "O" ring (71) from the centre plug.

(c) Thoroughly cleanse all components removed. Using a new washer provided, securely screw the needle valve into position.

(d) Having inspected the floats for damage or distortion, and rectified if required, refit the float assembly. Slide in the pivot pin and clip the assembly into position. To ensure correct fuel level, invert the instrument so that the tag closes the needle valve and measure from the face of the cover (i.e. with gasket removed) to the highest point of each float. Correct measurements are 16·0 to 17·0 mm.

(e) Using a new gasket, refit the float chamber by tightening the retaining screw securely from the centre, outwards. Fit a new "O" ring to the centre plug and screw this tightly into position.

(f) Using new gaskets, refit both carburettors to the induction manifold. Replenish the dash-pots with Zenith Lube-pack or the recommended grade of engine oil, to within ¼" of the top of the centre rod and refit the dampers. Re-connect the accelerator controls and reset the carburettors, as described on page 1·338.

Air Valve Assembly

(i) Remove the damper assembly (15), unscrew the four cover fixing screws (20) and carefully lift off the cover (19). Remove the air valve return spring (21), lift out the air valve (25) and drain the oil from the guide rod. Slacken the metering needle clamping screw (26) and withdraw the needle (27), placing this carefully to one side to avoid damage.

(ii) Take out the four diaphragm retaining screws (23) and remove the ring (22) and diaphragm (24). Locating its tag in the recess provided, position the new diaphragm on the air valve, followed by the ring and secure by firmly tightening the four screws.

(iii) Having checked to ensure that there is spring action in the housing at the top of the metering needle shank (27), insert this into the base of the air valve, lining up the flat portion with the locking screw (26). Using a narrow straight edge (approximately 1" wide) placed against the needle shoulder, push the needle into the air valve until the straight edge aligns the shoulder with the flat face inside the flange formed on the outer edge of the air valve. This position is extremely critical. Lightly tighten the locking screw to avoid crushing the needle biasing spring housing. When correctly fitted, the needle is biased away from the throttle and the shoulder of the needle is exactly flush with the air valve face.

(iv) Carefully enter the air valve and diaphragm assembly into the main body, guiding the metering needle into the jet with a finger in the air intake. Locate the outer tag of the diaphragm in a corresponding aperture on top of the body and look down the centre of the air valve to ensure that the two depression transfer holes are towards, and in line with, the throttle spindle. The metering needle should also be biased away from the throttle.

(v) Refit the air valve return spring and, holding air valve with finger or thumb in the air intake, slide on the cover and locate the screw holes: the damper ventilation boss must be towards the air intake. Refit the four cover screws, tightening them evenly and securely, then check movement of air valve. Freedom of movement is essential and when released from the uppermost position, the air valve should fall with a sharp metallic click on to the carburettor bridge.

Temperature Compensator Unit

(i) Take out the screws (10) and remove the temperature compensator unit (8).

(ii) Release the cover (11) by removing two screws (12) and check for freedom of valve movement by lifting it from its seat. When released, the valve should return freely. Do not strain the bi-metal blade or attempt to alter its tension adjustment. There should be a consistent radial clearance around the valve to allow for thermal expansion. If offset, slacken the fixing screw and move the blade laterally to centralise the valve. Provided the valve is free, replace the cover (11) and tighten the screw (12).

(iii) Using the new seals provided, replace the inner seal (14) in the carburettor body, and the outer seal (13) on the compensator unit. Refit the unit to the carburettor and tighten the two screws (10).

Throttle Spindle Seals

(i) Unscrew three screws (7) and lift off the by-pass valve assembly (5) and gasket (4).

(ii) Unscrew the throttle spindle nut (39), release the throttle spring (34) and take off the lever (35) and spring (34).

(iii) Pull or prise out the old throttle spindle seals (32) and replace with new seals. A small hole is provided in the face of the seal to facilitate removal.

(iv) Re-assemble the spring and lever to the throttle spindle and securely tighten and lock the nut (39).

(v) Using a new gasket (4), refit the by-pass valve to the carburettor body and securely tighten the three screws (7).

5. **48,000 Miles Service**

At this stage it is recommended that the 24,000 mile service is repeated or the old carburettor removed and rebuilt or substituted by a complete new exchange unit.

EVAPORATIVE CONTROL SYSTEM

Requirements

The fuel loss through evaporation must not exceed 6 grammes per test (as defined by the California Authorities for 1970 model year cars).

Description

The evaporative control system used on the 1970 model Spitfire III uses an activated carbon filter through which the fuel tank is vented.

From Fig. 73 it will be seen that:

(a) The fuel tank filler cap is sealed.

(b) An overflow tank allows for the expansion of fuel in high temperatures.

(c) The piping from the expansion tank to carbon filter canister is routed round the luggage compartment before being taken to the carbon canister at the front of the vehicle. This ensures that, at any vehicle angle, piping is always at a higher level than the tank, thus neat fuel is prevented from escaping to the carbon canister.

(d) The canister containing the activated carbon is vented to atmosphere via a gauze filter. The activated carbon is purged and prevented from a fuel vapour build up by a connection (1) to the constant depression area of the carburettor.

It will be appreciated that fuel overflowing into the expansion tank will be drawn back into the main fuel tank as the level of fuel drops and creates a depression.

All air drawn into the tank to replace used fuel is via the activated carbon and piping circuit.

The carburettor and associated equipment account for such small quantities of evaporated fuel that no special precautions are necessary providing all connections are kept tight and leak free.

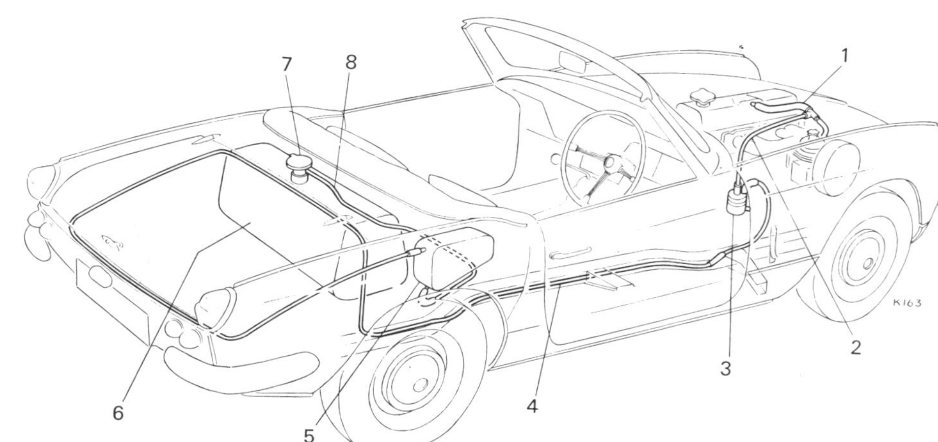

1 Pipe — Rocker cover to carburettor
2 Pipe — Canister purge
3 Activated carbon canister
4 Pipe — overflow tank to canister
5 Overflow tank
6 Main fuel tank
7 Sealed filler cap
8 Pipe — Filler tube to overflow tank

Fig. 73. Evaporative control system

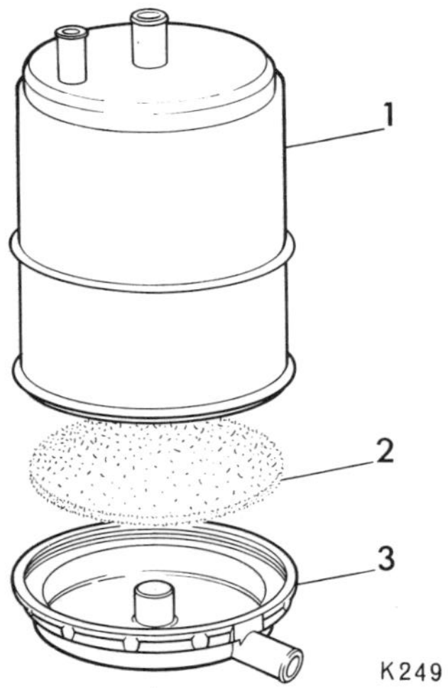

Fig. 74. Activated carbon canister

Servicing

Every 12,000 miles replace the filter in the carbon canister as follows:

Remove the inlet and purge tubes from the top of the canister.

Slacken the clip securing the canister to its mounting bracket.

Unscrew the base cover and remove the filter gauze.

Clean the base cover, fit a new gauze, replace cover and refit the canister.

Ensure that all piping is not chafing and is free from kinks.

Every 48,000 miles replace the canister adopting the method described above.

1 Gasket
2 Stud
3 Inlet and exhaust manifold
4 Manifold drain pipe
5 Drain pipe bracket
6 Stud
7 Nut
8 Washer
9 Clamp

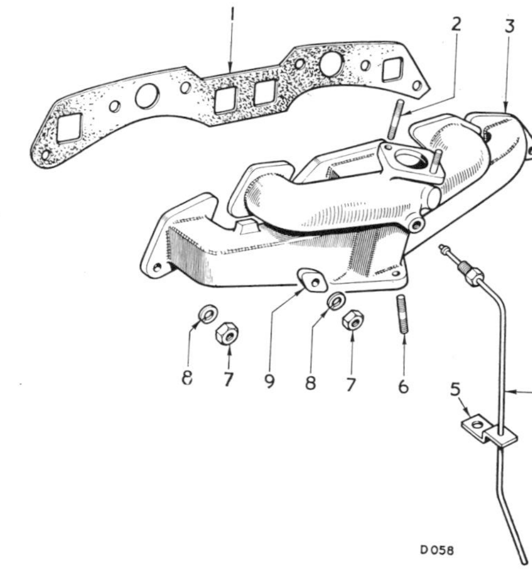

Fig. 1. Herald 1200 manifold details

1 Stud
2 Drain pipe assembly
3 Bracket
4 Stud
5 Nut
6 Spring washer
7 Clamp
8 Inlet and exhaust manifold
9 Gasket

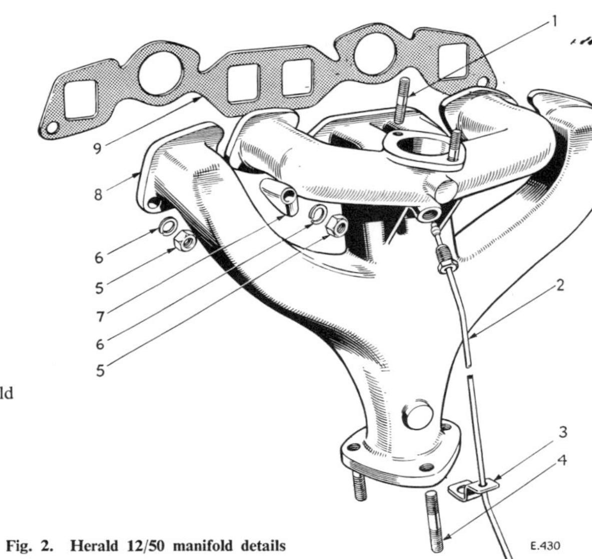

Fig. 2. Herald 12/50 manifold details

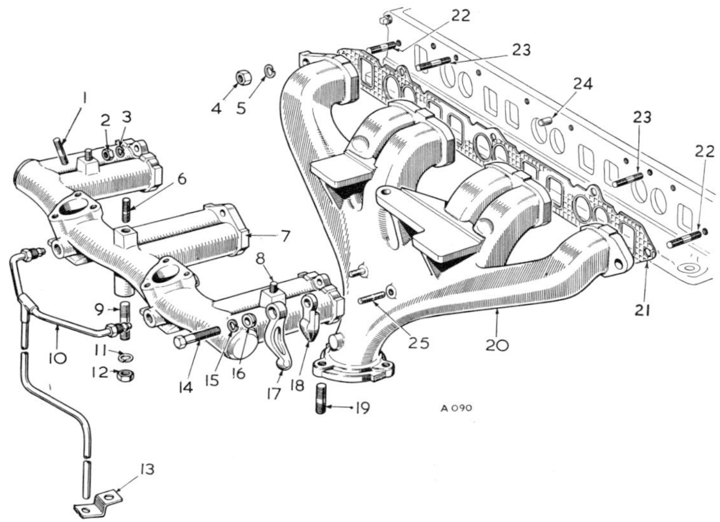

1 Stud—carburettor
2 Nut
3 Spring washer
4 Nut
5 Spring washer
6 Stud
7 Inlet manifold
8 Stud
9 Stud—inlet to exhaust manifold
10 Drain pipe
11 Spring washer
12 Nut
13 Clip
14 Bolt
15 Spring washer
16 Coned washer
17 Clamp
18 Clamp pivot
19 Stud—exhaust flange
20 Exhaust manifold
21 Gasket
22 Stud
23 Stud
24 Dowel
25 Stud—air cleaner bracket

Fig. 3. Vitesse manifold details

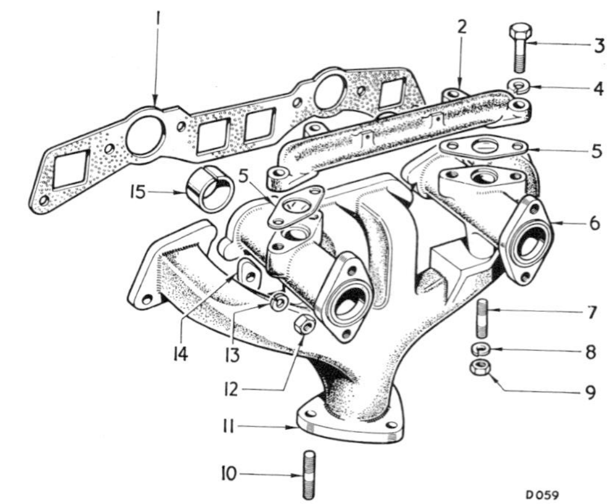

1 Gasket
2 Balance pipe
3 Bolt
4 Spring washer
5 Gasket
6 Inlet manifold
7 Stud
8 Spring washer
9 Nut
10 Stud
11 Exhaust manifold
12 Nut
13 Spring washer
14 Clamp
15 Location sleeve

Fig. 4. Spitfire manifold details

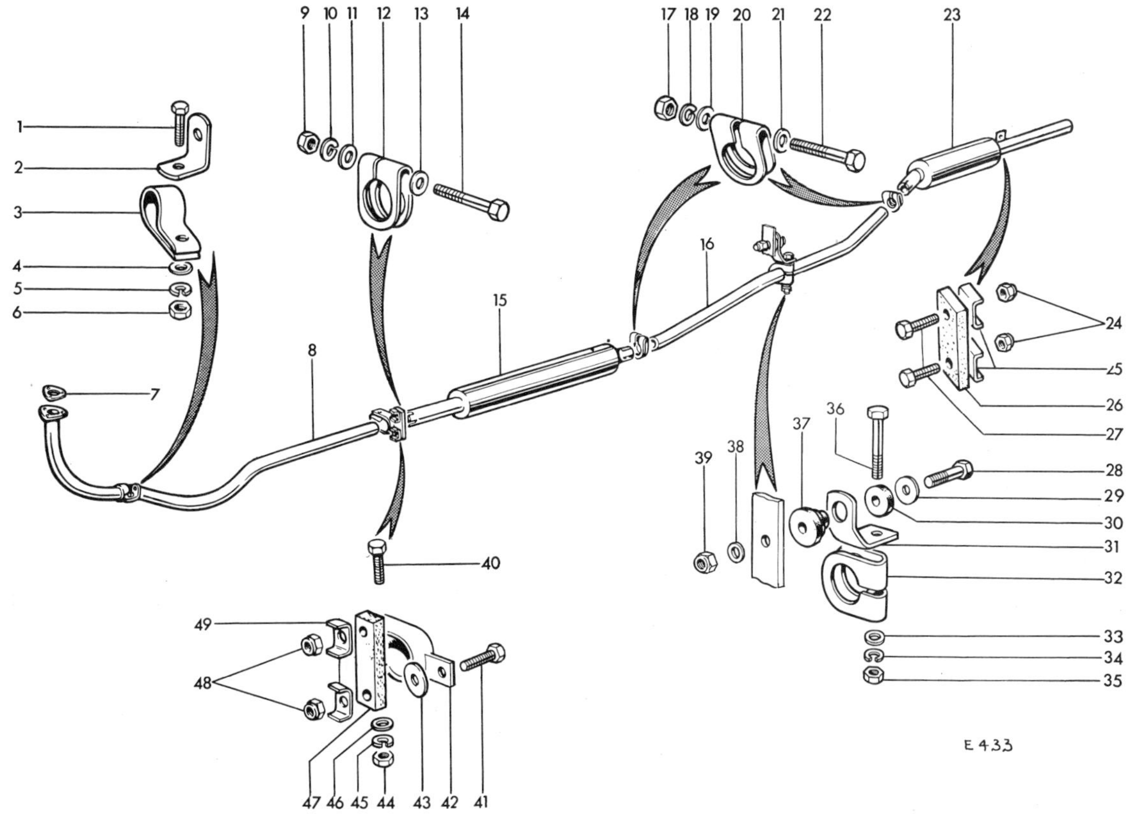

Fig. 5. Exploded view of Spitfire exhaust system

Key to Fig. 5

1	Bolt	18	Spring washer	34	Spring washer
2	Angle bracket to clutch housing	19	Plain washer	35	Nut
3	Pipe Clip	20	Clamp	36	Bolt
4	Plain washer	21	Plain washer	37	Grommet
5	Spring washer	22	Bolt	38	Plain washer
6	Nut	23	Secondary silencer	39	Nyloc nut
7	Gasket	24	Nyloc nut	40	Bolt
8	Front exhaust pipe	25	Plate	41	Bolt
9	Nut	26	Fabric strip	42	Clip and bracket
10	Spring washer	27	Bolt	43	Plain washer
11	Plain washer	28	Bolt	44	Nut
12	Clamp	29	Plain washer	45	Spring washer
13	Plain washer	30	Grommet washer	46	Plain washer
14	Bolt	31	Mounting bracket	47	Fabric strip
15	Main silencer	32	Clamp	48	Nyloc nut
16	Rear exhaust pipe	33	Plain washer	49	Plate
17	Nut				

NOTE: Items 9 to 14 and 28 to 39 .. .. Fitted from Commission No. FC.28017

Items 40 to 49 .. .. Fitted up to Commission No. FC.28016

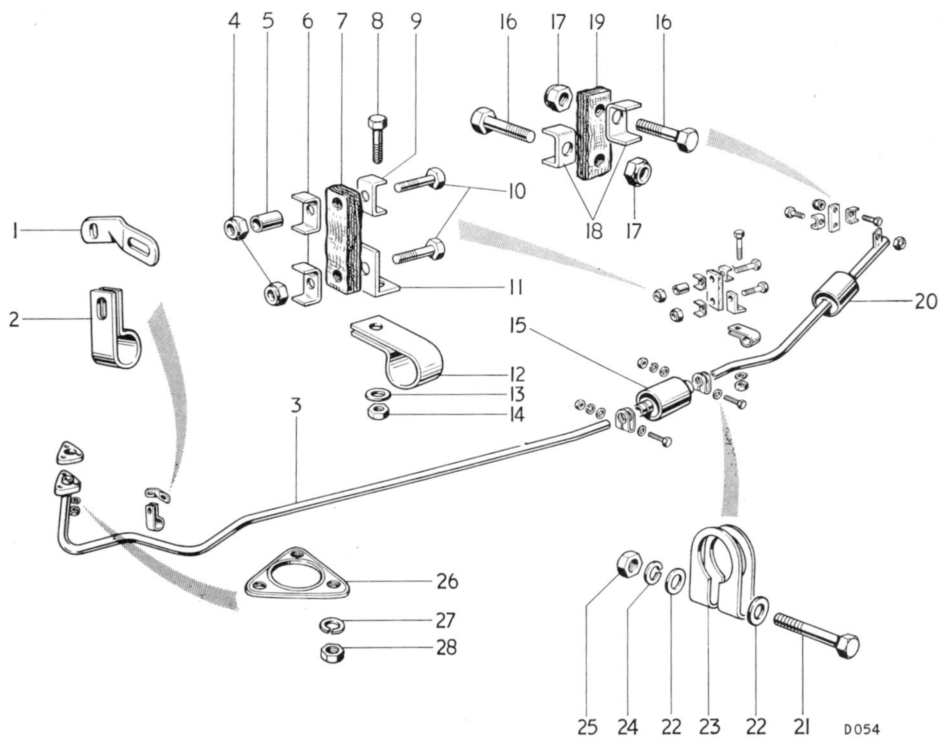

1	Bracket—front pipe to clutch housing	15	Intermediate silencer
2	Clip	16	Bolt
3	Front exhaust pipe	17	Nyloc nut
4	Nyloc nut	18	Plate
5	Distance piece	19	Fabric strap
6	Plate	20	Rear silencer and tail pipe
7	Fabric strap	21	Pinch bolt
8	Bolt	22	Plain washer
9	Plate	23	Clip
10	Bolts	24	Spring washer
11	Angle bracket	25	Nut
12	Pipe clip	26	Flange gasket
13	Washer	27	Spring washer
14	Nut	28	Nut

Fig. 6. Exploded view of Herald Mk. I exhaust system

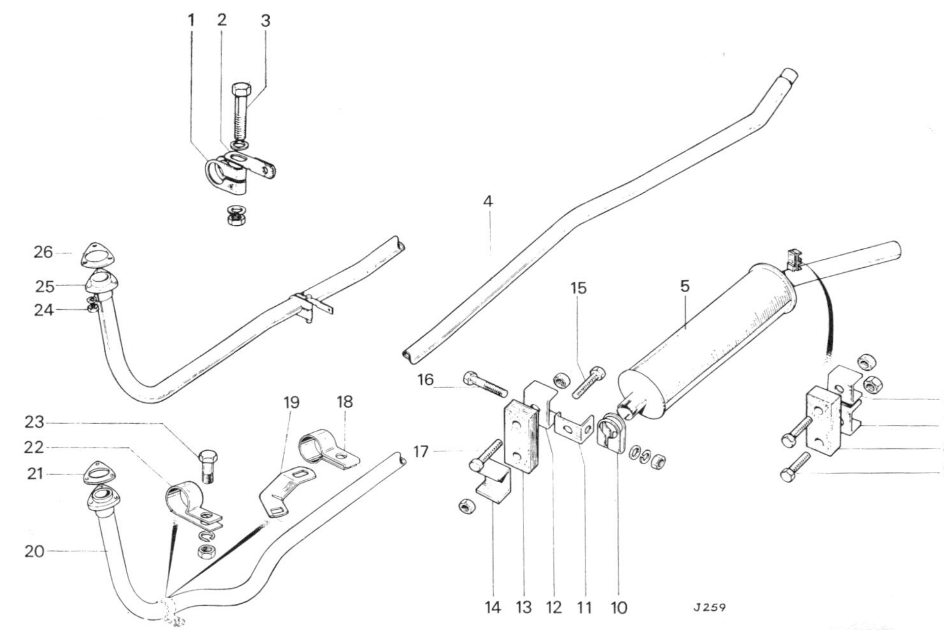

1	Pipe clip	14	Clamp plate
2	Bracket	15	Setscrew
3	Bolt	16	Bolt
4	Exhaust pipe	17	Setscrew
5	Exhaust silencer and rear pipe	18	Clip
6	Clamp plate	19	Bracket
7	Clamp plate	20	Front exhaust pipe
8	Flexible mounting strip	21	Gasket
9	Setscrew	22	Clip
10	Clip	23	Bolt
11	Mounting bracket	24	Nut
12	Clamp plate	25	Front exhaust pipe
13	Flexible mounting strip	26	Gasket

Fig. 7. Exhaust details 1200, 12/50, 13/60 and Vitesse 6

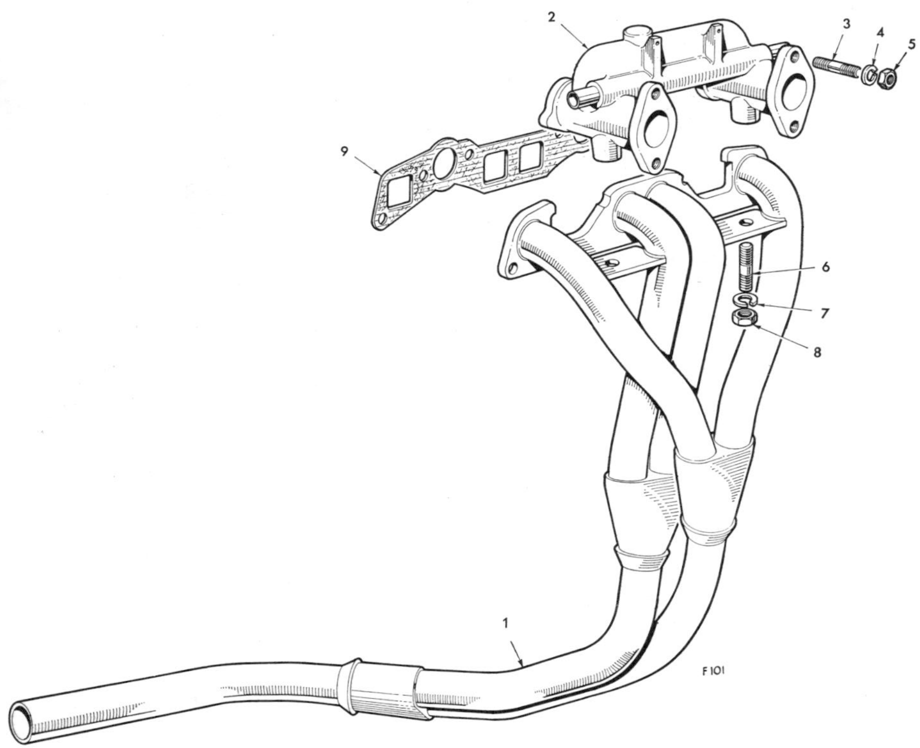

1 Exhaust manifold
2 Inlet manifold
3 Stud
4 Spring washer
5 Nut
6 Stud
7 Spring washer
8 Nut
9 Gasket

Fig. 8. Spitfire Mk. II manifold details

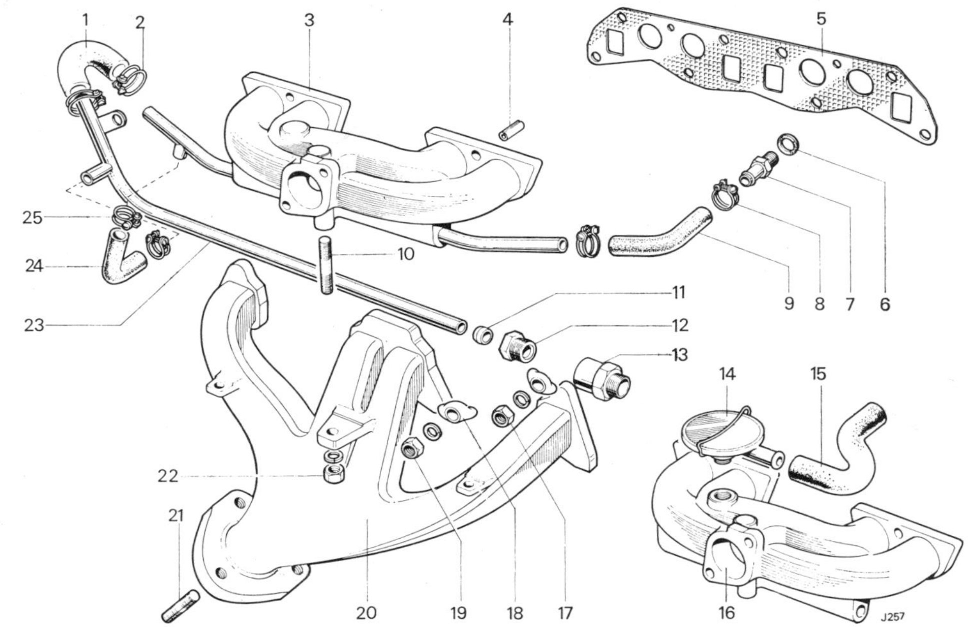

1 Hose (non-heater condition)
2 Clip
3 Inlet manifold
4 Mills pin
5 Manifold gasket
6 Gasket
7 Union
8 Clip
9 Hose
10 Stud
11 Olive
12 Union
13 Adaptor
14 Emission valve
15 Breather hose
16 Inlet manifold
17 Nut
18 Clamp
19 Nut
20 Exhaust
21 Stud
22 Nut
23 Heater pipe
24 Hose
25 Clip

Fig. 9. 13/60 Manifold details.

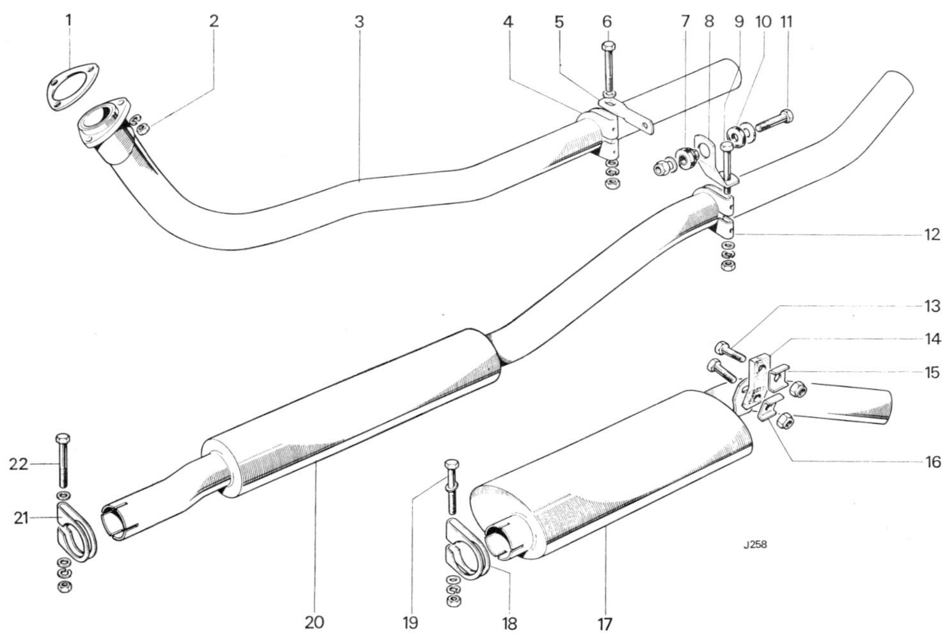

1	Gasket front pipe to manifold	12	Pipe clip
2	Nut	13	Bolt
3	Front exhaust pipe	14	Flexible strip
4	Clip	15	Clamp plate
5	Bracket	16	Clamp plate
6	Bolt	17	Rear silencer and tail pipe
7	Rubber grommet	18	Clip
8	Mounting bracket	19	Bolt
9	Bolt	20	Front silencer
10	Grommet washer	21	Clip
11	Bolt	22	Bolt

Fig. 10. Spitfire Mk. III exhaust details.

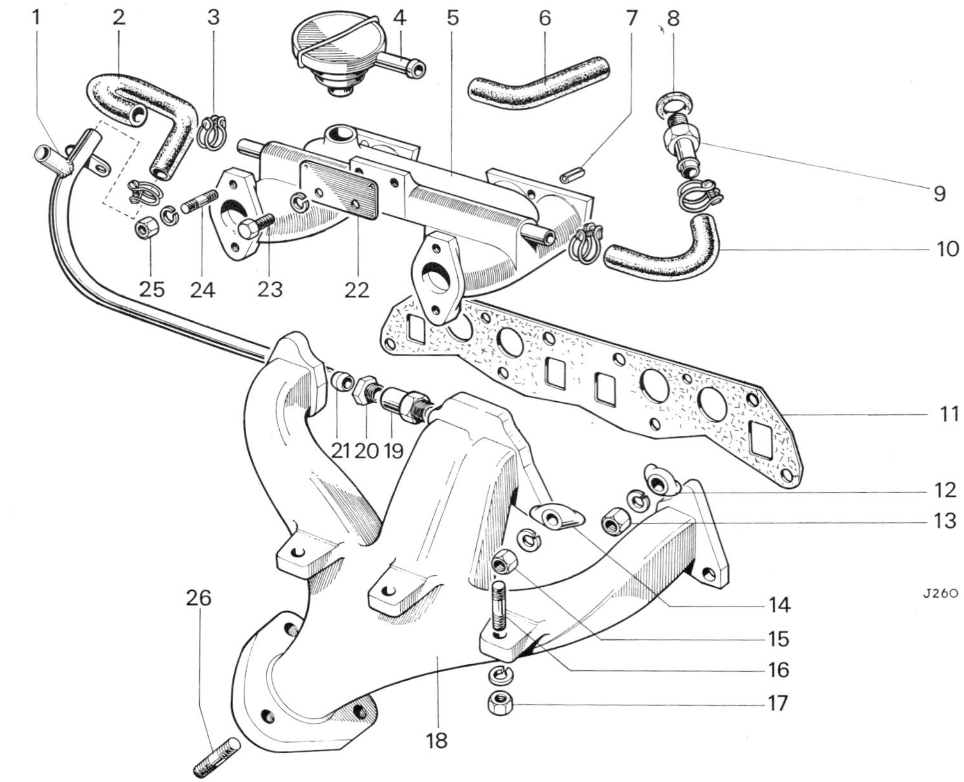

1	Heater pipe	14	Clamp
2	Hose	15	Nut
3	Clip	16	Stud
4	Breather valve	17	Nut
5	Inlet manifold	18	Exhaust manifold
6	Breather hose	19	Adaptor
7	Mills pin	20	Union
8	Gasket	21	Olive
9	Adaptor	22	Spring plate
10	Hose	23	Bolt
11	Manifold gasket	24	Stud
12	Clamp	25	Nut
13	Nut	26	Stud

Fig. 11. Spitfire Mk. III manifold details

TRIUMPH
HERALD, VITESSE 6
AND
SPITFIRE
WORKSHOP MANUAL

GROUP 2

Comprising :

TRIUMPH
HERALD, VITESSE 6
and
SPITFIRE

GROUP 2

CONTENTS

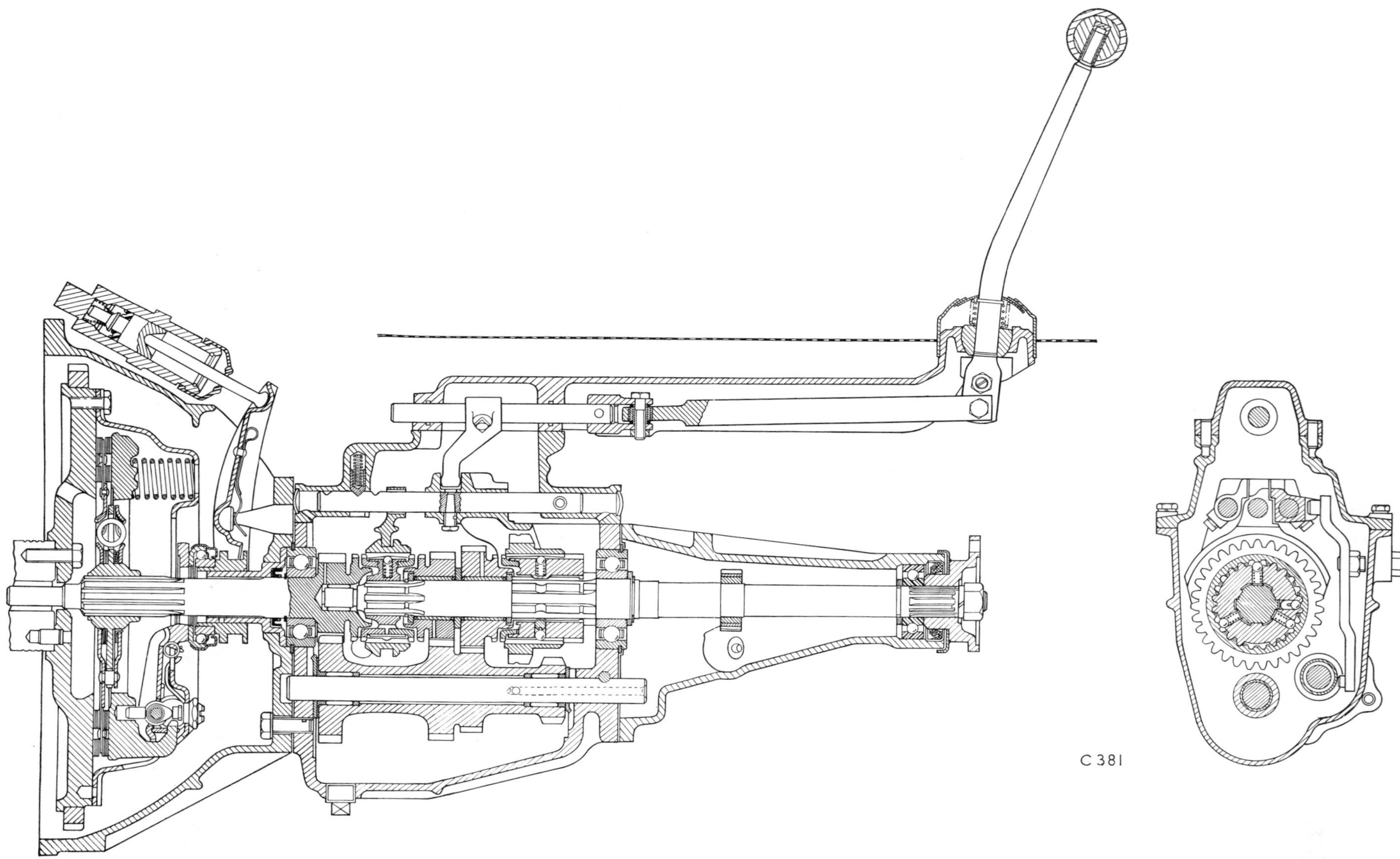

Fig. 2. Section of clutch (Vitesse) and gearbox unit. The gearbox is identical basically for the Herald 1200, 12/50, 13/60, Vitesse and Spitfire

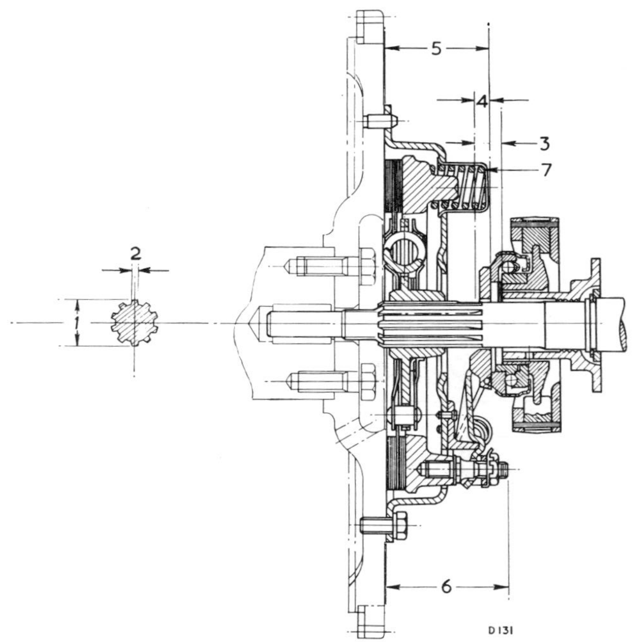

CLUTCH DATA

TYPE	6A "Single Dry Plate"
OPERATION	Hydraulic
ADJUSTMENT	Self adjusting
DRIVEN PLATE	Belleville washer type, cushioned by white/light green springs
FACINGS	Mintex M19
1. Spline diameter O/D	0·871"/0·873" (22·12/22·17 mm.)
2. Splines	0·875" (22·22 mm.) × 10 SAE splines
3. Maximum travel available	0·27" (6·86 mm.)
4. Minimum travel to release	0·24" (6·09 mm.)
5. Release lever plate height	1·83" (46·48 mm.) using 0·305" (7·797 mm.) gauge plate in place of driven plate
6. Maximum height of adjusters	2·22" (56·39 mm.) at full release
7. Thrust springs — 3 Dark Blue	90/100 lbs. (40·82/45·36 kgs.)
6 Red	75/85 lbs. (34/38·5 kgs.)

Fig. 1. Sectional view of the clutch, original condition (Herald 1200, 12/50 and Spitfire)

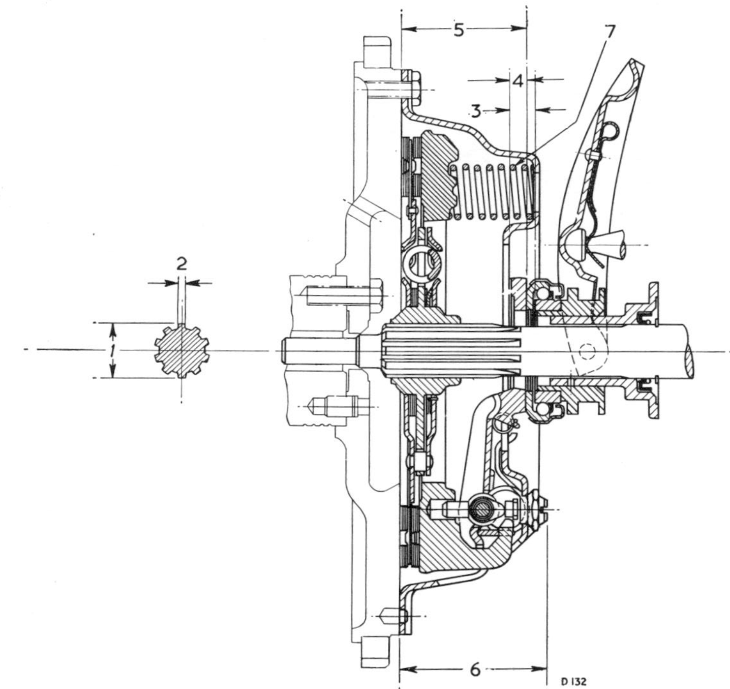

CLUTCH DATA

TYPE	8A6 "Single Dry Plate"
OPERATION	Hydraulic
ADJUSTMENT	Self adjusting
DRIVEN PLATE	Belleville washer type, cushioned by white/light green springs
FACINGS	Wound yarn (RY2)
1. Spline diameter (O/D)	0·996"/0·998" (25·3/25·35 mm.)
2. Splines	1·00" (25·4 mm.) × 10 SAE splines
3. Maximum travel available	0·42" (10·67 mm.)
4. Minimum travel to release	0·37" (9·4 mm.)
5. Release lever plate height	2·18" (53·54 mm.) using a 0·33" (8·38 mm.) gauge plate in place of driven plate
6. Maximum height of adjusters	2·70" (68·58 mm.)
7. Thrust springs — 6 Light Grey	195/205 lbs. (88·45/92·98 kgs.)

Fig. 3. Sectional view of the clutch (Vitesse)

MASTER CYLINDER OPERATION

A. Clutch Driving Condition

When the clutch pedal is released, the push rod (9) is returned to its stop (12) by the pedal return spring. This permits the plunger (7) to move rearwards under pressure of the spring (5). The flange on the end of the valve shank (4) contacts the spring retainer (6) and as the plunger continues to move rearwards, the valve shank (4) lifts the seal (1) from its seat on the end of the cylinder bore and compresses the spring (2). Hydraulic fluid can then flow past the three-legged distance piece (3) and seal (1) either to or from the reservoir.

B. Clutch Released Condition

Initial movement of the push rod (9) and plunger (7) releases the valve shank (4) and permits the spring (2) to press the valve shank (4) and seat (1) against its seat. This cuts off communication between the cylinder and reservoir. Continued movement of the plunger displaces fluid through the hydraulic pipelines and releases the clutch.

Maximum stroke available—
1·38″ (35·05 mm.)

Stroke position at maximum cut off—
0·099″ (2·5 mm.)

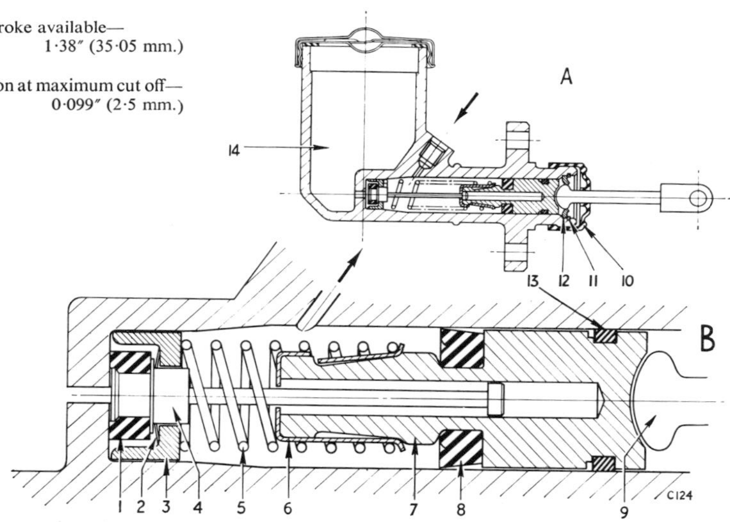

1 Valve seal	6 Spring retainer	11 Circlip
2 Spring (valve seal)	7 Plunger	12 Push rod stop
3 Distance piece	8 Plunger seal	13 Plunger seal
4 Valve shank	9 Push rod	14 Fluid reservoir
5 Plunger return spring	10 Dust cover	

Fig. 4. Section through clutch master cylinder

CLUTCH MASTER CYLINDER

To Remove (Fig. 5)

Proceed as follows:—

1. Empty the master cylinder through the clutch slave cylinder bleed nipple.
2. Pull back the rubber dust excluder.
3. Withdraw the clevis pin securing the push rod to the pedal.
4. Uncouple the hydraulic pipeline from the master cylinder.
5. Remove the bolts (16) from the master cylinder mounting flange and withdraw the unit from the bulkhead.

NOTE : Extreme cleanliness is essential when dealing with any part of the hydraulic system. Component parts should be cleaned in hydraulic fluid or alcohol.

To Dismantle (Fig. 6)

1. Remove the circlip (11) and the push rod stop (12) and push rod (9).
2. Withdraw the plunger (7) and recuperation valve assembly (19) from the cylinder bore.
3. Using a small screwdriver, lift the tag on the spring retainer (6) over the flanged end of the plunger (7) and detach the recuperating valve assembly.
4. Release the valve shank (4) from the spring retainer (6) by manoeuvring the flange on the stem through the eccentrically positioned hole in the end face of the spring retainer. The spring (5), distance piece (3) and spring (2) may now be withdrawn from the valve shank (4).
5. Remove the valve seal (1) from the shank (4) by carefully easing it off with the fingers.
6. Similarly, detach the rubber seals (8) and (13) from the piston grooves.

To Re-assemble

Reverse the dismantling procedure and note the following:—

1. When fitting the rubber seals, apply hydraulic fluid to ease their entry into the bore of the cylinder and ensure that their lips face forward.
2. Avoid trapping the spring (2) between the valve shank locating shoulder and the distance piece (3). The washer must be fitted with its domed side adjacent to the valve shank face.

To Refit

Reverse the removal operations, refill with hydraulic fluid and bleed the system as described on page 2·106.

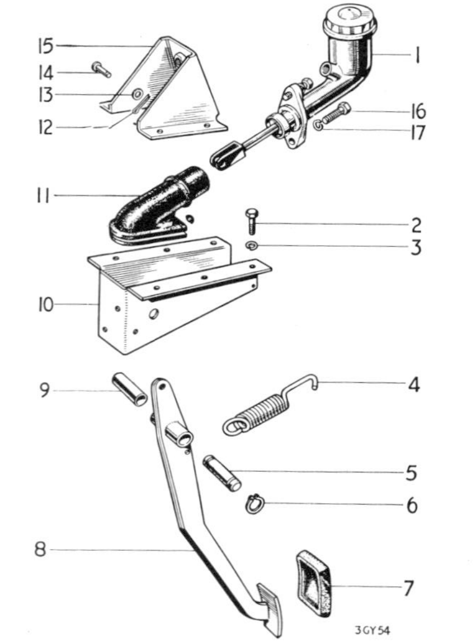

1 Master cylinder	10 Pedal bracket
2 Bolt	11 Rubber dust excluder
3 Spring washer	12 Split pin
4 Return spring	13 Plain washer
5 Pivot pin	14 Clevis pin
6 Circlip	15 Master cylinder bracket
7 Pedal rubber	16 Bolt
8 Pedal	17 Spring washer
9 Pedal pivot bush	

Fig. 5. Exploded clutch pedal and bracket assembly

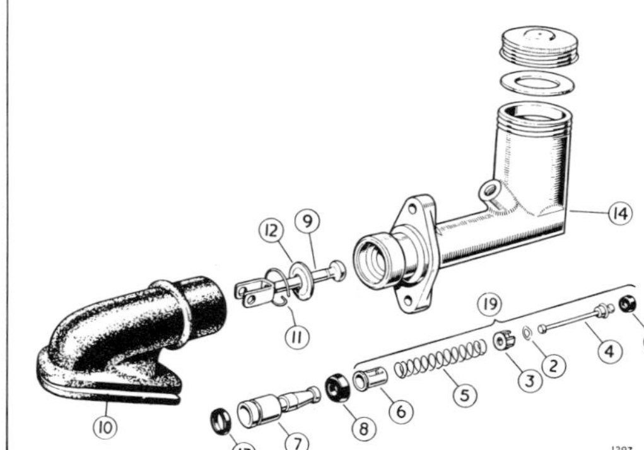

Fig. 6. Exploded clutch master cylinder
Annotations are given under Fig. 4.

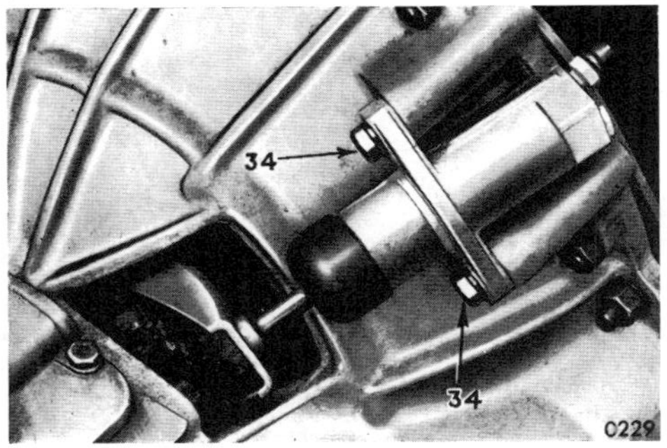

Fig. 7. Location of clutch slave cylinder (Vitesse)

Fig. 8. Clutch release bearing (Vitesse)

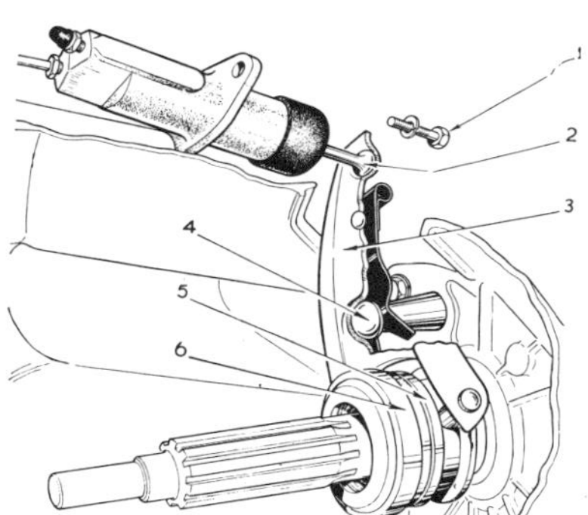

Fig. 9. Clutch release lever attachment (Vitesse)

SLAVE CYLINDER (Fig. 12)

To Remove

Drain the hydraulic system by attaching a tube to the bleed nipple (25) and pumping the clutch pedal. Remove the tube and disconnect the hydraulic feed pipe (26).

Release the slave cylinder by removing the bolt/s (34).

To Refit

Reverse the removal procedure, ensuring that the push rod is correctly engaged in the piston cup. Re-connect the hydraulic feed pipe, refill and bleed the system.

To Dismantle

Remove the cover (32), circlip (31) and shake out the piston (30) and spring (28). Detach the seal (29) from the piston.

To Re-assemble

Lubricate the components with hydraulic fluid and assemble the seal (29) to the piston (30), placing the sealing lip towards the closed end of the cylinder (27). Insert the spring (28) and piston (30) into the cylinder bore. Spring the circlip (31) into position and re-attach the rubber cover (32).

Bleeding the Hydraulic System

The presence of air in the system will prevent the proper functioning of the clutch and will necessitate bleeding to expel the air.

During the bleeding operation, keep the reservoir topped-up with new brake fluid and ensure that the level does not fall below half full. If the reservoir is allowed to empty, air will be drawn into the system, necessitating re-bleeding.

With the aid of a second operator, bleed the system as follows:—

Wipe the bleed nipple clean, attach a length of rubber tubing to the nipple and allow the end of the tube to hang in a glass jar partly filled with brake fluid.

Unscrew the bleed nipple about a quarter turn, and, giving fast full strokes with a slight pause between each stroke, pump the clutch pedal until the clutch fluid entering the glass container is free from air bubbles.

IMPORTANT. Ensure that the piston returns to its maximum travel at the end of each stroke. A sticking piston will be obvious from the feel of the pedal.

Finish with a few slightly faster applications of the pedal, using the bottom half of the stroke, until it is apparent that all air has been excluded. Close the bleed screw during the last pedal application, or with the pedal fully depressed.

CLUTCH RELEASE BEARING

To Remove

Referring to Fig. 11 for Herald 1200, 12/50, 13/60 and Spitfire vehicles: drive the pin (17) from the clutch housing and remove the operating lever (22). Drive out the pins (20) and release the bearing sleeve (15) by extracting the plugs (16). Withdraw the bearing (14) from the sleeve.

Referring to Fig. 9 for Vitesse vehicles:— remove the slave cylinder attachment bolts (1) and move the push rod (2) clear of the release lever (3). Unclip the lever from its spherical pivot pin (4), withdraw the bearing sleeve (5) and take off the bearing (6).

To Refit

Reverse the removal procedure.

CLUTCH

Removal

Remove the gearbox as described on page 2·205. Progressively unscrew the clutch attachment setscrews and detach the cover assembly and driven plate from the flywheel face.

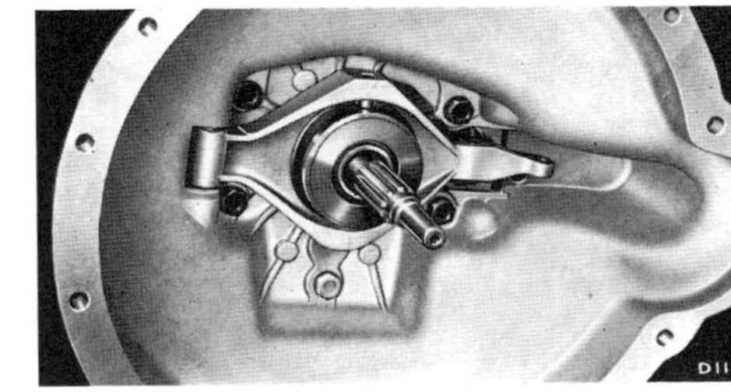

Fig. 10. Clutch release bearing and operating lever (Herald 1200, 12/50, 13/60 and Spitfire)

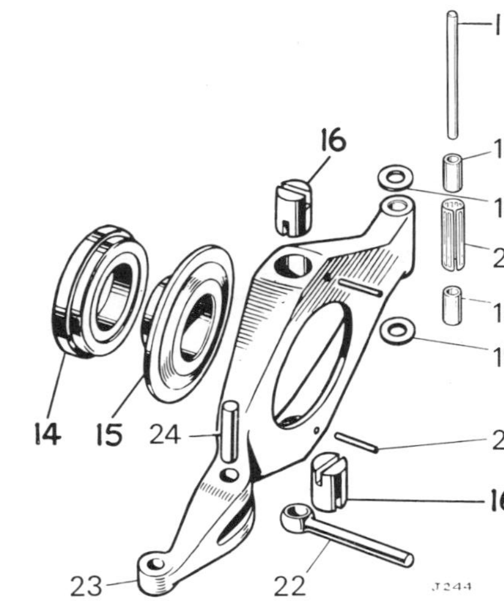

Fig. 11. Exploded operating lever assembly (Herald 1200, 12/50, 13/60 and Spitfire)

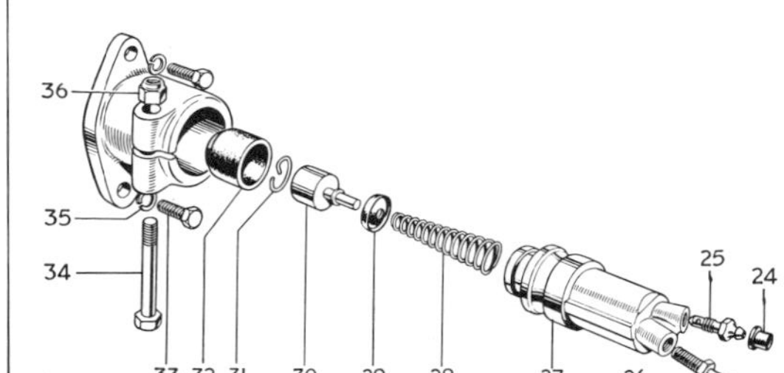

Fig. 12. Exploded slave cylinder details

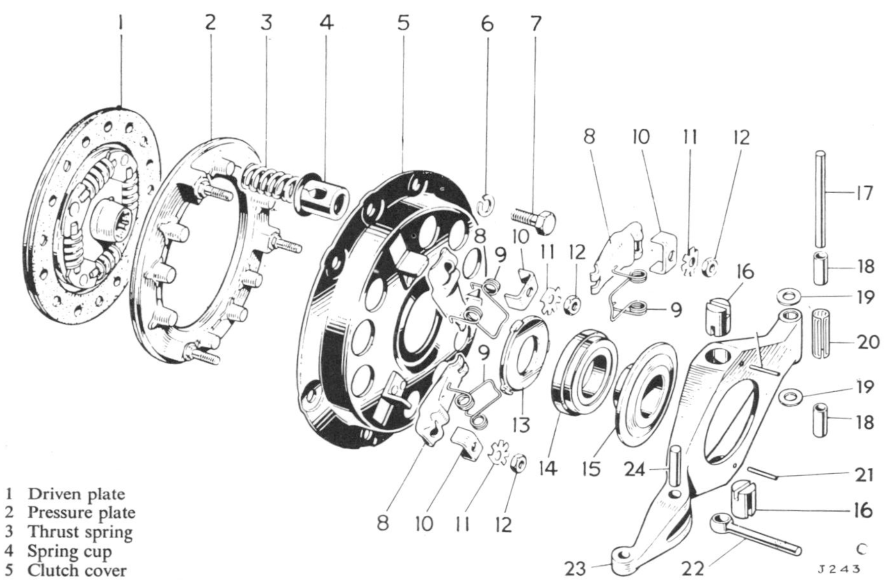

1 Driven plate
2 Pressure plate
3 Thrust spring
4 Spring cup
5 Clutch cover
6 Spring washer
7 Setscrew
8 Toggle
9 Retaining spring
10 Bridge piece
11 Lockplate
12 Adjusting nut
13 Release lever plate
14 Release bearing
15 Bearing carrier
16 Thrust plugs
17 Hinge pin
18 Bush
19 Spacer washer
20 Tolerance ring
21 Lock pin
22 Push rod
23 Operating lever
24 Push rod pin

Fig. 13. Exploded clutch unit (Herald 1200, 12/50 and Spitfire, condition prior to diaphragm type clutch)

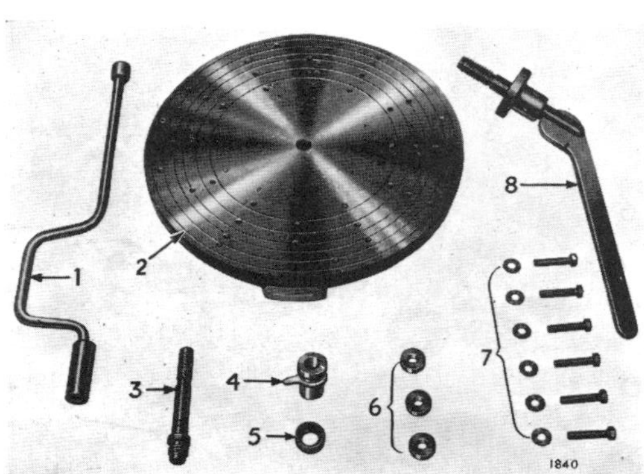

Fig. 14. Clutch assembly fixture No. 99A

Dismantling (Fig. 14)

The Churchill clutch assembly fixture No. 99A is recommended for servicing the clutch units fitted to early Herald 1200, 12/50, Spitfire and Vitesse models. The method of dismantling is as follows:—

1. Position the spacers (6) on the baseplate and place the clutch unit over the spacers, with the release levers as near as possible over the spacers.
2. Mark the pressure plate, cover and toggles to facilitate re-assembling them to their original positions. Fit the operating handle (8) to the baseplate, and clamp the clutch unit by levering the handle. Secure the unit to the baseplate with six setscrews (7). Remove the operating handle.
3. Referring to Fig. 13, hold the release lever plate (13) down and detach the retaining springs (9). Remove the release lever plate.

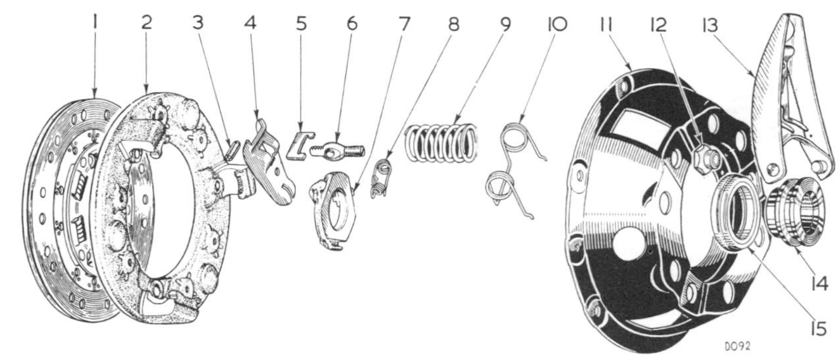

1 Driven plate
2 Pressure plate
3 Toggle pin
4 Toggle
5 Strut
6 Eyebolt
7 Release lever plate
8 Release plate retainer spring
9 Thrust spring
10 Anti-rattle spring
11 Clutch cover
12 Adjusting nut
13 Operating lever
14 Bearing sleeve
15 Release bearing

Fig. 15. Exploded clutch unit (Vitesse)

4. Continue to dismantle the clutch as follows:—
   (a) HERALD 1200, 12/50 AND SPITFIRE (Fig. 13)
   Release the lockplates (11) and remove the nuts (12), lockplates (11), bridge pieces (10) and toggle levers (8). Progressively slacken the setscrews retaining the cover to the baseplate and lift off the cover (5), retainers (4), springs (9) and pressure plate (2).
   (b) VITESSE (Fig. 15)
   Break the staking on the adjusting nuts (12) and remove them. Progressively release the baseplate setscrews and detach the cover (11), toggle levers (4), eyebolts (6), pins (3), struts (5) and springs (9). Detach the pressure plate (2).

Fig. 16 **Attaching clutch unit to Churchill fixture (Herald and Spitfire).**

Fig. 17 **Releasing lockplates (Herald and Spitfire).**

Fig. 18. Removing clutch cover assembly (Herald and Spitfire)

Fig. 19. Adjusting toggle height (Herald and Spitfire)

Fig. 20. Assembling toggles to pressure plate (Herald and Spitfire)

Fig. 21. Gauge finger fitted prior to adjusting toggle height (Vitesse)

Re-assembly

(a) HERALD 1200, 12/50 AND SPITFIRE

Position the pressure plate (2) on the baseplate, with the distance pieces positioned under the lever fulcrum studs. Fit the springs (3), cups (4) and cover (5). Tighten the cover down to the baseplate.

Assemble the toggle levers (8), bridge pieces (10), lockplates (11) and nuts (12). Fit the gauge finger (4), Fig. 14, with adaptor No. 5 and adjust the nuts (12) until the gauge finger just contacts the ends of each lever (8), Fig. 19. Remove the gauge and stud, fit the operating lever and operate the clutch a few times. Refit the stud and gauge, re-check the lever height and adjust if necessary. When correctly adjusted, bend up the lock-plates (11) against the nuts (12). Fit the release plate (13) and secure it with the springs (9). Check the run-out of the release plate with a clock gauge as shown on Fig. 23. This must not exceed 0·015″ (0·38 mm.). If satisfactory, remove the clutch from the baseplate.

(b) VITESSE

Position the pressure plate (2) on the baseplate with the distance pieces positioned under the lever fulcrum studs. Assemble the pressure plate (2), springs (9), eyebolts (6), pins (3), studs (5), toggles (4), anti-rattle springs (10) and fit the cover (11). Secure the cover to the baseplate with setscrews and fit the nuts (12) to the eyebolt threads (6).

Adjust the toggle height as described under "Adjustment" and fit the release plate (7) and springs (8). Check the run-out of the release plate with a clock gauge (Fig. 23). This must not exceed 0·015″ (0·38 mm.). If satisfactory, remove the clutch from the baseplate.

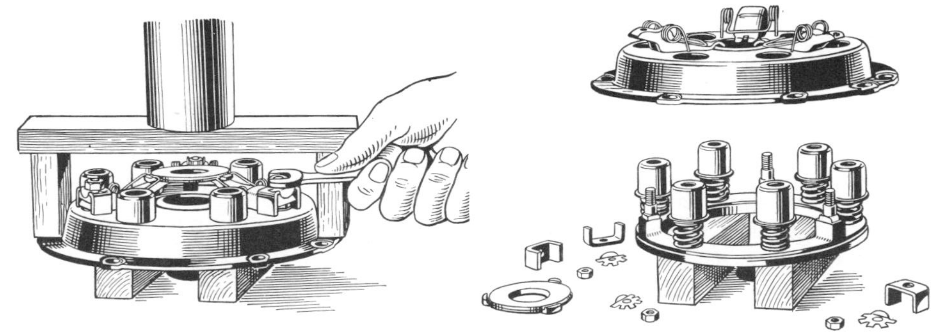

Fig. 22. Using a press and wood blocks as an alternative to Churchill fixture No. 99A

Refitting the Clutch Unit

Check the clutch driven plate for run-out by mounting it on a mandrel between lathe centres and rotating it slowly whilst the plunger of a dial indicator bears against the outside face of the friction lining.

The maximum run-out must not exceed 0·035″ (0·23 mm.). Prise the plate in the required direction until the run-out is within specified limits.

Check the flywheel clutch face for satisfactory condition, and refit the clutch unit as follows:—

With the longer boss of the splined hub towards the gearbox, offer the driven plate up to the flywheel and centralise it by using a special shaft which fits the splined bore of the hub and locates in a bush at the rear of the crankshaft. A discarded input shaft sawn off to suit can be conveniently used for this purpose.

Locate the cover assembly over the two dowels and secure the cover pressing by evenly tightening the setscrews to the correct torque. Remove the centralising shaft.

Fig. 23. Using a dial gauge to check run-out of release plate

Fig. 24. Centralizing the clutch driven plate

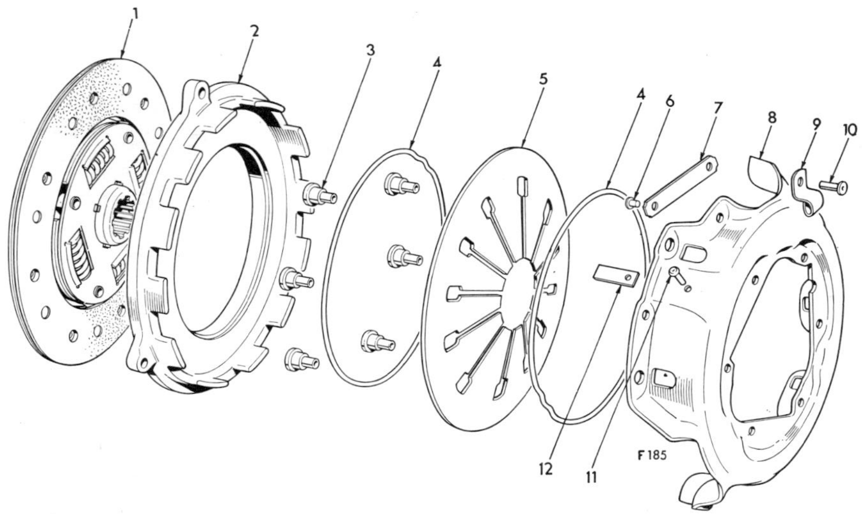

1 Driven plate
2 Pressure plate
3 Rivet
4 Fulcrum ring
5 Diaphragm spring
6 Rivet
7 Drive strap
8 Cover pressing
9 Retaining clip
10 Rivet
11 Rivet
12 Balance weight

Fig. 25. 6½" D.S. clutch details

DIAPHRAGM SPRING CLUTCH UNIT

The diaphragm spring clutch unit was introduced on Spitfire Mk. 2 and Herald 13/60 from 1st production and on Herald 1200 from Engine No. GA.204020E and GB.24121E; 12/50 GD. 44446E.

Under no circumstances must the diaphragm clutch unit be dismantled. Should any fault develop in the unit, a complete replacement assembly must be fitted.

DIMENSIONS AND TOLERANCES

PARTS AND DESCRIPTION	DIMENSIONS NEW ins.	DIMENSIONS NEW mm.	CLEARANCE NEW ins.	CLEARANCE NEW mm.	REMARKS
Input Shaft					
Input shaft spigot bush. Length . .	1·06	26·924			
Bore in crankshaft	0·754 0·753	19·1516 19·1262	0·002 0·0005	0·0508 0·0127	
Number of splines	10				
Dia. of journal for front ball race . .	1·0005 1·0001	25·4127 25·4025	—0·0008 —0·0001	—0·0103 —0·0025	
Input shaft spigot race ball dia. . .	0·688 0·687	17·475 17·449			Torrington needle roller bearing. Press fit in bore.
Mainshaft					
Spigot dia.	0·5000 0·4995	12·7 12·6873			Runs in Torrington needle roller bearing.
2nd/3rd gear bush journal dia. . .	0·8738 0·8733	22·1945 22·1818	0·0027 0·0012	0·0686 0·0305	
Centre ball race journal dia.	1·0004 1·0000	25·4101 25·4	+0·0002 —0·0002	+0·0051 —0·0051	Transition fit
Mainshaft 2nd/3rd gear circlip groove width	0·079 0·076	2·0066 1·9304	0·010 0·004	0·254 0·1016	
Mainshaft 2nd/3rd gear circlip groove bottom dia.	0·795 0·790	20·193 20·0660			
Mainshaft length between front end of 1st gear splines and front face of 2nd/3rd gear circlip groove . .	2·609 2·607	66·2686 66·2178			
Mainshaft rear ball race journal dia. . .	0·7504 0·7501	19·067 19·055	−0·0006 −0·0001	−0·0152 −0·0025	
Mainshaft Gears and Bushes					
3rd speed gear—I.D.	1·0945 1·0935	27·8003 27·7749	0·0037 0·0007	0·0940 0·0178	
Width of hub between thrust faces . .	0·996 0·998	25·2984 25·3492			
3rd speed bush—I.D.	0·876 0·875	22·2504 22·2250	0·0027 0·0012	0·0686 0·0305	
3rd speed bush—O.D.	1·0928 1·0908	27·7571 27·7063	0·0037 0·0007	0·0940 0·0178	
Length of bush	1·002 1·000	25·4508 25·4	0·002 0·006	0·0508 0·1524	End float of gear on bush.
2nd speed gear—I.D.	1·0945 1·0935	27·8003 27·7749	0·0027 0·0012	0·0686 0·0305	
Width of hub between thrust faces . .	1·121 1·123	28·4734 28·5242			
2nd speed bush—I.D.	0·876 0·875	22·2504 22·2250	0·0027 0·0012	0·0686 0·0305	
2nd speed bush—O.D.	1·0928 1·0908	27·7571 27·7063	—0·0037 —0·0007	—0·0940 —0·0178	

The minus sign indicates an interference fit

GEARBOX — DIMENSIONS AND TOLERANCES — continued

PARTS AND DESCRIPTION	DIMENSIONS NEW ins.	DIMENSIONS NEW mm.	CLEARANCE NEW ins.	CLEARANCE NEW mm.	REMARKS
HERALD 1200, 12/50 & SPITFIRE					
Countershaft gear cluster bore—both ends	0·7815	19·85			
	0·7805	19·825			
Depth of bore (rear)	1·53	38·862			
Depth of bore (front)	1·44	36·576			
VITESSE					
Countershaft gear cluster bore—both ends	0·8434	21·3224			
	0·8439	21·4351			
Depth of bore (rear)	1·025	26·035			
Depth of bore (front)	0·962	24·4348			
Clutch Release Bearing Details					
O.D. front cover extension	1·249	31·725	·0045	·1143	
	1·247	31·674	0·0015	0·0381	
Release bearing sleeve—I.D.	1·2515	31·788	0·0035	0·0889	
	1·2505	31·7627	0·0015	0·0381	
Release bearing sleeve journal—O.D.	1·5007	38·1177	−0·0012	−0·03048	
	1·5002	38·1051	−0·0002	−0·00508	
Clutch release bearing—I.D.	1·500	38·1	−0·0012	−0·03048	
	1·4995	38·0873	−0·0002	−0·00508	
Clutch release bearing—O.D.	2·625	66·675			
—Length	0·670	17·018			
Ball and Needle Roller Bearing Details			0·0035	0·0889	
Front and centre ball races—					
Hoffman MS. 10K.—O.D.	2·4995	63·487	Nil	Nil	
	2·4990	63·475	−·001	−·0254	
—I.D.	1·0002	25·405	+·0008	+·02032	
	0·9997	25·392	−·0001	−·00254	Transition fit.
Mainshaft spigot bearing—					
Torrington needle roller No. B.810 :					
I.D.	0·5	12·7			
O.D.	0·6875	17·4625			
Length	0·625	15·875			Stamped end must face outwards.
Depth of press fit into constant pinion shaft end face	0·47	11·938			
Rear extension ball race					
Hoffman LS.8—O.D.	1·8747	47·617	−0·001	−0·0254	
	1·8742	47·605	−0·000	−0·0000	
—I.D.	0·7502	19·055	−0·0006	−0·0152	
	0·7498	19·045	−0·0001	−0·0025	

GEARBOX — DIMENSIONS AND TOLERANCES — continued

PARTS AND DESCRIPTION	DIMENSIONS NEW ins.	DIMENSIONS NEW mm.	CLEARANCE NEW ins.	CLEARANCE NEW mm.	REMARKS
Mainshaft Gears and Bushes—continued					
Length of bush	1·127	28·6258	0·002	0·0508	End float of gear on bush.
	1·125	28·575	0·006	0·1524	
2nd/3rd gear thrust washer	0·154	3·9116			
	0·152	3·8608			
2nd gear thrust washer	0·124	3·1496			
	0·122	3·0988			
3rd gear circlip washer	0·124	3·1496			
	0·122	3·0988			
2nd/3rd gear mainshaft circlip thickness	0·072	1·8288	0·010	0·254	
	0·069	1·7526	0·004	0·1016	
2nd/3rd mainshaft circlip—I.D.	0·79	20·066			
2nd/3rd mainshaft circlip—O.D.	0·94	23·876			
Mainshaft maximum permissible end float of 2nd/3rd gears and bushes, thrust washers and circlip on mainshaft	0·004	0·1016	0·012	0·3048	Recommended end float 0·004″ to 0·010″ (0·1016 to 0·254 mm.). Obtain if necessary by selective assembly of components.
	0·019	0·4824	0·004	0·1016	
Hub width between thrust faces	0·849	21·5646			
	0·839	21·3106			
Reverse Gear					
Pinion—I.D. bush	0·6580	16·7132	0·003	0·0762	
	0·6573	16·6954	0·0018	0·04572	
Reverse gear spindle—Main dia.	0·6555	16·6497	0·003	0·0762	
	0·6550	16·6370	0·0018	0·04572	
End dia.	0·5618	14·2697	0·0015	0·0381	
	0·5613	14·2570	0·0002	0·0051	
Countershaft and Gears					
Countershaft—O.D.	0·6555	16·6497	0·003	0·0762	
	0·6550	16·6370	0·018	0·0457	
Countershaft—Length	8·75	222·25			
Countershaft bushes—Length	1·385	35·18			
	1·365	34·67			
I.D. Bushes—Countershaft gears	0·6580	16·713	0·003	0·0762	
	0·6573	16·6954	0·018	0·0457	
Distance between end thrust faces	5·971	151·6634			
	5·969	151·6126			
Thickness of front thrust washer	0·125	3·175			
	0·123	3·1242			
Thickness of rear thrust washer	0·068	1·7272			
	0·066	1·6764			
Thickness of rear rotating thrust washer	0·0665	1·6891			
	0·0635	1·6129			
Overall permissible end float			0·0125	0·3125	Obtain if necessary by selective assembly of thrust washers.
			0·0015	0·0381	

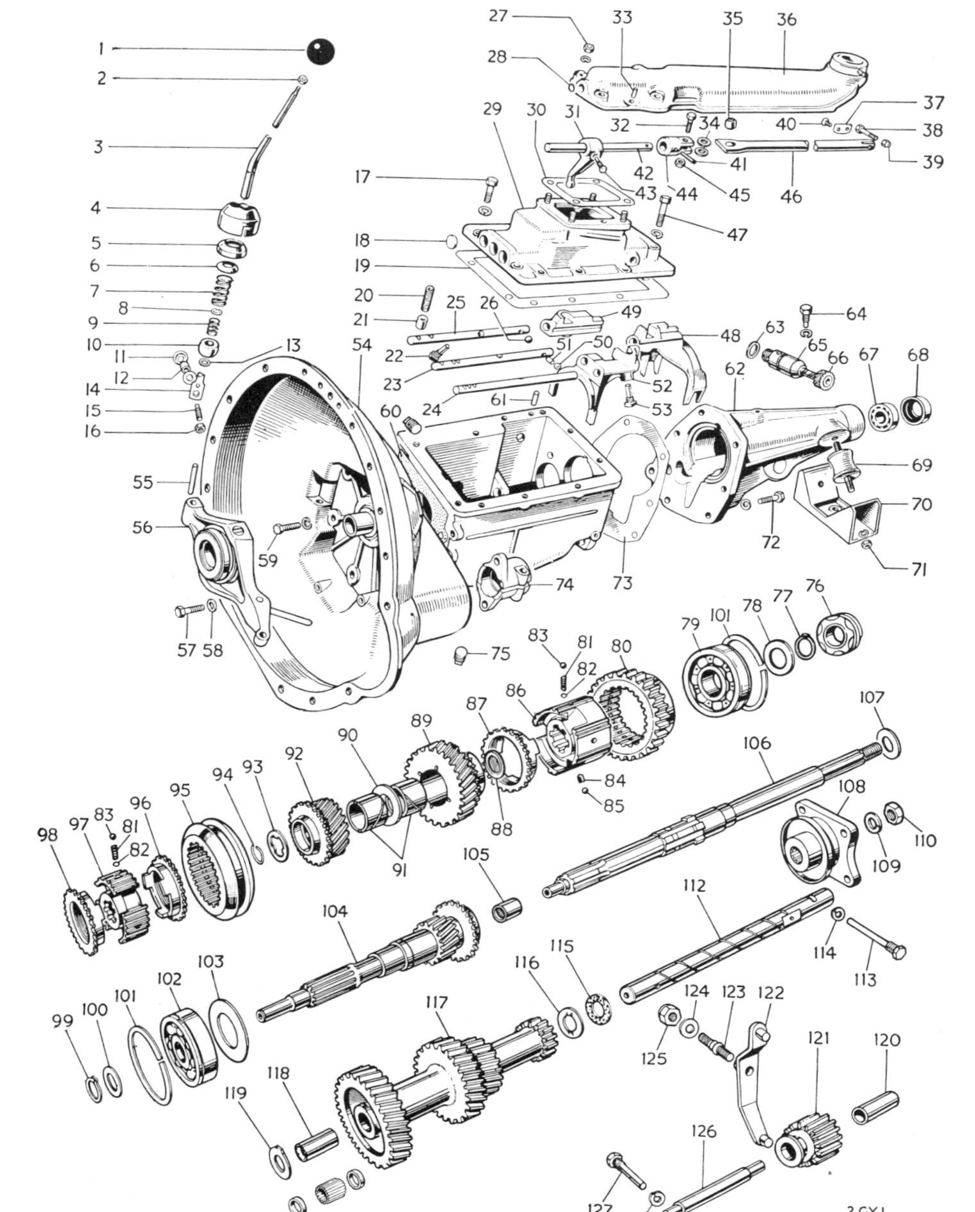

Fig. 1. Exploded Arrangement of Gearbox Details

Key to Fig. 1

1 Knob
2 Locknut
3 Gear change lever
4 Cover
5 Shield
6 Plate
7 Spring
8 Circlip
9 Spring
10 Nylon sphere
11 Stepped nylon washer
12 Bush
13 Washer
14 Lever end
15 Reverse stop pin
16 Locknut
17 Bolt
18 Welch plug
19 Gasket
20 Spring
21 Plunger
22 Taper locking pin
23 1st/2nd selector shaft
24 3rd/top selector shaft
25 Reverse selector shaft
26 Interlock ball
27 Nut
28 Rubber "O" ring
29 Top cover
30 Gasket
31 Selector ball-end
32 Bolt
33 Dowel
34 Washer
35 Bonded rubber bush
36 Gear change extension
37 Reverse stop
38 Bolt
39 Nyloc nut
40 Screw
41 Mills pin
42 Remote control shaft (front)
43 Taper locking pin
44 Fork
45 Nut
46 Remote control shaft (rear)
47 Bolt
48 1st/2nd selector fork
49 Reverse selector
50 Interlock ball
51 Interlock plunger
52 Top/3rd selector fork
53 Taper locking pin
54 Clutch housing
55 Pin
56 Clutch release mechanism
57 Wedgelock bolt
58 Plain washer
59 Bolt
60 Gasket
61 Dowel
62 Rear extension
63 Rubber "O" ring
64 Peg bolt
65 Speedo drive gear housing
66 Speedo drive gear
67 Extension ball race
68 Oil seal
69 Gearbox mounting rubber
70 Mounting bracket
71 Nut
72 Bolt
73 Gasket
74 Clutch slave cylinder bracket
75 Sump plug
76 Speedo driving gear
77 Circlip
78 Distance washer
79 Ball race
80 1st speed gear
81 Spring
82 Shim
83 Synchromesh ball
84 Plunger
85 Ball
86 2nd speed synchro hub
87 2nd speed synchro cup
88 Thrust washer
89 2nd speed mainshaft gear
90 Thrust washer
91 Bushes
92 3rd speed mainshaft gear
93 Thrust washer
94 Circlip
95 3rd/top synchro sleeve
96 3rd speed synchro cup
97 3rd/top inner synchro hub
98 Top synchro cup
99 Circlip
100 Distance washer
101 Circlip
102 Ball race
103 Oil deflector
104 Input shaft
105 Torrington needle roller bearing
106 Mainshaft
107 Distance washer
108 Driving flange
109 Spring washer
110 Nut
112 Countershaft
113 Peg bolt
114 Spring Washer
115 Rear fixed thrust washer
116 Rear rotating thrust washer
117 Countershaft gear cluster
118 Countershaft bush
119 Front fixed thrust washer (Vitesse has needle rollers and retaining rings)
120 Reverse gear bush
121 Reverse gear
122 Reverse gear actuator
123 Actuator pivot
124 Plain washer
125 Nyloc nut
126 Reverse gear shaft
127 Reverse shaft retaining bolt.
128 Spring washer

GEARBOX REMOVAL

Herald 1200, 12/50, 13/60, Vitesse and Spitfire

To Remove Gearbox Leaving Engine in Position

Raise the vehicle on a ramp or support it on axle stands. Isolate the battery, drain the gearbox and remove the front seats and carpets.

Referring to Fig. 2, release the casting (2), fitted only to the Spitfire, by removing the bolts (1) and (3) and by detaching the tachometer drive cable from the instrument.

The following instructions are common to all models:—

Remove the gear lever knob and grommet (4).

Release the gearbox cover (7) by removing the fasteners (5), and (6) and three screws on the engine side of the bulkhead.

Remove the attachments (8), withdraw the slave cylinder (9) and allow it to hang on its pipe (10).

Take out the bolts (11) and completely remove the propeller shaft.

Release the front exhaust pipe from the manifold and clutch housing.

Remove the starter motor and release the speedo drive (12) from the gearbox extension.

Remove the nuts (13), lift off gear change extension (14) and fit a cardboard cover to prevent the entry of foreign matter.

Remove the nuts (15), jack up under the sump until the gearbox extension clears the mounting bracket and take off the mountings (16).

Remove the clutch housing flange attachments (17) and withdraw the gearbox.

To Refit

Reverse the removal procedure.

IMPORTANT : Do not allow the gearbox to hang on the clutch spigot shaft whilst fitting it to the engine.

Refill the gearbox with oil.

Fig. 2. Spitfire facia support attachments

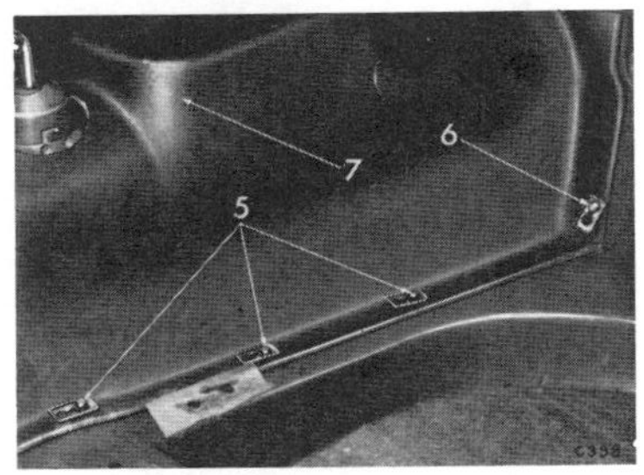

Fig. 3. Gearbox cover fixings

Fig. 4. Herald and Spitfire gearbox attachments

Fig. 5. Vitesse gearbox attachments

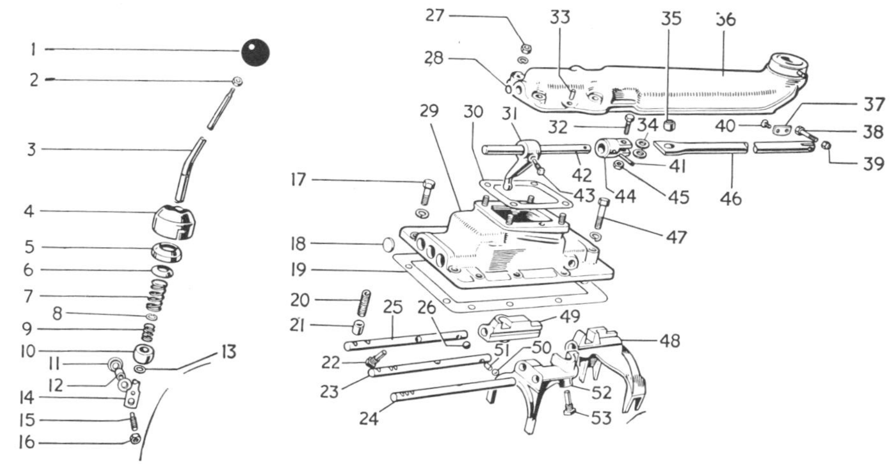

Fig. 6. Exploded top cover details

Fig. 7. Removing top cover

The following sub-assemblies may be removed and refitted in situ:

Top cover extension.

Top cover.

Rear extension.

Speedometer driver gear and bearing.

Speedometer cable.

DISMANTLING OPERATIONS

Top Cover

Withdraw the bolts (17), (47) lift off the top cover (29) and joint washer (19).

Remove the nuts (27) and the spring washers then lift off the extension (36) and the paper joint (30).

Remove the Nyloc nut (39) and bolt (38), releasing the shaft (46) from the gear change lever (3). Remove gear lever knob (1) by releasing locknut (2) and unscrewing knob.

Release cap (4) as shown on Fig. 9. Lift the lever assembly out of the extension and remove the cups (5) and (6), together with the outer spring (7).

Remove the snap ring (8) from the gear lever and detach the inner spring (9) and Nylon sphere (10). Detach the reverse stop plate (37) by removing the two countersunk screws (40). Unscrew reverse stop bolt (15) from gear lever.

Remove the threaded taper locking pin (43) and withdraw the shaft (42) from the extension casing (36) and selector (31).

Remove the rubber 'O' rings from the extension casing bore (Fig. 11).

Detach the locknut (45) and unscrew the pivot bolt (32) from the coupling fork (44). Withdraw the shaft (46) from the coupling, together with fibre washers (34).

Detach the coupling fork from shaft (42) by drifting out the hollow spring steel pin (41).

Dismantle the selector shaft and fork assemblies by driving out the Welch plugs (18) with a ⅛" (3·17 mm.) dia. pin punch as shown in Fig. 10 ensuring that the selector shafts are clear.

Remove the threaded tapered locking pins (53) and (22) from the selector shafts and forks.

Push the selector shaft (25) out of the cover, followed by items (23) and (24). Remove the two interlock balls (26), (50), plunger (51), three selector plungers (21) and three springs (20).

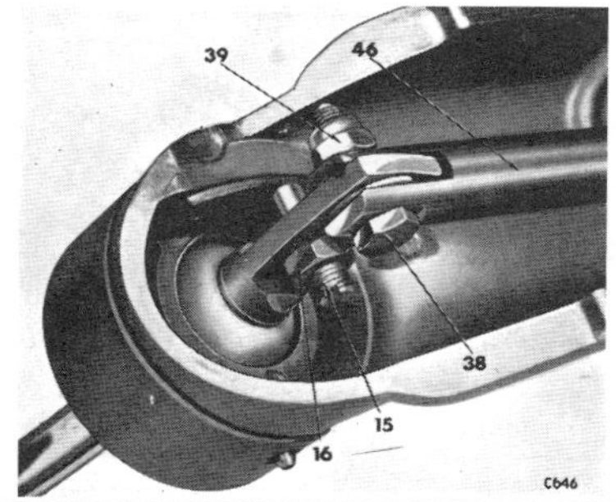

Fig. 8. **Control shaft to gearlever attachment details**

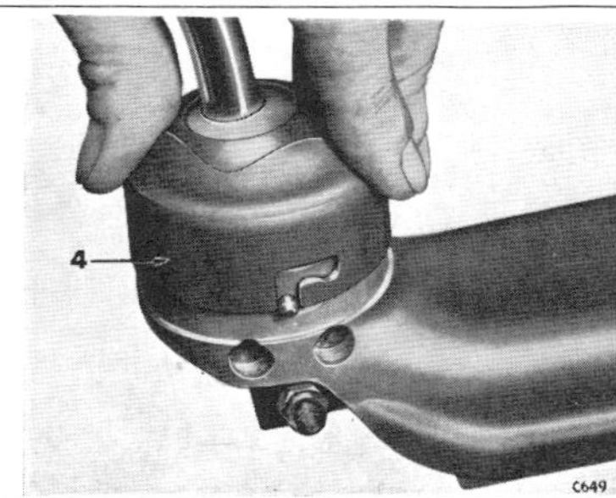

Fig. 9. **Turning the cover to release the gearlever assembly**

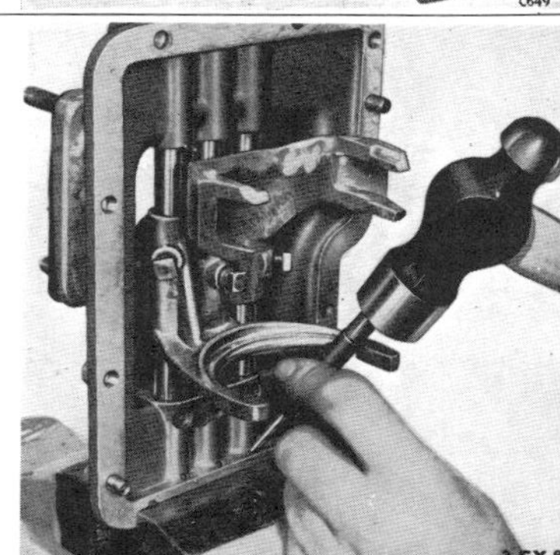

Fig. 10. **Removing selector shaft welch plugs**

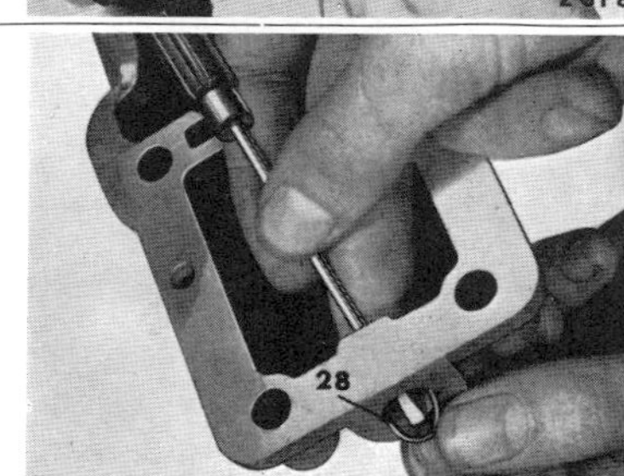

Fig. 11. **Removing rubber 'O' ring from extension**

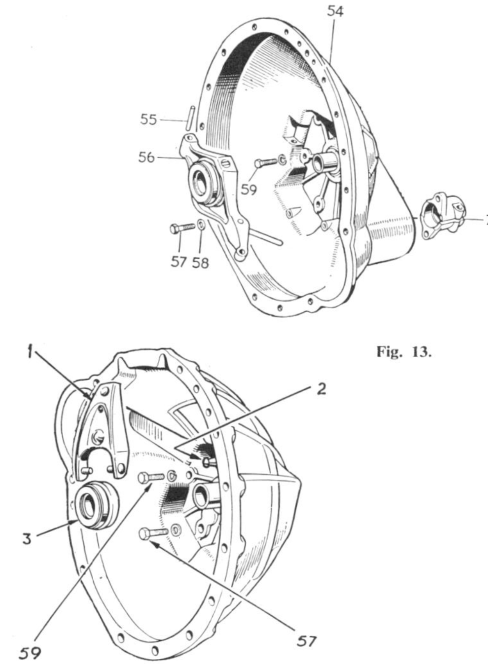

Fig. 13.

Fig. 14. **Withdrawing speedometer driving pinion**

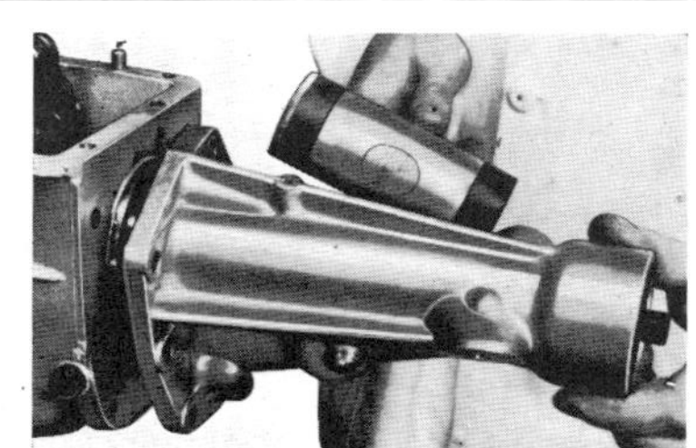

Fig. 15. **Removing rear extension**

Clutch Housing

HERALD 1200, 12/50, 13/60 and SPITFIRE

Drift out the pivot pin (55) from the clutch housing (54) and remove the operating lever assembly (56). Release the clutch housing by removing the slave cylinder bracket (74), four bolts (59) and one Wedgelock bolt (57).

VITESSE

Unclip the release lever pressing (1) from the pivot ball (2) and remove the lever and bearing (3). Remove the bolts (59) and (57) to release the clutch housing.

Rear Extension

Remove the nut (110), and spring washer (109) and withdraw the driving flange (108) from the mainshaft (106).

Withdraw six bolts (72) and one longer bolt securing the extension (62) to the gearbox. Remove the extension by lightly tapping the mounting lugs with a hide-faced hammer. Remove the paper joint washer (73) and distance washer (107) from the mainshaft.

Remove the peg bolt (64) and withdraw the housing (65) from the extension (62). Remove the gear and shaft from the housing and detach the rubber 'O' ring.

Eject the ball race (67) and oil seal (68) from the extension.

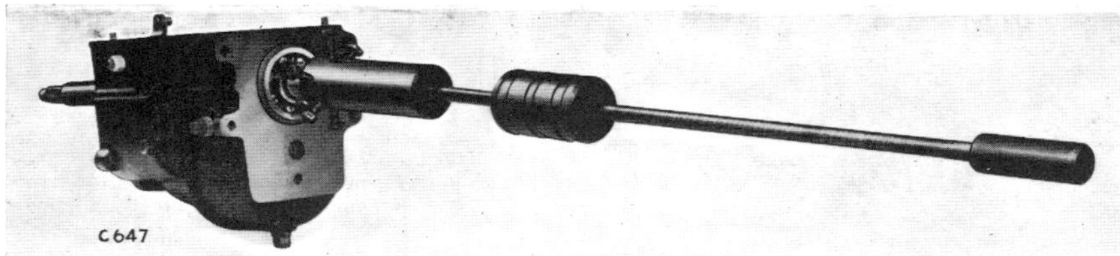

Fig. 16. Using Churchill main tool 4235A with adaptor S.4235A-2 to remove input shaft assembly

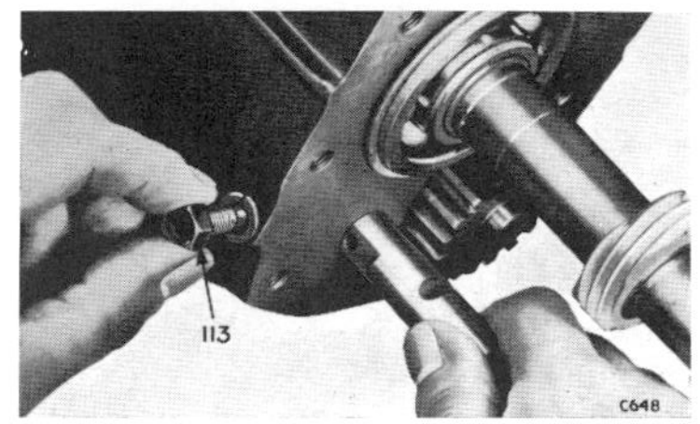

Fig. 17. Withdrawing the layshaft

Fig. 18. Using Churchill press and adaptors to remove input shaft bearing

Fig. 19. Tilting the mainshaft and removing synchro unit

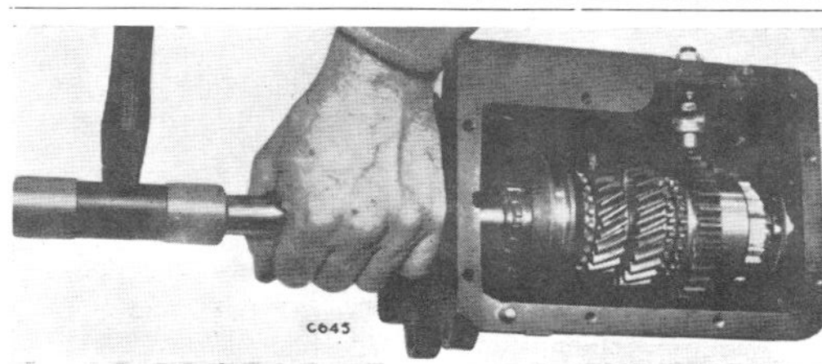

Fig. 20. Driving the mainshaft rearwards to allow the shaft to be tilted

Countershaft
HERALD 1200, 12/50, 13/60 and SPITFIRE

Extract the countershaft locating bolt (113) and eject the countershaft (112), permitting the countershaft gear cluster to drop clear of the mainshaft gear.

VITESSE

Eject the countershaft and retain the needle roller bearings by inserting a length of rod 0·655″ (16·64 mm.) dia. × 5·5″ (139·7 mm.) long.

Input Shaft

Utilizing Churchill tool as shown in Fig. 16, withdraw the input shaft assembly from the gearbox.

Remove the two circlips (99), (101), the distance washer (100), then place in a press and extract the ball race (102) and oil deflector (103), Fig. 18.

Mainshaft and Gears

Using a hollow drift, drive the mainshaft (106) rearwards, as shown on Fig. 20, until the rear ball race (79) is clear of its housing.

Tilt the mainshaft assembly (Fig. 19) and extract the synchro unit (92), (95) and the synchro cups (96) and (98).

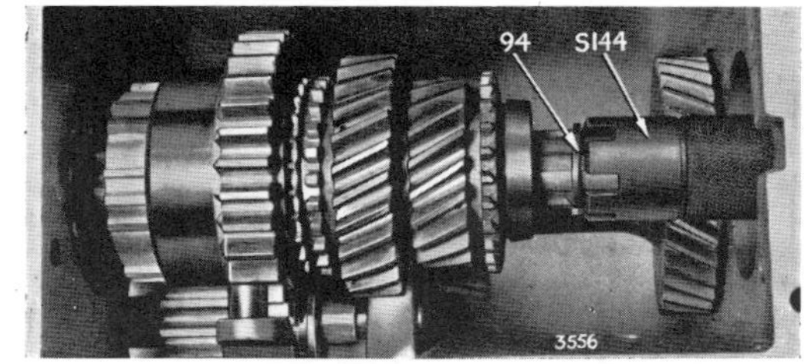

Re-position the mainshaft and, using a special extractor, remove the circlip (94).

Fig. 21. Using Churchill tool S.144 to remove mainshaft circlip

Again drive the mainshaft rearwards and as this is now being finally withdrawn remove the mainshaft details as they are released from the shaft.

Fig. 22. Removing mainshaft details

Completely dismantle the mainshaft by removing the nylon speedo driving gear (76), the circlips (77) and (101), distance washer (78) and ball race (79).

Fig. 23. Using Churchill press and adaptors to remove speedometer driving gear

Eject the reverse idler gear (121) rearwards. Remove the dowel bolt (127) and withdraw the reverse idler gear shaft (126).

Remove the rear thrust washer (115) and, after lifting the gear cluster (117) from the casing, remove the front thrust washer (119) and the rear rotating thrust washer (116).

Fig. 24. Ejecting the reverse pinion

Drift out worn countershaft bushes and fit new ones.

Fig. 25. Showing (left) **the Torrington needle roller bearings fitted to Vitesse countershaft and** (right) **the bushes fitted to Herald 1200, 13/60 and Spitfire.**

Complete the dismantling of the transmission case by unscrewing the nut (125) and removing the operating lever (122) and pivot pin (123).

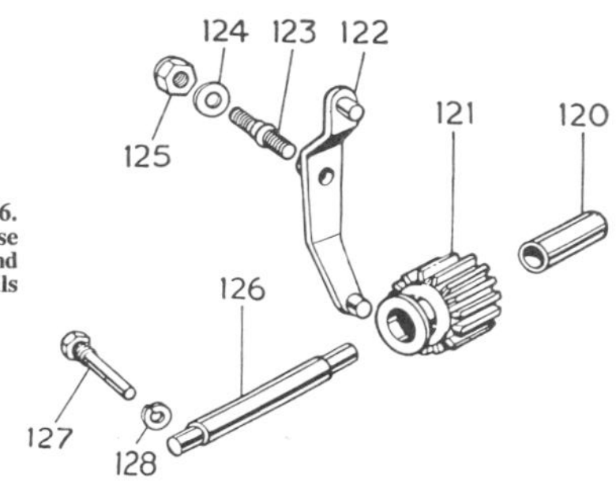

Fig. 26. Reverse pinion and lever details

Both synchro units are dismantled by withdrawing their outer synchro sleeves. It should be noted that spring-loaded balls are retained by these sleeves and to prevent losing any balls or springs it is advisable to cover each unit with clean rag whilst withdrawing its sliding member.

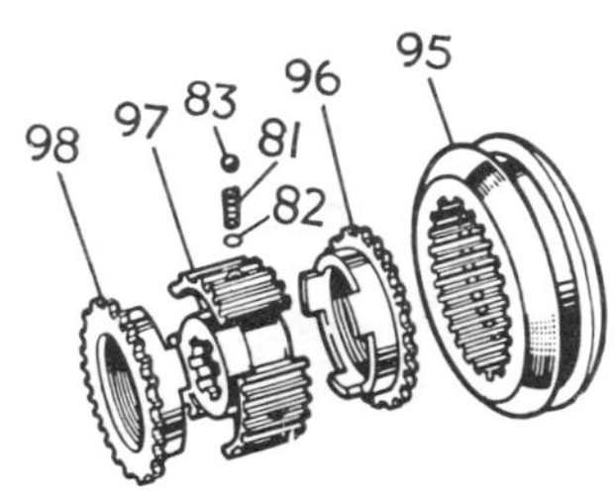

Fig. 27. Dismantled "Top" and "Third" synchro unit

In addition to the synchro balls and springs fitted to the second speed synchro unit, this is also provided with an interlock plunger and ball.

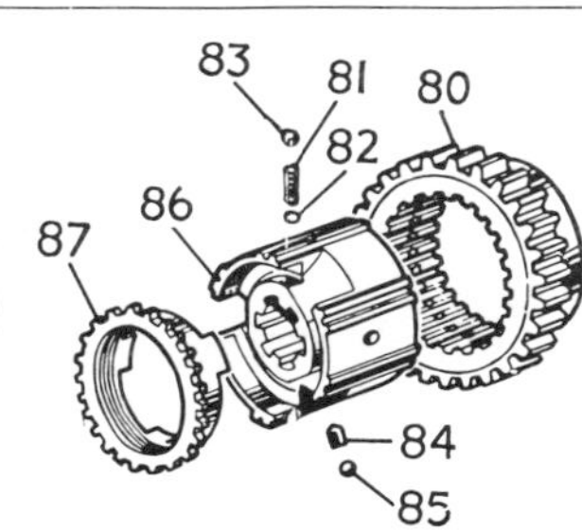

Fig. 28. Dismantled second gear synchro unit

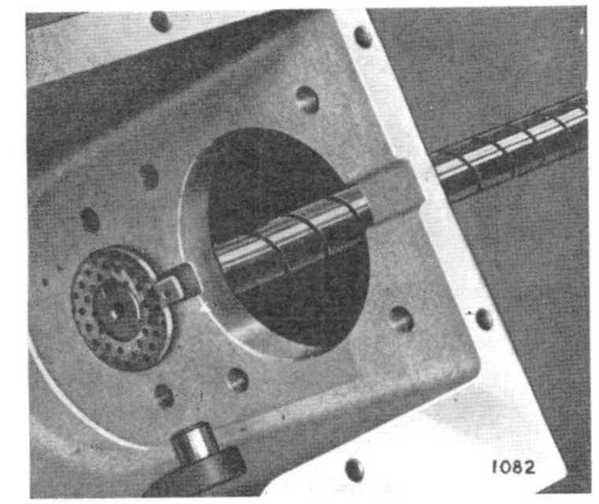

Fig. 29. Using the layshaft to centralise the front thrust washer

Fig. 30. Using feeler gauges to measure countershaft end float

Fig. 31. Inserting reverse pinion

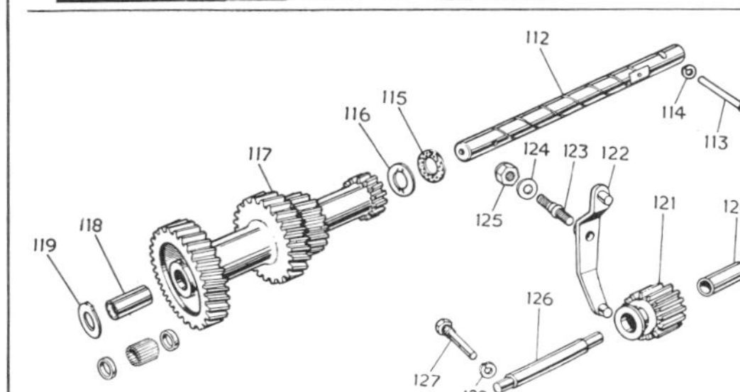

Fig. 32. Exploded countershaft and reverse pinion details

ASSEMBLY OPERATIONS

Having thoroughly cleaned and carefully examined the gearbox components, renew all defective and doubtful items and proceed to re-assemble them as follows:—

Countershaft

Using heavy grease to support it, smear the steel face of the front countershaft thrust washer (119) and locate this in the gearcase, placing the bronze face towards the gear with its tag in the recess provided. Centralise the washer by inserting the rear end of the countershaft (112) through the gearcase as shown on Fig. 29.

Attach the rear rotating thrust washer (116) in a similar manner, engaging its tags in the rear slotted face of the countershaft gear cluster, then lower the assembly into the casing.

Push the gear cluster towards the front thrust washer until this is nipped, then having smeared the rear thrust washer (115) with grease, insert this between the casing and the rotating thrust washer (116) and correctly position its tag in the recess provided.

To enable the countershaft gear end-float to be measured, it will now be necessary to align the thrust washers and the gear cluster with appropriate holes in the gearbox, then install the countershaft (112).

Using feeler gauges inserted between the rear fixed thrust washer (115) and the adjacent rotating washer (116) measure the gear end-float as shown on Fig. 30.

Although permissible limits of 0·0015″ to 0·0125″ (0·04 to 0·31 mm.) are quoted on page 2·203, an end-float of 0·006″ (0·15 mm.) is recommended. Adjust by selective assembly of available thrust washers. If it is necessary to reduce the thickness of any thrust washer, DO NOT REMOVE METAL FROM THE BRONZE FACE.

Eject the countershaft (112) allowing the gear cluster to drop to permit installation of the mainshaft assembly.

Reverse Idler Gear

Screw the pivot pin (123) into the reverse idler gear selector lever (122) until a thread protrudes through the attached boss on the lever, then assemble this in the gearcase and secure it with a nut (125) and plain washer (124).

Position the reverse idler gear shaft into the casing and, having aligned its locating hole, secure the shaft by inserting the locking pin (127) with lock washer (128) and tightening.

Slide the reverse idler gear (121) over the shaft and engage its annular groove with the pin attached to the lower end of the operating lever (122) as shown on Fig. 31.

Synchro Units

1. Assemble synchro springs (81), balls (83) and shims (82) to the 3rd/Top synchro hub (97). Fit the outer sleeve (95).
2. Repeat with 2nd synchro unit.
3. Test axial release load which should be:—
   3rd/Top: 19/21 lbs. (8·618/9·525 kg.);
   2nd: 19/21 lbs. (8·618/9·525 kg.).

NOTE : If the actual release loads differ from those specified, adjust the number of shims beneath each synchro spring to give the correct loading.

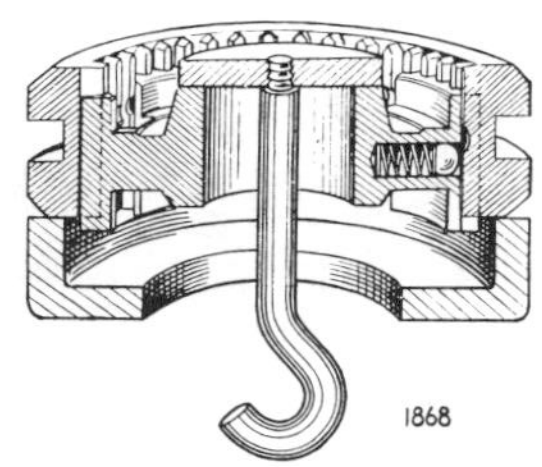

Fig. 33. Checking Top/3rd synchro release load. A spring balance is attached to the hook and the pull pressure increased to the point of release

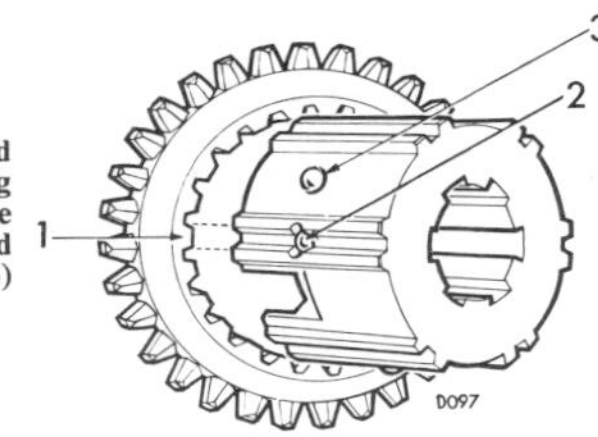

Fig. 34. Second speed synchro unit, showing "master" spline (1), the interlock ball (2) and the synchro ball (3)

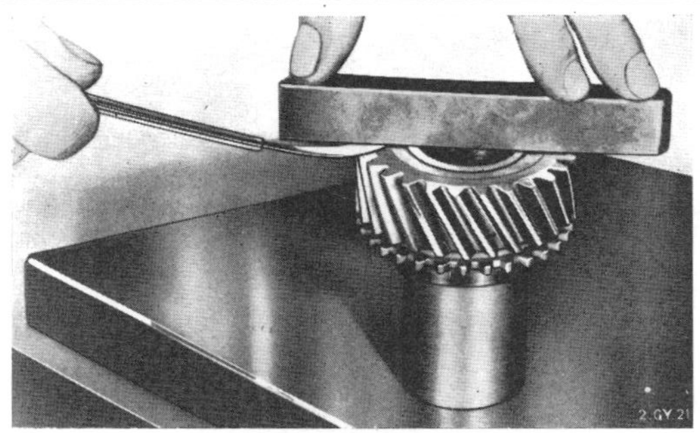

Fig. 35. Measuring gear end-float

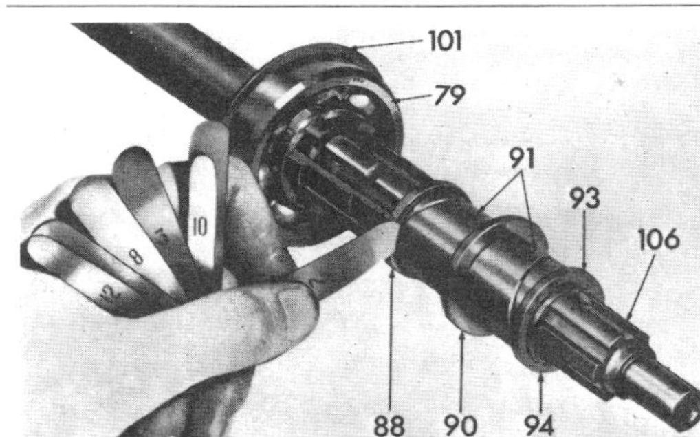

Fig. 36. Measuring overall bush end-float

2nd and 3rd Mainshaft Gear End Float on Bushes

Measure the end float of each gear on its respective bush as shown on Fig. 35. This should be 0·002″ to 0·006″ (0·05 to 0·1524 mm.). Fit a new bush to increase float; decrease float by reducing bush length.

CAUTION : Reduced bush length will increase end float of bushes on mainshaft.

Overall End Float of Bushes (Mainshaft)

Assemble the thrust washer (88), bush (91), washer (90), bush (91) and thrust washer (93) to the mainshaft. Secure the assembly with a discarded half-circlip (94) and measure the total end float of the bushes and thrust washers on the mainshaft. If necessary, adjust the end float by selective use of thrust washers to give 0·004″ to 0·010″ (0·1016 to 0·254 mm.).

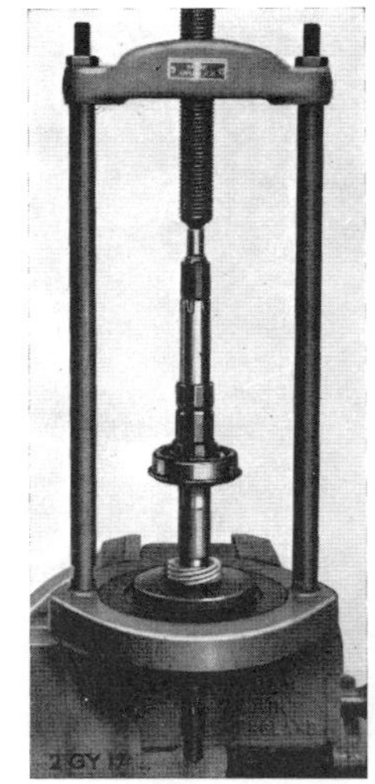

Fig. 38. Refitting the speedometer drive gear.

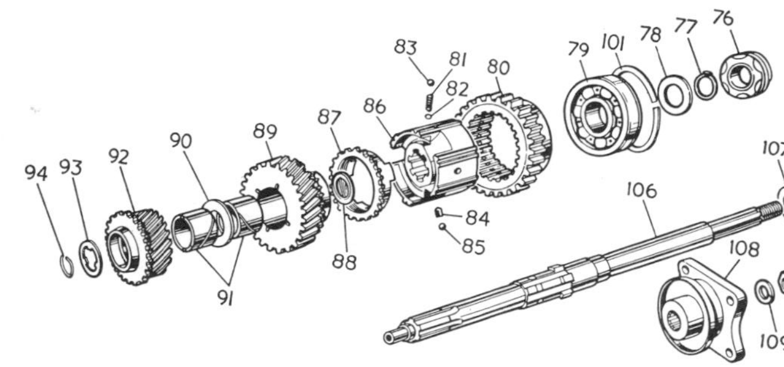

Fig. 37. Exploded mainshaft details

Fig. 39. Refitting the mainshaft bearing

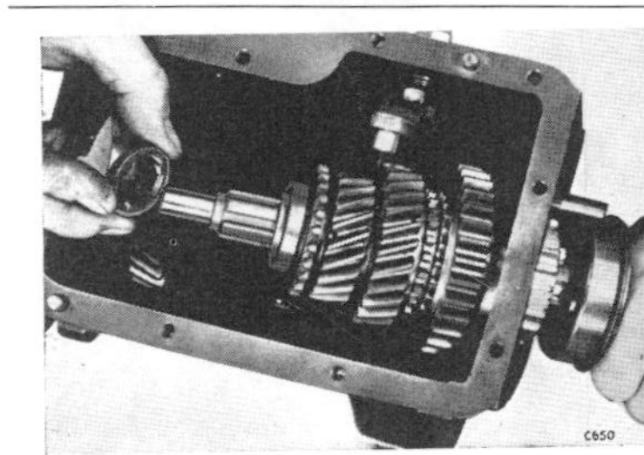

Fig. 40. Assembling the thrust washer with its scrolled face towards the gears

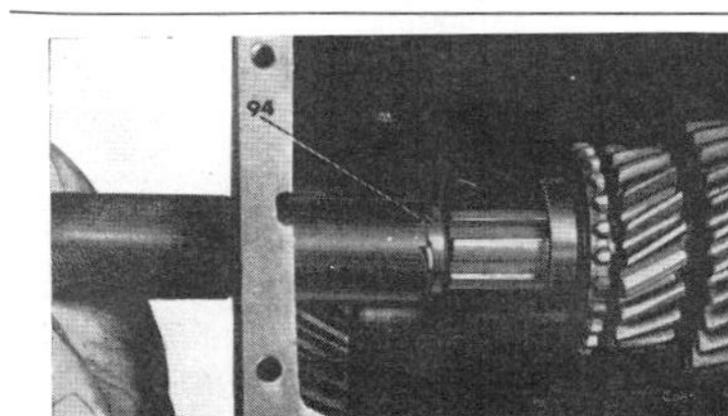

Fig. 41. Using Churchill tool S.145 to install the mainshaft circlip

Mainshaft Assembly

Placing the circlip groove to the rear, press the ball race (79) on the mainshaft (106), followed by the distance washer (78) and the Seeger circlip (77), which must be correctly located in the mainshaft groove.

Next press the speedo drive gear (76) on to the mainshaft as shown on Fig. 38 and spring the large circlip (101) into the ball race groove.

Pass the mainshaft through the gearbox and, holding it as shown on Fig. 40, thread the mainshaft components on to the shaft in this order:—

1. Second gear synchro unit assembly with gear portion forward (make sure that the interlock plug (82) and ball (83) are correctly located in this unit).
2. Second speed synchro cup (make sure that the three lugs locate in the synchro hub).
3. Rear thrust washer (88) with its scrolled face forward.
4. Second speed gear (89) and bush (91).
5. Centre thrust washer (90).
6. Third speed gear (92) and bush (91).
7. Front thrust washer (93) with its scrolled face rearward.

Utilising a special tool as shown on Fig. 41 install the circlip (94). Placing the longer boss of the inner synchro member forwards, slide the "top and third" synchro unit with baulk rings attached over the mainshaft and complete the installation by driving the rear ball race into its housing.

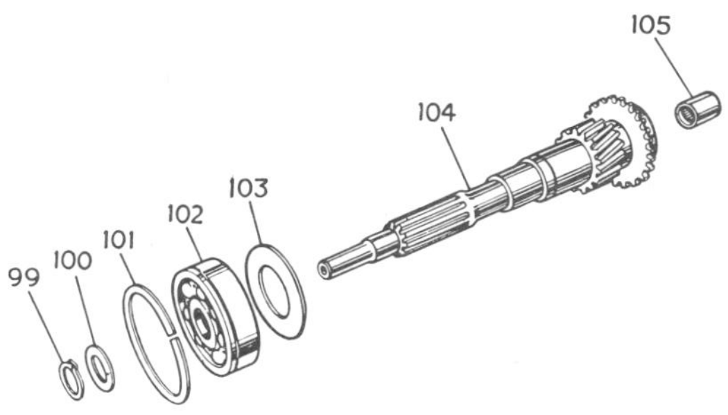

Fig. 42. Exploded input shaft details

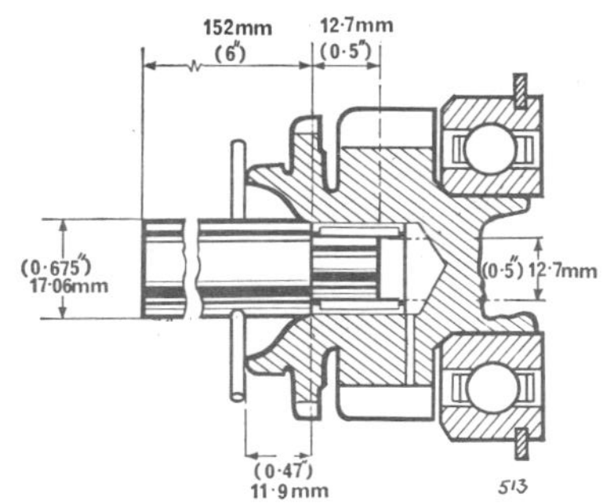

Fig. 43. Details of drift used for driving the needle bearing into the pinion

Input Shaft

Removal of the needle roller bearing (105) is not possible and necessitates replacement of the input shaft (104). Use a special drift, detailed on Fig. 43, to ensure that the new bearing is positioned at the correct depth.

Smear the oil deflector plate (103) with grease and place it over the spigot on the input shaft. Avoiding any disturbance of this plate, press the ball race (102) on to the shaft as shown on Fig. 44. Secure the ball race by fitting the distance washer (100) and the circlip (99) ensuring that the latter is correctly located in its annular groove in the shaft.

Having installed the large circlip (101) on the ball race outer member and placed the "top" synchro cup (93) over its cone on the input shaft, offer up the assembly and as the ball race is being driven into its housing, simultaneously locate the baulk-ring lugs in their respective slots in the synchro hub as shown on Fig. 45.

Countershaft

Align the thrust washers and countershaft gear cluster by pushing a 0·655" (16·64 mm.) dia. rod, having a short taper on one end, through the gearbox and countershaft assembly. Then eject this tool with the actual countershaft, taking care to maintain contact between the two shafts whilst the former is being driven out. Secure the shaft by aligning the lock pin holes and inserting the lock pin (113) with the lock washer (114).

Fig. 44. Pressing the ball race onto the input shaft

Fig. 45. Installing the input shaft assembly

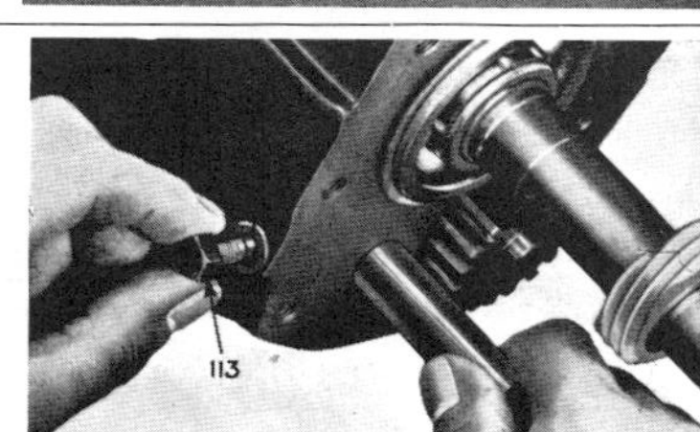

Fig. 46. Installing the layshaft and locking pin

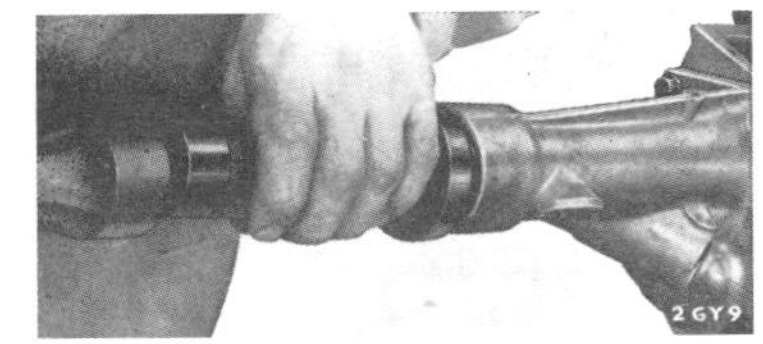

Fig. 47. Fitting the rear oil seal

Fig. 48. Using a torque wrench to tighten the driving flange nut

Fig. 49. Inserting the speedometer drive pinion

Fig. 50. Position of front cover oil seal (Vitesse)

Rear Extension

Drive the ball race (67) into its bore in the rear end of the housing, followed by the oil seal (68) with the sealing lip facing forward (see Fig. 47).

Lubricate the speedometer drive shaft and insert this into its housing (65). Renew the rubber 'O' ring (63) if it is torn or perished.

Insert the drive gear assembly into the rear extension, aligning the location hole with the corresponding hole in the extension. Insert and tighten the peg bolt (64) and spring washer as shown in Fig. 49.

Feed the distance washer (107) over the end of the mainshaft and, after smearing the joint washer (73) with grease, locate this on the rear face of the gearbox.

Using a hollow drift to drive the rear ball race over the mainshaft, install the extension and fit the securing setscrews (72) with lockwashers.

Fit the driving flange (108), spring washer (109) and nut (110), tightening the latter to the correct torque.

Front Cover Oil Seal (VITESSE)

If necessary, extract the front cover oil seal and drive in new seal, with its sealing lip facing the rear of the gearbox, into the recess in the clutch housing.

Coat the paper joint washer (60) with grease, then assemble the washer and clutch housing (54) to the gearbox. In the case of the Vitesse, protect the oil seal by wrapping the input shaft clutch splines with adhesive tape. Secure the cover with one wedge-lock bolt (57), plain washer (58) and 4 bolts (59) with spring washers.

Re-Assembly

To re-assemble the clutch housing and clutch release mechanism, reverse the removal sequence and note the following:—

To prevent oil leakage, fit a new copper plated steel washer (58) beneath the lower bolt (57).

Top Cover

Having inserted the plungers and springs into the cover (Fig. 51) slide the "third and top" selector shaft (24) into the front end of the cover (29) whilst feeding the shaft into position, press down on the selector plunger, thus enabling the shaft to pass over it and through the appropriate selector fork. Continue to insert the shaft until its middle indent registers with the plunger, *i.e.*, the neutral position.

Repeat the procedure with the "reverse" shaft (25) and selector (49) until this also has reached the neutral position.

Insert the interlock plunger (51) into the "first and second" speed shaft (23) and assemble this and its selector fork (48) into the cover by adopting a similar procedure, except that this shaft also passes through the "third and top" selector fork.

Before the shaft (23) has been pushed to its neutral position, insert the two interlock balls (50) and (26) into the transverse bore connecting the shaft bores at the rear of the casting as shown on Fig. 53 then push the shaft further into the cover until its selector plunger registers with the middle indent, and the interlock balls and plunger are retained by the shafts.

Secure the forks and reverse selector by inserting threaded tapered locking pins. Using sealing compound around the edges of the welch plugs (18) drift these into the ends of the selector shaft bores.

Ensure that all selectors and gears are in their neutral position, then place the joint washer and top cover assembly over the two dowels on the gearbox. Secure these items with setscrews and lockwashers, placing the longer ones at the rear.

Reverse Stop Adjustment
Adjust the reverse stop plate (37) and bolt (15) in the neutral position of the first/second gate as shown in Fig. 54.

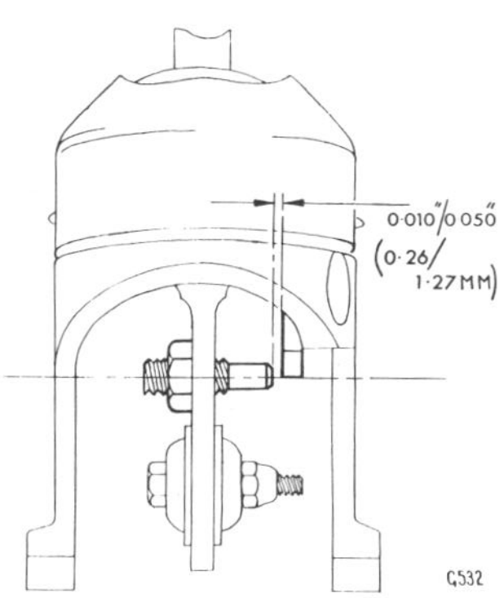

Fig. 54 Adjustment of reverse stop plate and bolt

Fig. 51. Fitting selector plunger and spring to top cover

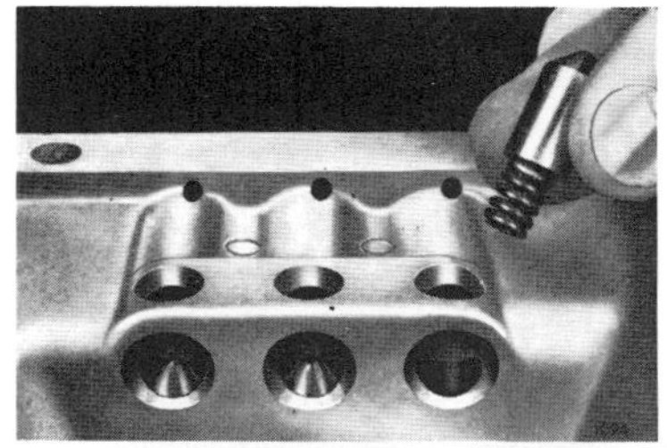

Fig. 52. Inserting 1st/2nd speed selector shaft showing interlock plunger at position (a)

Fig. 53. Lid cut away to show interlock plunger and balls

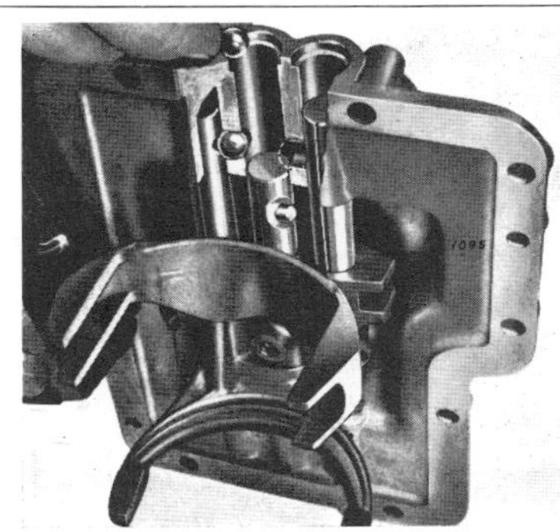

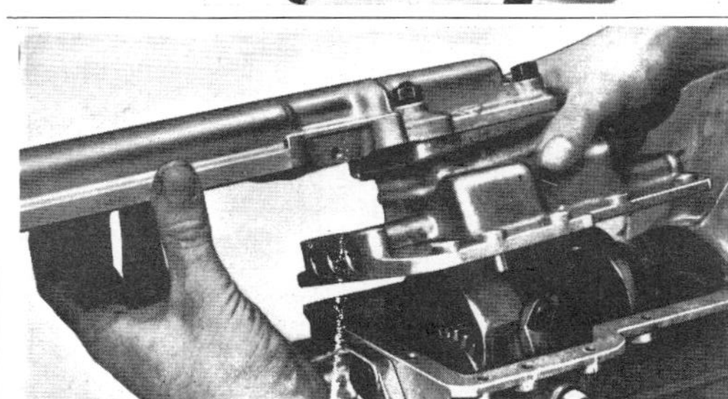

Fig. 55. Fitting top cover assembly to gearbox

1 Sliding yoke
2 Circlips
3 Bearing cups
4 Seals
5 Retainers
6 Spider
7 Flange

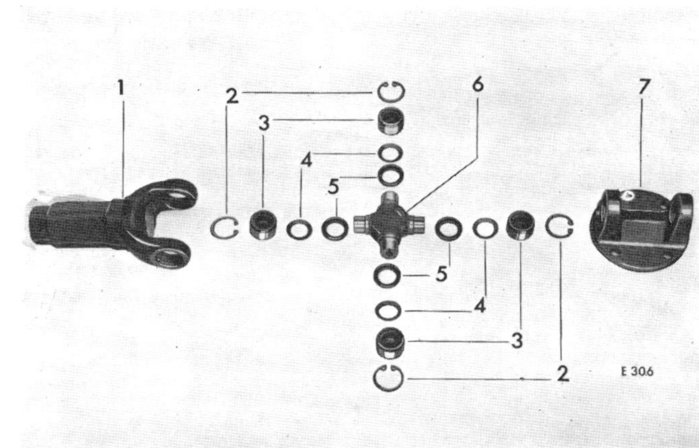

Fig. 1. Universal coupling details

VEHICLE AND STANDARD-TRIUMPH PART NUMBER	OVERALL LENGTH FACE TO FACE DIMENSION (1) in.	cm.	EXTENSION — DIMENSION (2) in.	cm.	MAXIMUM OUT OF BALANCE (AT EACH END)
Herald 1200/1250/1360					
207410 (BRD solid)	50·250	127·64	ZERO		— 0·5 in. ozs. at 5,000 r.p.m.
208033 (Hardy Spicer solid) . .	50·130	127·33			
209834 (BRD Frictionless) . .	49·94	126·84	0·50	1·27	— 0·4 in. ozs. at 3,500 r.p.m.
211143 (Hardy Spicer Sliding Joint)	50·19	127·48	0·75	1·91	— 0·4 in. ozs. at 3,500 r.p.m.
212549 (BRD Strap Drive) . .	50·19	127·48	ZERO		— 0·5 in. ozs. at 5,000 r.p.m.
Vitesse 6					
208942 (BRD ordinary sliding spline)	47·110 46·990	119·66 119·35	1·68 1·58	4·27 4·01	— 0·5 in. ozs. at 5,000 r.p.m.
Vitesse 6 with Overdrive					
208338 (BRD ordinary sliding spline)	43·650 43·530	110·87 110·57	1·68 1·58	4·27 4·01	— 0·5 in. ozs. at 5,000 r.p.m.
Spitfire					
209616 (BRD solid)	41·625	105·72	ZERO		— 0·4 in. ozs. at 3,500 r.p.m.
210508 (BRD Frictionless) . .	41·375	105·09	0·50	1·27	— 0·4 in. ozs. at 3,500 r.p.m.
Spitfire with Overdrive					
210985 (BRD Frictionless) . .	38·00	96·52	0·50	1·27	— 0·4 in. ozs. at 3,500 r.p.m.

For lubricating the rollers in the bearing cups (3), Fig. 1, use Shell Dentax 250 or Retinax A, or equivalent.

For lubricating splines, Sliding and Frictionless, use Duckham's grease Grade No. Q.5648 or Rocol Molytone 320, or equivalent.

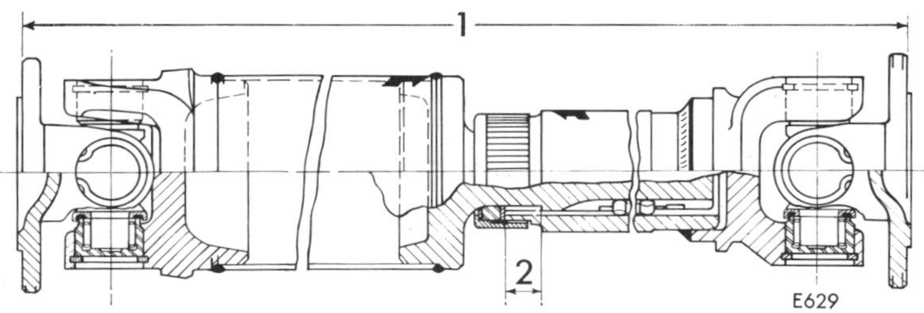

Fig. 2. Frictionless propeller shaft

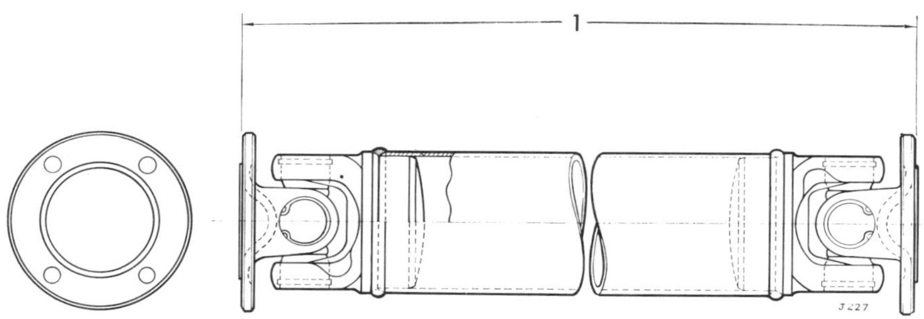

Fig. 3. Solid propeller shaft

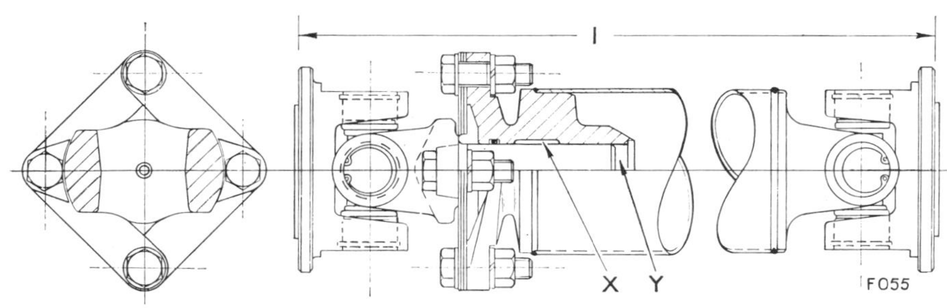

Fig. 4. Strap drive propeller shaft

PROPELLER SHAFT

To preserve the fine degree of balance throughout the transmission, should radial play develop in the propeller shaft universal couplings the complete assembly should be replaced with an exchange unit. Where exchange units are not available, proceed as follows:

To Remove — All models

Raise the vehicle on stands or a ramp.

Remove the facia support bracket, Spitfire only, and gearbox cover as described on page 2·205.

Remove the propeller shaft rearwards.

On Herald and Spitfire models, it may be necessary to lever the engine/gearbox unit forward to disengage the propeller shaft from the gearbox and axle driving flanges.

To Refit

Reverse the removal procedure, using new nyloc nuts if the original nuts can be screwed on to the bolts with finger pressure.

NOTE: The propeller shaft must be fitted with the sliding joint or strap drive at the rear end, if applicable, (see Figs. 12 and 13).

Dismantling — Universal Joints

Remove one circlip from the forked end of the shaft and tap the lug until the bearing cup emerges (Fig. 6). Finally remove the cup using grips. Repeat this operation on the opposite bearing and remove the companion flange from the propeller shaft.

Remove the two remaining circlips, and resting the two exposed trunnions on wooden block, tap the lugs of the flange or yoke to remove the remaining bearings and cups.

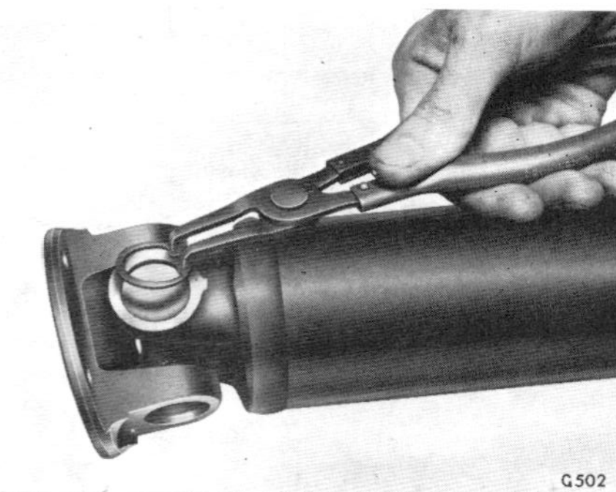

Fig. 5. Removing circlip

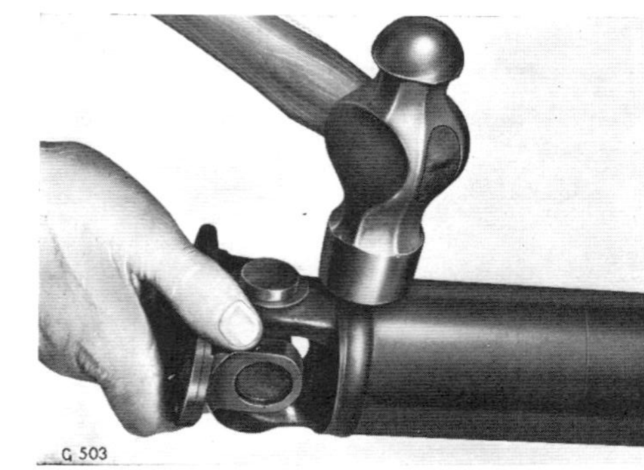

Fig. 6. Tapping bearing cups from yoke

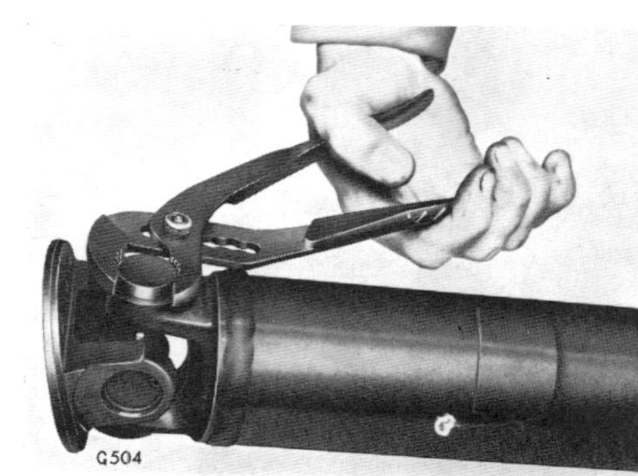

Fig. 7. Removing bearing cups

Fig. 8. Refitting bearing cups

Fig. 10. Refitting spider

Fig. 11. Location of grease plug

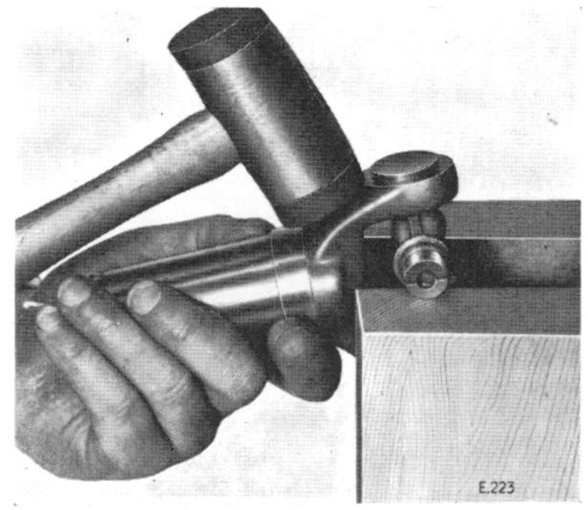

Fig. 9. Tapping cups from yoke

Re-assembly

Apply jointing compound to the journal shoulders on the new spider. Fit the oil seal retainers over the trunnions using a tubular drift. Fit the oil seals to the retainers.

Pass two trunnions of the spider through the bearing bores in the companion flange and fit the bearing cups and circlips, ensuring that these are properly seated.

The spider must be fitted with the lubrication boss towards the propeller shaft as shown in Fig. 11.

Pass the other pair of trunnions through the bearing bores in the forked end of the propeller shaft and fit the bearing cups and circlips.

Repeat the foregoing operations on the other universal coupling and refit the complete shaft assembly to the vehicle.

NOTE : The sliding joint should not be dismantled for any reason.

Dismantling — Strap Drive (Fig. 13)

Remove four bolts (3), nuts and washers securing the connector straps (1) to the end yoke (7) and tube coupling (6). Pull the end yoke clear of the tube coupling and when re-assembling lubricate as follows:

Repack the bore at "Y", Fig. 4, with Duckham Q.5648 grease and lubricate at "X" with Shell Dentax 250 or Retinax "A" or equivalent.

Re-assembly

Reverse the dismantling procedure and when refitting the connector straps (1) ensure that the straps are interleaved as shown on Fig. 4.

Serviceable Parts

Description	*S.T. Part No.*	*B.R.D. Part No.*
1. Connector strap	143215	—
2. "O" Ring — tube coupling	143213	245848
3. Bolt-end yoke	143214	—
4. Washer — plain	WP0036	—
5. Nut — Nyloc	YN2909	—

Non-Serviceable Parts

6. Tube coupling	212550	02/212300
7. End yoke	212551	02/206237

Fig. 12. Frictionless propeller shaft

Fig. 13. Strap drive propeller shaft

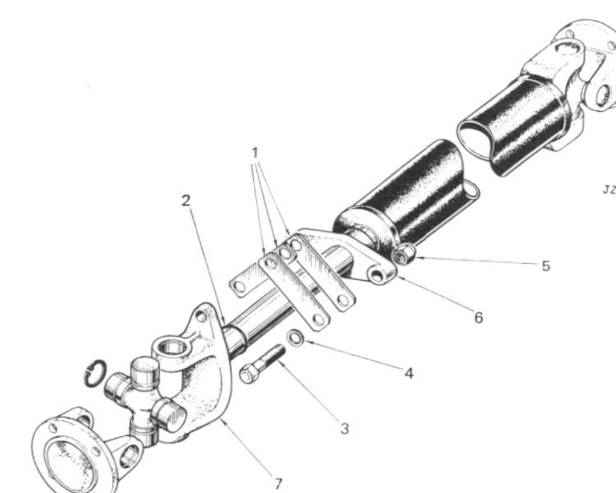

Fig. 14. Exploded arrangement of strap drive propeller shaft

OVERDRIVE UNIT

(OPTIONAL EQUIPMENT)

THE LAYCOCK DE NORMANVILLE OVERDRIVE UNIT DESCRIBED IN THIS SECTION IS FITTED TO VITESSE 6 AND SPITFIRE 4, MK2 AND MK3

DIMENSIONS, TOLERANCES AND SPECIAL TOOLS

PARTS AND DESCRIPTION	Dimensions New ins.	Dimensions New mm.	Clearances ins.	Clearances New mm.
Pump				
Plunger diameter	·3742 ·3746	9·504 9·514	·0002 ·0016	·005 ·041
Pump body bore	·3748 ·3758	9·52 9·545	·0002 ·0016	·005 ·041
Pin for roller diameter	·2497 ·2502	6·342 6·355	·0007 ·0022	·018 ·056
Roller bore diameter	·251 ·252	6·375 6·4	·0007 ·0022	·018 ·056
Pump Roller Bush				
Outside diameter of bush	·3736 ·3745	9·49 9·512	·0005 ·0023	·013 ·058
Inside diameter of roller	·375 ·3759	9·525 9·548	·0005 ·0023	·013 ·058
Inside diameter of bush	·251 ·2518	6·375 6·396	·0007 ·002	·018 ·051
Outside diameter of pin	·2497 ·2502	6·342 6·355	·0007 ·002	·018 ·051
Relief Valve				
Relief valve plunger diameter	·3122 ·3127	7·93 7·942	·0002 ·0013	·005 ·033
Relief valve body bore diameter	·3129 ·3135	7·958 7·963	·0002 ·0013	·005 ·033
Operating piston diameter	·8735 ·8742	22·187 22·205	·0003 ·002	·008 ·051
Operating piston bores	·8745 ·8755	22·212 22·237	·0003 ·002	·008 ·051
Operating valve diameter	·2494 ·2497	6·335 6·342	·0003 ·0012	·008 ·03
Operating valve bore	·25 ·2506	6·35 6·365	·0003 ·0012	·008 ·03
Gearbox Mainshaft				
Diameter at hub bush	·9236 ·9244	23·46 23·48	·004 ·006	·102 ·152
Bush internal diameter	·9284 ·9296	23·581 23·612	·004 ·006	·102 ·152
Diameter at sunwheel	·873 ·874	22·174 22·2	·003 ·005	·076 ·127
Inside diameter of sunwheel bush	·877 ·878	22·276 22·301	·003 ·005	·076 ·127
Diameter at steady bearing	·562 ·5625	14·275 14·287		
Planet pin diameter: 0·802 to 1 ratio (25%)	·4372 ·4375	11·105 11·112		
Miscellaneous				
Clutch movement from direct to overdrive	·04 ·06	1·016 1·524		
Hydraulic operation pressure	540-560 lb/sq. in. (37·962-39·368 kg/cm.)			
Ratio	25%			
Special Tools				
For special tools refer to page 0·111.				

LAYCOCK DE NORMANVILLE OVERDRIVE

The overdrive is an additional gear unit, mounted on the rear face of the gearbox in place of the normal extension. When in operation, the unit provides a higher overall gear ratio than is available with the standard transmission. Reduced engine speed, resulting from the higher ratio, will reduce fuel consumption, increase engine life, and ensure greater driving comfort, providing the unit is used correctly.

The overdrive is operated by an electrical solenoid, controlled by a switch mounted on the steering column. An inhibitor switch, fitted in the electrical circuit, prevents engagement of overdrive in reverse, first and second gears.

Suggested minimum engagement speeds are:	Top gear	40 m.p.h.
	Third gear	30 m.p.h.
Maximum disengagement speeds are:	Top gear	At driver's discretion.
	Third gear	70 m.p.h.

Disengagement of the overdrive at a speed higher than stated may cause damage from "over-revving".

WORKING PRINCIPLES

Overdrive Gears

The epicyclic gear train of the unit consists of a central sungear, meshing with three planet gears which in turn mesh with an internally toothed annulus.

Overdrive Disengaged (Fig. 1)

A cone clutch (A), mounted on the externally splined extension of the sungear (G) is spring-loaded, by four clutch springs (L), via a thrust ring (K) and bearing (M), against the annulus (E) thus locking the gear train and permitting over-run and reverse torque to be transmitted.

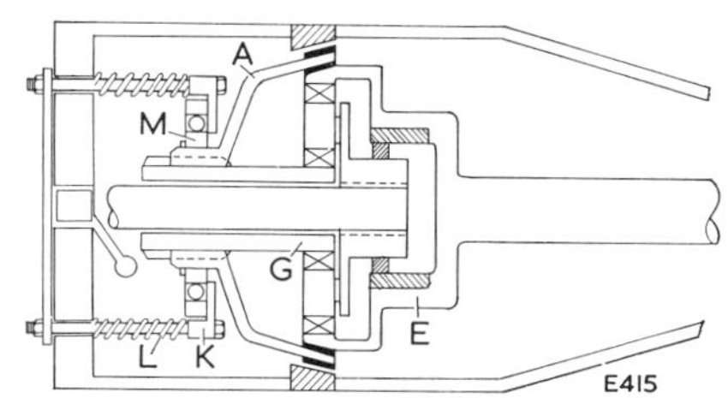

Fig. 1. Overdrive disengaged

Overdrive Engaged (Fig. 2)

When overdrive is selected, two hydraulically operated pistons (I) acting against bridge pieces (J), move forward and, overcoming the spring pressure, cause the cone clutch (A) to engage the brake ring (B) with sufficient load to hold the sungear (G) at rest. The planet carrier (D) can now rotate with the input shaft (H) causing the planet gears (F) to rotate about their own axis to drive the annulus at a faster speed than the input shaft, this being allowed by the free-wheeling action of the uni-directional clutch (C).

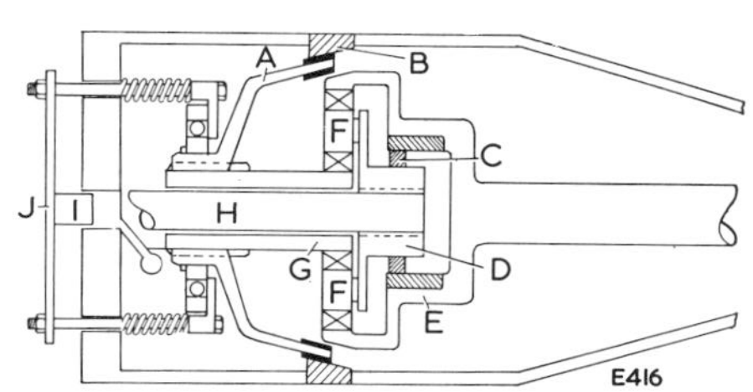

Fig. 2. Overdrive engaged

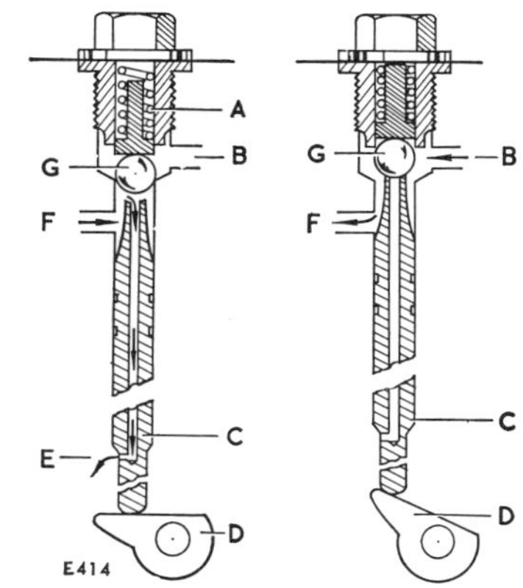

Fig. 3. Operating valve

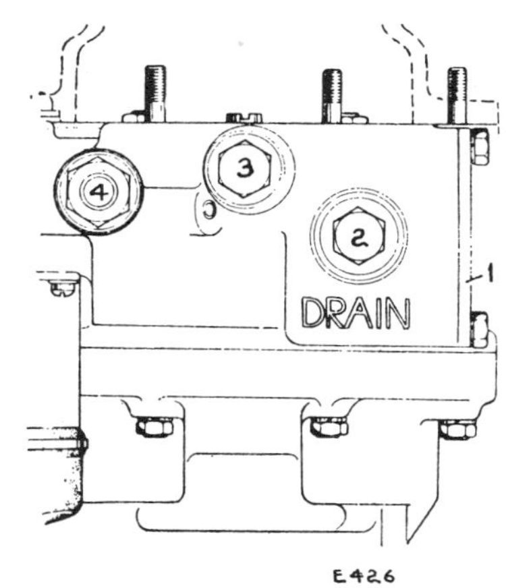

1 Filter cover plate
2 Drain plug
3 Non-return valve plug
4 Relief valve plug

Fig. 4. Front casing viewed from underneath

HYDRAULIC SYSTEM

Hydraulic pressure is developed by a plunger pump, cam operated, from the input shaft. The pump draws oil through a wire mesh filter and delivers it to the operating valve. A relief valve, incorporated in the system, controls the working pressure.

Operating Valve (Fig. 3)

In direct drive position, the ball valve (G) is seated in the casing thereby isolating the supply (B) from the operating cylinders (F).

When overdrive is selected, a solenoid causes cam (D) to rotate lifting the ball from its seat in the casing, and sealing the top of the valve, thus directing oil under pressure from port (B) to the operating cylinders (F).

When the valve is returned to the direct drive position, oil from the operating cylinders is exhausted down the hollow valve stem through the restrictor (E).

LUBRICATION

Being interconnected, the gearbox and overdrive unit have a common oil level, indicated by a plug on the side of the gearbox. When draining the oil, remove the overdrive unit drain plug and gearbox drain plug. Access to the gauze filter, which must be removed and cleaned prior to refilling with oil, is effected by removing plate (1) (Fig. 4) retained by four setscrews.

Spill oil, from the relief valve, is diverted through drilled passages to a bush in the front casing, then into the mainshaft and along a central drilling to the rear bearing in the annulus. From the bearing, oil is passed, due to centrifugal force, through the uni-directional clutch to an oil thrower, from which it is picked up by a catcher on the planet carrier and then to the planet gears via the hollow bearing pins.

NOTE: All gearbox and overdrive units fitted to new cars are filled with a special oil, formulated to give all necessary protection to new gears. Under normal circumstances, this oil should not be changed, but may be topped up with any of the approved oils. If a new unit is fitted, or parts of an existing unit are renewed, the unit should be replenished with new special oil, supplied with a new unit, or ordered separately from the Spares Division.

Should difficulty be experienced in obtaining the special oil, use one of the approved lubricants. ON NO ACCOUNT SHOULD ANTI-FRICTION ADDITIVES BE PUT INTO THE OIL.

After refilling the gearbox and running the car for a short distance, re-check and top up the oil level to replace the oil which has been distributed around the hydraulic system. Always use clean oil and take great care to prevent the entry of foreign matter when any part of the casing is opened.

SERVICING

The Operating Valve

Access to the valve plug, on top of the unit, is gained by removal of the gearbox cover (page 2·205, Fig. 3). Operate the solenoid several times to release the hydraulic pressure. Unscrew the valve plug and, with the aid of a small magnet, remove the spring, plunger and valve. Taking great care to avoid damage to the valve seat, remove the operating valve, by inserting a length of stiff wire down its centre and drawing it up. Ensure that the small hole at the bottom of the valve, breaking through to the central drilling, is not choked. This hole provides a passage for oil exhausted from the operating cylinders when the valve is moved to the "direct drive" position.

If necessary the ball can be reseated as follows:

Place the ball on a block of wood, position the seat of the valve on the ball and give the valve a sharp gentle tap. Clean the valve seat in the casing, locate the ball on its seat and gently tap the ball using a copper drift. Tapping the ball too hard will close the mouth of the valve seat and prevent valve re-assembly.

Adjustment of Solenoid Operating Lever

The operating valve, referred to above, is raised by a cam pinned on a transverse shaft. A solenoid-operated lever is attached to the opposite end of the shaft (Fig. 6).

Remove the cover plate from the solenoid housing, move the operating lever until a $\frac{3}{16}$" (4·762 mm.) setting pin, pushed through the hole in the lever aligns with a hole in the casing. With the solenoid energised, screw the adjusting nut until it just contacts the operating lever. Remove the setting pin and de-energise the solenoid. Energise the solenoid and re-check the alignment of the holes.

Check that the current consumption is approximately 2 amps. A reading of 20 amps. indicates that the solenoid plunger is not moving far enough to switch from the solenoid operating coil to the holding coil of the solenoid and the operating lever must be re-adjusted.

CONTINUOUS HIGH CURRENT WILL CAUSE PREMATURE SOLENOID FAILURE.

With the solenoid de-energised, re-align the setting holes and insert the setting pin. Hold the solenoid plunger against the blanking plug (Fig. 7) and check that dimension "A" is ·150" to ·155" (3·81 to 3·937 mm.). Obtain this dimension by varying the thickness of the washer between the blanking plug and the casing, as necessary.

Alternatively, on later units, adjust the position of the adjuster screw (32A) (inset Fig. 14).

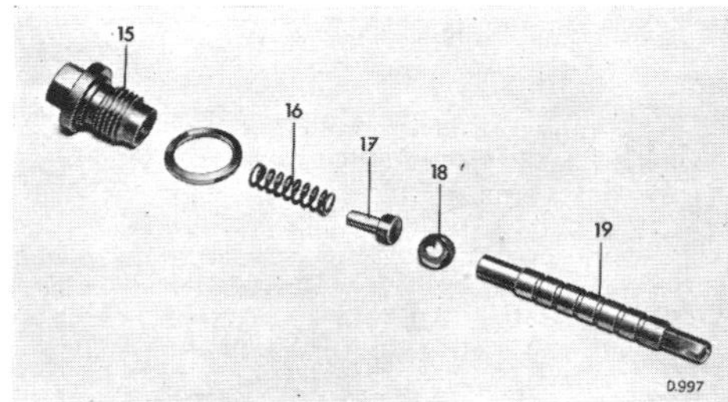

Fig. 5. Operating valve components

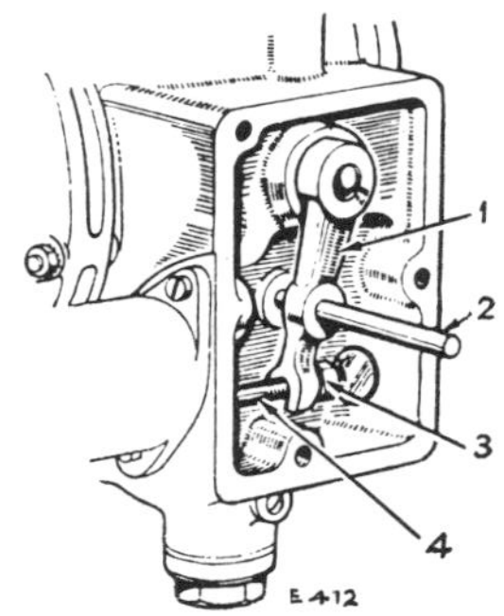

1 Operating lever
2 Setting pin
3 Adjusting nut
4 Solenoid plunger

Fig. 6. Adjustment of operating lever

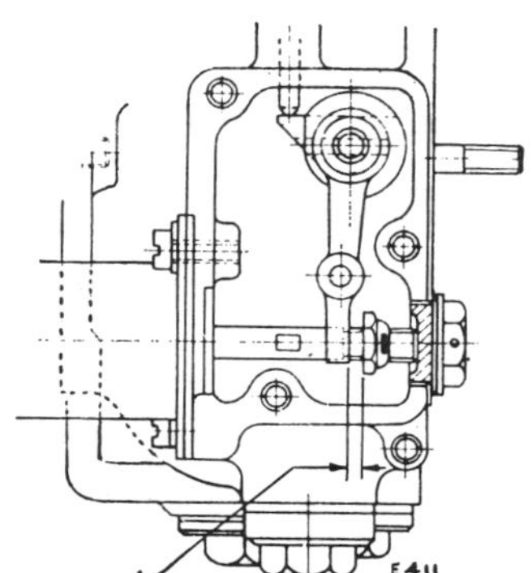

Fig. 7. Dimensional checks

Fig. 8. Testing oil pressure

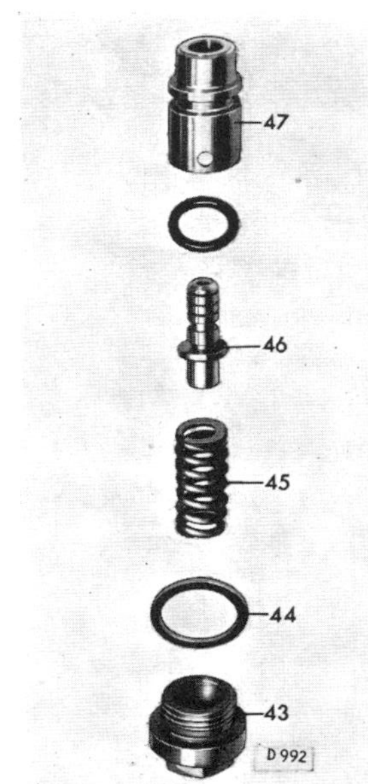

Fig. 9. Relief valve components

Testing Oil Pressure

Release the hydraulic pressure by switching on the ignition, engaging top gear and operating the overdrive switch several times, remove the operating valve plug and replace it with the hydraulic test equipment (Churchill Tool L.188).

Jack up the rear wheels of the car securely, start the engine and run up to about 20 m.p.h. on the speedometer. Check the hydraulic pressure in overdrive. See page 2·302.

Lack of pressure when overdrive is selected may indicate that the pump non-return valve requires cleaning and re-seating and/or the relief valve and filter cleaning.

Relief Valve

Access to the relief valve is gained by removing the plug at the bottom of the front casing adjacent to the solenoid housing cover plate. Remove the spring. The relief valve body can be withdrawn by inserting a length of stiff wire, shaped into a hook form, into the hole in the side of the body and pulling out.

The relief valve plunger can then be pushed out of the relief valve body.

Pump — Functional Check

To check that the pump is working, jack up the rear wheels of the car securely, remove the operating valve plug and start the engine. Engage top gear and with the engine running slowly, watch for oil being pumped into the valve chamber. If none appears the pump is not functioning and its non-return valve should be cleaned and re-seated. To re-seat FIRST REMOVE the valve body using Tool No. L.213, then, after cleaning, tap the ball sharply onto its seat. A flow of oil does not necessarily indicate that the hydraulic pressure is correct.

Sticking Clutch

If overdrive cannot be disengaged after carrying out the procedure outlined on page 2·305, the fault may result from a sticking cone clutch. This condition is more likely to occur on a new unit, due to insufficient "bedding in" of the clutch, than on a unit which has been in service for some time.

The clutch can usually be freed by giving the brake ring several sharp blows with a hide mallet from underneath when the car is on a hoist.

The Electrical Circuit

Because many operational failures are due to corroded terminals and faulty wiring, check the wiring and connections before dismantling any part of the overdrive unit.

Good earth connections are essential on all earthed components.

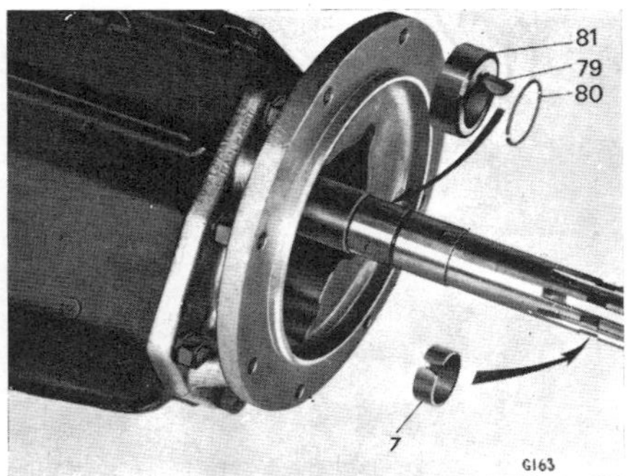

Fig. 10. Adaptor plate and mainshaft details

This applies particularly to the solenoid because of the heavy current passed momentarily each time the overdrive is engaged.

Incorrect adjustment of the solenoid, resulting in failure of the main winding contact to open, may cause damage to the solenoid and relay.

If the overdrive fails to operate after checking all the electrical connections, refer to Fig. 11, and proceed as follows:

1. Switch on the ignition and engage top gear. Set the column control switch (1) to overdrive position. Check that the battery voltage is present at terminals C.1 and W.2.
2. Short out the terminals on C.1 and C.2 on the relay unit (3). If the solenoid (4) operates then the relay unit, column switch and gearbox isolator switch are suspect. Remove short circuiting link from between terminals C.1 and C.2.
3. Earth terminal W.1 on the relay unit. If the overdrive solenoid operates, then the gearbox isolator switch is suspect. If the relay unit does not operate, renew the relay unit.
4. Earth the yellow/green cable on the switch. If the solenoid operates, renew the control switch.

OVERDRIVE UNIT

To Remove

Disconnect the connectors from the gearbox overdrive switch and overdrive solenoid, and remove the gearbox/overdrive unit from the vehicle in a similar manner to that described for gearbox removal on page 2·205.

Remove the nuts and spring washers securing the overdrive unit to the adaptor flange, and carefully withdraw the overdrive unit.

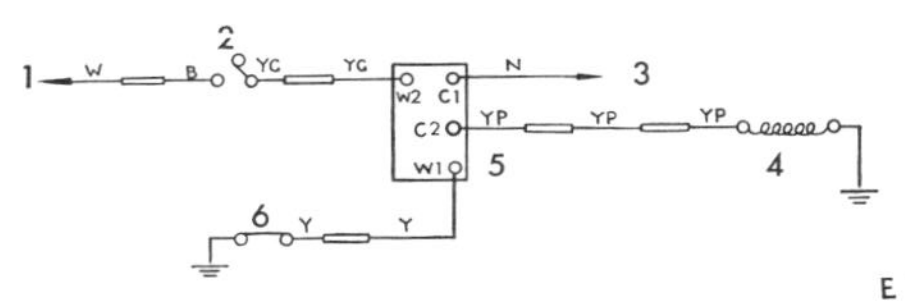

1 To SW on coil
2 Overdrive switch
3 To No. 1 on ignition switch
4 Solenoid
5 Relay
6 Gearbox isolator switch

Fig. 11. Overdrive circuit

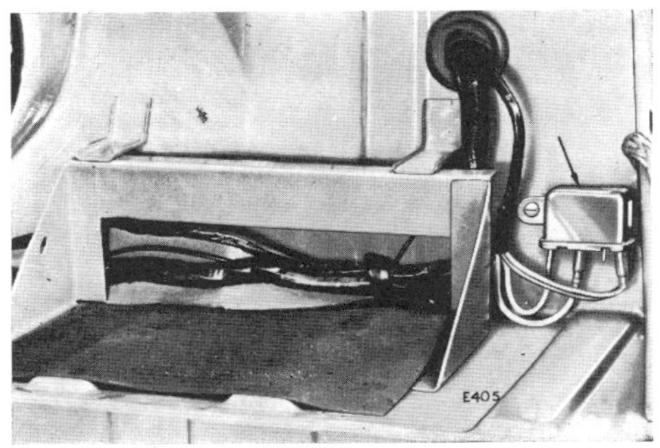

Fig. 12. Location of relay

Fig. 13. Location of (1) overdrive switch, (2) gearbox isolator switch

DISMANTLING (Fig. 14)

To prevent damage or faulty operation resulting from the inclusion of foreign matter, scrupulous cleanliness must be observed during all service operations. Prepare a clean area in which to lay out the dismantled unit and clean containers to receive the smaller parts.

With the front casing uppermost, secure the unit in suitably protected vice jaws. Release the tab washers securing the four bridge piece retaining nuts, remove the nuts, washers, bridge pieces (27) and, from the operating piston bores, remove the bias springs (28).

Loosen the two solenoid securing screws to prevent the rubber solenoid cover fouling during front casing removal.

Progressively loosen, to ensure gradual release of the clutch spring loading, the eight nuts securing the front casing (21) and brake ring (51) to the rear casing (56). Remove the nuts, spring washers and lift off the front casing. If the brake ring remains with the rear casing, tap gently to remove.

Remove the four clutch return springs (29) and withdraw the clutch sliding member complete with thrust bearing (11), thrust ring (10), retaining plate (12) and sungear (9).

Operating Valve and Relief Valve

Remove as detailed on pages 2·305 and 2·306 respectively.

Pump

IMPORTANT: Remove the pump locating screw (33) before extracting the pump body.

Remove the pump plug (42), non-return valve spring (40) and ball (39), and the pump locating screw (33), see note above. Unscrew the non-return valve body (38) using tool L.213. Using tools L.183A, L.183A2 and adaptor L.205, extract the pump body as follows (Fig. 15):—

Screw the spindle into the pump body, position the adaptor against the casing and screw the wing nut down.

Filter

Remove the cover plate (23), retained by four setscrews and withdraw the filter (24), three magnetic rings (25), and the rubber/steel bonded sealing washer (26).

Operating Pistons

Withdraw the operating pistons (30) from their respective housings using tool L.252.

Sliding Clutch Member

Remove the sungear retaining circlip (14) from its groove in the sungear extension and withdraw the sungear (9).

Remove the thrust bearing retaining plate (12), bearing circlip (13) from its groove on the cone clutch hub and press the hub from the bearing (11) and thrust ring (10). Extract the bearing from the thrust ring using tool L.210A.

Fig. 15. Extracting pump body

Fig. 16. Clutch sliding member assembly

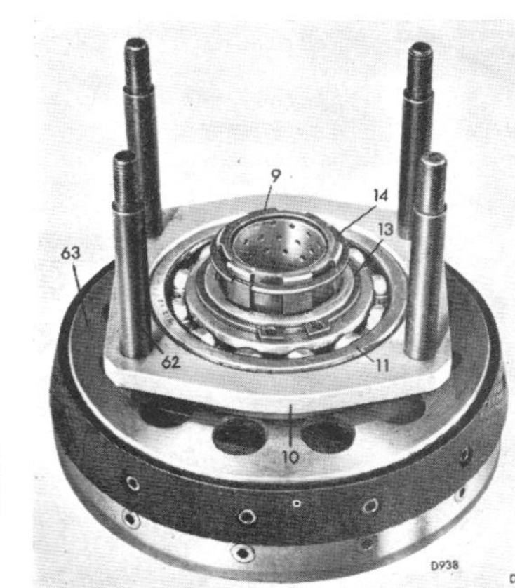

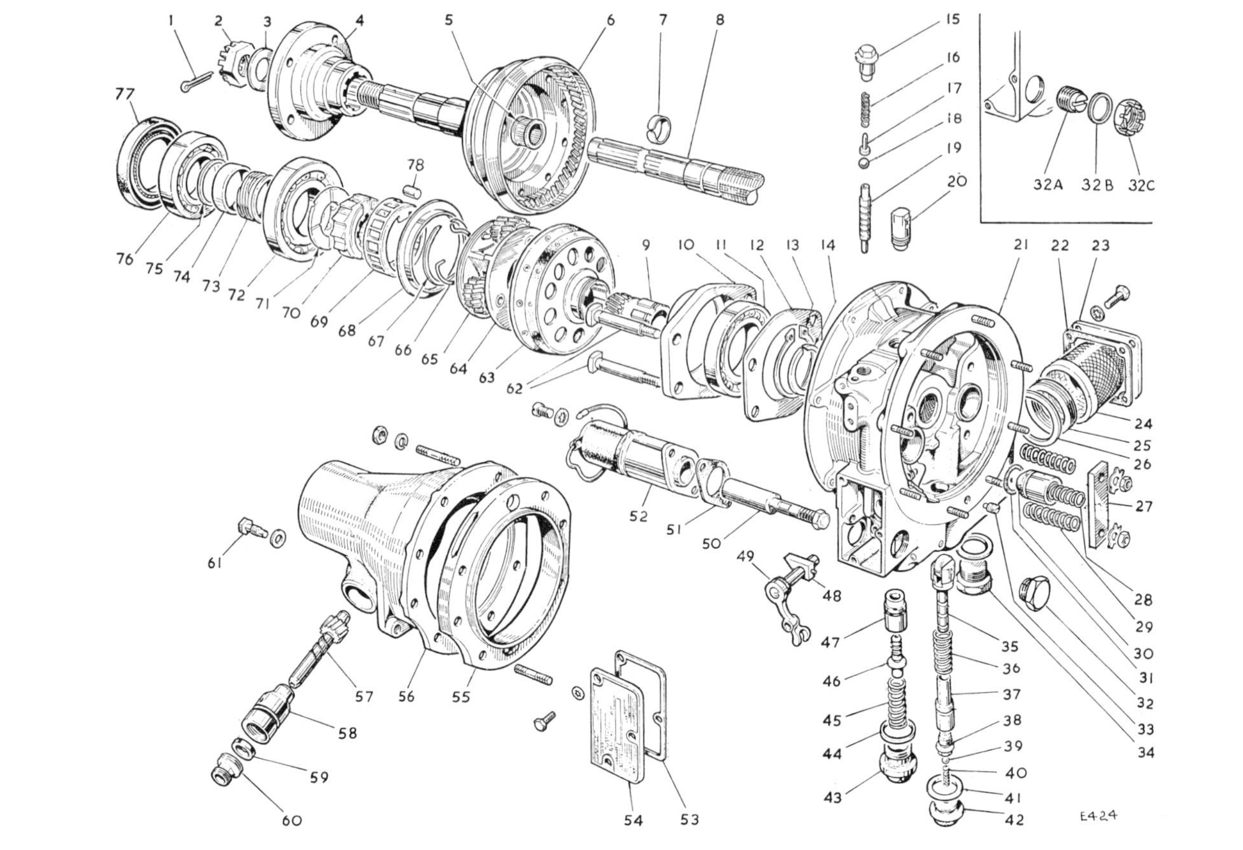

Fig. 14 Overdrive unit (Inset shows later condition of item 32.)

KEY TO FIG. 14

1 Split pin
2 Nut
3 Washer
4 Coupling flange
5 Needle bearing
6 Annulus
7 Spring
8 Main shaft
9 Sungear
10 Thrust ring
11 Thrust bearing
12 Retaining plate
13 Circlip
14 Circlip
15 Plug
16 Spring
17 Plunger
18 Ball
19 Operating valve
20 Lubrication bush
21 Front casing
22 Gasket
23 Cover plate
24 Filter
25 Magnetic rings
26 Rubber/Steel washer
27 Bridge piece
28 Bias spring
29 Clutch return spring
30 Piston
31 Piston 'O' ring
32 Plug
32A Adjuster screw } These items replace item 32 on later units
32B Locknut
32C Fibre washer
33 Pump locating screw
34 Plug
35 Pump plunger
36 Return spring
37 Pump body
38 Non-return valve body
39 Ball
40 Spring
41 Washer
42 Plug
43 Plug
44 Washer
45 Spring
46 Relief valve plunger
47 Relief valve body
48 Cam
49 Operating lever
50 Solenoid plunger
51 Gasket
52 Solenoid
53 Gasket
54 Cover plate
55 Brake ring
56 Rear casing
57 Speedometer pinion
58 Speedometer pinion bush
59 Seal
60 Screwed end
61 Locating screw
62 Bolts
63 Cone clutch
64 Planet carrier assembly
65 Planet gear
66 Spring
67 Circlip
68 Oil thrower
69 Cage
70 Inner member
71 Thrust washer
72 Front bearing
73 Speedometer drive gear
74 Distance piece
75 Spacer
76 Rear bearing
77 Oil seal
78 Roller
79 Woodruff key } Refer to Fig. 10
80 Ring spring
81 Cam

Fig. 17. View of unit from right-hand side showing solenoid cover removed

Fig. 18. Planet carrier assembly and oil pick-up ring

Fig. 19. Removal of coupling flange nut

Fig. 20. Removing needle bearing from annulus

Solenoid

Remove the cover plate (54), retained by four setscrews, blanking plug (32), and unscrew the adjusting nut. Unscrew the two solenoid retaining screws and remove the solenoid (52) and plunger (50).

Planet Carrier Assembly

Inspect the gear teeth for damage and wear and check for excessive movement indicating needle bearing or retaining pin wear.

If necessary, renew the complete carrier assembly (64).

Annulus, Removal from Rear Casing

Remove the speedometer bush locating screw (61) and, to avoid damage to threads, use tool L.214 to extract speedometer drive bush (58) and pinion (57) from the rear casing.

Remove the split pin (1) and nut (2) securing the coupling flange (4) and press the annulus forward out of the rear case (56). The rear bearing (76) and oil seal (77) will remain in situ while the front bearing (72), speedometer drive gear (73), distance piece (74) and spacer washer (75) will be withdrawn with the annulus.

Remove circlip (67) and brass oil thrower ring (68) and withdraw the uni-directional clutch from the annulus.

The needle bearing (5) in the centre of the annulus may be withdrawn using tool L.208 as follows:—

Withdraw the central bolt from the tool and locate the outer part of the tool inside the bearing, ensuring the four tangs register behind it. Insert the central bolt and screw against the annulus.

Tap out the oil seal and rear bearing from the rear casing.

RE-ASSEMBLY (Fig. 14)

Renew gaskets, "O" rings, seals and tab washers, as necessary, during re-assembly operations.

Operating Valve

Locate the operating valve (19) within its orifice in the front casing and check that its hemispherical end abuts the flat of the operating cam (48). Position the steel ball (18), plunger (17) and spring (16) and secure with blanking plug (15).

Relief Valve

Insert the relief valve plunger (46) in the relief valve body and locate the assembly within its orifice at the base of the front casing. Insert the spring (45), locating it on the boss of the plunger, and secure with the relief valve blanking plug (43).

Pump

Assemble the pump plunger (35), spring (36) and body (37) and locate the assembly within its orifice in the front casing, locating the flat of the plunger roller fork against the thrust button situated below the centre bush. Press the pump body home, using tool L.206A, until the annular groove in the pump body is in alignment with the locating screw orifice. Insert the dowelled locating screw and tighten, ensuring that the dowel locates in the groove.

Screw in the non-return valve body (38), using tool L.213, position the ball (39) and spring (40) in the body and fit the retaining plug, ensuring that the spring locates correctly in the plug recess.

Filter

Position the three magnetic rings (25) in the mouth of the filter (24) and the bonded steel/rubber sealing ring (26) in the filter housing with its steel face against the casing.

Locate the filter in its housing, open end against the rubber surface of the bonded washer, fit the cover plate (23) and secure with the four retaining setscrews. Fit the drain plug (34).

Operating Pistons

Replace the pistons with the open end of the piston bore facing forward, carefully easing the sealing rings into the cylinder bores.

Fig. 21. View of front casing showing pump installed

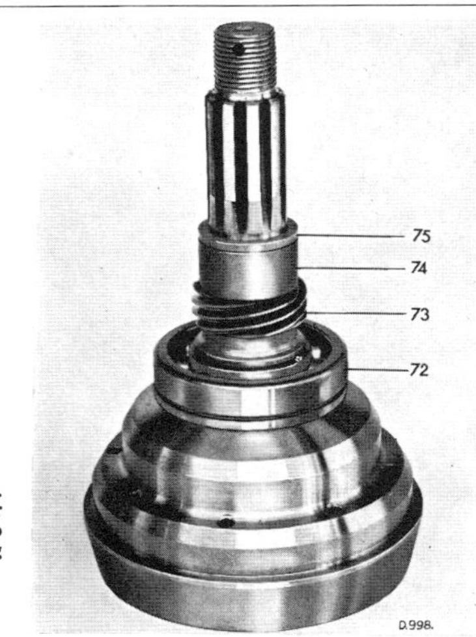

Fig. 22. Annulus prior to fitting to rear casing

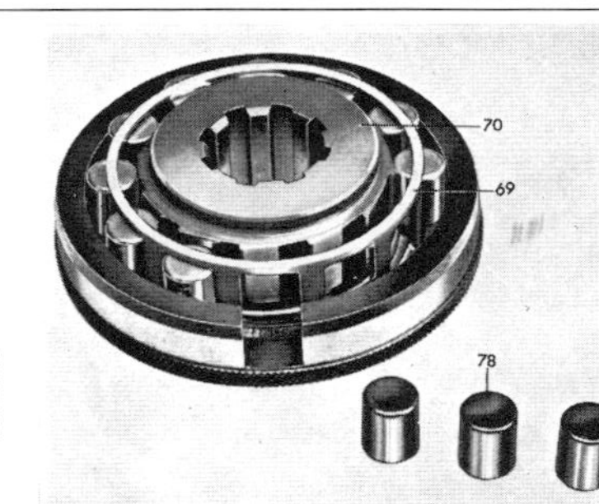

Fig. 23. Fitting rollers to uni-directional clutch

Fig. 24. Fitting uni-directional clutch to annulus

Fig. 25. Uni-directional clutch in position

Fig. 26. Planet gear alignment

Annulus and Rear Casing

Locate the front bearing (72) over the annulus tail shaft and press into position against the locating shoulder at the rear of the annulus.

Position the speedometer drive gear (73), distance piece (74), and, if fitted, the spacing washer (75) on the tail shaft. Fit the assembly to the rear casing.

NOTE : Where new parts have been fitted, make a dimensional check between the distance piece and abutment shoulder for the rear bearing. Fit spacing washers, as required, to give a ·005″ to ·010″ (·1270 to ·254 mm.) end float between the rear bearing and the casing.

Press the rear bearing (76) on the tail shaft and into the rear casing simultaneously. Fit the oil seal (77) using tool L.212.

Press the rear coupling flange (4) on the tail shaft, locate the washer (3) and secure with nut (2) and split pin (1).

Insert the speedometer drive pinion (57) and bush (58) turning the annulus as necessary to engage the gear. Align the bush and casing holes and fit the dowelled locating screw (61).

Insert the needle bearing (5) in the centre of the annulus using Tool L.209.

Fit the spring (66) in the roller cage (69) of the uni-directional clutch, engaging one end in the cage. Insert the inner member (70), engaging the opposite end of the spring, and ensure that the slots of the inner member engage the tongues of the cage.

Place the assembly, front face down, in the assembly tool L.178 (Fig. 22) and fit the rollers. Check that the spring rotates the cage to drive the rollers up the inclined faces of the inner member.

Refit the thrust washer (71) and uni-directional clutch (Fig. 24) transferring the clutch direct from the assembly tool. Fit the brass oil thrower ring (68) and secure with circlip (67).

Planet Gears

Rotate the gears until the ETCHED lines on the gear and carrier coincide (Fig. 26). NOTE: On one of the three gears the etched line occurs on the same tooth as the centre pop mark. Insert the sungear and recheck the etched lines for alignment. Position the assembly within the annulus and remove the sungear.

Clutch Sliding Member

Press the thrust bearing (11) into the thrust ring and fit the four bolts ensuring the heads are correctly positioned. Press the assembly on the cone clutch hub and secure with circlip (13). Fit the retaining plate (12).

Insert the sungear (9) in the splined bore of the cone clutch and secure with circlip (14). Locate the assembly within the annulus and fit the four clutch return springs (29).

Front Case to Rear Case

Position the brake ring, both faces coated with suitable jointing compound, on the rear face of the front case, ensuring the kidney-shaped slot in the brake ring is located at the bottom (Fig. 27).

Fit the front casing to the rear casing. Clutch spring pressure will now be felt and it will be necessary to exert a slight pressure to bring the two casings together sufficiently to start the nuts. Tighten diametrically opposed nuts until the two faces meet.

Locate the bias springs (28) within the piston bores, fit the bridge pieces (27) and secure with nuts and tab washers.

Position the solenoid plunger (50) in the fork of the operating lever (49) and screw on the adjusting nut, replace the solenoid and secure with the two setscrews. Adjust as detailed on page 2·305 and, on completion, refit cover plate (54) and blanking plug (32).

OVERDRIVE UNIT

To Refit

Align the splines of the planet carrier and uni-directional clutch using a long screwdriver. Check the alignment by inserting dummy mainshaft (Tool No. L.201) (Fig. 28).

Rotate the gearbox mainshaft and position the pump operating cam with its highest point uppermost. Check that the spring clip (7) is correctly located in its groove on the mainshaft and does not protrude above the splines.

NOTE : It is essential that rotation of gearbox mainshaft and overdrive coupling flange is avoided until the unit is fitted to the gearbox.

Remove the dummy mainshaft and fit the unit to the gearbox, secure with spring washers and nuts.

To refit the gearbox/overdrive unit to the vehicle, reverse the removal procedure.

Fig. 27. Offering front case to rear case

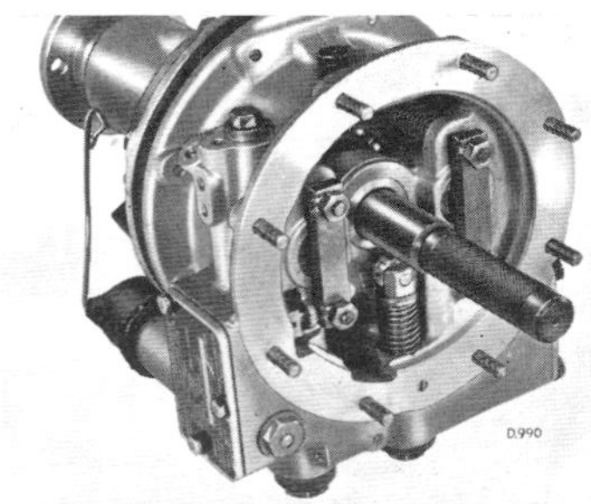

Fig. 28. Alignment check using Tool No. L201

Fig. 29. Overdrive support bracket (1) and flexible mounting (2)

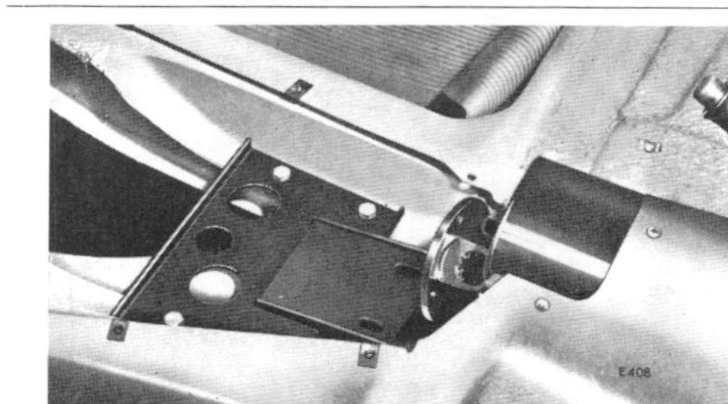

Fig. 30. Overdrive mounting platform

TRIUMPH
HERALD, VITESSE 6
AND
SPITFIRE
WORKSHOP MANUAL

GROUP 3

Comprising :

TRIUMPH
HERALD, VITESSE 6
and
SPITFIRE

GROUP 3

CONTENTS

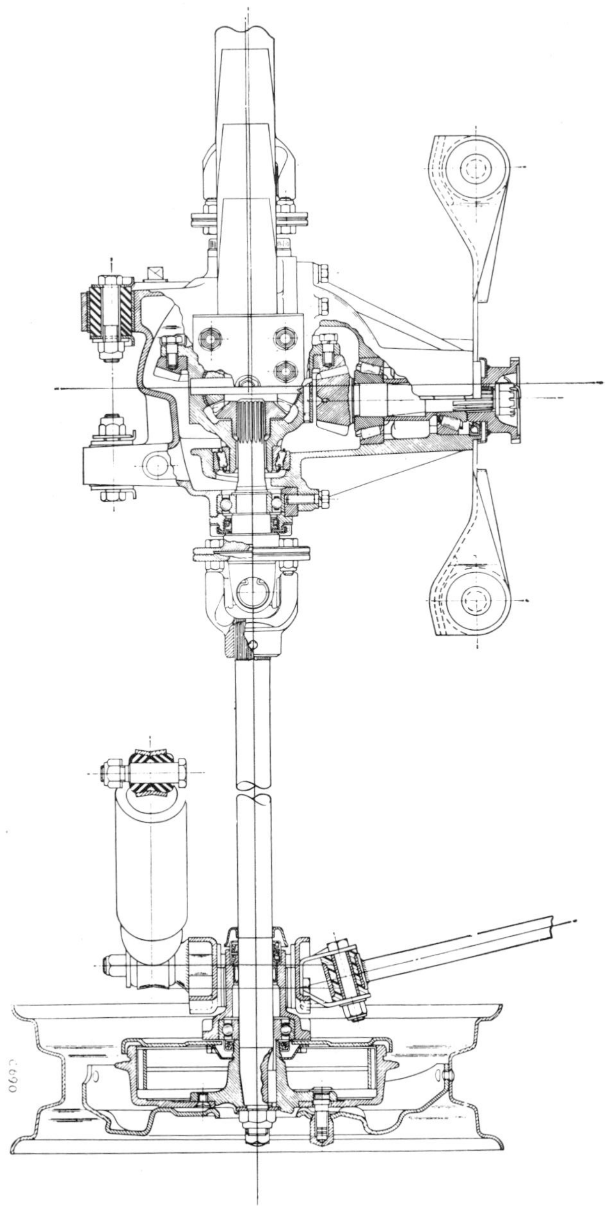

Fig. 1. Rear axle arrangement

REAR AXLE — DIMENSIONS AND TOLERANCES — 1200, 12/50, 13/60, VITESSE and SPITFIRE

PARTS AND DESCRIPTION	DIMENSIONS NEW		CLEARANCES NEW		REMARKS
Axle Ratio	4·1 : 1				No change in ratio when over-drive is fitted to Vitesse 6 or Spitfire
Track	4 ft. (122 cms.)				
Crown Wheel	in.	mm.	in.	mm.	
Number of teeth	37				
Locating diameter	3·6875 3·6885	93·662 93·687	0·001 0·003	0·025 0·076	
Maximum permissible backlash	0·003	0·076	0·004 0·006	0·101 0·152	Achieved by shimming between differential side bearing and casing.
Pinion					
Number of teeth	9				
Diameter of journal — for pinion head bearing	1·0006 1·0011	25·415 25·428			Bearing press-fit on pinion.
for pinion tail bearing	0·7504 0·7509	19·06 19·073			
Spline diameters — Maximum	0·719 0·728	18·263 18·491			
— Minimum	0·6424 0·6439	16·317 16·355			Driving flange locating diameter.
Thread dimensions	$\frac{3}{16}$" × 18 t.p.i. U.N.F.				
Hypoid Housing	in.	mm.			
Internal diameter for—					
Pinion head bearing outer ring	2·6860 2·6870	68·2244 68·2498			
Pinion tail bearing outer ring	2·1235 2·1245	53·937 53·962			Ring is press-fit in bore.
Differential bearing outer ring	2·4418 2·4428	61·996 62·022			
Width between differential bearing outer ring abutment	5·120 5·128	130·048 130·251			
Maximum spreading load for: entry of assembled differential unit	3360 lbs. (1524 kg.)				
***Inner Axle Shafts**	in.	mm.			
Bearing journal diameter	0·8754 0·8759	22·215 22·228			Bearing press-fit on inner axle shaft.
Number of serrations	18				*Fitted to all 12/50 and Vitesse 6 models and up to and including comm. Nos. T.1200 GA. 237600 and GB57201, Spitfire FD22570.
External diameter of serrations	0·7877 0·7917	20·007 20·109			
Oil seal journal diameter	1·130 1·135	28·702 28·829			

REAR AXLE — DIMENSIONS AND TOLERANCES — 1200, 12/50, 13/60, VITESSE and SPITFIRE — cont.

PARTS AND DESCRIPTION	DIMENSIONS NEW	CLEARANCES NEW	REMARKS
†Inner Axle Shafts	in. mm.		
Bearing journal diameter	0·9847 25·011 0·9852 25·024		Bearing press-fit on inner axle shaft.
Number of serrations	20		†Fitted from 1st production 13/60 and from comm. Nos. T1200 GA237601 and GB57202; Spitfire Mk. 3, FD 22571.
External diameter of serrations	0·870 22·098 0·875 22·225		
Oil seal journal diameter	1·130 28·702 1·135 28·829		
Outer Axle Shafts	in. mm.		
Shaft length	18·53 470·662		
Shaft end to centre	0·880 22·352		
Line of universal coupling			
Number of serrations	24		
Mills pin — Type — Length	G.P.3 1·63 41·402		
Keyway width	0·1865 4·737 0·1875 4·762		
Driving key dimensions — Width	0·1875 4·762 0·1885 4·788		
— Depth	0·250 6·35 0·251 6·38		
Pinion Setting Dimensions	in. mm.	in. mm.	
Distance from head bearing abutment face on pinion to centre of crown wheel bearings	3·03125 76·994		
Pinion centre-line "offset" below crown wheel centre line	0·7445 19·037 0·7505 19·063		
Pinion bearing pre-load (without oil seal)	12-16 lbs/in. (0·0138- 0·185 mkg.)		
Length of bearing spacer	1·450 36·83 1·455 36·96		Alternative spacer length 1·544/1·549 in. (39·22/39·34 mm.)
Backlash between pinion and crown wheel		0·004 ·102 0·006 ·152	
***Differential Carrier**	in. mm.		
Crown wheel locating spigot diameter	3·6855 93·726 3·6865 98·751		*Fitted to all 12/50 and Vitesse 6 models and up to and including comm. Nos. T.1200, GA237600 and GB57201; Spitfire, FD22570
Bore for cross-shaft	·4993 12·682 ·5000 12·700		
Bore for sun gear spigot	1·126 28·600 1·128 28·651		
Side bearing spigot O.D.	1·251 31·788		
Max. permissible run-out	·003 0·076		

REAR AXLE — DIMENSIONS AND TOLERANCES — 1200, 12/50, 13/60, VITESSE and SPITFIRE — cont.

PARTS AND DESCRIPTION	DIMENSIONS NEW	CLEARANCES NEW	REMARKS
Differential Carrier	in. mm.		
Crown wheel locating spigot diameter	3·6855 93·726 3·6865 98·751		†Fitted from 1st production 13/60 and from comm. Nos. T.1200, GA237601 and GB57202; Spitfire Mk. 3, FD22571.
Bore for cross-shaft	·6245 15·862 ·6255 15·888		
Bore for sun-gear spigot	1·251 31·775 1·253 31·826		
Side bearing spigot O.D.	1·251 31·788		
Max. permissible run-out	·003 0·076		
***Differential Gears**	in. mm.	in. mm.	
Differential sun gear — Number of teeth	16		
Spigot diameter	1·1235 28·537 1·1243 28·557	0·0017 0·043 0·0045 0·114	Clearance of gear spigot in carrier
Number of internal serrations	18		
Internal diameter	0·725 18·415 0·729 18·517		*Fitted to all 12/50 and Vitesse 6 models and up to and including comm. Nos. T.1200, GA237600 and GB57201; Spitfire FD22570.
Differential planet gear —			
Number of teeth	10		
Diameter of bore	0·5000 12·7 0·5015 12·738	0·0005 0·013 0·0025 0·064	
Backlash between any two pairs of gears		0·004 0·102	
Diameter of cross-shaft	0·4990 12·600 0·4995 12·610		
†Differential Gears			
Differential sun gear —	in. mm.	in. mm.	
Number of teeth	16		
Spigot diameter	1·2485 31·798 1·2485 31·798	0·0017 0·043 0·0045 0·114	Clear of gear spigot in carrier.
Number of internal serrations	20		
Sun gear thrust washer thickness	0·0345 0·876 0·0375 0·952		†Fitted from 1st production 13/60 and comm. Nos. T.1200, GA237601 and GB257202; Spitfire Mk. 3 FD22571.
Differential planet gear —			
Number of teeth	10		
Diameter of bore	0·625 15·815 0·625 15·913	0·0008 0·020 0·0028 0·071	
Backlash between any two pairs of gears		0·002 0·051 0·004 0·102	
Diameter of cross-shaft	0·6237 15·842 0·6242 15·855		

REAR AXLE — DIMENSIONS AND TOLERANCES — 1200, 12/50, 13/60, VITESSE and SPITFIRE — cont.

PARTS AND DESCRIPTION	DIMENSIONS NEW		CLEARANCES NEW		REMARKS
	in.	mm.	in.	mm.	
Hubs (Rear)					
Inner hub assembly — Internal dia. for —					
Needle roller bearing	1·2508 1·2498	31·750 31·775	0·0005 0·0015	0·0137 0·038	
Hub bearing outer ring and outer grease seal	2·2493 2·2499	57·132 57·147			
Inner grease seal	1·4990 1·5000	38·075 38·100			
Diameter of hub bearing outer ring	2·2490 2·2495	57·125 57·137			
External diameter of needle roller bearing	1·2495	31·737			
Dimension from face of needle roller bearing to inner face of hub	0·500	12·700			

PART No.	THICKNESS in.	THICKNESS mm.	REMARKS
DIFFERENTIAL BEARING SHIMS			
123813	0·0085/0·00095	0·216/0·241	
123814	0·012/0·013	0·300/0·330	
123815	0·014/0·015	0·350/0·381	
123816	0·016/0·017	0·406/0·432	
123817	0·019/0·021	0·483/0·533	
PLANET GEAR — THRUST WASHERS			
145282	0·033/0·035	0·838/0·889	Fitted to all 12/50 and Vitesse 6 models, and up to and including Commission Nos. T.1200, GA237600 and GB57201; Spitfire FD22570.
104572	0·035/0·037	0·889/0·939	
145262	0·037/0·039	0·939/0·990	
108935	0·039/0·041	0·990/1·041	
142167	0·041/0·043	1·041/1·092	
108936	0·043/0·045	1·092/1·143	
142168	0·045/0·047	1·143/1·193	
108937	0·047/0·049	1·193/1·244	
108938	0·051/0·052	1·295/1·320	
108939	0·055/0·057	1·397/1·447	
PLANET GEAR — THRUST WASHERS			
138440	0·026/0·028	0·660/0·711	Fitted from 1st production 13/60 and from Commission Nos. T.1200, GA237601 and GB57202; Spitfire Mk. 3 FD22571.
147249	0·028/0·030	0·711/0·762	
134076	0·030/0·032	0·762/0·812	
147250	0·032/0·034	0·812/0·863	
138441	0·034/0·036	0·863/0·914	
147251	0·036/0·038	0·914/0·965	
138442	0·038/0·040	0·965/1·016	
158805	0·040/0·042	1·016/1·066	
147252	0·042/0·044	1·066/1·117	
PINION HEAD BEARING SHIMS			
100562	0·003	0·0762	
100563	0·005	0·127	
100564	0·010	0·254	
PINION TAIL BEARING SHIMS			
104562	0·003	0·0762	
104563	0·005	0·127	
104561	0·010	0·254	

Unless otherwise stated, all operations contained in this Rear Axle Section, appertain to Herald 1200, 12/50, 13/60, Vitesse 6 and Spitfire.

HUB AND OUTER AXLE SHAFT ASSEMBLY

To Remove

Jack up the rear of the vehicle, support it on chassis stands and remove the nave plate, wheel nuts and road wheel.

Disconnect the flexible brake hose (1) from the chassis bracket (2) and pipe (3).

Disconnect the handbrake cable from the lever (4).

Using a jack to relieve the damper of load, remove the bolt (5) to release the radius arm.

Remove four bolts (6) and nyloc nuts (7) to release the axle shaft coupling flange.

Remove the nyloc nut (8) and washer from the damper lower attachment eye and pull the bottom of the damper clear of its mounting pin.

Remove the jack from beneath the vertical link plates, and whilst supporting the brake assembly by hand, remove the nut (9) bolt from the road spring eye.

Withdraw the hub and outer axle shaft assembly from the vehicle.

To Refit

Assemble the vertical link to the road spring eye, leaving the nyloc nut semi-tight at this stage.

Carefully jack up the vertical link plate and secure the extended damper to its lower attachment.

Re-attach the radius arm to the vertical link bracket and secure with bolt (5) and nut.

Secure the outer axle shaft to the flange of the inner axle shaft and remove the jack.

Load the vehicle to a "Static Laden" condition and tighten the nyloc nut securing the vertical link to the road spring.

Re-connect the handbrake cable to the handbrake lever (4).

Re-connect the flexible brake pipe to the chassis bracket (2) and pipe union (3).

Adjust and bleed the brake system.

Fit the road wheel, nuts and nave plate.

Fig. 3. Rear damper and brake pipe attachments

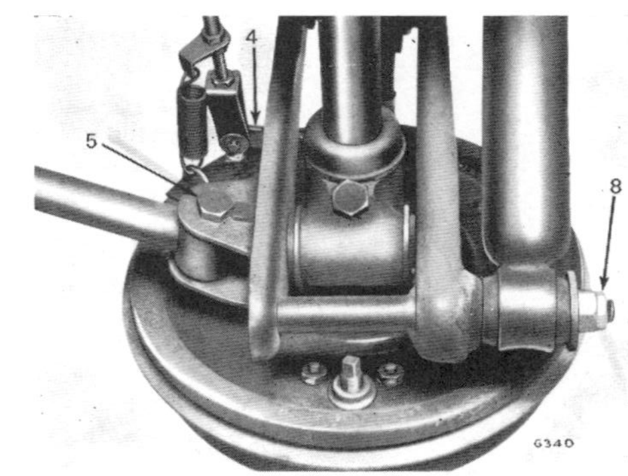

Fig. 4. Handbrake cable and radius arm attachments

Fig. 5. Axle shaft coupling

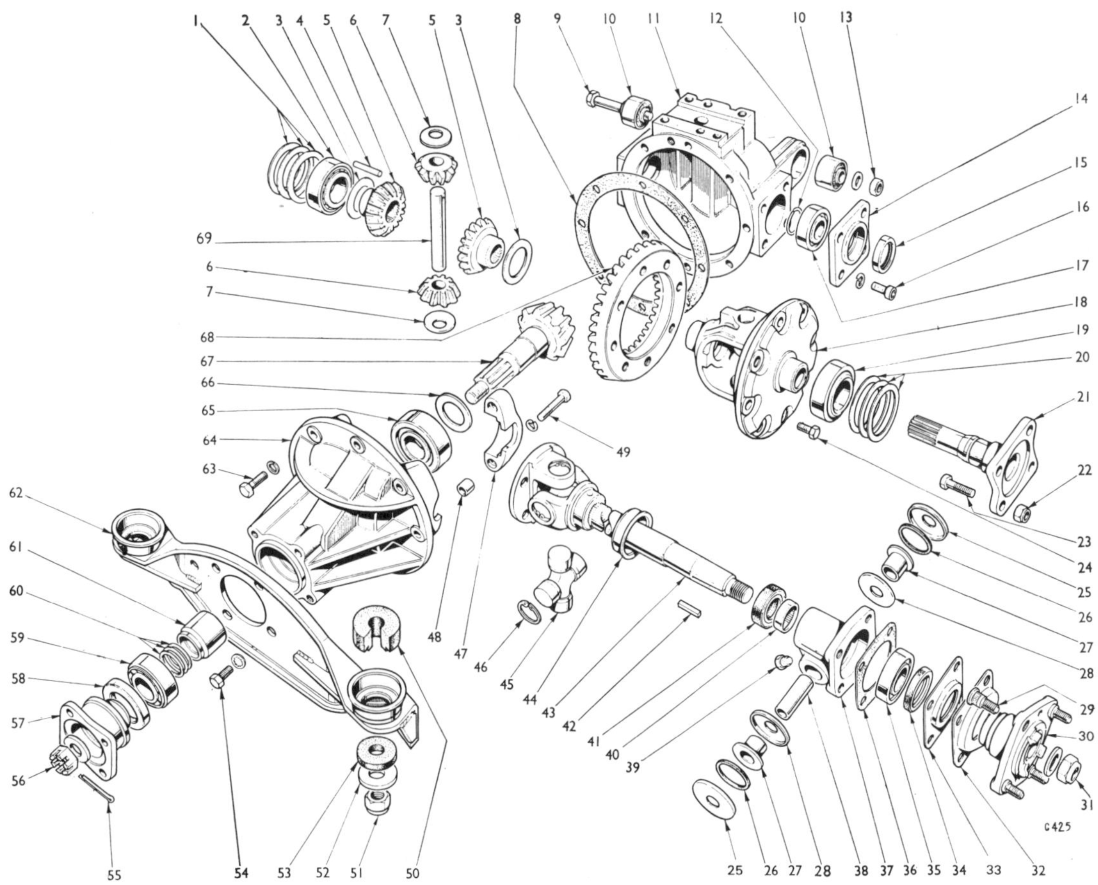

Fig. 2. Rear axle details

Key to Fig. 2.

1 Shims
2 Differential side bearing
3 Thrust washer
4 Cross-shaft locking pin
5 Sun gear
6 Planet gear
7 Thrust washer
8 Joint washer
9 Rear mounting bolt
10 Metalastik bush
11 Hypoid rear casing
12 Circlip
13 Nyloc nut
14 Seal housing plate
15 Oil seal
16 Hexagon socket screw
17 Ball race
18 Differential carrier
19 Differential side bearing
20 Shims
21 Inner axle shaft
22 Nyloc nut
23 Bolt
24 Bolt
†25 Shim
†26 Rubber sealing ring
†27 Nylon bush
†28 Shim
29 Stud
30 Hub
31 Nyloc nut
32 Grease trap
33 Outer seal housing
34 Seal
35 Ballrace
36 Joint washer
37 Trunnion housing
38 Distance tube
39 Grease plug
40 Needle roller bearing
41 Inner oil seal
42 Key
43 Outer axle shaft
44 Grease flinger
45 Universal joint assembly
46 Circlip
47 Bearing cap
48 Tubular dowel
49 Bolt
50 Mounting rubber
51 Nyloc nut
52 Plain washer
53 Rubber pad
54 Bolt
55 Split pin
56 Slotted nut
57 Coupling flange
58 Oil seal
59 Pinion tail bearing
60 Shims
61 Spacer
62 Mounting plate
63 Bolt
64 Hypoid nose piece casing
65 Pinion head bearing
66 Spacer
67 Pinion
68 Crownwheel
69 Cross-shaft
70 Bolt
71 Lockplate
72 Brake backplate
73 Bolt
74 Nyloc nut
75 Vertical link

Note. †New trunnion sealing details introduced from Commission No. Herald 1200, GA184442 and GB36051; Herald 12/50, GD36956; Spitfire, FC62167; Vitesse 6, HB28055.

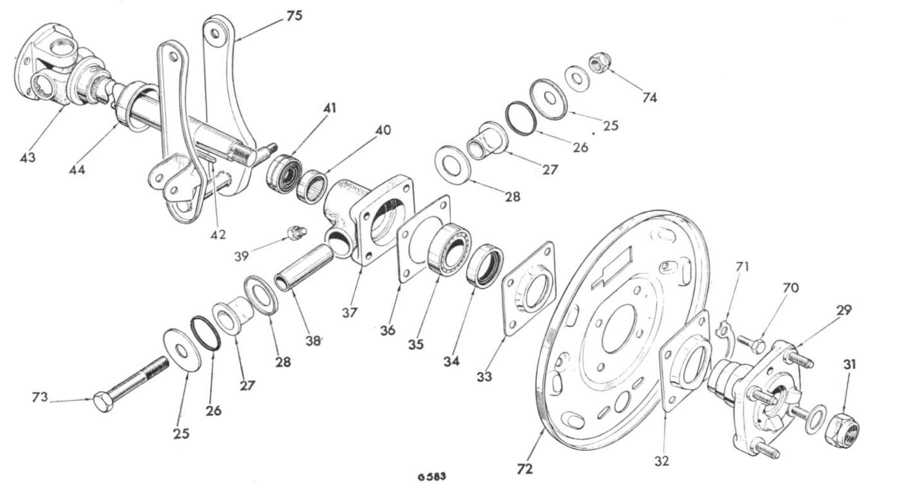

Fig. 6. Outer axle shaft and hub assembly details
(annotations are given under Fig. 2)

Fig. 7. Using Tool No. S109C to remove rear hub

Fig. 8. Pressing the axle shaft through the trunnion assembly

OUTER AXLE SHAFT (Fig. 6)

Dismantling

Remove the countersunk screws and detach the brake drums.

Remove the hub nut (31), plain washer and extract the hub (30) and key (42) using Churchill Tool No. S109C.

Remove the nyloc nut (74) and withdraw the bolt (73). Detach the vertical link (75) from the trunnion, remove the shims (25 and 28), rubber seals (26), steel bush (38) and nylon inserts (27) from the trunnion.

Release the lockplates (71), withdraw four bolts (70) and remove the grease trap (32), brake backplate (72), seal housing (33), and joint washer.

Remove the oil seal (34) from its housing (33).

Remove the ball race (35), trunnion housing (37) and flinger (44) together, using Churchill Tool No. S4221A with adaptors S4221A/14.

Extract the inner oil seal (41) and needle roller bearing (40) from the trunnion.

Re-assembly

Using Churchill Tool No. S300A, fit the needle roller bearing (40) into the trunnion (37), (pressing on the lettered end) to a depth of 0·5″ (12·7 mm.) from the trunnion face.

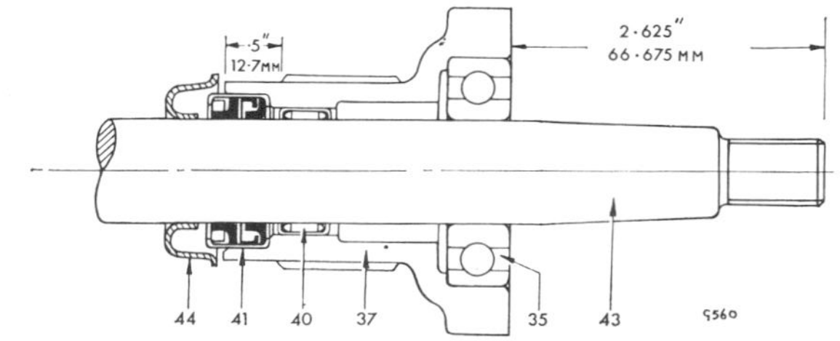

Fig. 9. Section through rear hub

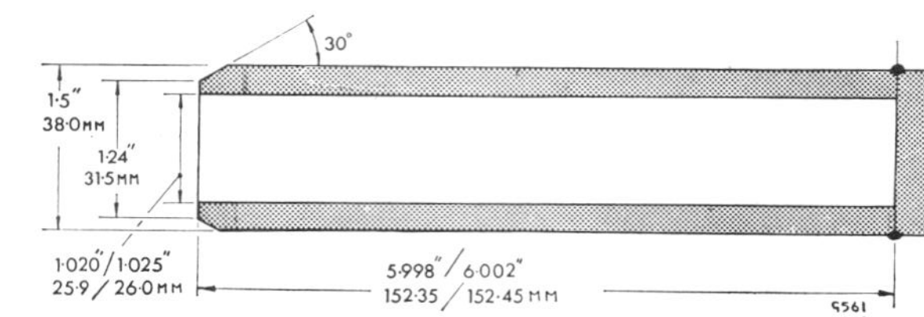

Fig. 10. Dimensions of tool for fitting flinger

With the sealing lips trailing, drift the inner oil seal (41) into the trunnion.

Drive the flinger (44) on to the axle shaft using the tool shown on Fig. 10.

Pack the needle rollers with grease and pass the axle shaft through the trunnion, taking care not to damage the inner oil seal.

Secure the axle shaft in the protected jaws of a vice, pack the ballrace with grease and drift it onto the shaft, using Churchill Tool No. S304, as shown on Fig. 12.

With the sealing lip trailing, press a new seal (34) into the seal housing (33). Coat a new paper joint (36) with grease, position it on the trunnion outer face, and assemble the seal housing, brake backplate assembly (72) (with wheel cylinder at the top) and grease trap (32) (with duct to bottom). Secure the assembly with bolts (70) and new lockplates (71).

Insert the key (42) into its keyway in the axle shaft and, ensuring that the tapers are clean, fit the hub (30) and secure it with a plain washer and new nyloc nut (31).

Secure the brake drums with the countersunk screws.

Complete the trunnion assembly by fitting the nylon bushes (27), steel sleeve (38), shims (28 and 25), rubber seals (26) and vertical link (75).

Fig. 11. Pressing the needle roller bearing into the trunnion

Fig. 12. Driving the ballrace onto the shaft

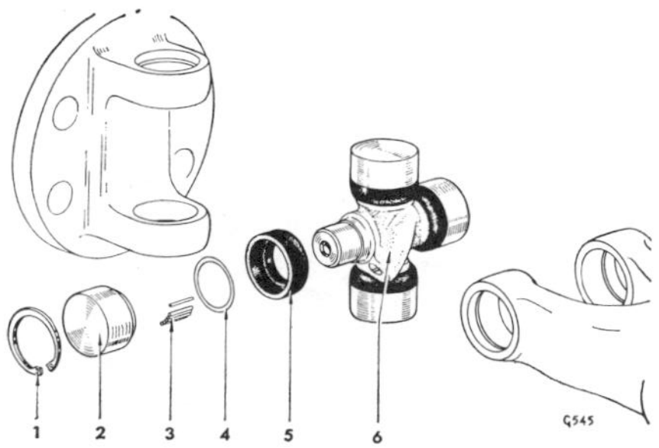

1	Circlip	4	Washer
2	Cup	5	Seal
3	Needle rollers	6	Spider

Fig. 13. Coupling details

Fig. 14. Coupling attachment

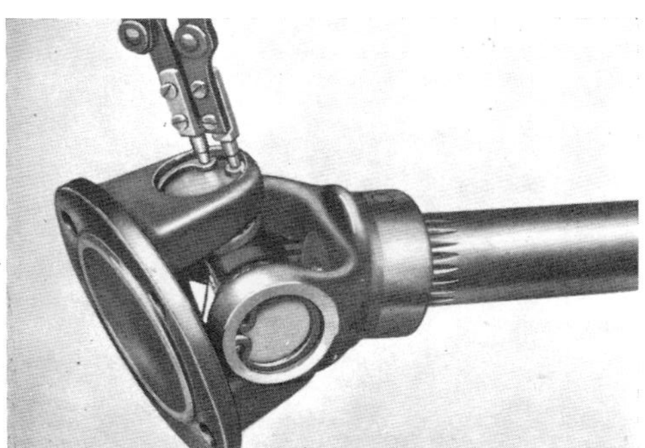

Fig. 15. Removing circlips

OUTER AXLE SHAFT COUPLINGS

Inspection

Jack up the rear of the car and support it on chassis stands. Remove the nave plates and road wheels.

Place a trolley jack under the vertical link and raise it until the assembly assumes its normal operating position.

Remove the bolts securing the coupling to the inner axle shaft. Taking care not to damage the flange faces, lever the flanges apart, easing the vertical link outwards on the jack.

Holding the axle shaft firmly, move the flange yoke axially along the spider journals. If end float exists, renew the spider and cup assemblies. This will necessitate removal of the outer axle shaft assembly as described on page 3·105.

Repeat the inspection procedure on the other axle shaft coupling.

Dismantling (Fig. 13)

Secure the axle shaft in a vice and remove the circlips (1) retaining the roller cups (2).

Support the flange yoke and tap it with a hide-faced mallet (Fig. 16) to partially eject the cup from the yoke. Completely withdraw the cup using grips (Fig. 17). Repeat the operation with the opposite cup.

Detach the flange yoke from the spider and remove the cups as described above. Remove the spider from the outer yoke.

NOTE: A tight cup may be removed by gripping it in the jaws of a vice and tapping the yoke with a hide faced mallet.

Replacement of Parts

The needle rollers, cups, spiders, seals and circlips are supplied only as a complete package. The occurrence of wear in the bores of a universal joint yoke will necessitate its removal. The outer yoke is attached to the axle shaft and can only be obtained as an assembly.

Re-assembly

Carefully fit the seals (5) and washers (4) onto the cups (2). Manoeuvre the spider into the outer yoke. Press the cups squarely into the yoke ensuring that the needle rollers engage with the spider journals. Repeat with the flange yoke.

Secure the cups in the yokes by inserting the circlips in their grooves.

Circlips are obtainable in the following sizes:

Part Number	*in.*	*mm.*
128651	·058/·059	1·473/1·498
128652	·059/·060	1·498/1·524
128653	·060/·061	1·524/1·549
128654	·061/·062	1·549/1·574

Fig. 16. Tapping cup from flange yoke

Fig. 17. Using grips to remove needle roller cup

Fig. 18. Fitting cup and needle rollers

Fig. 19. Unscrewing hexagon socket screws

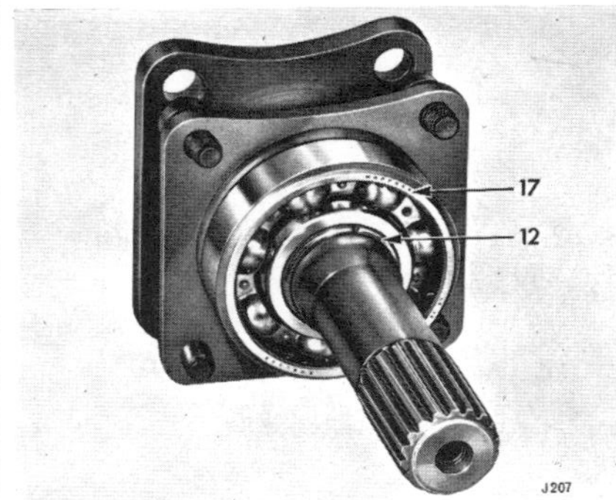

Fig. 20. Inner axle shaft assembly

Fig. 21. Pressing out inner axle shaft

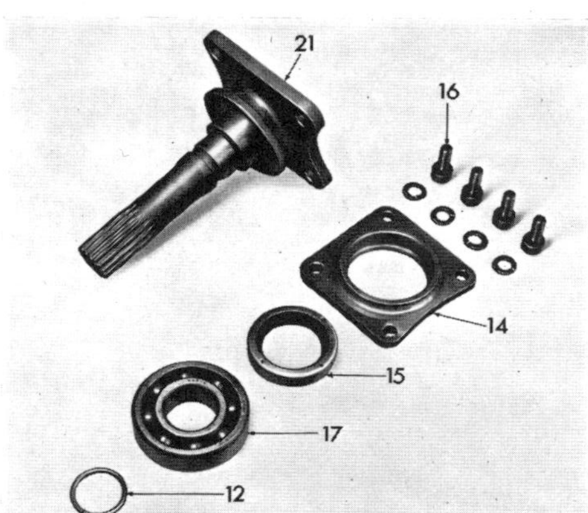

Fig. 22. Inner axle shaft details

INNER AXLE SHAFT AND BEARING ASSEMBLIES

To Remove (Fig. 19)

Referring to page 3·105, remove the hub and outer axle shaft assembly.

Drain rear axle oil.

Utilising a $\frac{3}{16}$ in. (6·763 mm.) hexagon socket key, as shown on Fig. 19, remove the socket screws from the hypoid casing. On Vitesse 6 models, the screws cannot be completely withdrawn.

To Dismantle (Fig. 22)

Remove the circlip (12) (Fig. 20) and, using a Churchill Press and Adaptor Set No. S4221A-7B, withdraw the race from the inner axle shaft, shown on Fig. 21.

Detach the seal housing plate (14) and drive out the oil seal (15).

To Re-assemble (Fig. 23)

With the lip of the seal leading, drive a new seal into the housing plate (14).

With the sealing lip trailing, slide the housing onto the inner axle shaft, taking care not to damage the seal as it passes over the serrations.

Press the ballrace onto the axle shaft, as shown on Fig. 24.

Fit the circlip (12) to the inner axle shaft groove.

To Refit

Insert the inner axle shaft into the hypoid housing and secure it with the four hexagon socket screws (16).

Refill the hypoid housing with oil and refit the outer axle shaft.

PINION OIL SEAL

To Replace (Fig. 25)

Drain the hypoid unit, remove the exhaust tail pipe and disconnect the rear end of the propeller shaft. Withdraw the split pin (55), unscrew the nut (56) and remove the driving flange (57).

Lever out the old seal (58) and drive a new one into position.

Refit the driving flange (57), washer, nut (56) and split pin (55). Reconnect the propeller shaft and refit the exhaust pipe.

Refill the hypoid housing unit with oil.

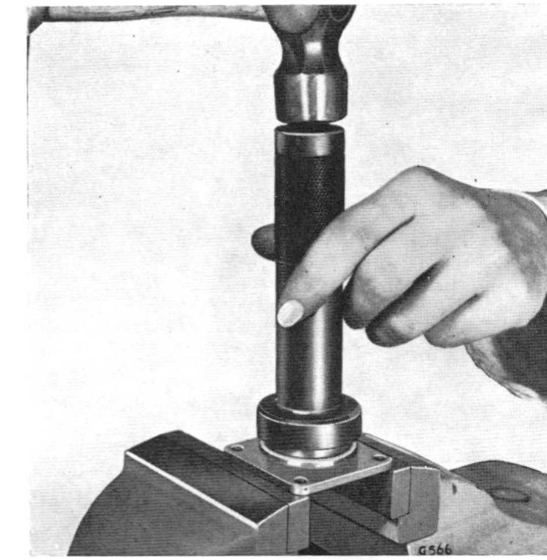

Fig. 23. Fitting inner axle shaft oil seal

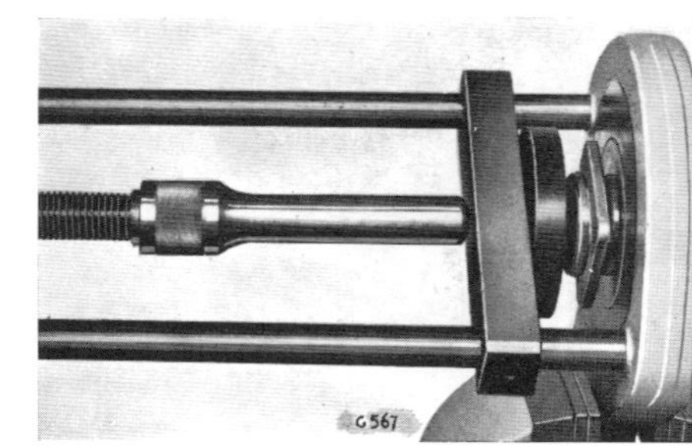

Fig. 24. Pressing inner axle shaft through bearing and housing

Fig. 25. Driving pinion oil seal into position

Fig. 26. Underside view of hypoid unit

Fig. 27. Cover removed to show rear road spring attachment

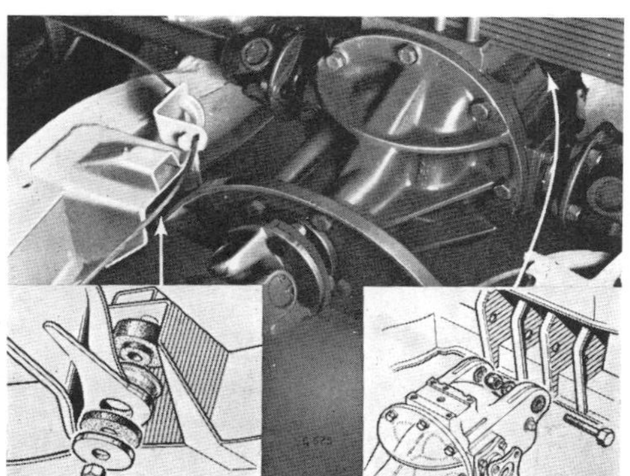

Fig. 28. Hypoid unit attachments

HYPOID UNIT

To Remove

Jack up the rear of the vehicle, place on stands and drain the hypoid unit.

Remove the nave plates, if fitted, and the road wheels.

Support the vertical links with screw jacks to relieve the dampers of spring load.

Remove the nyloc nuts and washers from the damper lower attachment eyes and pull the bottom of the dampers clear of the mounting pins.

Remove the exhaust silencer and tail pipe from the vehicle.

Disconnect the inner shaft couplings and the rear end of the propeller shaft from the hypoid unit.

Take out the rear seat assembly and remove the spring access plate from the floor.

Release the spring retaining plate and remove the three rear studs from the axle casing (Fig. 26).

Release the rear attachment by removing the nyloc nuts (13), plain washers and withdrawing the bolts (9).

With an assistant taking the weight of the hypoid unit, release the front nose mounting plate by removing the nyloc nuts (51), large plain washers (52) and rubber pads (53).

Manoeuvre the hypoid unit forward and down from beneath the vehicle.

To Refit

Offer up the hypoid unit to its rear mounting points and locate the bolts through the rear mounting lugs and fit the nyloc nuts (13) hand tight.

Fit the front rubber pads (53) ensuring that the upper ones locate in the corresponding holes in the front mounting plate. Fit the plain washers (52) and tighten the nyloc nuts (51) and the rear mounting nyloc nuts (13).

Refit the three rear spring attachment studs, the spring plate, plain washers and tighten the nyloc nuts.

Jack up each vertical link and refit the axle shaft couplings.

Refit the dampers and tighten the attachments.

Reconnect the propeller shaft and refit the exhaust tail pipe and silencer.

Refill the unit with oil, and adjust the brakes.

Refit the road wheels, remove the stands, and tighten the wheel nuts and refit nave plates.

HYPOID UNIT

General Recommendations

Scrape existing joint material from the joint faces and clean the axle components, preferably in a trichlorethylene degreasing plant, giving particular attention to the bearings.

Examine all joint faces and bearing locations for burrs and other damage likely to affect proper seating of the components and rectify as necessary.

Avoid the intermixing of bearing components and keep all shim packs intact. Assess the serviceability of all components by careful examination and by checking the measurement of worn surfaces against the maximum worn tolerances given on page 3·102.

When re-building the unit, use new joint washers and spring washers and renew damaged studs, nuts, bolts and unserviceable components. Use Hylomar, Wellseal or Hermetite for all gasket joints.

Tighten all nuts, bolts and studs to the appropriate torque figures listed on page 0·113.

To Remove Differential Housing from Casing

Clean the unit with paraffin, and place it on a clean bench. Remove the inner axle shafts as described on page 3·110. Remove the bolts (63) and spring washers and turn the pinion until the two chamfered portions on the edge of the differential carrier permit withdrawal of the differential housing.

To Refit

Reverse the removal procedure, ensuring that the differential housing and casing flange faces are clean. Fit a new paper joint, coated with grease, between the two faces.

Removal of Differential Carrier

Remove the bearing cap bolts (49) and detach the bearing caps (47). Assemble the Churchill spreading tool on the housing face as shown on Fig. 31. Spread the fixture by turning the double-ended tensioner screw until it is hand tight, then complete the spread by moving it a further half-turn with a spanner.

IMPORTANT: DO NOT OVER-SPREAD BY EXCEEDING THIS AMOUNT OR THE HOUSING WILL BE DAMAGED BEYOND REPAIR.

Lift the differential carrier from the housing. If the bearings are to be re-used, suitably identify them or, preferably, tie the bearing outer rings and shims to their respective inner races.

Fig. 29. Removing inner axle shaft from hypoid unit

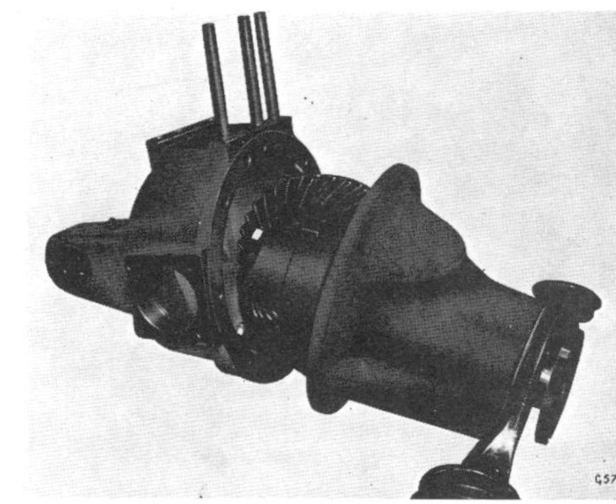

Fig. 31. Using spreading tool to release differential carrier

Fig. 30. Hypoid unit removed from rear casing

Fig. 32. Unscrewing crownwheel attachment bolts

Fig. 33. Checking differential carrier flange run-out

Fig. 34. Withdrawing differential side bearing

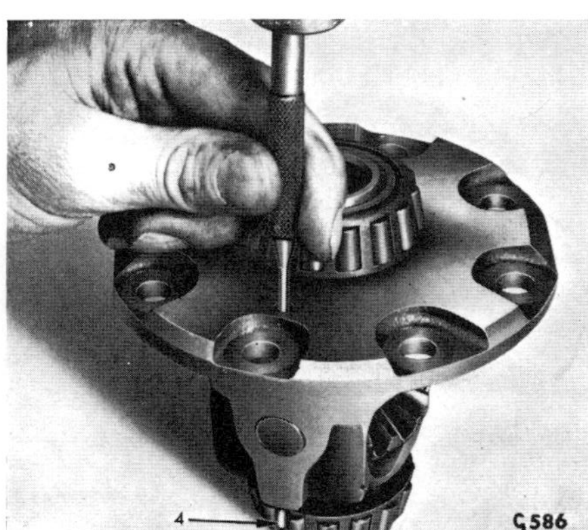

Fig. 35. Driving out cross-shaft locking pin

Dismantling the Differential Unit

Remove the bolts (24) and detach the gear (68) from the carrier. Refit the differential assembly, complete with bearings and shims but without the crown wheel, into the pinion housing and release the Churchill spreading tool.

With a dial indicator gauge mounted on the housing and the plunger operating squarely against the carrier face, slowly rotate the carrier and check the "run-out". Maximum "run-out" must not exceed 0·003 in. (0·076 mm.).

Remove the differential carrier assembly and the spreading tool. Using Churchill Tool No. S4221A-8C, withdraw the bearings (19) as shown on Fig. 34.

Drive out the cross-shaft locking pin (4) (Fig. 35) and remove the cross-shaft (69), differential gears (5), (6) and thrust washers (3), (7).

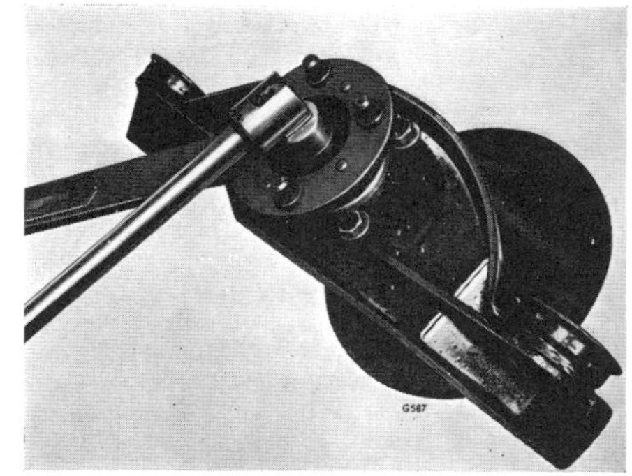

Fig. 36. Unscrewing pinion flange nut

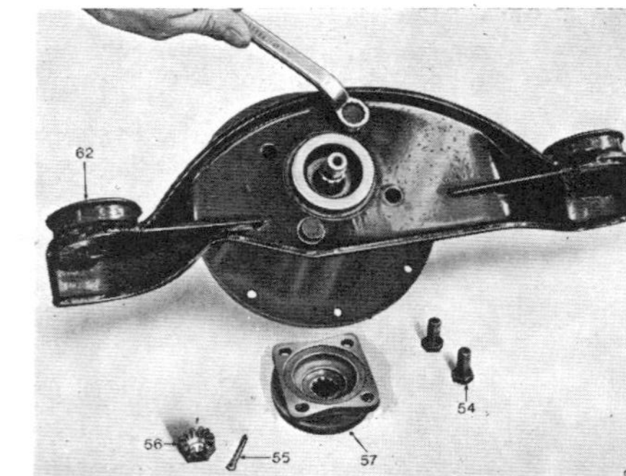

Fig. 37. Removing front nose mounting plate

Removing Pinion

Remove the split pin (55), nut (56) and plain washer. Withdraw the flange (57) from the pinion (67) and drive the pinion from the casing. Carefully keeping all shims intact, remove these and the spacer (61) from the pinion. Extract the pinion head bearing and selective spacer (66) using Tool No. S4221A-4A as shown on Fig. 39.

Drive out the pinion tail bearing outer race, the oil seal (58) and the head bearing outer race. See Fig. 38.

Remove the four "Wedgelok" setscrews (54) and front mounting plate (62).

Examination of Pinion Housing

Before proceeding to re-assemble the axle components, check the bearing housing for burrs or other damage likely to prevent correct seating of the bearings.

Fig. 38. Driving out pinion bearing outer races

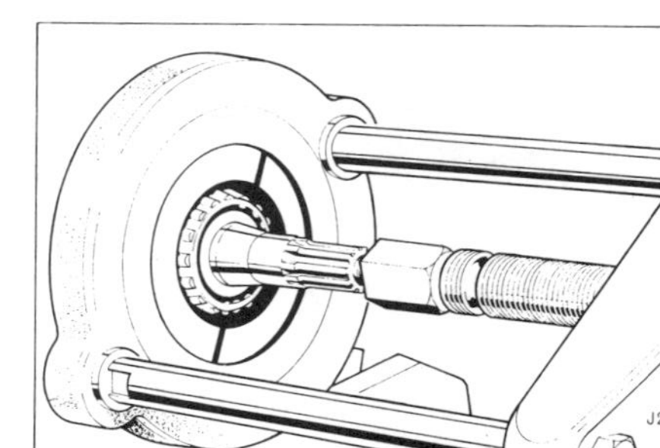

Fig. 39. Withdrawing pinion head bearing

Fig. 40. Fitting pinion head bearing

Fig. 41. Measuring pinion height

Fig. 42. Crownwheel and pinion markings

RE-ASSEMBLY

Carefully examine all components and decide which items require renewal. If slight damage to the crown wheel or the pinion necessitates replacement, discard both items and fit a new matched pair. These gears are lapped together during manufacture and etched with similar marking to identify them as a pair, therefore, before fitting, ensure that each gear is similarly marked as shown on Fig. 42.

Installing Pinion and Bearings

Locate the pinion bearing outer races in the differential housing (64). Omitting the selective spacer (66), at this stage, lightly oil the head bearing (65) and press it on to the pinion (67).

Install the pinion into the housing and omitting the spacer (61), shims (60) and oil seal (58) assemble the tail bearing (59), driving flange (57), plain washer and nut (56). Tighten the nut to the required torque given on page 0·113.

IMPORTANT: To ensure correct location of the bearing rollers, spin the pinion whilst tightening the flange nut.

Adjusting Pinion Height

Using the ground button, depress the dial gauge plunger to its limit and "zero" the gauge.

Place the gauge in the axle casing with the plunger contacting the pinion (Fig. 41).

Exerting downward pressure on the gauge, obtain a maximum reading. This indicates the thickness of shims required between a normal pinion and head bearing.

A pinion of normal height bears the letter "N" on the top face of the pinion. Hypoid pinions not marked in this manner bear a number preceded by a plus or minus sign as shown in Fig. 42. These symbols indicate the amount which must be added to, or subtracted from the figure derived from gauge reading.

e.g. Gauge reading ·013 in.
Marking on pinion head "+1"
Selective spacer required = 0·013 in.
+0·001 „
=0·014 in.

Having determined the requisite spacer thickness, remove the pinion, bearings and driving flange from the housing but leave the bearing outer rings in place. Assemble the spacer (66) to the pinion and refit the head bearing.

Adjusting Pinion Bearing Pre-load

Assemble the spacer (61) and the shim pack (60) to the pinion shaft and fit the assembly into the housing.

NOTE: The thickness of the shim pack (60) may require re-adjusting to give correct preloading.

Drive the bearing (59) on to the pinion shaft and fit the driving flange (57), plain washer and nut (56). Tighten the nut to the required torque given on page 0·113.

Attach a pre-load gauge to the driving flange as shown in Fig. 44. Slowly move the weight along the graduated scale and note the point at which it falls. The gauge should read 12-16 lb/in.

Higher readings require a thicker shim pack between the tail bearing and spacer, lower readings require a thinner shim pack.

NOTE: One thousandth of an inch shim thickness = 4 lb/in. torque (approx.).

When the pre-load is correct, remove the driving flange and fit a new oil seal. Re-attach the flange, plain washer and nut. Tighten the nut and secure it with a split pin.

Measure the flange 'run-out' as shown in Fig. 45. Maximum 'run-out' must not exceed 0·002 in. (0·05 mm.).

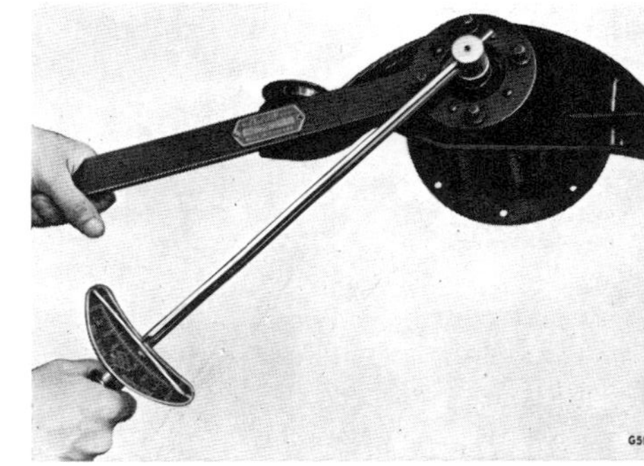

Fig. 43. Tightening pinion flange nut

Fig. 44. Using Tool No. S98A to measure pinion bearing preload

Fig. 45. Measuring pinion flange run-out

Fig. 46. Differential gears

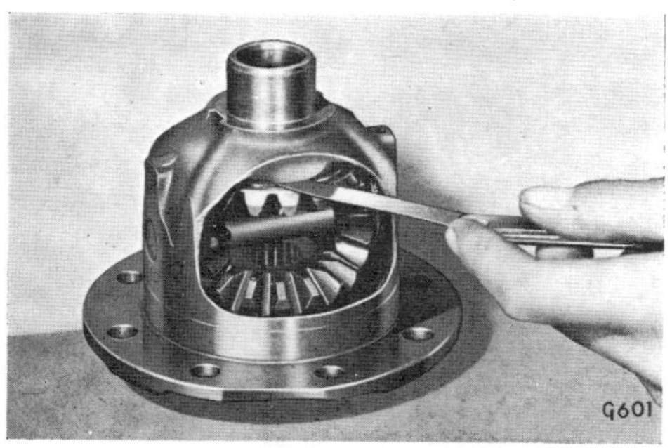

Fig. 47. Measuring differential gear backlash

Fig. 48. Fitting differential side bearings

Differential Gears (Fig. 46)

Assemble the sun gears (5), planet gears (6) and thrust washers (3), (7) into the differential carrier (18).

Insert the cross-shaft (69) into the carrier and check the planet gear backlash. By selection of planet gear thrust washers, reduce the end float to give minimum backlash consistent with freedom of rotation.

Insert the cross-shaft locking pin (4) and secure it by peening the metal over the end of the pin.

Measuring Total Differential Float

Fit the differential bearings to the carrier journals and place the assembly in the housing, omitting the shims.

Attach a dial gauge to the housing so that the dial plunger operates squarely against the crown wheel mounting face of the carrier (Fig. 49). Pressing both bearing outer rings towards each other, move the assembly away from the gauge and "zero" the dial.

Similarly, move the assembly towards the gauge, and note the dial reading. This indicates the total side float and is referred to as dimension "A" (see Fig. 51).

Remove the dial gauge and the differential carrier from the hypoid housing.

Crown Wheel—Measuring "In and Out" of Mesh

Ensuring that the mounting faces are clean and free from burrs, attach the crown wheel (68) to the carrier (18) and secure with new bolts (24).

NOTE: Thoroughly clean the carrier flange, crownwheel and bolts in a degreasing plant and apply 2 drops of "Loctite Studlok" to the threads of the bolts. Tighten the bolts to the required torque given on page 0·113.

Refit the differential unit in the hypoid casing and position the dial gauge as shown on Fig. 50.

Move the differential unit away from the gauge, to the "Full Mesh" position and "zero" the dial.

Move the differential unit towards the gauge and note the dial reading. This is the "in and out" of mesh dimension used in the following calculations and is referred to as dimension "B" (see Fig. 51).

Lift the differential carrier from the housing taking care not to mix the bearing out rings.

Differential Bearing Pre-load

By substituting correct measurement in place of those used in the following examples, calculate the thickness of both shim packs as follows:

Example

Total float "A"	0·060″
Plus 0·003″ pre-load..	0·003″
Total thickness of shims required ..	0·063″
Shim thickness at "Y":	
In/Out of mesh clearance "B" ..	0·025″
Subtract specified backlash ..	0·005″
Shim pack thickness required at "Y"	0·020″
Shim thickness at "X":	
Total shim thickness	0·063″
Minus shim pack thickness at "Y"..	0·020″
Shim pack thickness required at "X"	0·043″

Fig. 49. Measuring total side float

Fig. 50. Measuring in/out of mesh

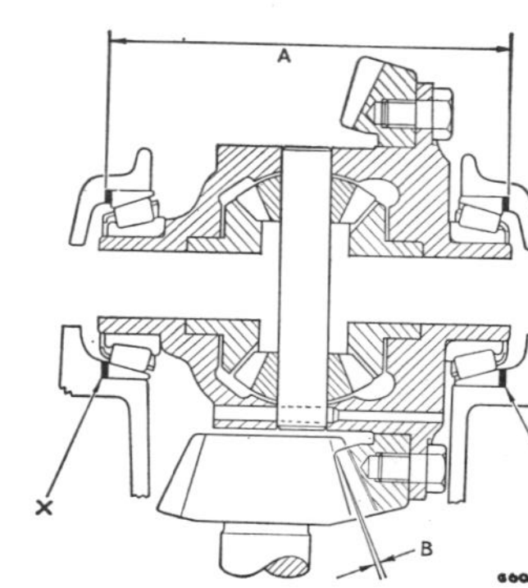

Fig. 51. Diagram for calculating shim pack thicknesses

Fig. 52. Tightening bearing cap bolts

Fig. 53. Measuring crownwheel/pinion backlash

Fig. 54. Painting crownwheel teeth to check pinion meshing

Using the axle spreading tool, and again taking care not to overspread, insert the differential carrier complete with shims into the casing. Remove the axle spreader, assemble the caps to their respective bearings and tighten the securing bolts.

Crown Wheel Backlash

Mount the dial gauge on the casing (Fig. 53) and by moving the crown wheel in either direction, take up the free movement, noting the readings on the dial gauge. Measure this backlash at several positions, each of which should be within the limits of 0·004″ to 0·006″ (0·1 to 0·15 mm.).

Should the backlash be excessive, reduce the thickness of the shim pack at "X", (Fig. 51) and add an equal amount to "Y". If the backlash is insufficient, reverse the procedure.

Tooth Markings

After setting the backlash to the required figure, use a small brush to lightly smear eight or ten of the crown wheel teeth with engineers' blue. Move the painted gear in mesh with the pinion to obtain a good tooth impression.

(a) **Correct Markings** (Fig. 55)

When the gear meshing is correctly adjusted the markings obtained should closely approximate those shown at (a), this being the ideal contact.

The area of contact is evenly distributed over the working depth of the tooth profile and is located slightly nearer to the TOE than the heel.

(b) **High Contact**

The markings shown at (b) are those produced by high contact, i.e., when the tooth contact is heavy on the crown wheel face or addendum and caused by the pinion being too far out of mesh. To rectify, move the pinion deeper into mesh by adding shims between the pinion and head bearing. To maintain the existing pinion bearing preload, an equal amount of shims must also be added between the tail bearing inner cone and the bearing distance piece.

(c) **Low Contact**

Fig. 55 (c) shows heavy markings on the crown wheel flank or dedendum this being the opposite to that shown in (b). Rectification of this condition necessitates moving the pinion out of mesh by removing an equal amount of shims from the positions described in (b).

NOTE: When correcting for (b), the new position will tend to move the tooth contact towards the toe on drive and the heel on coast, whilst correcting for (c) will tend to move the tooth contact towards the heel on drive and the toe on coast. In either case it may be necessary, after correcting the pinion mesh, to re-adjust the crown wheel as described in (d) and (e).

(d) **Toe Contact**

The markings shown on Fig. 55 (d) result when the tooth contact is concentrated at the small end of the tooth. To rectify this condition, move the crown wheel out of mesh, i.e., increase backlash by transferring shims from the crown wheel side of the differential to the opposite side.

(e) **Heel Contact**

Fig. 55 (e) shows the markings obtained when the tooth contact is concentrated at the large end of the tooth. This condition is rectified by reducing backlash, i.e., by transferring shims in the opposite direction as for (d).

IMPORTANT: Whatever corrections are necessary, it is most important that the backlash at all times is within the specified limits.

(i) BACKLASH. When adjusting for backlash, always move the crown wheel as this member has more direct influence on backlash.

(ii) CROWN WHEEL MOVEMENT. Moving the gear out of mesh has the effect of moving the tooth contact towards the heel and raising it slightly towards the top of the tooth.

(iii) PINION MOVEMENT. Moving the pinion out of mesh raises the tooth contact on the face of the tooth and slightly towards the heel on drive, and towards the toe on coast.

Having assembled the differential unit, refit it to the casing (as described on page 3·113 and attach the assembly to the vehicle (as described on page 3·112).

Refill the axle with one of the recommended lubricants.

ADDENDUM — Pitch line to tooth tip.

DEDENDUM — Pitch line to tooth root.

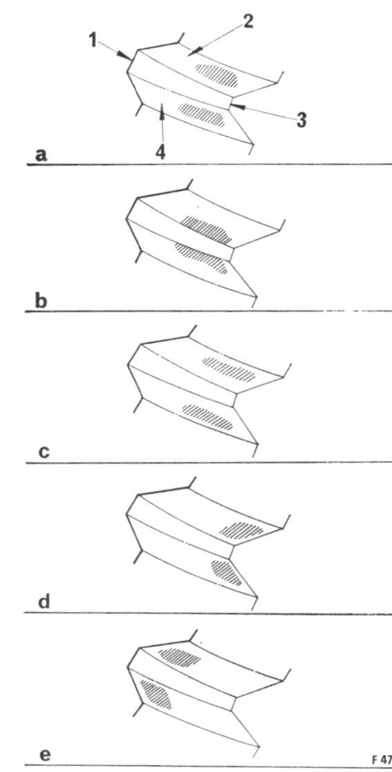

1 Heel (thick end)
2 Coastside (concave)
3 Toe (thin end)
4 Drive side (convex)

Fig. 55. Crownwheel tooth markings

BRAKE PIPE LAYOUT

BRAKE DATA

System .. .. .. Girling Hydraulic

	HERALD 1200	SPITFIRE, 12/50, 13/60	VITESSE 6
Front	Drum 8″ × 1¼″	Disc 9″	Disc 9″
Rear	Drum 7″ × 1¼″	Drum 7″ × 1¼″	Drum 8″ × 1¼″
Total Swept Area ..	118 sq. in.	199 sq. in. (12P calipers) 205 sq. in. (14LF calipers)	207 sq. in.

Adjustment .. .. Disc, self-adjusting; Drums, front two adjusters, rear one adjuster

Handbrake .. .. Centrally mounted hand lever operating rear brakes mechanically.

Disc Pad Material .. Herald 1200, 12/50, Spitfire and Vitesse 6, Don 55 (with 12P calipers)

Herald 1200, 12/50 13/60 and Spitfire, Don 212 (with 14LF calipers)

Shoe Lining Material

Front .. .. Herald 1200, Ferodo M.S.I

Rear .. .. Herald 1200, 12/50, Spitfire, Ferodo M.S.I (with 12P calipers)

Rear .. .. Vitesse 6, Don 24 (with 12P calipers)

Rear .. .. Herald 1200, 12/50, 13/60 and Spitfire, Don 242 (with 14LF calipers)

Fluid Type .. .. Castrol, Girling, Brake Fluid Crimson. Where this proprietary brand is not available, other fluids which meet SAE.70R3 specification may be used.

Discs .. .. .. Maximum permissible run-out, ·004″

14LF CALIPERS

NOTE. Type 14LF calipers were introduced on Production from first Spitfire Mk. 3 and first Herald 13/60 and from Commission Nos.: Herald 1200, GA.229455; 1200 Export, GB.53670; 12/50, GD.54349 with the exception of the following numbers:

1200 — GA.229488, 229509 and 229539

12/50 — GD.54358, 54365 and 54379

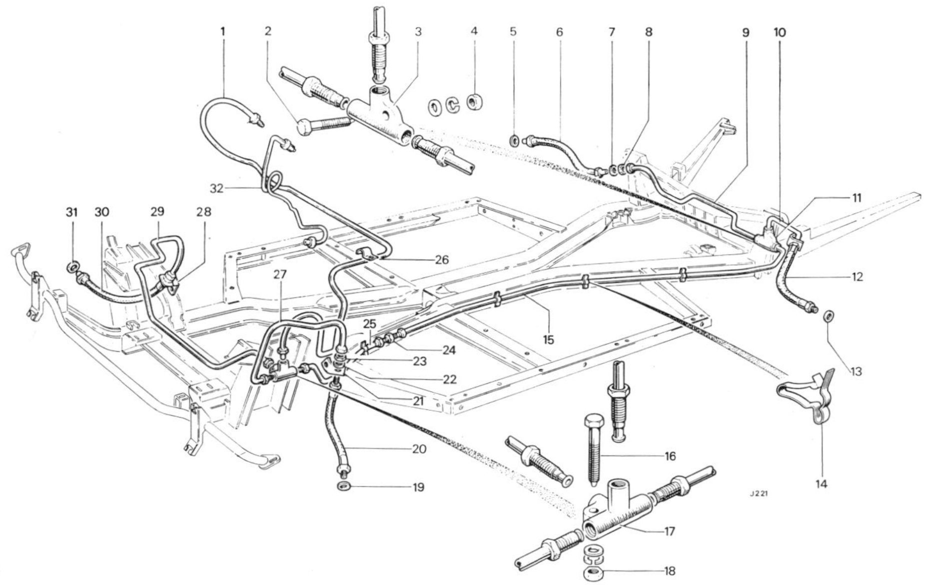

1 Pipe—master cylinder to four-way connection (R.H. steering)
2 Bolt—three-way piece attachment
3 Three-way piece
4 Nut—three-way piece attachment
5 Gasket—hose
6 Rear hose assembly
7 Shakeproof washer—hose attachment
8 Nut—hose attachment
9 Pipe—three-way to hose—R.H.
10 Pipe—three-way to hose—L.H.
11 Three-way piece
12 Rear hose assembly
13 Gasket—hose
14 Clip—pipe to frame
15 Pipe—three-way to double end union
16 Bolt—four-way piece attachment
17 Four-way piece
18 Nut—four-way piece attachment
19 Gasket—hose
20 Hose—high pressure—front
21 Hose mounting bracket
22 Shakeproof washer—hose attachment
23 Nut—hose attachment
24 Double end union—connector
25 Pipe—four-way to double end union
26 Clip—brake pipe attachment
27 Pipe—four-way to front hose—L.H.
28 Hose—mounting bracket
29 Pipe—four-way to front hose—R.H.
30 Hose—high pressure—front
31 Gasket—hose
32 Pipe—clutch master cylinder to slave cylinder

Fig. 1. Brake Pipe Layout (13/60)

MASTER CYLINDER OPERATION

A. Brakes Released Condition

When the brake pedal is released, hydraulic pressure created by the brake shoe pull-off spring, plus the plunger return spring (5), causes the plunger (7) to return to its rear stop (12). The last $\frac{1}{32}$" (0·794 mm.) of movement withdraws the valve shank (4) rearwards, lifting the seal (1) from its seat on the end face of the cylinder, thus permitting recuperation of the hydraulic fluid to the reservoir via the drilled passage.

B. Brakes Applied Condition

Pressure applied to the push-rod (9) by operation of the pedal, forces the plunger (7) forward. This in turn allows the valve shank (4) to move forward under the influence of the spring (5) until the valve spacer contacts the end face of the cylinder. The spring washer (2) then forces the valve shank and seal (1) forward until the seal contacts the end face and closes the passage to the reservoir.

Continued movement of the piston displaces fluid through the hydraulic pipe lines and applies the brakes, the valve shank (4) passing further into the hollow centre of the piston as the latter moves down the cylinder bore.

Maximum stroke available—
1·38" (35·05 mm.)

Stroke position at maximum cut off—
0·099" (2·5 mm.)

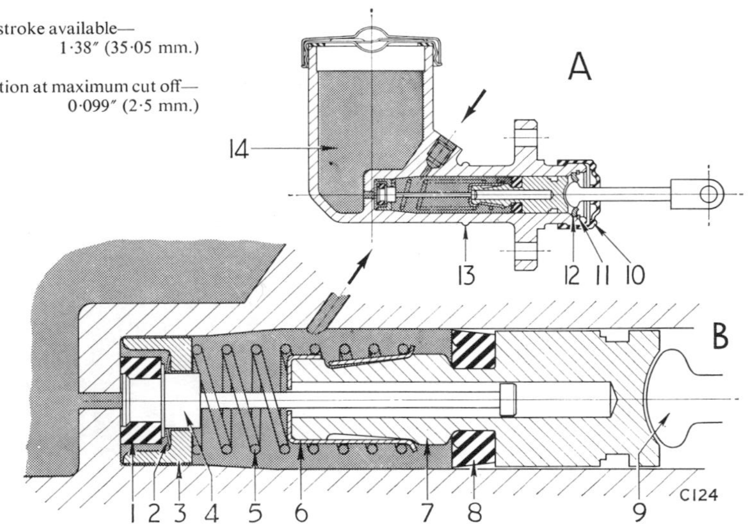

1 Valve seal
2 Spring (valve seal)
3 Distance piece
4 Valve shank
5 Plunger return spring
6 Spring retainer
7 Plunger
8 Plunger seal
9 Push rod
10 Dust cover
11 Circlip
12 Push rod stop
13 Identification ring(s)
14 Fluid reservoir

Fig. 2. Section through brake master cylinder

BRAKE MASTER CYLINDER

Removal (Fig. 3)

1. Empty the brake hydraulic system.
2. Pull back the rubber dust excluder (11) and withdraw the clevis pin (14) securing the push rod to the pedal.
3. Detach the fluid pipe from the master cylinder.
4. Remove the two bolts (16) which secure the master cylinder to its mounting bracket (15) and withdraw the unit from the bulkhead.

Dismantling (Fig. 2)

1. Depress the push rod (9), remove the circlip (11) and withdraw the push rod and return stop plate (12).
2. Shake out the plunger (7) and the recuperation valve assembly. If necessary, apply low pressure compressed air to the outlet union to eject the plunger assembly.
3. Lift the locating clip on the spring retainer (6) and remove the retainer from the plunger (7) with the valve and spring assembly.
4. Detach the valve shank (4) by passing it through the offset hole in the retainer. Remove the spring (5), distance piece (3) and spring (2) from the valve shank. Using fingers, detach the seal (1) from item (4) and the seal (8) from item (7).

Re-Assembly (Fig. 2)

1. Refit the seals (1) and (8) to items (4) and (7).
2. Fit the spring (2), distance piece (3) and spring (5) to the valve shank (4), attach the spring retainer (6) and fit the assembly to the plunger (7). Lubricate the assembly with clean hydraulic fluid and insert it in the master cylinder bore. Fit the push rod (9) with stop plate (12) and the circlip (11).

To Refit (Fig. 3)

Secure the master cylinder to its mounting bracket. Using a new split pin, refit the clevis pin securing the push rod to the pedal. Refit the rubber dust excluder and the fluid pipe to the cylinder and refill and bleed the system as described on page 3·204.

BRAKE PEDAL

To Renew Pivot Bush

1. Pull back the rubber dust excluder (11) and withdraw the clevis pin (14).
2. Detach the pedal return spring (4), remove the circlip (6), push the pivot pin (5) from the bracket and pedal and withdraw the pedal from the bracket.
3. **Renew the pivot bush and re-assemble by reversing the dismantling sequence.**

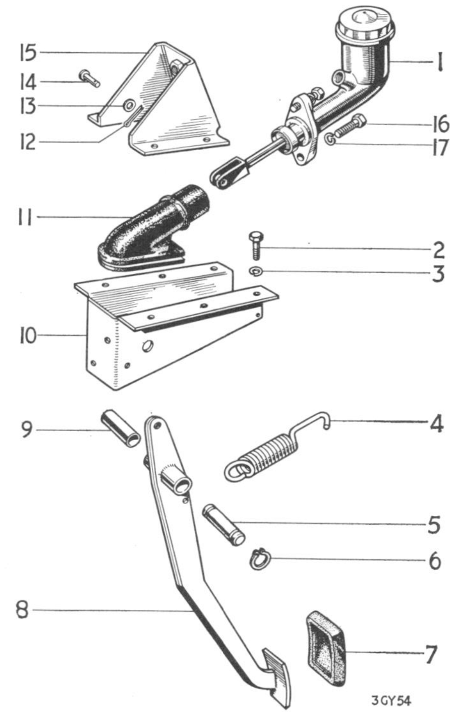

1	Master cylinder	10	Pedal bracket
2	Bolt	11	Rubber dust excluder
3	Spring washer	12	Split pin
4	Return spring	13	Plain washer
5	Pivot pin	14	Clevis pin
6	Circlip	15	Master cylinder bracket
7	Pedal rubber	16	Bolt
8	Pedal	17	Spring washer
9	Pedal pivot bush		

Fig. 3. Exploded brake pedal and bracket assembly

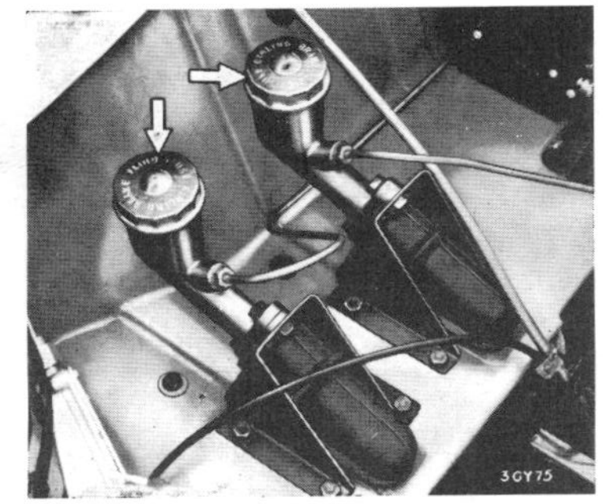

Fig. 4.

Brake and clutch master cylinder filler caps

Fig. 5.

Rear drum brake adjusters and bleed nipple

Fig. 6.

Front drum brake adjusters and bleed nipple

Fig. 7.

Bleeding disc brakes

BLEEDING THE HYDRAULIC SYSTEM

Air is compressible, and its presence in the system will prevent the correct functioning of the brakes. Therefore, if a pipe joint has been uncoupled, or if air has been admitted for other reasons, the system must be bled to expel this air.

With the aid of a second operator, proceed as follows :

1. During the bleeding operation, keep the reservoir topped-up with new brake fluid and ensure that the level does not fall below half full. If the reservoir is allowed to empty, air will be drawn into the system, necessitating re-bleeding.
2. Turn the rear brake adjusters clockwise to lock the drums.
3. Commencing with the rear wheel cylinder furthest from the master cylinder, wipe the bleed nipple clean, attach a length of rubber tubing to the nipple and allow the end of the tube to hang in a glass jar partly filled with brake fluid.
4. Unscrew the bleed nipple about a quarter turn, and, giving fast full strokes with a slight pause between each stroke, pump the brake pedal until the fluid entering the glass container is free from air bubbles.
5. **Important.** Ensure that the piston returns to its maximum travel at the end of each stroke. A sticking piston will be obvious from the feel of the pedal.
6. Finish with a few slightly faster applications of the pedal, using the bottom half of the stroke, until it is apparent that all air has been excluded. Close the bleed screw during the last pedal application, or with the pedal fully depressed.
7. Repeat the procedure for the three remaining brakes, finishing with the front wheel cylinder nearest to the master cylinder. If bleeding of any cylinder continues without success for a considerable time, it may be that air is being drawn in past the bleed screw threads. In such instances, the bleed screw should be tightened at the end of each downward stroke of the pedal, allowing the piston to return fully before re-opening of the bleed screw, close the bleed screw finally during the last pedal application.
8. Adjust all brakes in the normal manner and, whilst applying pressure to the brake pedal, check for leaks at all pipe joints and unions, flexible hose connections, wheel cylinders and master cylinder.

NOTE : When replenishing the system, particularly where disc brakes are fitted, use only new fluid that has been stored in a container sealed from the atmosphere. Immediately bleeding is completed, re-seal residual fluid in the container, before it is again stored, as exposure to atmosphere lowers the fluid boiling point.

BRAKES

Front Brakes (VITESSE, HERALD 12/50, 13/60 AND SPITFIRE)

Self-adjusting front brakes consists of Girling 9″ discs with double acting caliper units, each containing two quickly detachable friction pads.

Friction Pad Replacement

1. Jack up the car and remove the front road wheels.
2. Release two spring retainers (9) and remove the pad retainer pins (10).
3. Lift the friction pads (4) from the caliper and renew them if worn. Do not attempt to re-line worn pad assemblies.
4. Before fitting new pads, push the pistons (6) back to the full extent of their travel. Refit the pads and insert the retainer pins (10) securing them with the spring retainer clips (9).

Caliper Cylinder Maintenance

To replace piston sealing rings or dust excluders, dismantle as follows :—

1. Release the rigid pipe and locknut at the support bracket. Unscrew the flexible hose from the caliper.
2. Remove two bolts (21) securing the caliper to its support bracket.
3. Remove the caliper and withdraw the pistons from the body.
4. Carefully remove the rubber sealing ring (7) from its recess.
5. Clean the piston, cylinder and rubbers with clean brake fluid ONLY.
6. Examine all components for serviceability and renew where necessary.

Re-Assembly

1. Fit a new piston seal (7) into the recess in the cylinder.
2. Locate the projecting lip of the rubber dust excluder (8) in its recess in the cylinder.
3. Insert the piston (6), closed end leading, into the cylinder, taking care not to damage the polished surface. Push the piston fully home and engage the outer lip of the dust excluder with the recess in the piston. Replace the friction pads.
4. Assemble the caliper over the disc, and refit to the mounting bracket.
5. Refit the flexible brake hose and bleed the system.

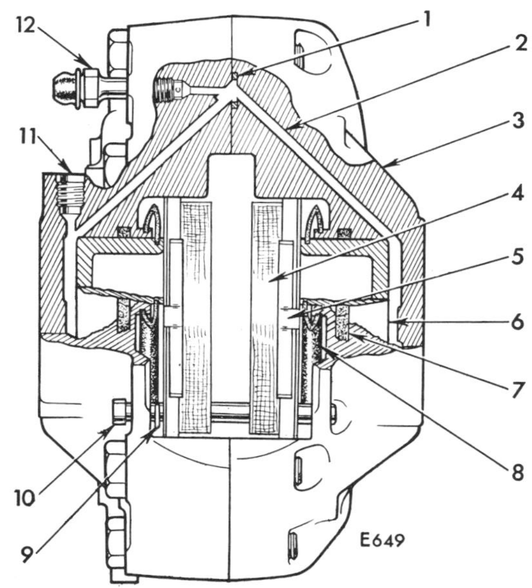

1 Rubber "O" ring	7 Piston sealing ring
2 Fluid transfer channels	8 Dust cover
3 Caliper body	9 Retaining clip
4 Brake pad	10 Retaining pin
5 Anti-squeal plate	11 Flexible hose connection
6 Piston	12 Bleed nipple

Fig. 8. Section through caliper assembly

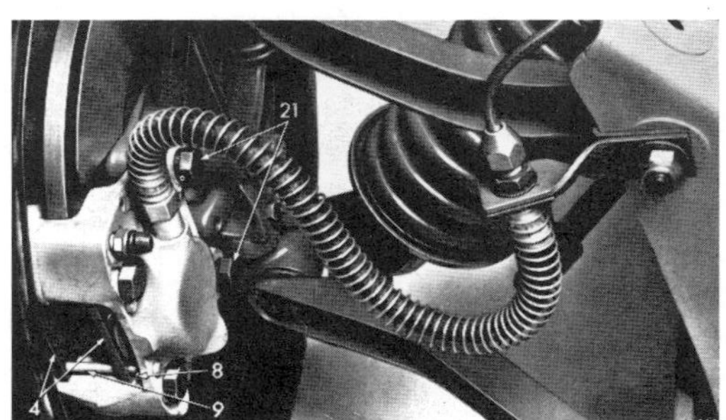

Fig. 9. Location of caliper attachments, bolts and brake pad details

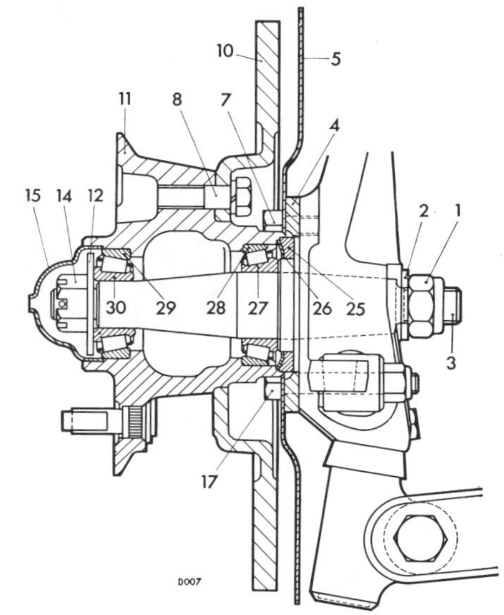

Fig. 10. Section through hub

Fig. 11. Measuring disc run-out

Disc and Hub Removal (Figs. 10 and 12)

1. Remove caliper assembly (19).
2. Remove the grease retaining cap (15) from the hub by screwing through it a No. 10 U.N.F. setscrew (supplied in tool kit).
3. Remove the split pin, slotted nut (14) and plain washer (12) from the stub axle (3).
4. Withdraw the hub (11) complete with the outer race (30) and the outer part of the inner race (28).
5. Detach the brake disc (10) from the hub (11) and degrease the hub components.

If new bearings are required, drift the old bearing outer rings and the oil seal (25) with retainer (26) from the hub. New bearings should only be fitted as complete sets.

Re-Assembly

1. Fit the bearing outer rings (28) and (29) with their tapers facing outwards. Refit the disc (10), securing with bolts (8) and washers (9).
2. Assemble the inner races (27) and (30) and fit the hub and disc to the stub axle. Fit the washer (12) and slotted nut (14) and, whilst rotating the hub, tighten the nut (14) with finger pressure only. Slacken the nut back to the nearest split pin hole and mark its position by centre punching the end of the nut and stub axle. The hub should have 0·003″ to 0·005″ (·076 mm. to 0·127 mm.) end float. If slackening back the nut produces excessive end float, remove the nut and file the rear face so that when refitted the correct end float is provided.
NOTE: Maximum permissible run-out on the friction faces of the disc is ·002″ (0·0508 mm.).
3. Remove the nut (14), washer (12), hub (11) and races (27) and (30). Pack the races and hub with an approved grease.
4. Secure a new hub sealing felt (25) to the seal retainer (26) with jointing compound. Allow the compound to dry, then soak the seal in engine oil and squeeze out surplus oil.
5. Fit the races (27) and (30) and seal retainer (26) to the hub, with the felt seal facing inwards.
6. Fit the hub assembly to the stub axle, securing it with the washer (12) and nut (14). Tighten the nut until the centre punch marks correspond, and secure the nut with a new split pin (13).
7. Fit the cap (15). Secure the caliper assembly with bolts (21) and spring washers (20).

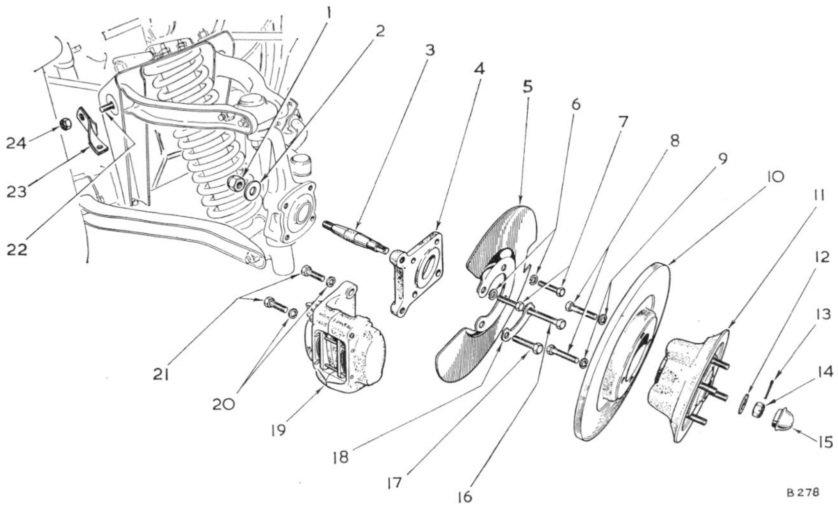

1 Nyloc nut	9 Spring washers	17 Bolt
2 Washer	10 Disc	18 Lock plate
3 Stub axle	11 Hub	19 Caliper assembly
4 Caliper mounting bracket	12 Washer	20 Spring washer
5 Disc shield	13 Split pin	21 Bolts
6 Spring washers	14 Slotted nut	22 Bolt
7 Bolts	15 Cap	23 Bracket
8 Bolts	16 Bolt	24 Nyloc nut

Fig. 12. Exploded disc brake components

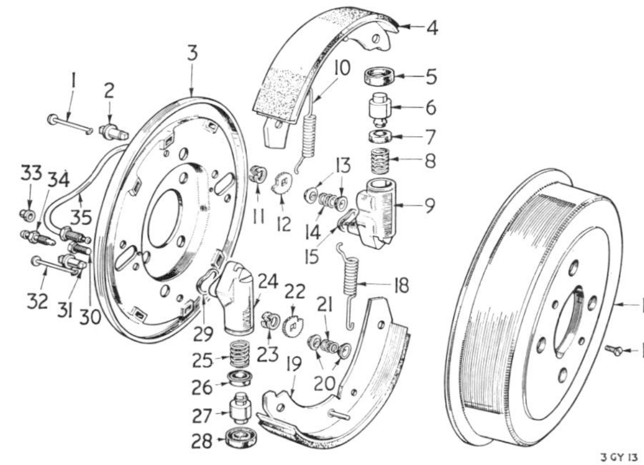

1 Steady pin	18 Return spring
2 Adjuster shank	19 Brake shoe
3 Backplate	20 Steady pin cups
4 Brake shoe	21 Spring
5 Dust excluder	22 Adjuster cam
6 Piston	23 Spring
7 Seal	24 Wheel cylinder
8 Spring	25 Spring
9 Wheel cylinder	26 Seal
10 Return spring	27 Piston
11 Spring	28 Dust excluder
12 Adjuster cam	29 Seal
13 Steady pin cups	30 Screw
14 Spring	31 Adjuster shank
15 Seal	32 Steady pin
16 Brake drum	33 Dust cap
17 Countersunk screw	34 Bleed screw
	35 Bridge pipe

Fig. 13. Exploded front brake assembly (L.H. side)

Fig. 14.

Arrangement of brake shoes and pull-off springs (front right-hand side)

Fig. 15.

Front drum brake shoe adjusters

DRUM BRAKES

Front Brake Shoes (HERALD 1200 ONLY)

To Remove

Jack up the front of the car and place it on chassis stands. Remove the nave plate, road wheel, and turn both adjusters anti-clockwise to the off position.

Remove the brake drum (16), release the anchor pins (1), cups (13) and springs (14).

Detach the return springs (10) and (18) by lifting the shoes (4) and (19) from their abutments.

Manoeuvre the shoes and springs clear of the backplate (3) ensuring that the lower piston (27) does not fall from its cylinder.

Secure the piston in position with a rubber band, wire or string.

Re-Assembly

Apply white grease sparingly to the adjuster cam faces and shoe ends. Do not contaminate the linings with grease.

Assemble the shoes, pull-off springs and shoe anchor pins to the backplate, and remove the rubber band retaining the lower piston.

Refit the brake drum, adjust the brake as follows :—

Adjustment

Each front brake has two adjusters. Operating each adjuster separately, turn it fully clockwise to lock, and turn it back by single notch increments until the drum is free to rotate.

Refit the road wheel, remove the chassis stands, tighten the wheel nuts and refit the nave plate.

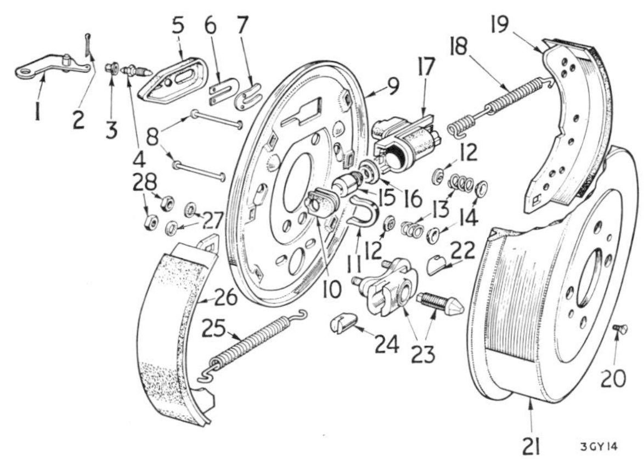

1 Handbrake lever
2 Split pin
3 Dust cap
4 Bleed nipple
5 Dust excluder
6 Retaining clip
7 Retaining clip
8 Steady pins
9 Backplate
10 Dust excluder
11 Clip
12 Steady pin cups
13 Springs
14 Steady pin cups
15 Piston
16 Seal
17 Wheel cylinder
18 Return spring
19 Brake shoe
20 Countersunk screw
21 Brake drum
22 Adjuster tappet
23 Adjuster wedge and body
24 Adjuster tappet
25 Return spring
26 Brake shoe
27 Shakeproof washers
28 Nuts

Fig. 16. Exploded rear brake assembly (L.H. side)

Rear Brake Shoes (All Models)

To Remove

Jack up the rear of the car and place it on chassis stands. Remove the nave plate, road wheel, brake drum and turn the adjuster anti-clockwise to the off position.

Withdraw the split pin (2), release the anchor pins (8), cups (12) and (14) and springs (13).

Detach the return springs (18) and (25) by lifting the shoes out of their abutments, disengaging the front shoe from the handbrake lever, and manoeuvring the shoes until the tension of the return springs is released.

Re-Assembly

Lightly smear the shoe steady posts and the ends of the shoe webs with white (zinc base) grease, taking care not to contaminate the linings.

Assemble the springs to the shoes, as shown on Fig. 17, engage the front shoe with its abutments, ensuring that the handbrake lever enters the slotted shoe web ; then manoeuvre the rear shoe into position.

Fit a new split pin (2) to the handbrake lever (1).

Refit the brake drum and adjust the shoe clearances as follows :—

Adjustment

Each rear wheel brake is provided with one adjuster which is turned fully clockwise to lock. Turn the adjuster anti-clockwise by single notch increments until the drum is free to rotate.

Refit the road wheel, remove the chassis stands, tighten the wheel nuts and refit the nave plate.

Fig. 17.

Arrangement of brake shoes and pull-off springs (rear right-hand side)

Fig. 18.

Rear brake shoe adjuster

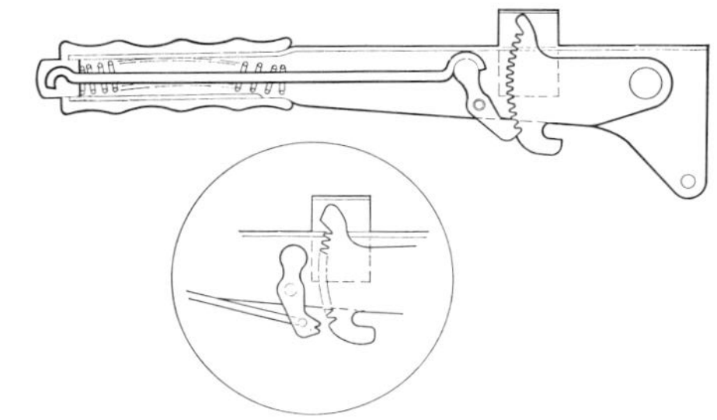

Fig. 20. Arrangement of Herald 1200, 12/50 and Vitesse handbrake lever ratchet and pawl. Inset shows Spitfire arrangement

Fig. 21. Primary cable adjuster

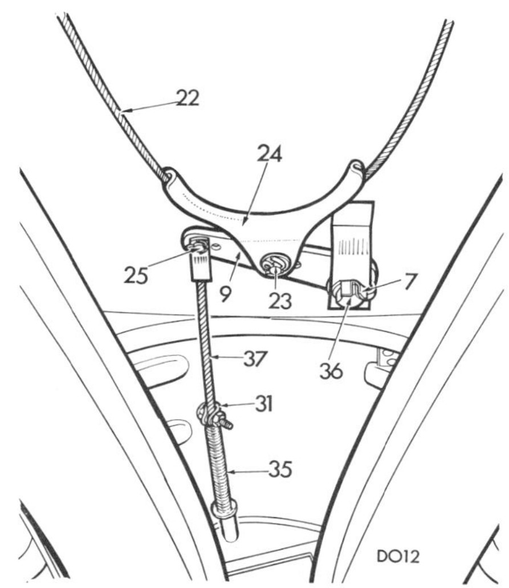

Fig. 22. Handbrake relay lever and compensator

HANDBRAKE MECHANISM

Handbrake Lever
To Remove and Dismantle

Remove the front seats and the centre carpet. Take out four screws to release the combined cover/gaiter and manoeuvre it clear of the handbrake lever.

Release the handlever by removing the circlip (2), washer (3), pivot pin (6) and the clevis pin (41). Take out the ratchet (44) and withdraw the pawl release rod (1), spring (46) and pawl (45).

To Re-Assemble and Refit

Reverse the foregoing procedures.

Primary Cable
To Remove

Take out the pivot pin (6), lift the handlever from its bracket and withdraw the clevis pin (41).

Unscrew the clevis fork (40) and pull the free end of the cable through the floor. Withdraw the clevis pin (25) and remove the clamp (31) from the cable.

To Refit

Reverse the removal procedure and, with the handlever in the off position, adjust the cable to position the relay as shown on Fig. 25.

Moving the clamp (31) against the spring (35), compress the spring approximately 1″ (25·4 mm.) and tighten the clamp. Ensure that the spring does not become coil bound when the handbrake is fully applied.

Relay Lever
To Remove

Take out the clevis pin (25), unscrew the pivot bolt (36) and withdraw the relay clear of the propeller shaft. Remove the clevis pin (23) and, if necessary, renew the bearing (10).

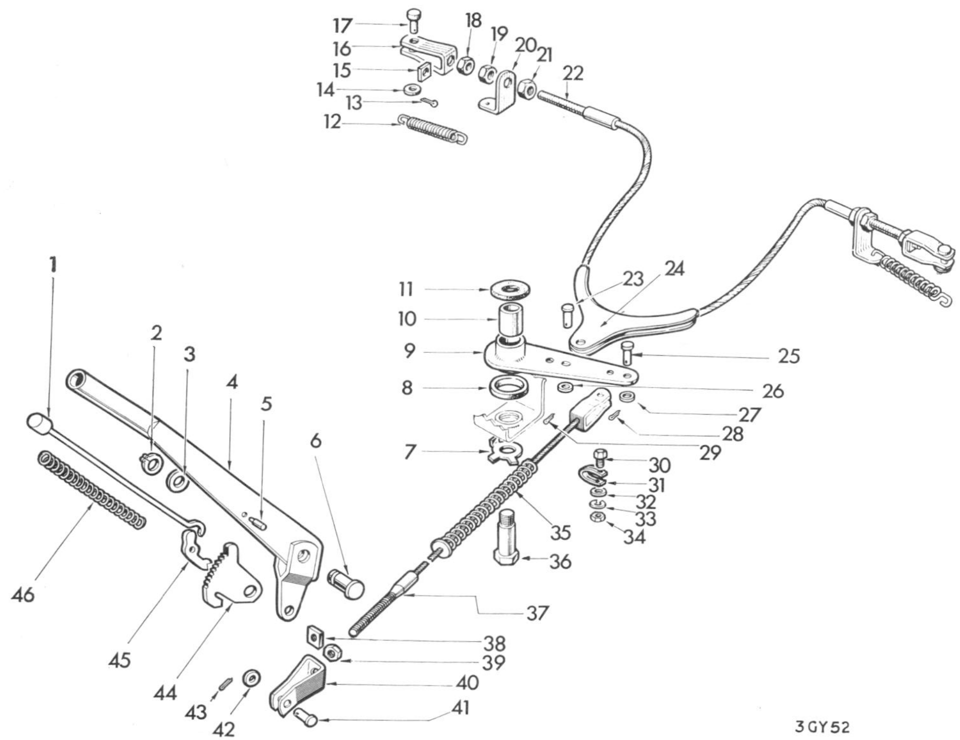

1 Pawl release rod
2 Circlip
3 Plain washer
4 Handbrake lever
5 Pawl pivot pin
6 Pivot pin
7 Lock plate
8 Rubber seal
9 Relay lever
10 Bush
11 Felt seal
12 Pull-off spring
13 Split pin
14 Plain washer
15 Square nut
16 Clevis
17 Clevis pin
18 Locknut
19 Adjusting nut
20 Adjustable spring anchor
21 Locknut
22 Secondary cable
23 Clevis pin
24 Compensator sector
25 Clevis pin
26 Plain washer
27 Plain washer
28 Split pin
29 Split pin
30 Clamp bolt
31 Clamp
32 Plain washer
33 Spring washer
34 Nut
35 Spring
36 Pivot bolt
37 Primary cable
38 Square nut
39 Locknut
40 Clevis
41 Clevis pin
42 Plain washer
43 Split pin
44 Ratchet
45 Pawl
46 Pawl spring

Fig. 19. Arrangement of Handbrake components

To Refit

Insert the clevis pin (23), securing the compensator sector (24) to the relay lever (9), and fit plain washer (26) and split pin (29).

Attach the primary cable clevis fork to the outer hole of the relay lever (9). Smear the relay lever bush (10) and the pivot bolt (36) with grease, and assemble the lever to the body floor bracket, placing the felt seal (11) above the lever and the rubber seal (8) below, as shown on Fig. 19.

Insert the pivot bolt (36) with its tab washer (7) through the relay lever and floor bracket. Tighten the bolt and lock with the tab washer.

Secondary Cable

To Remove

Release the cable "pull-off" springs (12) from the cable brackets (20) and remove the clevis pins (17).

Release the tab washer (7), remove the pivot bolt (36), lower the relay lever (9) and remove the clevis pin (23).

Lift off the compensating sector (24) and remove the cable by pulling it through the curved guides shown on Fig. 24.

To Refit

Feed the threaded ends of the cable through the left- and right-hand guides.

Assemble the compensating sector (24) over the cable and secure it to the relay lever (9) with the clevis pin (23). Refit the relay lever.

Whilst the cable is still slack, apply grease liberally to the cable guides and compensator sector, working the cable backwards and forwards to distribute the grease.

Re-assemble and connect both ends of the cable to the brake levers as shown on Fig. 23.

Handbrake Adjustment

Under normal circumstances, adjustment of the rear brakes will automatically provide satisfactory handbrake adjustment. Stretched cables will necessitate further adjustment as follows:—

1. Jack up the rear wheels, release the handbrake and lock the brake drums by screwing each brake adjuster fully in.
2. Disconnect the pull-off spring (12) and remove the clevis pin (17) from the brake lever.
3. Adjust the clevis (16) at each end of the cable by equal amounts to reduce the cable slackness. The cables are too tight if the clevis pins cannot be easily inserted without straining the cables.
   Secure the clevis pins, re-connect the spring (12) and readjust the cable brackets (20) to provide slight spring tension. Turn each rear brake adjuster back by one notch increments until the wheels are free to rotate. Lower the vehicle and remove the jack.

Fig. 23. Handbrake secondary cable arrangement

Fig. 24. Secondary cable guides

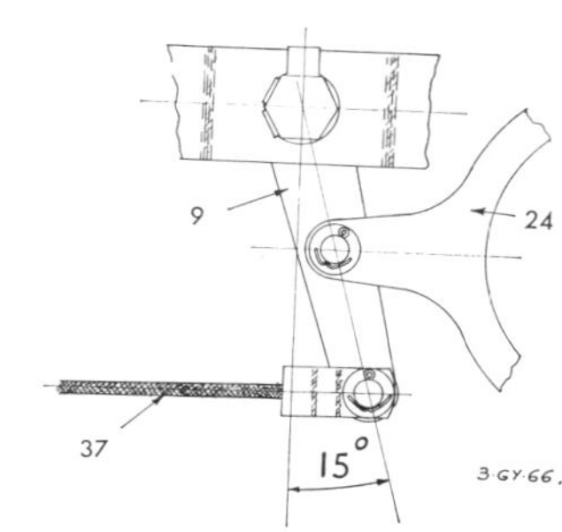

Fig. 25. Showing the correct angular position of the relay lever when the brakes are released

Fig. 26. Removing retaining plate from rear wheel cylinder

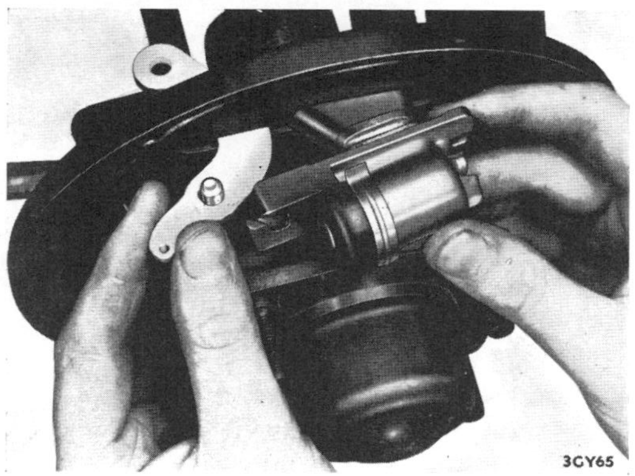

Fig. 27. Removing rear wheel cylinder

Fig. 28 Churchill brake efficiency recorder

FRONT WHEEL CYLINDERS

Removal

1. Drain the hydraulic system through the brake bleed nipple, and remove the brake shoes.
2. Disconnect the flexible brake hose from the steel pipe and its support bracket. Unscrew the hose from the cylinder.
3. Detach the bridge pipe from the two wheel cylinders, remove the setscrews and withdraw the cylinders from the backplate.

To Refit

Reverse the removal procedure, adjust the brakes and bleed the hydraulic system.

REAR WHEEL CYLINDERS

Removal

1. Repeat operations 1 and 2 above.
2. Disconnect the handbrake cable clevis from its lever.
3. Remove the dust excluder, retaining plate and spring clip, and withdraw the cylinder from the backplate.

To Refit

Reverse the above procedure.

TO RENEW PISTON SEALS

1. Remove the rubber dust excluder and withdraw the piston.
2. Remove the old seal from the piston and, using fingers only, fit the new seal with its lip towards the bottom of the cylinder.
3. Lubricate the seal with hydraulic fluid, fit the piston into the cylinder and refit the dust excluder.

TANDEM BRAKING SYSTEM (Spitfire Mk. 3 U.S.A.)

Hydraulic System
Description

The foot operated hydraulic braking system employs a tandem master cylinder for transmitting pressure to independent front and rear braking systems. Both systems are connected to opposing sides of a pressure differential warning actuator (P.D.W.A.) which operates an electrical switch when a pressure drop on one side of the valve causes a shuttle to move from its mid-position. The P.D.W.A. switch operates a warning light on the facia which is series/parallel connected with the oil warning light. Thus when the brakes are working correctly, the brake warning light and the oil warning light are both extinguished as the engine speed is increased from idle (giving regular assurance that the brake warning light is functioning). In the event of a partial brake failure the brake warning system is earthed directly, causing the warning light to glow brightly.

Bleeding the Hydraulic Braking System
General

If air has entered either of the hydraulic braking systems then only the system affected need be bled. During bleeding, exercise care, as described in the following procedure, to avoid moving the shuttle from its mid-position. However, if the shuttle has moved during bleeding or subsequent to a fault condition, centralise the shuttle by performing operations 5 to 9 below.

Preparation for Bleeding

Before commencing to bleed the brakes ensure that all the bleed nipples are clean, and, taking care to avoid dirt entering the fluid reservoir, remove its filler cap and top-up with new hydraulic fluid. During the bleeding operation keep the level of fluid above the dividing partition in the reservoir. Do not use fluid bled from the system for topping-up.

Use new fluid from a sealed container, resealing the container after use.

Procedure

Commence with the brake, of the pair being bled, farthest from the master cylinder. If both systems are to be bled, bleed the rear brakes first. When bleeding the rear brakes, release the handbrake and turn the brake adjusters to lock the shoes against the drums. When the bleeding is completed adjust the brakes as detailed on page 3·209.

1. Attach a rubber tube of approx. ¼″ (6 mm.) bore to the brake bleed nipple allowing the other end of the tube to hang submerged in a jar containing a quantity of clean brake fluid.
2. Unscrew the bleed-screw enough to allow the fluid to be pumped out (half a turn is normally sufficient).
3. Depress the brake pedal and allow it to return slowly noting that only a LIGHT pedal effort is required and the pedal must NOT be pushed through the end of the stroke. (In addition, never "try" the pedal until all air has been dispelled and the system is fully bled, as either action will cause the shuttle to move and actuate the switch.) Pausing between each depression of the pedal, continue pumping until all air has been dispelled from the bleed-screw (denoted by the absence of bubbles in the fluid being pumped into the jar).
4. With the pedal depressed, close the bleed-screw nipple and repeat the operation on the other brake.

Procedure for Re-centralising the P.D.W.A. Piston

If, for reasons described above, the P.D.W.A. shuttle requires to be re-centralised, adopt the following procedure.

5. Fit a rubber tube, as described in 1 above, to a brake bleed-screw at the opposite end of the car to that which has just been bled.
6. Open the bleed-screw.
7. Switch the ignition on but DO NOT START THE ENGINE. (The brake warning light will glow but the oil warning light will remain extinguished.)
8. Exert a steady pressure on the brake pedal until the brake light dims and the oil light glows (A click should be felt on the pedal as the shuttle returns to its mid-position.)
9. Tighten the bleed screw.
   NOTE: If the pedal has been pushed too hard the shuttle will move to the other side of the valve, thus requiring the procedure to be repeated on a brake at the opposite end of the car.

MASTER CYLINDER

General

The Spitfire Mk. 3 (U.S.A.) employs a tandem master cylinder which consists of two independent and complete hydraulic cylinders in series, one operating on the front brakes and the other on the rear. Both cylinders are supplied by a common reservoir divided by a partition.

Different tandem master cylinders have varying volume ratios (70-30 to 50-50) it is, therefore, of paramount importance to use only the correct replacement parts or cylinders.

Operation of the T.V. C.V. Master Cylinder (Fig. 27)

Application of pressure on the push rod moves the primary plunger up the cylinder bore and allows a spring loaded tipping valve to return to centre. The primary supply port is closed by the valve and further movement of the primary plunger results in hydraulic pressure being transmitted to the wheel cylinders of the front brakes. At the same time the pressure created acts in conjunction with the increasing force of the intermediate spring to overcome the stronger secondary spring, thus actuating the secondary plunger.

Initial movement of the secondary plunger closes off the centre valve supply port and the hydraulic pressure is transmitted to the wheel cylinders of the rear brakes.

In case of failure of either chamber or circuit, mechanical contact takes place within the cylinders and the remaining chamber builds up the normal pressure to operate the brakes that it controls.

Regular Maintenance

Every week check the level of fluid in the brake master cylinder reservoir. The fluid level is visible through the translucent casing of the reservoir, **do not remove the cap.** A gradual lowering of the level over a long period is caused by brake pad wear and does not require topping-up. A sudden appreciable drop in the level must be investigated, the cause ascertained and rectified immediately.

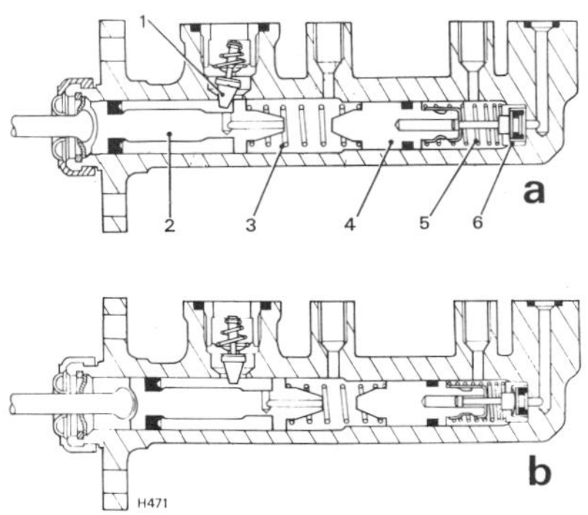

1	Tipping valve	5	Secondary spring
2	Primary plunger	6	Centre valve
3	Intermediate spring	a	Brake off
4	Secondary plunger	b	Brake applied

Fig. 27. Operation of the master cylinder

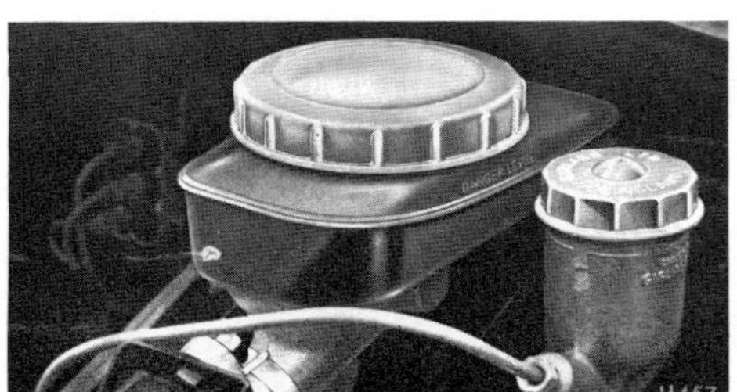

Fig. 28. Showing the danger line on the side of the master cylinder

Do not allow the level to drop below the danger line on the side of the casing (see Fig. 28).

To avoid dirt entering the system ensure that the reservoir is clean externally before removing the cap. Use only new fluid from a sealed container and re-seal the container after use. Replace the reservoir cap immediately after filling.

Removing

1. Detach both fluid pipes from the cylinder body, plug the open ports of the master cylinder to prevent fluid draining onto the paintwork.
2. Withdraw the rubber dust cover to expose the master cylinder push rod and clevis pin.
3. Remove the clevis pin, secured by a split pin, attaching the push rod to the brake pedal.
4. Remove the bolts attaching the master cylinder to the bulkhead and lift off the unit.

Dismantling (Fig. 31)

IMPORTANT: Before carrying out work on the brake master cylinder, see "General" on page 3·213.

1. Drain and discard the master cylinder fluid.
2. Remove four screws (12) attaching the reservoir to the cylinder body.
3. Depress the push rod (11), remove the circlip (10) and withdraw the push rod together with abutment plate (9) and circlip (10).
4. With an Allen key unscrew the tipping valve securing nut (5) and remove the seal (7).
5. Depress the primary plunger and remove the tipping valve (6).
6. Remove the internal parts either by applying low air pressure to the end inlet orifice or by shaking the cylinder body.
7. Separate the plunger and intermediate spring.
8. Lift the leaf spring of the spring retainer (insert Fig. 31) and remove the spring and centre valve sub-assembly from the secondary plunger (16).
9. Remove the spring (19), valve spacer (20) and spring washer (21) from the valve stem (22), and remove the valve seal (23) from the valve head.
10. Remove the seals from the primary (14) and secondary (16) plungers.
11. Lever out the baffle (2) and remove the cap washer (3) from the filler cap.

Cleaning Examination

Replace all seals with those contained in the service kit. Clean all the remaining parts and the cylinder thoroughly with hydraulic cleaning fluid.

Examine the bore of the cylinder and the plunger for visible score marks, ridges or corrosion. The slightest imperfection of the bore will necessitate the fitting of a new master cylinder.

Assembling

Prior to assembly lubricate all parts with new hydraulic fluid.

1. Assemble the seals to the primary and secondary plungers.
2. Referring to inset on Fig. 31, fit the valve seal (23) smallest diameter leading, on to the valve head (22).
3. Position the spring washer (21) on the valve stem so that it 'flares' away from the valve stem shoulder and follow with the valve spacer (20), legs first.
4. Attach the spring retainer (18) to the valve stem, keyhole first.
5. Slide the secondary spring (19) over the spring retainer, then position the sub-assembly on the secondary plunger (16).
6. The spring must now be compressed whilst the leaf of the spring retainer is pressed down behind the head of the plunger. To do this, position the sub-assembly between the jaws of a bench vice and, to prevent possible contamination, place a clean piece of paper between each end of the sub-assembly and the vice jaws (Fig. 29). Close the vice to compress the spring until it is almost coil bound. Use a small screwdriver to press the spring retainer right back against the secondary plunger (Fig. 29). Using a pair of pointed nose pliers (Fig. 30), depress the leaf of the spring retainer behind the head of the plunger. Ensure that the retainer leaf is straight and firmly located behind the plunger head as shown on Fig. 31 inset.
7. Fit the intermediate spring (19) into position between the primary and secondary plunger.
8. Lubricate the cylinder bore and plunger seals with hydraulic brake fluid.
9. Insert the plunger assemblies into the bore, valve-end leading, easing the entrance of the plunger seals.
10. Press the primary plunger down the bore and fit the tipping valve, securing nut and seal. Tighten to a torque of 35 to 40 lb/ft.
11. Fit the cap washer and baffle to filler cap. Screw the cap on the reservoir.
12. Fit the reservoir seals (24 and 7), position the reservoir on the cylinder and secure with the retaining screws.
13. Fit the push rod (11) with the abutment plate (9) and circlip.

Refitting

Refitting is the reversal of removing, ensure that the fluid pipes are securely tightened. Bleed the system as described on page 3·213.

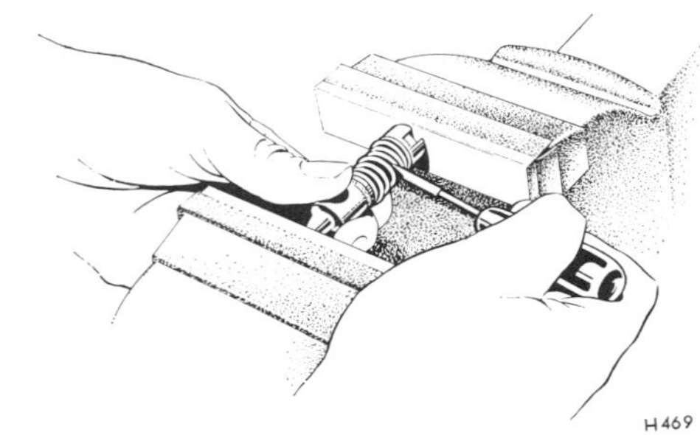

Fig. 29. Pressing the spring retainer back against the secondary plunger

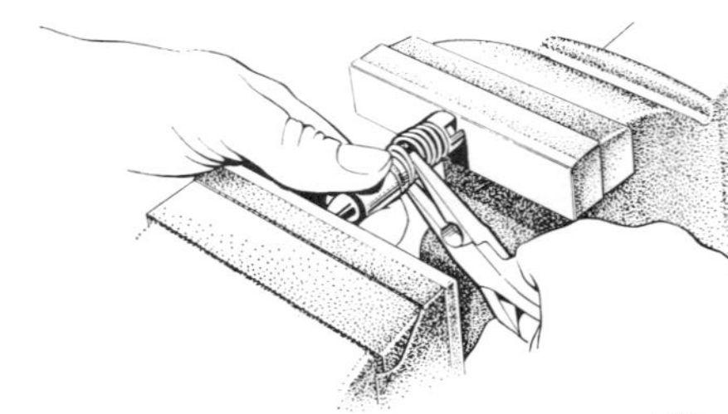

Fig. 30. Depressing the leaf of the spring retainer behind the head of the plunger

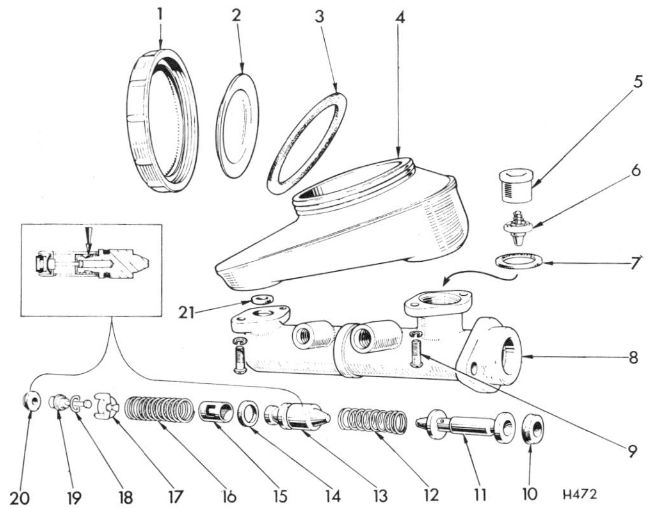

1 Cap	12 Intermediate spring
2 Baffle plate	13 Secondary plunger
3 Seal	14 Seal
4 Reservoir	15 Spring retainer
5 Tipping valve securing nut	16 Secondary spring
6 Tipping valve	17 Valve spacer
7 Seal reservoir to body	18 Spring washer
8 Body	19 Valve
9 Screw—reservoir to body	20 Seal
10 Seal	21 Seal—reservoir to body
11 Primary plunger	

Fig. 31. Exploded view of master cylinder

PRESSURE DIFFERENTIAL WARNING ACTUATOR (P.D.W.A.)

General

The P.D.W.A. is an 'inline' hydraulic valve through which both brake fluid lines are routed. The purpose of the device is to detect failure in either of the systems and to transmit, electrically, warning of the failure to a light on the facia.

From Fig. 32 it will be appreciated that the shuttle valve (2 and 5) is held in mid-position in the body by equalised pressure in the fluid lines; the switch is in contact with a peripheral groove in the shuttle valve. Lack of pressure in either line allows the pressure in the other line to displace the shuttle and force the plunger to actuate the switch.

For ease of assembly the shuttle valve is made in two parts.

Removing and Refitting

1. Remove the electrical connection.
2. Disconnect the two inlet and two outlet pipes, plug all inlet and outlet ports to prevent loss of fluid and ingress of dirt to the system.
3. Remove the bolt securing the P.D.W.A. to the bulkhead and lift off the unit.

Refitting is a reversal of removing: ensure that all connections are securely tightened before bleeding and, if necessary, recentralise the P.D.W.A. as described on page 3·213.

After bleeding check for fluid leaks with the pedal fully depressed and with the system at rest.

Dismantling (Fig. 32)

1. Remove the unit from the vehicle.
2. Remove the end plugs (4 and 7) from the unit and discard the copper washers (1).
3. Remove the nylon switch (8 or 10), double pin switches use a ball (9) as an actuating plunger, collect it.
4. Carefully push out the valves taking care not to damage the bore.
5. Remove the seals (3 and 6) taking care not to score the shuttle valves.

Examination

Replace the seals and copper washers with new parts from a Girling Service Kit.

Thoroughly clean the remaining parts in clean brake fluid. Dry the parts thoroughly and inspect the bore of the body and the shuttle valves for scoring or imperfections. The unit must be replaced if these items are found defective.

To test the nylon switch assembly, reconnect the warning light circuit and actuate the plunger at the base of the switch by pressing it against the earthed frame of the vehicle.

Re-assembling

1. Lubricate the valve pistons, seals and bore with unused brake fluid.
2. Using the fingers only, fit the new seals onto the pistons with the lips facing outwards, i.e., facing the slots in the end of the valve pistons.
3. Insert the longer piston (5) into the bore (slotted end outermost) until the radiused groove is opposite the switch plunger aperture. Insert the ball (where fitted) and screw in the switch plunger, tightening to a torque of 2 to 2·5 lb/ft. Ensure that the piston seals are never pushed across the central aperture in the valve body as this will damage the seals and require them to be replaced.
4. Insert the shorter piston into the bore (slotted end outermost).
5. Ensuring that the seating faces on the body and plugs are clean and undamaged, fit new copper washers and screw in the plugs, tightening to a torque of 16 to 20 lb/ft.
6. Refit the unit to the vehicle as detailed above.

1 Copper gasket
2 Piston (short)
3 Seal
4 End plug
5 Piston (long)
6 Seal
7 End plug
8 Switch—single pin
9 Ball—double pin
10 Switch—double pin

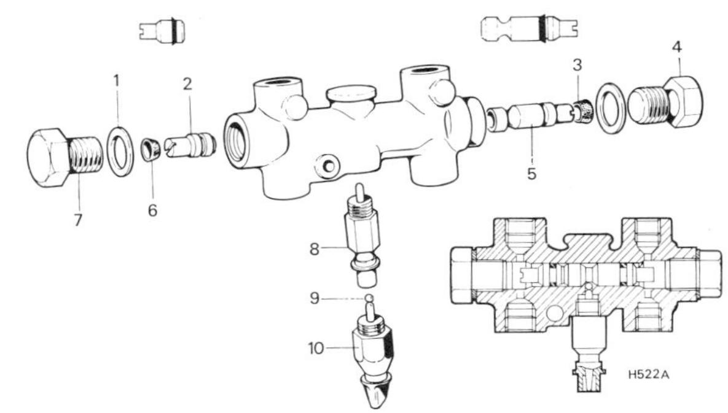

Fig. 32. Pressure differential warning actuator exploded view

MODEL			HERALD 1200, 12/50, 13/60 Convertible/ Coupé/Saloon		HERALD 1200, 13/60 Estate Car		VITESSE Convertible/ Saloon		COURIER VAN		SPITFIRE			
WHEEL RIM			3½D		4½J		4½J		4½J		3½D DISC or 4½J WIRE WHEEL			
TYRE SIZE			5·20 × 13 in.		5·60 × 13 in.		5·60 × 13 in.		5·60 × 13 in.		5·20S × 13 in. or 145SR × 13 in. CROSS-PLY		RADIAL-PLY	
PRESSURES			lb/in.²	kg/cm.²	lb/in.²	kg/cm.²	lb/in.²	kg/cm.²	lb/in.²	kg/cm.²	lb/in.²	kg/cm.²	lb/in.²	kg/cm.²
	2 UP	Front	21	1·48	21	1·48	22	1·55	15	1·06	18	1·26	21	1·48
		Rear	24	1·7	25	1·75	24	1·7	25	1·76	24	1·7	26	1·83
	4 UP	Front	21	1·48	21	1·48	22	1·55	—	—	—	—	—	—
		Rear	28	1·97	30	2·1	26	1·83	—	—	—	—	—	—

COURIER VAN PRESSURES	SEMI LADEN				FULLY LADEN (4 Ply Tyres)				FULLY LADEN (6 Ply Tyres)			
	FRONT		REAR		FRONT		REAR		FRONT		REAR	
	lb/in.²	kg/cm.²	lb/in.²	kg/cm.²	lb/in.²	kg/cm.²	lb/in.²	kg/cm.²	lb/in.²	kg/cm.²	lb/in.²	kg/cm.²
	15	1·06	25	1·76	15	1·06	32	2·25	15	1·06	36	2·53

NOTE. All Models. The maintenance of the pressure differential between front and rear tyres is essential for correct steering behaviour

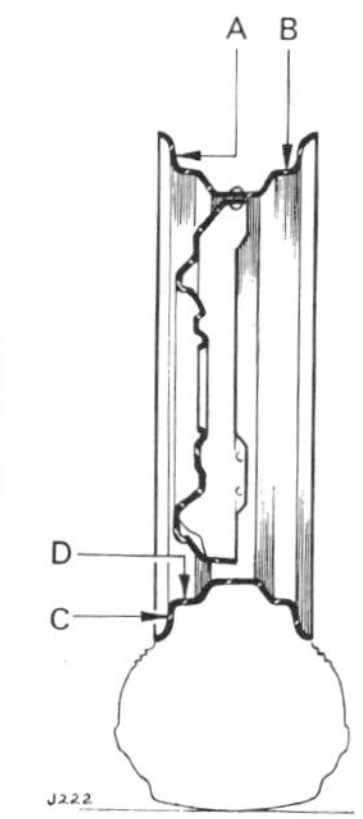

Fig. 1.
Measure lateral wobble at A without tyre or C with tyre. Measure radial lift at B without tyre, D with tyre

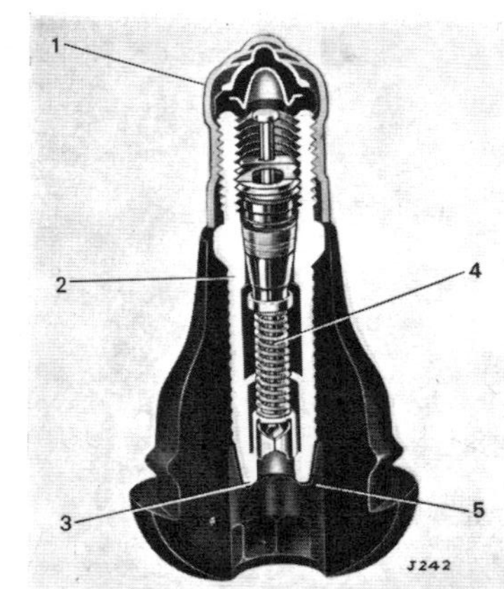

1 Cap with doubly reinforced swivel seal
2 Solid brass insert; rubber covered
3 Rounded and free insert end
4 Interchangeable valve core
5 Free-floating, tapering insert giving "ball and socket" action

Fig. 2. Tubeless tyre valve

WHEELS AND TYRES

General

The wheels and tyres, their correct types and pressures, are an integral part of a vehicle's design. Thus the regular maintenance of the tyres contributes not only to the safety but to the designed functioning of the vehicle, as road holding, steering and braking are especially vulnerable to the use of incorrectly pressurised, badly fitted or worn tyres.

Radial-ply and Cross-ply tyres

It is both dangerous and, in the U.K., illegal to use, on the public roads, a vehicle fitted with unsuitable combinations of tyres. The following recommendations should therefore be observed.

1. Do not mix radial-ply and cross-ply tyres on the same axle.
2. Do not fit radial-ply tyres to the front wheels and cross-ply tyres to the rear wheels.
3. With suitable tyre pressure adjustments it may be possible to obtain acceptable handling with cross-ply tyres on the front wheels and radial-ply tyres on the rear wheels, but this combination is not recommended.

Winter Tyres

Winter tyres are designed primarily to give improved traction and braking in mud and snow. Their performance on hard surfaces may, however, be inferior to normal road tyres and extra care is required when using them under normal conditions.

Wheel Tolerances

The tolerances for wheel construction laid down by the Society of Motor Manufacturers and Traders are as follows:

A. **Wobble,** i.e., the lateral variation, measured on the vertical inside face of the flange (point A, Fig. 1): Not to exceed
   Disc wheels — 0·07 in. (1·78 mm.)
   Wire wheels — 0·05 in. (1·27 mm.)

B. **Lift,** i.e., the difference between the high and low points of a rotating wheel measured at any point on either bead seat (point B, Fig. 1): Not to exceed
   Disc wheels — 0·07 in. (1·78 mm.)
   Wire wheels — 0·05 in. (1·27 mm.)

Measurements A and B above should be used when the tyre is removed, points C and D may be used when the tyre is fitted.

Lateral and radial inaccuracies outside these limits contribute dynamic and radial unbalance respectively.

Severe eccentricity intermittently increases the load on the tyre and results in irregular wear. Static and dynamic balancing will not rectify this condition and a new wheel must be fitted.

Valve

Whenever a new tubeless tyre is fitted it is essential to fit a new Schrader snap-in valve, part number 414—Rim Hole Dia. ·453″ (11·41 mm.) as shown on Fig. 2. Before fitting, the valve should be lubricated with a soap solution. The lever mounting tool, part number 992, is screwed on to the valve thread, as shown in Fig. 3, and the notched handle locates on the wheel rim to provide leverage and assistance in aligning the valve.

Tyre Care

Check at frequent intervals that the tyre pressures are correct.

Ensure that the tyres are cold when checking the pressures. Never bleed air out of a warm tyre in order to achieve the recommended pressure, since when the tyre cools it will be under-inflated.

If oil or grease have been in contact with a tyre wipe the affected area with a cloth lightly moistened with petrol or trichlorethylene. Remove any flints or road debris from the tyre tread as soon as possible as these tend to accelerate tyre wear.

Puncture Repair

The use of the 'plug' type repair should be reserved for emergency only, the tyre should then be repaired by a garage or tyre specialist as soon as possible to effect a permanent repair.

Wheel Alignment

Settings for front and rear wheel alignment are given in Group 4. Excessive misalignment caused by kerb impact or other accidental damage will result in severe tyre wear and faulty steering.

Pressed Steel Wheel Maintenance

Ensure that the bead seats and flange faces are kept free from rust and dirt and that wheels having damaged or elongated stud holes are replaced.

Locally damaged flanges may be corrected by careful hammering, but a buckled wheel, i.e., one which no longer conforms to the tolerances quoted, must be replaced.

Changing Pressed Steel Wheels

1. Firmly apply the handbrake and chock the wheel diagonally opposite the one being lifted.
2. Remove the spare wheel from the luggage compartment and make sure that its tyre pressure is correct.
3. To prevent damage, insert the lever (Fig. 4) into the slot formed on the inner periphery of the wheel trim, behind the nave plate. Twist the lever to remove the nave plate, lift off the wheel trim and loosen the wheel nuts one turn.

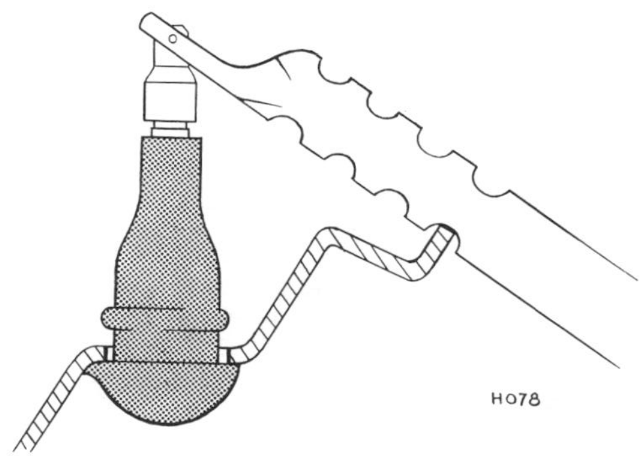

Fig. 3. Inserting a new valve

Fig. 4. Removing nave plate and wheel trim

Fig. 5. Locating wheel jack

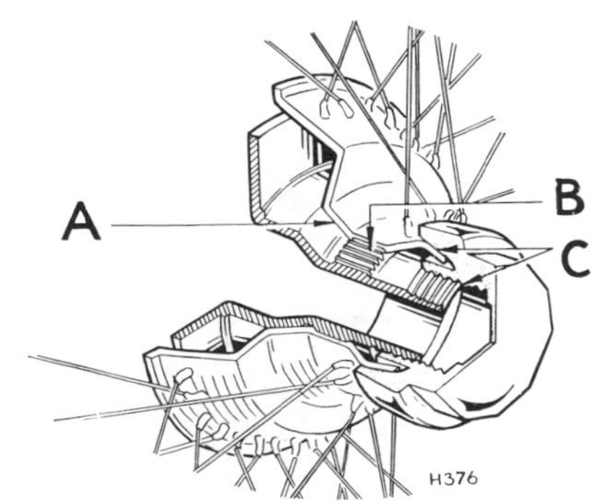

Fig. 6. Tightening hub nuts

4. Place the jack in position and lift the wheel clear of the ground. Should it be necessary to lift the vehicle whilst it is on sloping ground, exercise the greatest care.
5. Completely remove the wheel nuts, exchange the road wheels and replace the nuts.
6. Lower the jack and give the wheel nuts a final tighten. Refit the wheel trim and secure the nave plate by placing its edge over the wheel projections and giving the plate a sharp tap with the hand to spring it into position.

Changing Wire Spoked Wheels

A soft faced hammer and special wheel nut spanner are provided with vehicles equipped with wire spoked wheels to facilitate wheel nut removal. Turn the wheel nuts on the right-hand side of the car clockwise and the wheel nuts on the left-hand side of the car anti-clockwise to remove them. Detach the wheels by pulling them from the splined hubs.

Examination of Wheels and Adaptors

Before fitting the wheels to the vehicle refer to Fig. 6 and check that the following are clean and undamaged:

A. Wheel hub inner taper and mating adaptor taper.
B. Wheel hub and adaptor splines.
C. Screw threads, wheel hub outer taper and wheel nut taper.

It is particularly important to ensure that areas B and C are not contaminated with paint.

Burrs and bruising on the tapered face will prevent correct seating of the retaining nut. Such damage should be carefully dressed. The wheels should always be handled carefully and not carelessly set down on the tapered face. (NOTE: Should the wheels be stored for a period, they should be suitably protected against corrosion and the risk of damage.)

Failure to observe these precautions, can result in the tapered faces binding, causing premature tightening of the nut against the wheel outer taper but failing to clamp the wheel against the inner adaptor taper. Such a condition would prevent the wheel from seating correctly and lead to damaged splines and subsequent loss of drive.

It is most important that the splined hub adaptors are fitted to the correct side of the vehicle. The left-hand threaded adaptors are fitted to the right-hand side of the vehicle and the right-hand threaded adaptors to the left-hand side of the vehicle as viewed from the driver's seat.

WARNING: Should the adaptors be fitted to the wrong sides of the vehicle, the wheel retaining nuts are liable to work loose, thereby causing serious damage and possibly endangering life. Wheel nuts used to retain "Pressed Steel Wheels" are unsuitable for securing the splined adaptors. Adaptor retaining nuts are torque tightened to 45 lb/ft. (6·2 kg/m.).

To Refit the Wheels

Examine the wheels and adaptors as described opposite and liberally coat areas A, B and C with special P.B.C. grease.

Note. P.B.C. grease is obtainable from Triumph dealers under the following part numbers:

1 oz. (28 grm.) Tube Part Number 153245
4½ oz. (127 grm.) Tube Part Number 153317

Slide the wheel on to the adaptor and pushing against the wheel hub centre to maintain concentric location, simultaneously screw on the retaining nut by hand until the wheel is felt to seat on the adaptor taper.

RESTRAINING THE WHEEL WITH ONE HAND, CONTINUE TO TIGHTEN THE WHEEL WITH A SPANNER. GRIP TYRE AT DIAMETRICALLY OPPOSITE AREAS OF ITS CIRCUMFERENCE AND ATTEMPT TO ROCK THE WHEEL ON ITS ADAPTOR. IF FREE PLAY (OTHER THAN THAT DUE TO HUB BEARING CLEARANCE) IS APPARENT, RELEASE CENTRE LOCK NUT AND RE-TIGHTEN WHILST PUSHING WHEEL ONTO ADAPTOR.

Lower the wheel to the ground and finally tighten (Fig. 8).

Check that each wheel retaining nut tightens in the opposite direction to the wheel rotation. The foregoing instructions apply each time a wheel is removed and replaced.

Maintenance

When the wheels are built the spokes are tightened to a pre-determined torque loading. A wheel should maintain this torque loading throughout its life and spoke tightening should be unnecessary. If, however, a wheel sustains damage, as, for example, from curb impact, looseness of spokes may result.

If a wheel is used in this condition additional loading is imposed on other spokes in the assembly, with the result that these in turn will also become loose. This condition would permit the wheel to distort and result in increased tyre wear. It is, therefore, recommended that wheels be checked periodically and loose spokes tightened. This will necessitate removing the tyre and tube and filing the spoke ends flush with the retaining nipples.

Unless trained personnel and wheel equipment are available, such work should be entrusted to specialists.

Fig. 7. Wire wheel adaptor nuts

Fig. 8. Wire wheel nut tapers

Fig. 9. Tyre wear resulting from under-inflation

Under-inflation causes fast wear, excessive heating, and can bring about tyre failure through blow-out.

Fig. 10. Tyre wear resulting from over-inflation

This causes the fabric to be easily damaged, and seriously shortens tyre life by rapidly wearing the centre of the tread.

Fig. 11. The results of excessive front wheel camber

Possibly caused by wear or impact damage to the suspension unit.

FACTORS AFFECTING TYRE LIFE

Inflation Pressures

There is an average loss of 13% tread mileage for every 10% reduction in inflation pressure below the recommended figure.

Severe and persistent under-inflation produces unmistakable evidence on the tread (Fig. 9). It also causes structural failure due to excessive friction and temperature within the casing.

Pressure higher than those recommended reduce tread life by concentrating the load on a small tread area. Excessive pressures overstrain the casing cords, cause rapid wear, and make the tyres more susceptible to impact fractures and cuts (see Fig. 10).

Effect of Temperature

Air expands with heating and tyre pressures increase as the tyres warm up. Pressures increase more in hot weather than in cold weather and as a result of high speed.

Pressure in warm tyres should not be reduced to standard pressure for cold tyres. "Bleeding" the tyres increases their deflections and causes their temperatures to climb still higher. The tyres will also be under-inflated when they have cooled.

The rate of tread wear may be twice as fast at 50 m.p.h. (80 k.p.h.) as at 30 m.p.h. (50 k.p.h.).

High speed causes increased temperatures due to more deflections per minute and a faster rate of deflection and recovery. The resistance of the tread to abrasion decreases with increased tyre temperature.

Camber, Castor and King Pin Inclination

These angles normally require no attention unless they have been disturbed by a severe impact or abnormal wear of front end bearings. It is always advisable to check them if steering irregularities develop.

Wheel camber, usually combined with road camber, causes a wheel to try to turn in the direction of lean, due to one side of the tread attempting to make more revolutions per mile than the other side. The resulting increased tread shuffle on the road and the off-centre tyre loading tend to cause rapid and one-sided wear (Fig. 11). Unequal cambers introduce unbalanced forces which try to steer the car one way or the other. This must be countered by steering in the opposite direction which increases tread wear.

Castor and king pin inclination by themselves have no direct bearing on tyre wear but their measurement is often useful for providing a general indication of the condition of the front end geometry and suspension.

TRIUMPH
HERALD, VITESSE 6 AND SPITFIRE
WORKSHOP MANUAL

GROUP 4

Comprising :

TRIUMPH
HERALD, VITESSE 6 and SPITFIRE MODELS

GROUP 4

CONTENTS

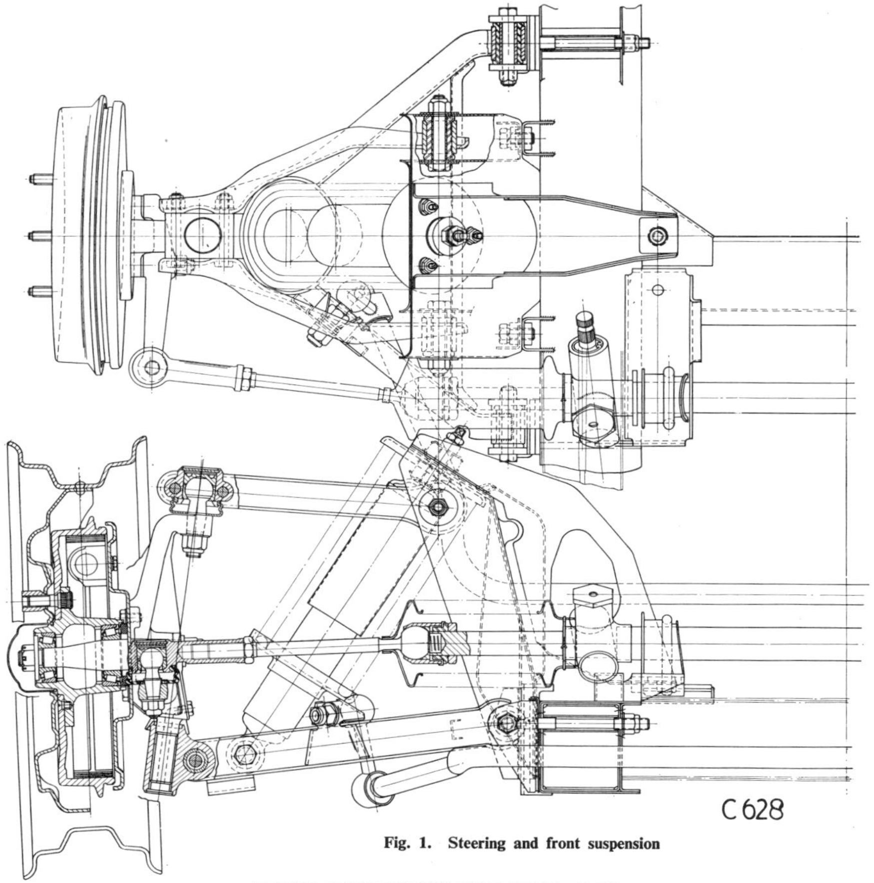

Fig. 1. Steering and front suspension

FRONT SUSPENSION GEOMETRY DATA

ITEM	DESCRIPTION	DIMENSIONS
Upper Wishbone	Inner fulcrum centre to outer fulcrum centre	7·75″ (19·685 cm.)
Lower Wishbone	Inner fulcrum centre to outer fulcrum centre	10·13″ (25·433 cm.)
Steering Axis Inclination	.. ..	6¾°
Toe-in (front & rear)	Static laden (See Page 4·201)	0″ to $\frac{1}{16}$″ (1·6 mm.)
Track at Ground Level	Distance between wheel centres at ground level (static laden)	Drum brakes 48″ (121·9 cm.) Disc brakes 48·94″ (124·3 cm.)
Camber angle Herald 1200 Herald 12/50 Vitesse	See Page 4·203 (Static laden)	Front 2° pos. Rear 2° neg.
Castor angle	See Page 4·203 (Static laden)	4° pos.
Spitfire Camber Angle	See Page 4·203 (Static laden)	Front 2° pos. Rear 3° neg.

FRONT ROAD SPRINGS

MODEL	PART No.	FREE LENGTH Approx.	FITTED LENGTH	FITTED LOAD	RATE	IDENTIFICATION
Herald Heavy Duty and Courier Van	209033	10·97″ 278·6 mm.	8·18″ ± ·09″ 207·8 mm. ± 2·29 mm.	790 lbs. 358·7 kg.	284 lb/in. 5071 kg/m.	Yellow
Spitfire	209685	12·59″ 319·8 mm.	7·80″ ± ·09″ 198·1 mm. ± 2·29 mm.	718 lb. 325·97 kg.	150 lb/in. 2875 kg/m.	Green
	210566	12·21″ 310·2 mm.	7·42″ ± ·09″ 188·5 mm. ± 2·29 mm.	718 lbs. 325·97 kg.	150 lb/in. 2875 kg/m.	Light blue
Herald Interchangeable	208056	12·08″ 306·8 mm. 12·11″ 307·6 mm.	8·18″ ± ·09″ 207·8 mm. ± 2·29 mm. 8·18″ ± ·09″ 207·8 mm. ± 2·29 mm.	790 lb. 358·7 kg. 790 lb 358·7 kg.	203 lb/in. 3624 kg/m. 201 lb/in. 3590 kg./m.	White
Vitesse	209009	12·49″ 317·3 mm.	8·18″ ± ·09″ 207·8 mm. ± 2·29 mm.	940 lb. 426 kg.	229 lb/in. 4089 kg/m.	Brown
Herald (Competition)	209013	10·47″ 282 mm.	7·68″ ± ·09″ 193 mm. ± 2·29 mm.	790 lb. 358·7 kg.	284 lb/in. 5071 kg/m.	Black

Spring packings, Part Number 125441 fitted between upper spring plate and suspension brackets on both sides of vehicle when equipped with heavy duty springs. Fitted to L.H. steering vehicles with normal spring on L.H. side only. (Except Heavy Duty springs, Estate Cars and Courier Van.)

REAR ROAD SPRINGS

MODEL	PART No.	BLADE THICKNESS	No. OF BLADES	LADEN CAMBER	LOAD	RATE
Courier Van	305686	0·3125″ 7·94 mm.	8	1·75″ Neg. ± ·13″ 44·45 mm. ± 3·3 mm.	1910 lb. 903 kg.	552 lb/in. 9855 kg/m.
Herald Estate Car	304860	0·31″ 7·87 mm.	7	1·63″ Neg. ± ·13″ 41·4 mm. ± 3·3 mm.	1735 lb. 817·7 kg.	510 lb/in. 9106 kg/m.
Herald Coupé & Vitesse	303724	0·2188″ 5·56 mm.	8	0·93″ Neg. ± ·13″ 23·62 mm. ± 3·3 mm.	1010 lb. 458·54 kg.	202 lb/in. 3607 kg/m.
*Herald & Vitesse Convertibles also Saloons from Commission Nos. quoted below	305945	0·2188″ 5·56 mm.	11	1·94″ Neg. ± ·13″ 49·28 mm. ± 3·3 mm.	1420 lb. 664·7 kg.	270 lb/in. 4821 kg/m.
*Herald & Vitesse Saloon Up to Commission Nos. quoted below	303727	0·2188″ 5·56 mm.	11	1·54″ Neg. ± ·13″ 39·12 mm. ± 3·3 mm.	1420 lb. 664·7 kg.	270 lb/in. 4821 kg/m.
Spitfire	305894	0·2188″ 5·56 mm.	7	1·88″ Neg. ± ·13″ 38·9 mm. ± 3·3 mm.	945 lb. 429·1 kg.	166 lb/in. 2964 kg/m.
Herald Saloon and Estate Competition	305544	0·31″ 7·87 mm.	7	2·25″ Neg. ± ·13″ 57·2 mm. ± 3·3 mm.	1735 lb. 817·7 kg.	510 lb/in. 9106 kg/m.
Herald Saloon, Coupé, Convertible Competition	305543	0·2188″ 5·56 mm.	12	2·5″ Neg. ± ·13″ 63·5 mm. ± 3·3 mm.	1420 lb. 644·68 kg.	295 lb/in. 5267 kg/m.
Herald & Vitesse Saloon, Convertible Heavy Duty	305288	0·2188″ 5·56 mm.	12	1·54″ Neg. ± ·13″ 39·12 mm. ± 3·3 mm.	1420 lb. 644·68 kg.	295 lb/in. 5267 kg/m.

*From Commission Nos.: Vitesse HC.1420; Herald 1200 GA.223682; 12/50 GD.51956; 13/60 All Models; Herald Export GB.50849, rear road spring Part No. 303727 is replaced by Part No. 305945.

DAMPERS — FRONT

MODEL	DAMPER PART NUMBER	DAMPER AND SPRING UNIT PART NUMBER
Herald Saloon, Coupé, Convertible	206262	208176
Vitesse HEAVY DUTY	134635	134811
Herald Estate Car	208022	208178
Courier Van and Herald HEAVY DUTY	208022	209317
Herald Saloon, Coupé, Convertible, Estate Car, Courier Van	134635	209679
Spitfire	206262	209766
Vitesse and Herald Competition	209021	209030

DAMPERS — REAR

MODEL	DAMPER PART NUMBER
Herald and Vitesse Saloon, Coupé, Convertible	123100
Spitfire	123100
Herald and Vitesse and Courier and Heavy Duty for Saloon, Coupé, Convertible	132111
Herald and Vitesse Competition	209022

FRONT HUB BEARINGS

	HERALD & SPITFIRE	VITESSE
Outer		
Standard Part No.	100536	129897
British Timken Part No. — Cone	03062	LM.11949
— Cup	03162	LM.11910
Bore	0·6255″ (15·89 mm.) 0·6250″ (15·875 mm.)	0·75005″ (19·051 mm.) 0·750″ (19·050 mm.)
O.D.	1·6256″ (41·293 mm.) 1·6250″ (41·275 mm.)	1·782″ (45·245 mm.) 1·781″ (45·244 mm.)
Inner		
Standard Part No.	100573	129897
British Timken Part No. — Cone	07100S	L.44649
— Cup	07210X	L.44610
Bore	1·0006″ (27·415 mm.) 1·0000″ (25·4 mm.)	1·0633″ (27·008 mm.) 1·0625″ (26·98 mm.)
O.D.	2·0006″ (50·815 mm.) 2·0000″ (50·8 mm.)	1·981″ (50·26 mm.) 1·980″ (50·292 mm.)

FRONT SUSPENSION

General

Before disturbing any part of the front suspension assembly, jack up the front of the vehicle and lower it on to stands placed under the chassis sidemembers, rearward of the front cross-member. Remove the road wheels and dismantle either R.H. or L.H. suspension unit as follows:—

Suspension Sub-Assembly—Removal

1. Open bonnet.
2. Slacken the impact clamps (see Page 4·212) and withdraw steering column from coupling (only necessary when removing sub-assembly on driver's side).
3. Empty the hydraulic system and disconnect the hydraulic brake flexible hose from the bracket or side valance (Fig. 2).
4. On Herald 1200, Mk. II, 12/50 and Vitesse models, remove the nut and bolt securing each valance to the sub-frame.
5. Disconnect the anti-roll bar link (2) from the lower wishbone (Fig. 9).
6. Remove the nyloc nut, plain washer, and using an extractor (Fig. 3), detach the tie rod end from the steering arm.
7. Note the number and position of shims (31) between the chassis frame and front and rear lower wishbone fulcrum brackets (32). Remove the nyloc nut (29) and washer (30) securing each fulcrum bracket to the chassis.
8. Remove 4 bolts (1) Fig. 4, spring and plain washers and tapping plates from the outer face of the sub-frame and one bolt (2), spring and plain washer securing the inner end of the sub-frame to the chassis frame.
9. Remove the suspension sub-assembly from the chassis frame.

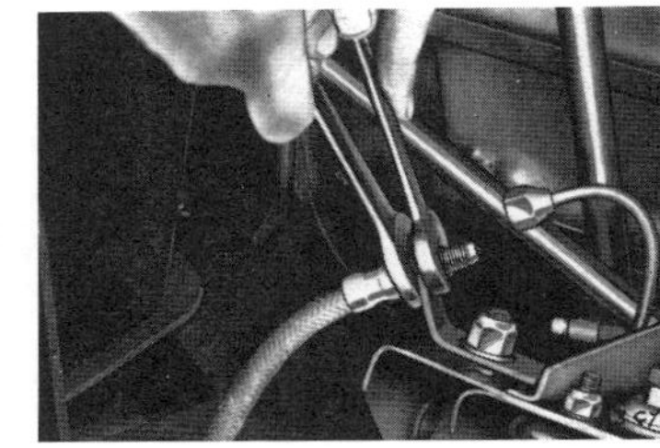

Fig. 2. **Disconnecting Hydraulic brake hose**

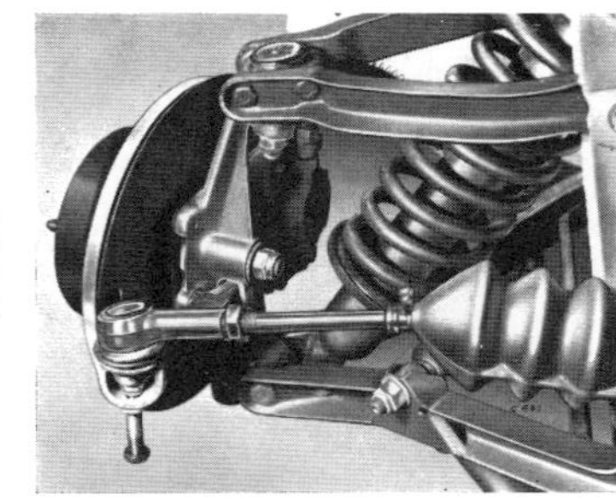

Fig. 3. **Using Tool No. S.160 to remove tie-rod end from steering lever**

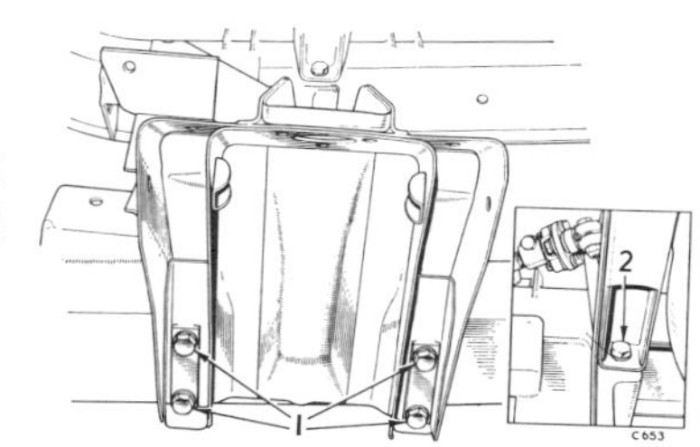

Fig. 4. **sub-frame attachment points**

1 Outer bolts
2 Inner bolts

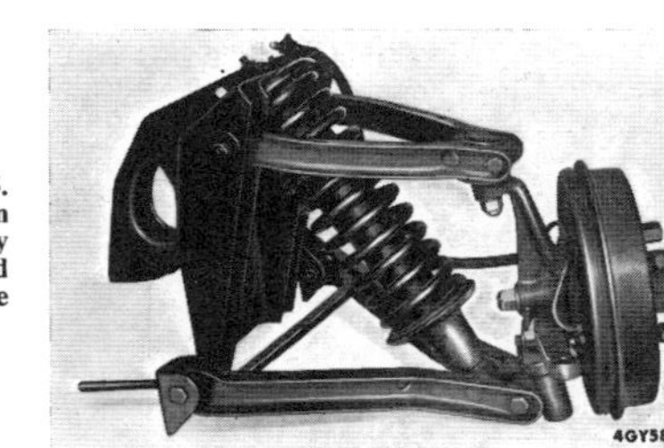

Fig. 5. **Suspension sub-assembly detached from frame**

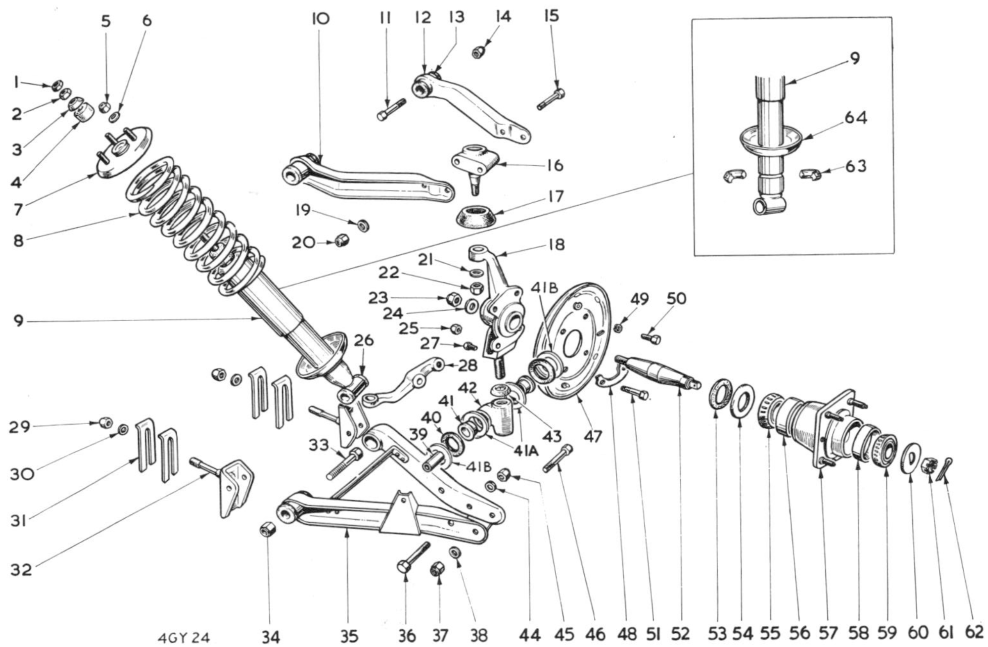

- 1 Locknut
- 2 Nut
- 3 Washer
- 4 Rubber bush
- 5 Nyloc nut
- 6 Plain washer
- 7 Upper spring pan
- 8 Road spring
- 9 Damper
- 10 Front upper wishbone arm
- 11 Bolt
- 12 Rear upper wishbone arm
- 13 Rubber bush
- 14 Nyloc nut
- 15 Bolt
- 16 Ball joint
- 17 Rubber gaiter
- 18 Vertical link
- 19 Plain washer
- 20 Nyloc nut
- 21 Plain washer
- 22 Nyloc nut
- 23 Nyloc nut
- 24 Plain Washer
- 25 Nyloc nut
- 26 Rubber bush
- 27 Plug
- 28 Steering arm
- 29 Nyloc nut
- 30 Plain washer
- 31 Shim
- 32 Inner fulcrum bracket
- 33 Fulcrum bolt
- 34 Nyloc nut
- 35 Lower wishbone assembly
- 36 Suspension unit fulcrum bolt
- 37 Nyloc nut
- 38 Plain washer
- 39 Steel bush
- 40 Rubber seal
- 41 Nylon bush
- 41A Washer
- 41B Washer
- 42 Lower trunnion
- 43 Rubber seal
- 44 Plain washer
- 45 Nyloc nut
- 46 Fulcrum bolt
- 47 Brake backplate
- 48 Locking plate
- 49 Spring washer
- 50 Setscrew
- 51 Bolt
- 52 Stub axle
- 53 Felt seal
- 54 Seal retainer
- 55 Taper roller bearing—inner
- 56 Roller bearing outer ring
- 57 Hub
- 58 Roller bearing outer ring
- 59 Taper roller bearing—outer
- 60 "D" washer
- 61 Slotted nut
- 62 Split pin
- 63 Spring retaining collet
- 64 Spring cup

Fig. 6. Exploded front suspension. Inset Woodhead-Monroe type

Fig. 7. Tightening sub-frame attachment bolts

Fig. 8. Fitting shims between lower fulcrum bracket and chassis frame

Fig. 9. Anti-roll bar attachment to lower wishbone

To Refit

1. Insert the lower inner fulcrum bracket studs through the holes in the chassis frame and secure with washers (30) and nyloc nuts (29). Insert the shims (31) between the brackets (32) and chassis frame, ensuring that they occupy their original positions. Tighten the nyloc nuts (29).
2. Offer up the sub-frame and secure it with the inner attachment bolt, spring and plain washer, and four outer bolts, spring and plain washers (Fig. 7) and two tapping plates. Finally tighten the bolts.
3. Refit the steering tie rod end to the steering arm.
4. Secure the valance or radiator stay to the sub-frame.
5. Re-connect the anti-roll bar link (2) to the lower wishbone and secure with a washer (3) and nyloc nut (4), Fig. 9.
6. Re-connect the flexible hose, refill and bleed the hydraulic system.
7. If necessary, re-connect the steering column to the flexible coupling and re-tighten the impact clamp.
8. Fit the road wheels and nuts.
9. Remove chassis stands and lower vehicle to ground.
10. Check and if necessary adjust the castor and camber angles and front wheel alignment.

Dismantling Suspension (Fig. 6)

The front suspension may be dismantled with the sub-frame either on or off the chassis frame, as follows:—

1. Remove the front road spring assembly as described on page 4·112. Dismantle the spring and damper as described on page 4·113.
2. Remove the two screws and detach the brake drum (Herald 1200 drum brakes).
   Remove bolts, Fig. 10, and detach the brake caliper assembly from its bracket (Herald 1200, Spitfire or Vitesse disc brakes). If the sub-frame is left in position, tie the caliper unit or brake assembly to the chassis frame, or detach the back plate.
3. Remove the grease cap, split pin (62), slotted nut (61) and washer (60), then detach the hub assembly from the stub axle (52). Dismantle the hub as described on page 4·116.
4. Release the tabwasher (48) and remove four bolts, tabwasher, washers and nyloc nut securing the steering arm (28), brake backing plate (47), or caliper mounting bracket and dust shield to the vertical link (18).
5. Remove nyloc nuts (14) and bolts (11) securing the inner ends of the upper wishbones to the sub-frame.
6. Release the anti-roll bar from the lower wishbone (Fig. 9). Remove nyloc nuts (29) and washers (30) and detach the lower wishbone brackets (32) from the chassis frame. Note the number and disposition of the shims (31).
7. Detach the vertical link and wishbone assembly from the chassis sub-frame.
8. Remove the nyloc nut (22), washer (21) and, using an extractor (Fig. 12), separate the upper ball joint (16) from the vertical link (18).
9. Remove the bolts (15), nyloc nuts (20) and detach the ball joint (16) from the outer ends of the wishbone arms (10) and (12).
10. Remove the nyloc nut (37), bolt (46) and detach the lower wishbone assembly (35) from the lower trunnion (42), followed by the steel bush (39), shouldered nylon bushes (41) and dust seals (40) (see Fig. 13).
11. Unscrew the vertical link (18) from the lower trunnion (42) and remove the dust seal (43).
12. Remove the nyloc nut (23), plain washer (24) and press the stub axle (52) from the vertical link (18).
13. If necessary, press the rubber bushes (13) from the inner ends of the upper and lower wishbone arms.

Fig. 10. Disc brake caliper attachment bolts

Fig. 11. Drum brake backplate attachments

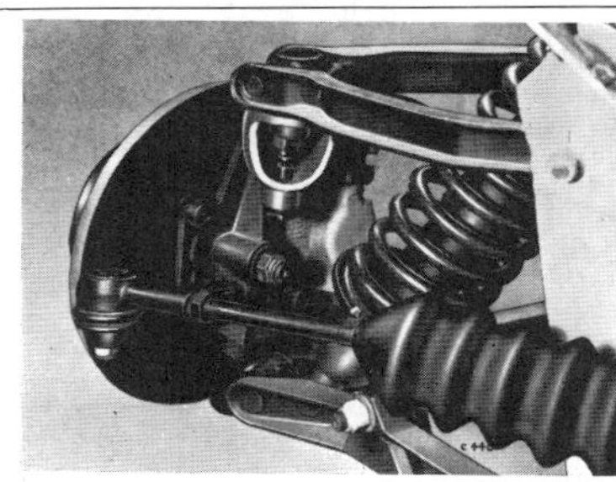

Fig. 12. Using extractor No. S166A to remove upper wishbone ball joint assembly

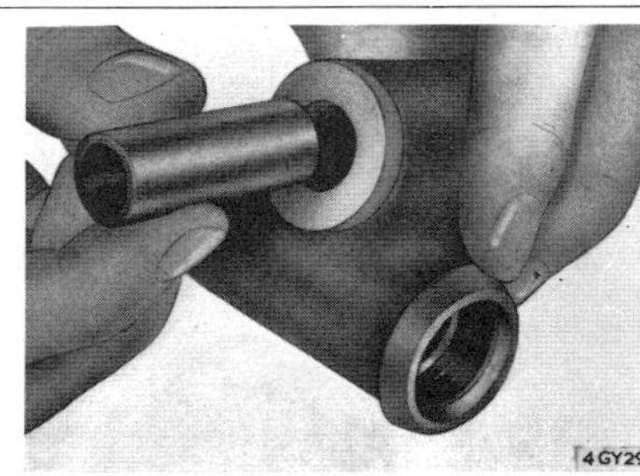

Fig. 13. Removing steel bush from lower trunnion

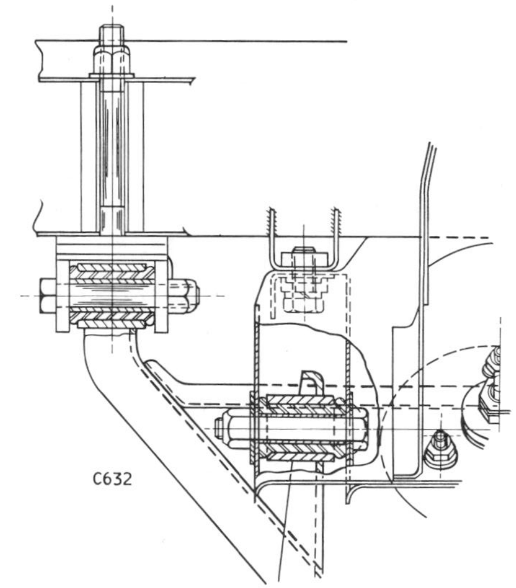

Fig. 14. Cross section of upper and lower inner fulcrum pivots

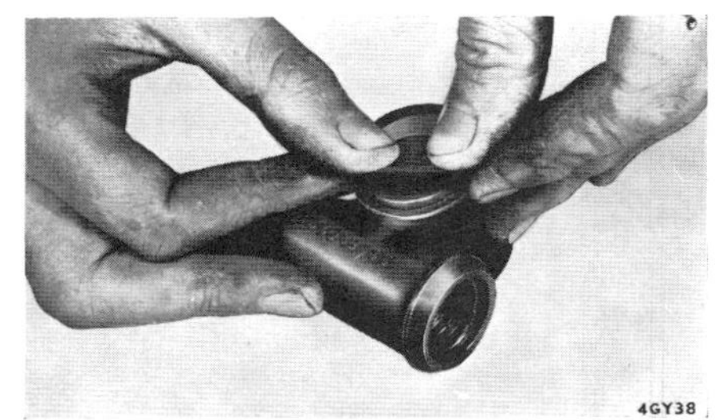

Fig. 15. Fitting seals to lower fulcrum nylon bushes

Fig. 16. Fitting rubber seal to vertical link

Front Suspension Re-Assembly (Fig. 6)

1. Using a suitable press and pilot tool, press the rubber bushes (13) into the eyes at the inner ends of the upper wishbones (10) and (12) and lower wishbones (35) until they protrude equally either side of the wishbone eyes as shown on Fig. 14.
2. Fit the stub axle (52) to the vertical link (18), with the split pin hole in its outer end horizontal. Secure the stub axle with the plain washer (24) and nyloc nut (23).
3. Fit two nylon bushes (41) with a washer (41A) beneath the flange, steel sleeve (39) and spring the rubber dust excluders (40) over the nylon bush flanges on the lower trunnion (42) (see Fig. 15).
4. Fit the rubber seal (43) to the vertical link (Fig. 16), screw the vertical link into the bronze trunnion (42) as far as possible, then unscrew it to the first working position.

NOTE : The L.H. threaded vertical link and trunnion must be fitted to the L.H. side of the vehicle and the R.H. threaded components to the R.H. side of the vehicle. The R.H. threaded trunnion has a reduced diameter at its lower end for identification (see Fig. 17).

5. Fit the washers (41B) and insert bronze trunnion (42) between the outer ends of the lower wishbone (35); retain in position with the bolt (46), washer (38) and nyloc nut (37). (Fig. 18).

6. Fit the brackets (1) and (2) (Fig. 19) to the inner eyes of the lower wishbone arms. Note that the bracket fitted to the front wishbone must have the longest portion below the chassis attachment stud centre line and the bracket fitted to the rearmost wishbone arm must have its longest portion above the stud centre line.

7. Fit the ball joint assembly (16) between the outer ends of the upper wishbone arms (10) and (12) and secure with bolts (15), washers (19) and nyloc nuts (20).

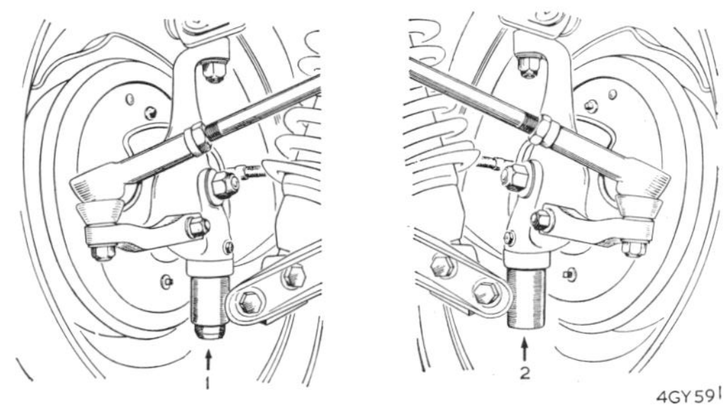

Fig. 17. Identification of R.H. lower trunnion by reduced dia. at lower end

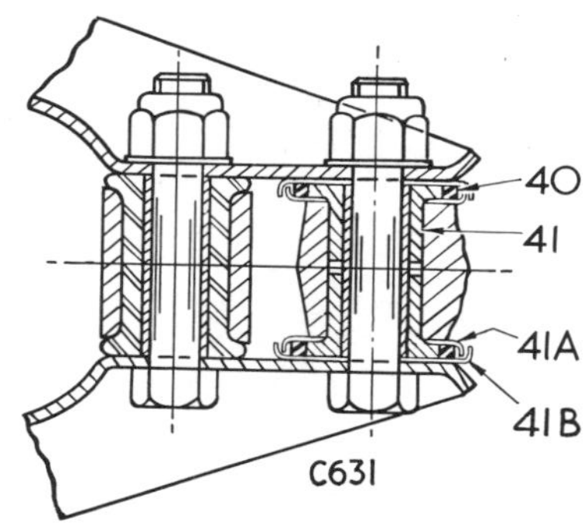

Fig. 18. Cross section of lower wishbone attachments to lower trunnion and damper/spring unit

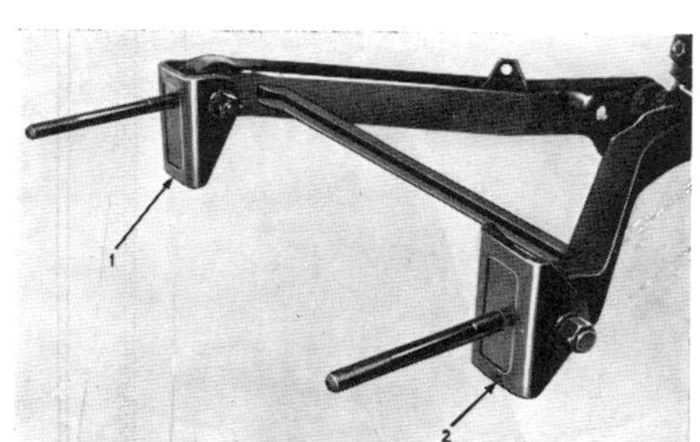

Fig. 19. Positions of lower fulcrum brackets, (1) front, (2) rear

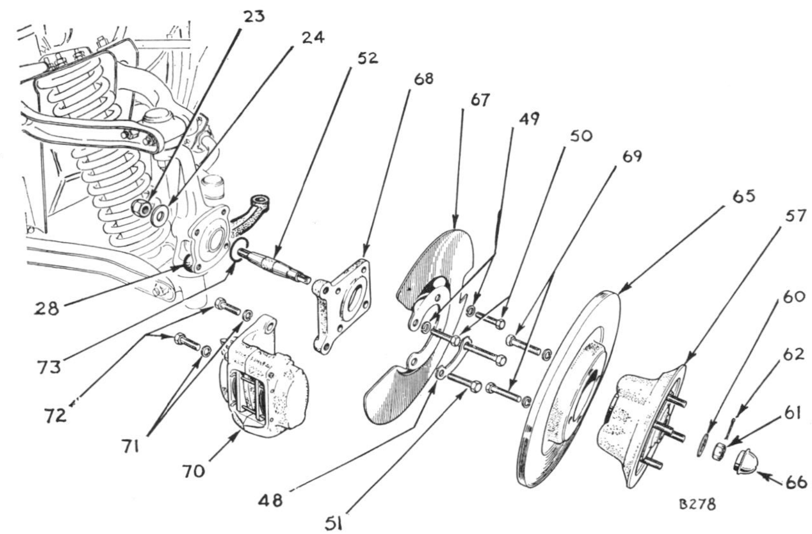

Fig. 20. Exploded disc brake components

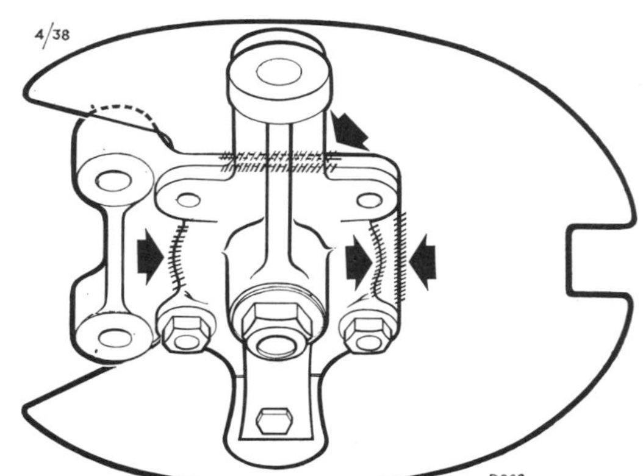

Fig. 21. Positions of Expandite Seal-a-Strip between disc brake caliper bracket and vertical link

8. Assemble the ball joint tapered shank to the vertical link (18) and fit the nyloc nut (22) and washer (21).

9. Assemble the steering arm (28) and brake backing plate (47) to the vertical link (18). On disc brake models, assemble the dust shield and caliper bracket as shown on Fig. 21, sealing the dust shield to the vertical link and caliper bracket with Expandite Seal-a-Strip (105 S) Part No. 554420.

NOTE : Vehicles with Commission Nos. from G.A.99486 (Herald 1200), F.C.2393 (Spitfire), H.B.7082 (Vitesse) and G.D.215 (Herald 12/50) have a rubber seal (73), Fig. 33, fitted between the recessed face of the caliper bracket and the vertical link.

Secure the components with bolts (51), spring washers (49), nyloc nut (25) and a new tab-washer (48). Tighten the bolts and nyloc nut to the torques quoted on page 23. Secure the tabs against the two lower bolt heads as shown on Fig. 22.

10. Assemble and adjust the hub assembly as instructed on page 4·116.

11 Secure the upper (10 and 12) and lower wishbone (35) and inner fulcrums (32) to the chassis and sub-frame, ensuring that· the shim packs are correctly located between the fulcrum brackets and chassis frame as shown on Fig. 23. Do not tighten bolts 36, 11 and 33, Fig. 6, at this stage.

12. Assemble and fit the damper/spring unit to the front suspension as described on page 4·112.

13. Fit the tie rod end to the steering arm and secure with nyloc nut and washer.

14. Refit the brake drum or caliper assembly, ensuring that any shims between the caliper and bracket are refitted. Adjust the brake shoe clearance in the drum as described on page 3·208.

15. Lubricate the vertical link lower trunnion (see page 0·204).

16. Refit the road wheels and lower the vehicle to the ground. To allow the rubber bushes to assume their correct working position, load the car before tightening the inner fulcrum bolts (11 and 33) and the damper lower attachment bolt (36). Check the castor, camber and front wheel alignment.

Fig. 22. Locking tabs securing backing plate and steering arm bolts

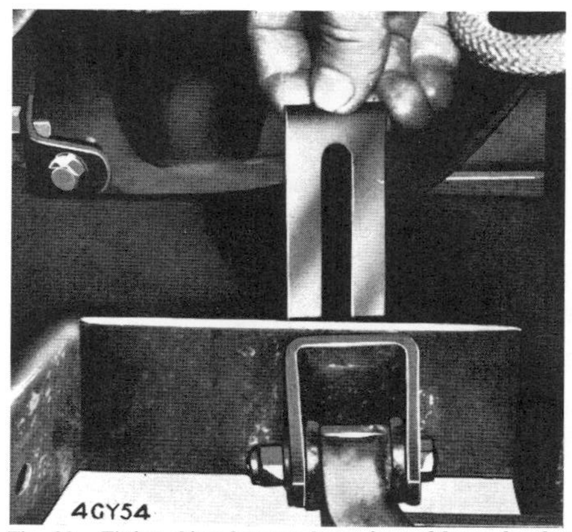

Fig. 23. Fitting shims between lower inner fulcrum bracket and chassis frame

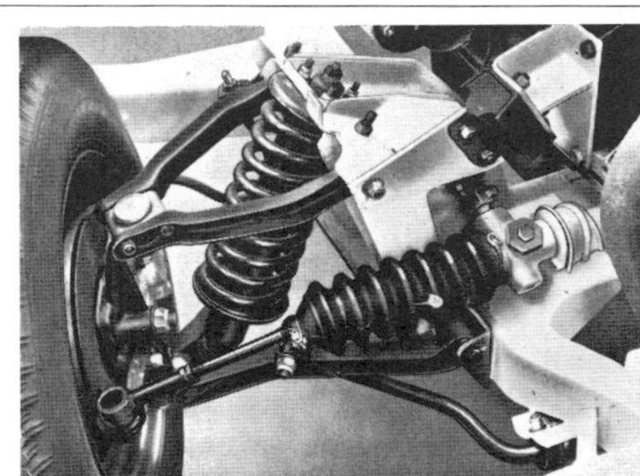

Fig. 24. Upper and lower wishbone attachments

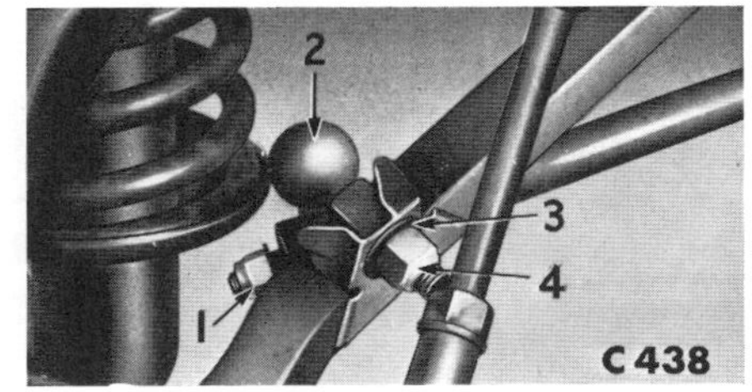

Fig. 25. Anti-roll bar attachment to lower wishbone

Fig. 26. Spring and damper attachments to chassis sub-frame

Fig. 27. Removing spring and damper assembly from front suspension

Front Road Spring Assembly (Fig. 28)

Removal

1. Jack up front of vehicle and support on chassis stands.
2. Open bonnet.
3. Remove hub disc, wheel nuts and road wheel.
4. Disconnect anti-roll bar from lower wishbone.
5. Remove the three nuts (4) and washers (6) that secure the upper spring pan (7) to the chassis sub-frame (see Fig. 26).
6. Remove the nut (18), plain washers (17) and (15) and bolt (14) from the damper lower attachment eye.
7. Support the brake drum assembly and withdraw the road spring assembly, Fig. 27.

Fitting

1. Support the brake drum assembly and enter the road spring assembly from beneath, passing the three studs of the upper spring pan through the holes in the chassis sub-frame.
2. Secure the damper lower eye to the wishbone with the bolt (14), plain washers (15) and (17) and nyloc nut (18).
3. Secure the upper spring pan to the chassis sub-frame with three washers (6) and nyloc nuts (4). A packing piece is fitted between the upper spring pan and chassis sub-frame on the left-hand side of left-hand drive vehicles.

4. Attach the anti-roll bar to the lower wishbone (Fig. 25).
5. Fit road wheel, wheel nuts and hub disc.
6. Close bonnet.
7. Jack up front of vehicle, remove chassis stands and lower vehicle to ground.

Dampers (Fig. 28)

Removal

1. Remove road spring and damper assembly
2. Using a press, compress as many coils as possible of the road spring just sufficient to relieve the load from the damper top nuts, Fig. 29.
3. Remove the locknut (1), nut (2), washer (3) and rubber (5) from the top of the damper.
4. Carefully release the load from the road spring and withdraw the assembly from the press.
5. Withdraw the damper (11) from the upper spring pan (7) and road spring (10).
6. Remove the lower spring pan (12) and collets (13) from the damper (Woodhead-Monroe type only).

Refitting

1. Fit the washer (9) and rubber (8) to the top of the damper (11).
2. Fit the collets (13) and lower spring pan (12) to the damper (Woodhead-Monroe type only).
3. Extend the damper (11) and insert it into the road spring (10) and upper spring pan (7).
4. Using a press, compress the road spring sufficient to enable the completion of the damper attachment to the upper spring pan, Fig. 29.
5. Fit the rubber (5), the washer (3), nut (2) and locknut (1).

1 Locknut
2 Nut
3 Washer
4 Nyloc nut
5 Rubber bush
6 Washer
7 Upper spring pan
8 Rubber bush
9 Washer
10 Road spring
11 Damper
12 Lower spring pan
13 Collets
14 Bolt
15 Washer
16 Metalastik bush
17 Washer
18 Nyloc nut

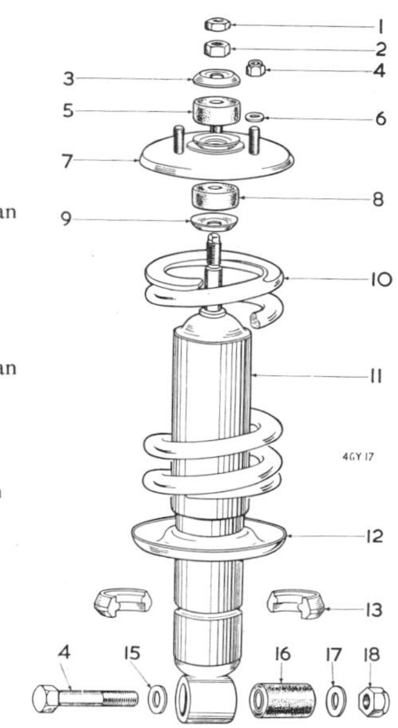

Fig. 28. Exploded view of front road spring and damper assembly

Fig. 29. Using press S.4221A with adaptor S.4221A-5 to compress the front road spring

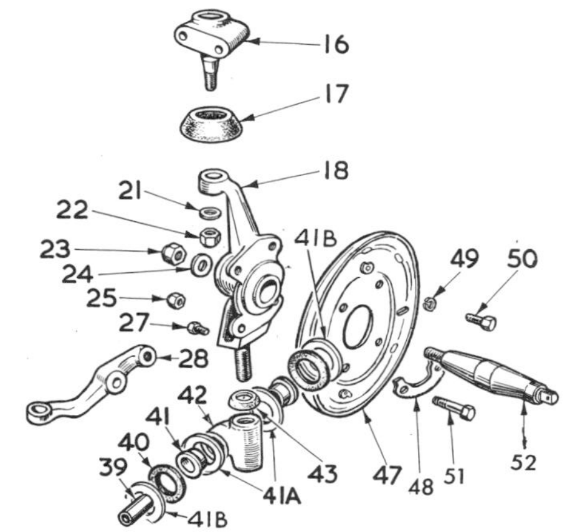

Fig. 30. Vertical link, steering arm and associated details

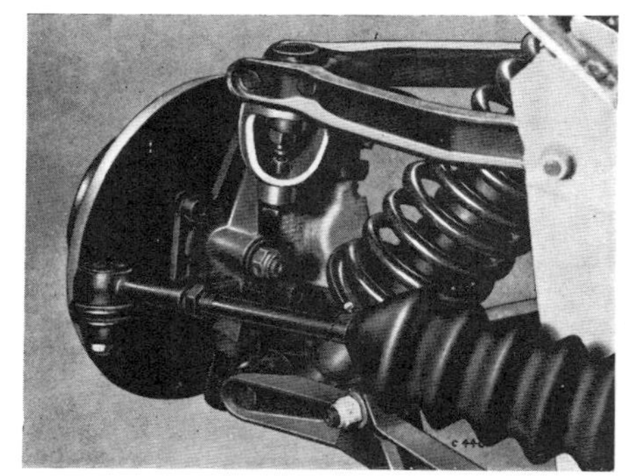

Fig. 31. Using tool No. S.166A to release top ball joint from vertical link

Fig. 32. Removing rubber seal from vertical link

Vertical Link

Removal

1. Open bonnet.
2. Remove the two screws and the brake drum, or detach the caliper unit from its bracket (disc brakes).
3. Remove the grease cap, split pin, slotted nut, washer and hub assembly from the stub axle.
4. Release the locktabs, remove four bolts (50) and (51), tabwasher (48), washers and one nyloc nut (25) securing the brake backing plate (47) and steering lever (28) to the vertical link (18). On disc brake models remove the dust shield and caliper bracket. Remove the brake backing plate (47) and tie it to the chassis frame to prevent it hanging on the flexible hose.
5. Remove the nyloc nut (22) and washer (21) and, using an extractor, separate the vertical link (18) from the tapered pin of the ball joint (16) as shown on Fig. 31.
6. Unscrew the vertical link (18) from the trunnion (42) and withdraw the seal (43) see Fig. 32. The vertical link fitted to the left-hand side of the vehicle has a left-hand thread and the vertical link fitted to the right-hand side of the vehicle has a right-hand thread.
7. Remove the nyloc nut (23) and plain washer (24) and, using a press, remove the stub axle (52) from the vertical link (18).

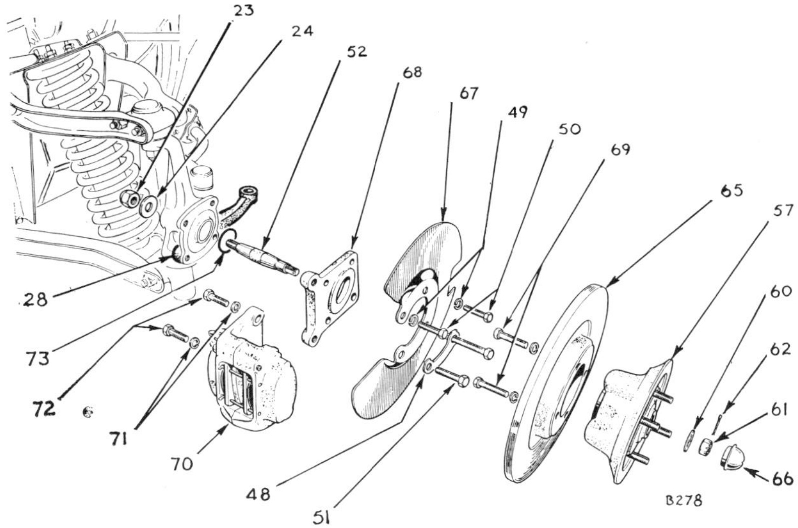

Fig. 33. Exploded details of disc brake components

Refitting

1. Insert the stub axle (52) into the vertical link (18) with the split pin hole in its outer end horizontal. Fit the washer and nyloc nut securing the stub axle to the vertical link.
2. Fit the rubber seal (43) to the vertical link, Fig. 32. Screw the vertical link into the bronze trunnion as far as possible then unscrew it to the first working position, *i.e.*, so that it does not bottom when the road wheel is turned to full front or back lock.
3. Insert the tapered pin of the ball joint (16) into the tapered hole in the top of the vertical link (18) and retain in position with the washer (21) and nyloc nut (22).
4. Untie the brake backing plate assembly from the chassis frame and locate it in position on the vertical link. Insert the steering lever (28) through the aperture in the vertical link (18). Retain the brake backing plate (47) or caliper bracket dust shield and steering lever (28) in position by fitting the tabwasher, washers, bolts and nyloc nut. On disc brakes, seal the dust shield to the vertical link and caliper bracket with expandite seal-a-strip (105 S) Part No. 554420.
   Turn up tabs of the locking plate against the side of the bolt heads, Fig. 34.
5. Assemble and adjust the hub assembly as instructed on pages 4·116 and 4·117.
6. Adjust the brake shoe/drum clearance as instructed on page 3·208.
8. Lubricate the vertical link lower bronze trunnion as instructed on page 0·204.
9. Close bonnet.

Fig. 34. Securing the heads of steering attachment bolts with lock tabs

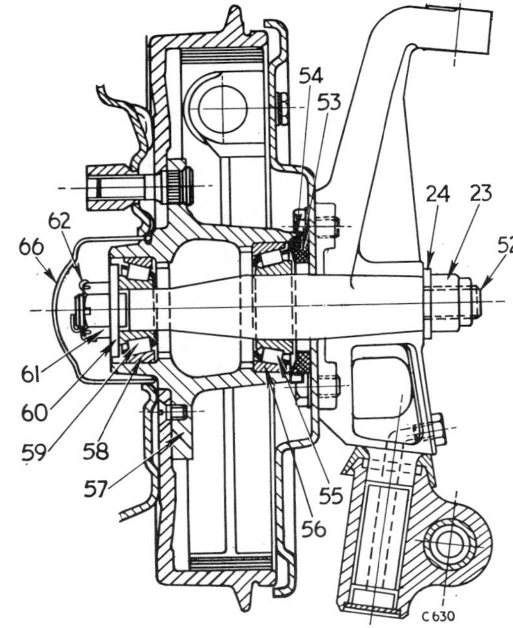

Fig. 35. Cross section of Herald 1200 drum brake and hub assembly

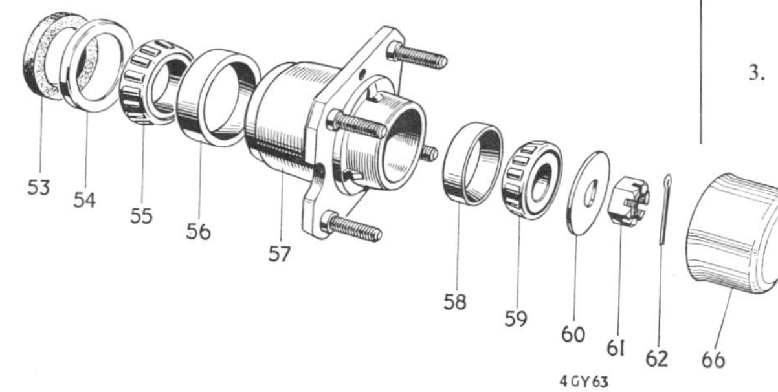

Fig. 36. Exploded view of drum brake hub bearing details

Hubs

Removal

1. Remove the two screws and the brake drum, or detach the brake caliper unit (disc brakes).
2. Remove the grease cap (66), split pin (62) slotted nut (61) and washer (60) then pull the hub assembly from the stub axle.

Dismantling

1. Remove the outer roller bearing inner member (59) from the hub.
2. Using a soft metal drift, tap the inner roller bearing inner member (55) and felt seal assembly (53) and (54) from the hub (57).
3. Tap the outer rings (56) and (58) of the outer and inner roller bearings from the hub.
4. If necessary, remove the bolts (69), Fig. 37, and detach the disc (65) from the hub (57).

Assembly

1. Obtain the correct adjustment by assembling the hub bearings dry, as follows :—Press the roller bearing outer rings (56) and (58) into the hub until they contact their respective seatings. Fit the bearings and the hub to the stub axle and retain by the washer and the slotted nut. Whilst rotating the hub by hand, tighten the nut only sufficiently to remove slackness. Slacken the nut back to the nearest split pin hole and record its position by marking the washer and the nut.
2. Remove the hub assembly and pack the space between the outer rings with grease and smear grease over the outer rings.
3. Coat the rollers of the inner roller bearing inner member (55) with grease and insert it into its outer ring.

4. Tap the felt seal retainer (54) into the hub. Oil the felt seal (53), squeeze out surplus oil and fit the seal to the retainer (54). On disc brake models ensure that the disc registers are clean and free from burrs before fitting the disc to the hub, and securing with bolts and spring washers.

5. Fit the hub assembly to the stub axle.

6. Coat the rollers of the outer roller bearing inner member (59) with grease and insert it into its outer ring in the hub (57).

7. Fit the washer (60) and slotted nut (61), tightening the nut until the marks correspond. Secure the nut with a new split pin and refit the grease cap.

8. Fit the brake drum and retain with two screws, or refit the caliper unit.

Adjustment in Service

1. Whilst spinning the hub, tighten the slotted nut to 5 lb/ft. (0·7 mkg.) then unscrew the slotted nut one flat to give 0·002″ to 0·008″ (0·05 mm. to 0·2 mm.) end float of the hub.

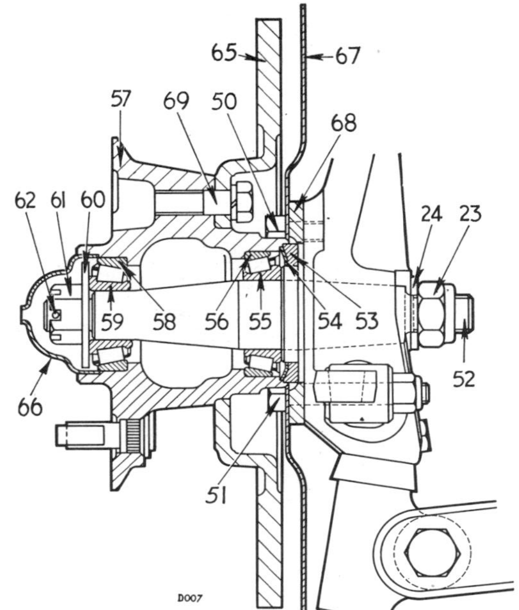

Fig. 37. Cross section of disc brake and hub assembly

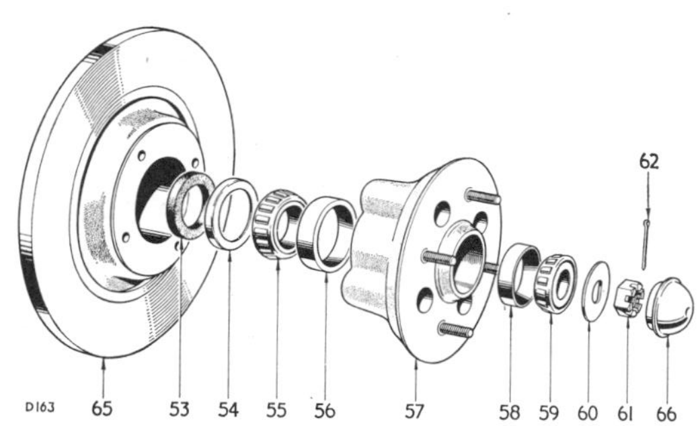

Fig. 38. Exploded view of disc brake hub bearing details

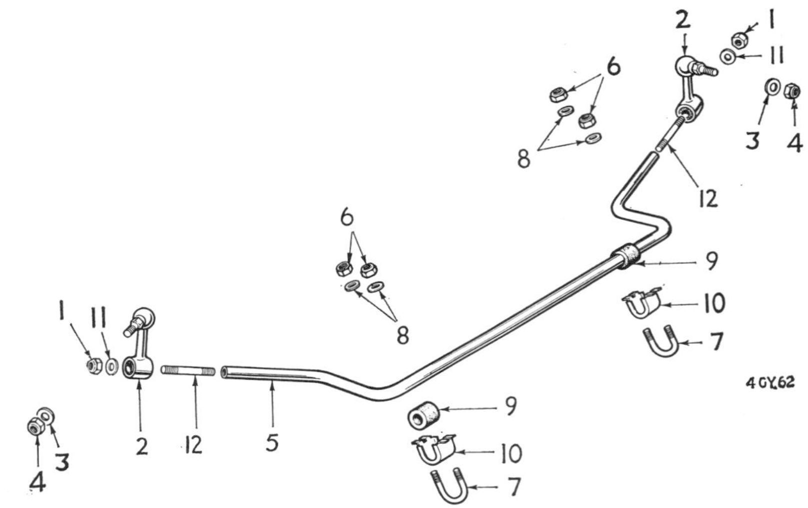

1 Nyloc nut	4 Nyloc nut	7 "U" bolt	10 Clamp
2 Link	5 Anti-roll bar	8 Plain washer	11 Plain washer
3 Plain washer	6 Nyloc nut	9 Rubber bush	12 Stud

Fig. 39. Exploded details of anti-roll bar

Fig. 40. Anti-roll bar link attachments to lower suspension wishbone

Anti-Roll Bar

Removal

1. Remove the nyloc nuts (4) and plain washers (3).

2. Remove the nyloc nuts (6), plain washers (8), clamps (10) and "U" bolts (7) and withdraw anti-roll bar (5). If necessary remove the nuts (1), washers (11) and detach links (2) from anti-roll bar (5).

Replacement

1. Fit the clamps over the rubber bushes (9) on the anti-roll bar (5) and attach to the chassis crossmember with "U" bolts (7), plain washers (8) and nyloc nuts (6).

2. Assemble the links (2) to the anti-roll bar (5) with washers (11) and nuts (1).

3. Engage the links in the lower wishbone bracket and fit the nyloc nuts (4) and plain washers (3).

4. Tighten all nuts with the vehicle in the static laden condition.

REAR SUSPENSION

Before carrying out any work on the rear suspension, jack up the rear of the vehicle and support it on chassis stands. Remove the road wheels.

REAR ROAD SPRING

To Remove

1. Disconnect each brake hose from its steel pipe and chassis bracket by unscrewing the union nut (56), Fig. 41, and removing the nut (58) whilst holding the flexible pipe (57).
2. Disconnect the handbrake cable (64) from the backplate lever by withdrawing the clevis pin (61). Disconnect the spring (63), Fig. 42.
3. Jack up the vertical link (10), as shown on Fig. 43, to relieve the dampers of load. Remove nuts (47), bolts (43), Fig. 45, and disconnect the axle shaft couplings.
4. Slacken the damper upper attachment bolt (44), Fig. 41, remove the nyloc nut (13) and washer (14) from the lower attachment and pull the damper (9) clear of its lower fulcrum. Remove the jack from the vertical link.
5. Supporting the vertical link (10), remove the bolt (46) from the road spring eye as shown on Fig. 46.
6. Take out the rear seat and squab and remove the spring access cover.
7. Remove the six nyloc nuts (4), plain washers (5), detach the spring clamp plate (3) and unscrew the three rear studs (42) from the axle casing (Fig. 47).
8. Withdraw the road spring from the vehicle (Fig. 48).

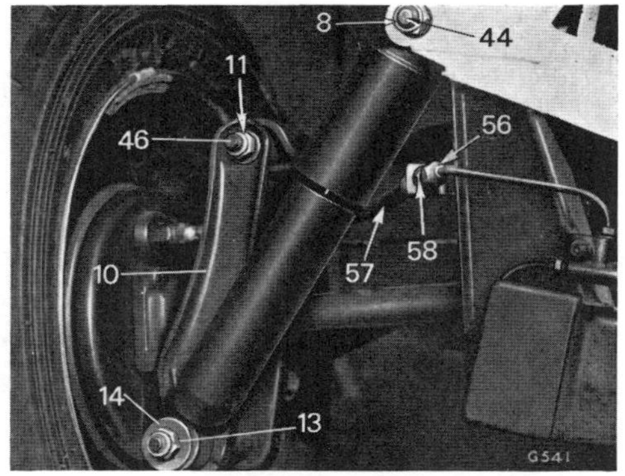

Fig. 41. Rear suspension, vertical link, brake pipe and damper attachments

Fig. 42. Handbrake connections

Fig. 43. Using jack beneath vertical link

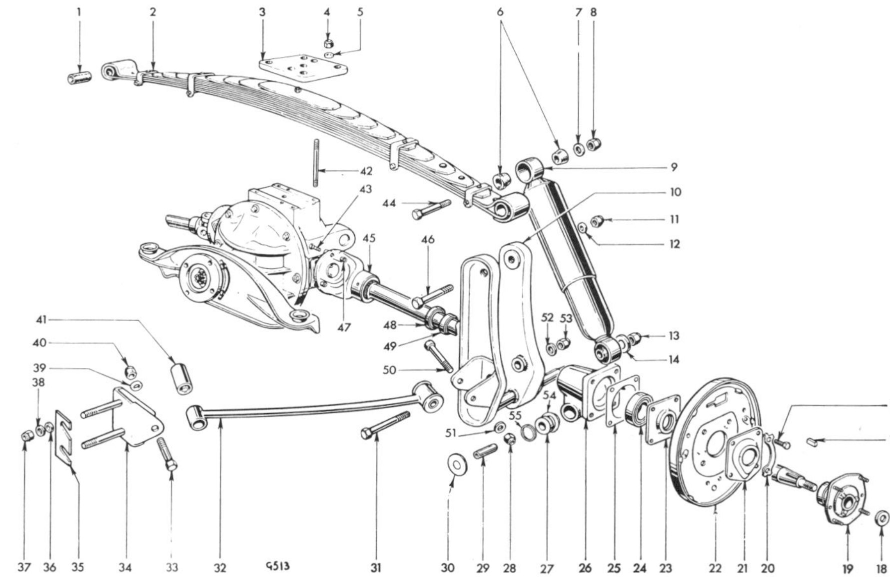

1	Spring eye bush	20	Locktab	39	Washer
2	Road spring	21	Grease retainer	40	Nut
3	Spring clamp plate	22	Brake backplate	41	Rubber bush
4	Nut	23	Seal housing	42	Stud
5	Washer	24	Bearing	43	Bolt
6	Rubber bush	25	Gasket	44	Bolt
7	Washer	26	Trunnion housing	45	Axle shaft coupling
8	Nut	27	Nylon bush	46	Bolt
9	Damper	28	Nut	47	Nut
10	Vertical link	29	Steel bush	48	Flinger
11	Nut	30	Dust seal	49	Seal
12	Washer	31	Bolt	50	Bolt
13	Nut	32	Radius arm	51	Washer
14	Washer	33	Bolt	52	Washer
15	Bolt	34	Radius arm bracket	53	Nut
16	Key	35	Shim	54	Dust seal
17	Nut	36	Washer	55	Rubber ring
18	Washer	37	Nut		
19	Hub	38	Washer		

Fig. 44. Exploded view of rear suspension

Fig. 45. Axle shaft universal joint connections

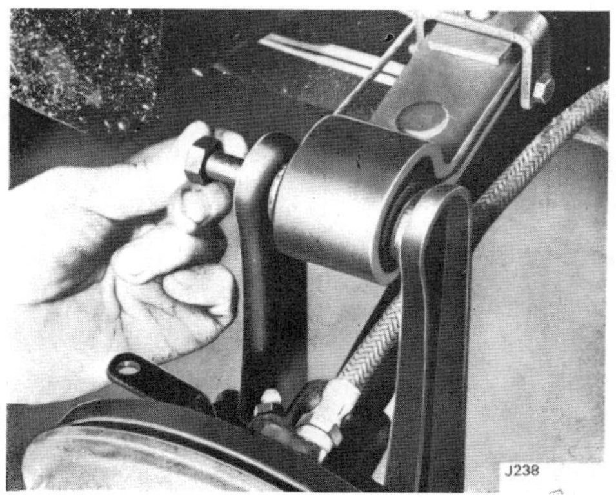

Fig. 46. Removing spring eye bolt

Fig. 47. Spring clamp plate attachments

To Refit

1. Fit the road spring into its recess in the axle casing with the centre bolt spigoting in its locating hole. The spring is marked "FRONT" for correct location.

2. Refit the three studs (42) with the shorter threaded portion leading, into the axle casing. Refit the spring clamp plate (3) and tighten the nyloc nuts (4).

3. Apply "Prestik" sealer to the edge of the access plate, refit the plate, securing with two screws, and liberally apply "Seelastik" to the joint. Replace the seat and squab.

4. Attach the vertical links (10) to the spring eyes using bolts (46), washers (12) and nyloc nut (11). Do not tighten the nut (11) at this stage.

5. Jack up the vertical links (10), fit the dampers and reconnect the axle shaft couplings.

6. Connect the handbrake cable to the backplate lever, refit the pull-off spring (63), Fig. 42, and reconnect the flexible brake hose. Adjust and bleed the brakes.

7. Place a trolley jack under the differential casing, remove the chassis stands and, with the vertical links supported at their running height, load the car and lower its rear end until the axle shafts assume their static laden operating position. This is to allow the rubber bushes to assume their correct working position before tightening the nuts (11), (8) and (13).

DAMPERS

To Remove

1. Jack up the vertical link (10) to relieve the damper (9) of load, as shown on Fig. 50, remove the bolt (44) from the upper attachment and the nyloc nut (13) from the lower damper eye.

2. Pull the damper clear of its attachment points.

To Refit

Bleed air from the damper by holding it in a vertical position and operating the damper over its full stroke. Maintaining the unit in a vertical position, refit the damper by reversing the removal procedure, fitting new rubber bushes if necessary.

RADIUS ARMS

To Remove

Proceed as for removal of dampers, adjusting the jack beneath the vertical link (10) until the radius arm attachment bolts (33) and (50) can be easily withdrawn.

If the rubber bushes (41) are perished, worn or cut, use a press to remove them, and press in new bushes. If the radius arm chassis attachment brackets (34) are removed, ensure that on re-assembly the same number of shims (35) are refitted.

To Refit

Refit the radius arm (32), tighten the attachment bolts and nuts (50) and (28), (33) and (40), remove the jack from the vertical link.

Rear Wheel Alignment

Check, and if necessary, adjust the rear wheel alignment. Removing an equal number of shims from both sides (35) Fig. 44 increases the rear wheel toe-in and the addition of shims decreases the rear wheel toe-in.

Fig. 48. Removing road spring

Fig. 49. Radius arm attachment

Fig. 50. Jacking vertical link

Fig. 51. Axle shaft universal joint connections

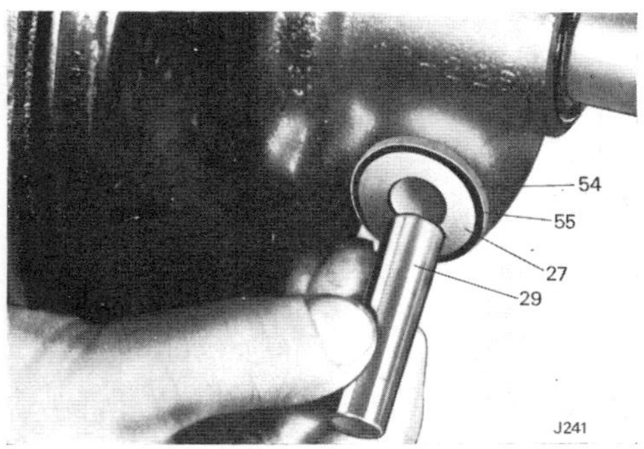

Fig. 52. Removing steel bush from nylon bushes in trunnion housing

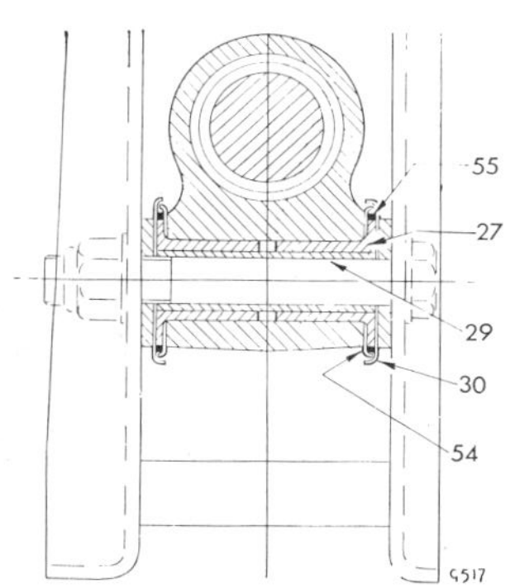

Fig. 53. Sectioned view of trunnion bushes

VERTICAL LINK ASSEMBLY

To Renew Trunnion Housing Bushes

1. Jack up under the vertical link to relieve the damper of load as shown on Fig. 50.

2. Disconnect:—
   — the brake hose (57) from its steel pipe and chassis bracket;
   — the handbrake cable (64) from the back-plate lever, and return spring (63) Fig. 42;
   — the axle shaft coupling, Fig. 51;
   — the radius arm from the vertical link.

3. Remove the damper (9), lower and remove the jack.

4. Supporting the brake assembly, remove the bolt (46) from the road spring eye, Fig. 46, and place the brake/axle shaft assembly on a clean bench.

5. Remove the bolt (31), Fig. 44, and withdraw the vertical link (10) from the trunnion housing (26). Remove the steel bush (29), Fig. 52.

6. Examine and if necessary replace the seals and bushes as Fig. 53.

   NOTE: Sufficient grease (Shell, Retinax "A" or approved alternative) must be used during assembly of these bearings to ensure that the space around the bearings is full.

7. Fit the vertical link assembly (10) to the trunnion housing (26) and to the road spring eye bush (1). Do not, at this stage, fully tighten the spring eye bolt (46).

8. Jack up beneath the vertical link and fit the damper (9), radius arm (32) and the axle shaft coupling (45).

9. Place a trolley jack under the differential casing, remove the chassis stands and, with the vertical link supported at its running height, load the car and lower its rear end until the axle shaft assumes its static laden operating position. This is to allow the rubber bushes to assume their correct working position before tightening the nuts (11), (8), (13) and (28).

10. Connect the brake hose and handbrake cable. Adjust and bleed the brakes.

ASSESSMENT OF ACCIDENTAL DAMAGE

The following dimensioned illustrations assist in the assessment of accidental damage.
It is suggested that any components which have sustained damage or are suspect in any way, should first be removed from the vehicle as instructed, then cleaned and accurately measured on a surface table.
The measurements obtained should then be compared with those given in the appropriate illustration and the serviceability of the components determined

Dimension	Ins.	mm.
1	5·19	131·8 mm.
2	1·88	47·75 ,,
3	10·13	254·33 ,,
4	5·88	149·35 ,,
5	1·5	38·1 ,,

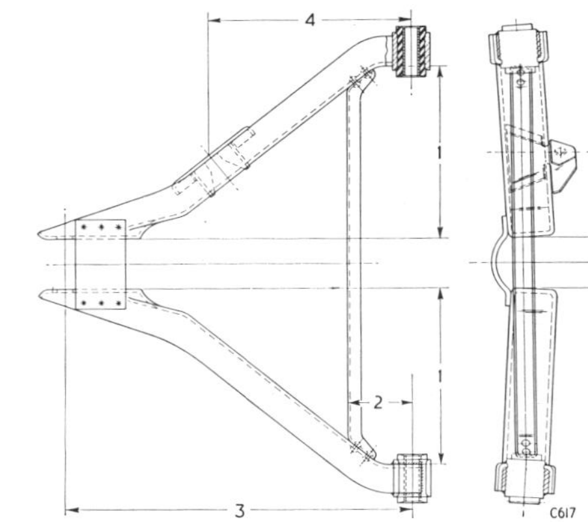

Fig. 60. Lower wishbone arm assembly

Dimension	Ins.	mm.
1	1·5	38·1 mm.
2	7	177·8 ,,
3	2·13	54·1 ,,

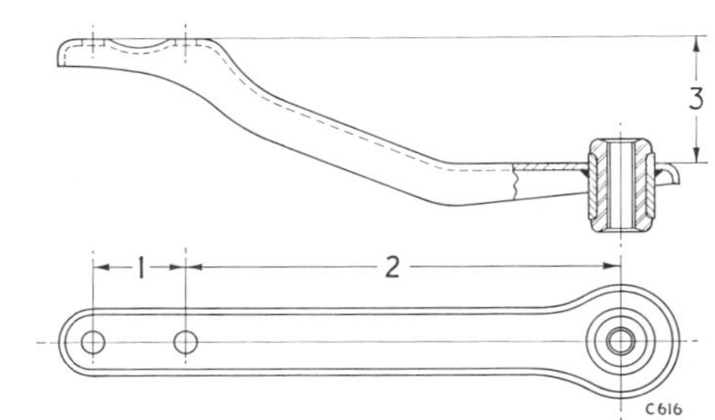

Fig. 61. Upper wishbone arm

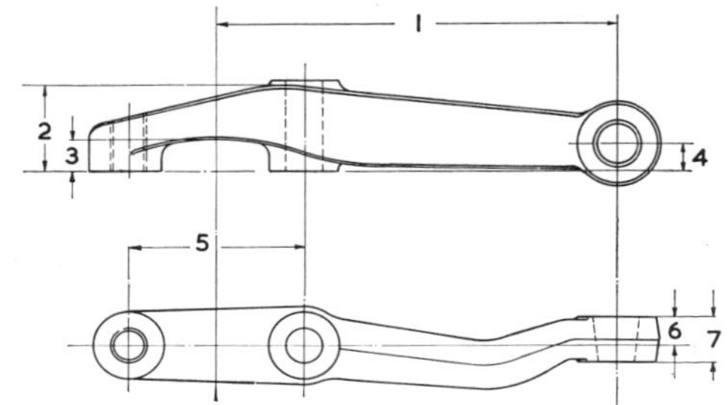

Up to and including the following commission numbers:—

Spitfire	.. ..	FC 15575
Herald 1200..	..	GA 127238
12/50..	.. ..	GD 12253

Dimension	Ins.	mm.
1	4·375	111·13
2	0·99	25·14
3	0·39	85·32
4	0·367	9·32
	0·377	9·57
5	1·936	49·17
	1·94	49·28
6	0·31	7·87
7	0·5	12·7

Fig. 62. Right-hand steering lever (early type, now used on Vitesse only)

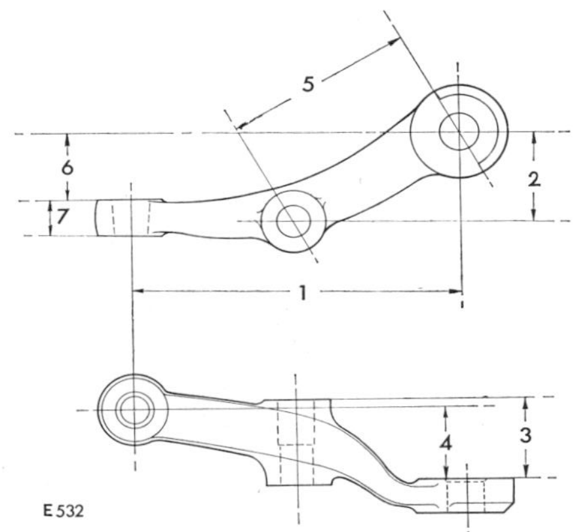

Dimension	Ins.	mm.
1	4·375	111·13
2	1·26	32
3	1·107	28·12
	1·117	28·37
4	0·955	24·26
	0·965	24·51
5	2·543	64·59
	2·553	64·84
6	0·914	23·2
7	0·5	12·7

Fig. 63. Right-hand steering lever (late type)

Fitted from the following commission numbers (inclusive):—

Spitfire	.. ..	FC 15576
Herald 1200..	..	GA 127239
Herald 12/50	..	GD 12254
Herald 13/60	..	All models

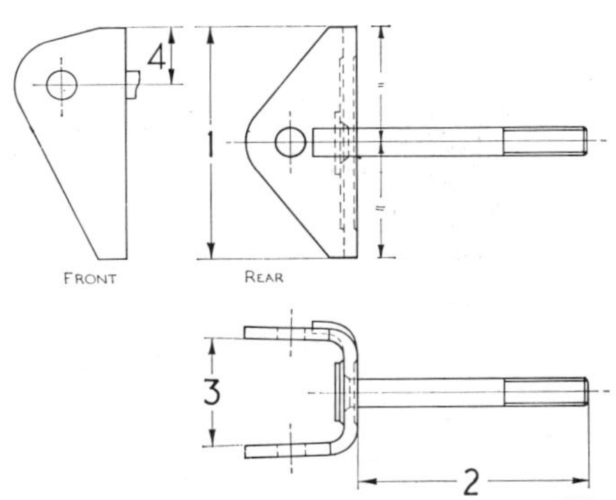

Dimension	Ins.	mm.
1	3·25	82·5
2	3·13	79·5
3	{ 1·445	36·7
	1·460	37·1
4	0·74	18·8

Fig. 64. Lower wishbone fulcrum bracket

Dimension	Ins.	mm.
1	1·83	46·48
2	0·335	8·51
	0·345	8·76
3	0·875	22·2
4	0·245	6·22
	0·255	6·48
5	5·44	138·18
6	0·963	24·46
	0·973	24·7
7	0·9995	25·387
	1·0005	25·413
8	0·13	3·3
9	2·25	57·15
10	4·44	112·8
11	3·12	79·25
	3·13	79·5
12	1·936	49·17
	1·940	49·28
13	9 degrees	
14	2 degrees	

For Vitesse, dimension 7 is 1·062/1·063 in. (26·975/27·000 mm.).

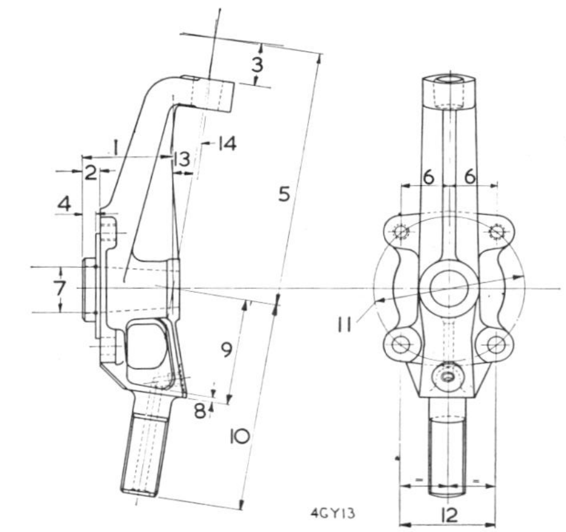

Fig. 65. Vertical link (early Herald type, now used on Vitesse only)

Dimension	Ins.	mm.
1	1·83	46·48
	0·825	20·955
2	0·815	20·701
3	0·875	22·2
4	0·245	6·22
	0·255	6·48
5	5·44	138·18
6	1·6257	41·293
	1·6242	41·255
7	0·9995	25·387
	1·0005	25·413
8	1·94	49·28
9	2·25	57·15
10	4·44	112·8
11	3·2515	82·588
	3·2485	82·512
12	1·964	49·88
	1·960	49·78
13	9 degrees	
14	2 degrees	

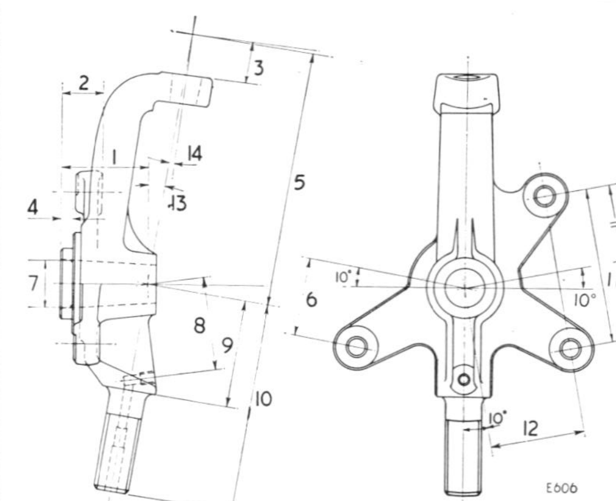

Fig. 66. Vertical link (late type)

Dimension	Ins.	mm.
1	12·5	317·5 mm.

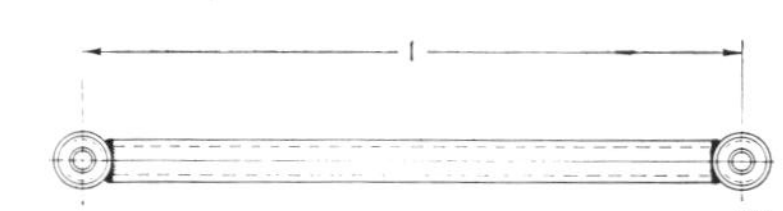

Fig. 67 Spitfire Rear suspension radius rod.

Dimension	Ins.	mm.
1	15·88	403·3 mm.

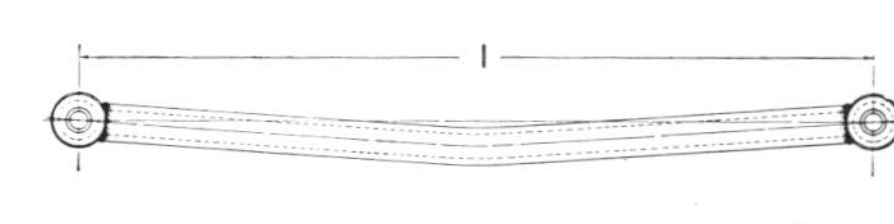

Fig. 68. Herald 1200, 12/50, 13/60 and Vitesse rear suspension radius rod

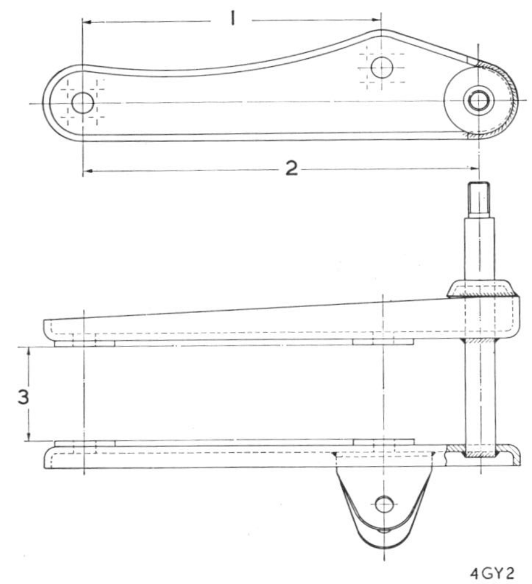

Dimension	Ins.	mm.
1	6·185	157·1
	to 6·195	to 157·35
2	8·185	207·9
	to 8·195	to 208·15
3	2	50·8

Fig. 69. Rear suspension vertical link plate assembly

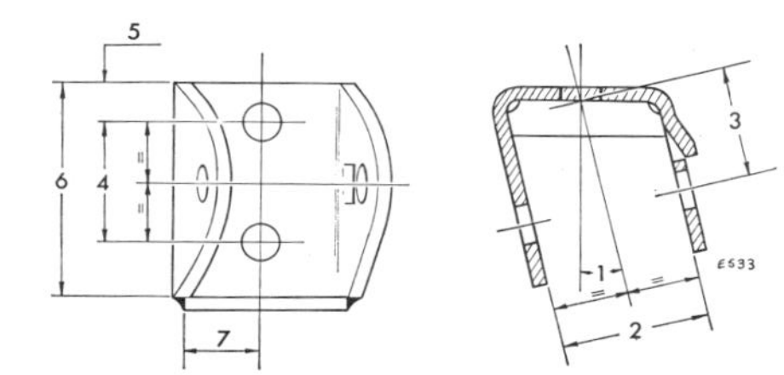

Dimension	Ins.	mm.
1	14 degrees	
2	1·44	36·58
3	1·06	26·92
4	1·182	30·02
	1·192	30·28
5	0·38	9·65
6	2·13	54·1
7	0·75	19·05

Fig. 70. Rear suspension radius rod chassis bracket

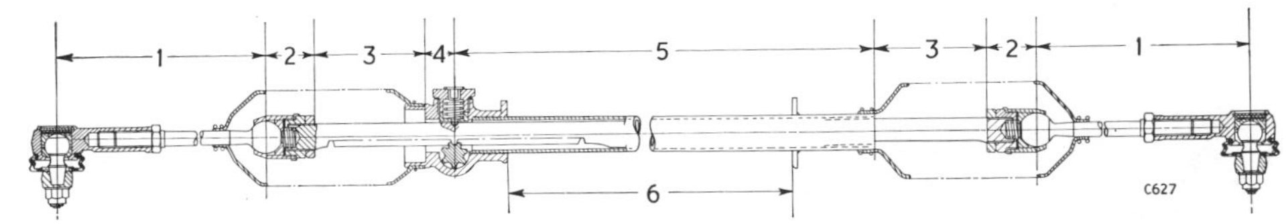

1 8·715″ (221·36 mm.)	3 3·325″ (84·45 mm)	5 16·875″ (428·63 mm.)
2 1·42″ (36·07 mm.)	4 0·875″ (22·23 mm.)	6 12·78″ (324·62 mm.)

Fig. 1. Steering unit dimensions

STEERING MEASUREMENTS AND ADJUSTMENTS

Before carrying out measurements and adjustments on the front suspension and steering, inflate the tyres to the correct pressures and position the vehicle on a smooth, level surface. Place a load of 150 lb. (68 kg.) on each seat.

A. Checking Steering Locks

NOTE : The back and front lock angles are equal to each other only when the wheels are set at 20° from the straight-ahead position.

Position the front wheels on Weaver or similar wheel turning gauges, and place wood blocks of equivalent thickness to that of each gauge under the rear wheels.

Set the front wheels straight ahead and zero the gauges. Turn each wheel to 20° front lock and read the opposite gauge. Repeat the procedure with 20° back lock. If the front and back lock angles do not conform to 20°, damage to suspension components must be assumed.

B. Lock Stop Adjustment

Limitation of the steering lock is controlled by the locknut (33) Fig. 4, contacting the rack tube. Thus dimension (3) Fig. 1 is particularly important. Providing that this dimension is accurate and the steering unit is centrally mounted on the chassis, correct steering locks should result.

C. Track Adjustment (Figs. 2, 3 and 4)

Centralize the steering unit and measure the front wheel alignment, using Dunlop or similar wheel alignment equipment. If adjustment is required, slacken the locknuts (43) Fig. 4, the clips (42) and rotate the tie-rods (38) until alignment is correct. Note the reading. Roll the vehicle forward to rotate the wheels 180°, and take a second reading. Adjust the tie-rods to a mean of the two readings thus allowing for wheel rim run-out.

Tighten the tie-rod locknuts and gaiter clips.

Fig. 2. Using Dunlop optical wheel alignment gauge

Fig. 3. Tie-rod end locknut and gaiter clip

EXPLODED STEERING UNIT

Castor and Camber Measurement

The following instructions for measuring castor and camber are applicable to the Weaver instrument.

Run the front wheels on to Weaver or similar wheel turning radius gauges as shown on Fig. 5 and place wood blocks of equivalent thickness to that of each gauge under the rear wheels. Zero the gauges with the front wheels in the straight ahead position.

Remove the hub cap from the hub.

Ensuring that the split pin does not foul it, place the spacer washer (4), Fig. 5, with flange outwards, and engage the claws of the adaptor (3) on the stub axle thread between two of the nut slots. Secure the spirit level unit (1) to the adaptor and tighten the knurled nut (2).

With the wheels in the straight ahead position, measure the camber from the L.H. Scale.

Turn the wheel to 20° back lock and zero the bubble on the R.H. scale.

Turn the wheel to 20° front lock and read the castor angle from the R.H. scale.

Repeat the operations on the opposite wheel. Compare the camber and castor angles with those given on page 4·102. Appreciable differences indicate distorted suspension components, worn suspension bushes or settled front springs.

Castor and Camber Adjustments

Adjustment of camber and castor angles is accomplished by altering the number of shims assembled between the chassis and the lower inner fulcrum brackets.

Before adjustments are made, jack up under the spring to relieve side loading on the fulcrum brackets. Loosen the bracket from the chassis to permit manipulation of the shims.

After each adjustment is made, tighten the brackets to the chassis, remove the jack and measure the angles.

Castor Angles

To decrease, add shims to the front bracket or remove shims from the rear.
To increase, reverse the procedure.

Camber Angles

To decrease, add an equal number of shims to both brackets.
To increase, reverse the procedure.

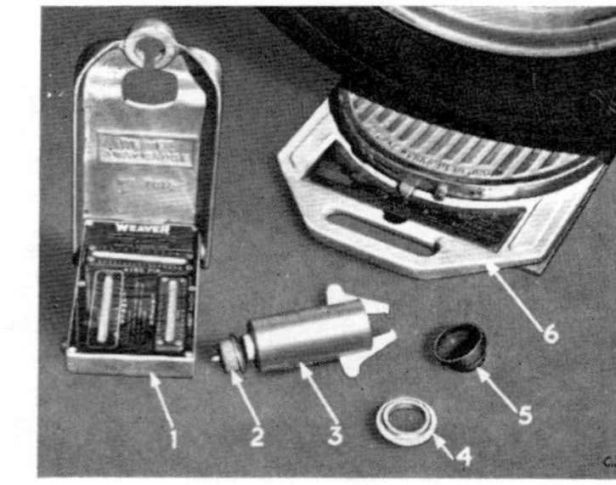

1 Spirit level
2 Knurled nut
3 Adaptor
4 Spacer washer
5 Hub cap
6 Turning gauge

Fig. 5. Weaver Measuring Equipment

Fig. 6. Using Weaver equipment to measure castor angle

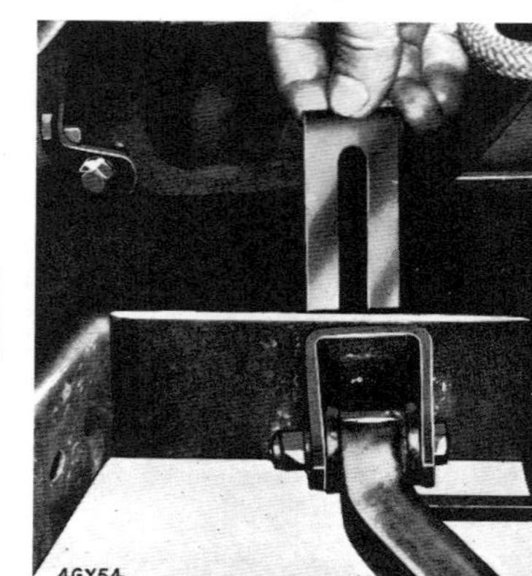

Fig. 7. Positioning of shims between fulcrum bracket and frame

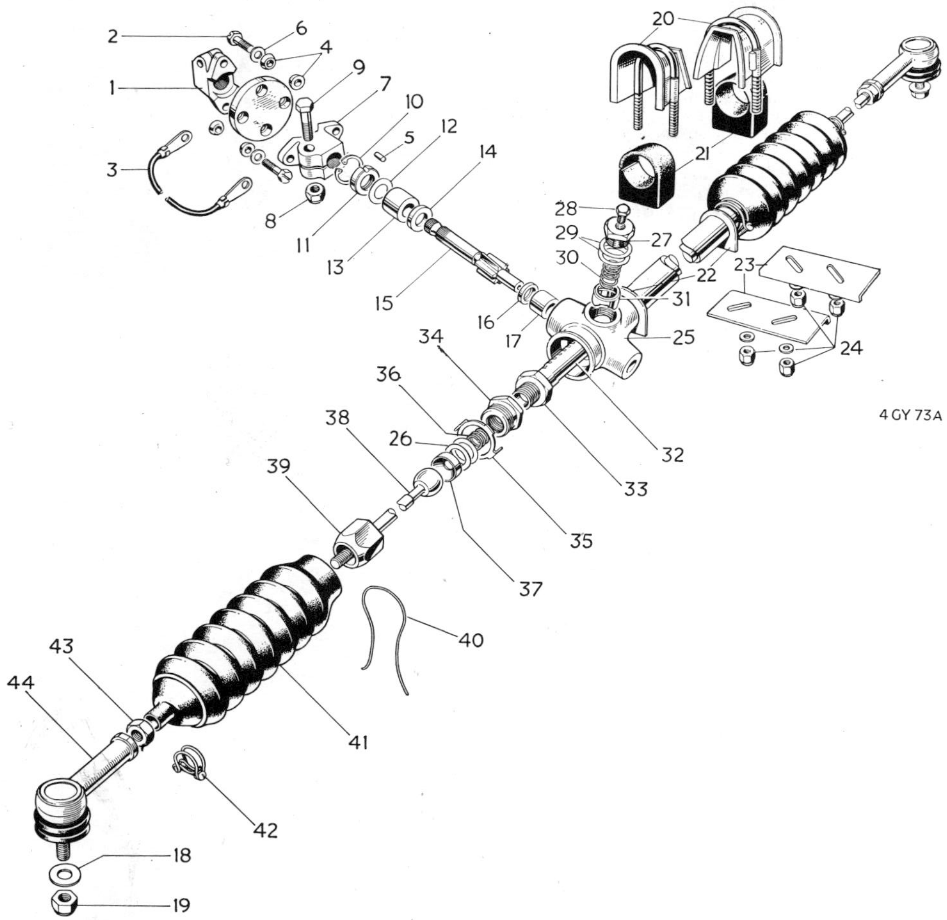

Fig. 4. Exploded steering unit

Key to Fig. 4

1	Steering coupling (upper)	23	Locating plates
2	Bolt	24	Nyloc nuts
3	Earth cable	25	Rack assembly
4	Rubber bushes	26	Shims
5	Dowel	27	Cap
6	Washer	28	Grease plug
7	Steering coupling (lower)	29	Shims
8	Nyloc nut	30	Spring
9	Pinch bolt	31	Plunger
10	Circlip	32	Rack
11	Retaining ring	33	Locknut
12	Shims	34	Sleeve nut
13	Bush	35	Lock tab
14	Thrust washer	36	Spring
15	Pinion shaft	37	Cup
16	Thrust washer	38	Tie-rod
17	Bush	39	Cup nut
18	Washer	40	Locking wire
19	Nyloc nut	41	Rubber gaiter
20	"U" bolts	42	Clip
21	Rubber bushes	43	Locknut
22	Abutment plates	44	Tie-rod end

Fig. 8. Steering unit attachments

Steering Unit

Removal (Fig. 8)

1. Remove item (9) from the coupling (7). Disconnect the earth strap, secured by item (28) at one end, from the bolt securing it to the chassis frame.

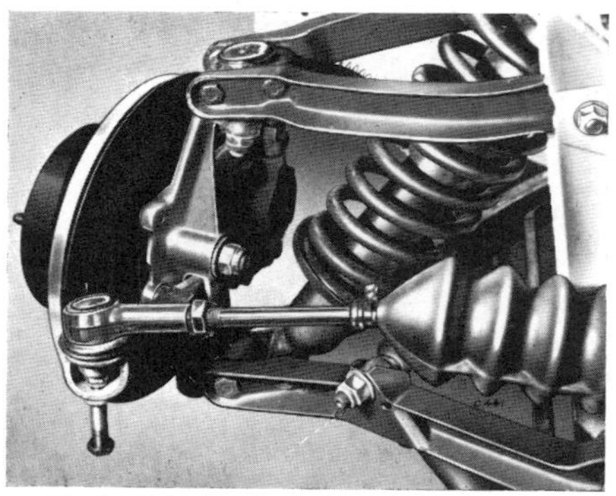

Fig. 9. Releasing tie-rod end with tool No. S.160

2. Referring to Fig. 9, extract the tie-rod ends from the steering arms, after removing the securing nuts and washers.

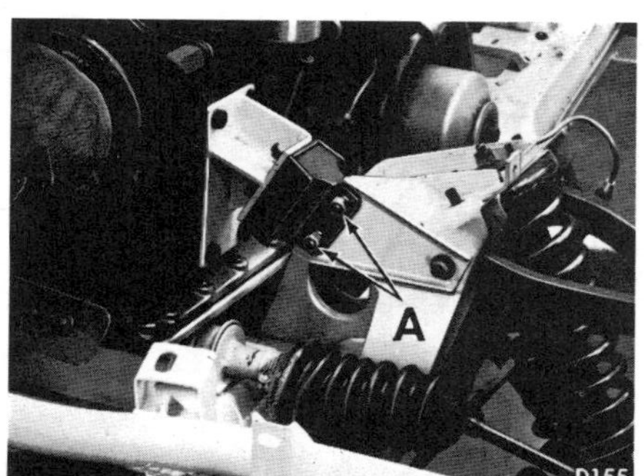

Fig. 10. Engine mounting bolts "A"

3. Referring to Fig. 4, remove in the following order, items (24), (23), (20) and (21).
4. Using a sling and hoist, relieve the vehicle of the weight of the engine, and remove the bolts (A) Fig. 10; then raise the engine approximately ¾" (19 mm.) (Vitesse only).
5. Move the steering unit forward to disengage the coupling from the steering column, and manoeuvre the unit from the vehicle, via the valance aperture on the driver's side.

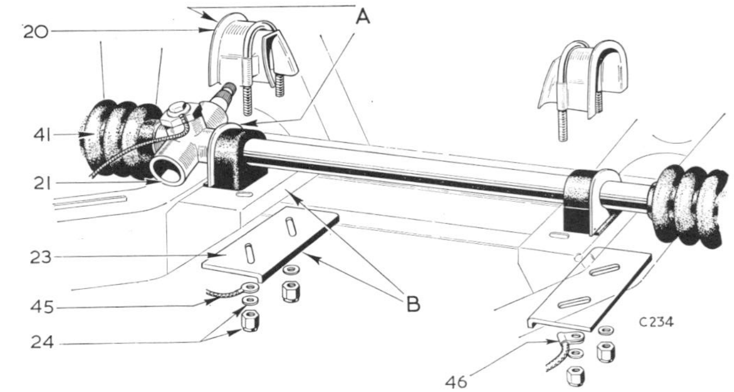

A Distance between flanges must be ⅛" (3·17 mm.)

B Flange of item (23) must contact innermost flange of frame.

20 "U" bolt

21 Rubber bush

23 Locating plates

24 Nyloc nuts

41 Rubber gaiter

45 Steering column earth cables

46 Engine earth cable

Fig. 11. Steering unit attachments

Refitting

1. Referring to Figs. 1 and 11, ensure that the steering unit is assembled to the dimensions given.
2. Rotate the pinion shaft from lock to lock, counting the number of revolutions. Turn the pinion shaft back half this number of rotations ; thus centralizing the rack in relation to the pinion.
3. Position the steering wheel in the straight ahead position, *i.e.*, with the spokes horizontal and beneath the wheel boss centre.
4. Manoeuvre the steering unit through the wing valance aperture on the driver's side of the vehicle (Herald and Vitesse) and engage the steering column in the flexible coupling.
5. Fit the rubber bushes (21) to the steering unit. Assemble the "U" bolts (20) as shown on Fig. 11 and loosely secure them with the plates (23) and nyloc nuts (24).
6. Push the "U" bolt assemblies outwards until a ⅛" (3·175 mm.) clearance exists between the flange plates welded on the rack tube and the retainers welded to the "U" bolts.
7. Hold the "U" bolts in the position achieved in (6), whilst an assistant slides the plates (23) inwards to abut their flanged faces against the chassis frame flange. Tighten the nuts.
8. Fit the nyloc nut (8) and bolt (9) to the steering coupling (7).
9. Re-connect the earth strap from the steering unit to the chassis frame.
10. Refit the tie-rod ends (44) to the steering arms and secure with plain washers (18) and nyloc nuts (19).
11. Check the front wheel alignment as described on page 4·201.

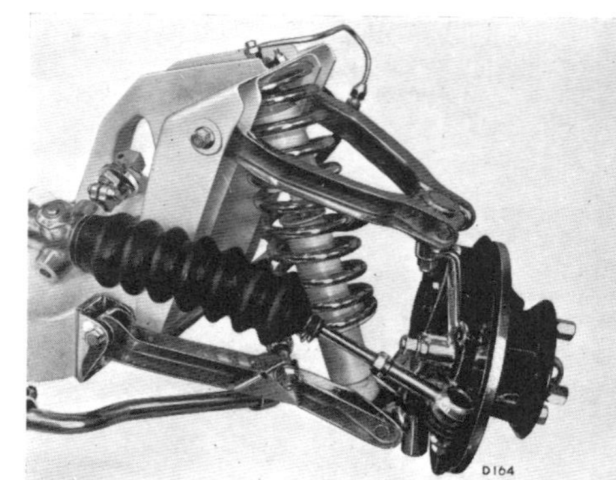

Fig. 12. Tie-rod attachments

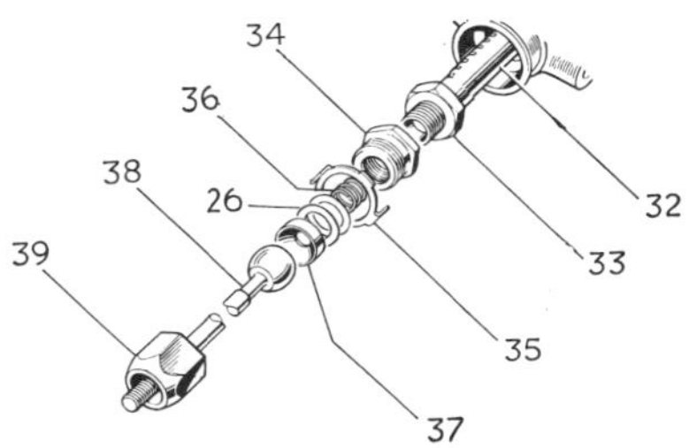

Fig. 13. Tie-rod inner ball joints

Steering Unit (Fig. 4)

Dismantle

Release the clips (42) and (40), and slide both bellows towards the outer ball joints. Slacken the locknuts (33) and unscrew both outer tie rod assemblies from the rack (32). Withdraw the coil spring (36) from each end of the rack.

Release the tabwasher (35), unscrew the sleeve nut (34) and remove the tabwasher (35), shims (26) and cup (37). Slacken the locknuts (43) and unscrew the outer ball joint assemblies (44) from the tie rods (38).

Remove the locknuts (43), rubber bellows (41), clips (42) and cup nut (39) from each outer tie-rod (38).

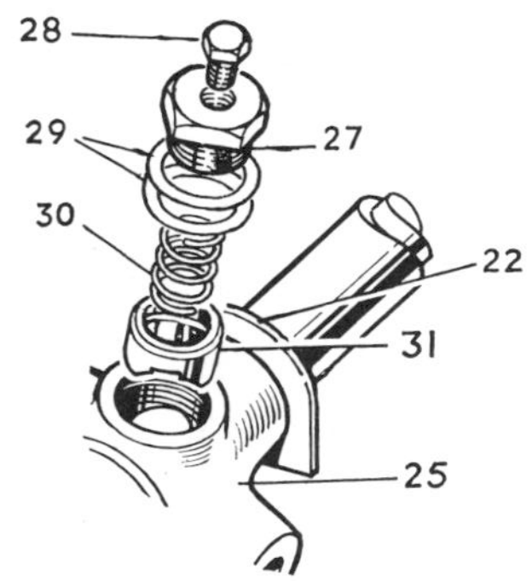

Fig. 14. Pinion thrust pad assembly

Remove the locknuts (33) from the ends of the rack. Unscrew the cap (27) and remove the shims (29), spring (30) and pressure pad (31) from the housing.

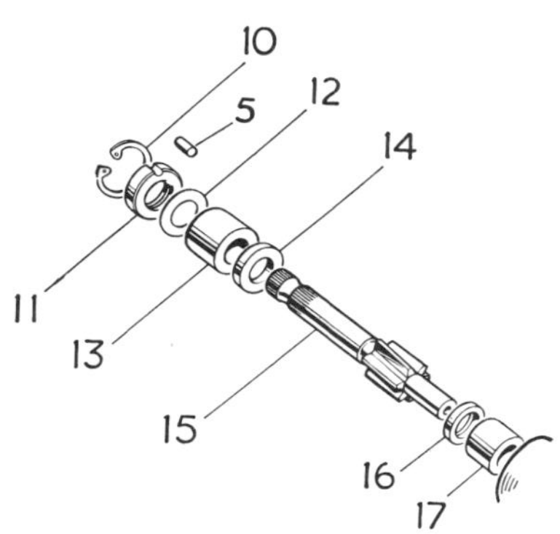

Fig. 15. Pinion assembly

Remove the circlip (10) and withdraw the pinion assembly, taking care not to lose the dowel peg (5). Remove the retaining ring (11), shims (12), bush (13) and thrust washer (14). Detach the rubber "O" ring from the annular groove in the retaining ring (11).

Withdraw the rack (32) from the tube (25) and remove the thrust washer (16) and bush (17) from the pinion housing.

Assembly

Insert the rack (32) into the tube (25) and place the bush (17) and thrust washer (16) into the pinion housing.

Adjust the pinion end float as follows:—

1. Assemble the thrust washer (14), bush (13) and retaining ring (11) to the pinion (15). Insert the assembly into the pinion housing and secure the pinion with the circlip (10).
2. Mount a dial gauge on the tube as shown on Fig. 17. Push the pinion down to its limit and zero the dial gauge. Lift the shaft until the retaining ring contacts the circlip and note the dial reading. This represents the total pinion shaft end float. Remove the circlip (10) and withdraw the pinion shaft assembly. Remove the retaining ring (11) and renew its rubber "O" ring.
3. Make up a shim pack to give minimum end float consistent with free rotation of the pinion shaft. Shims are available in 0·004″ (0·102 mm.) and 0·010″ (0·254 mm.) thickness.
4. Assemble the shim pack (12) and retainer ring (11) to the pinion. Re-insert the assembly into the housing and finally secure it by fitting the dowel (5) and circlip (10).

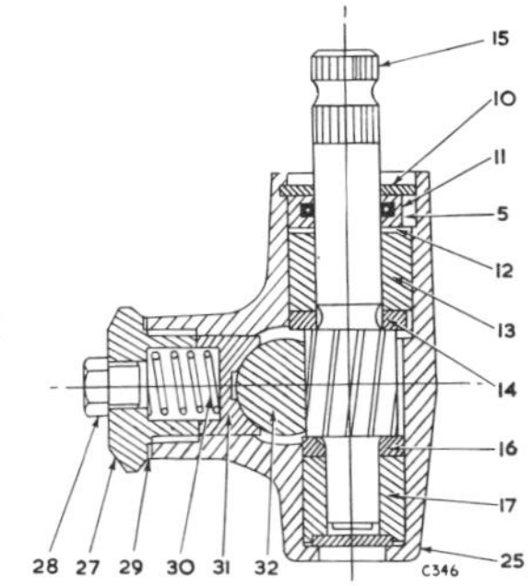

Fig. 16. Cross-section through steering unit

Fig. 17. Measuring pinion end float

Adjust the pinion pressure pad as follows:—

5. Fit the plunger (31) and cap nut (27) to the rack tube (25). Tighten the nut to eliminate all end float and, using feeler gauges, measure the clearance between the nut and the rack tube faces as shown on Fig. 18. Remove the cap nut (27) and plunger (31).
6. Make up a shim pack equal to the cap housing clearance plus 0·004″ (0·1 mm.) nominal end float.
7. Pack the unit with grease and assemble the cap nut (27), shim pack (29), spring (30) and plunger (31) to the housing (25) and tighten the cap nut.
8. When the unit is correctly adjusted, a force of 2 lb. (0·91 kg.) is required to rotate the pinion shaft at a radius of 7·9″ (20·3 cm.) see Fig. 19. Check and re-adjust the unit, if necessary, by adding or subtracting shims from beneath the cap nut (27).

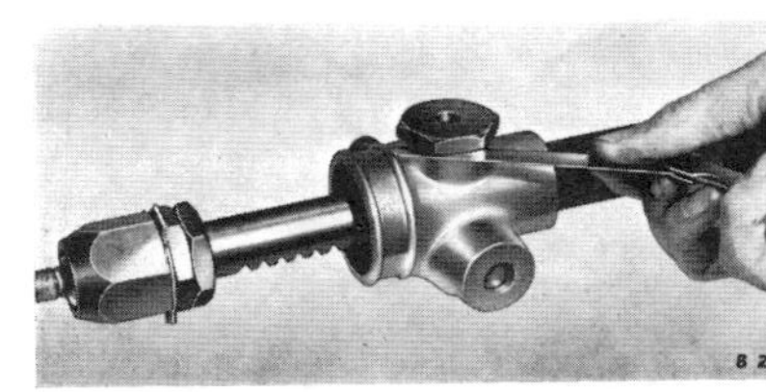

Fig. 18. Using feeler gauge to determine shim thickness required under cap nut

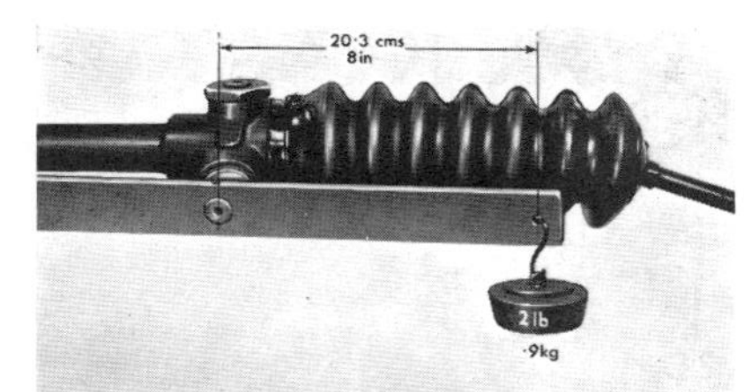

Fig. 19. Measuring load required to rotate pinion

EXPLODED ARRANGEMENT OF STEERING COLUMN

Assembling and Adjusting Tie-rod Inner Ball Joints

1. Slide the cup nut (39) over the tie-rod (38) and insert the cup (37) into the cup nut (39).

2. Position the lock tab (35) over the sleeve nut (34) and screw this fully into the cup nut (39). With the cup nut held in a vice, move the tie-rod (38) axially to determine the approximate shim pack thickness required. Remove the assembly from the vice and remove sleeve nut (34).

3. Prepare a shim pack (26) in excess of the estimated ball end movement and insert this in the cup nut behind the cup (37).

4. Screw the sleeve nut (34) with lock tab (35) fully into the cup nut (39).

5. Using feeler gauges, measure the gap between the sleeve nut flange, lock tab (35) and cup nut face (39). This dimension, plus 0·002″ (0·05 mm.) is the amount by which the trial shim pack must be reduced to give correct ball end movement.

6. Dismantle the ball joint and re-assemble it with the correct shim pack determined in (5). Test adjustment by applying a load of 1½ lb. (0·681 kg.) at the outer end of the tie-rod (38), when the tie-rod should articulate freely. If necessary, adjust the shim pack until correct operation is obtained. Shims are obtainable in 0·002″ (0·05 mm.) and 0·010″ (0·254 mm.) thickness.

7. When adjustment is correct, lock the assembly by bending the lock tab (35) over the sleeve nut (34) and cup nut (39).

Refitting Ball Joint to Steering Rack

1. Screw the locknut (33) on to the end of the rack (32) so that its position corresponds with dimensions 3 + 4 + 5 + 3 on Fig. 1, *i.e.*, 24·40″ (619·76 mm.) between inner locknut faces.

2. Insert the spring (36) into the end of the rack and screw the ball joint assembly as far as possible up to the locknut (33).

3. Repack the bellows (41) with grease (½ oz. Retinax "A" from dry) before securing them in position with clips (42) and wire (40).

4. Fit the locknuts (43) and outer tie-rod ends (44) to the tie-rods (38), adjusting them so that they correspond with dimensions 1 + 2, Fig. 1, *i.e.*, 10·13″ (257·43 mm.).

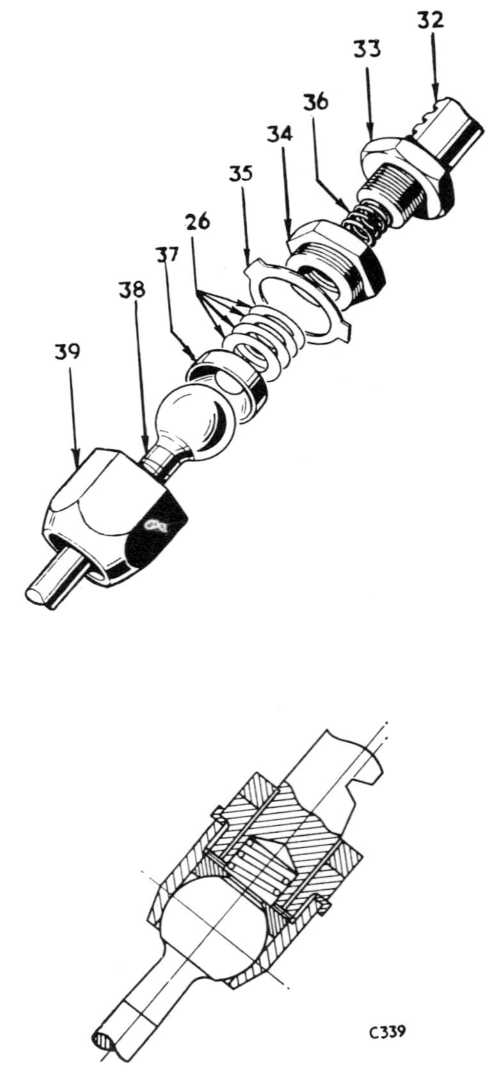

Fig. 21. Tie-rod coupling details

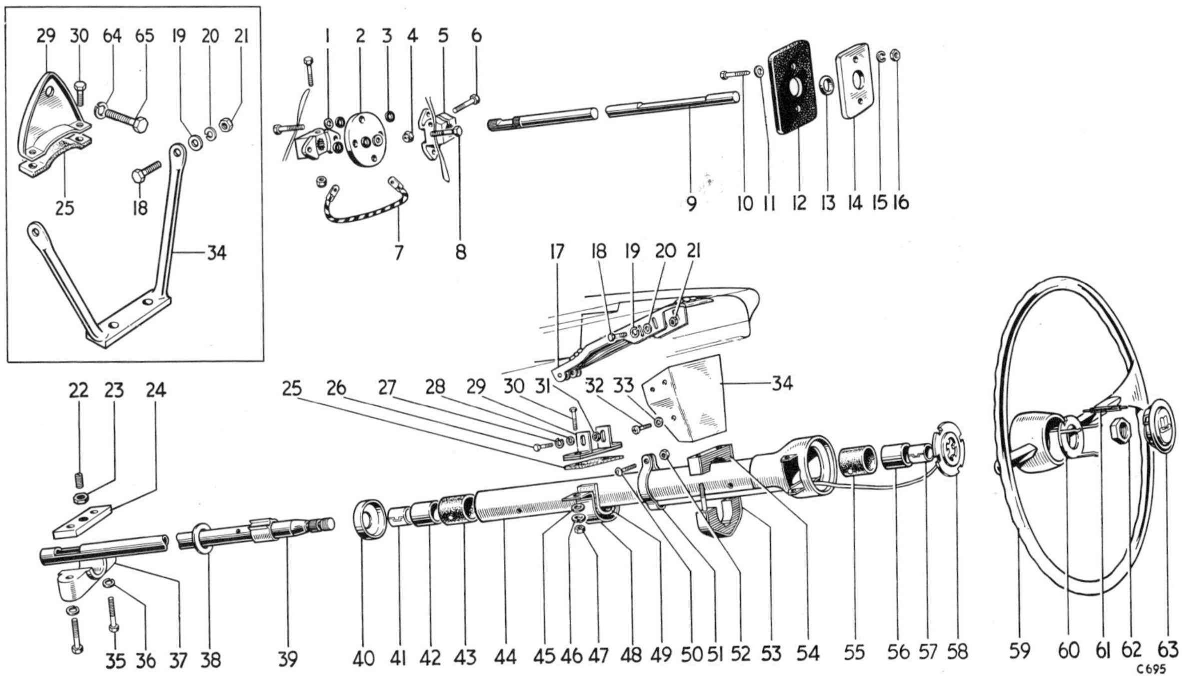

Fig. 20. Exploded arrangement of steering column

Key to Fig. 20

1 Washer
2 Disc
3 Rubber washer
4 Nyloc nut
5 Adaptor
6 Pinch bolt
7 Earth cable
8 Bolt
9 Lower steering column
10 Bolt
11 Washer
12 Rubber seal
13 Washer
14 Retaining plate
15 Spring washer
16 Nut
17 Support bracket
18 Bolt
19 Spring washer
20 Washer
21 Nut
22 Socket screw
23 Nut
24 Clamp plate
25 Felt pad
26 Bolt
27 Spring washer
28 Washer
29 Bracket
30 Bolt
31 Nut
32 Screw
33 Washer
34 Bracket
35 Bolt
36 Spring washer
37 Clamp
38 Nylon washer
39 Upper inner steering column
40 End cap
41 Nylon bush
42 Steel bush
43 Rubber bush
44 Outer upper column
45 Washer
46 Spring washer
47 Nut
48 Lower outer column clamp
49 Felt pad
50 Screw
51 Cable trough clip
52 Nut
53 Upper clamp (lower half)
54 Upper clamp (upper half)
55 Rubber bush
56 Steel bush
57 Nylon bush
58 Horn contact ring
59 Steering wheel
60 Clip
61 Horn contact brush
62 Nut
63 Horn push
64 Spring washer
65 Bolt

Inset shows upper outer column clamp attachment
on Herald 1200, 12/50 and Vitesse.

Fig. 22. Steering column lower coupling

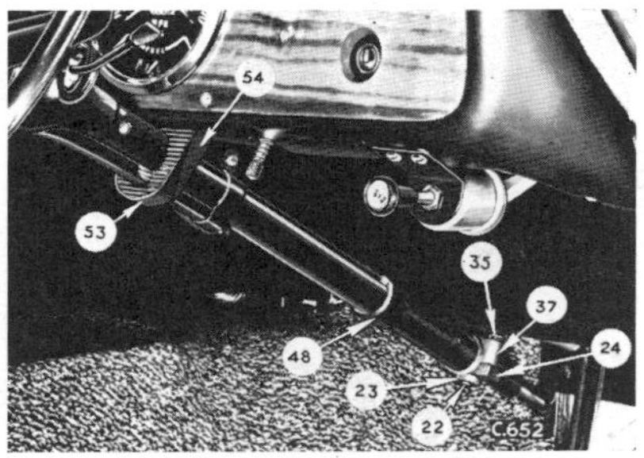

Fig. 23. Steering column attachments (HERALD 1200, 12/50 AND VITESSE)

Fig. 24. Removing flasher and lighting switches

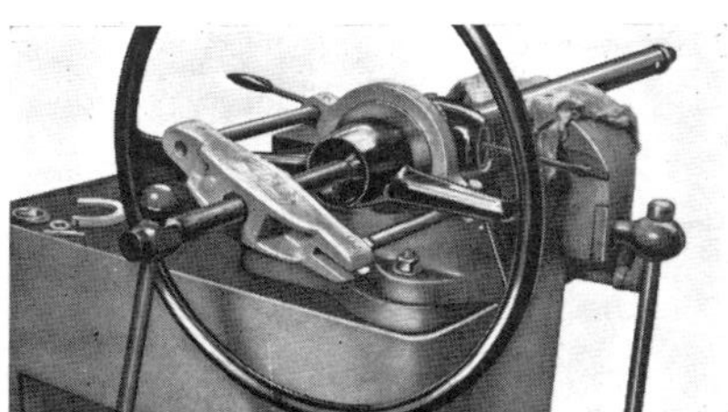

Fig. 25. Using Tool No. S3600 to remove steering wheel

STEERING COLUMN

Removal

1. Remove the bolt (9) from the steering coupling (7), Fig. 22.

2. Disconnect the steering head cables at their snap connectors beneath the facia, and note the colours to facilitate re-assembly.

3. Referring to Figs. 20 and 23, remove the outer column support clamp (48) (lower) and the lower portion of the steering column upper clamp (53).
   NOTE : On Spitfire models remove the driver's side glove box to obtain access to the nuts.

4. Withdraw the steering column assembly from the vehicle.

To Dismantle

1. Remove the cable trough (51).

2. Prise the horn push assembly (63) from the steering wheel boss and withdraw the contact brush (61).

3. Remove the switch covers and detach each switch from the column (Fig. 24).

4. Remove the bolts (35), spring washers (36), and detach the halves of the impact clamp (37) and (24). Withdraw the lower column (9) downwards and detach the nylon washer (38). Remove the upper inner column (39) with the steering wheel (59) in an upwards direction.

5. Hold the column (39) in the protected jaws of a vice and remove the nut (62) and spring clip (60). Use an extractor as shown on Fig. 25 to remove the wheel from the column.

6. Remove the end cap (40) and depress the protrusions on the rubber bushes (43) and (55) as shown on Fig. 26. Using a length of bar, eject the bushes from the outer column (44). Remove the metal inserts (42) and nylon bushes (41) from the rubber bushes.

Re-Assembly

1. Assemble the nylon bush (41) and steel sleeve (42) to each rubber bush (43) and push the assembly into the bottom of the outer column (44) engaging the locating lugs with the holes as shown on Fig. 27. Ensure that the metal reinforcement ring at the end of the bush is positioned towards the lower end of the column. Repeat the procedure with the upper bush assembly.

2. Fit the end cap (40) to the lower end of the column (44).

3. Fit the steering wheel to the inner column (39), aligning the direction indicator cancelling lugs on the column to correspond with the steering wheel spokes as shown on Fig. 28. Fit the clip (60) and secure with the nut (62). Peen the metal of the nut to the inner column to prevent it unscrewing.

   NOTE : When replacing an old flasher switch with a new switch, the new cancellation clip and setscrew must also be fitted.

4. Insert the inner column (39) into the outer column (44), taking care not to dislodge the bushes.

5. Pass the cables of the direction indicator and lighting switches through the apertures in the upper end of the outer column, and fit the switches and covers.

6. Insert the horn contact plunger (61) into the steering wheel boss and fit the horn button assembly (63).

7. Fit the lower column (9) and assemble the impact clamp (37), leaving the bolts (35) slack at this stage.

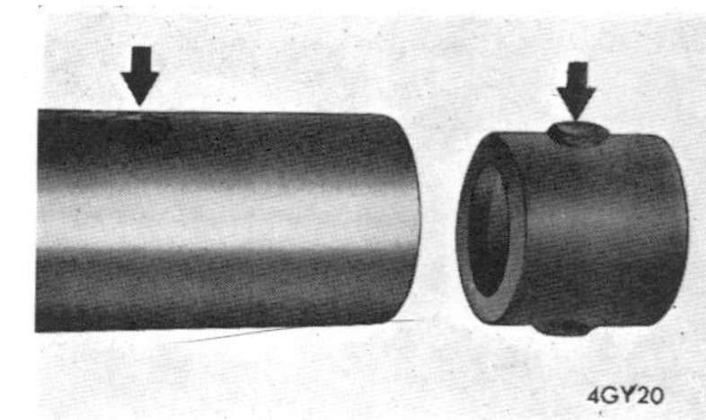

Fig. 26. Protrusions on rubber bushes and corresponding holes in steering column

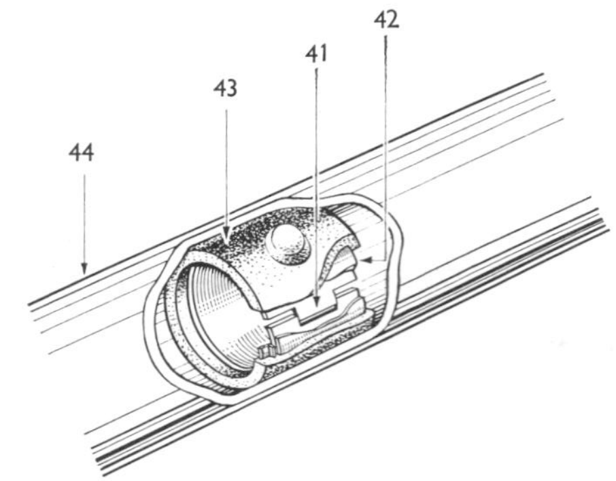

Fig. 27. Steering column bush assembly

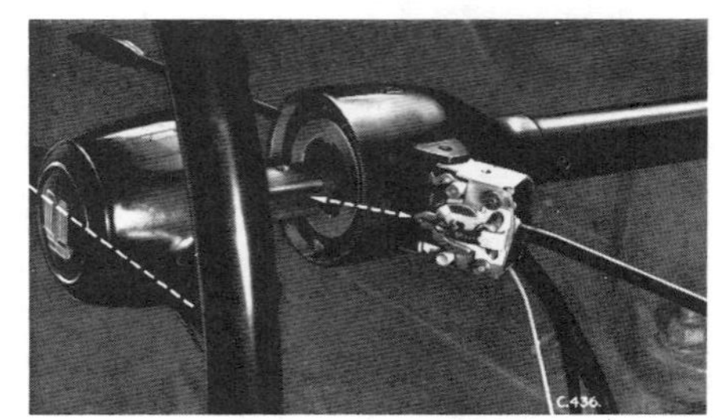

Fig. 28. Position of direction indicator cancelling lugs in relation to the steering wheel

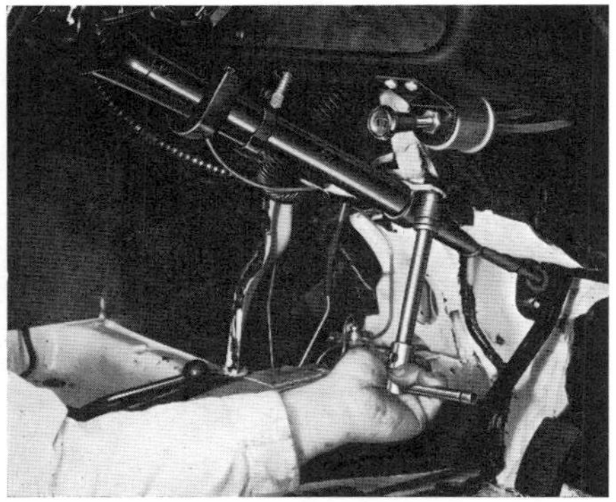

Fig. 29. Tightening lower column clamp nuts

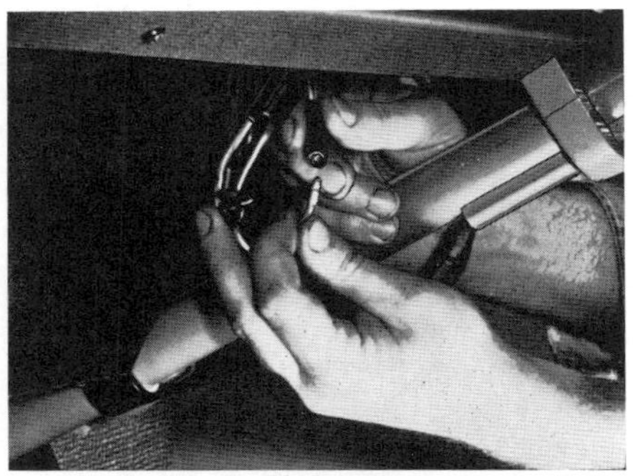

Fig. 30. Reconnecting cables at snap connectors

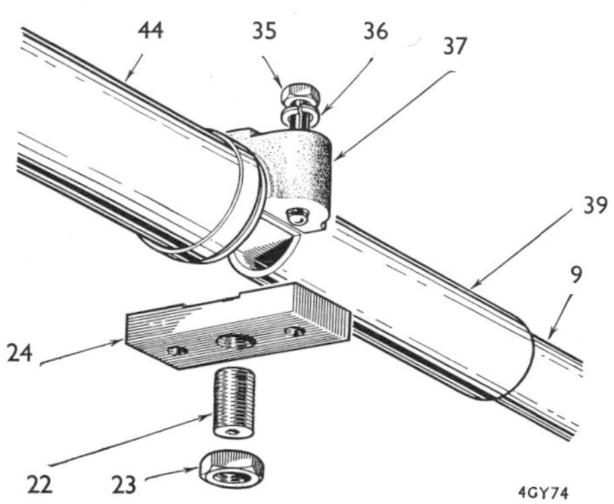

Fig. 31. Exploded view of steering column impact clamp

To Refit the Column Assembly

1. Fit the steering column assembly to the vehicle, passing the column through the rubber grommet in the bulkhead.
2. Fit the cable trough and the lower half of the upper support clamp (53).
3. Fit the lower clamp (48) with felt (49) and secure with nuts (47) and washers (45) and (46).
4. Position the steering wheel at the desired height and tighten the clamps (53) and (48).
5. With the steering wheel and road wheels in the straight ahead position, engage the lower column (9) with the steering coupling and secure with the pinch bolt (6) and nut (4).
6. Re-tighten the bolts (35) on the impact clamp (37). Using a socket key tighten the screw (22), Fig. 31, by hand as much as possible without bending the wrench. Tighten the locknut (23).

   NOTE : The column will be unable to telescope if adjusted to its lowest position.
7. Re-connect the horn, traffic indicator and lighting cables at the snap connectors and re-clip the cables beneath the facia.
8. Refit the driver's side glove box, if previously removed.

COLUMN ALIGNMENT
SPITFIRE ONLY

To align the steering column in relation to body mounting, limited adjustment is permitted by slots in items (17) and (29), Fig. 20.

STEERING

Steering Geometry and Suspension Geometry

The term "steering geometry" refers to the layout of the steering mechanism and any of its dimensions, linear or angular, which contribute to the required behaviour of the steering system. The steering system is always designed to comply with the specification of the front suspension, in order that the best possible steering behaviour is obtained under all conditions.

For example, Toe-in and Camber are classed as suspension geometry; K.P.I. and Castor are classed as steering geometry.

Departure from any steering/suspension dimensions may result in unsatisfactory steering and/or abnormal wear of tyres, steering and suspension components.

NOTE : Poor steering and tyre wear is often caused by unbalance of the tyres themselves.

To avoid using jigs for rear wheel alignment, it is recommended that optical equipment (*e.g.*, Optiline, Optoflex, etc.) be used, enabling the front and rear wheels to be aligned simultaneously. This equipment projects a beam of light in a plane at right angles to each individual wheel axle, on to a graduated screen. The various angles and dimensions may be read directly and accurately off the screens.

Steering Axis Inclination (Fig. 32)

This is the angle in front elevation between the steering axis "A" and the vertical line "B". The steering axis is the continuation of the lower trunnion centre line through the centre point of the upper ball swivel, and it is about this axis that the wheel pivots as it is turned for control of vehicle direction.

Camber (Fig. 32)

Positive camber is the amount in degrees that the front wheels are tilted outwards at the top "C", from the vertical line "B".

Castor (Fig. 33)

Castor is the angle in side elevation between the steering axis "A" and the vertical line "B". It is considered positive when the steering axis is inclined rearwards.

Wheel Alignment

To ensure parallel tracking when the vehicle is moving, the recommended static setting is parallel to $\frac{1}{16}$" (1·6 mm.) toe-in.

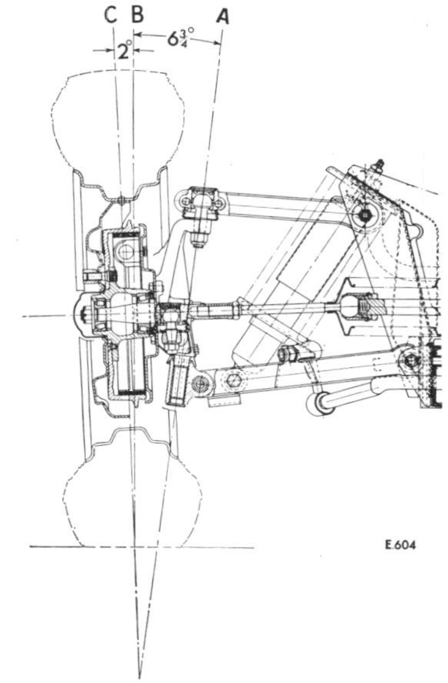

Fig. 32. Steering axis inclination and camber angle

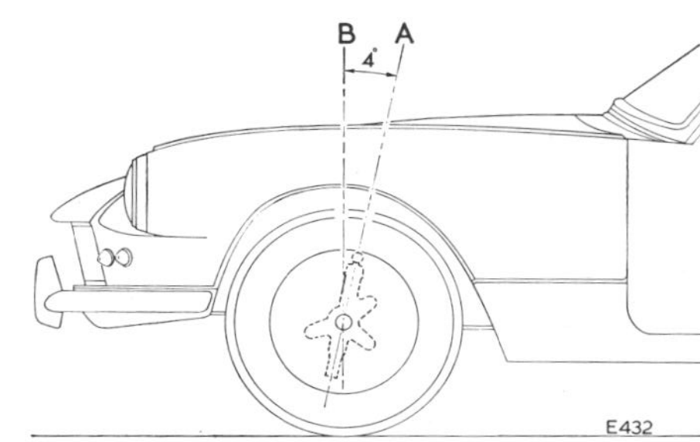

Fig. 33. Castor angle

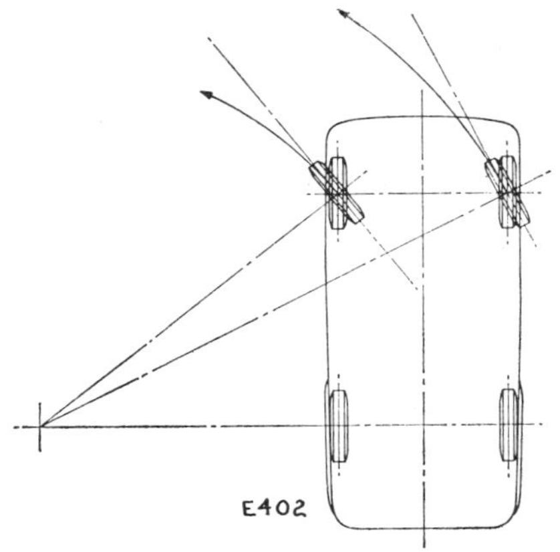

Fig. 34. Showing the relative angles of the front wheels when making a turn

Turning Radius Angles

Inside Wheel	Outside Wheel
20 degrees 48° max.	20 degrees 50° 30′ max.

Toe-out on Turns (Fig. 34)

This is the alignment of the front wheels relative to each other as they are turned to the left or right.

To eliminate scuffing when the vehicle is making a turn, each front wheel must be at right angles to the radius from its point of contact with the road to the centre of the turning circle. Thus the inner wheel toes-out relative to the outer wheel.

Unfortunately, using simple steering mechanisms, it is not possible to obtain the exact toe-out at every position through the complete turn from straight-ahead to full lock. However, scuffing can be minimised by careful positioning of the steering components.

Static Laden

The steering dimensions illustrated on Figs. 32 and 33 apply to a vehicle when static laden.

This condition is obtained by placing a 150 lb. (68 kg.) weight on each front seat and two similar weights on the rear seat.

OPTICAL ALIGNMENT EQUIPMENT

General Recommendations

To obtain the greatest accuracy from optical alignment equipment, it is necessary to comply with the following instructions:—

(a) Assemble the equipment in accordance with the manufacturer's instructions.
(b) Set the screen parallel and at right angles to a level floor.
(c) Set the car square to the screen with the centre of the front wheels 5 ft. 7 in. from the face of the screen.
(d) Adjust the tyre pressures and load the vehicle to the static laden condition.

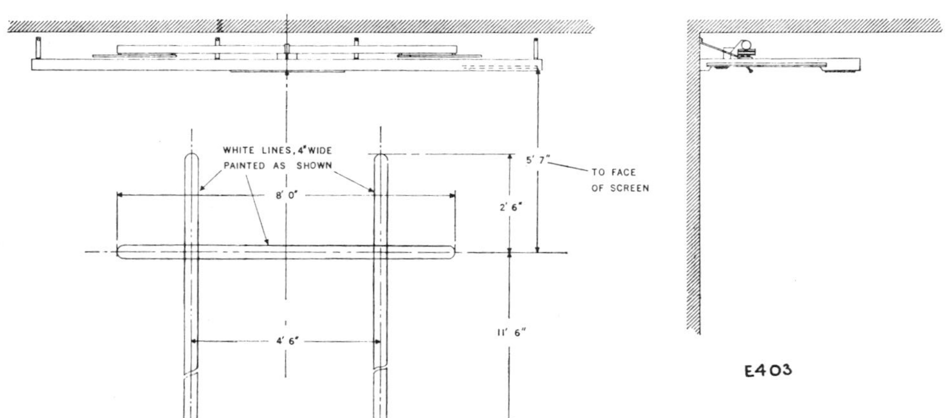

Fig. 35. Suggested floor markings relative to the optical screen face

Attaching the Projectors

Attach the wheel clamps by resting the lower support (6) on the edge of the wheel rim and pushing the upper support (4) until the cut-screws touch the inside of the upper wheel rim. Whilst pressing the upper support against the wheel rim edge, turn the cam lock (3) to secure the clamp.

Jack up the front wheels and ensure that the wheel clamp is clear of obstructions when rotating the wheel. Loosen the projector cam lock (5) centre the projector pivot (7) on the rods and retighten the cam lock (5). Slide the projector on to its pivot and tighten the clamping bolt (9). Repeat the procedure on the opposite front wheel.

Compensating for Wheel Run-out

The projector pivot mountings are provided with three large diameter milled edged compensating screws (2) for adjusting the projector beams to the true axis of the road wheels. Compensation for wheel run-out is effected as follows:—

Connect the projectors to the control panel and, by sliding the telescopic projector lens (8) backwards or forwards, focus the light beam on the vertical line trueing scale immediately above the mirror hole in the screen.

Slacken the projector clamp screw (9) and, holding the projector (10) to keep the light image within the trueing scale, slowly rotate the road wheel. Note the extent of movement made by the light image across the scale and stop turning the wheel when the image reaches one extreme position.

Adjust the rearmost compensating screw (2) to bring the image to the centre of its movement. If two screws point to the rear, adjust both evenly. Repeat as necessary until the light image remains laterally stationary during wheel rotation.

Lower the wheels on to the centre of the turntables and apply the brake pedal depressor. Take hold of the bumper and jolt the car up and down a few more times. Unlock the turntables and jolt the car a few more times.

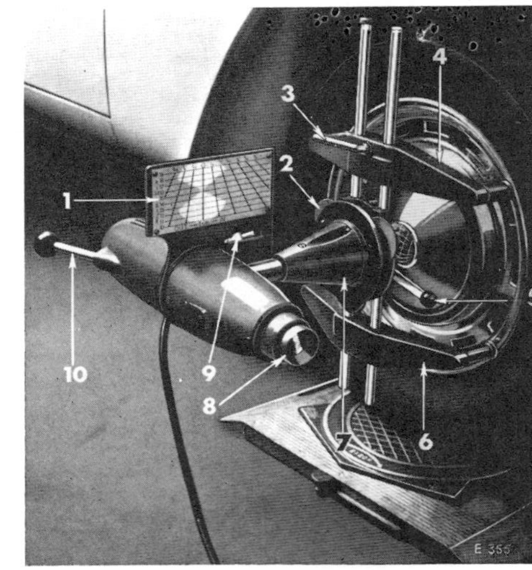

Fig. 36. Projector attachment

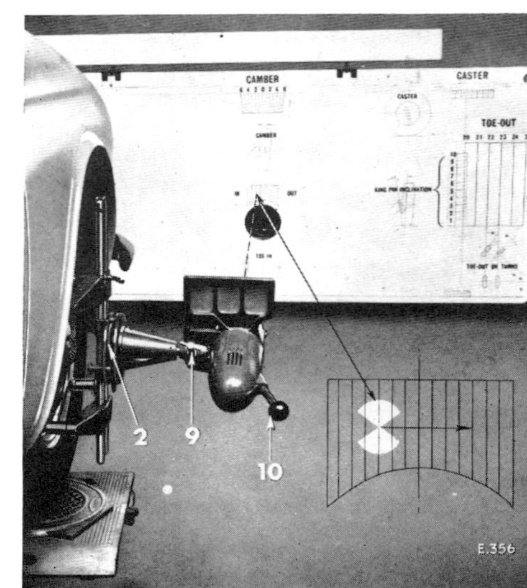

Fig. 37. Checking wheel run-out

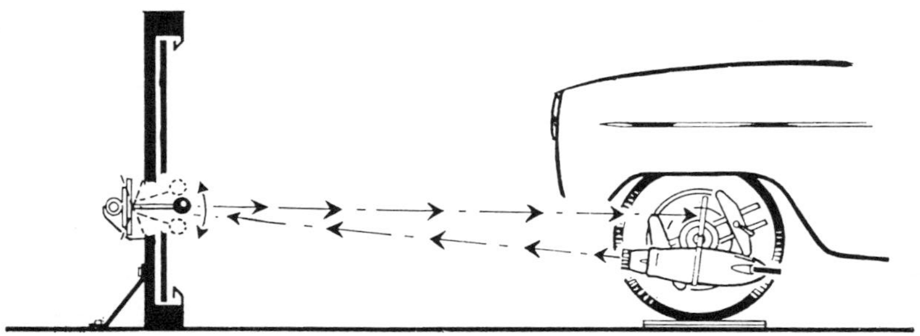

Fig. 38. Aligning mirrors to re-direct light image to the toe-in scale

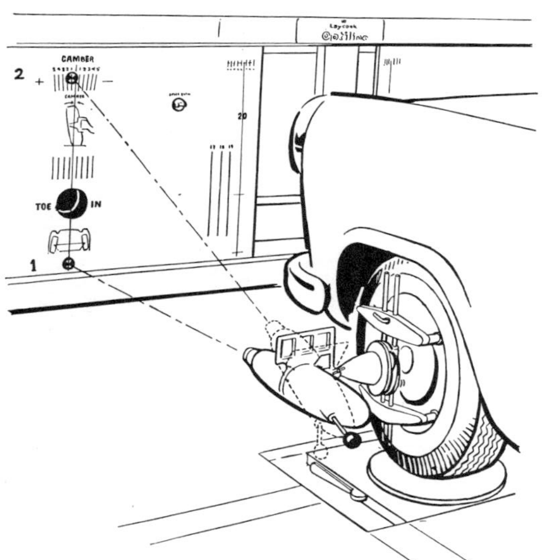

Fig. 39. Checking front wheel camber angle

TAKE CARE TO ENSURE THAT THE SCREENS REMAIN IN THIS POSITION FOR ALL FURTHER OPERATIONS.

Toe-in

To check toe-in condition, aim the light image at the centre of the mirror and, by tilting the mirror up or down, re-direct and focus the image on to the toe-in scale (1), Fig. 36, attached to the top of the projector. Turn the steering to align the light image with the zero line on the scale. In this position the road wheel is at right angles to the mirror.

Aim the opposite projector at the centre of its mirror and focus the reflected image on the toe-in scale. A direct reading of the toe-in condition can now be read from this scale.

Centre Steering

When toe-in checks have been completed, turn the steering to equalize the readings on both projector toe-in scales and check the position of the steering wheel spokes. These should be perfectly horizontal.

Camber — Straight ahead position

IMPORTANT: Before taking a camber reading it is essential that the wheel is in the straight-ahead position (this applies for both L.H. and R.H. front wheels).

To check the camber of either front wheel, aim the light image at the centre of the mirror and, by tilting the mirror up or down, re-direct and focus the image on to the toe-in scale attached to the top of the projector. Turn the steering to align the light image with the zero line on the scale. In this position the road wheel is at right angles to the mirror.

By traversing the screen horizontally and tilting the projector, aim and refocus the light image on the measuring cross below the mirror. Tilt the projector to bring the image into the camber scale and note the reading.

Repeat the procedure on the opposite wheel.

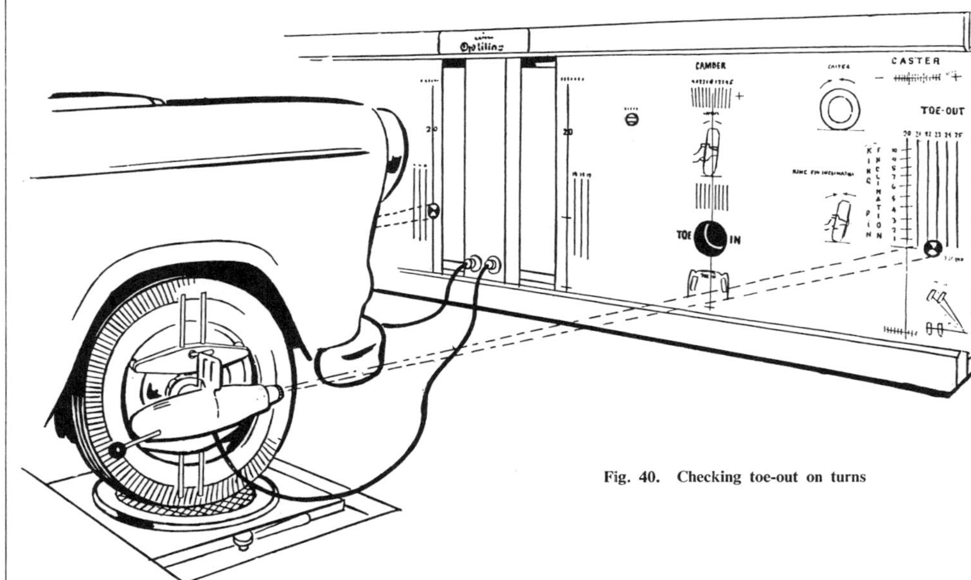

Fig. 40. Checking toe-out on turns

King Pin Inclination and Castor (Fig. 41)

Turn the wheel inwards and tilt the projector to focus the light image on the lower measuring cross (Position 1). Tilt the projector to bring the image into Position 2 **and note the reading on the Castor index scale.**

Tilt the projector to focus the image on the measuring cross (Position 3) and tighten the projector clamping screw. Turn the wheel 20° outwards and **note the reading on the K.P.I. scale (Position 4).**

Slacken the projector clamping screw and, by turning the road wheels and tilting the projector as necessary, focus the light image on the lower Castor index scale (Position 5) to the same value noted in Position 2.

Tilt the projector to bring the image into Position 4 and **note the reading on the Castor scale.**

Toe-out on Turns (Fig. 40)

Turn the L.H. wheel inwards and focus the light image on the mean measuring cross on the 20° line nearest the inner edge of the L.H. screen. Tilt the projector on the opposite wheel and focus the light image on the base line of the Toe-out scale, nearest to the outer edge of the R.H. screen. **This will indicate R.H. wheel toe-out on turns.**

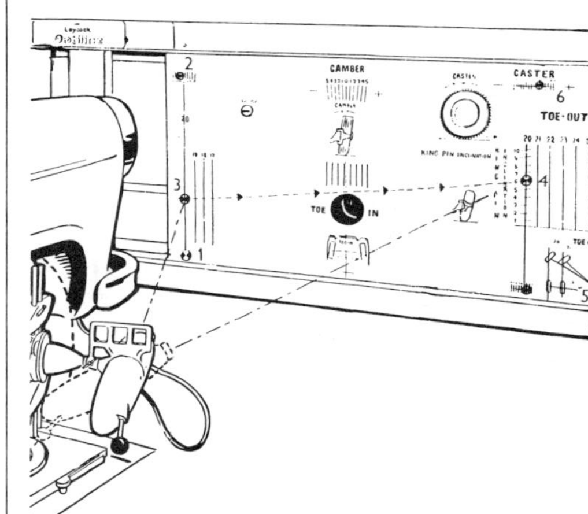

Fig. 41. Measuring castor and king pin inclination

Fig. 42. Scales fitted to the rear wheels

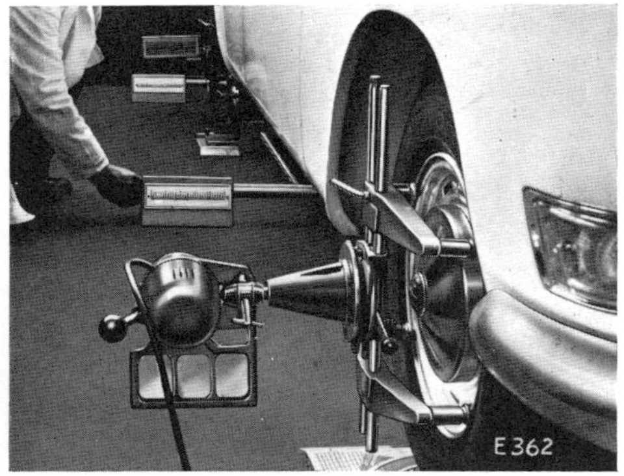

Fig. 43. Centralising the front measuring rod

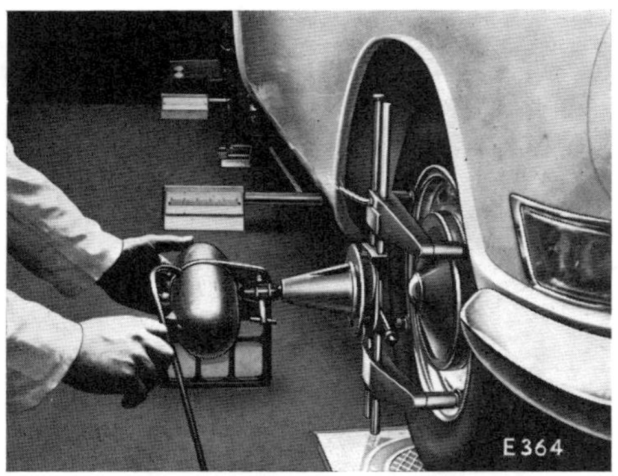

Fig. 44. Centralising the rear measuring rod

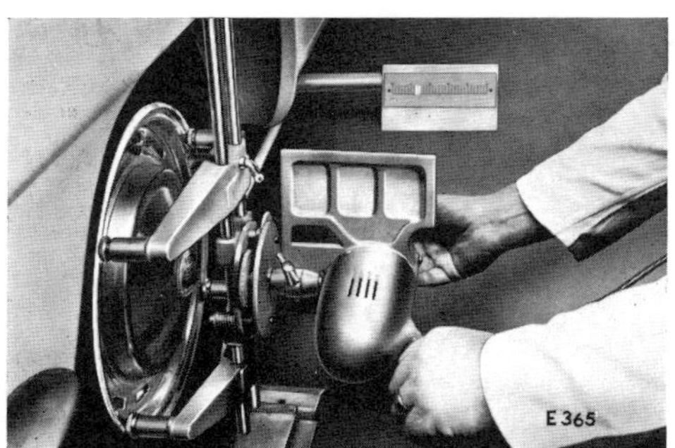

Fig. 45. Checking rear wheel toe-in

Rear Wheel Toe-in

Attach wheel clamps and scales to the rear wheels by following the procedure on page 4·215, for "attaching the projectors", but substituting scales for projectors.

Turn the projectors on the front holders through 180° until the beams of light appear on the scales mounted on the rear holders. Turn the steering wheel until the same reading is obtained on both right and left rear wheel scales.

Mount the distance rods onto the measuring rods; place the assemblies on the floor in front and behind the rear axle with the distance rod plates resting against the wheels.

Focus both beams of light onto the front measuring rod scales, move measuring rods sideways until the same reading is obtained on the right- and left-hand scales; repeat this operation for setting the rear measuring rod.

Remove the projectors from the front holders and fit them in place of the rear wheel scales on the rear holders. Focus the beam of light on both front and rear measuring rods in turn, taking note of the readings obtained; by subtracting one from the other a toe-in value is obtained for each rear wheel.

Rear Wheel Camber (Fig. 46)

1. With the projectors mounted on the rear holders, focus the beam of light onto the main screens and, by traversing the screens horizontally, focus the light image on the measuring cross (Position 1).

2. Tilt the projector to bring the image into the camber scale (Position 2) and note the reading. Repeat the procedure on the opposite side.

Chassis Alignment

When the rear end check is completed, check chassis alignment by placing the wheel indicator scales on the front holders (without disturbing the wheels, as they are set in the straight-ahead position). Readings taken direct from the wheel indicator scales will give an indication of the chassis and axle condition.

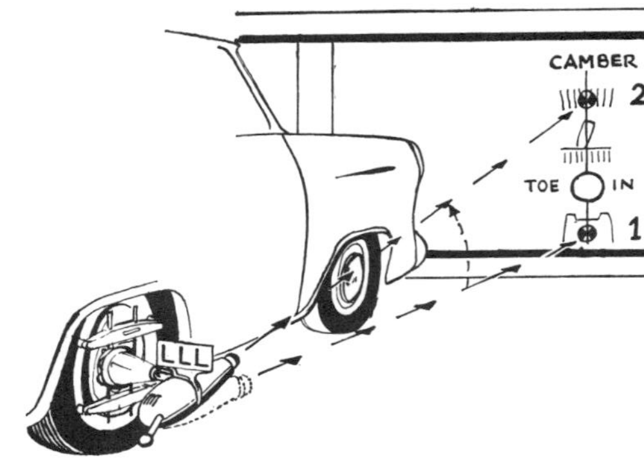

Fig. 46. Checking rear wheel camber

TRIUMPH
HERALD, VITESSE 6
AND
SPITFIRE
WORKSHOP MANUAL

GROUP 5

Comprising :

HERALD RANGE

SPITFIRE RANGE

TRIUMPH
HERALD and VITESSE 6

GROUP 5

CONTENTS

TRIUMPH
SPITFIRE

GROUP 5

CONTENTS

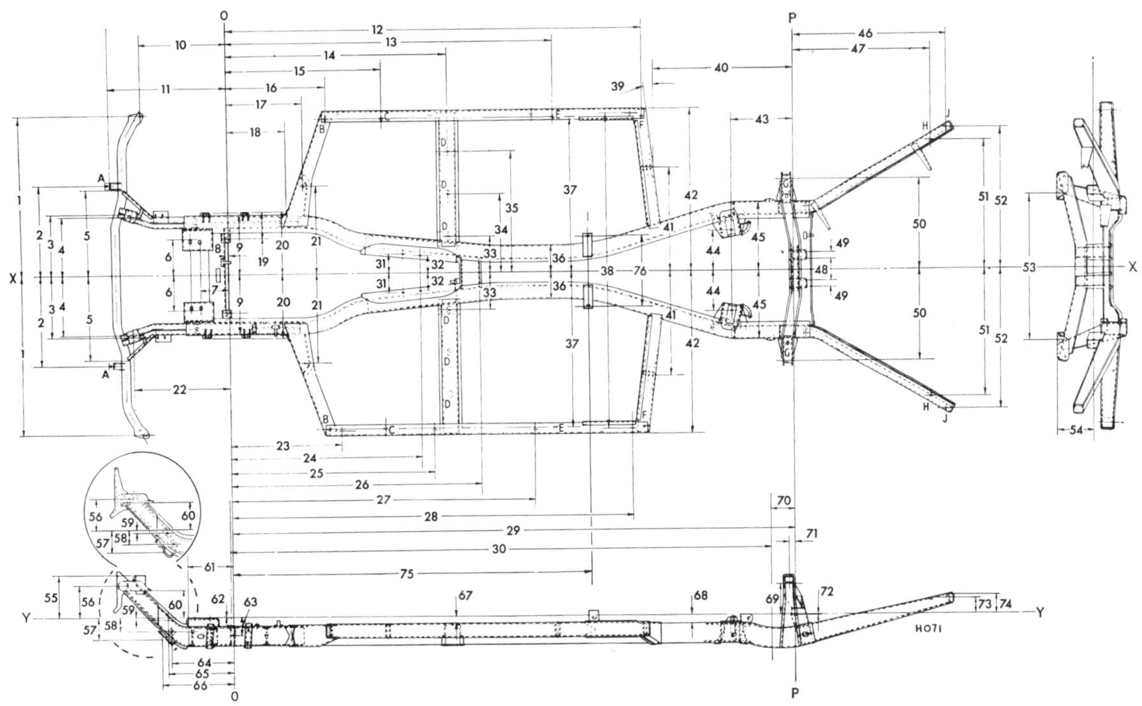

Fig. 1. Chassis Frame – Herald 1200, 12/50, 13/60 and Vitesse 6 (Herald 1200 and 12/50 condition shown inset)

Key to Fig. 1

	Inches	*Centimetres*
1	26·09	66·27
2	14·75	37·47
3	10·07	25·58
	9·94	25·25
4†	9·78	24·84
	9·72	24·69
5	13·50	24·09
	13·38	33·99
6	5·53	14·05
	5·50	13·97
7	4·82	12·24
	4·76	12·09
8	0·50	1·27
9	9·78	24·84
	9·72	24·69
10	14·70	37·34
11	20·06	50·95
	19·94	50·65
12	70·00	177·80
13	55·00	139·70
14	37·37	94·92
	37·25	94·62
15	26·10	66·29
16	16·81	42·69
	16·69	42·39
17	12·78	32·46
	12·72	32·31
18	9·81	24·92
19	4·32	10·97
	4·30	10·92
20	10·32	26·21
21	14·52	36·88
	14·49	38·81
22†	16·56	42·06
	16·44	41·76
23	18·75	47·63
24	32·64	82·91
	32·48	82·49
25	34·50	87·63

	Inches	*Centimetres*
26	42·19	107·16
	41·94	106·53
27	51·50	130·81
28	68·00	172·72
29	95·69	243·05
	95·44	242·42
30	91·76	233·07
31	3·23	8·20
	3·21	8·15
32	2·92	7·42
	2·89	7·34
33	6·03	15·32
	5·97	15·16
34	13·00	33·02
35	20·00	50·80
36	4·25	10·79
37	25·35	64·39
	25·28	64·21
38	51·63	131·14
39	7°27′	7°27′
40	23·54	59·79
	23·42	59·49
41	16·91	42·95
	16·85	42·79
42	26·50	67·31
43	10·70	27·18
	10·65	27·03
44	6·64	16·87
	6·61	16·79
45	11·28	28·65
	11·22	28·49
46	25·94	65·89
47	23·30	59·18
	23·18	58·88
48	3·25	8·26
	3·22	8·18
49	1·51	3·84
50	14·75	37·47
51	21·07	53·52

	Inches	*Centimetres*
	20·94	53·19
52	23·08	58·62
53	24·00	60·96
54	6·22	15·79
55	7·03	17·86
	6·97	17·70
56	5·5	13·97
57†	3·00	7·62
	2·88	7·32
58	1·94	4·93
59	0·25	0·64
60	4·81	12·22
	4·69	11·91
61	7·44	18·89
62	0·20	0·51
	0·18	0·46
63	2·63	6·68
64	10·19	25·88
65	10·78	27·38
66	12·06	30·63
	11·94	30·33
67	1·03	2·62
	0·97	2·46
68	1·13	2·87
69	5·00	12·70
	4·88	12·39
70	4·06	10·31
71	1·12	2·85
	1·00	2·54
72	0·15	0·38
73	2·97	7·54
	2·85	7·24
74	3·47	8·81
75	61·31	155·72
	61·19	155·42
76	10·78	27·38
	10·66	27·07

†13/60 and Vitesse 6 only

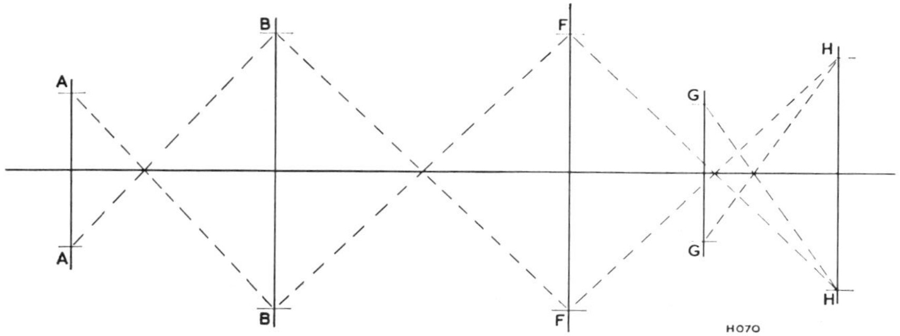

Fig. 2

CHASSIS

Assessment of Damage

Severe damage to a chassis is obvious; damage of a less serious nature can cause distortion which may not be visually apparent.

If a check on the steering and suspension geometry reveals distortion of the chassis, check for twist and squareness.

Checking for Twist

With the vehicle on a clean level floor, place a jack under each jacking point and raise the vehicle sufficiently to enable the road wheels to be removed.

Adjust the jacks until the following conditions are achieved:—

Points "A" are 25·53 in. (64·81 cm.) and points "E" are 24·94 in. (63·35 cm.) above the floor.

This condition sets the datum 20 in. (50·8 cm.) above the floor.

If the heights of both points "A" are unequal, then the chassis is twisted, the amount of twist being the difference in height between points "A".

Checking for Squareness

Position the vehicle as previously described and, referring to Fig. 1, transfer the lettered points to the floor, using a plumb-bob and fine cord.

Letter the transferred points and connect each pair by drawing a straight line between them, as Fig. 2.

Mark the central point of each line and place a straight edge along these mid-points. The frame may be considered true when the straight edge passes through all of these points.

Continue a further check for squareness as follows:—

Using a straight edge mark the diagonals as shown dotted in Fig. 2. If the frame is square then each pair of opposite diagonals must be of equal length and the points of intersection must lie on the same straight line.

Chassis distortion is assessed by the amount and direction which any central point on the transverse line and/or the point of intersection of any pair of diagonals deviates from the centre line.

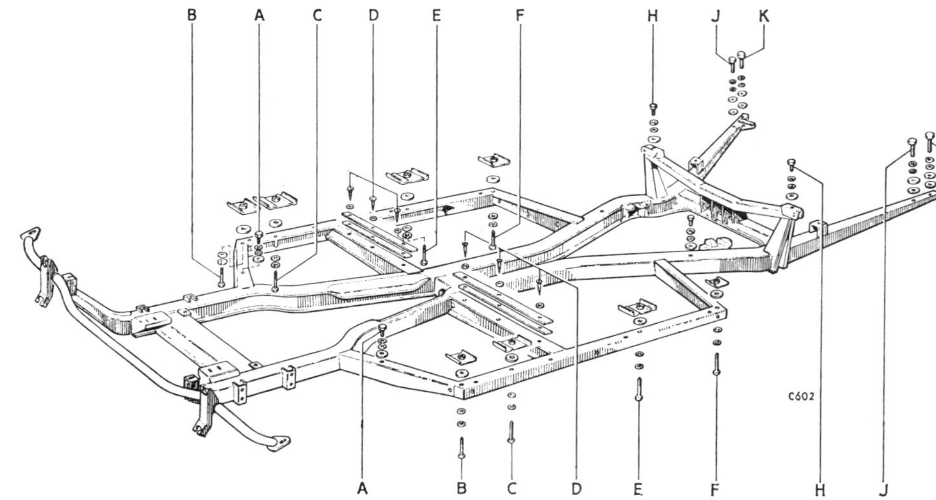

Fig. 1. Body mounting points

The design and construction of the *Herald* and *Vitesse 6* body permits use of conventional chassis and separate body units, so enabling removal and replacement of body sections when accident repair is necessary.

The main units are as follows:—

1. Bonnet
2. Front valance
3. Rear quarter and centre valances
4. Sills
5. Roof
6. Rear end section
7. Centre section
8. Doors

The centre section is the key section and is attached to the frame at six points, A, B and C.

Close tolerance holes in the centre section are provided to enable accurate location of the bolts in the frame at point "D".

Wide tolerance holes in the rear section are provided to enable adequate body adjustment at points "D" (reference page 5·227).

Fig. 2. Dashpanel to front outrigger mounting bolts

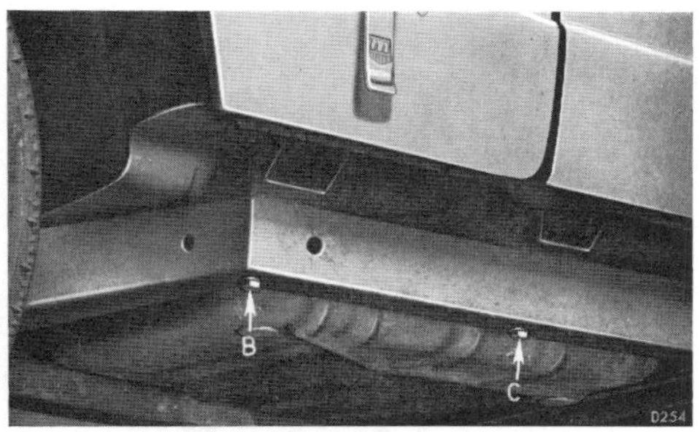

Fig. 3. Front floor to side channel mounting bolt

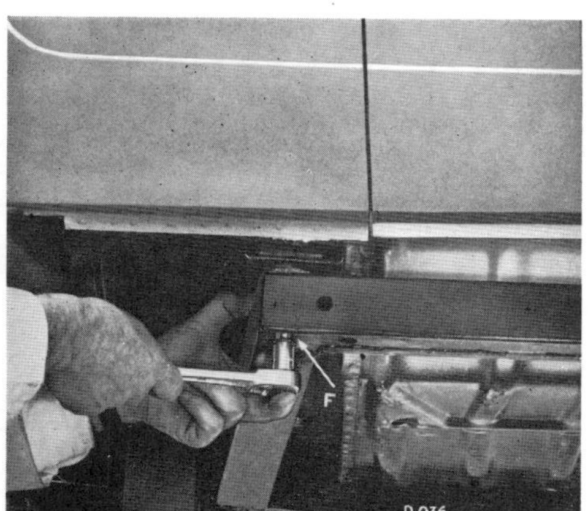

Fig. 4. Rear seat pan side channel mounting bolts

BODY REMOVAL

1200, 12/50, 13/60 and Vitesse 6

Remove the battery, drain the engine coolant and carry out the following:

Disconnect

- lighting cables at bonnet (Fig. 8);
- cables from temperature gauge transmitter, oil pressure switch, generator and coil;
- tachometer drive cable from distributor (*Vitesse* only from Commission No. HB 15001);
- choke and accelerator controls;
- fuel pipe from the tank;
- heater pipes and control cable at water valve (Fig. 114);
- speedometer drive cable from speedo head and pull the cable into the engine compartment.
- handbrake cable at compensator pin.

Remove

- bonnet (page 5·205);
- engine bay side valances (page 5·209);
- brake hydraulic pipe between master cylinder and four-way connector;
- seats (page 5·258);
- gearbox cover (page 5·225);
- floor covering (page 5·257).

Remove both sill panels (page 5·208). Fit reinforcement bracket (Fig. 5) using four ¼″ bolts with nuts and washers.

Referring to page 4·210 slacken the steering column impact clamp, release the clamp bolt from the lower steering coupling and push the inner column upwards, clear of the front suspension.

Remove twenty-two bolts securing the body to the chassis (Fig. 1). The bolts are located as follows:

- two in engine compartment, adjacent to dash panel (A) (Fig. 2);
- eight at frame side channel, adjacent to sill panels (B), (C), (E), (F) (Figs. 3 and 4);
- six at frame intermediate outrigger, through front and rear floor (D);
- four at frame rear extension, through luggage floor (J) and (K).

Lift the body from the frame. The method of lifting the body will be determined by the equipment available. Fig. 5 shows two hoists in use.

To refit, reverse the removal procedure and note the adjustment procedures given on page 5·227.

Reinforcement bracket dimensions:

		Inches	Millimetres
A	..	0·75	19·0
B	..	3·375	85·0
C	..	6·625	168·3
D	..	0·50	12·7
E	..	1·00	25·4

Material: 1″ (25·4 mm.) angle iron

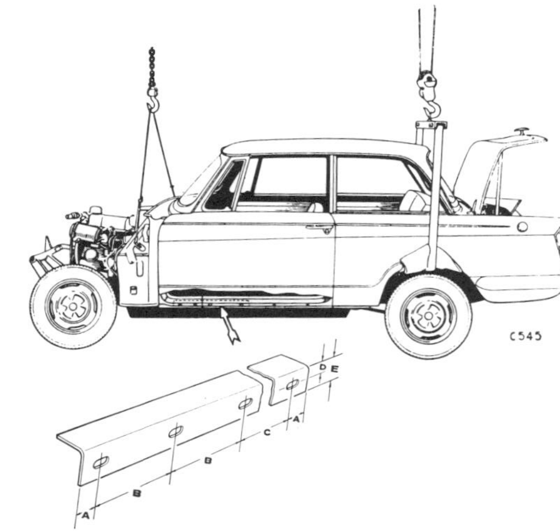

Fig. 5. Lifting body (arrow indicates position of sill reinforcement bracket)

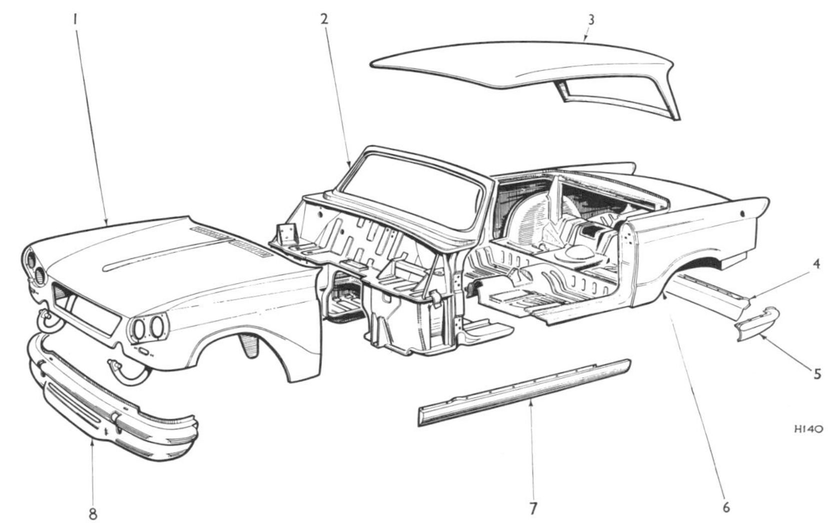

1 Bonnet assembly	3 Roof panel	5 Quarter valance	7 Sill panel
2 Centre section	4 Rear valance	6 Rear end section	8 Front valance

Fig. 6. Body sub-assemblies (Vitesse 6)

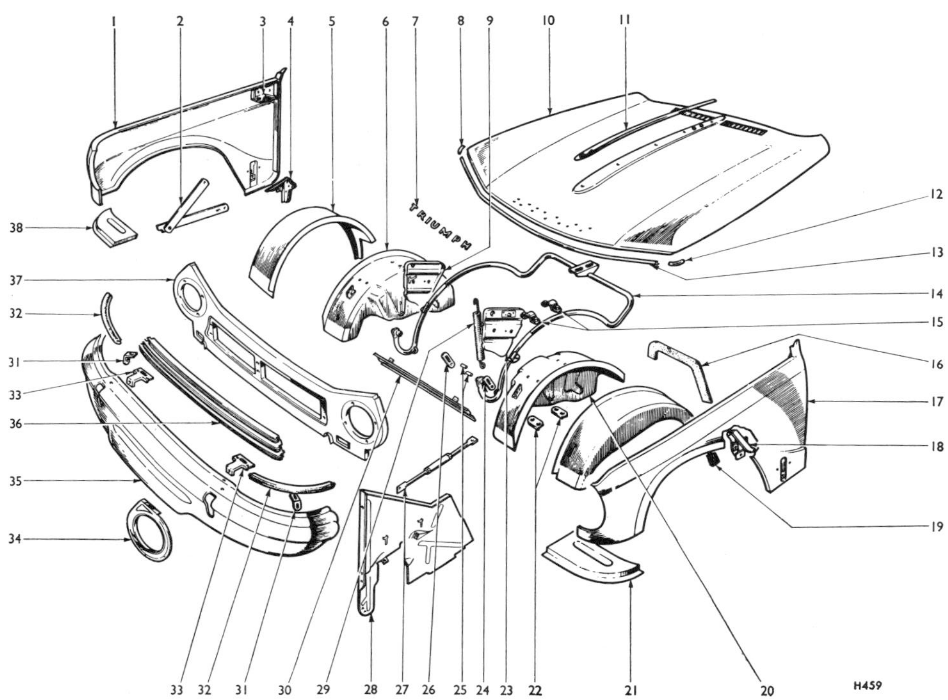

1	Side assembly—front wing	20	Wheelarch inner
2	Stay—bonnet	21	Panel filler piece
3	Bracket—bonnet pin	22	Plate—hinge tube
4	Bonnet catch	23	Stiffener—wheelarch
5	Wheelarch—outer	24	Bonnet link
6	Wheelarch—inner	25	Spacer
7	TRIUMPH letters	26	Bonnet link
8	Moulding—bonnet corner	27	Rod—adjustable
9	Stiffener—wheelarch	28	Engine bay valance
10	Top assembly—bonnet	29	Counterbalance spring
11	Moulding—bonnet top	30	Horn support bracket
12	Moulding—bonnet corner	31	Bracket front valance
13	Moulding—bonnet front edge	32	Seal—front valance
14	Hinge tube assembly	33	Bracket valance support
15	Bracket—hinge tube	34	Headlamp bezel
16	Seal—wheelarch to dash	35	Front valance
17	Side assembly—front wing	36	Front grille
18	Bonnet catch	37	Grille surround
19	Wheelarch outer	38	Panel filler piece

Fig. 7. Bonnet, front valance and grille details (Herald 13/60)

BONNET ASSEMBLY

1200, 12/50, 13/60 and Vitesse 6

To Remove

Isolate the battery.

Disconnect the front lighting and horn cables at the snap connectors on the top centre of grille (Fig. 8).

1200 and 12/50 only (Fig. 9)

Remove the overriders by unscrewing items (3), (4) and (7). Note distance piece fitted to *1200* models only. Take out bolt (8) (Fig. 11) and support the bonnet as the hinge bolts (5) and (6) are being withdrawn.

Lift off bonnet.

13/60 and Vitesse 6 only (Fig. 10)

Remove both overriders by unscrewing items (4) and (7), take out bolt (8) (Fig. 11) and support the bonnet as the hinge bolts (5) and (6) are being withdrawn.

Lift off bonnet.

To Refit

Reverse the removal procedure and refer to bonnet adjustment procedure as follows:

Height Adjustment

Condition "A" (Fig. 12) – **1200 and Vitesse 6**

Slacken two screws (shown arrowed) securing the bonnet stop to the scuttle panel and raise or lower the stop to achieve the requisite bonnet height. Retighten the screws. Re-adjust the bonnet catch plate on the dash side panel accordingly.

Condition "B" (Fig. 13) – **1200 and Vitesse 6**

Slacken the locknut securing the cone-shaped buffer to the bonnet. Screw the buffer in or out to respectively lower or raise the bonnet rear edge. Re-adjust the bonnet catch plate on the dash side panel accordingly.

Condition "C" (Fig. 14) – **1200, 12/50, 13/60 and Vitesse 6**

Slacken the locknut (1) securing the cone-shaped buffer to the mounting bracket (2) on the scuttle panel. Screw the buffer in or out to respectively lower or raise the bonnet rear edge. Re-adjust the bonnet catch plate (3) on the dash side panel accordingly.

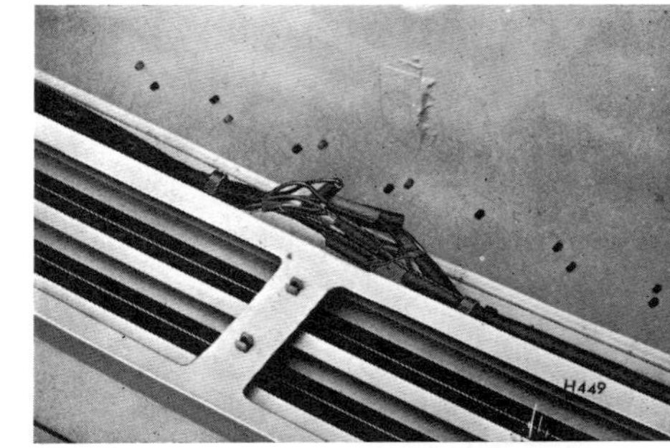

Fig. 8. Bonnet snap connectors

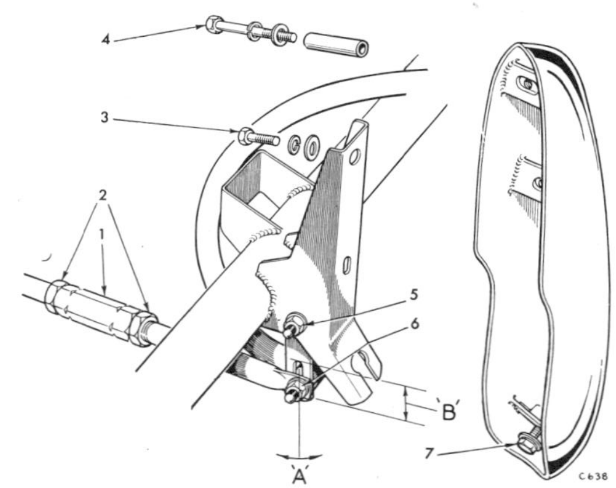

Fig. 9. Bonnet adjustment points (1200 and 12/50)

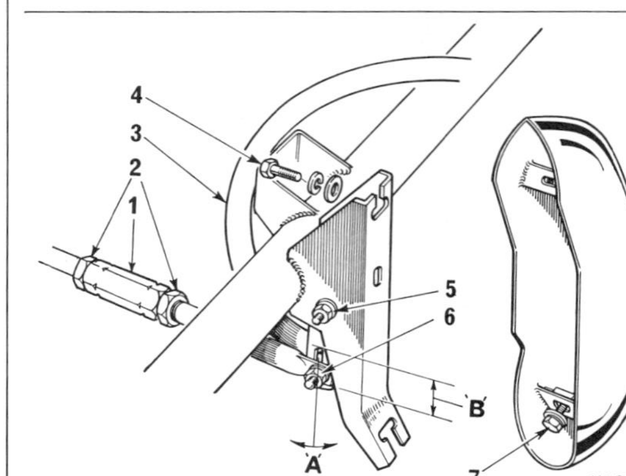

Fig. 10. Bonnet adjustment points (13/60 and Vitesse 6)

Fig. 11. Bonnet stay attachment

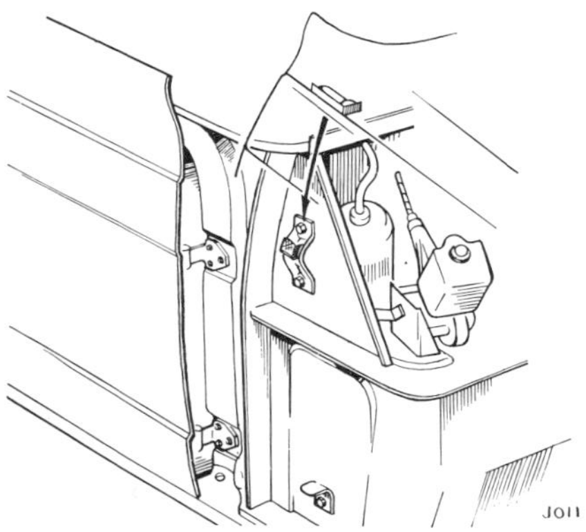

Fig. 12. Bonnet height adjusters (condition "A")

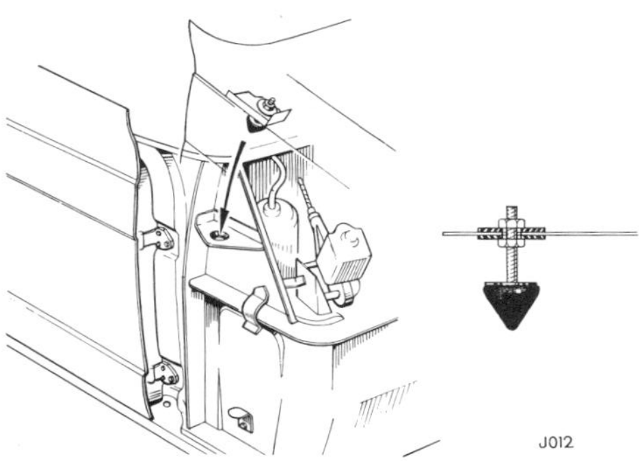

Fig. 13. Bonnet height adjusters (condition "B")

Horizontal Adjustment

1200, 12/50, 13/60 and Vitesse 6

If slight adjustment is required to achieve a parallel clearance of $\frac{3}{16}''$ (5 mm.) between the bonnet and scuttle panel, slacken the locknuts (2) and turn the sleeve nut (1) (Figs. 9 and 10) on either side as necessary.

Appreciable horizontal or vertical movement will necessitate the removal of both overriders (see page 5·208).

Vertical Adjustment (Figs. 9 and 10)

1200, 12/50, 13/60 and Vitesse 6

Slacken the link bolts (5) and (6) and lift or lower the front of the bonnet until parallel clearance between the bonnet and the door is achieved. During this movement the bonnet will pivot on the rear stops. Re-tighten the link bolts when adjustment is completed.

FRONT GRILLE

Herald 1200

To Remove

Unscrew 12 cross/recess screws securing the grille mesh to the grille surround. To release the grille surround, remove the uppermost overrider attachment bolts (4) shown in (Fig. 9).

To Refit

Reverse the removal procedure.

Herald 12/50

To Remove

Unscrew four screws, two each side securing the upper part of the grille to the engine bay valances and four screws securing the lower part of the grille to the front valance.

Fig. 14. Bonnet height adjusters (condition "C")

To Refit

Reverse the removal procedure.

13/60 and Vitesse 6

To Remove (Figs. 15 and 16)

For *Vitesse 6* take out eight screws with washers (arrowed Fig. 15).

For *13/60* take out six screws with washers (arrowed Fig. 16).

To Refit

Reverse the removal procedure.

FRONT VALANCE

To Remove

1200 and 12/50

Referring to Fig. 9, open the bonnet and release the overriders by removing bolts (3) and (4) and slacken lower bolts (7). Remove the overriders from the mounting brackets. Remove four cross/recess screws (2), Fig. 18, and four hex/headed screws (1) and (3).

13/60 and Vitesse 6

Referring to Fig. 10, open the bonnet and release the overriders by removing bolts (7) and slacken upper bolts (4). Remove the overriders from the mounting brackets. Remove four cross/recess screws (2), Fig. 18, and four hex/headed screws (1) and (3) and pull the valance clear.

To Refit

Reverse the removal procedure.

Fig. 15. Front grille attachment (Vitesse 6)

Fig. 16. Front grille attachment (13/60)

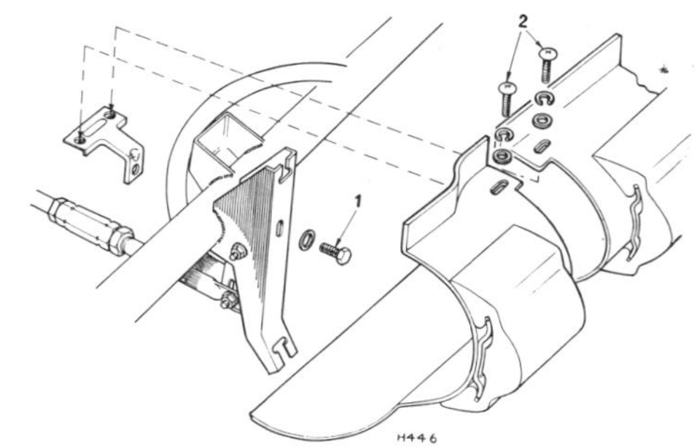

Fig. 17. Front valance retaining bracket

Fig. 18. Front valance attachment

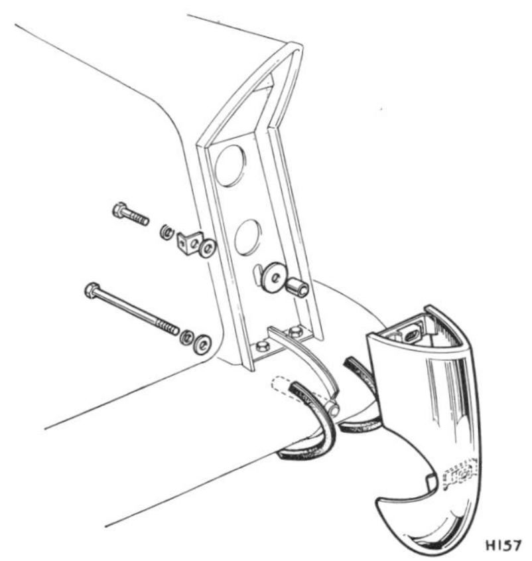

Fig. 19. Rear overrider attachments

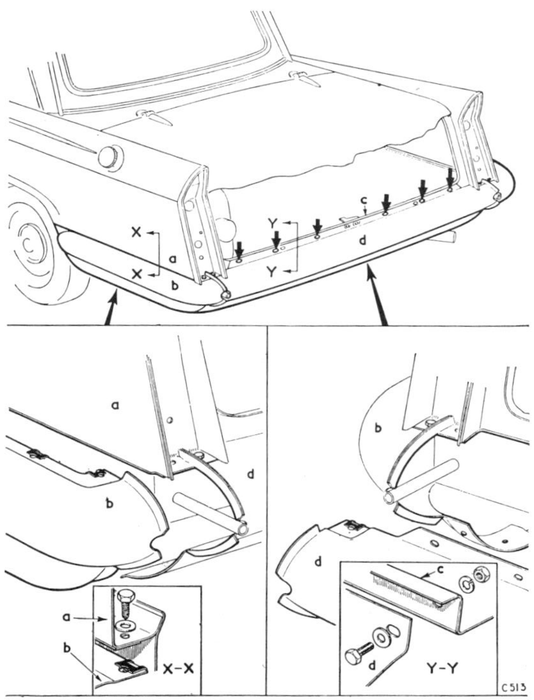

Fig. 20. Rear valance attachments

REAR AND QUARTER VALANCES

1200, 12/50, 13/60 and Vitesse 6

Rear Valance

To Remove (Fig. 20)

Remove the lens from the stop/tail lamps (page 6·136) and remove the fuel tank (page 5·263). Remove both overriders.

Remove the luggage compartment lock striker plate (two screws, item 9, Fig. 28). Take out 12 acme hex/headed screws and remove the rear valance.

To Refit

Reverse the removal procedure and reseal in accordance with instructions given on page 5·301.

Quarter Valance

To Remove (Fig. 20)

Remove the lens from the stop/tail lamps, page 6·136 and remove the fuel tank (left-hand side valance only), page 5·263.

Remove overriders.

Take out 12 acme hex/headed screws, (six at each side) and remove quarter valance.

To Refit

Reverse the removal procedure and reseal in accordance with instructions on page 5·301.

OVERRIDERS

Front

Herald 1200 and 12/50

To Remove

Open the bonnet and referring to Fig. 9 (pages 5·205) remove bolts (3) and (4) and slacken lower bolts (7). Remove the overrider.

Key to Fig. 20

A – Tonneau side panel
B – Rear quarter valance
C – Luggage floor panel
D – Rear centre valance

Herald 13/60 and Vitesse 6

To Remove

Open the bonnet and referring to Fig. 10 (page 5·205), slacken the upper bolt (4), remove the lower bolt (7) and remove the overrider.

To Refit

Reverse the removal procedure

Rear

1200, 12/50, 13/60 and Vitesse 6

To Remove (Fig. 19)

Referring to page 6·136, remove the lens from the stop/tail lamp.

Remove the fuel tank as described on page 5·262 (left-hand side only).

Release each overrider from the body by removing two bolts.

To Refit

Reverse the removal procedure.

ENGINE BAY VALANCES

Herald 1200, 12/50 and 13/60

To Remove (Fig. 21)

— four nuts (1) (two each side) and washers securing valance to radiator;
— four nuts (2) (two each side) and washers securing horn support bracket to valance;
— four bolts (3) (two each side) securing valance to frame.

Remove four bolts (4 and 5) (two each side) and washers and nyloc nuts securing valance to front suspension mounting brackets.

Pull engine bay valance clear of the engine compartment.

Vitesse 6

To Remove

Referring to Fig. 22, remove two nyloc nuts (1) (one each side) and washers valance to radiator and four screws (2) (two each side) valance to frame.

Referring to Fig. 23, remove four bolts (3) and (4) (two each side) and washers and nyloc nuts securing valance to front suspension mounting brackets. Pull engine bay valance clear of the engine compartment.

To Refit

Reverse the removal procedure.

Fig. 21. Engine bay valance attachment (1200, 12/50 and 13/60)

Fig. 22. Engine bay valance front attachment (Vitesse 6)

Fig. 23. Engine bay valance rear attachment (Vitesse 6)

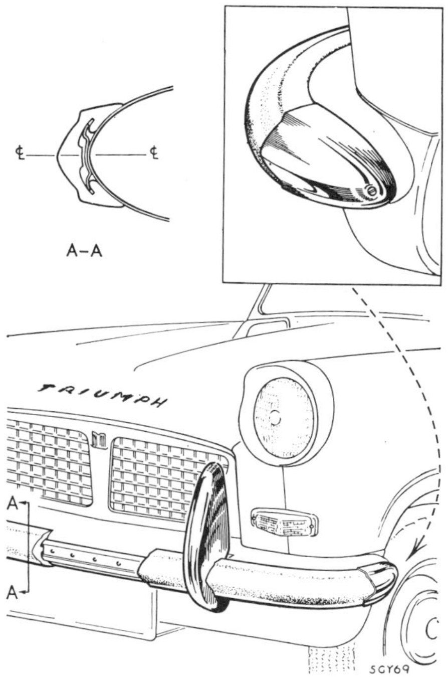

Fig. 24. Bumper rubber attachment

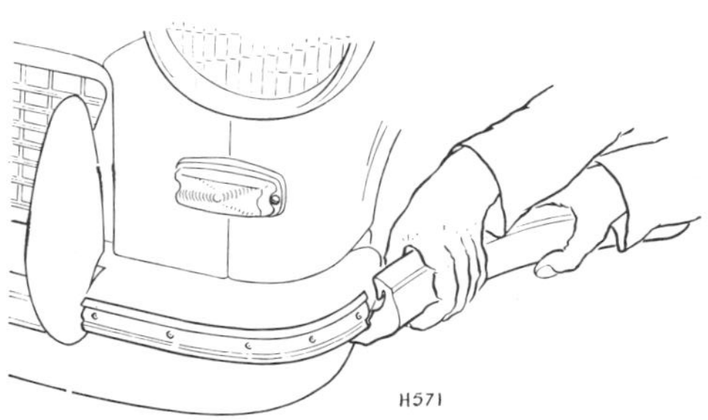

Fig. 25. Fitting bumper rubber

BUMPER RUBBERS

1200, 12/50 and 13/60 (excluding Courier)

The bumper rubbers are self-supporting on metal flanges spot welded to the valances. The outer end of each rubber is held by a cover plate which is secured to the valance by a single self-tapping screw.

Front and Rear
To Remove (Fig. 24)
Take off cover plates (arrowed). Pull the lower edge of the rubber sufficiently to release it from the metal flange shown on inset (A.A.).

To Refit (Fig. 25)
Apply soapy solution on the inner flanges of the rubber. Enter the lower flange of the rubber over the lower edge of the retainer and bend the rubber outwards sufficiently to permit its upper edge to fit the retainer.

BUMPER FINISHERS

Vitesse 6

The bumper finishers each comprise three sections and are secured to the valance by rivets.

Front and Rear
To Remove (Fig. 26)
Using a ⅛″ (3 mm.) diameter drill, remove two rivets from each of the front sections and three rivets from each of the rear.

To Refit
Secure the sections with ⅛″ (3 mm.) pop rivets.

Fig. 26. Bumper finisher attachment (Vitesse 6)

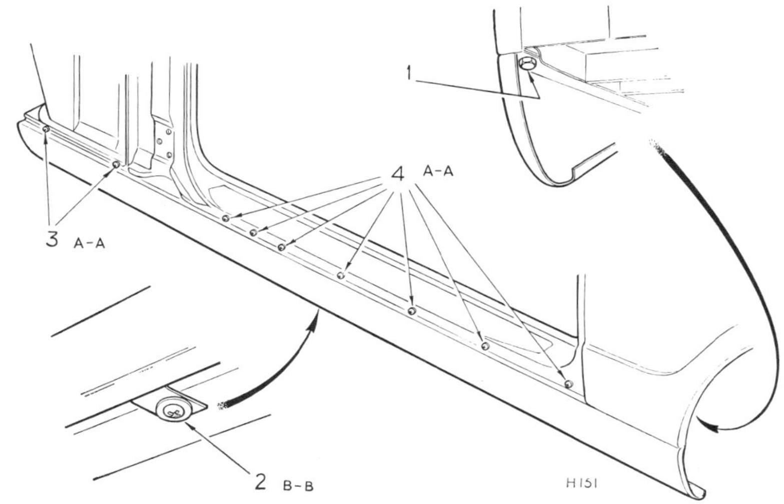

SILLS

1200, 12/50, 13/60 and Vitesse 6

To Remove (Fig. 27)
Lift the bonnet and open the door.

1 Remove one hex/headed screw (1) and lock-washer securing the underside of the sill to the tonneau side panel.

2 Remove four cross/recess screws (2) and plain washers securing the brackets on the underside of the sill assembly to the chassis frame.

3 Take out two cross/recess screws (3) and lock-washers fixing the sill to the dash side panel.

4 Take out seven cross/recess screws (4) and lockwashers securing the sill assembly to the floor panels.

5 Pull the sill clear.

To Refit
Reverse the removal procedure.

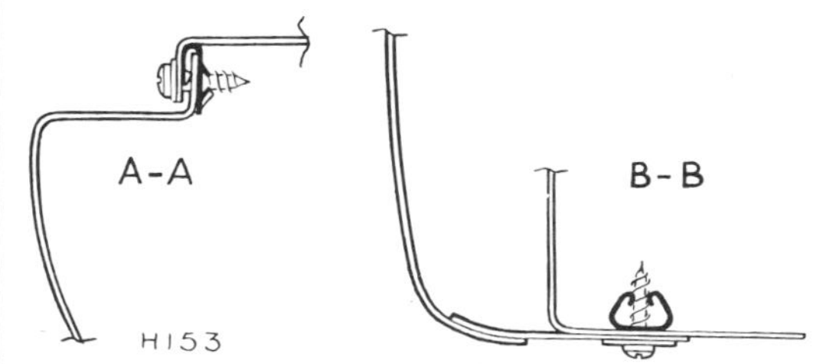

2-B-B Sill panel to chassis frame
3-A-A Sill panel to dash side panel
4-A-A Sill panel to floor panel

Fig. 27. Sill panel attachments

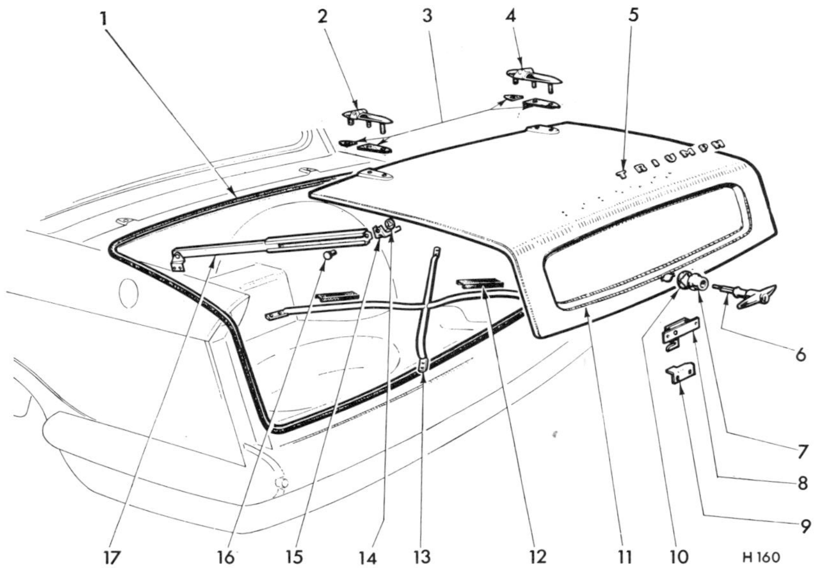

1	Weatherstrip	7	Escutcheon	13	Lid reinforcement
2	Hinge	8	Lock	14	Clip
3	Gasket	9	Striker plate	15	Bracket support
4	Hinge	10	Seal	16	Pivot
5	Letters	11	Trunk lid	17	Support stay
6	Locking handle	12	Packing rubber		

Fig. 28. Luggage compartment details

LUGGAGE COMPARTMENT LID

1200, 12/50, 13/60 and Vitesse 6

To Remove (Fig. 28)

Isolate the battery. Support the lid in the open position and disconnect the cables from the number plate lamp. Withdraw the cables from the compartment lid.

Release the upper end of the stay (17) from the bracket (15) and remove the securing nut from the forward stud of each hinge. Lift the lid, complete with hinges from the body.

If necessary, release the hinges (2) and (4) from the lid and note the position of the sealing washers (3).

To Refit

Reverse the removal procedure leaving the hinge nuts semi-tight.

Oversize holes permit limited adjustment. Move the lid as required to effect a close fit and finally tighten the hinge nuts.

Lock

To Remove

Raise the luggage lid, remove the nut from the inner end of the handle (6) and withdraw the handle from the lock (8). Release the lock (8) by removing two securing screws.

To Refit

Reverse the removal procedure.

Striker

Oversize holes in the striker plate (9) permit limited adjustment.

Sealing

Refer to "Dust and Water Sealing," page 5·301.

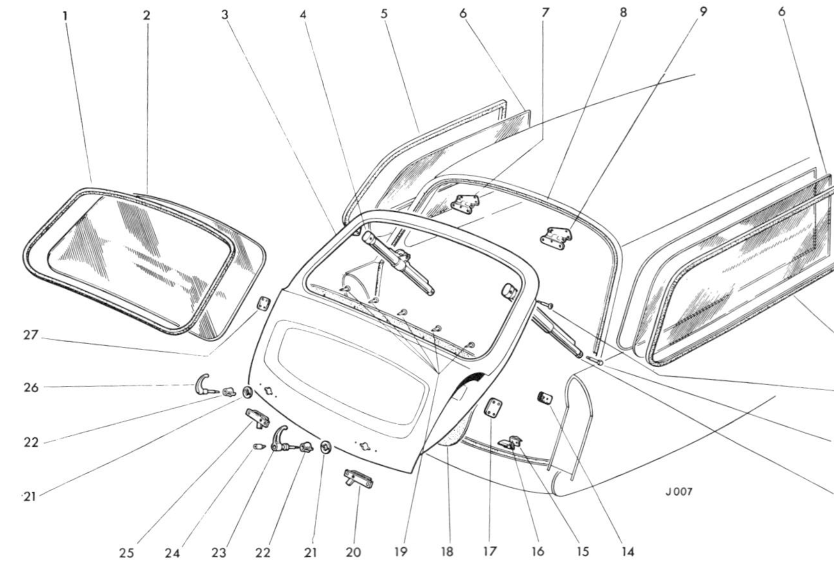

1	Weatherstrip	10	Weatherstrip—R.H.	19	Trim buttons
2	Rear door glass	11	Upper pivot bolt	20	Budget lock—R.H.
3	Rear door assembly	12	Lower pivot bolt	21	Seating washer
4	Spring stay assembly—L.H.	13	Spring stay assembly—R.H.	22	Escutcheon—door handle
5	Weatherstrip—L.H.	14	Rubber dovetail block	23	Locking door handle—R.H.
6	Quarterlight glass—L.H.	15	Catch plate	24	Locking barrel
7	Hinge	16	Protection plate	25	Budget lock—L.H.
8	Rear door—Sealing rubber	17	Rubbing plate—dovetail	26	Non-locking door handle
9	Hinge	18	Rear door trim pad	27	Rubbing plate—dovetail

Fig. 29. Tail gate details

TAIL GATE

1200 Estate Car and Courier and 13/60 Estate Car

The tail gate is hinged at its upper end and is supported in the open condition by two spring-loaded check arms. A cam-operated stop is incorporated in the left-hand side check arm.

To Remove (Fig. 29)

Isolate the battery.

Open the tail gate and remove the number plate and the trim panel.

Disconnect the cables from the number plate lamp and withdraw the cables from the tail gate.

Exercising care, remove the upper pivot bolts (11) from each support stay (13).

The right-hand stay is in three separate sections, which will spring apart when released. With the aid of a second operator to support the tail gate, take out three screws from each hinge and lift the tail gate clear. Finally, remove the hinges from the body.

To Refit

Reverse the removal procedure.

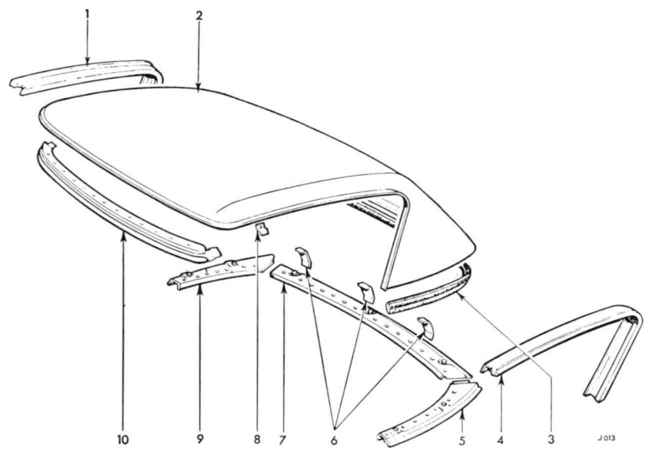

1 Cantrail assembly—R.H.
2 Roof panel assembly
3 Sealing rubber—roof to deck
4 Cantrail assembly—L.H.
5 Side reinforcement
6 Backlight aperture—tie plate
7 Roof panel reinforcement
8 Rail mounting—listing rail
9 Side reinforcement
10 Header panel

Fig. 30. Roof panel details, 1200 coupé

1 Roof panel assembly
2 Pillar assembly—rear outer R.H.
3 Panel—rear inner pillar—R.H.
4 Panel—rear inner pillar—L.H.
5 Mounting bracket—courtesy light
6 Pillar assembly—rear outer —L.H.
7 Sealing rubber—rear pillar —L.H.
8 Sealing rubber—rear pillar —R.H.
9 Cantrail assembly—L.H.
10 Cantrail assembly—R.H.

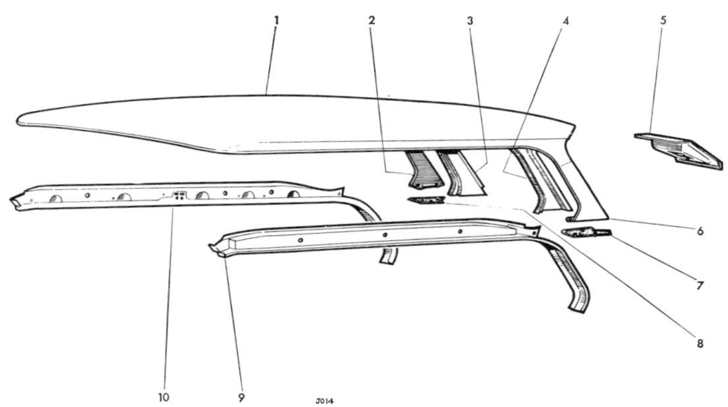

Fig. 31. Roof panel details, Estate car

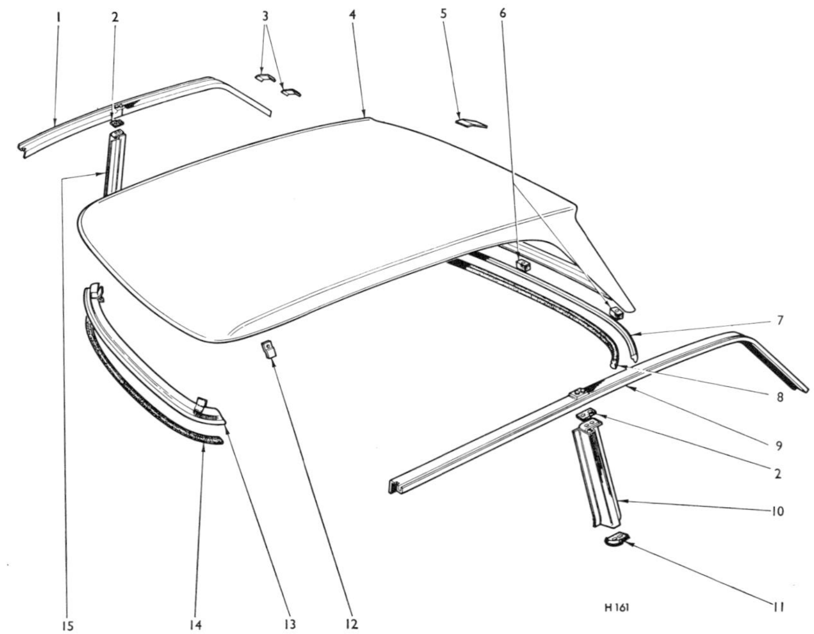

1 Cantrail assembly—R.H.
2 Sealing rubber—quarter pillar
3 Tie plate—upper and lower roof
4 Roof panel assembly
5 Reinforcement—backlight
6 Distance piece—roof
7 Finisher—seal—roof to deck
8 Seal—roof to deck
9 Cantrail assembly—L.H.
10 Pillar—quarter light
11 Sealing rubber—quarter pillar
12 Bracket—listing rail
13 Panel—header rail
14 Weatherstrip—leader rail
15 Pillar—quarter light

Fig. 32. Roof panel details, Saloon

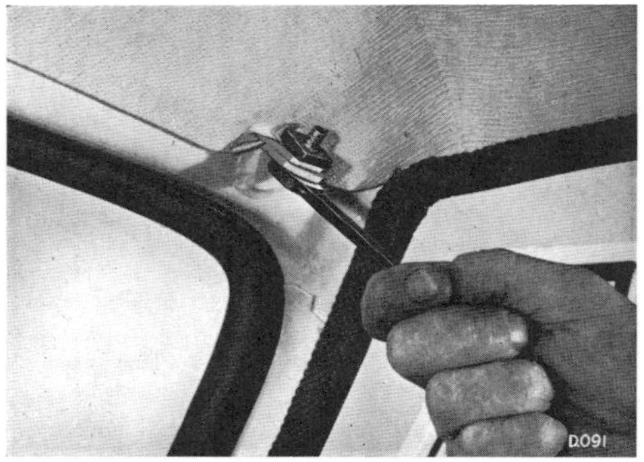

Fig. 33. Releasing roof header rail fixing

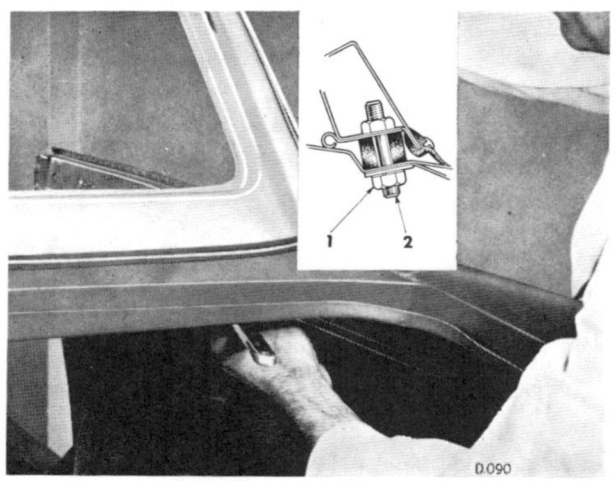

Fig. 34. Releasing roof rear deck fixing, saloon

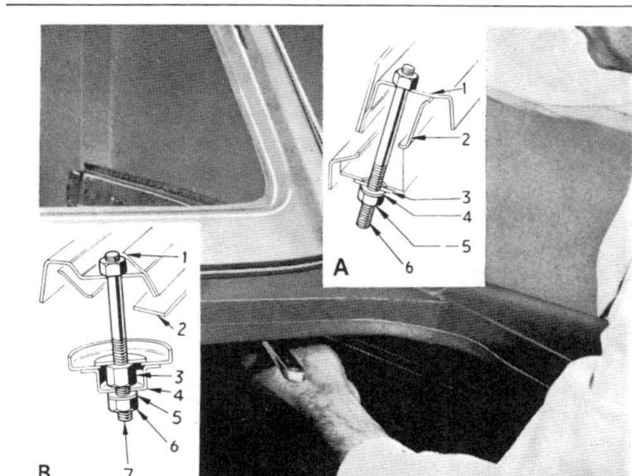

Fig. 35. Releasing roof rear deck fixing, coupé

ROOF PANEL

1200, 12/50, 13/60 and Vitesse 6 All Models

To Remove

Isolate the battery and remove the sun visors. Take out two bolts securing the roof panel to the header rail (Fig. 33). Remove the draught welt from both door apertures.

1200, 12/50, 13/60 and Vitesse 6 Saloon Models

Remove the quarter lights and the backlight, page 5·237. Detach the trim from the centre pillar. Release the roof panel by removing four screws (two at each side), securing the centre pillar to the roof, and three nuts (1) from the studs (2) shown on inset (Fig. 34) securing the rear lower edge of the roof to the body.

Vitesse 6 Saloon only

Disconnect the roof lamp (purple and purple with white cables) at the snap connectors, located adjacent to the upper forward edge of the fuel tank in the luggage compartment (Fig. 36).

As the roof panel is lifted, withdraw the roof lamp cables from the luggage compartment. Note that three rubber blocks are used between the rear edge of the roof panel and the body

Herald 1200 Coupé only

To Remove

Remove the occasional seat, if fitted, and take out the rear trim panel (6 screws). Remove the quarter trim panel by inserting a screwdriver between the forward edge of the trim panel and the body. Gently prise the retaining clips from the body.

Remove four nuts (two at each side) shown (Fig. 35, inset A) and three nuts with cup washers (inset B). These are accessible from inside the luggage compartment.

Lift the roof clear and note the position of the two rubber blocks between the roof and body side panels.

1200 Estate and Courier Van and 13/60 Estate Car

The procedure for roof removal and refitting is identical for the Estate Car and Courier Van, except that the centre pillars and quarter lights on the Estate Car are replaced by side panels welded to the roof for the van. A roof lining is not fitted on the van.

To Remove – Estate Car

Remove the tail gate, page 5·213 and the side windows. Detach the trim from the centre pillar and remove the roof lining, page 5·219. Release the rear quarter trim panels and disconnect the cables from the tail lamp at the snap connectors located adjacent to the lamps. Unscrew four nuts (two each side) and washers securing the rear pillars to the body (Fig. 40).

To Remove – Courier Van

Remove the tail gate, page 5·213. Release the wooden side panels and disconnect the cables from the tail lamp at the snap connectors located adjacent to the lamps. Remove 14 bolts (seven at each side) securing the lower edge of the metal side panels to the body. Unscrew four nuts (two each side) and washers securing the rear pillars to the body (Fig. 40).

To Remove – Estate Car and Courier Van

Lift the roof and as it is being lifted the cables which pass through the rear pillars and above the tailgate to connect the tail lamps, will be withdrawn (Fig. 40). Note the position of the rubber seals and washers between the lower ends of the rear pillar and the body, and the seal between the roof and windscreen header rail.

1200, 12/50, 13/60 and Vitesse 6 Saloon Models

To Refit

1 Clean off the old sealing compound from the roof panel, windscreen header rail and rubber weatherstrips. Examine the rubber and renew, if necessary.

2 Liberally coat the upper edge of the header rail with Seelastik. Attach the rubber weatherstrip and apply Seelastik to the upper surface of the rubber.

3 Position the sealing rubbers at the base of the roof rear pillar and seal with Seelastik.

4 Apply adhesive to the lower rear edge of the roof panel and to the rubber weatherstrip channel. When tacky, refit the weatherstrip.

5 Apply Seelastik to the contact faces and assemble a small rubber block over each of the three studs on the rear of the roof. Place the roof in position and secure it to the header rail by refitting the two outer bolts (Fig. 33).

6 Lift the rear end of the roof panel, attach a rubber seal to the top of each centre pillar and for *Vitesse 6* only, pass the cables from the rear lamp through the rear deck into the luggage compartment.

7 Lower the roof and secure the rear end with three nuts. Align the top of each centre pillar and secure it to the roof with two screws.

8 Refit the quarter lights, page 5·238, and the backlight, page 5·237, and for *Vitesse 6* only, re-connect the roof lamp cables in the luggage compartment.

9 Refit the battery cables and sun visors. For sealing operations refer to "Dust and Water Sealing" section, page 5·301.

Fig. 36 – Roof lamp snap connectors (Vitesse 6)

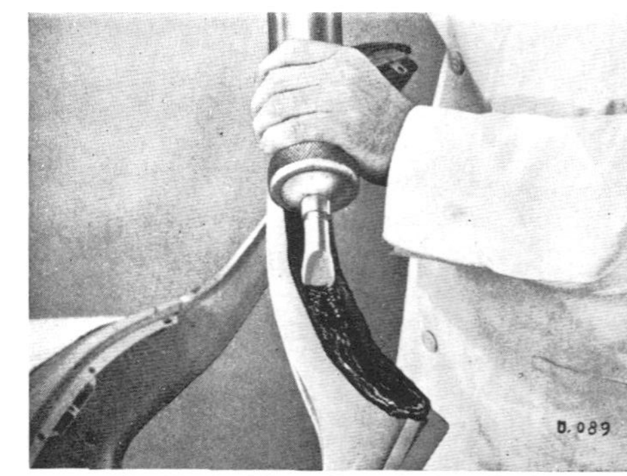

Fig. 37. Applying sealer to header rail rubber

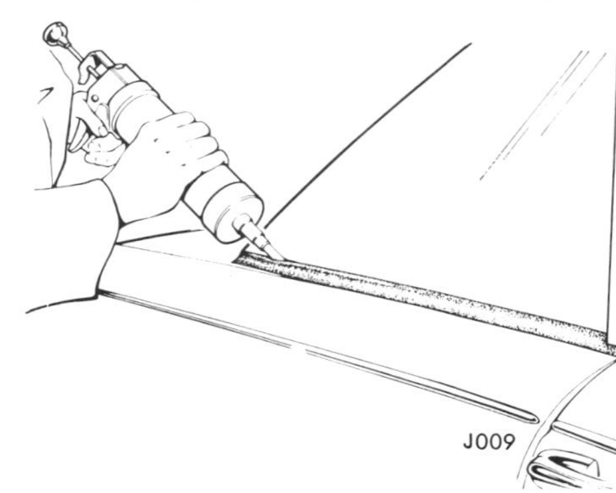

Fig. 38. Sealing weatherstrip to roof panel

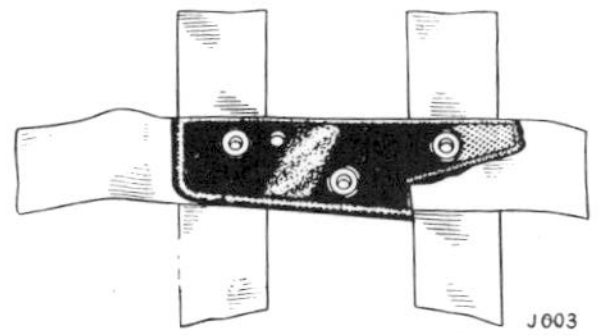

Fig. 39. Position of sealing rubbers on tape

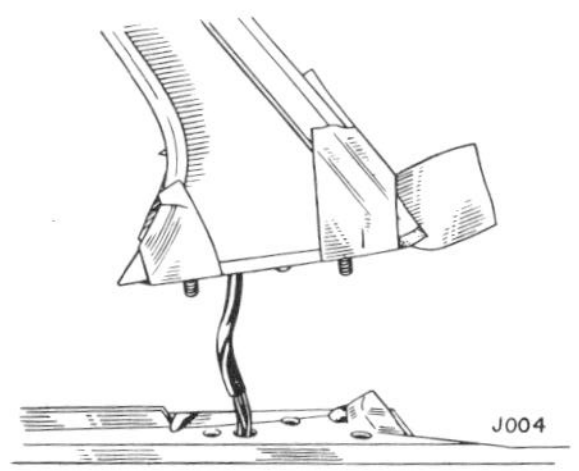

Fig. 40. Sealing rubber secured by tape to rear pillar

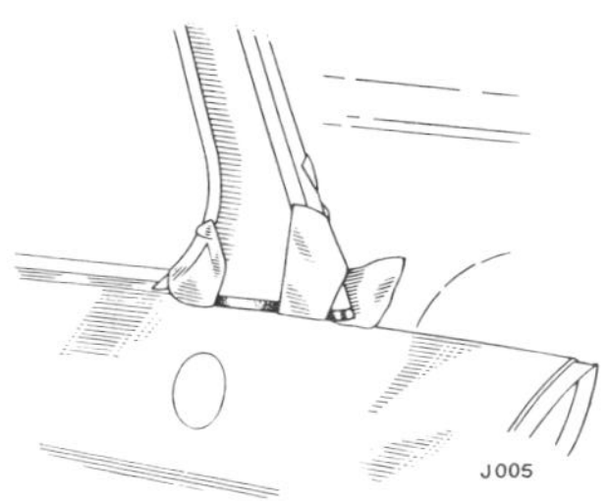

Fig. 41. Rear pillar seal

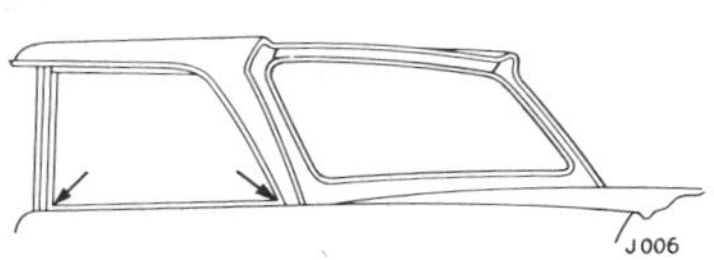

Fig. 42. Plugging quarter light corners

Herald 1200 Coupé only

To Refit

1 As saloon operation 1. } See page 5·217
2 As saloon operation 2. }
3 As saloon operation 3. }
4 Placing the wide end of each spacer block towards the front, and the chamfered edge face downwards with the narrow side nearer to the centre of the car apply Seelastik to the lower block face and attach it to the body side panel, between the stud holes.
5 Attach the roof panel, align the roof and body flanges and loosely secure the panel at the rear centre position.
6 Refit the two rear outer bolts and two bolts securing the roof panel to the header rail. Refit the nuts and washers to the roof-to-body side panel fixing studs and fully tighten.
7 Turn the adjusting nuts on each side of the studs across the rear of the car until the nut contacts the body. Refit the cup washers and fully tighten (Fig. 35).
8 As saloon operation 9. - See page 5·217

1200 Estate Car and Courier Van and 13/60 Estate Car

The following instructions relating to the Estate Car may, by deleting reference to the centre pillar and roof lining, be applied to the Courier Van.

To Refit

1 As saloon operation 1. } See page 5·217
2 As saloon operation 2. }
3. Coat both sides of a rubber seal with Seelastik and attach it to the upper end of the centre pillar. Apply Seelastik to the upper surface of the rear pillar sealing rubbers.
4 Assemble the rubber to the base of each pillar. This operation is facilitated by placing the rubber on black adhesive tape which is then used to hold the rubber in position on the pillar (Figs. 39 and 41).
5 Place the roof into position and loosely secure it to the windscreen header rail. Raise the rear end of the roof and pass the cables into the body. Apply Seelastik to the contacting surfaces of the rubber and body, lower the roof and fully tighten the roof to windscreen head rail securing bolts.
6 Refit nuts and washers to the rear pillar studs and fully tighten. Refit two bolts to each centre pillar and seal the screw located inside the channel with MR roofing compound.
7 Refit 14 bolts (seven on each side) and secure the roof and side panels to the body (on Courier van only).
8 Refit the battery cables and sun visors, tail gate, roof lining and quarter lights, page 5·238. Re-connect the tail lamps and refit the trim panel. For sealing operations refer to "Dust and Water Sealing" page 5·301.
9 Cut off the surplus black tape (Fig. 41) flush with the sealing rubber to provide a neat appearance.

ROOF LINING

1200, 12/50, 13/60 and Vitesse 6

Maintenance

Maintenance is restricted to cleaning the material with warm soapy water. Obstinate grease marks may be removed using a cloth moistened in white spirit. The edges of the lining are secured to the roof panel with a rubber solution, and in consequence damage will result from the careless use of adhesive solvents.

1200 Saloon and Coupé, 12/50, 13/60 and Vitesse 6 Saloon

To Remove

Remove the roof panel as described on page 5·216. Release the edges of the lining from the panel, taking care, if the lining is to be subsequently refitted.

Press the ends of the listing rails inwards to release them from their locations in the cantrails. Withdraw the rails from the lining.

To Refit

1 Using an adhesive solvent, remove all trace of adhesive from the flange of the roof panel and lining.
2 Assemble the listing rail to the lining and ensure that they are correctly located by referring to the individual colour coding of each rail.
The colour code is as follows:
(Numbered from the front of the vehicle):
Saloon: No. 1 Green, No. 2 White, No. 3 Black, No. 4 Grey, No. 5 Double section – no colour.
Coupé: No. 1 Red, No. 2 Yellow, No. 3 Blue.
3 Apply a fresh coating of adhesive to the roof flange and lining.
4 Commencing at the rear, assemble the rails to the roof panel cantrail. Secure the front rail No. 1 behind two retaining clips (Fig. 43). Gently pull the lining to the rear and lightly secure it to the roof flange only (Fig. 44).
Lightly secure the lining to the front edge of the roof panel (Fig. 45). Working outwards from the centre of the lining, smooth out wrinkles and seal lining to the edge of the roof panel.
If a new lining is being fitted, cut the edges to within ⅛″ (3 mm.) of the turnover. The cuts should be approximately ½″ (13 mm.) apart.
5 Refit the roof panel.

1200 and 13/60 Estate Car

The instructions for removing and refitting the roof lining are basically similar to those given for the saloon and coupé models. The lining, however, is fitted after the roof panel is fitted to the car.

The colour coding of the listing rails is as follows:

(Numbered from the front of the vehicle). No. 1 Green, No. 2 White, No. 3 Brown, No. 4 Orange, No. 5 Purple, No. 6 Double section – no colour.

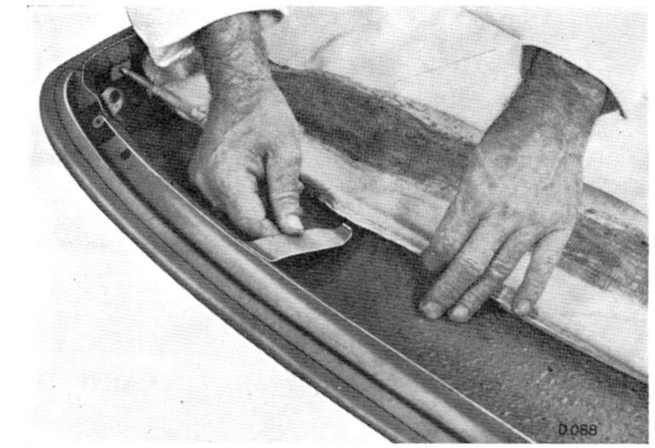

Fig. 43 Assembling listing rail No. 1 to the retaining clips

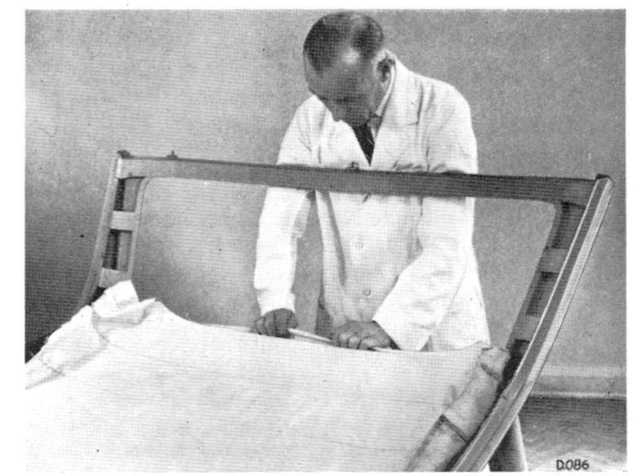

Fig. 44. Securing rear edge of roof lining

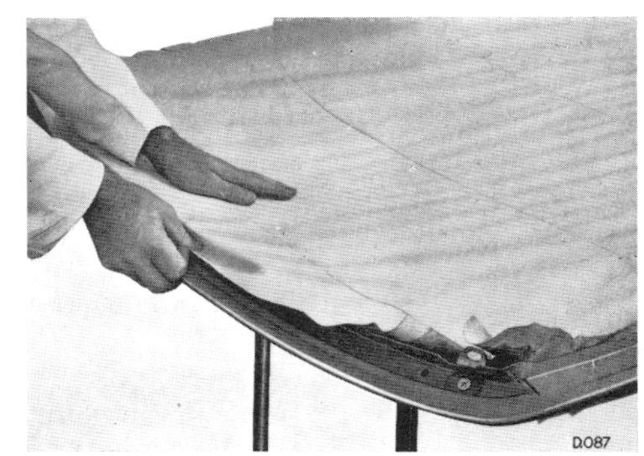

Fig. 45. Fitting front edge of lining

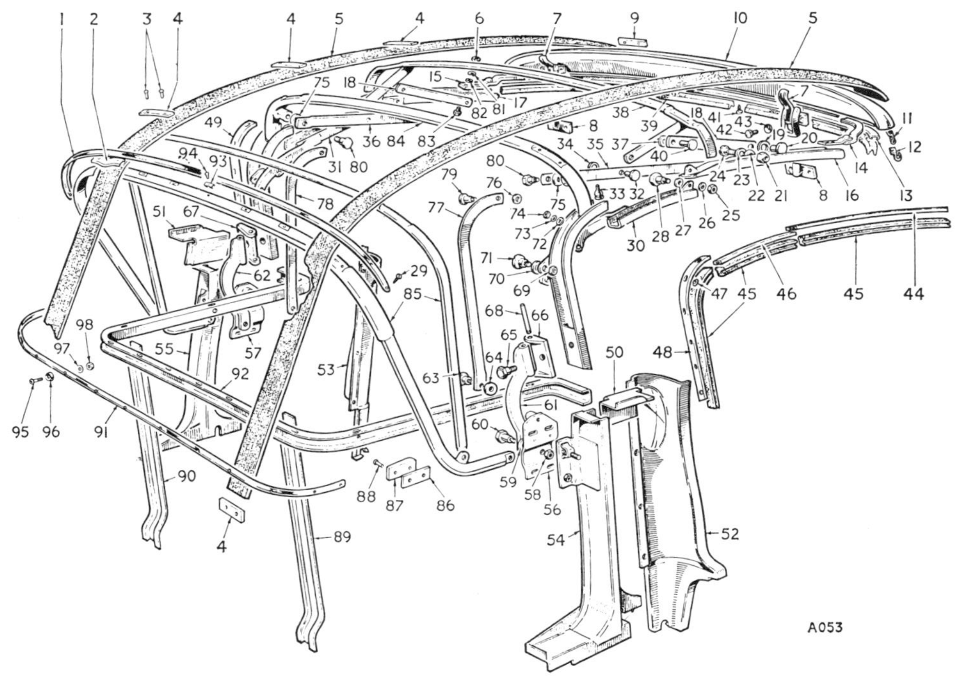

1 Finishing strip—rear hood stick
2 Webbing retaining plate
3 Rivets
4 Webbing retaining plate
5 Webbing
6 Nut
7 Head catch assembly—front hood stick
8 Head catch assembly—screen header
9 Webbing retaining plate
10 Front stick assembly
11 Roof header finisher
12 Front hood stick end finisher
13 Weather strip retainer
14 Pivot bracket assembly—R.H.
15 Pivot bracket assembly—L.H.
16 Cantrail assembly—R.H.
17 Cantrail assembly—L.H.
18 Front cantrail link
19 Plain washer
20 Rivet
21 Nyloc nut
22 Nut
23 Plain washer
24 Shoulder bolt
25 Nut
26 Plain washer
27 Plain washer
28 Shouldered bolt
29 Finisher strip retaining screw
30 Cantrail rear assy.—R.H.
31 Cantrail rear assy.—L.H.
32 Rivet
33 Rubber buffer
34 Plain washer
35 Front cantrail link—R.H.
36 Front cantrail link—L.H.
37 Plain washer
38 Front intermediate hood stick assembly
39 Front hood stick weather strip
40 Rivet
41 Screw
42 Screw
43 Washer
44 Front cantrail weather strip retainer
45 Weather strip
46 Rear cantrail weather strip retainer
47 Screw
48 "B" post—upper—R.H.
49 "B" post—upper—L.H.
50 "B" post filler panel—R.H.
51 "B" post filler panel—L.H.
52 "B" post closing panel—R.H.
53 "B" post closing panel—L.H.
54 "B" post inner panel assembly—R.H.
55 "B" post inner panel assembly—L.H.
56 Pivot mounting bracket—R.H.
57 Pivot mounting bracket—L.H.
58 Nut
59 Plain washer
60 Shouldered bolt
61 Hinge link—R.H.
62 Hinge link—L.H.
63 Shouldered bolt
64 Plain washer
65 Shouldered bolt
66 "B" post hinge—R.H.
67 "B" post hinge—L.H.
68 Pivot pin
69 Nut
70 Plain washer
71 Shouldered bolt
72 Plain washer
73 Shakeproof washer
74 Nut
75 Plain washer
76 Plain washer
77 Rear cantrail control link—R.H.
78 Rear cantrail control link—L.H.
79 Shouldered bolt
80 Shouldered bolt
81 Spring washer
82 Plain washer
83 Bolt
84 Intermediate hood stick, and "B" post upper assy.
85 Rear hood stick and intermediate stick assembly
86 Packing piece
87 Nylon guide block
88 Rivet
89 Tonneau support strut—R.H.
90 Tonneau support strut—L.H.
91 Head cloth finishing strip
92 Tonneau support rail
93 Finishing strip retaining clips
94 Rivet
95 Screw
96 Snap fastener
97 Rubber washer
98 Nut

Fig. 46. Convertible soft-top frame details

SOFT TOP ADJUSTMENTS

1200, 13/60 and Vitesse 6 CONVERTIBLE MODEL ONLY (Fig. 46)

CONDITION	ADJUSTMENT
Cantrail low in the centre causing it to foul the door glass.	Remove and re-set the curved section of the rear cantrail assembly (30 and 31).
Upper edge of door glass fouls the cantrail.	Adjust door glass stop until satisfactory clearance is obtained.
Rear corner of door glass fouls curved section of rear cantrail assembly.	Remove pivot mounting bracket (56 and 57) and elongate the holes to provide sufficient vertical adjustment. Use oversize washers when refitting the securing screws.
"B" post weatherstrip does not form an effective seal at the rear edge of door glass.	Two adjustments are available: 1. Slacken the pivot bracket (56 and 57) securing bolts and move the bracket forward. If hood material between the "B" post weather-deck is now subject to undue stress, remove the "B" post and rear strip and release the hood material as necessary. 2. Remove the weatherstrip and hood material from "B" post. Insert suitable packing between the hood material and "B" post. Refit the hood material and weatherstrip.
Hood stitching broken away at the base of the "B" post.	Remove the bolts securing the pivot mounting bracket (56 and 57) to the body and insert suitable packing between the bracket and body to obtain a clearance of approximately ¼″ (6·3 mm.) between the hoodsticks and the body outer panel.
Small holes in hood 4″ to 6″ (10·16 cm. to 15·24 cm.) above the body outer panel and to the rear of the "B" post are caused by the hood material being trapped between the hoodsticks when the hood is lowered.	Shorten the bolts securing the weatherstrip to the "B" post. Remove the fourth bolt, counting from the bottom, and discard it.

HOOD FASTENER ADJUSTMENTS

CONDITION	ADJUSTMENT
Hood peak rail out of line with windscreen header rail	Slacken the screws securing the head catch (7) to the peak rail and centralize. Re-tighten the screws.
Incorrect tension on hood fasteners.	Slacken the screws securing the retainer plate (8) to the windscreen header rail and raise or lower the plate to obtain correct tension. Re-tighten the screws.

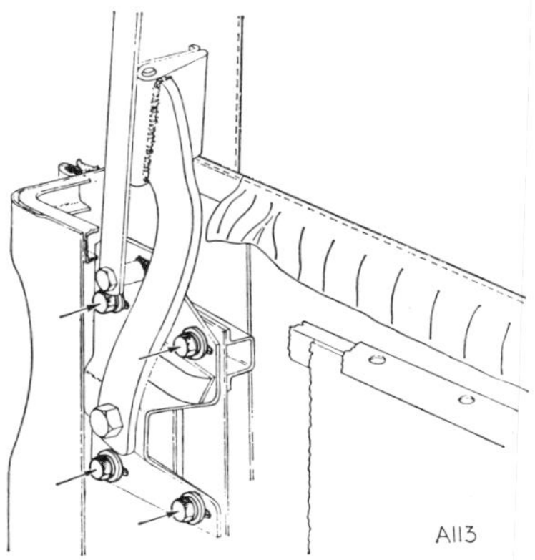

Fig. 47. Soft-top pivot mounting

Fig. 48. Sliding roof

CONVERTIBLE HOOD ASSEMBLY

1200, 13/60 and Vitesse 6

To Remove (Fig. 46)

1 Remove twelve screws (95), fasteners (96), washers (97) and nuts (98).

2 Detach the finisher strip (91), release the hood material from the body and drill out twelve rivets (3) retaining the plates (4) and the webbing (5) to the hood sticks and rear deck flange.

3 Release the head catch assemblies (7) on the screen rail and two snap-on clips securing the hood to the body side flanges.

4. Remove the trim quarter panels to gain access to the pivot mounting brackets (56) and (57). Release the bracket by removing the four securing bolts arrowed (Fig. 47).
Lift the hood assembly from the body.

To Refit

Reverse the removal procedure and make adjustments as required in accordance with the conditions listed on page 5·221.

SLIDING ROOF ASSEMBLY

Standard Fitment on 12/50; Optional Extra on 1200, 13/60 and Vitesse 6

To Remove (Fig. 48)

With the sliding roof in the half-open position, hold one side steady and pull the other side forward. This releases the nylon sliders from the metal runners. Repeat the operation until all the sliders are clear.

Remove four screws at the rear of the sliding roof and lift clear.

To Refit

Reverse the above procedure.

Adjustment

The four screws (30) pass through elongated holes to enable the fabric to be slackened or tensioned as necessary to improve appearance.

Any stiffness in the sliding action may be relieved by applying Ambersil Silicone Formula 1 spray to the runners.

Should it be necessary to service the sliding roof catch mechanism, remove the sliding roof assembly complete. Pull the ends of the front listing rail clear of the fabric, pull the fabric clear of the front box-section. Remove two screws (6) (Fig. 49) and lift the metal section clear.

To re-assemble, reverse the above procedure.

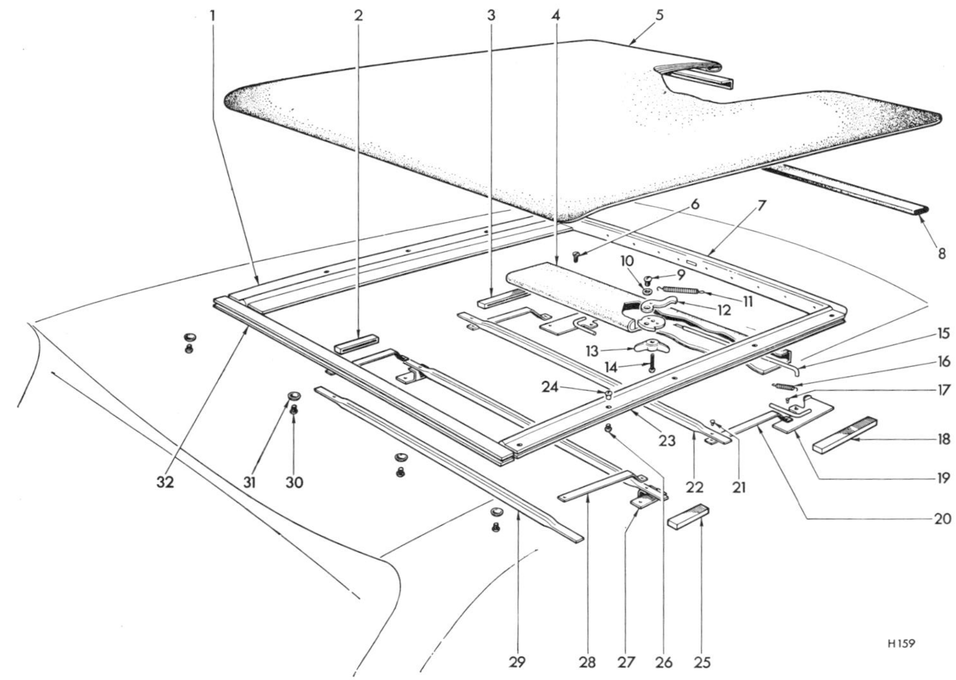

1 Side rail	17 Rivet
2 Slide—intermediate	18 Slide—front
3 Slide—front	19 Front side assembly
4 Listing rail assembly—intermediate	20 Spring—lifting
5 Cover assembly, sliding roof	21 Rivet—listing rail
6 Screw—front cover plate	22 Listing rail
7 Front angle assembly	23 Side rail
8 Rubber strip—front	24 Sleeve—side rail to roof
9 Screw—hook to cam	25 Slide—intermediate
10 Washer—hook to cam	26 Screw—side rail to roof
11 Tension spring	27 Listing rail assembly—intermediate
12 Hook—locking	28 Spring—lifting
13 Handle	29 Listing rail
14 Screw—handle to control box	30 Set screw—rear cover plate
15 Push-rod	31 Washer
16 Spring—front slide	32 Rear rail

Fig. 49. Sliding roof details

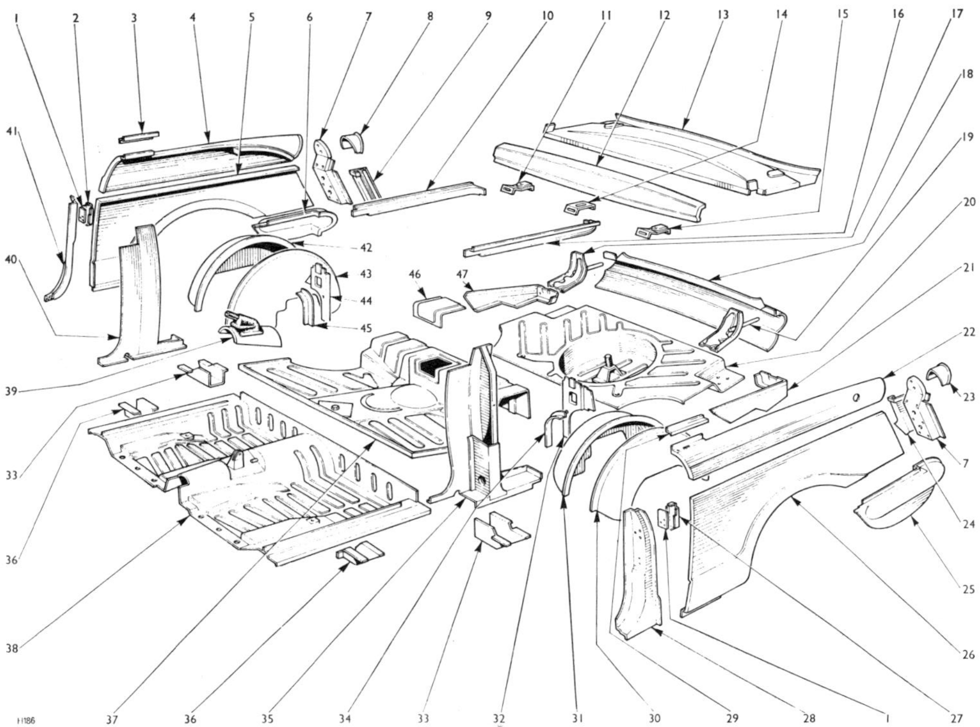

1	Tapped plate	17	Mounting bracket—luggage floor	32	Stiffener—wheelarch to tonneau side
2	Retainer—tapped plate	18	Rear valance	33	Mounting bracket—"B" post
3	Filler panel—tonneau upper	19	Mounting bracket—luggage floor	34	Angle support—squab side
4	Upper panel—tonneau side	20	Luggage floor	35	Inner panel—"B" post
5	Lower panel—tonneau side	21	Luggage floor—side panel	36	Mounting bracket—rear floor
6	Quarter valance	22	Upper panel—tonneau side	37	Rear seat pan
7	Closing panel lower—tonneau side	23	Closing panel—tonneau end	38	Rear floor panel
8	Closing panel—tonneau end	24	Side panel—trunk aperture	39	Handbrake cover and grommet
9	Side panel—trunk aperture	25	Quarter valance	40	Inner panel—"B" post
10	Waist rail	26	Lower panel—tonneau side	41	"B" post
11	Reinforcement—roof fixing	27	Retainer—tapped plate	42	Outer wheelarch
12	Reinforcement—rear deck	28	"B" post panel	43	Inner wheelarch
13	Rear deck	29	Filler panel—tonneau upper	44	Stiffener—wheelarch to tonneau side
14	Reinforcement—roof fixing	30	Outer wheelarch	45	Angle support—squab side
15	Reinforcement—roof fixing	31	Inner wheelarch	46	Cover—spring access
16	Waist rail			47	Luggage floor side panel

Fig. 50. Rear end section details

REAR END SECTION

Herald 1200, 12/50, 13/60 and Vitesse 6

To Remove

Isolate the battery and release the accelerator cable or linkage from the carburettor and pedal.

Remove

— Seats (page 5·258);
— Floor covering (page 5·257);
— Rear quarter trim (page 5·257);
— Doors (page 5·230);
— Both sill panels (page 5·211);
— Roof panel (page 5·216);
— Luggage compartment lid or
— tailgate (page 5·213);

Remove the floor covering or wooden floor from the luggage compartment and take out the spare wheel. Drain and remove the fuel tank (page 5·263). Disconnect the rear brake cable at the compensator (page 3·211).

Remove the dash side trim panel from the left-hand side of the car (three screws) and disconnect the cables to the rear of the vehicle at the snap connectors under the facia.

Take off the knob from the change speed lever and remove the gearbox cover by unscrewing eleven screws. Eight of the screws (4 at each side) are accessible from the driving compartment (Fig. 51), the remaining three screws are located below the heater unit in the engine compartment.

Remove two hex/headed screws with washers, one each side of the vehicle, positioned in front of the outboard seat runners.

Referring to Fig. 1, release the rear end section from the chassis frame by removing

— Six bolts (D), positioned transversely across the vehicle in front of the seat runners;
— Two bolts (G) located rear of the seat pan;
— Four bolts (H) and (J) accessible from inside the luggage compartment;
— Eight bolts (B), (C), (E) and (F) located beneath the frame side members.

Lift the rear section and note the location of mounting pads between the body and the chassis frame.

To Refit

Remove the old sealing compound from the rear and centre section joint faces and apply new lengths of "Everseal" strip to the outer face of the centre section (1) Fig. 53, and rubberised canvas between the centre and rear section joints (2).

Position and secure the mounting pads to the chassis, using Bostik 1261. The pads are ¼" (6·3 mm.) thick. On some vehicles, two pads ⅛" (3 mm.) are used in place of a single pad.

Refit the rear end section by reversing the removal procedure.

Referring to page 5·227, adjust the rear end section to achieve an even clearance of the doors.

Refit the roof panel (page 5·216), rear quarter glass (page 5·238) and re-connect the electrical system and the handbrake mechanism.

Refit seats, carpets and remaining components.

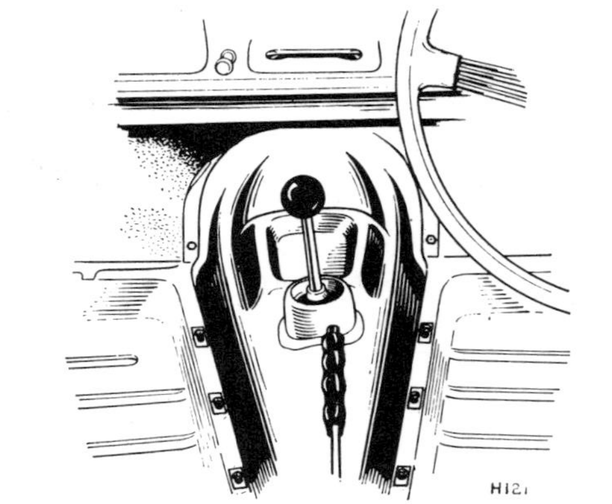

Fig. 51. Location of gearbox cover

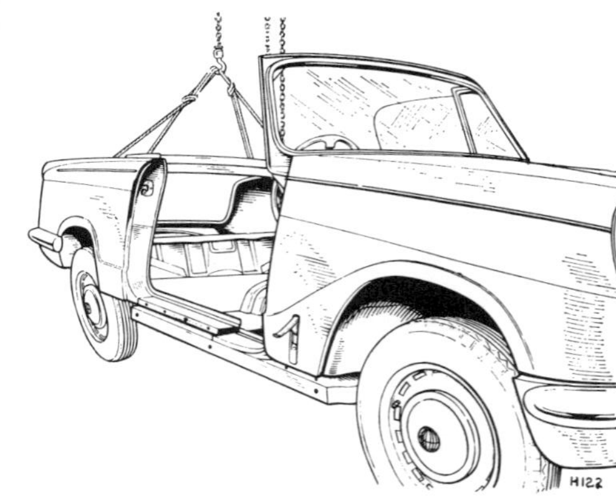

Fig. 52. Lifting rear end section

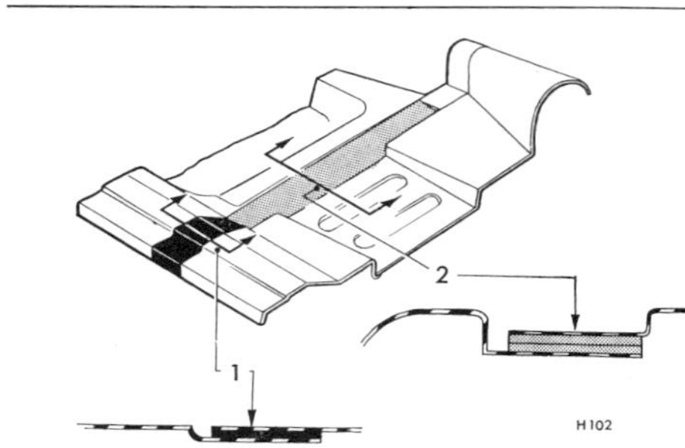

Fig. 53. Location of floor panel sealing strips

CENTRE SECTION DETAILS

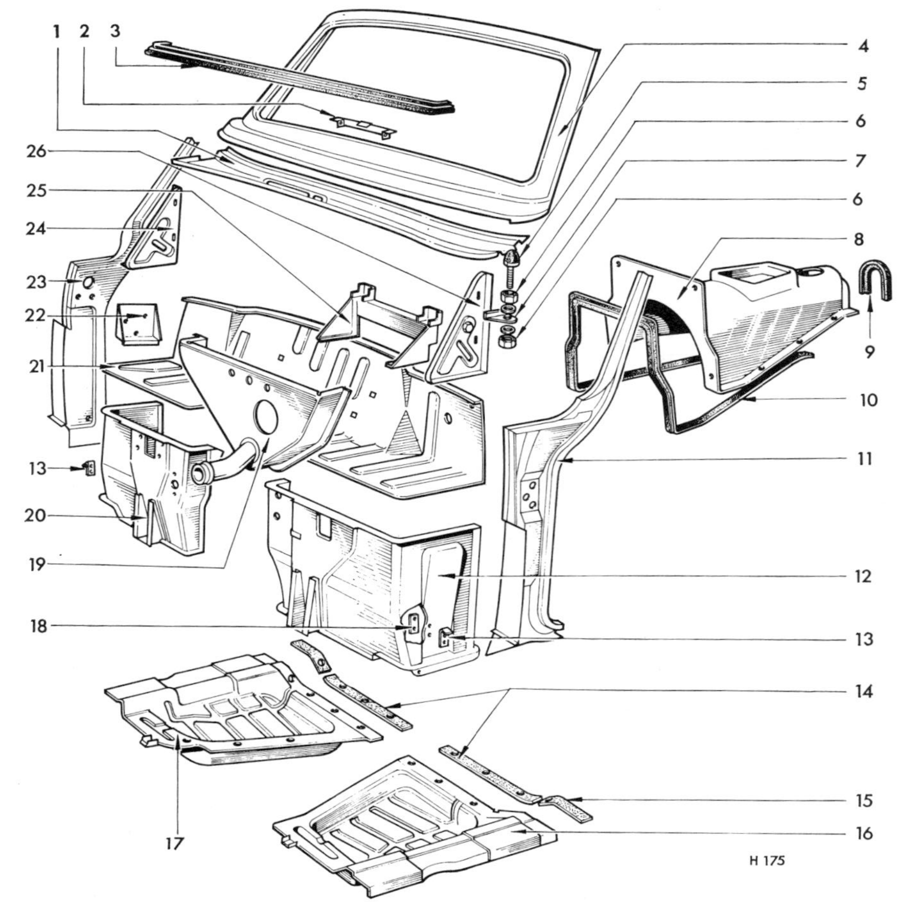

1 Front deck
2 Bracket—demister support
3 Rubber seal
4 Panel—screen surround
5 Bonnet locator pin
6 Lock nut
7 Mounting plate
8 Nut
9 Seal—gearbox cover
10 Seal—gearbox cover
11 "A" post panel
12 Panel—dash side
13 Bonnet catch plate
14 Sealing strip
15 Sealing strip
16 Front floor L.H.
17 Front floor R.H.
18 Stiffener plate
19 Air box panel
20 Panel—dash side
21 Dash shelf panel
22 Bracket—wiper motor
23 "A" post panel
24 Gusset panel
25 Bracket assembly—battery
26 Gusset panel

Fig. 54. Centre section details

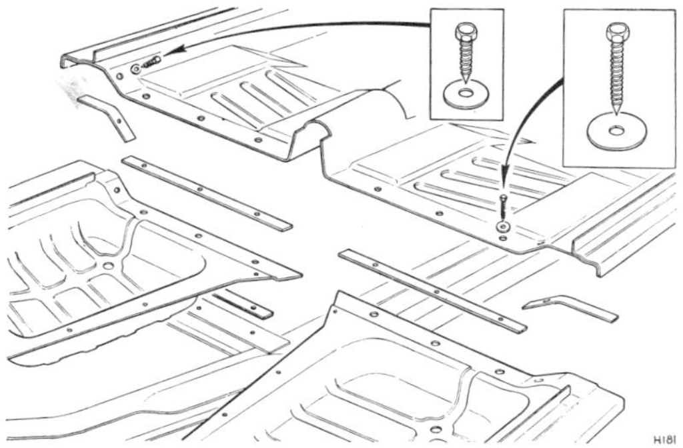

Fig. 55. Front to rear floor attachment

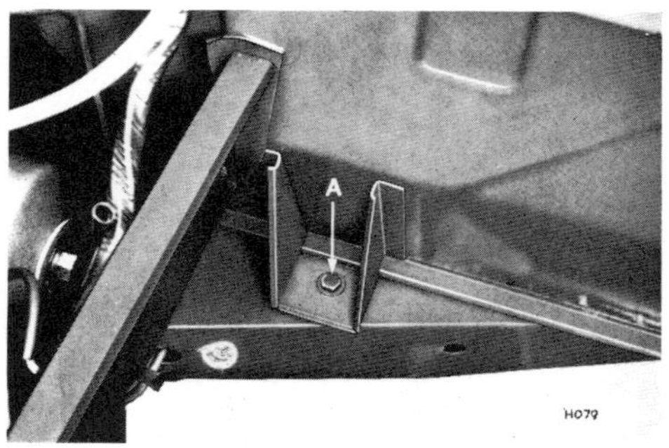

Fig. 56. Dash panel mounting to chassis frame

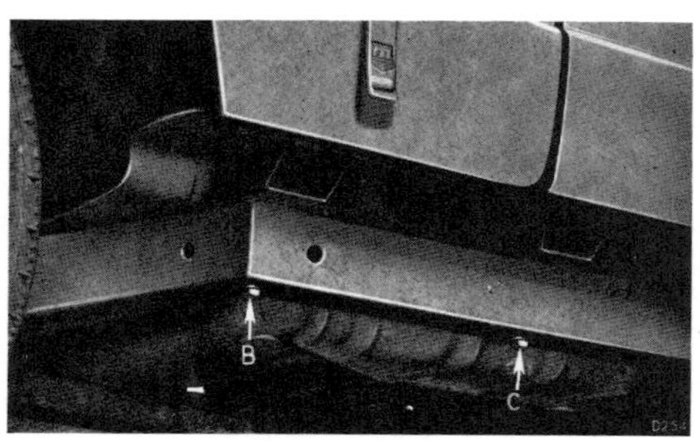

Fig. 57 Centre section to frame side channel assembly

CENTRE SECTION

Herald 1200, 12/50, 13/60 and Vitesse 6

To Remove

Isolate the battery, drain the engine coolant and disconnect both water hoses from the heater unit.

Remove the rear end section (page 5·225). Remove the engine bay side valances (page 5·209). Disconnect the front lighting, and horn cables at the snap connectors on top centre of the grille (Fig. 8), and unclip the cable harness from the chassis frame.

Disconnect the cables from the generator, coil and temperature gauge transmitter, if fitted. Remove the steering column (page 4·210).

Drain the clutch and brake hydraulic systems and disconnect the pipes from the master cylinders.

Disconnect the speedometer drive (all models), and the tachometer drive on *Vitesse 6* models from Commission No. HB 15001 and pull the cables into the engine compartment.

Referring to page 5·202, release the centre section from the chassis frame and remove two bolts in the engine compartment, adjacent to the dash panel (A) (Fig. 56).

To Refit

Reverse the removal procedure, using Bostik 1261 to attach all the body mounting pads to the centre and rear sections.

Lift the centre section into position and secure it to the chassis frame using two bolts located in the engine compartment (A) (Fig. 56). Referring to page 5·225, refit the rear end section.

Re-connect the hydraulic and electrical systems. Bleed the brake and clutch systems and road test the car.

BODY ADJUSTMENT

Herald 1200, 12/50, 13/60 and Vitesse 6

A uniform clearance of approximately $\frac{3}{16}$″ (5 mm.) should exist between the bonnet, door and rear section.

Bonnet adjustments are given on page 5·205. Should normal door adjustment fail to produce a satisfactory clearance, move the rear section of the body as required. Limited movement without disturbance to the roof on side windows is effected as follows:

Insufficient Clearance (Fig. 60)

Remove the sill panel (page 5·211) from the side requiring adjustment and slacken the body mounting bolts D, E, F, G, H and J (Fig. 1).

Insert a hardwood wedge between the shut face of the door and rear section as shown. Close the door to spread the sections sufficiently to produce a satisfactory clearance.

Re-tighten all body mounting bolts. Remove the wedge, check the clearance and refit the sill.

Excessive Clearance (Fig. 58)

Remove the sill panel (page 5·211) from the side of the car requiring adjustment, and slacken the body mounting bolts D, E, F, H and K (page 5·201).

Insert two hardwood wedges between the frame and the rear floor approximately 2″ (5·1 mm.) inward of body mounting point "F". Gently hammer the wedges in, as shown, until satisfactory clearance is achieved.

Re-tighten body mounting bolts. Remove the wedges, check the clearance and refit the sill.

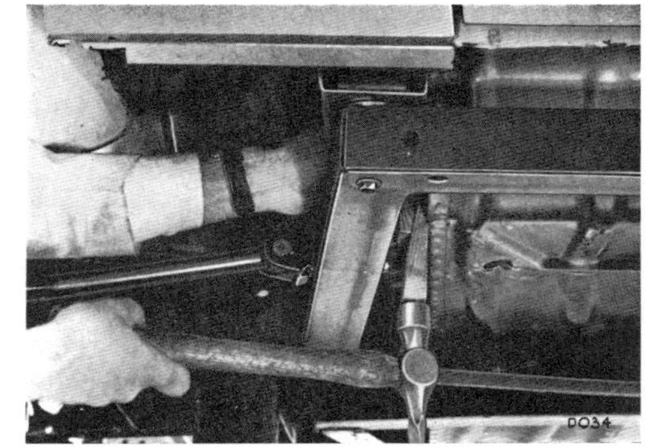

Fig. 58. Inserting wedges to reduce gap

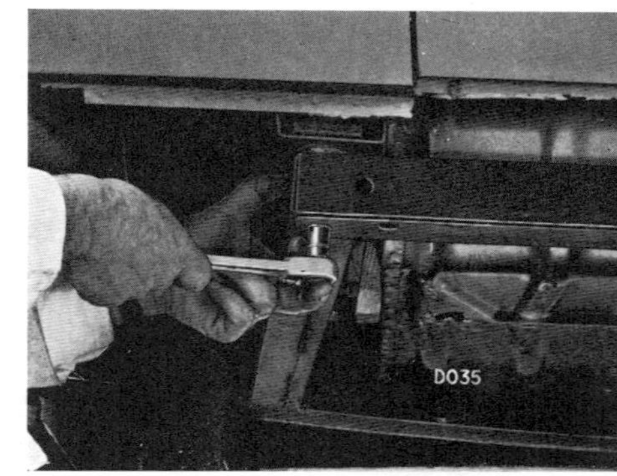

Fig. 59. Re-tightening body mounting bolts

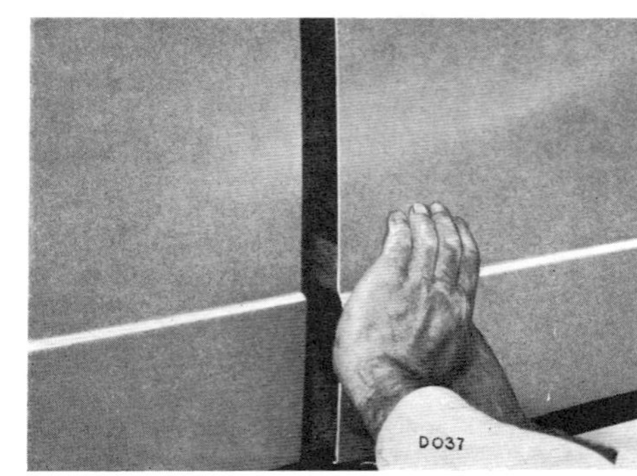

Fig. 60. Inserting wedges to increase gap

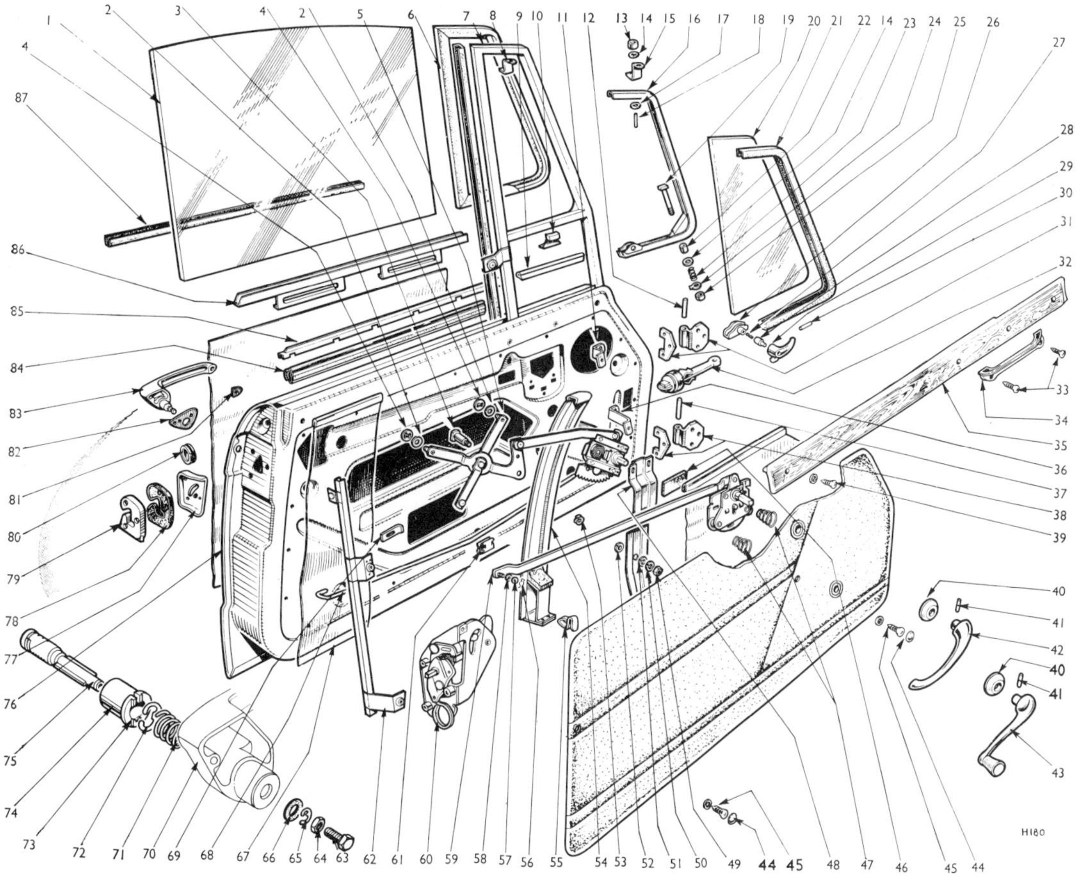

Fig. 61. Door details

Key to Fig. 61

1 Glass—door
2 Washer—leather
3 Pivot—regulator mounting
4 Clip—retainer
5 Window regulator assembly
6 Weatherstrip
7 Outer frame
8 Bracket—top pivot, outer
9 Finisher—waist forward, inner
10 Plate—catch
11 Bracket—vent support
12 Pin—door hinge
13 Washer—thick
14 Washer—thin
15 Bracket—top pivot, inner
16 Inner frame—assembly
17 Washer—thin
18 Rivet—semi-tubular
19 Shaft assembly—bottom pivot
20 Glass—vent
21 Strip—glazing
22 Spacing piece
23 Spring
24 Washer—tab
25 Nut
26 Bracket assembly—handle
27 Spring
28 Button—push
29 Handle—locking
30 Pin—locking
31 Hinge—door
32 Check link assembly—door
33 Screw
34 Handle—door pull
35 Capping—veneer
36 Bracket—vent support assembly
37 Pin—door hinge
38 Hinge—door
39 Screw—capping veneer
40 Escutcheon—inside handle
41 Pin—handle fixing
42 Handle—remote control
43 Window regulator handle
44 Cap—door trim
45 Screw—door trim
46 Felt pad
47 Spring—regulator
48 Reinforcement—regulator pivot
49 Nut
50 Washer—lock
51 Washer—plain
52 Washer—plain (thin)
53 Washer—special
54 Stiffener assembly—anti-drum
55 Clip—trim panel to door
56 Clip
57 Washer—waved
58 Washer—plain
59 Remote control mechanism
60 Cam lock assembly
61 Clip—tie rod attachment
62 Channel—glass assembly
63 Bolt—lock adjusting
64 Nut—lock adjusting
65 "E" clip—securing push button in handle
66 Washer—rubber
67 Weather curtain
68 Rod—tie, glass channel, bottom
69 Window regulator stop bracket
70 Body—door handle, outside
71 Spring—button return
72 "E" clip—locking handle only
73 Plunger—locator
74 Button—push, locking handle only
75 Barrel—locking (plunger), locking handle only
76 Door assembly
77 Plate—dove tail, cam lock
78 Rubber sealing—striker, cam lock
79 Striker assembly—cam lock
80 Grommet—rubber
81 Washer—seating, small
82 Washer—seating, large
83 Door handle assembly—outside
84 Strip—sealing, waist, door inner
85 Strip—sealing, waist, door outer
86 Channel assembly—window regulator
87 Strip—glazing channel

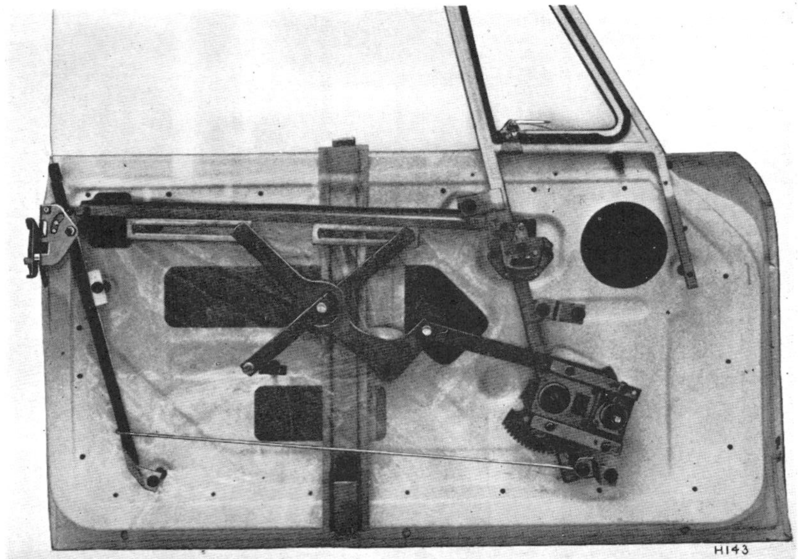

Fig. 62. Door components

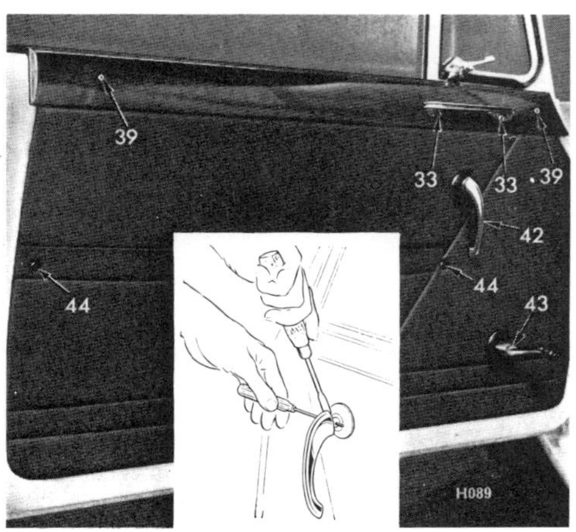

Fig. 63. Trim panel attachments

DOORS

Lubrication

Before refitting the door casing and other items ensure that all moving parts are adequately greased. After assembly and once a month introduce a few drops of thin machine oil into the outside key slots and into the latch slot.

IMPORTANT: The private lock cylinders must not under any circumstances be lubricated with grease or graphite.

1200, 12/50, 13/60 and Vitesse 6

A. TRIM PANEL

1. **To Remove** (Fig. 63)
   (a) Remove four screws (33) and (39) securing the wood cappings to the door (*Vitesse 6* only).
   (b) Lever off two buttons (44), unscrew the exposed screws (48) and remove the washers (*Vitesse 6* only).
   (c) Remove two interior handles (42 and 43) by pressing the escutcheons (40) firmly against the trim panel and pushing out the retaining pins (41).

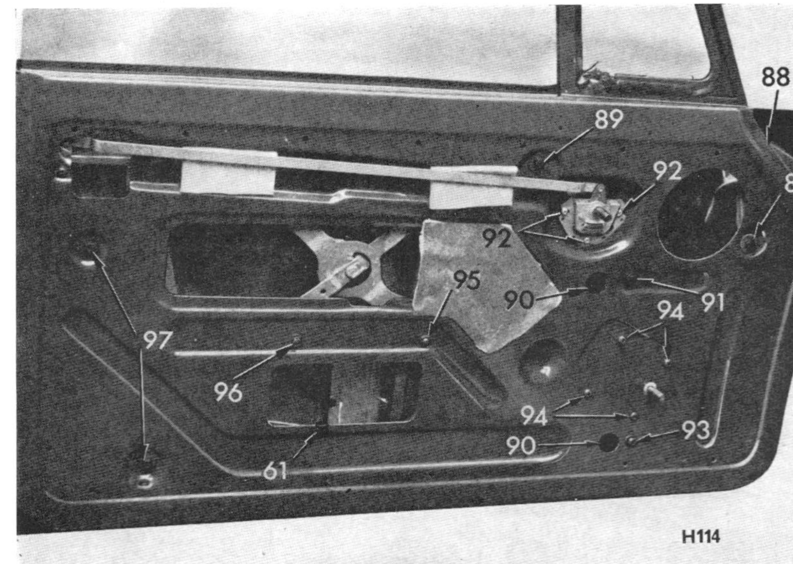

Fig. 64. Door component attachment

   (d) Prise the edge of the trim panel from the door.
   (e) Remove the coil springs (47) from the spindles.

2. **To Refit:** Reverse the removal procedure.

B. REMOTE CONTROL

1. **To Remove** (Figs. 61, 64 and 66)
   (a) Perform operation A1.
   (b) Refit the remote control handle and retain it in the door open position.
   (c) Remove the spring clip (56) with waved washer (57) and release the link arm from the lock assembly.
   (d) Take out three screws (92) and remove the remote control mechanism (59) from the door.

2. **To Align the Unit** (Fig. 64)
   (a) Perform operation A1.
   (b) Slacken three screws (92) and slide the remote control towards the lock until the lock lever comes in contact with its stop. The holes in the remote control unit are elongated for adjustment purposes.

Fig. 65. Releasing the trim panel

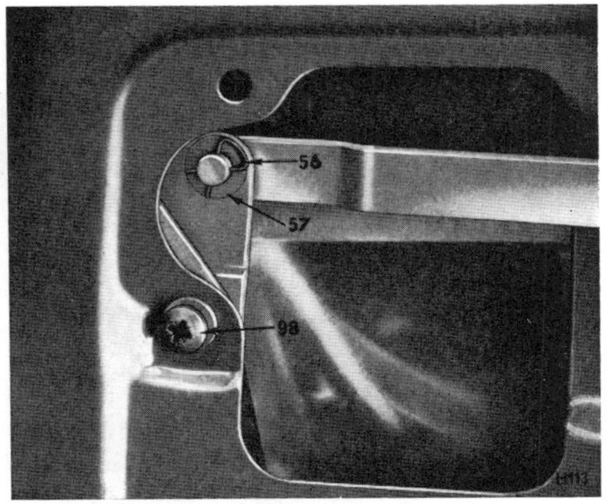

Fig. 66. Remote control link attachment to lock

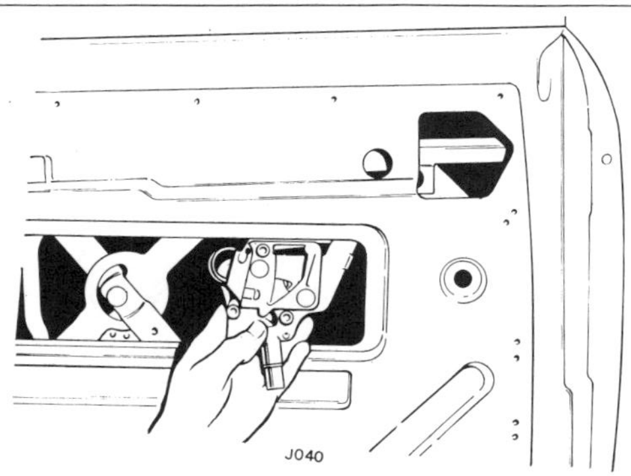

Fig. 67. Removing/fitting early type of lock

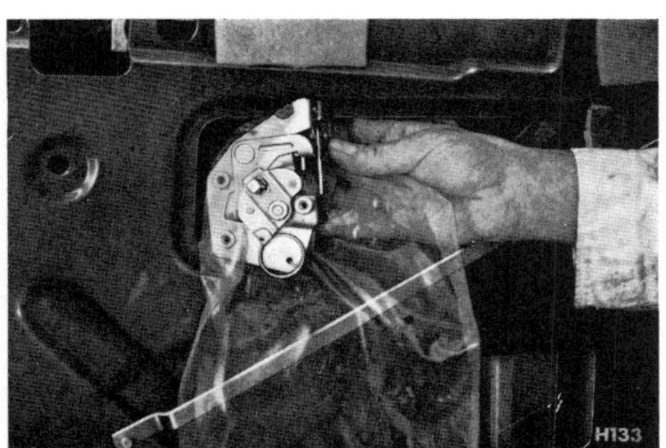

Fig. 68. Removing/fitting latest type of lock

(c) Finally tighten the three securing screws.

3. **To Refit:** Reverse the removal procedure.

C. GLASS RUN CHANNEL

1. **To Remove** (Figs. 61 and 64)
   (a) Perform operation A1.
   (b) Loosely refit the regulating handle and raise the glass to the fully closed position.
   (c) Remove the rubber grommet (80) and take out the exposed hex/headed bolt with washer.
   (d) Remove two hex/headed bolts (97) with washers. Pull the lower end of the channel (62) away from the tension wire (68).
   (e) Lower the channel into the bottom of the door and manoeuvre it through the lower door aperture.

2. **To Refit:** Reverse the removal procedure.

D. DOOR LOCK

A re-designed door lock unit was introduced from Commission Nos. GA51185LH and GA51163RH *1200* convertible; GA51546LH and GA50639RH *1200* saloon; HB4 *Vitesse 6* (see Fig. 67 for early condition and Fig. 68 for latest condition).

1. **To Remove** (Figs. 66 and 69)
   (a) Perform operation C1.
   (b) Perform operation B1 (c).
   (c) Remove three cross/recess screws (100) securing the lock and dovetail to the door and remove one cross/recess screw (98).
   (d) Referring to Figs. 67 and 68, remove the lock. Do not use levers for this operation or serious distortion of the mechanism may result.

IMPORTANT: In the event of there being insufficient clearance the lower edge of the small aperture in the door inner panel may cut away slightly.

2. **To Refit:** Reverse the removal procedure, taking care to position the polythene curtain correctly as shown in Fig. 68.

E. EXTERIOR DOOR HANDLE

1. **To Remove** (Figs. 69 and 70)
   (a) Perform operation A1.
   (b) Loosely refit the regulating handle and raise the glass to the fully closed position.

   (c) Release the handle by unscrewing two screws, one (99) is situated adjacent to the dovetail plate shown in Fig. 69, the other screw is located on the inside of the door panel at the forward end of the handle.

2. **To Adjust Push Button** (Fig. 70)
   (a) Perform operation E1.
   (b) Slacken the locknut (64) and adjust the bolt (63) to give a clearance of $\frac{1}{16}''$ between the bolt head and the lock lever. Finally re-tighten the locknut (64).

3. **To Refit:** Reverse the removal procedure.

F. WINDOW REGULATOR MECHANISM

1. **To Remove** (Figs. 61, 64 and 71)
   (a) Perform operation A1.
   (b) Loosely refit the regulating handle and lower the glass until the operating arms are accessible through the large aperture in the door inner panel.
   (c) Remove the clips (4) and leather washer (2). Spring the arms clear of the channel and lift the glass to its highest position.
   (d) Remove the nut (49) with spring washer (50) securing the regulator pivot (3) to the inner panel.
   (e) Remove the pivot (3) and the double coil spring washer (55) which is fitted between the regulator and the door inner panel.
   (f) Take out two hex/headed bolts (89) and two cross/recess screws (90) which are accessible through circular holes in the door panel. Remove one screw (88) and lift the ventilator assembly approximately 2″ (50 mm.).
   (g) Take out four cross/recess screws (94) securing the regulator to the door inner panel and pass the assembly through the large aperture.

2. **To Refit:** Reverse the removal procedure and when refitting the ventilator assembly ensure that the screw (90) secures the forward end of the tension wire (68).

G. DOOR GLASS

1. **To Remove** (Fig. 71)
   (a) Perform operation C1 and F1 (b).
   (b) Remove the spring clips (4) and leather washers (2). Disconnect the arms from the operating channel on the bottom edge of the glass and lower the glass.

Fig. 69. Dovetail plate/lock attachment

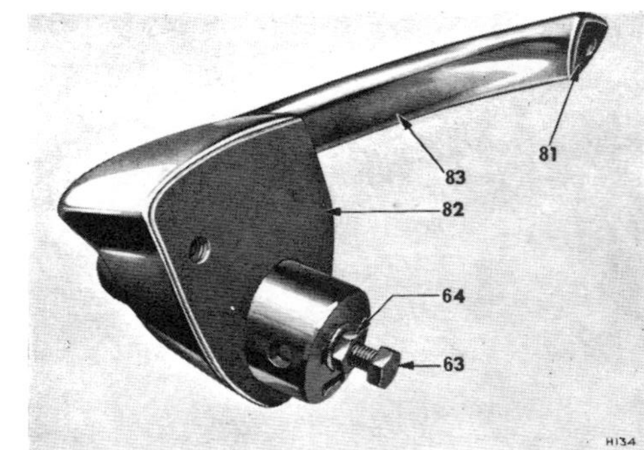

Fig. 70. Exterior handle details

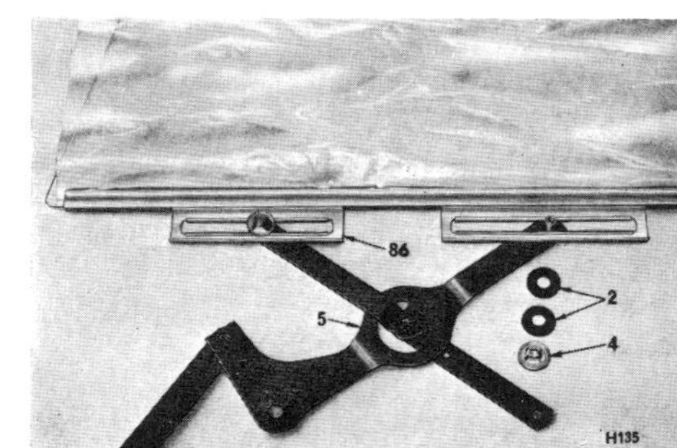

Fig. 71. Regulator arms

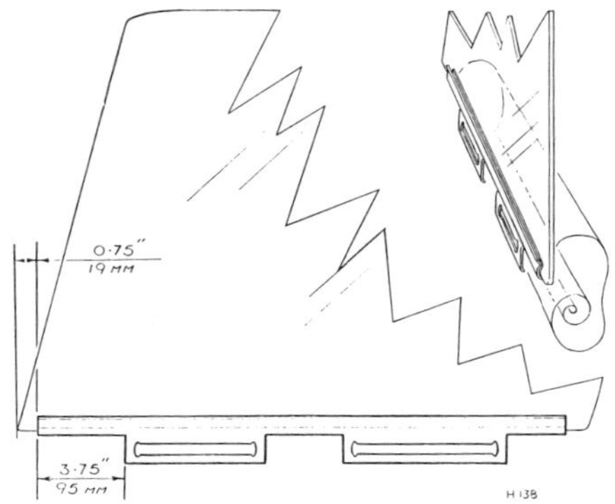

Fig. 72. Door glass/channel

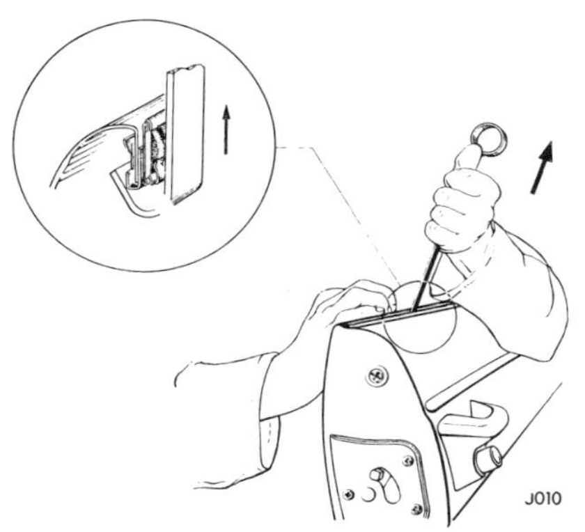

Fig. 73. Fitting weatherstrip

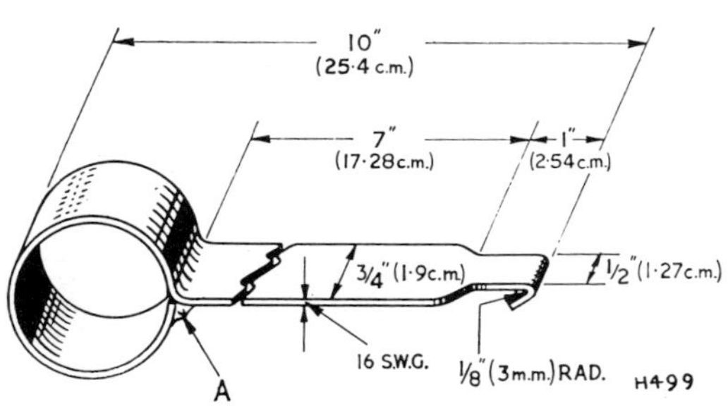

Fig. 74. Weatherstrip fitting tool

(c) Perform operation H1.
(d) Perform operation F1 (f).
(e) Lift out the glass by tilting it as required, taking care not to damage the water deflector panel which is attached to the glass by the channel.

2. **To Refit**
(a) Fold the deflector flat against the inner side of the glass and place the glass into the door.
(b) Lower the glass and reverse operation F1 (f).
(c) Reverse operation G1 (b).
(d) Reverse operation F1 (b), C1 (b), (c), (d) and (e).
(e) Perform operation H2.

3. **To Refit:** Door glass to channel
(a) Place one end of the polythene sheet together with the rubber weatherstrip over the channel run (Fig. 72).
(b) Position the glass, as shown on Fig. 72, and compress the glass into the channel.

H. INNER AND/OR OUTER WEATHER-STRIP

1. **To Remove** (Fig. 61)
(a) Perform operation A1 and lower the door glass.
(b) Remove the weatherstrip (84) and (85) by pressing the retaining clips downwards with a screwdriver.

2. **To Refit**
An easily made tool (Fig. 74) is required for refitting the weatherstrip from inside the door panel as follows:
(a) The inner weatherstrip (85) can be refitted with the door glass in the normal down position.
(b) To refit the outer weatherstrip (84) remove the stiffener bracket (54) from the door inner panel and lower the door glass as far as possible. The stiffener bracket is retained by two cross/recess screws, located below the bracket on the underside of the door.
(c) Holding the weatherstrip in position locate the spring clip over the edge of the door panel and weatherstrip. Using the hooked tool shown in Fig. 73 pull the clip firmly onto the door flange and repeat with the remaining clips. The hooked tool may be used to fit any clip which requires renewing.
(d) Perform operation A2.

J. QUARTER VENT

1. **To Remove** (Fig. 64)
(a) Perform operation G1.
(b) Lift out the vent.

2. **To Dismantle the Ventilator Assembly** (Fig. 61)
(a) Bend back the tag on the washer (24). Remove the nut (25), washer (14) and spring (23) from the bottom swivel (19).

(b) Remove the rivet (18) and spacer (13) from the upper swivel. Push the upper edge of the inner frame of the vent outward and withdraw the assembly from the outer frame.
(c) Tap out the retaining pin (30) and remove the vent locking handle (29) and push button (28).

3. **To Refit**
(a) Perform operation G2.
(b) For remaining operations, reverse the removal procedure.

K. LOCK STRIKER PLATE

1. **To Remove** (Fig. 75)
(a) Remove three screws (101) and release the striker plate (78) from the "B" post.

2. **To Adjust**
(a) Slacken three securing screws (101).
(b) Correct position of the striker plate is carried out by a process of trial and error, proved by checking the door closing action and its position when closed. Ensure that the striker is in the horizontal plane relative to the axis of the door movement.
(c) Finally re-tighten the securing screws (101).

3. **To Refit:** Reverse the removal procedure.

L. DOOR ASSEMBLY

1. **To Remove** (Figs. 61 and 76)
(a) Remove the rivet securing the check arm (32) to the "A" post.
(b) Take out three bolts (102) securing each hinge to the "A" post and lift the door from the vehicle.
Each hinge is secured to the door by two bolts and one cross/recess screw.

2. **To Refit:** Reverse the removal procedure.

M. CHECK STRAP BRACKET

1. **To Remove** (Fig. 77)
(a) Remove all components from the door.
(b) Perform operation L1.
(c) Drill through the spot welds securing the bracket to the door panel.

2. **To Refit**
(a) Secure the bracket to the door with four ⅛" (3·0 mm.) dia. cheese headed steel rivets
(b) Perform operation L2.
(c) Refit all door components.

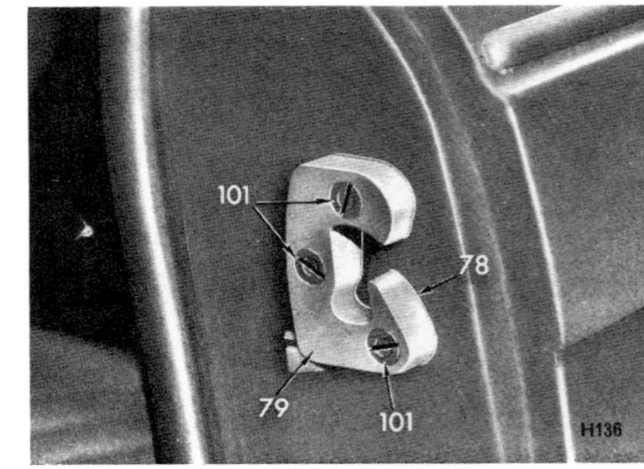

Fig. 75. Door lock striker plate

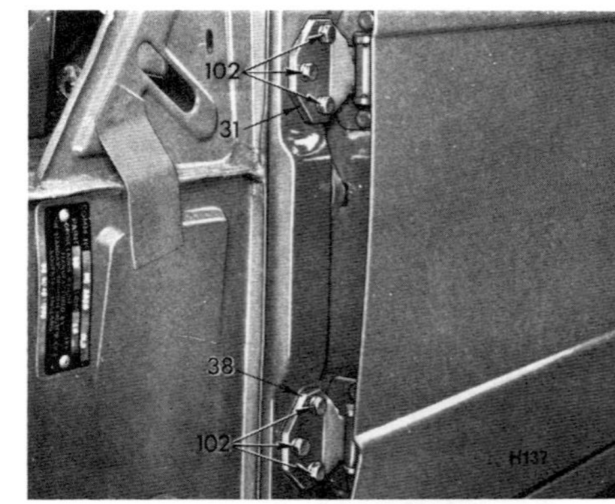

Fig. 76. Door hinge attachment

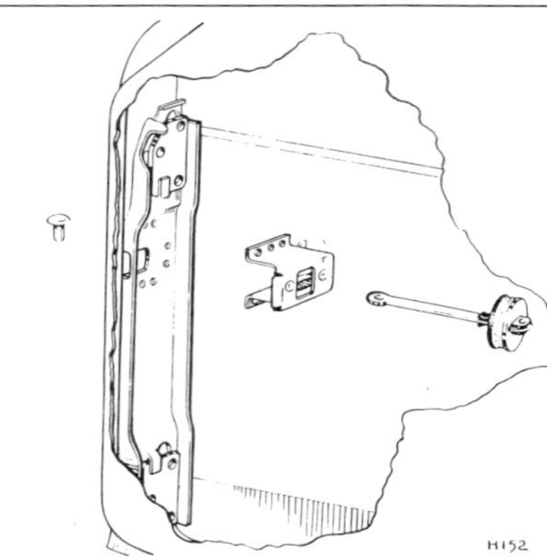

Fig. 77. Check strap bracket

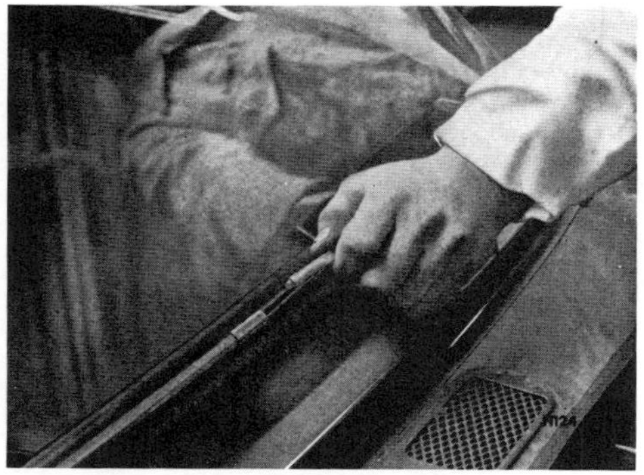

Fig. 78. Removing windscreen mouldings

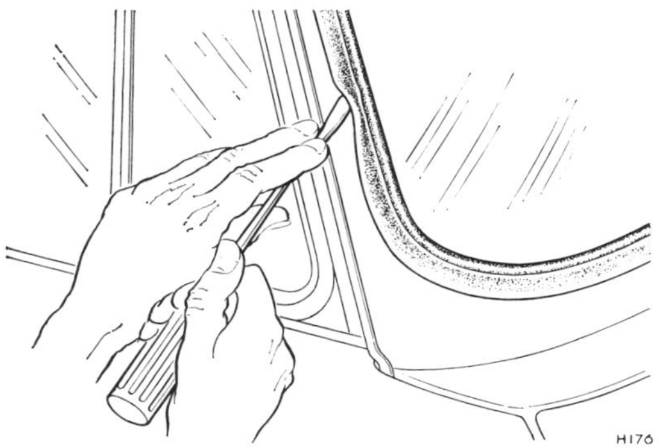

Fig. 79. Breaking weatherstrip seal

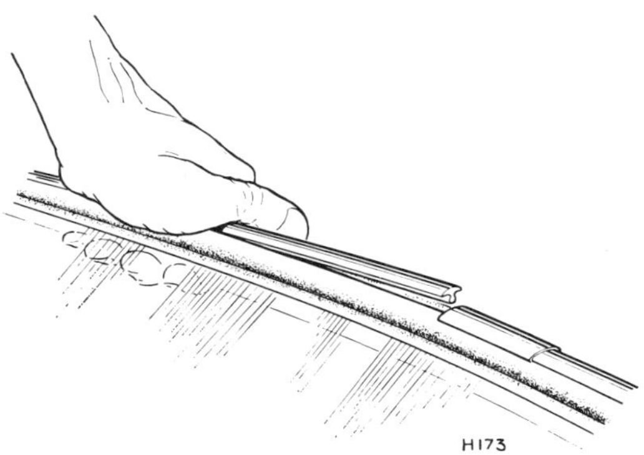

Fig. 80. Fitting windscreen moulding

WINDSCREEN

1200, 12/50, 13/60 and Vitesse 6

To Remove

Remove both windscreen wiper arms, sun visors and rear view mirror.

Using a small screwdriver from which all sharp edges have been removed, break the sealing between the rubber weatherstrip and the body flange (Fig. 79).

Avoid damage to the surrounding paintwork by keeping the tool pressed firmly under the lip of the rubber while breaking the seal. Commencing at one of the lower corners, apply hand pressure from inside the car and force the windscreen outward, whilst a second operator, working outside the car, takes the weight of the glass as it is released.

Release the moulding by sliding the upper and lower cover plates away from the moulding joint and remove both sections from the rubber (Fig. 78).

ALL MODELS EXCEPT COUPÉ

To Refit (Weatherstrip to glass)

1. Remove all trace of old sealing compound from the glass and weatherstrip.
2. Assemble the weatherstrip to the glass and re-seal with Seelastik.
3. Using a small screwdriver, clear all obstructions from the channel in the weatherstrip, into which the moulding is to be fitted.
4. Press both sections of the moulding into place and secure them by sliding the cover plates over the ends of the moulding (Fig. 80).

1200 COUPÉ ONLY

To Refit (Weatherstrip to glass)

Installation of the moulding to the weatherstrip requires the use of a small tool (Fig. 84).

1. Remove all trace of old sealing compound from the glass and weatherstrip.
2. Assemble the weatherstrip to the glass and re-seal with Seelastik.

3. Using the rounded end of the tool, clear all obstructions and burrs from the lip of the moulding channel. Apply a solution of soft soap and water.
4. Position the moulding on the weatherstrip as shown on Fig. 85. Dip the hooked end of the tool in the soapy solution, push it under the moulding and lift up the lip of the channel. Draw the tool around the moulding, simultaneously keeping it pressed firmly into the channel. Refit the cover plates to the moulding.

1200, 12/50, 13/60 and Vitesse 6

To Refit (Glass to body)

1. Insert a length of strong cord into the inner channel of the rubber, positioning the loose ends at the lower centre of the glass (Fig. 81).
2. Apply a coating of Seelastik to the outer channel of the weatherstrip and to the outer flange of the aperture.
3. Pass the ends of the cord into the vehicle and with the aid of a second operator, maintaining steady pressure on the outside of the glass, pull the ends of the cord to bring the lip of the rubber over the body flange. It may be necessary to strike the outside of the weatherstrip with a rubber-faced hammer to seat the windscreen properly (Fig. 83).
4. Withdraw the cord completely and seal the weatherstrip to the body by pressing the strip firmly into contact. Remove surplus sealing compound using a cloth moistened with petrol or white spirit. Do not allow any excess liquid to seep into the joint and destroy the bond.

BACKLIGHT

1200, 12/50, 13/60 and Vitesse 6

To Remove and Refit

Instructions for removing and refitting the backlight are identical to those given for the windscreen except reference to wiper arms, rear view mirror and sun visors.

For sealing operations, refer to "Dust and Water Sealing", page 5·301.

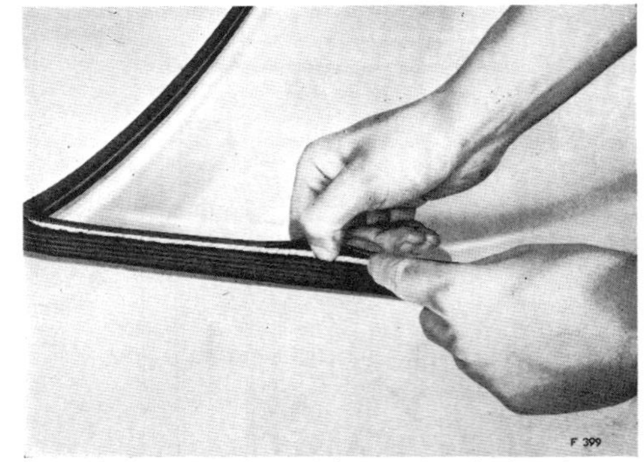

Fig. 81. Inserting cord into weatherstrip channel

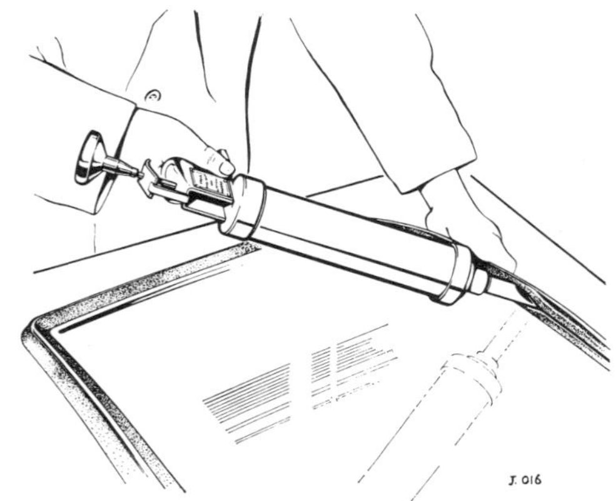

Fig. 82. Sealing window rubber

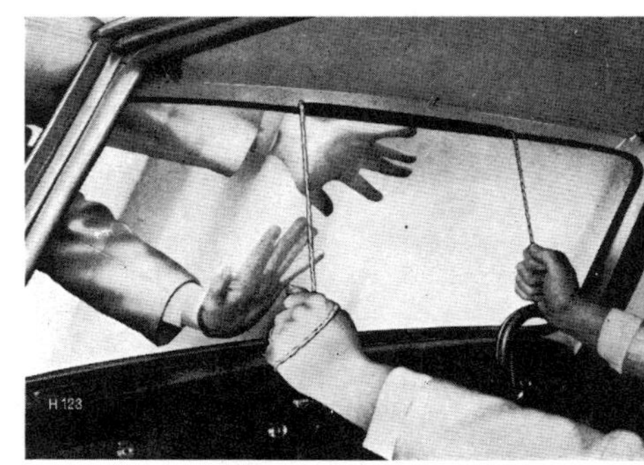

Fig. 83. Fitting windscreen

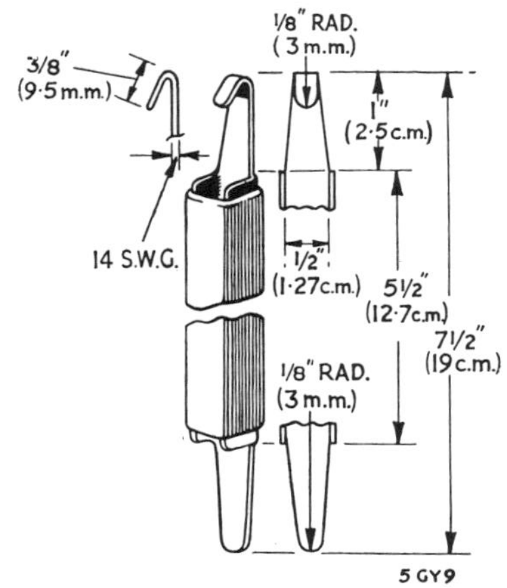

Fig. 84. Special tool details

Fig. 85. Fitting mouldings to coupé windscreen

Fig. 86. Fitting quarter light

QUARTER LIGHTS

1200, 12/50, 13/60 and Vitesse 6

To Remove

Using a small screwdriver from which all sharp edges have been removed, break the seal between the rubber and the body and, starting at the lower corner, force the quarterlight outward, whilst a second operator, working outside the car, takes the weight of the glass as it is released.

Remove the moulding and weatherstrip.

To Refit

1. Use an adhesive solvent to remove the old sealing compound from the glass weatherstrip and body flanges. Examine the rubber for cracks or other defects and renew if necessary.
2. Plug the gaps between the lower edge of the roof rear pillar and the body, and at a corresponding position at the base of the roof centre pillar (Fig. 42).
3. Fit the weatherstrip to the glass, insert the moulding and use Seelastik to seal the rubber to the glass.
4. Insert a length of strong cord into the inner channel around the periphery of the weatherstrip and permit the ends to protrude from the bottom edge of the weatherstrip.
5. Offer the quarterlight up to the body and pass the free ends of the cord into the car. Maintain firm pressure on the corner and side of the glass, as a second operator, working inside the car, withdraws the cord to turn the lip of the rubber over the body flange. It may be necessary to gently strike the glass with a rubber mallet or the palm of the hand as near as possible to its edge (Fig. 86).
6. Seal the rubber to the body with Seelastik. Remove surplus sealing compound using a cloth moistened with petrol or white spirit. Do not allow any excess liquid to seep into the joint and destroy the bond. For sealing operations, refer to "Dust and Water Sealing", page 5·301.

INSTRUMENTS, SWITCHES AND CONTROLS

NOTE: Before disturbing any part of the facia isolate the battery. When refitting any of the lucar connectors described in the following procedures, refer to Group 6—Facia Connections.

INSTRUMENTS

1200, 12/50 and Vitesse 6

Speedometer and Tachometer (Fig. 87)

To Remove

Disconnect the drive cable and pull out the illumination bulb holders. From the speedometer and voltage stabiliser, disconnect the trip reset cable and disconnect the Lucar connectors. Remove two knurled ends (E), spring washers, one earth lead from speedometer or two leads from tachometer, and clamps (F). Push the instrument out through the front of the facia, simultaneously removing the reinforcing ring from behind.

To Refit

Ensuring that the rubber ring is undamaged and located adjacent to the rim, mount the instrument on the facia and secure it from behind by fitting the reinforcing ring, clamps (F), earth lead/s, spring washers and knurled nuts (E). Push the illumination bulb holders into position and re-connect the drive cable. To the speedometer and voltage stabiliser re-connect the trip reset cable and Lucar connectors.

Flasher Warning Light

To Remove

Pull the bulb holder from the body, unscrew the body and, if required, push the lens out through the front of the facia.

To Refit

Reverse the removal procedure.

Vitesse 6

Fuel Contents and Water Temperature Gauge (Fig. 88)

To Remove

Pull off the Lucar connectors and illumination bulb holder from the gauge. Remove the knurled nut (C), spring washer, clamp (D) and earth lead. Push out the gauge through the front of the facia, simultaneously removing the reinforcing ring from behind.

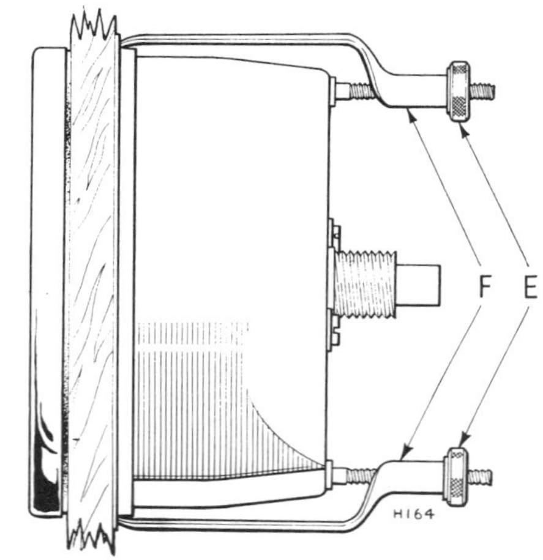

Fig. 87. Speedometer/tachometer (1200, 12/50 and Vitesse 6)

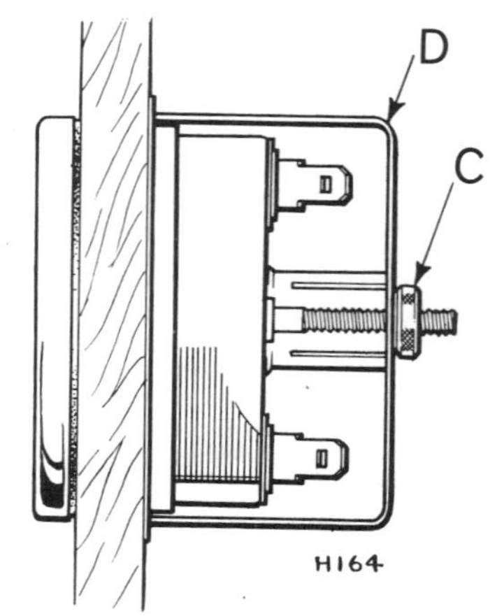

Fig. 88. Fuel/temperature gauge (Vitesse 6)

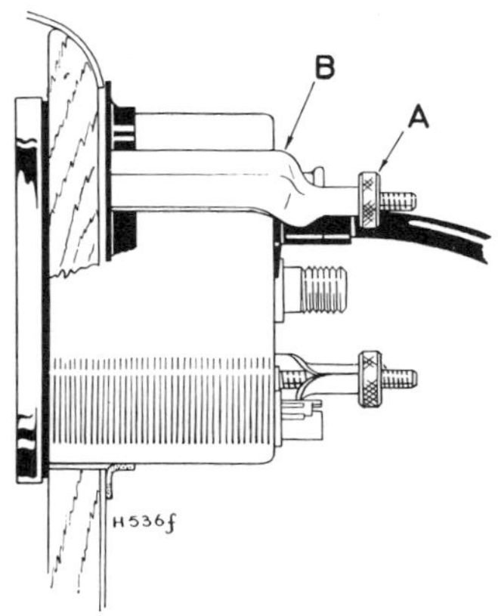

Fig. 89. Speedometer (13/60)

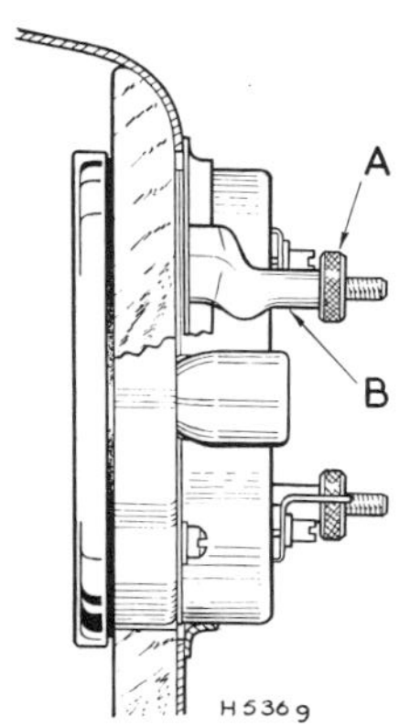

Fig. 90. Temperature/fuel gauge (13/60)

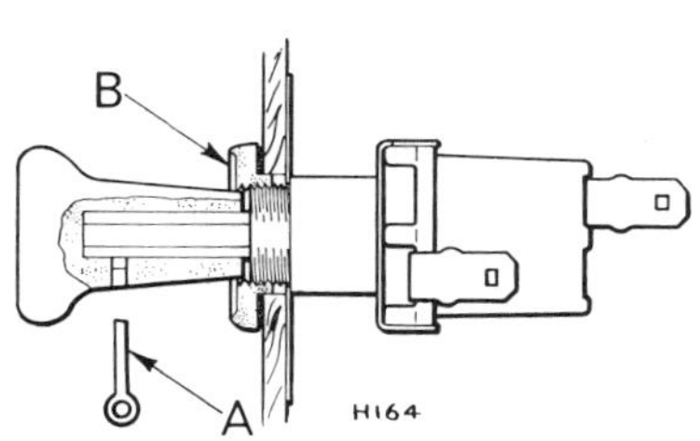

Fig. 91. Lighting switch (1200, 12/50 and Vitesse 6)

To Refit

Ensuring that the rubber ring is undamaged and located adjacent to the rim, mount the gauge on the facia and secure it from behind by fitting the reinforcing ring, clamp (D), earth lead, spring washer and knurled nut. Push the illumination bulb holder into position and re-connect the Lucar connectors.

13/60

Speedometer (Fig. 89)

To Remove

Disconnect the drive cable and pull out the illumination bulb holders, unscrew the trip reset cable and disconnect the lucar connectors. Remove the two knurled nuts (A) with the spring washers and clamps (B). Push the instrument out through the front of the facia, simultaneously removing the reinforcement ring from behind the facia.

To Refit

Ensuring that the rubber ring is undamaged and located adjacent to the rim, mount the instrument on the facia and secure it from behind by fitting the reinforcement ring, clamps (B), earth leads, spring washers and knurled nuts (A). Push the illumination bulb holders into position and re-connect the drive cable. Re-connect the trip reset cable and lucar connectors.

Temperature/Fuel Gauge (Fig. 90)

To Remove

Pull off the lucar connectors and the illumination bulb holder from the gauge. Remove the knurled nuts (A), spring washers, clamps (B) and earth lead. Push out the gauge through the front of the facia, simultaneously removing the reinforcement ring from behind the facia.

To Refit

Ensuring that the rubber ring is undamaged and located adjacent to the rim, mount the gauge on the facia and secure it from behind by fitting the reinforcement ring clamp (B), earth lead, spring washer and knurled nut (A). Push the illumination bulb holder into position and re-connect the lucar connectors.

SWITCHES

1200, 12/50 and Vitesse 6

Windscreen Wiper and Lights (Fig. 91)

To Remove

Depress the spring plunger by pushing a suitable pin (A) into the hole and pull off the knob. Unscrew the bezel (B), withdraw the switch from behind the facia and pull off the Lucar connectors.

To Refit

With the spring plunger on the knob spindle lowermost, locate the switch on the facia and secure it by tightening the bezel (B). Push on the knob to engage with the spring and re-attach the Lucar connectors.

Heater Blower (Fig. 92)

To Remove

Pull the Lucar connectors from the switch, unscrew the bezel and take out the switch from behind the facia.

To Refit

With the angled connector blade pointing downward, locate the switch on the facia and secure it by tightening the bezel. Re-attach the Lucar connectors.

13/60

Ignition/Starter Switch (Fig. 93)

To Remove

Pull off the Lucar connectors from the switch, unscrew the bezel (D) and withdraw the switch from behind the facia.

To Refit

Reverse the removal procedure and refer to Group 6—Facia Connections.

Master Light Switch (Fig. 94)

To Remove

Depress the spring plunger by pushing a suitable pin (C) into the hole and pull off the knob. Unscrew the bezel (D), withdraw the switch from behind the facia and pull off the Lucar connectors.

To Refit

Locate the switch on the switch panel and secure it by tightening the bezel, re-attach the Lucar connectors. Push on the knob to engage with the spring plunger.

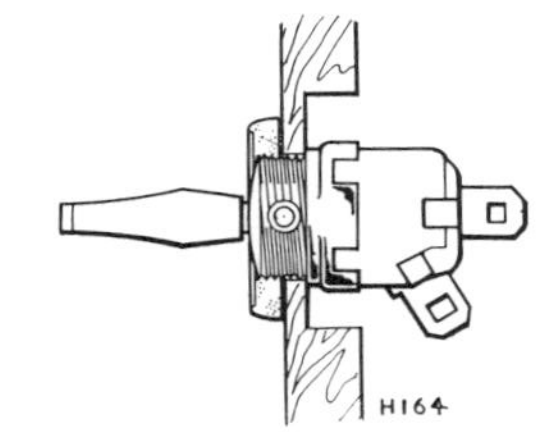

Fig. 92. Heater blower switch (1200, 12/50 and Vitesse 6)

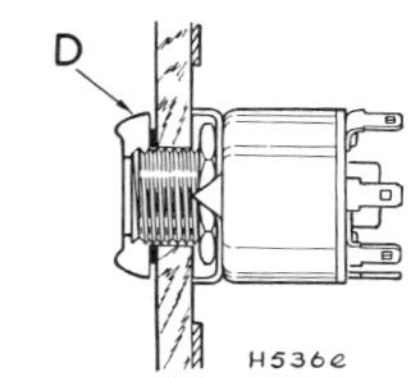

Fig. 93. Ignition/starter switch (13/60)

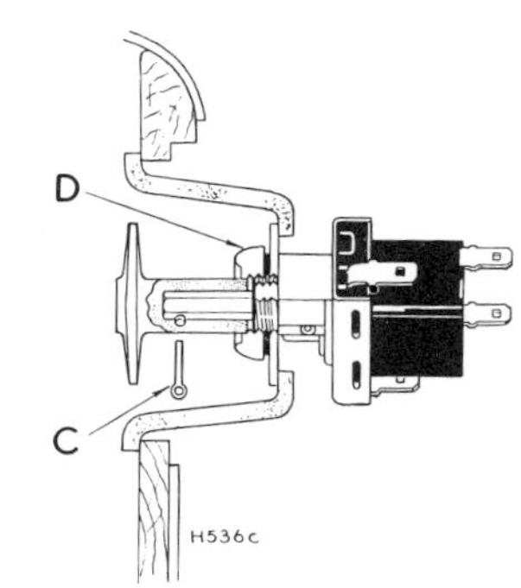

Fig. 94. Light switch (13/60)

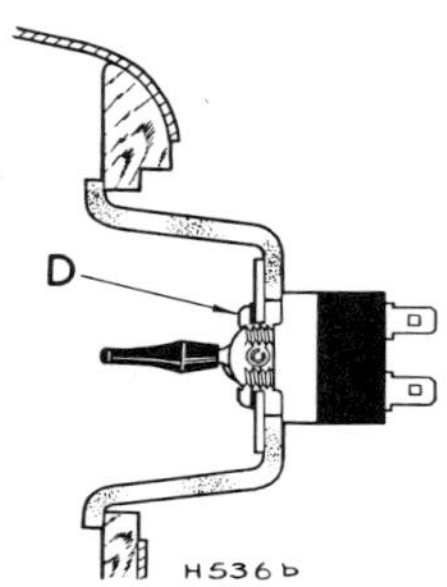

Fig. 95. Heater blower switch (13/60)

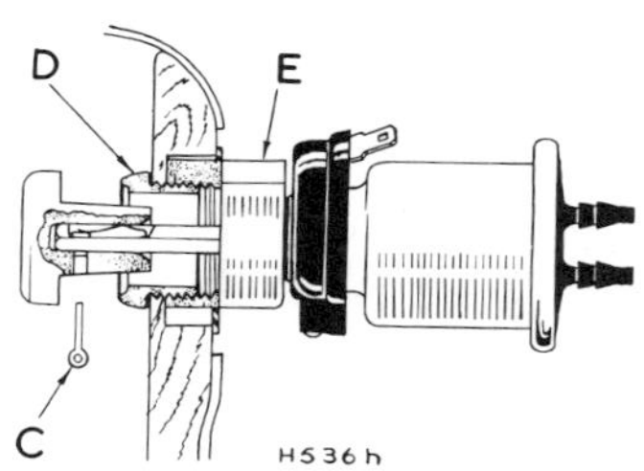

Fig. 96. Windscreen washer/wiper control (13/60)

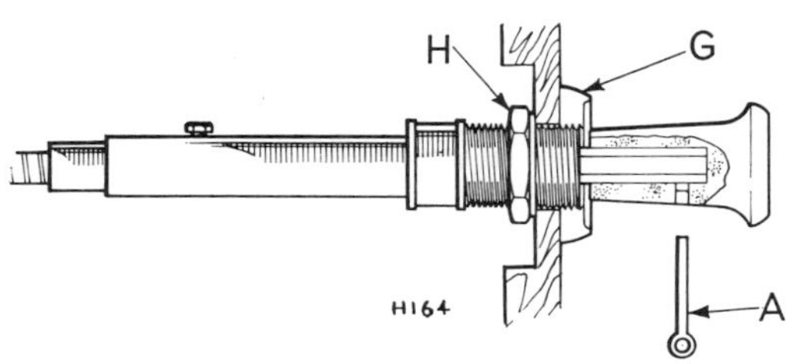

Fig. 97. Control cable (1200, 12/50 and Vitesse 6)

Heater Blower Switch (Fig. 95)

To Remove

Pull off the Lucar connectors from the switch, unscrew the bezel (D) and withdraw the switch from behind the facia.

To Refit

Reverse the removal procedure and refer to Group 6—Facia Connections.

Windscreen Washer/Wiper Control (Fig. 96)

To Remove

Depress the spring plunger by pushing a suitable pin (C) into the hole and pull off the knob. Unscrew the bezel (D), withdraw the switch from behind the facia and pull off the nylon washer pipes and the Lucar connectors.

To Refit

Working behind the facia, locate the keyway (E) on the switch body into the cutout in the metal support, attached to the veneered panel and secure the switch by tightening the bezel (D). Push on the knob to engage with the spring and re-attach the nylon pipes and Lucar connectors.

CONTROL CABLES

1200, 12/50 and Vitesse 6

Heat Control and Air Distribution (Fig. 97)

To Remove

Depress the spring plunger by pushing a suitable pin (A) into the hole and pull off the knob. Unscrew the bezel (G) and withdraw the cable.

To Refit

With the spring plunger lowermost, attach the cable to the facia by screwing on the bezel (G) until flush with the threaded end of the cable. Tighten the locknut (H) and push on the knob to engage with the spring plunger.

Choke Pull

To Remove

Disconnect the inner and outer cables from the carburettors and pull the choke knob complete with inner cable from the front of the facia. Unscrew the bezel and withdraw the outer cable.

To Refit

Feed the outer cable through the facia, screw on the bezel until flush with the threaded end of the cable and insert the inner cable. Rotate the outer cable in the facia to correctly position the emblem and tighten the locknut. Re-connect the opposite end of the cables to the carburettors.

13/60

Choke Control (Fig. 98)

To Remove

Disconnect the inner and outer cables from the carburettor and pull the choke knob complete with inner cable from the front of the facia. Unscrew the bezel (D) and withdraw the outer cable.

To Refit

Feed the outer cable complete with support bracket through the switch panel, screw on the bezel until flush with the threaded end of the cable and insert the inner cable. Rotate the outer cable in the switch panel to correctly position the knob and tighten the locknut (F). Re-connect the opposite end of the cables to the carburettors.

Heat Control and Air Distribution (Fig. 99)

To Remove

Disconnect the control cables from the water valve and heater unit. Depress the spring plunger by pushing a suitable pin (C) into the hole and pull off the knob. Unscrew the bezel (D) and withdraw the cable.

To Refit

Attach the cables to the switch panel by screwing the bezel (D) until flush with the threaded end of the cable. Push on the knob to engage with the spring plunger. Re-connect the opposite end of the cables to the water valve and heater unit.

Vitesse 6

Windscreen Washer Pump (Fig. 100)

To Remove

Unscrew the knob and collar (J) and disconnect the pipes from the rear of the pump. Unscrew the nut (K) and withdraw the pump body rearwards. If necessary unscrew the bezel (L) and remove the nut (M).

To Refit

Secure the distance piece (N) and bezel to the panel and screw the nut (M) onto the pump body, fit the pump body and secure with the nut (K). Refit the knob, collar and pipes.

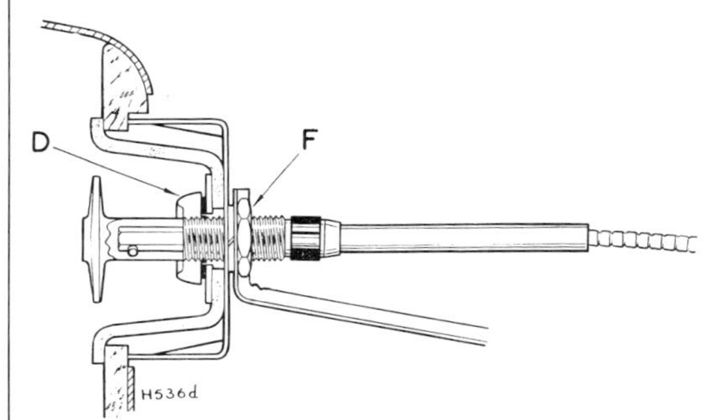

Fig. 98. Choke control (13/60)

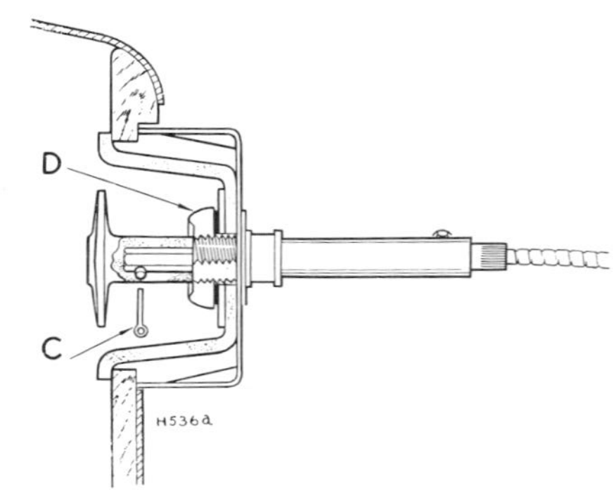

Fig. 99. Heat/Air control (13/60)

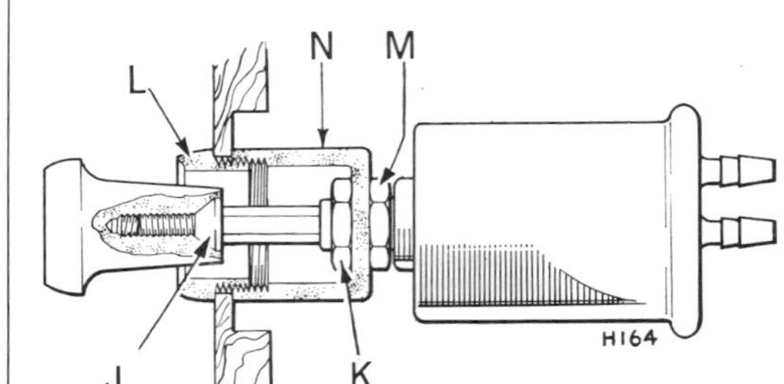

Fig. 100. Windscreen washer (Vitesse 6)

FACIA PANEL DETAILS
VITESSE 6

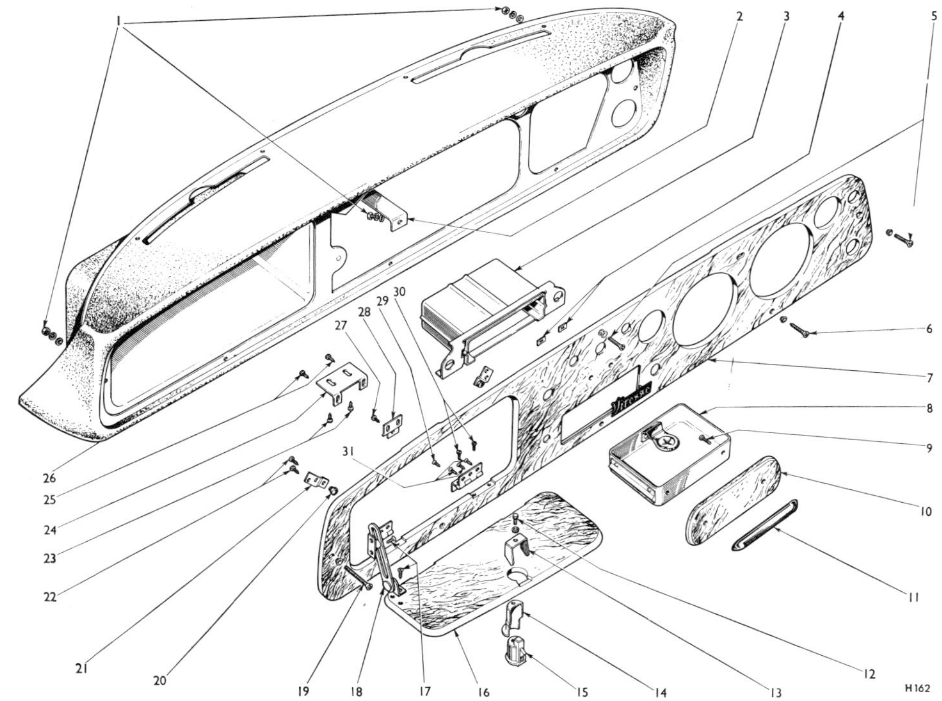

1	Nut—panel attachment.	17	Screw—link attachment
2	Bracket—centre attachments	18	Check link
3	Ash tray housing	19	Screw—facia attachment
4	Clips	20	Rubber—buffer
5	Screw—panel attachment	21	Buffer—bracket
6	Screw—panel attachment	22	Screw—bracket attachment
7	Veneered panel	23	Screw—tie bracket
8	Ash tray bowl	24	Tie bracket
9	Screw—capping attachment	25	Screw—tie bracket
10	Ash tray capping	26	Trimmed facia
11	Pull handle	27	Screw—striker bracket
12	Screw lock clamp	28	Striker bracket
13	Lock clamp	29	Screw—hinge to lid
14	Finger pull	30	Screw—hinge to panel
15	Glove box lock	31	Screw—hinge to lid
16	Glove box lid		

Fig. 101. Facia panel details (Vitesse 6 from Commission No. HB15001)

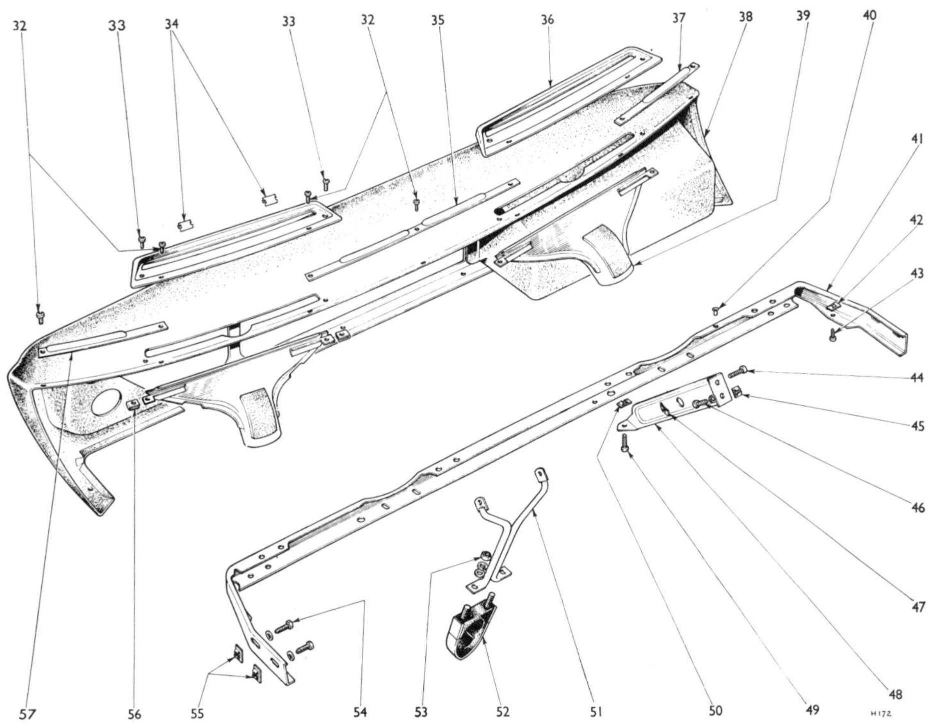

32 Screw—facia attachment
33 Screw—demister finisher attachment
34 Clips—demister finisher attachment
35 Finisher—top edge—centre
36 Finisher—demister vent
37 Finisher—top edge L.H.
38 Trimmed facia
39 Demister vent
40 Rivet
41 Facia rail
42 Fix nut
43 Screw—facia to rail
44 Screw—glove box bracket
45 Fix nut
46 Screw—bracket to bulkhead
47 Fix nut
48 Bracket—glove box support
49 Screw—bracket to facia
50 Fix nut
51 Steering column support bracket
52 Steering column clamp
53 Nut
54 Bolts—facia rail to dash sides
55 Fix nuts
56 Fix nuts
57 Finisher—top edge R.H.

Fig. 102. Facia attachment (Vitesse 6 from Commission No. HB15001)

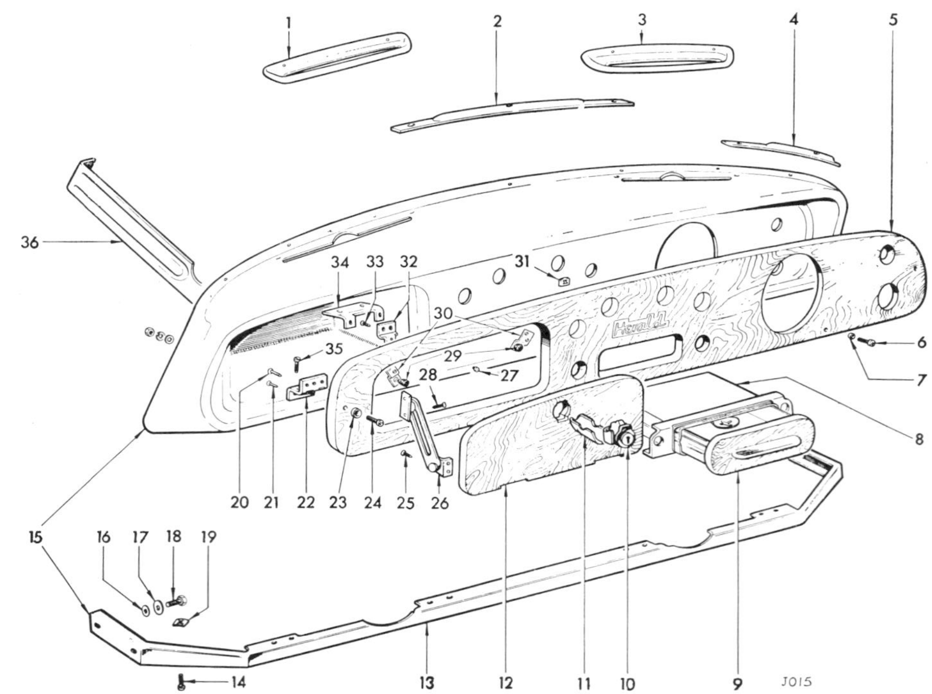

1 Finisher—Demister vent
2 Finisher—top edge—centre
3 Finisher—demister vent
4 Finisher—top edge—L.H.
5 Veneered panel
6 Screw—panel attachment
7 Cup washer—panel attachment
8 Ash tray—support bracket
9 Ash tray
10 Glove box lock
11 Finger pull
12 Glove box lid
13 Facia rail
14 Screw—facia to rail
15 Facia panel assembly
16 Washer }
17 Washer } Facia rail to dash sides
18 Bolt }
19 Fix nut }
20 Screw—hinge to lid
21 Screw—hinge to lid
22 Glove box—hinge
23 Cup washer } panel
24 Screw } attachment
25 Screw—link attachment
26 Check link
27 Screw
28 Screw—link attachment
29 Rubber buffer
30 Buffer bracket
31 Clip
32 Striker bracket
33 Screw—striker bracket
34 Tie bracket
35 Screw—hinge to panel
36 Bracket—glove box support

Fig. 103. Facia arrangement (1200, 12/50 and Vitesse 6 prior to Commission No. HB15001)

FACIA PANEL DETAILS
13/60

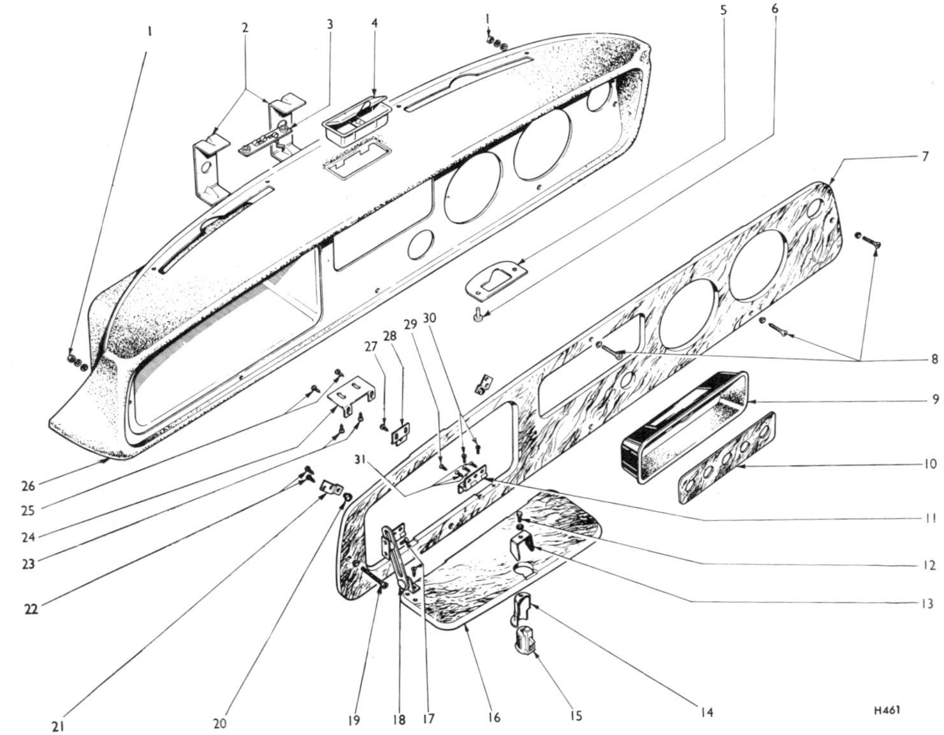

1	Nut—panel attachment
2	Switch panel—saddle bracket
3	Facia—light switch
4	Ash tray
5	Light switch—cover plate
6	Nylon stud—light switch
7	Veneered panel
8	Screw panel—attachment
9	Switch panel
10	Finisher plate
11	Hinge—glove box
12	Screw—lock clamp
13	Lock clamp
14	Finger pull
15	Glove box lock
16	Glove box lid
17	Screw—link attachment
18	Check link
19	Screw—facia attachment
20	Rubber—buffer
21	Buffer—bracket
22	Screw—bracket attachment
23	Screw—tie bracket
24	Tie bracket
25	Screw tie bracket
26	Trimmed facia
27	Screw—striker bracket
28	Striker bracket
29	Screw—hinge to lid
30	Screw—hinge to panel
31	Screw—hinge to lid

Fig. 104. Facia panel details (13/60)

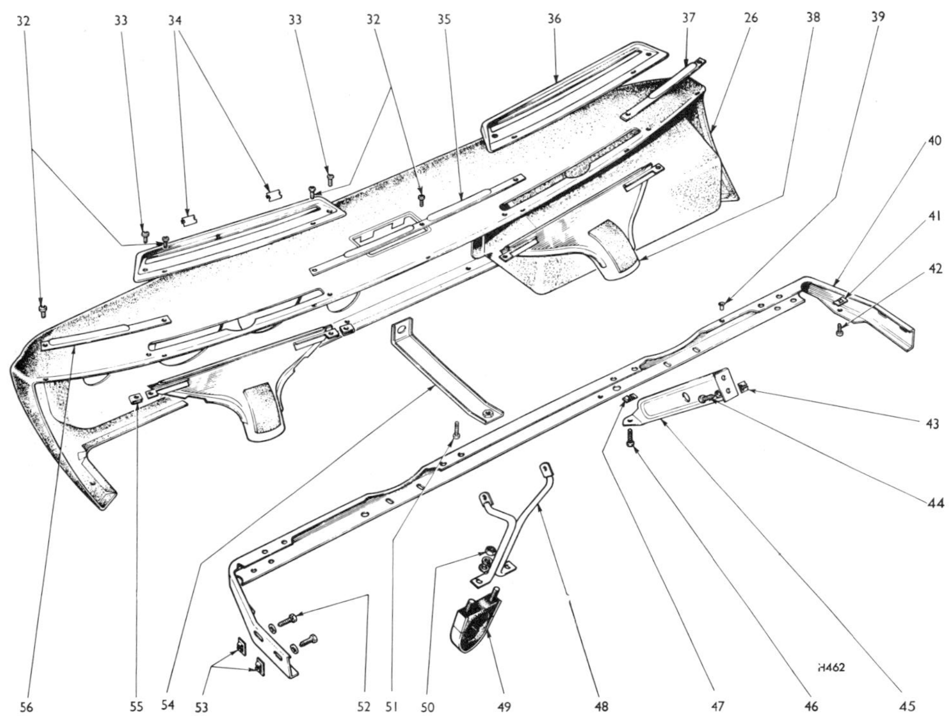

32 Screw—facia attachment
33 Screw—demister finisher attachment
34 Clips—demister finisher attachment
35 Finisher—top edge—centre
36 Finisher—demister vent
37 Finisher—top edge—L.H.
38 Demister vent
39 Pop rivet
40 Facia rail
41 Fix nut
42 Screw—facia to rail
43 Fix nut
44 Screw—bracket to bulkhead
45 Support bracket
46 Screw—bracket to facia
47 Fix nut
48 Steering column support bracket
49 Steering column clamp
50 Nut
51 Screw—choke bracket attachment
52 Bolts—facia rail to dash side
53 Fix nuts
54 Choke—support bracket
55 Fix nuts
56 Finisher—top edge R.H.

Fig. 105. Facia attachments (13/60)

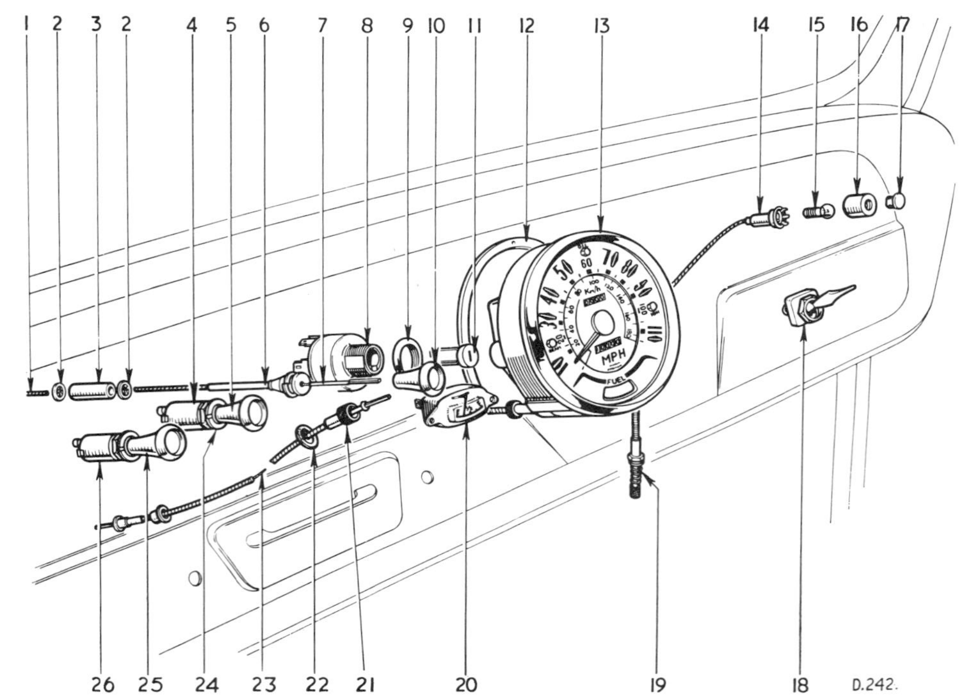

1 Choke control outer cable
2 Clip
3 Sleeve
4 Switch
5 Knob
6 Choke control outer cable
7 Choke control inner cable
8 Starter ignition switch
9 Bezel
10 Knob
11 Lock barrel
12 Reinforcement ring
13 Speedometer
14 Bulb holder
15 Bulb
16 Lamp housing
17 Lens
18 Blower switch
19 Trip cancelling cable
20 Fuel gauge
21 Speedometer drive outer cable
22 Grommet
23 Speedometer drive inner cable
24 Bezel
25 Knob
26 Switch

Fig. 106. Switches and instruments (1200, 12/50 and Vitesse 6 prior to Commission No. HB15001)

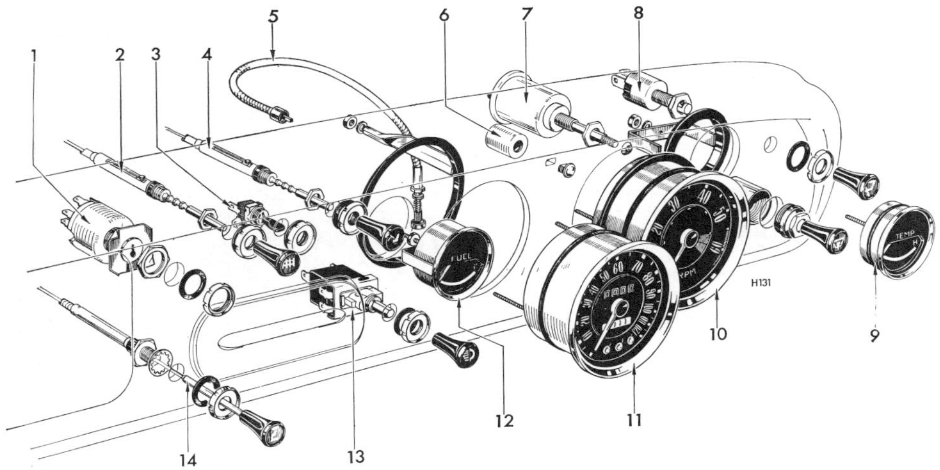

1 Ignition/Starter switch
2 Heater control cable
3 Heater blower switch
4 Air distribution control cable
5 Odometer trip release cable
6 Flasher warning light body
7 Windscreen washer pump
8 Windscreen wiper switch
9 Temperature gauge
10 Tachometer
11 Speedometer
12 Fuel gauge
13 Lighting switch
14 Choke cable

Fig. 107. Switches, instruments and controls (Vitesse 6 from Commission No. HB15001)

FACIA ASSEMBLY

1200, 12/50, 13/60 and Vitesse 6

To Remove (Figs. 101 and 102)

Isolate the battery. Release the clips securing the wiring harness to the bulkhead panel and disconnect the harness leads from the stop lamp switch, wiper motor and steering column switches.

Release the control cables from the carburettor, water valve and heater air distribution flap.

Unscrew the drive cable from the speedometer and remove the air hoses from the demister vents (38). Disconnect the plastic pipes from the windscreen washer pump. Unscrew the drive cable from the tachometer (*Vitesse 6* only from Commission No. HB 15001).

Release the steering column assembly (as described on page 4·210) and withdraw it from the car.

Excluding *13/60*, take out two screws (46) securing the glove box bracket (48) to the bulkhead (Fig. 102) and remove seven screws (32) securing facia top edge and finishers to windscreen lower rail (Fig. 110). Remove four screws (54), two each side securing the facia rail (41) to the dash sides (Fig. 102).

For *13/60* only, take out two screws (44) securing the facia rail support (45) to the bulkhead (Fig. 109) and one screw (51) securing the choke control support bracket (54) to the bulkhead.

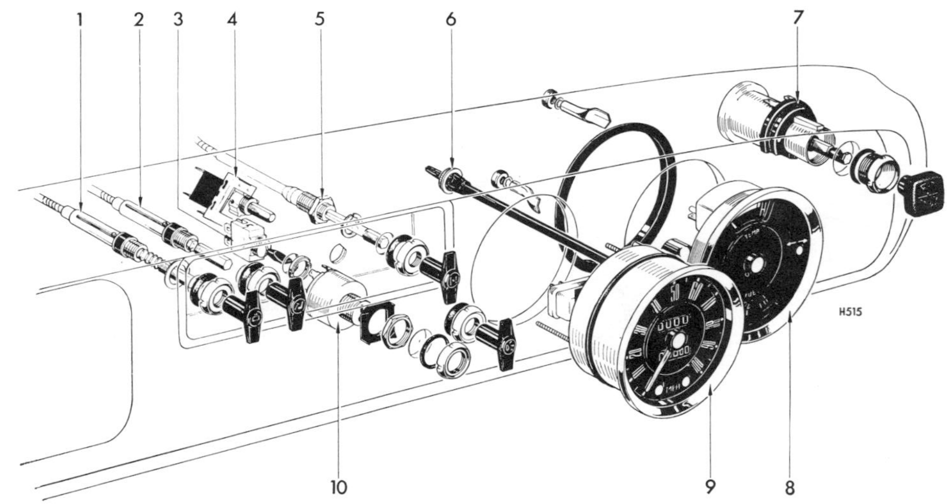

Remove seven screws (32) securing facia top edge and finishers to the windscreen lower rail (Fig. 110). Remove four screws (52) two each side securing the facia rail (40) to the dash sides (Fig. 111).

For all models carefully withdraw the facia assembly and disconnect the wiring harness from the switches, instruments and facia lamp.

To Refit

Reverse the removal procedure, and refer to Group 6—Facia Connections. Road test the vehicle and check the operation of all instruments and controls.

FACIA RAIL

1200, 12/50 and Vitesse 6

To Remove (Figs. 101 and 102)

Remove the facia assembly from the vehicle. Working on the bench, open the glove box lid and drill out the pop rivet (40). Release the trip cancelling control from the facia rail. Take out the screw (49) and slacken the three lower screws (6) securing the veneered panel to the facia pressing. Remove the screws (43) and (49) and withdraw the facia rail (41) and bracket (48).

1 Heater control cable
2 Air distribution control
3 Heat blower switch
4 Lighting switch
5 Choke control
6 Trip cancelling control
7 Windscreen washer/wiper control
8 Temperature/Fuel instrument
9 Speedometer
10 Ignition/Starter switch

Fig. 108. Switches, instruments and controls (13/60)

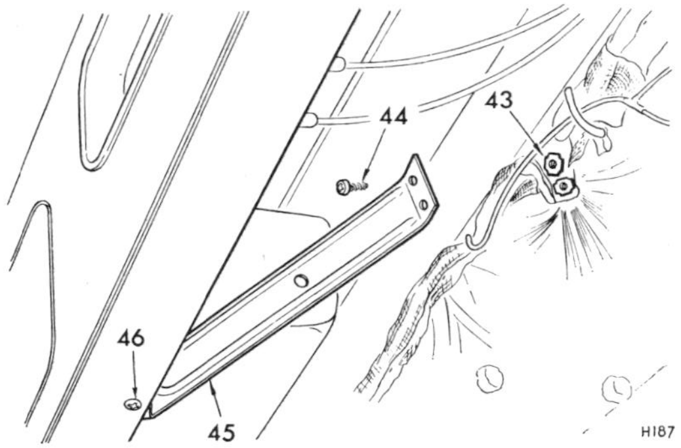

Fig. 109. Facia rail support attachment

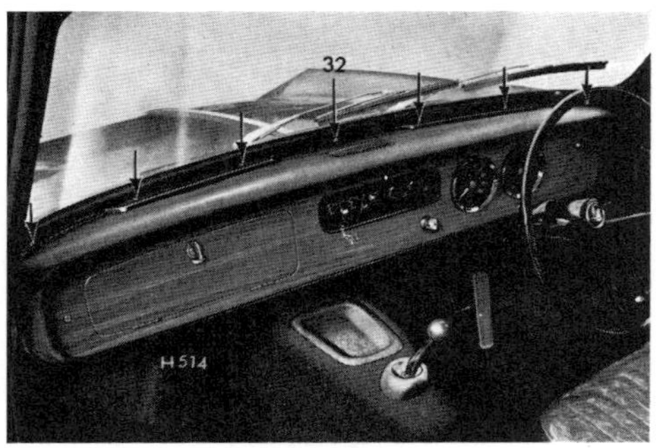

Fig. 110. Facia top edge attachment

Fig. 111. Facia rail to dash sides

13/60 only

To Remove (Figs. 104 and 105)

Remove the facia assembly from the vehicle. Working on the bench, open the glove box lid and drill out the pop rivet (39). Release the trip cancelling control from the facia rail. Take out the screw (46) and remove the bracket (45). Slacken the three lower screws (8) securing the veneered panel to the facia rail (40). Remove four screws (42) securing the fibre trimmed facia to the facia rail and withdraw the rail.

To Refit

Reverse the removal procedure.

VENEERED PANEL

1200, 12/50 and Vitesse 6

To Remove (Fig. 101)

Remove the facia assembly from the vehicle. Working on the bench, pull out the ashtray, depress the spring and withdraw the ashtray assembly from the facia. Take out the screw (9) and separate the ashtray bowl (8), capping (10) and pull handle (11).

Remove the instruments, switches, controls and ashtray housing (3) from the facia panel.

Take out the screws (5), (6), (19) and (23), and remove the veneered panel assembly.

Pull off the clips (4) and remove the badge.

Take out the screws (22), (27) and (25) and remove the buffer brackets (21), striker plate (28) and tie bracket (24).

Take out the screw (12) and remove the lock assembly (15), clamp (13) and finger pull (14).

Take out the screws (17), (29), (30) and (31) and remove the check link assembly (18) and hinges (7).

13/60 only

To Remove (Fig. 104)

Remove the facia assembly from the vehicle. Working on the bench remove the instruments, switches, controls and switch panel (9) from the facia panel. Take out eight screws (8), (19) and (23) and remove the veneered panel assembly (7).

Take out the screws (22), (27) and (25) and remove the buffer brackets (21), striker plate (28) and tie bracket (24).

Take out screw (12) and remove the lock assembly (15), clamp (13) and finger pull (14).

Take out the screws (17), (29), (30) and (31) and remove the check link assembly (18) and hinge (11).

To Refit

Reverse the removal procedure.

WINDSCREEN WASHER

The screen washer is manually operated by depressing a knob and plunger fitted to the facia panel on *13/60* and *Vitesse 6*, and to a bracket below the facia on *1200* and *12/50* models.

1200, 12/50, 13/60 and Vitesse 6

To Remove (Fig. 112)

Isolate the battery.

Remove the water container cap, located on the right-hand side of the car under the bonnet adjacent to the wiper motor, and lift the water container (8) clear of its retaining clip (7).

Release the feed tube (9) from the pump and pull the tube through the aperture in the dash panel into the engine compartment. Remove the knob and plunger as described on page 5·242 and 5·243.

Release the dash millboard trim panel and pull the water delivery tubing (5), (6) and (10) away from the jet nozzles and the plunger.

Remove the nut (4) and washer (3) from the jet assembly under the windscreen surround panel.

Withdraw the jet assembly together with the fibre washer (2) from the top side of the windscreen surround panel.

To Refit

Reverse the removal procedure.

WINDSCREEN WIPER WHEELBOXES

1200, 12/50, 13/60 and Vitesse 6

Wheelboxes (Fig. 113)—**To Remove**

Remove the wiper arms and locknuts.

Remove four screws arrowed, accessible from behind the facia panel, and release the wheelbox outer casings from the wheelbox main body.

Manoeuvre the wheelbox main body from behind the facia panel.

To Refit

Reverse the removal procedure, refer to "Dust and Water Sealing", page 5·301.

Wheelbox Drive Cable—To Remove

Remove the wiper arms from the spindles. Referring to page 6·139, remove the connecting rod from the wiper motor and pull the drive cable clear of the dash panel.

To Refit

Feed the drive cable through the wheelbox tubing.

Attach a suitable spring scale to hole in cross-head and check the force required to move the cable.

Maximum permissible force to move cable rack in tubing is 6·0 lb.

Install the connecting rod to the wiper motor, page 6·139.

Refit the wiper arms to the spindles.

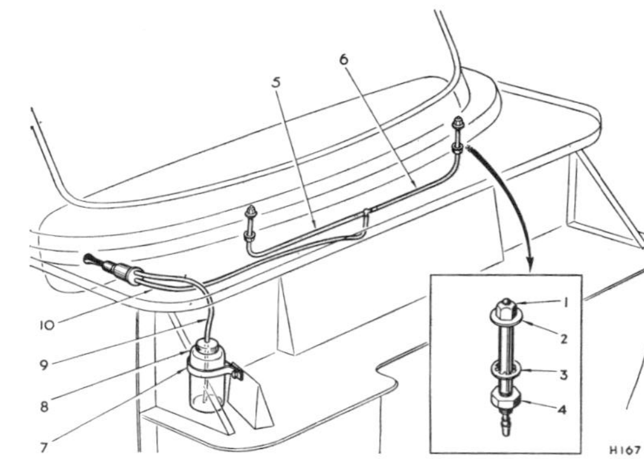

1 Jet
2 Fibre washer
3 Washer
4 Nut
5 Delivery—tubing
6 Delivery—tubing
7 Retaining clip—container
8 Cap—water container
9 Fuel tubing
10 Delivery—tubing

Fig. 112. Windscreen washer

Fig. 113. Wiper wheelbox attachment

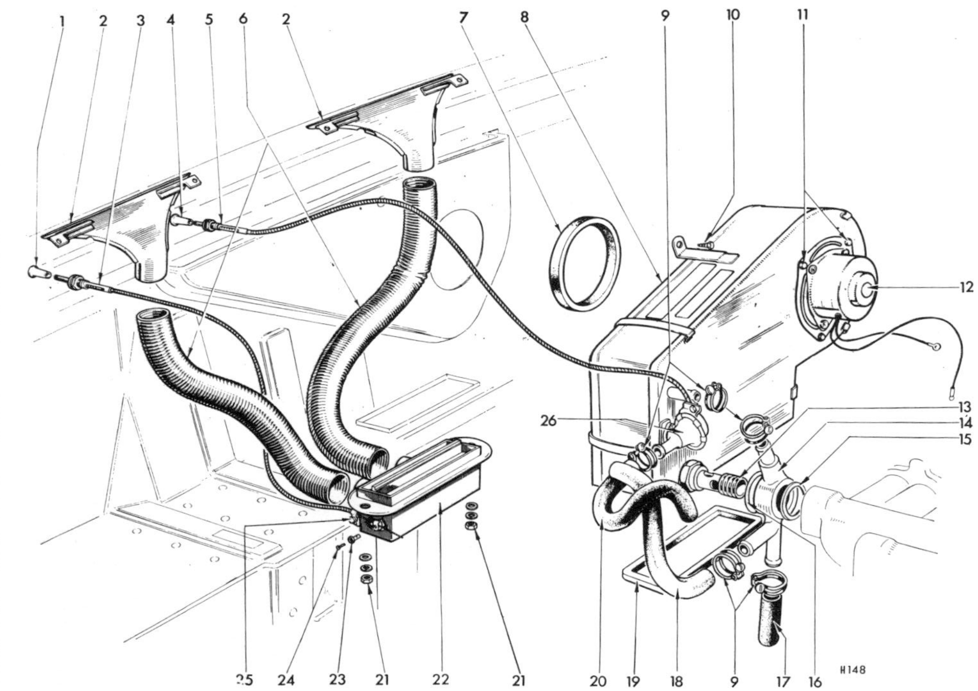

1	Control knob	20	Adaptor/water valve hose	39	Hose clip
2	Demister duct	21	Nuts	40	Adaptor
3	Air distribution control cable	22	Air distribution box	41	Water pipe
4	Control knob	23	Trunnion	42	Hose clip
5	Temperature control cable	24	Securing bolt	43	Water valve trunnion
6	Demister hoses	25	Securing bracket	44	Trunnion screw
7	Sealing rubber	26	Water valve	45	Hose clip
8	Heater unit	27	Hose clip	46	Water hose
9	Hose clips	28	Water hose	47	Water hose
10	Spire screw	29	Hose clip	48	Manifold—water pipe
11	Blower motor attachment screws	30	Water pipe	49	Hose clip
12	Heater blower	31	Adaptor	50	Hose clip
13	Banjo bolt	32	Hose clip	51	Hose clip
14	Adaptor	33	Water hose	52	Spire screws
15	Washer	34	Hose clip	53	Demister vent finisher
16	Washer	35	Hose clip	54	Water control valve lever
17	Bottom hose	36	Hose clip	55	Trunnion screw
18	Adaptor/heater unit hose	37	Water hose	56	Air distribution flap.
19	Seal	38	Water hose		

Fig. 114. Heater system details (Vitesse 6 from Commission No. HB27986) (Smiths)

HEATER AND VENTILATION SYSTEM (SMITHS)

1200, 12/50, 13/60 and Vitesse 6

To Remove Heater Unit (Fig. 114)

Drain the cooling system and isolate the battery. Release the temperature control cable (5) from the water control valve (26). Remove the water hoses from the heater unit, refer to Figs. 114, 115, 116 and 117). Disconnect the blower motor leads and take out the screw (10) securing the heater support bracket to the dash panel.

Working inside the car release the dash millboard and disconnect the air distribution control cable (3) from the air distribution box (22).

Disconnect the demister hoses from the air distribution box and remove two nuts (21) with washers to release the box from the heater unit. Lift the heater unit from the bulkhead.

NOTE: It may be necessary to disconnect the choke cable from the carburettor to facilitate removal of heater unit.

To Refit (Fig. 114)

1. Remove the old sealing compound and apply a liberal coating of "Seelastik S.R.51" to the contact faces of the rubbers (7) and (19) and the bulkhead panel.
2. Locate the heater unit studs through the holes in the bulkhead and the air distribution box.
3. Secure the top centre support bracket with one screw (10) and working inside the car refit the two nuts (21) with washers to the studs on the heater unit. Re-connect the demister hoses.
4. Re-connect the air distribution control cable (3) and the temperature valve control cable (5).
5. Viewed from the right-hand side of the car adjust the controls as follows:

   Push the control knobs to the fully "In" position.

   Slacken the trunnions securing the inner cables.

   Turn the water control valve (54), Fig, 121, fully clockwise and tighten the trunnion (55). Turn the air distribution control fully counter-clockwise and tighten the screw.

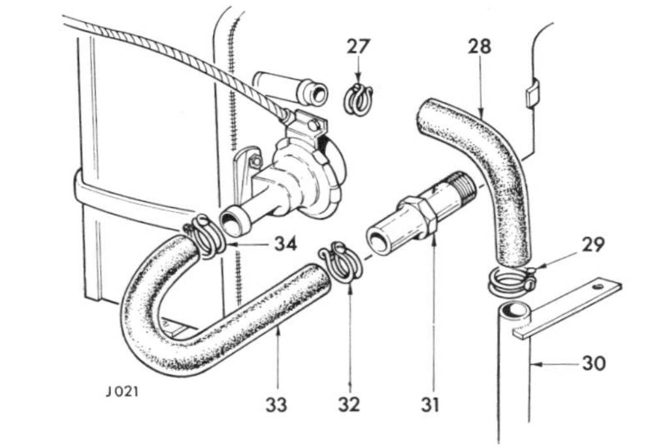

Fig. 115. Water hoses (Vitesse 6 condition up to Commission No. HB27985)

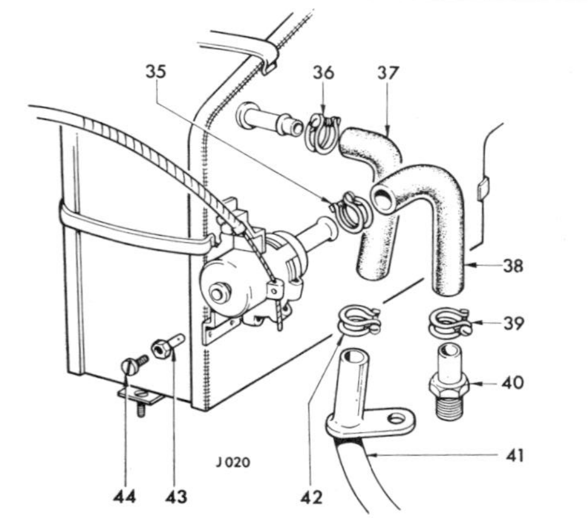

Fig. 116. Water hoses (1200 and 12/50)

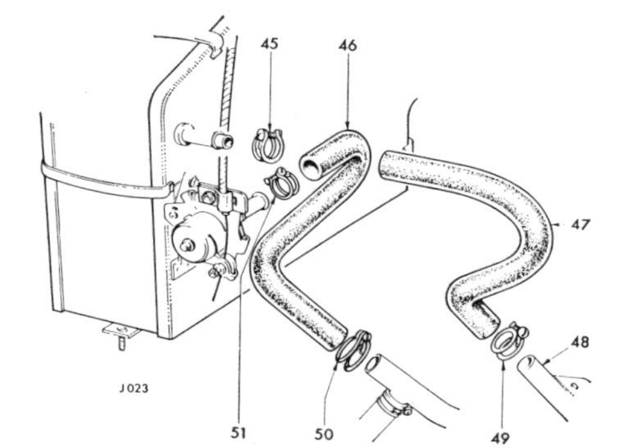

Fig. 117. Water hoses (13/60)

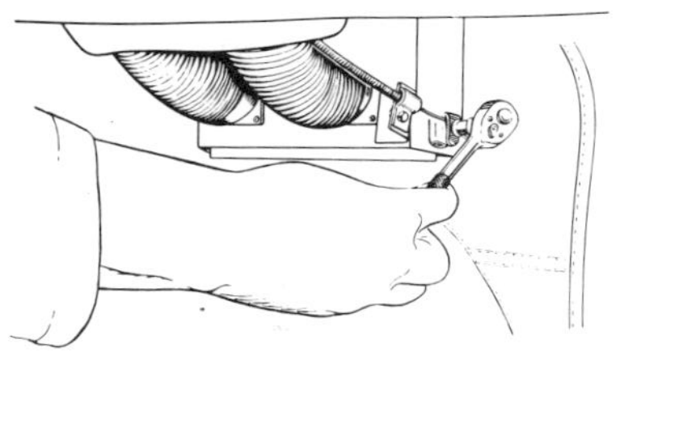

Fig. 118. Disconnecting air distribution control

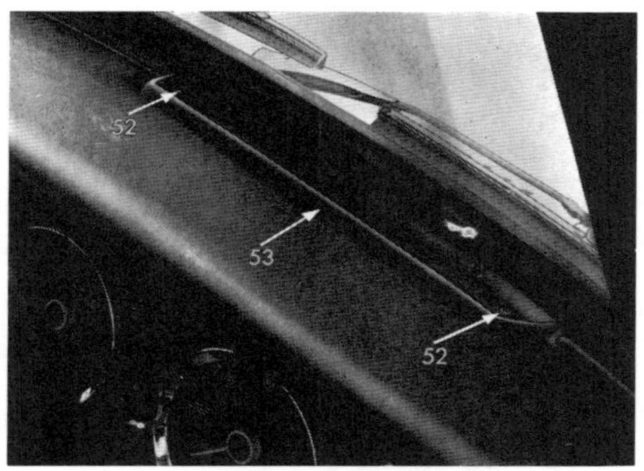

Fig. 119. Demister vent attachment

6. Re-connect the battery, blower motor, water hoses and refill the cooling system. Align and clip the dash millboard into position. Start the engine and check for leaks.

Air Distribution Box and Demisting System

To Remove (Figs. 114 and 118)

Unclip the dash millboard (Item 25, page 5·259).

Pull the demister hoses (6) from the air distribution box (22) and the demister ducts (2). Disconnect the control cable (3) from the air distribution box, remove two nuts (21) with washers and take off the box.

To remove either demister duct from the facia assembly remove the two spire screws (52), Fig. 119, from the extremities of the heater unit finisher (53) and manoeuvre the duct (2) from the facia.

To Refit

Push the control knob (1) fully in and secure the inner and outer cables as shown on Fig. 114. Ensure that the air distribution flap (56) is turned fully anti-clockwise before tightening the securing bracket (25) and trunnion (23).

Position the demister duct underneath the facia assembly, align the holes with those in the extremities of the heater vent finisher (53) and secure with two screws (52).

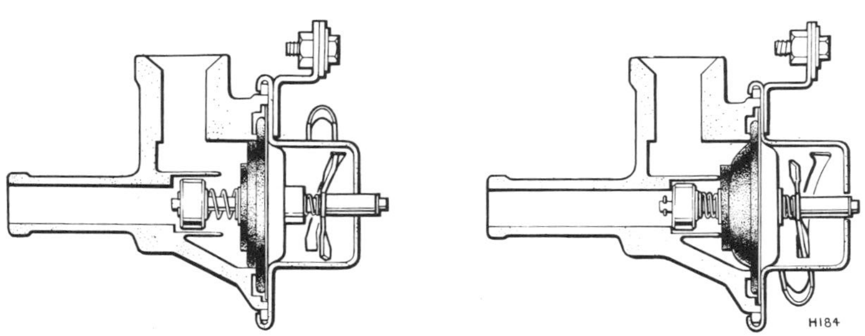

Fig. 120 Water control valve operation (Smiths)

Water Control Valve

To Remove (Figs. 114 and 121)

Drain the cooling system. Disconnect the hose and temperature control cable (5) from the water valve (26) and remove the two nuts and serrated washers retaining the water valve to the body of the heater. Remove the valve from the studs ensuring that the sealing rubber ring is not misplaced. Refer to Fig. 120 for the operation of the water control valve.

To Refit

Reverse the removal procedure, referring to refitment of the heater unit, when re-connecting the control cable.

NOTE: The water control valve is serviced only by replacement.

Heater Blower Motor

To Remove (Figs. 114 and 123)

Isolate the battery and disconnect the heater blower leads. Remove three retaining screws (11) and washers and take out the blower motor assembly (12).

Loosen the brass nut in the centre of the impellor and withdraw the impellor from the blow motor shaft. (Fig. 124)

To Refit

Reverse the removal procedure.

NOTE: The blower motor assembly is serviced only by replacement.

Fig. 121. Water valve (Smiths)

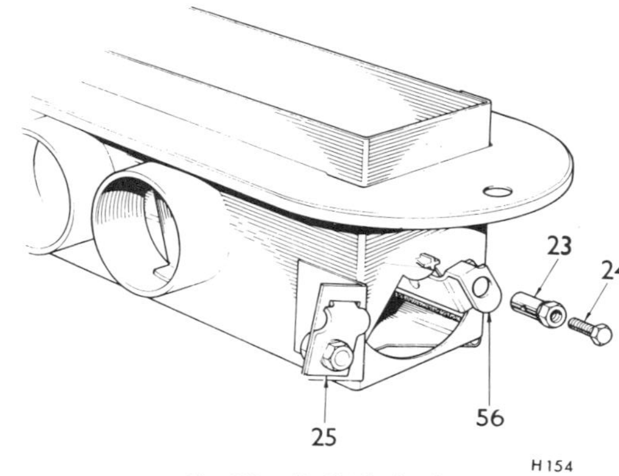

Fig. 122. Air distribution flap

Fig. 123. Blower attachment (Smiths)

Fig. 124. Fan attachment (Smiths)

Fig. 125. Water control valve (Delaney Gallay)

Fig. 126. Heater Unit (Delaney Gallay)

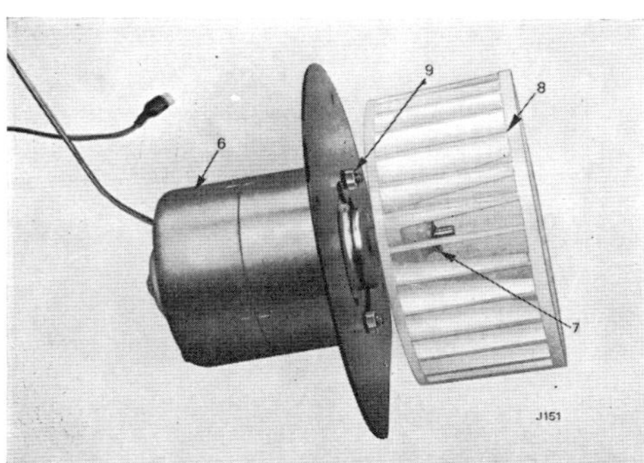

Fig. 127. Fan attachment (Delaney Gallay)

HEATER AND VENTILATION SYSTEM (DELANEY GALLAY)

1200, 12/50 and 13/60

The instructions for removing and refitting the Delaney Gallay heater unit are basically similar to those given for the "Smiths" heater unit (see page 5·253). However, there is a physical difference in the water control valve, and the heater blower motor. The removing and refitting procedure is as follows:

Water Control Valve

To Remove (Fig. 125)

Drain the cooling system. Disconnect the hoses and temperature control cable from the water valve (1) and remove two screws (2) retaining the water valve to the body of the heater.

To Refit

Reverse the removal procedure, referring to refitment of the heater unit, when re-connecting the control cable.

To Adjust

The heat control shut-off adjusting screw (4) (Fig. 126) on the water valve is pre-set by the manufacturer prior to delivery. If adjustment is necessary, proceed as follows:

Disconnect the heat control cable at the water valve and move the water valve lever (3) (Fig. 125) fully clockwise. Screw the adjusting screw (4) (Fig. 126) down onto its stop. Re-connect the heat control cable and tighten the trunnion. Finally, test the operation.

NOTE: The water control valve is serviced only by replacement.

Heater Blower Motor

To Remove (Fig. 126)

Isolate the battery and disconnect the heater blower leads. Remove four retaining screws (5) and washers and take out the blower motor assembly (6).

Release the clip (7) (Fig. 127) retaining the impellor to the blower motor shaft and pull the impellor (8) away from the shaft. Remove two nuts (9) retaining the motor to the mounting plate.

To Refit

Reverse the removal procedure.

NOTE: The blower motor assembly is serviced only by replacement.

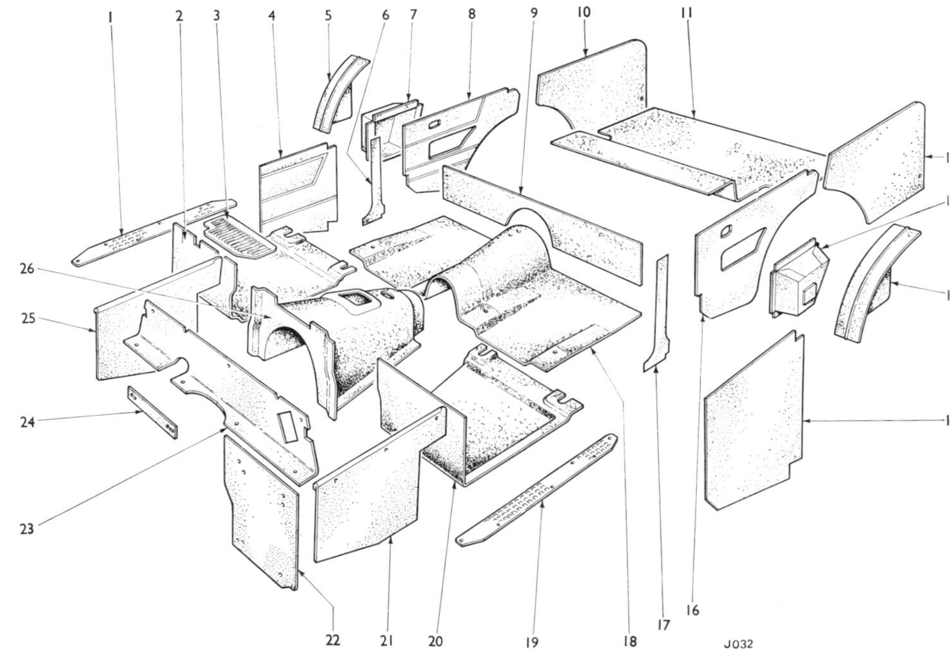

1	Tread plate sill	14	Cover wheelarch
2	Carpet front floor	15	Trim pad rear quarter—Convertible
3	Heel mat	16	Trim pad rear quarter—Saloon
4	Trim pad rear quarter—Convertible	17	Cover "B" post trim
5	Cover wheelarch	18	Carpet rear floor
6	Cover "B" post trim	19	Tread plate sill
7	Pocket assembly rear quarter	20	Carpet front floor
8	Trim pad rear quarter—Saloon	21	Millboard dash side
9	Mat heelboard	22	Millboard dash lower
10	Luggage compartment trim	23	Millboard dash upper
11	Luggage compartment mat	24	Strip sound deadening
12	Luggage compartment trim	25	Millboard deadening
13	Pocket assembly rear quarter	26	Carpet gearbox cover

Fig. 128. Floor coverings and trim panels (Vitesse 6)

SEAT DETAILS

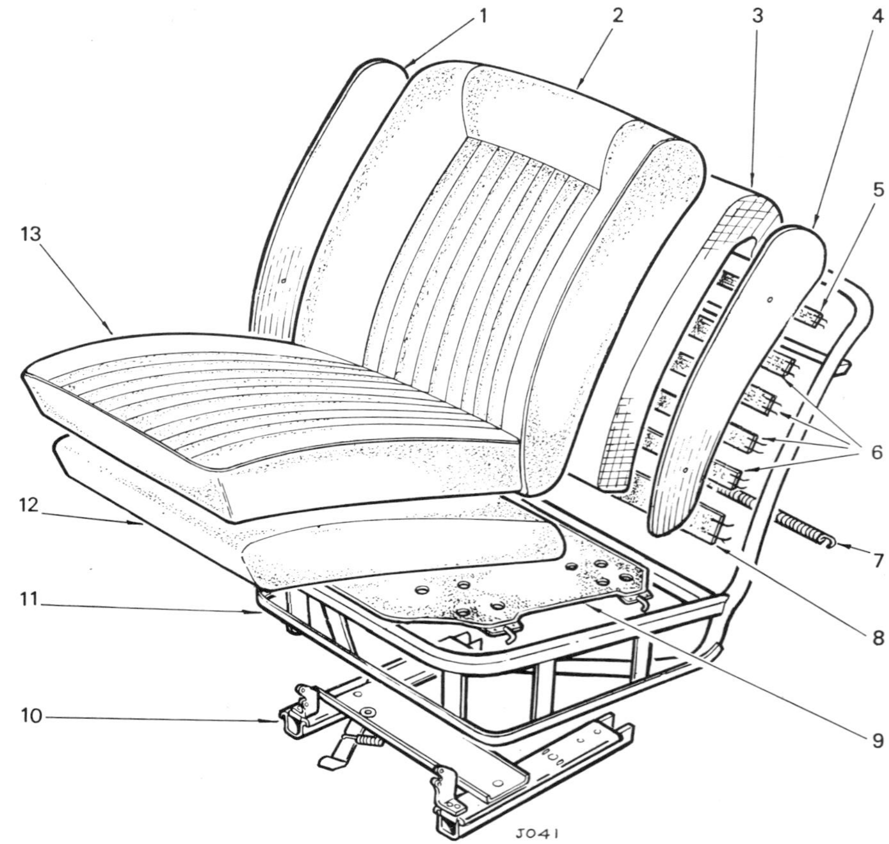

1 Squab side millboard—R.H.
2 Squab cover assembly
3 Squab pad
4 Squab side millboard—L.H.
5 Strap assembly—upper
6 Strap assembly—centre
7 Cushion tension—spring
8 Strap assembly—lower
9 Seat base—diaphragm assembly
10 Slide assembly
11 Seat frame
12 Seat cushion-pad
13 Cushion cover assembly

Fig. 129. Front seat details (13/60)

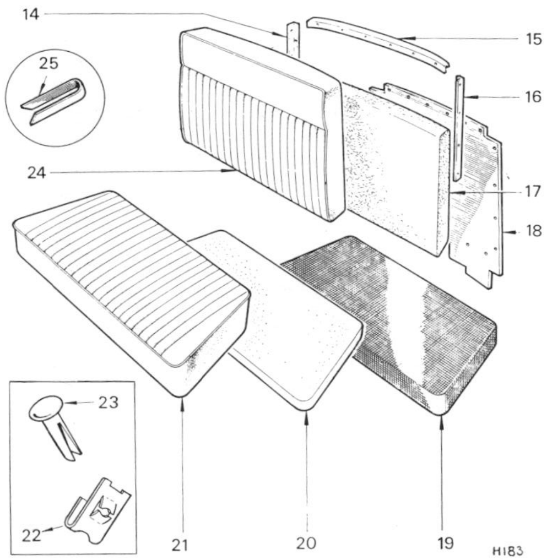

14 Trim angle
15 Trim channel
16 Trim angle
17 Hair pad
18 Squab board
19 Spring case cushion
20 Pad—rear seat cushion
21 Cushion cover assembly
22 Fix nut
23 Pop-rivet
24 Squab cover assembly
25 Staple

Fig. 130. Rear seat details (Convertible)

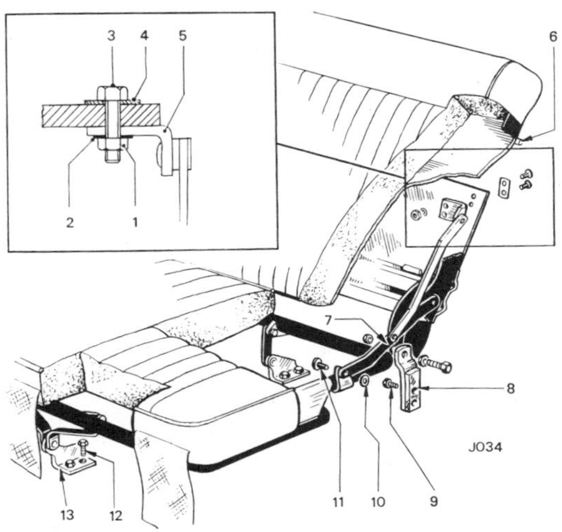

1 Nut
2 Shakeproof washer
3 Setscrew
4 Plate washer
5 Squab bracket
6 Squab shoot bolt
7 Squab link arm
8 Squab pivot bracket
9 Setscrew
10 "Salter" clip
11 Stud—link arm
12 Bolt
13 Cushion brackets

Fig. 131. Rear seat attachments (Estate car)

SEATS

1200, 12/50, 13/60 and Vitesse 6

Front Seats
To Remove (Fig. 132)
Move the seat fully forward and remove one bolt from the rear of each channel. Push the seat fully rearwards and remove one bolt (1) from the front of each channel. Lift the seat clear, complete with seat slide channel.

To Refit
Reverse the removal procedure.

Fore and Aft – Adjustment
The drivers and passengers seats are adjustable for leg reach by moving the lever at the front of each seat as shown on Fig. 132 to the desired position. Some additional seat movement may be necessary to ensure positive location of the nearest adjustment notch.

Height Adjustment (Fig. 133)
By attaching the seat frame to either of the two locations "A" or "B" at the front of the seat runners, alternative seat height positions are possible.

Back Rest – Adjustment (Fig. 133)
The driver's seat is adjusted for rake by turning the rubber blocks "C" to the most suitable of the four numbered positions.

Rear Seats
To Remove – Saloon
Lift out the seat cushion.
Remove two bolts, washers and nuts, accessible from the luggage compartment.
Lift the squab clear of the two retainers on the rear bulkhead and remove the squab from the car.

To Refit
Reverse the removal procedure.

To Remove – Convertible (Fig. 134)
Lift out the seat cushion.
Drill out six pop rivets (1) with No. 30 (3·30 mm.) drill. Remove four acme screws (2), two each side. Lift the squab clear and remove the squab from the car.

To Refit
Reverse the removal procedure.

To Remove – Estate Car (Fig. 131)
1. Remove four screws securing the cushion apron to floor heelboard.
2. Remove eight bolts (12) and washers securing the cushion brackets (13) to the seat pan floor.
3. Disconnect the link arms (7) from the rear squab by removing two "Salter" clips (10) and two studs (11).
4. Lift the seat cushion from the car.
5. Release the shoot bolts (6) from the "B" post reinforcement and remove four screws (3) plate washers (4), shakeproof washers (2) and nuts (1) retaining the closing board to the squab bracket (5).
6. Remove four screws (9) and washers securing the squab pivot bracket and rubber seal (8) to the wheelarch.
7. Lift the rear seat squab from the car.

To Refit
1. Position the rear squab in the car and attach the pivot brackets (8) to the wheelarch panels with four setscrews (9) and washers, leaving them fingertight at this stage.
2. With the squab in the upright position push the shoot bolts into the wheelarch retainers and fully tighten the pivot brackets (8).
3. Move the squab to the down position, adjust the end brackets on the "B" post reinforcement to align with the shoot bolts, secure the end brackets and move the squab to the upright position.
4. Position the rear seat cushion in the car, re-connect the link arms (7) from the squab with two studs (11) and "Salter" clips, using a suitable tool to fit the clips.
5. Secure the cushion brackets (13) to the seat pan floor with eight bolts (12).
6. Re-attach the closing board to the squab bracket (5) with four screws (3), plate washers (4), shakeproof washers (2) and nuts.
7. Finally secure the cushion apron to the heelboard with four screws.

Fig. 132. Front seat attachment

Fig. 133. Front seat adjustment

Fig. 134. Rear seat attachment (Convertible)

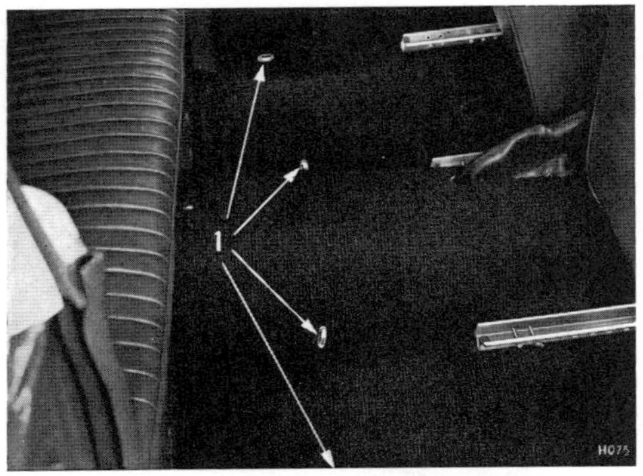

Fig. 135. Floor eyebolt attachment

Fig. 136. Waist Rail attachment (13/60 Saloon)

Fig. 137. Wheelarch attachment (Convertible)

SAFETY HARNESS ANCHORAGES

3 Point Fixing — Front

HERALD RANGE AND VITESSE 6

Saloon and Estate Car

To Remove

1. Release the latched hooks on the safety belt from the eye bolts 1 (Fig. 135).

2. Unscrew the pivot bolt and remove the waved washer and the pivot bolt spacer from the veneered capping—rear waist rail 2 (Fig. 136).

To Refit

1. Pass the pivot bolt through the belt strap attachment plate, waved washer and spacer. Refit the assembly to the waist rail.

2. Reconnect the latched hooks to the eye bolts.

Convertible

To Remove

1. Release the latched hooks on the safety belt from the eye bolts 1 (Fig. 135).

2. Unscrew the pivot bolt and remove the waved washer and pivot bolt spacer from the rear wheelarch 3 (Fig. 137).

To Refit

1. Pass the safety belt through the aperture in the rear quarter trim panel as shown. Pass the pivot bolt through the belt strap attachment plate, waved washer and spacer. Refit the assembly to the wheelarch.

2. Reconnect the latched hooks to the eye bolts.

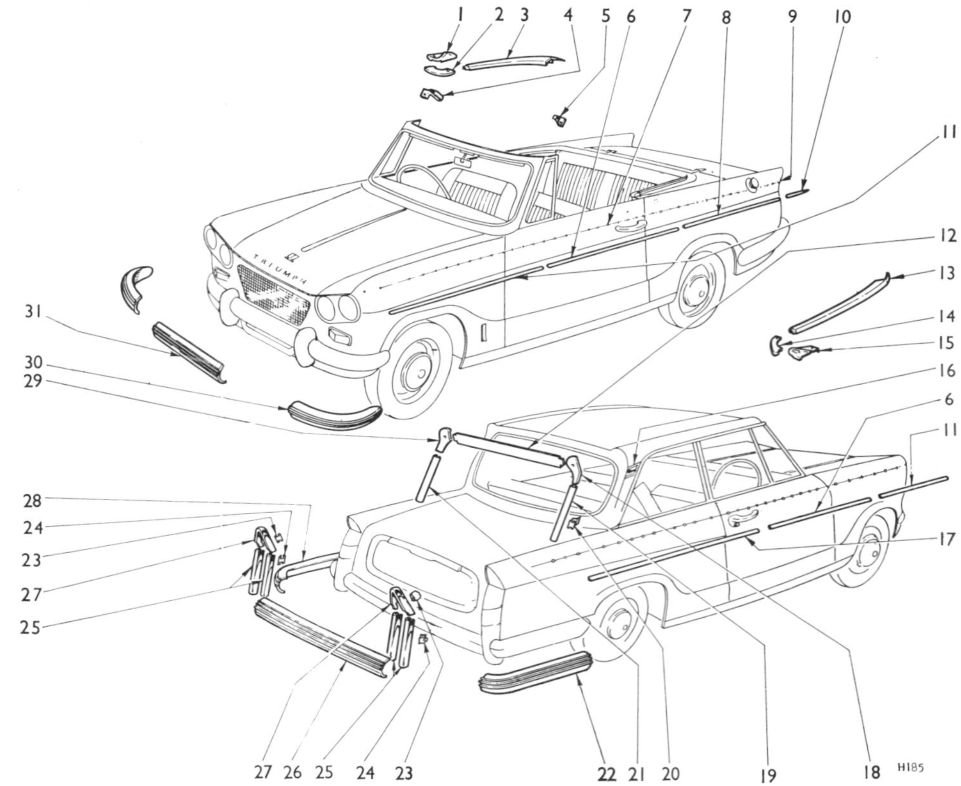

1	Finisher hoodstick	12	Finisher roof/rear	22	Finisher bumper
2	Finisher hoodstick	13	Squab rail	23	Clip
3	Squab rail	14	Finisher hoodstick	24	Clip
4	Finisher "A" post—R.H.	15	Finisher hoodstick	25	Moulding rear lamp
5	Finisher "A" post—L.H.	16	Badge	26	Finisher bumper
6	Door moulding	17	Tonneau side moulding	27	Finisher tail lamp
7	Clip—moulding	18	Finisher roof corner	28	Finisher bumper
8	Tonneau side moulding	19	Finisher	29	Finisher roof corner
9	Retainer—moulding	20	Clip	30	Finisher bumper
10	Tonneau side moulding	21	Finisher roof/rear	31	Finisher bumper
11	Bonnet moulding				

Fig. 138. Exterior mouldings, finishers and bumpers (Vitesse 6)

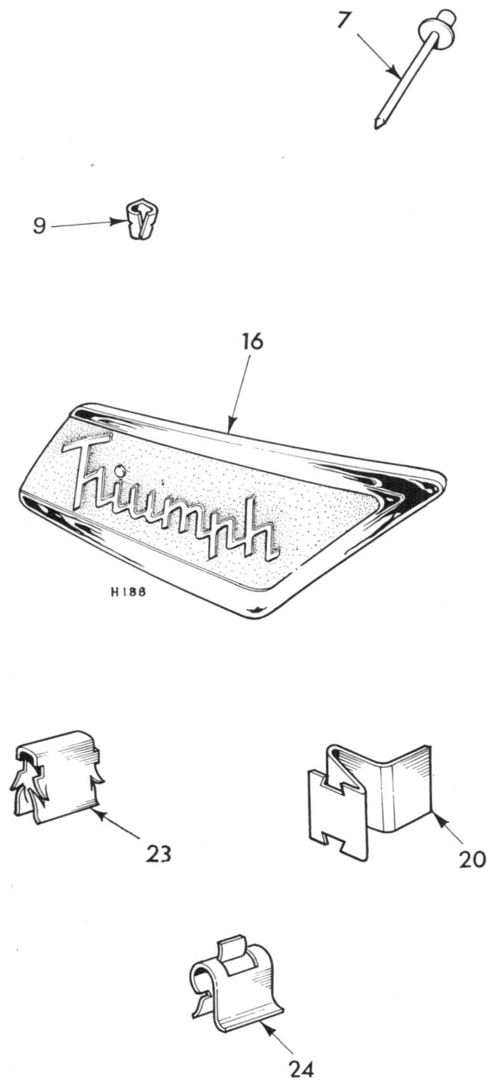

Fig. 139. Exterior moulding fixings details

FINISHER MOULDINGS

1200, 12/50, 13/60 and Vitesse 6

Waistline Mouldings

The waistline mouldings are retained by clips riveted to the bonnet, door and tonneau side panels.

To Remove

Using a small screwdriver from which all sharp edges have been removed, gently lever the mouldings from the panels.

To Refit

Place the mouldings on to the clips and applying firm hand pressure, snap the mouldings into position.

Stop/Tail Lamp Surround

The stop/tail lamp surround comprises three sections, which are retained to the rear end of the tonneau side panel by barbed clips.

To Remove

Using a small screwdriver from which all sharp edges have been removed, gently lever the surround off the clips.

To Refit

The clips are forced into position with light blows from a mallet and the surround pushed on to the clips.

Backlight Surround – Saloon Only

To Remove

Take out one screw from each corner section and three screws from the upper section. Using a piece of hardwood as a drift, remove both side sections, and note the position of the clips in the channel.

To Refit

Using a hide mallet force the side section into position. Apply Seelastik to five screw holes along the top and refit the upper and corner sections.

Backlight Surround – Estate Car and Courier Van

Using a piece of hardwood as a drift, remove the cover plate, which is located at the top centre of the surround.

Remove both halves of the upper section and both side sections by using a hardwood drift and a small hammer. Note the position of the clips in the channel.

Drill out one rivet from each corner section and remove both sections.

To Refit

Space the clips evenly along each side section and using a hide mallet force the sections into position. Refit the corner sections and secure them with "Imex" rivets.

Refit the upper sections.

FUEL TANK

1200, 12/50, 13/60 and Vitesse 6 Saloon, Coupé and Convertible

To Remove (Fig. 140)

Isolate the battery.

Remove the luggage compartment floor covering. Disconnect the cables from the tank unit. Drain the fuel tank. The drain plug is accessible from under the vehicle behind the left-hand side of the rear wheelarch.

Disconnect the fuel pipe by pulling the rubber connector (4) from the upper forward corner of the tank. Remove four acme screws (1 and 2). Remove one bolt securing the fuel tank to luggage floor (3) (*Vitesse* 6 only). Supporting the trunk lid in the open position, take out two cross/recess screws securing the bracket between the trunk lid stay and the tank.

Take off the filler cap and manoeuvre the tank from the luggage compartment.

To Refit

Reverse the removal procedure.

1200 and 13/60 Estate Car and 1200 Courier

To Remove (Fig. 141)

Isolate the battery, remove the rear quarter trim. Release the clips (3) and (8) and detach the filler hose and air relief pipe from the tank.

Up to and including Commission Nos. GA 192253 and GB 38351 (separate spare wheel cover), remove the spare wheel cover and disconnect the floor extension from the lower edge of the rear seat. Remove seventeen screws and lift the floor panel from the car.

Fig. 140. Fuel tank fixings (Saloon, Coupé and Convertible)

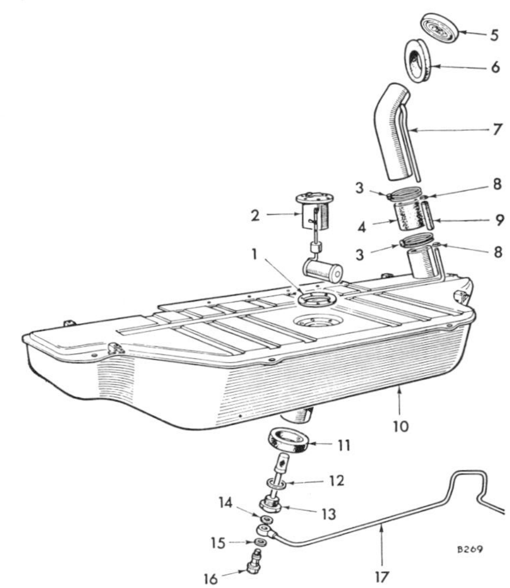

1 Gauge unit—washer
2 Bi-metal gauge unit
3 Hose clip
4 Filler pipe—connection
5 Filler cap
6 Fuel filler—grommet
7 Filler pipe assembly
8 Hose clip
9 Vent pipe—connection
10 Fuel tank assembly
11 Sealing ring
12 Sealing washer
13 Pipe assembly
14 Adaptor washer
15 Adaptor washer
16 Adaptor bolt
17 Pipe assembly

Fig. 141. Fuel tank details (Estate Car and Courier Van.

Fig. 142. Removing fuel tank (Estate Car and Courier Van)

From Commission Nos. GA 192254 and GB 38352 (one-piece floor cover), disconnect the floor extension from the lower edge of the rear seat. Remove eighteen screws and lift the floor panel from the car.

Disconnect the cable from the tank unit (2). The green cable is connected to the terminal on the unit.

Disconnect the fuel pipe (17) from the underside of the tank and drain the fuel. Take out two cross/recess screws and four acme screws and lift the tank from the car.

To Refit

Reverse the removal procedure.

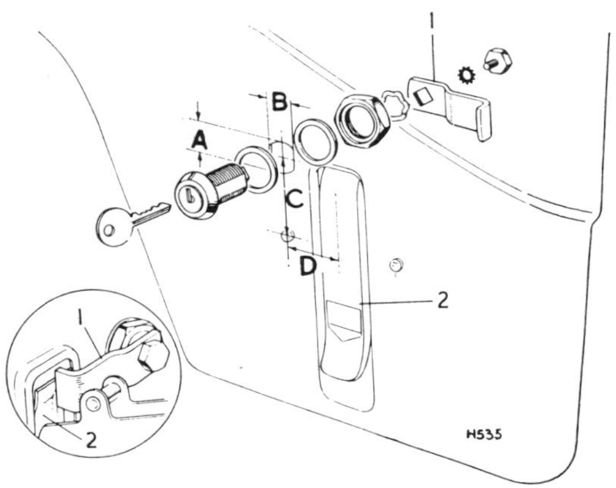

		Inches	Millimetres
A	..	0·75	19·05
B	..	0·66	16·80
C	..	1·75	44·45
D	..	1·25	31·75

Fig. 143. Exploded arrangement of bonnet lock details

BONNET LOCK

1200, 12/50, 13/60 and Vitesse 6

A bonnet lock is available as a special accessory in kit form comprising two lock assemblies.

Fitting Instructions (Fig. 143)

Cover the area, forward of the bonnet catch lever, with white masking tape. Use a pencil to mark the position of a hole as shown and dimensioned. Open out the hole to ⅝″ (15·9 mm.) diameter, and shape the hole as dimensioned. Remove the tape and paint the edge of the metal to prevent rust formation.

Assemble the bonnet lock details in the sequence shown.

DUST AND WATER SEALING

HERALD RANGE AND VITESSE 6

The following notes and diagrams indicate the locations of sealed joints and serve to familiarise dealers with the necessary materials and techniques employed to render the body shell dust and water proof.

The list of approved sealing compounds has been broken down into sections, appertaining to the progressive body build. The diagrams showing the location of sealed joints (heavy lines) show, in some cases, seams which are sealed with compounds which require curing in heated atmosphere. These compounds are listed under the general term "Plastisol" and are not suitable for application in service. In every case where Plastisol compounds have been used and the seal has failed, Hermetal "Double Bond" Metallic Cream, Docker's Compound or Hermetal Plastic Metal Filler should be used.

The scrap sections in the following pages correspond with the numbers on the diagram showing the complete car.

SEALING COMPOUNDS

COMPOUND	MANUFACTURER	COMPOUND	MANUFACTURER
Glasticon 303 Glasticord 305 and 400 Kelseal 3/315M. Kelseal 305.	Kelseal Ltd., Vogue House, Hanover Square, London, W.1.	Seelastik SR.51 Seelastrip LS.105	Expandite Ltd., Cunard Road Works, London, N.W.10.
Docker's Compound	Docker Bros. Ltd., Rotton Park Street, Birmingham, 16.	Boscoseal B.B. Plastisol Putty S.106.46	B.B. Chemicals, Ulverscroft Road, Leicester.
Supra Dedseal	Supra Chemical & Paint Ltd., Hainge Road, Tipton, Staffs.	Hermetal "Double Bond" Metallic Cream Hermetal Plastic Metal Filler	The Kenilworth Mfg. Co. Ltd., West Drayton, Middlesex.
3M's EC 1168 Mastic Sealer	Minnesota Mining and Manufacturing, 3M House, Wigmoore Street, London, W.1.	Dunlop D5.5035/S Sealer	Dunlop Chemical Division, Chester Road, Erdington, Birmingham, 24.

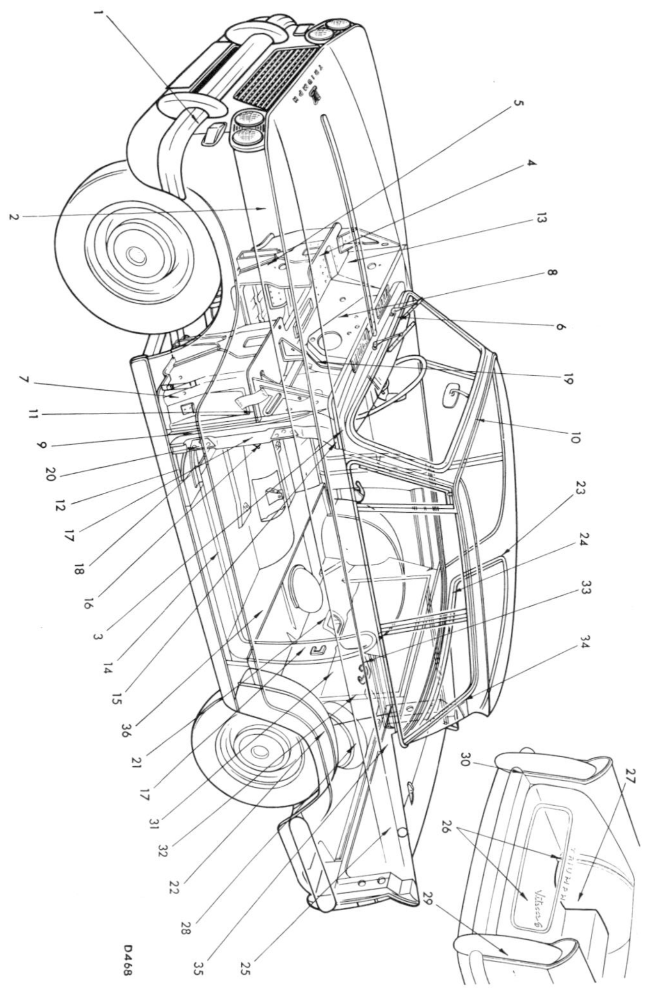

Fig. 1. Location of sealed joints

NOTE: The locations given above relate to those numbered in the following pages.

APPROVED SEALING MATERIALS — BODY IN WHITE (UNPAINTED)

APPLICATION	MASTICS	STRIP SEALERS
Spotweld Sealers	553938 Expandite Seelastik (Natural) 559357 3 M's EC 1168	569630 Expandite Seelastrip LS.105 571214 Glasticord $\frac{1}{2} \times \frac{1}{2}$ 400 Strip Sealer
Plugging small holes		569630 Expandite Seelastrip LS.105 554422 Glasticon 303
Pre-Phosphate Sealer	566800-BB. Chemical S.23/206	

PAINT SHOP

APPLICATION	GUN APPLIED SEALERS	PUTTIES	PLASTISOL	REMARKS
Internal joints	514697–Plus Products PD 18/11 562959 Supraseal 574270–Expandite–Heat Gel Sealer 607/1 574699–Plus Products HG9 574700–Dunlop Chemical Products DS5035/S			To be pumped with Graco equipment
External joints			560563 Kelseal 3/315 m. 574701–Expandite Plastisol 869	Low temperature cure
Plugging small holes		554422 Glasticon 303	564159–B.B. Plastisol Putty S.106.46 564158 Expandite Plastisol Putty	

APPROVED SEALING MATERIALS — TRIM AND FINISH

APPLICATION	MASTICS	STRIP SEALERS	PUTTIES	REMARKS
Windscreen sealers, rubber weatherstrips, plugs and grommets	566600 Seelastik SR.51			
Bolted metal to metal joints, metal mouldings, small holes, screw fixings, etc.	566600 Expandite Seelastik SR.51	Prestik Expandite Seelastrip LS.105 Kelseal Strip 305 B.B. Chem. P41.228 563615 $\frac{3}{4}$" × $\frac{1}{16}$" Glasticord Strip Sealer	554422 Glasticon 303	Strip sealers have Part Nos. allocated according to section
Special Purpose *i.e.* paper to metal		Glasticord 400		

AFTER PAINT REPAIRS

APPLICATION	MISCELLANEOUS
External Joints	Docker's Compound Hermetal Double Bond

BODY UNDERSIDE PROTECTORS

APPLICATION	SOLVENT BASED
Sealing external joints and protection of vulnerable areas on underside of body	554419 SUPRA DEDSEAL 557167 BOSCOSEAL 9010 567815 BOSCOSEAL 9020 Plus Products LCHM 10

1. 1 Wing side to wing front panels (use approved Plastisol).

   2 Side and flasher lamp rubber and lamp to bonnet (use approved Mastics).

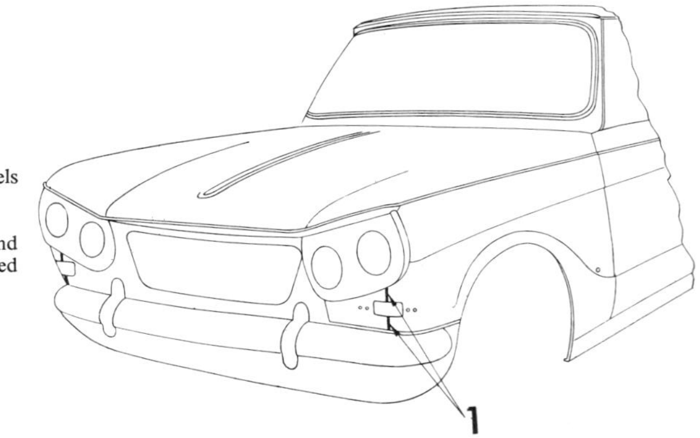

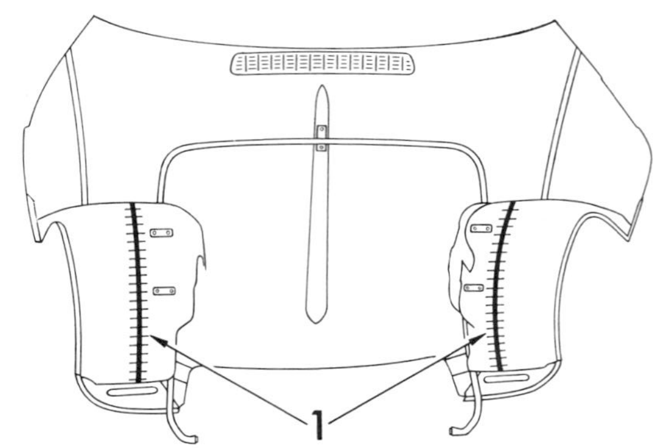

2. 1 Wheelarch inner to wheelarch outer (use approved Plastisol).

3. 1 Windscreen pillar drip channel (use approved Plastisol).

   2 Top finisher front edge to screen (use approved Plastisol). (Convertible only).

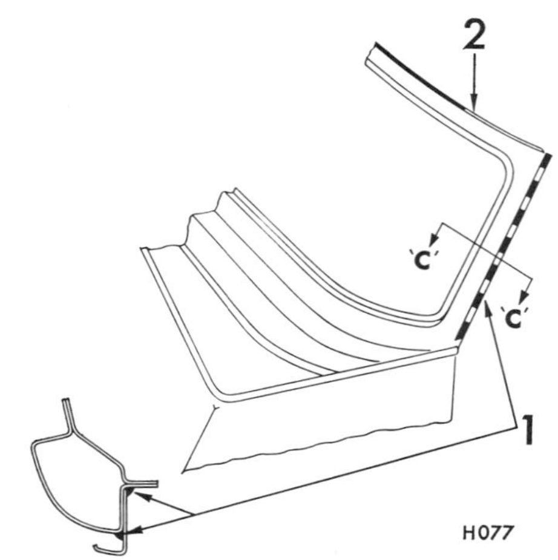

H077

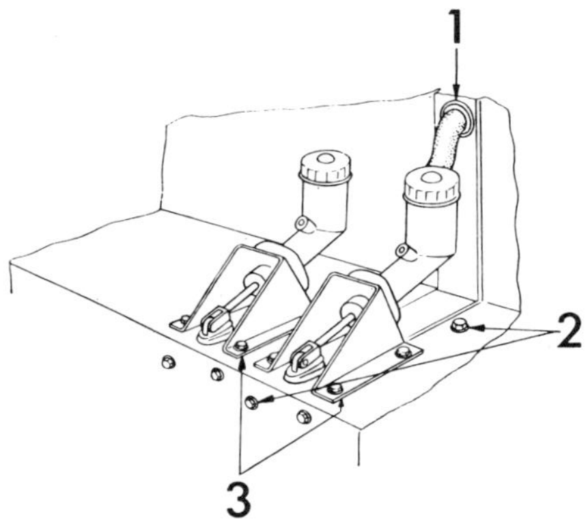

4. 1 All rubber grommets to components attached to the dash panel, including those on the inside of the car (use approved Mastics).

2 Master cylinder fixing bolts (use approved Mastics).

3 Underside of master cylinder brackets before assembly
(use approved Mastics).

4 Master cylinder rubber covers to dash (use approved Mastics).

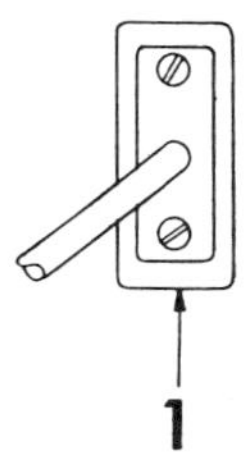

5. 1 Steering column to rubber grommet and grommet to dash panel (use approved Mastics).

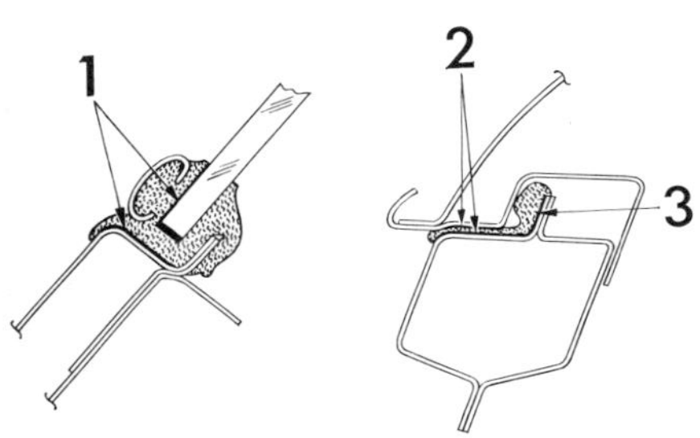

6. 1 Windscreen to glazing rubber and rubber to body (use approved Mastics).

2 Roof panel weatherstrip to screen header rail and roof (use approved Mastics).

3 Roof panel weatherstrip to screen header (Plus products 6/63D).

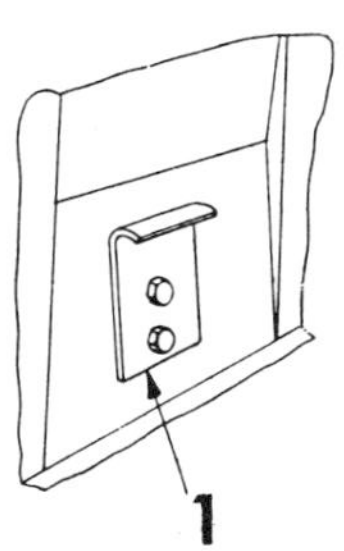

7. 1 Catch plate bonnet to dash side panel (use approved Mastics).

8. 1 Facia stay bracket to dash side panel (use approved Mastics).

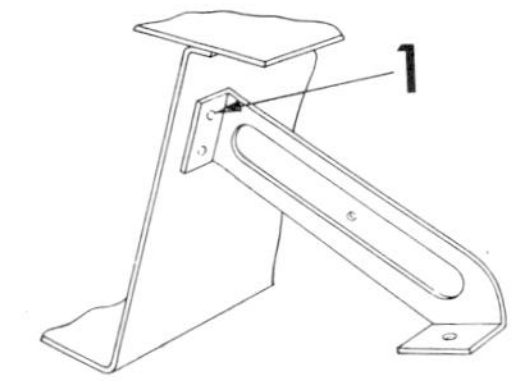

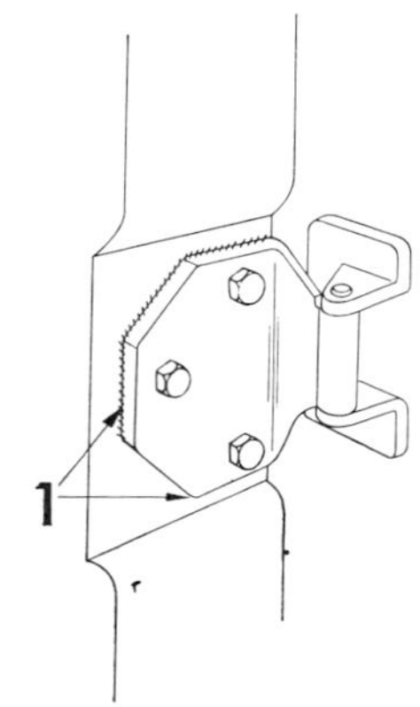

9. 1 Door hinge to "A" post (use approved Mastics).

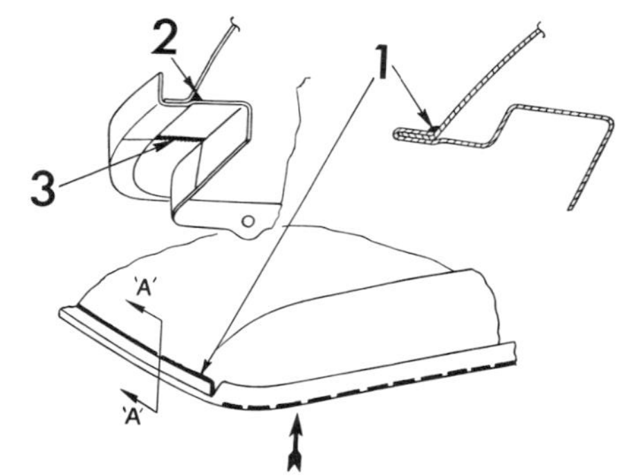

10. 1 Roof panel, joint edge of flange to cantrail inside of water channel (use approved Plastisol).

2 Cantrail to roof panel (use approved Mastics).

3 Cantrail and header panel joint (use approved Plastisol).

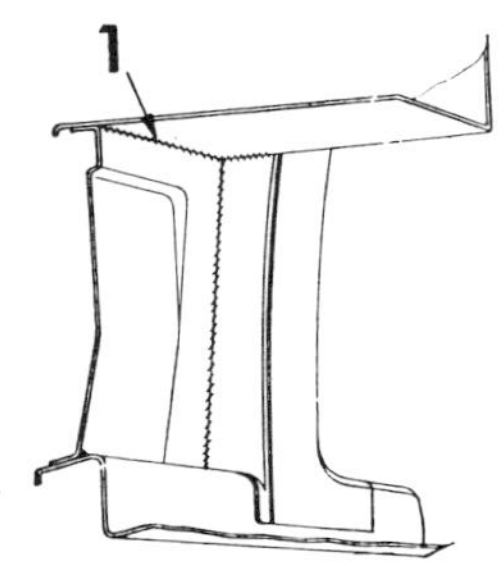

11. 1 "A" post inner panel to dash side panels (use approved Mastics).

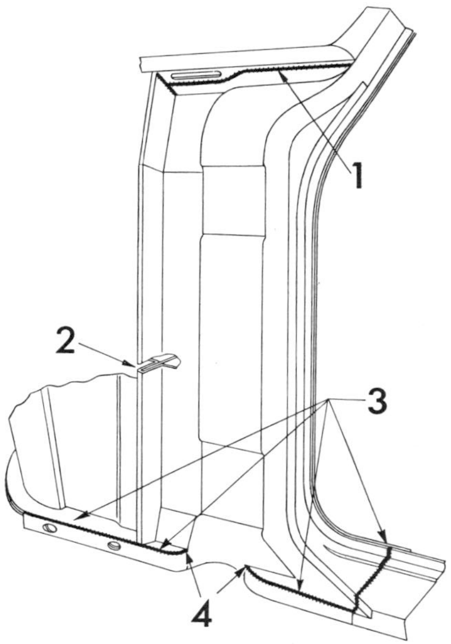

12. 1 Dash shelf panel to front deck panel (use approved Plastisol).

2 Front deck panel to dash shelf panel (use approved Plastisol).

3 Outer "A" post to front floor panels (use approved Plastisol).

4 Plug two corner holes at the base of the "A" post (Glasticon 303).

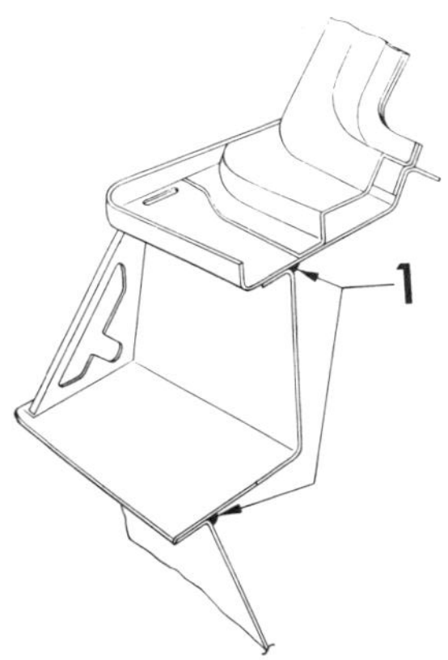

13. 1 Dash side front to dash shelf and dash shelf to Panel deck front (use approved gun-applied sealers).

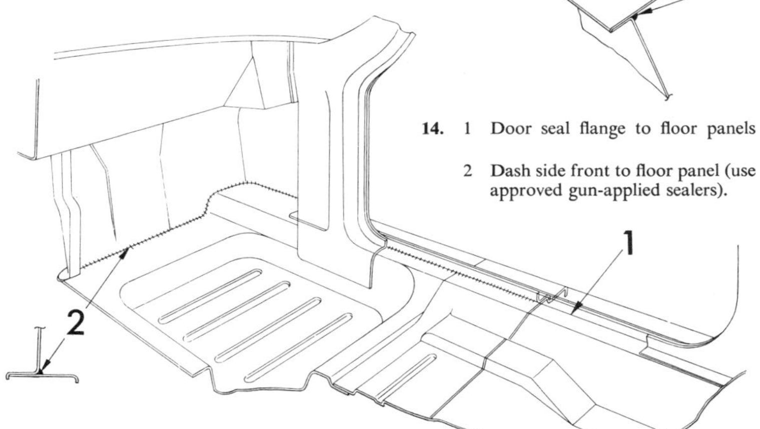

14. 1 Door seal flange to floor panels

2 Dash side front to floor panel (use approved gun-applied sealers).

15. 1 Seal opening between draught ventilator and door panel (Glasticon 303).

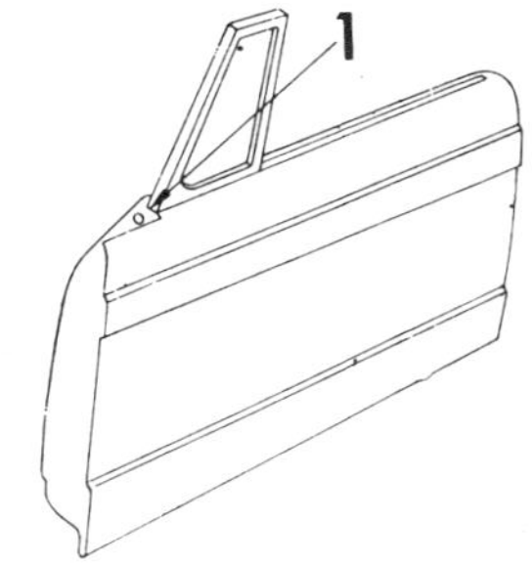

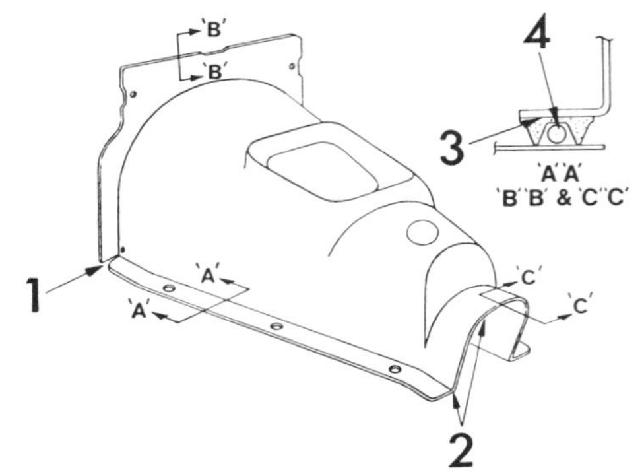

16. 1 Gearbox cover corner (Glasticon 303).

2 Gearbox cover rear corners and over tunnel, double application of (approved Mastics).

3 Seal to gearbox cover (Bostik 8GC.122).

4 Apply to sealing rubber before fitting cover ⅛" bead of (approved Mastics).

17. 1 Striker plate to "B" post (use approved Mastics).

2 Courtesy switch to "A" post (use approved Mastics).

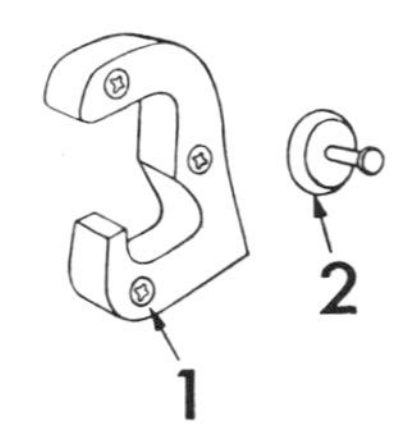

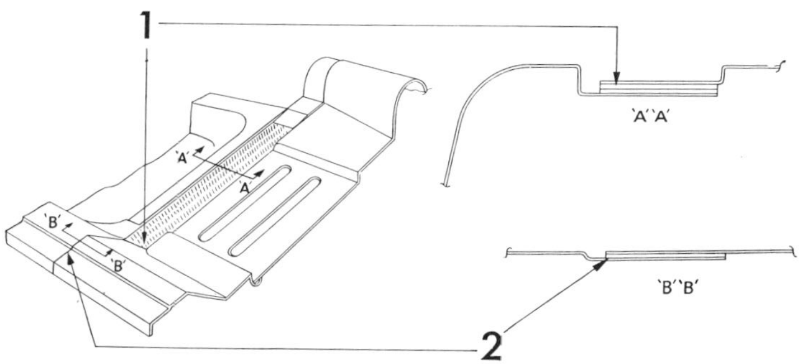

18. 1 Rear floor to front floor panel centre (Rubberised canvas).

2 Rear floor to front floor panel outer (Everseal strip).

19. 1 Air distribution box to dash panel (use approved Plastisol).

2 Heater control and choke cables to grommet and dash panel (use approved Mastics).

3 Cover plate to be sealed when heater is not fitted (use approved Mastics).

4 Cover plate to be sealed when heater is not fitted (use approved Mastics).

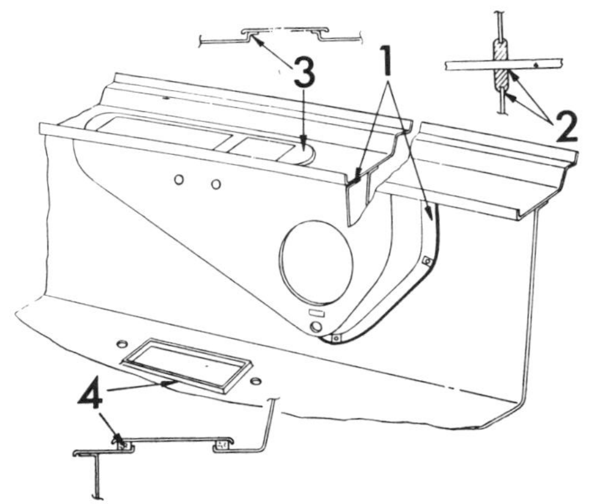

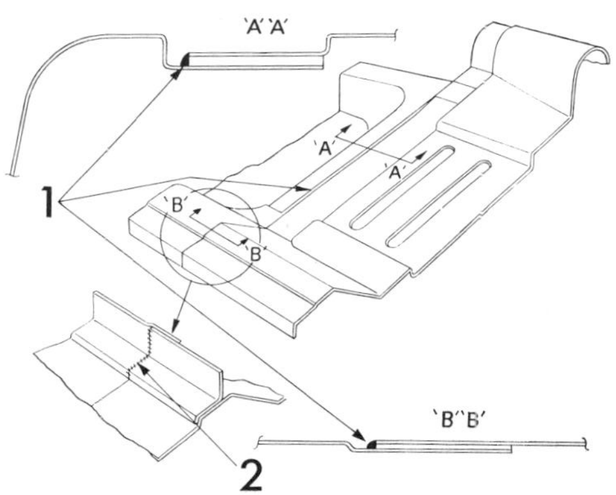

20. 1 Rear floor to front floor panel joint (use approved Mastics).

2 Sill panel angle joints (use approved Plastisol).

21. 1 Seal cover—rear spring access hole (Prestik $\frac{1}{2}'' \times \frac{1}{16}''$)

2 Cover spring access to rear of seat pan (use approved Mastics).

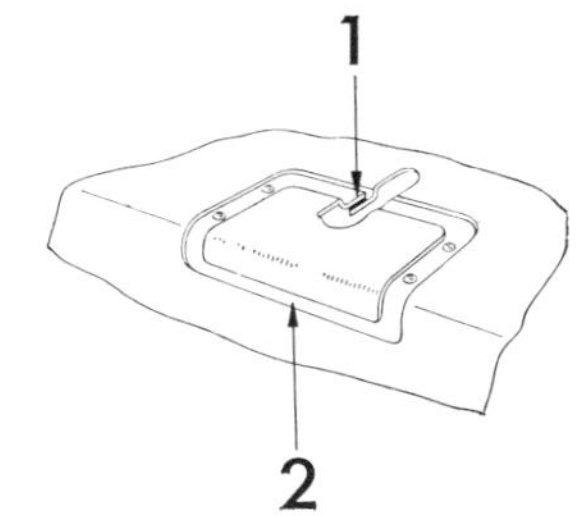

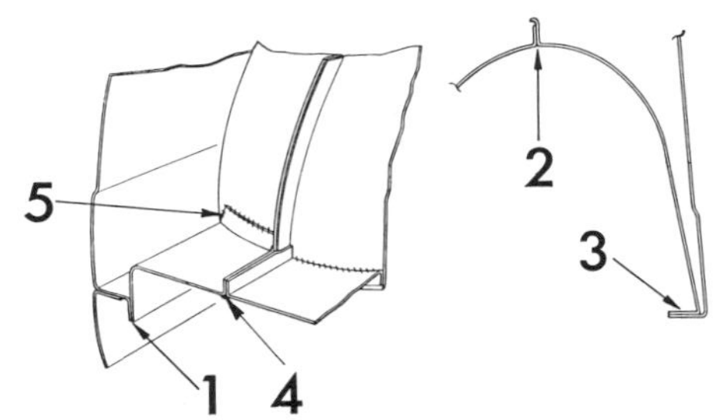

22. 1 Panel side rear seat pan to tonneau side (Seelastik interweld).

2 Wheelarch outer panel to wheelarch inner panels (use approved Mastics).

3 Wheelarch outer panel to tonneau side panel (Seelastik interweld).

4 Rear seat pan to panel side (top and underside) (use approved Mastics).

5 Corner holes plugged at the joints between outer wheelarch, tonneau lower side and seat panel (Glasticon 303).

23. 1 Backlight weatherstrip to glass and roof panel (use approved Mastics).

2 Backlight sealing rubber to roof (use approved Mastics).

3 Sealing rubber to be fixed firmly to panel (Bostik 1261).

4 Plug hole at roof to screen panel joint (use approved sealer).

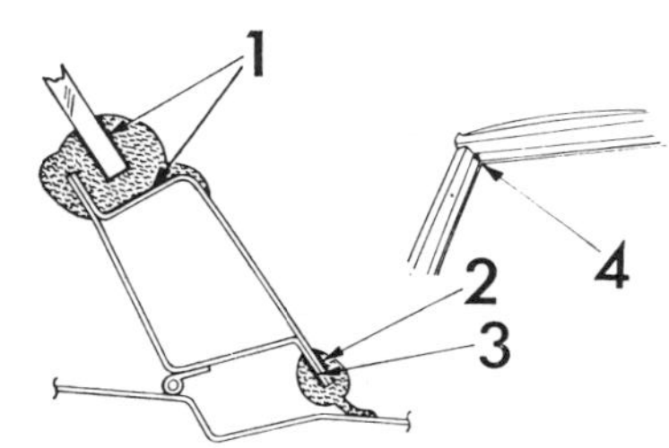

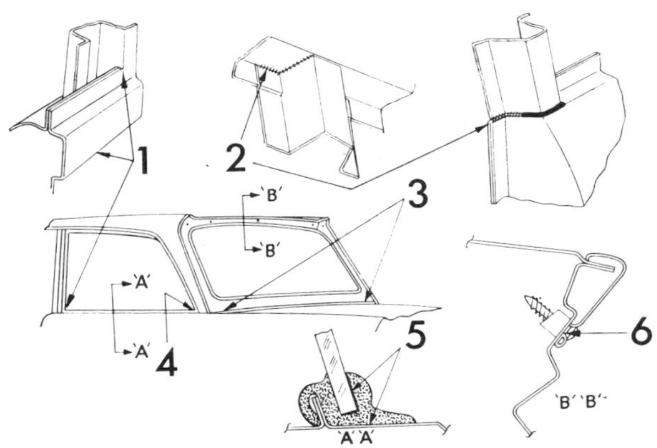

24. 1 Plug hole from interior of the body (Glasticon 303).

2 Quarter light pillar (Glasticon 303).

3 Seal roof rubber to deck 3″ each side (Glasticon 303).

4 Seal corner of roof to tonneau side before fitting quarter light rubber (Glasticon 303).

5 Seal all round quarter light glazing strip to glass and body (use approved Mastics).

6 Seal roof capping fixing to body (use approved Mastics).

25. 1 Seal round petrol tank filler neck grommet and body panel (use approved Mastics).

2 End fixing of tonneau side moulding (Glasticon 303).

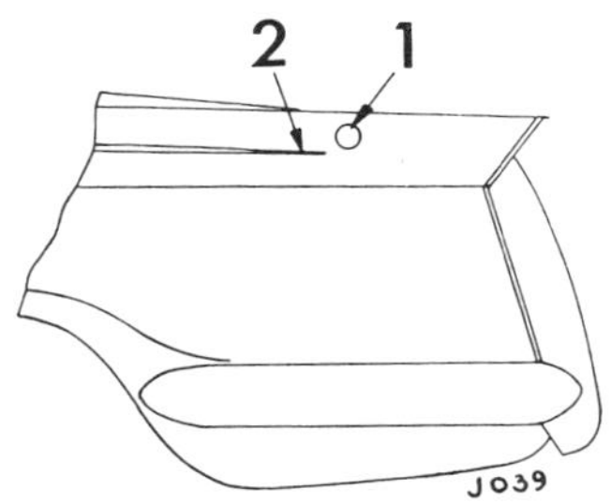

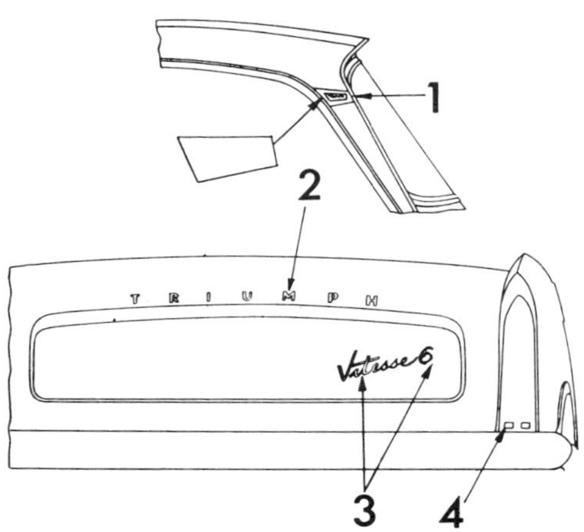

26. 1 Triumph badge to roof panel (Glasticon 303).

2 Triumph letters to luggage compartment lid (Glasticon 303).

3 Vitesse 6 badge to luggage compartment lid depression (use approved Mastics).

4 Seal holes with Dalmas Klingfast C10 tape 1″ wide.

27. 1 Corner holes between the wheelarch outer panel and luggage floor side panel and between the inner and outer wheelarch panels and luggage floor (Glasticon 303).

2 Outer wheelarch tonneau side panel and rear valance side panel (use approved Mastics).

3 Luggage floor panel to seat pan. Seat pan to inner wheelarch panel. Inner wheelarch to floor panel. Wheelarch to luggage floor side panel. (use approved Mastics).

4 Spare wheel tray to luggage floor (use approved Plastisol).

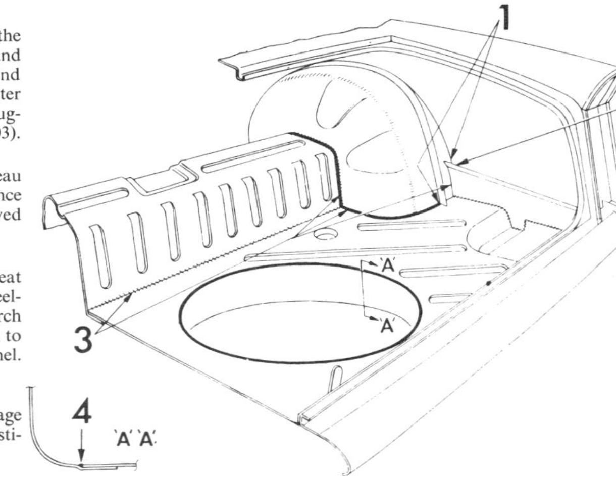

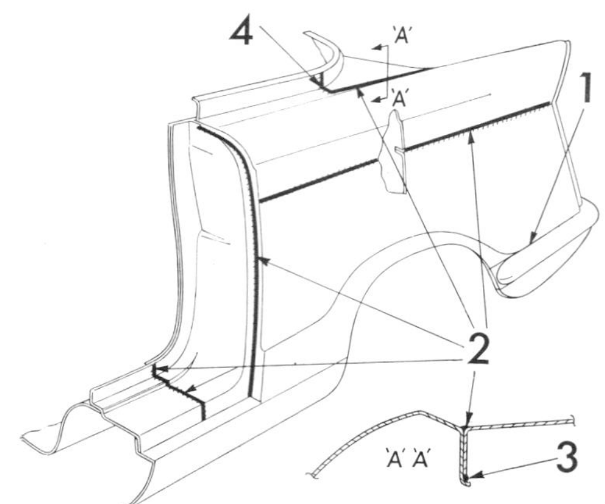

28. 1 Luggage compartment to valance fixings (use approved Plastisol).

2 "B" post outer panel to tonneau side, "B" post outer panel to sill, Tonneau side upper to lower panel, Rear deck to tonneau upper panel (use approved Plastisol).

3 Rear deck to tonneau side panel (use approved Mastics).

4 Seal hole in rear deck as shown (Glasticon 303).

29. 1 Tonneau side rear end closing panel (use approved Plastisol).

2 Inside edge of tail lamp apertures (use approved Plastisol).

3 Rear deck to tonneau side (Glasticon 303).

4 Water channel—rear deck to tonneau side (use approved Plastisol).

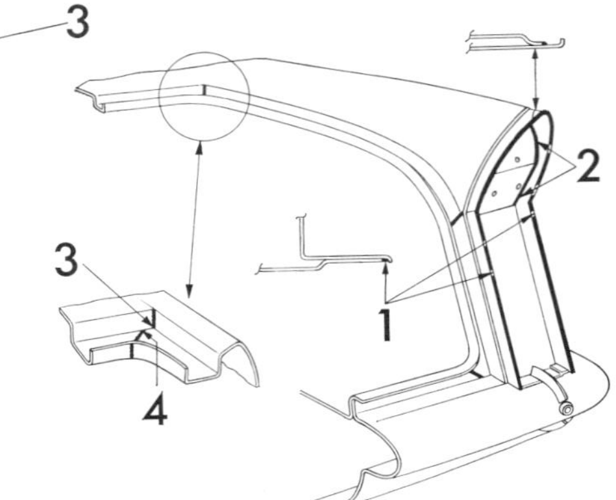

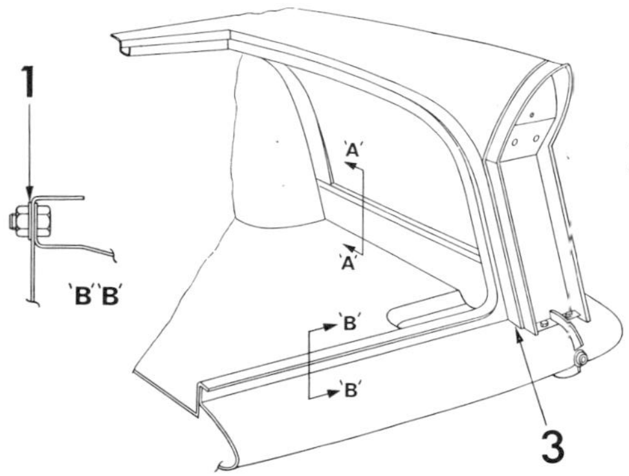

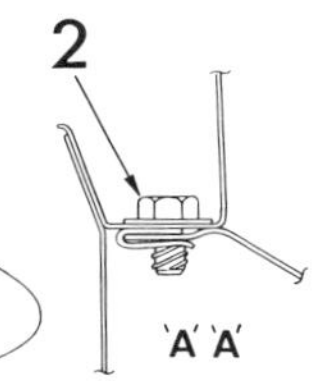

30. 1 Seal valance fixings on inside of body (use approved Mastics).

2 Seal side valance fixings on inside of body (use approved Mastics).

3 Lower ends of tail lamp aperture before assembly of valance panels (use approved Strip Sealer).

31. 1 Seal between rear valance centre and luggage floor panel side (Seelastik interweld).

2 Seal between rear valance side panel and luggage floor panel side (Seelastik interweld).

3 Seal luggage compartment floor joint as shown (Seelastik interweld).

4 Trunk lid stay fixings (Seelastik interweld).

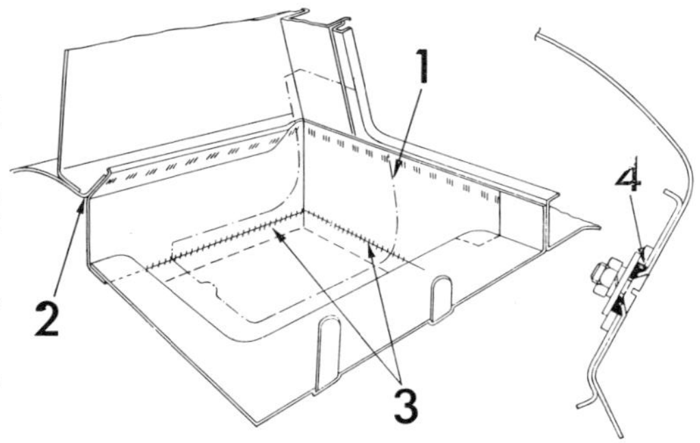

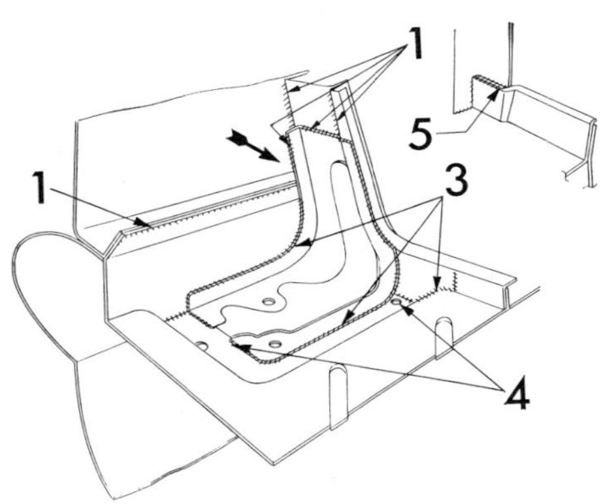

32. 1 Luggage floor side to tonneau side lower panel (use approved Mastics).

2 Rear body mounting bracket to tonneau closing panel (use approved Mastics).

3 Rear body mounting bracket to luggage compartment floor and rear valance (use approved Mastics).

4 Corner holes plugged (Glasticon 303).

5 Tonneau side panel lower corner holes (use approved Mastics).

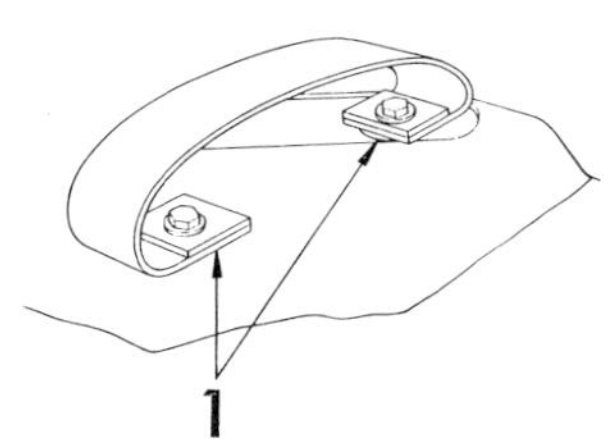

33. 1 Seal tool kit strap to luggage floor panel (use approved Mastics).

2 Trunk lid seal to be fixed firmly in position (Plus Products 6/63D).

34. 1 Roof top to lower panel (Plastisol 53).

2 Panel roof top to panel lower roof (Expandite 607/1).

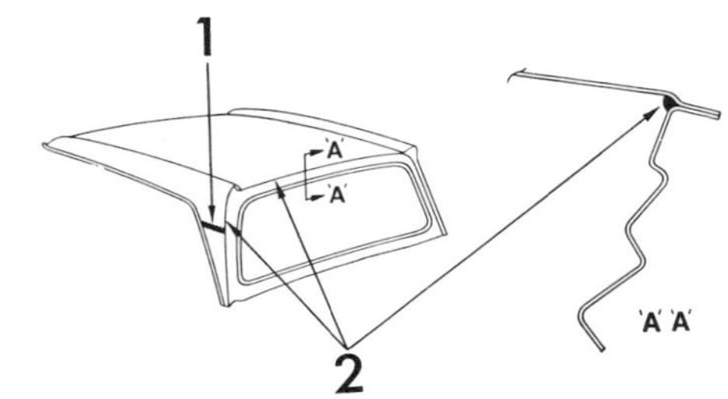

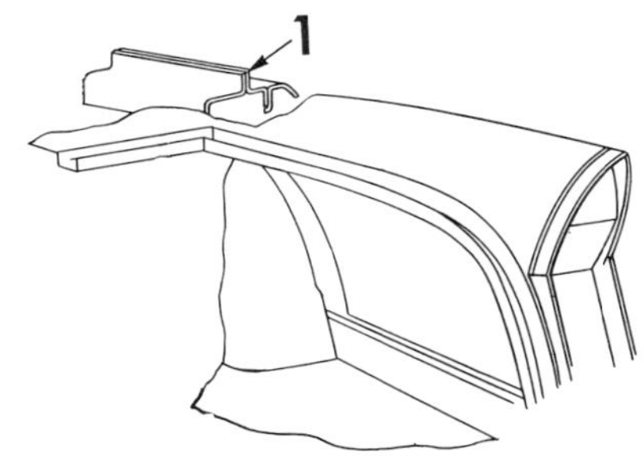

35. 1 Joint between waist rail and deck panel (use approved Plastisol, approx. ½" each side).

36. 1 Wheelarch to seat pan (use approved Plastisol).

2 Seal holes at base of "B" post (use approved Mastics).

3 Rear floor panel to heelboard (use approved Mastics).

4 Heelboard panel to rear seat pan (use approved Mastics).

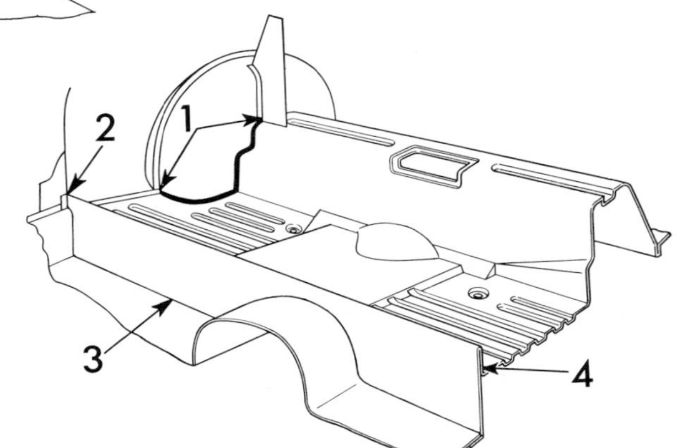

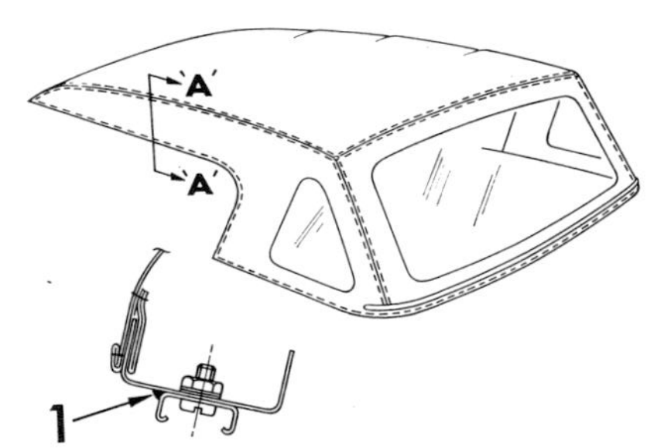

37. 1 Rubber retainer to cantrail after setting with (cream Seelastik).

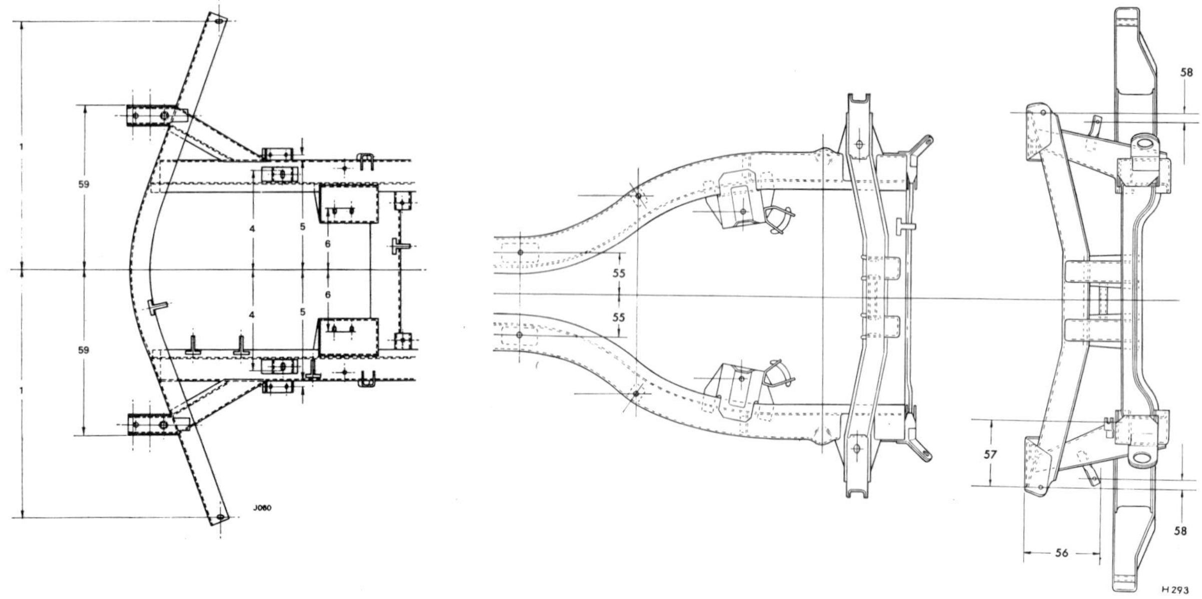

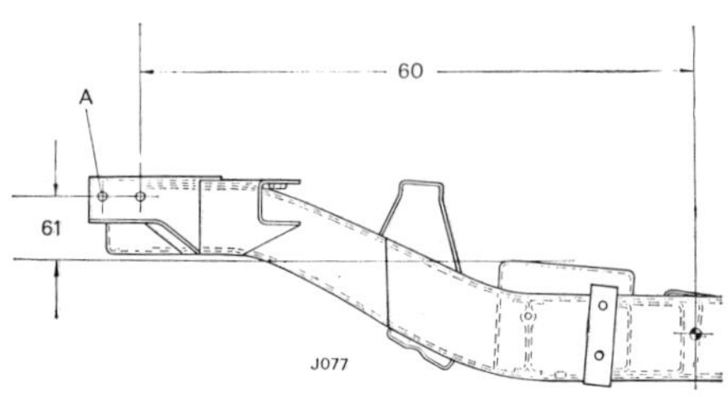

Location of Checking Points

A Bonnet to frame mounting, see Fig. 14

B Toe board mounting to frame, see Fig. 4

C Seat well mounting to frame, see Fig. 5

D Rear seat mounting to frame, see Fig. 6

E Rear damper mounting to frame

Fig. 2. Chassis frame dimensions (Spitfire Mk. 3) Refer to page 5.403 for dimensions

CHASSIS FRAME DIMENSIONS

SPITFIRE 4 AND MK. 2

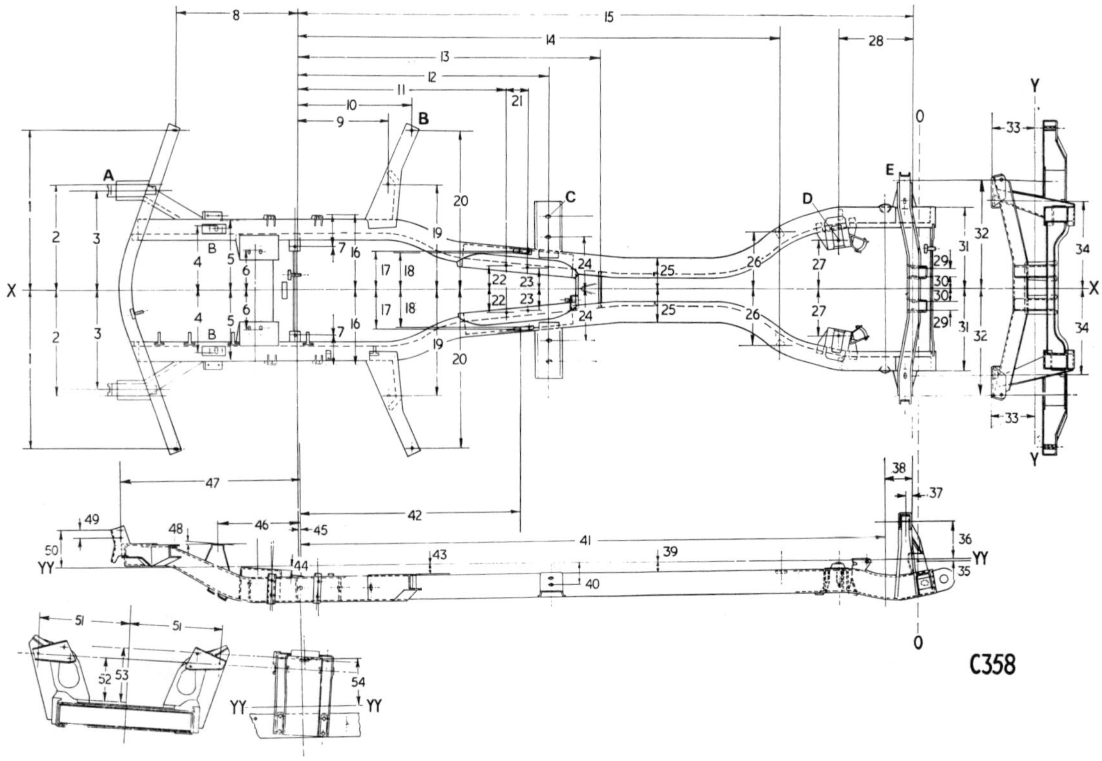

Location of Checking Points

A Bonnet to frame top mounting, see Fig. 13
B Toe board mounting to frame, see Fig. 4
C Seat well mounting to frame, see Fig. 5
D Rear seat mounting to frame, see Fig. 6
E Rear damper mounting to frame

Fig. 1. Chassis frame dimensions Refer to page 5·404 for Spitfire Mk. 3

Key to Fig. 1

	Inches	Centimetres		Inches	Centimetres		Inches	Centimetres
1	22·15	59·69	19	14·51	36·86	39	1·13	2·87
	22·10	58·42		14·48	36·78	40	2·80	7·11
2	14·56	36·98	20	21·03	53·39	41	83·26	211·48
3	13·78	35·00		20·97	53·27	42	31·45	79·88
	13·72	34·85	21	3·02	7·67		31·39	77·73
4	8·64	21·89		2·98	7·56	43	1·06	2·69
5	9·78	24·84	22	3·23	8·20	44	4½°	4½°
	9·72	24·69		3·12	8·15	45	0·26	0·66
6	5·55	14·05	23	2·91	7·37	46	11·69	29·69
	5·50	13·97		2·89	7·24		11·56	28·36
7	4·32	10·97	24	7·19	18·26	47	25·59	65·00
	4·30	10·92		7·13	18·11		25·47	64·69
8	17·37	44·12	25	4·25	10·80	48	4½°	4½°
	17·25	43·91	26	7·83	19·86	49	1·00	2·54
9	12·78	32·36		7·80	19·81	50	5·32	12·76
	12·72	32·31	27	6·64	16·87		5·26	12·77
10	16·09	40·87		6·61	16·79	51	13·06	33·17
	16·03	40·72	28	10·70	27·18		12·94	32·87
11	29·62	75·13		10·65	27·05	52	5·91	15·01
	29·50	74·77	29	1·51	3·83	53	7·31	18·50
12	36·56	92·86	30	1·63	4·14	54	6·29	15·97
	36·44	92·56		1·61	4·09		6·17	15·67
13	42·19	107·16	31	11·78	29·92	55	6·71	17·06
	41·94	104·83		11·72	29·77		6·59	16·74
14	68·22	173·28	32	14·75	37·46	56	6·22	15·80
	68·10	172·97	33	6·22	15·80	57	5·13	13·01
15	87·19	221·46	34	12·00	30·48	58	·78	1·98
	86·93	220·80	35	0·15	0·38	59	14·53	36·90
16	10·32	26·21	36	5·00	12·70		14·47	36·76
17	5·39	13·69		4·88	12·40	60	23·31	59·21
	5·36	13·61	37	1·12	2·87		23·19	58·90
18	5·23	13·28		1·00	2·54	61	2·95	7·50
	5·20	13·20	38	4·06	10·31		2·82	7·08

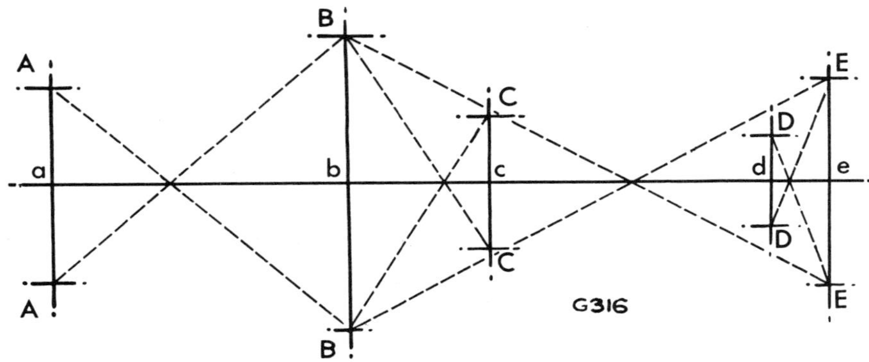

Fig. 3. Diagonal checking diagram

ASSESSMENT OF DAMAGE

Severe damage to the chassis is apparent; however, damage of a less serious nature may cause distortion of the frame which may not be detected visually.

If a check on the steering and suspension geometry reveals a fault which cannot be attributed to anything other than distortion of the chassis, then check for twist and squareness.

Checking for Twist

With the vehicle on a clean level floor, place a jack under each jacking point and raise the vehicle sufficiently to enable the road wheels to be removed.

Adjust the jacks until the following conditions are achieved:

Spitfire 4 and Mk. 2 Points 'A' are 25·29 in. (64·23 cm.) and Points 'E' are 24·94 in. (63·35 cm.) above the floor.

Spitfire Mk. 3 Points 'A' are 22·87 in. (56·76 cm.) and Points 'E' are 24·94 in. (63·35 cm.) above the floor.

This condition sets the datum 20 in. (50·8 cm.) above the floor.

If it is impossible to equalise the height of Points "A", then the chassis is twisted, the amount of twist being the difference in height of points "A".

Checking for Squareness

Position the vehicle as previously described and, referring to Fig. 1., transfer the lettered points to the floor using a plumb-bob and fine cord.

Letter the points on the floor and connect each pair by drawing a vertical line between them, as Fig. 3.

Mark and letter the central point of each line and place a straight-edge along these mid-points.

Make a further check for squareness as follows:

Using a straight-edge, mark the diagonals as shown in Fig. 3. If the frame is square then each pair of opposite diagonals must be equal in length and the points of inter-section must lie on the same straight line.

Chassis distortion is assessed by the amount and direction which any central point on the transverse line and/or the point of intersection of any pair of diagonals deviates from the centre line.

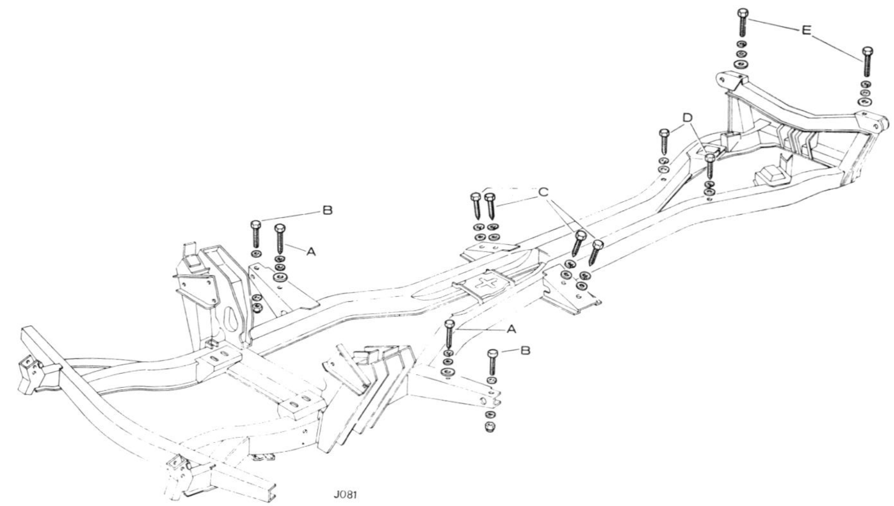

Fig. 1. Body mounting bolts

Fig. 2. Lifting the body

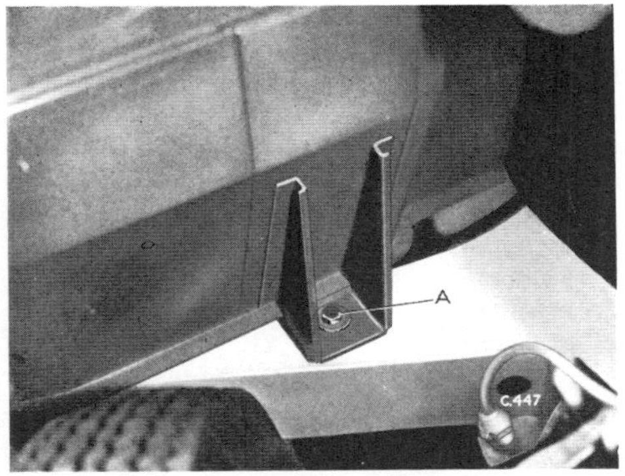

Fig. 3. Engine bay mounting points

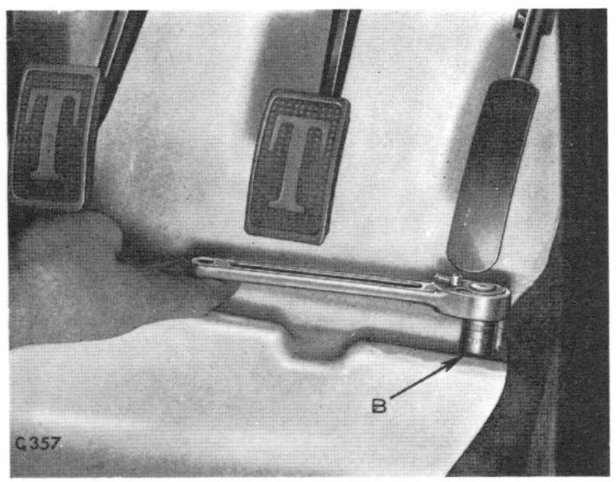

Fig. 4. Toe board mounting points

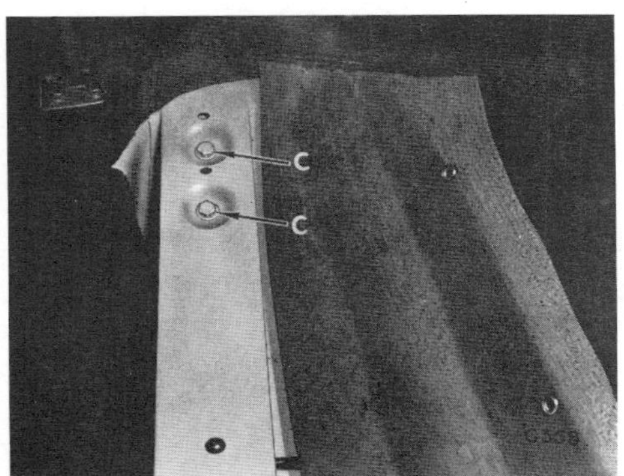

Fig. 5. Seat well mounting points

BODY REMOVAL

SPITFIRE 4, MK. 2 AND MK. 3

Remove the battery, drain the engine coolant and carry out the following:

Disconnect:

- lighting cables at bonnet (Fig. 11);
- cables from temperature gauge transmitter, oil pressure switch, generator and coil;
- tachometer drive cable from the Distributor;
- speedometer drive cable from the speedo head and pull the cable into the engine compartment;
- choke and accelerator controls at the carburettor;
- engine earth cable from top of the clutch housing;
- heater hoses from the engine;
- handbrake cable compensator from the relay lever (1 joint pin, cotter pin and washer);
- throttle operating rod from the accelerator operating lever;
- exhaust tail pipe from the body.

Remove:

- bonnet (page 5·505);
- engine bay side valance (page 5·507) fitted to models from Commission No. FC. 20753;
- brake hydraulic pipe between the master cylinder and fourway;
- seats (page 5·533);
- four bolts securing the facia support bracket to the floor (page 5·529);
- floor covering (page 5·534);
- spare wheel (page 5·511);
- fuel tank (page 5·535);

Release all clips securing the cable harness to the chassis.

Pass the cable harness under the outer left hand side tie rod and withdraw the harness clear of the engine.

Referring to Group 4, slacken the steering column clamp, release the clamp bolt from the lower steering coupling and push the inner column upwards, clear of the front suspension.

Disconnect the rear suspension radius arms from the body (one bolt in each), (Fig. 6).

Remove twelve bolts securing the body to the chassis frame (Fig. 1).

The bolts are located as follows:

- two in engine compartment, adjacent to dash panel (A) (Fig. 3);
- one each side of the front toe board (B) (Fig. 4);
- two each side of the body in line with the rear end of the gearbox cover (C) (Fig. 5);
- one each side of the front end of the rear seat pan (D) (Fig. 7);
- one each side of the spring access cover (E) (Fig. 8);

the bolts are concealed by rubber grommets.

Make up two lifting brackets to the dimensions shown in Fig. 9.

Remove the bonnet catch brackets (Fig. 15) and secure the lifting brackets to the body.

Protecting the body against chafing, attach lifting tackle to the lifting brackets (Fig. 2) and to the safety harness eyebolts adjacent to the rear wheel arches.

Lift the body clear of the chassis.

To Refit

Reverse the removal procedure.

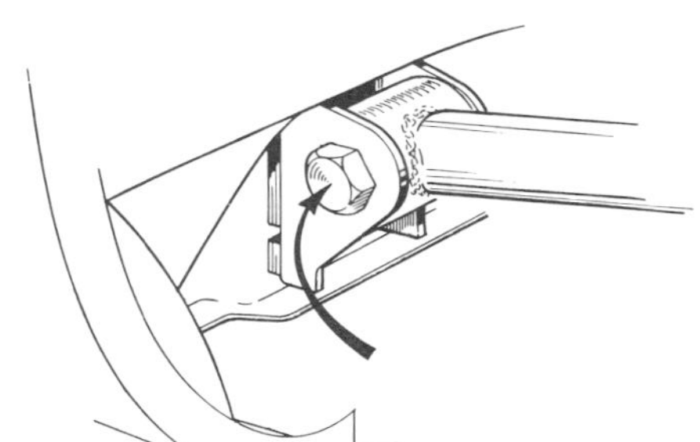

Fig. 6. Radius arm attachment to body

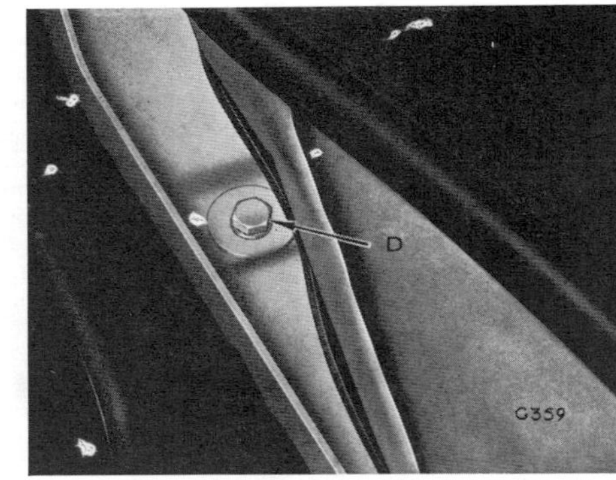

Fig. 7. Rear seat pan mounting points

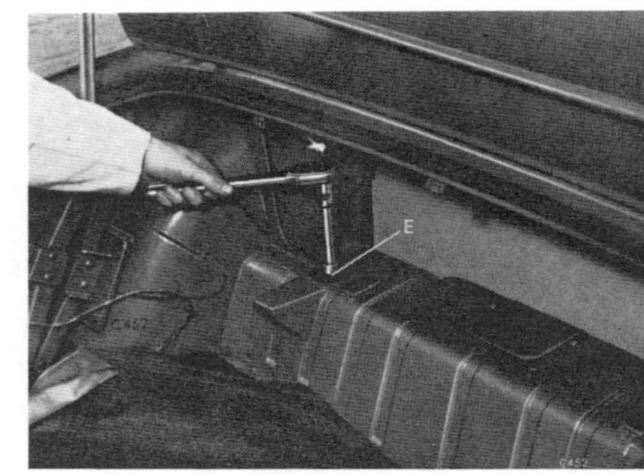

Fig. 8. Spring tunnel mounting points

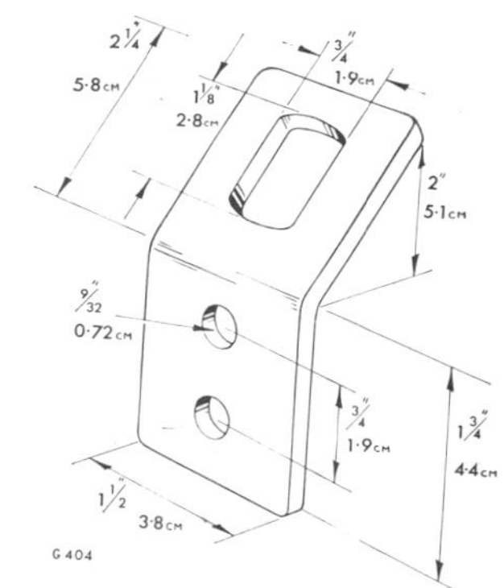

Fig. 9. Lifting bracket dimensions

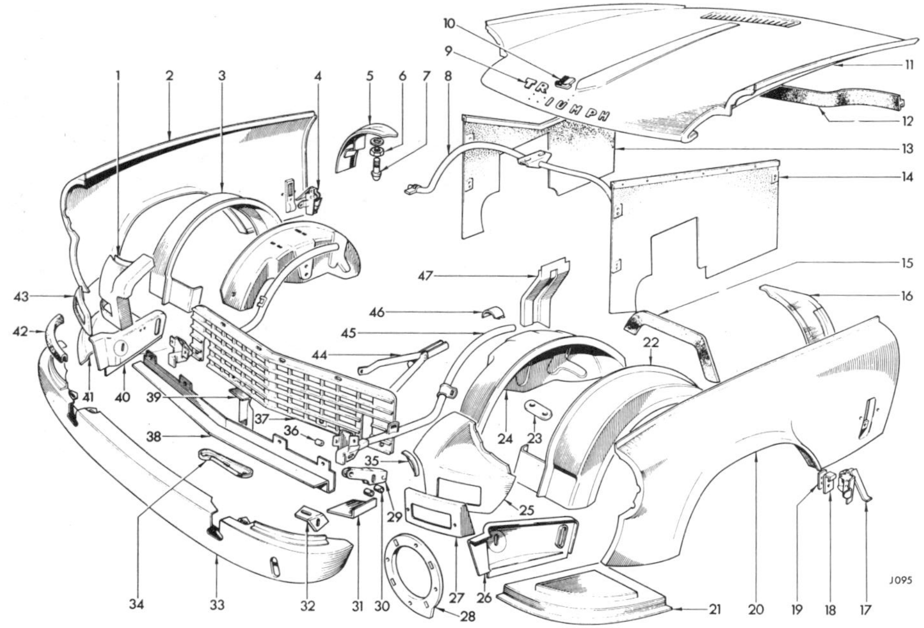

1	Nose panel — R.H.	17	Bonnet catch assembly	33	Front valance
2	Front wing side panel	18	Bonnet catch plate	34	Support bracket — front valance
3	Outer wheelarch panel	19	Tapping plate	35	Nose panel reinforcement
4	Bonnet catch	20	Front wing side panel	36	Bonnet hinge tube — spacer
5	Front wing reinforcement	21	Nose filler panel	37	Front grille assembly
6	Locknut	22	Outer wheelarch panel	38	Grille mounting
7	Bonnet location peg	23	Backing plate	39	Grille reinforcement
8	Rear support tube	24	Inner wheelarch panel	40	Grille aperture closing panel
9	Triumph lettering	25	Nose panel — L.H.	41	Nose filler panel
10	Bonnet badge	26	Closing panel assembly	42	Bonnet seal
11	Bonnet top assembly	27	Side/flasher plinth — L.H.	43	Side/flasher plinth — R.H.
12	Bonnet sealing rubber	28	Headlamp mounting bracket	44	Support stay
13	Engine bay valance — R.H.	29	Bonnet hinge bracket assembly	45	Bonnet hinge tube
14	Engine bay valance — L.H.	30	Distance piece	46	Tube packing piece
15	Wheelarch rear seal	31	Valance bracket	47	Wing support
16	Front wing reinforcement	32	Front valance support		

Fig. 10. Bonnet, front valance and grille details

BONNET ASSEMBLY

SPITFIRE 4, MK. 2 AND MK. 3

To remove

Isolate the battery.

Disconnect the front lighting and horn cables at the snap connectors on the top centre of the grille (Fig. 11)

Remove both overriders (Page 5·507).

Disconnect the bonnet stay from the front suspension mounting bracket (Fig. 12).

Close the bonnet and take out two bolts (1), (Fig. 13 and (2), Fig. 14).

Lift the bonnet away.

To Refit

Reverse the removal procedure and refer to bonnet adjustment procedure as follows:

Horizontal adjustment

Slacken the bolts (1) and (2), Fig. (13) for Spitfire 4 and Mk. 2 and (2), (Fig. 14) for Spitfire Mk. 3; move the bonnet forwards or rearwards to achieve a parallel gap of $\frac{3}{16}$" (5 mm.) between the bonnet, scuttle and doors.

Retighten the bolts.

Height Adjustment, Front (Figs. 13 and 14)

Slacken the bolts (1) and raise the bonnet to achieve a parallel gap between the rear vertical edge and the doors.

Re-tighten the bolts.

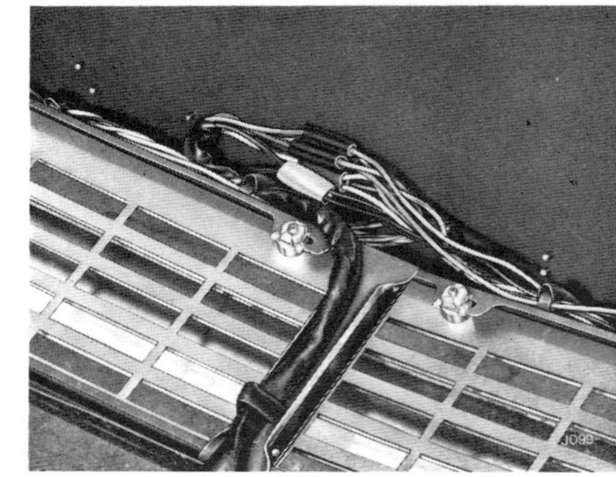

Fig. 11. Bonnet snap connectors

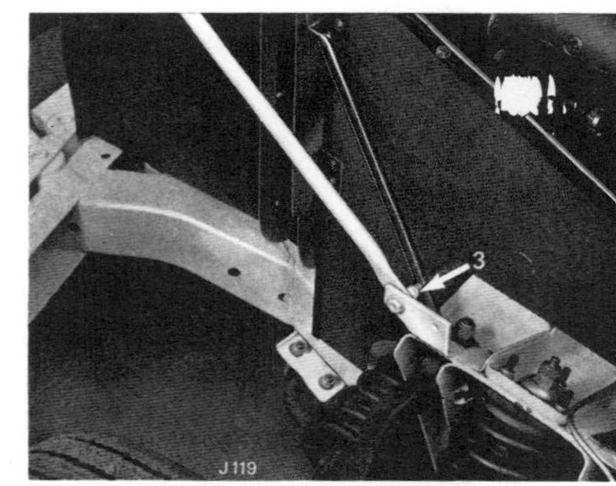

Fig. 12. Bonnet stay

Fig. 13. Bonnet adjustment (Spitfire 4 and Mk. 2)

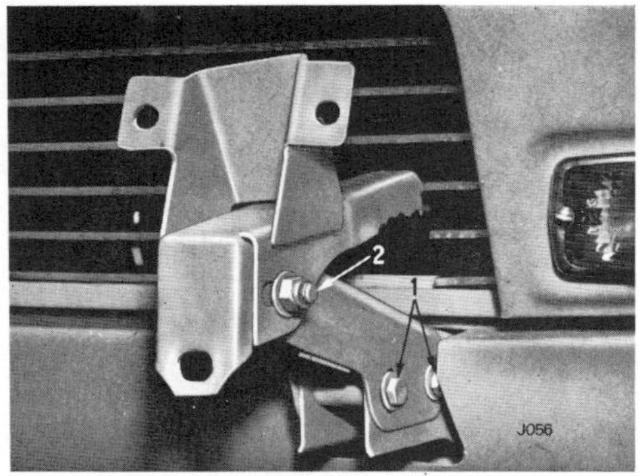
Fig. 14. Bonnet adjustment (Spitfire Mk. 3)

Fig. 15. Bonnet height adjustment

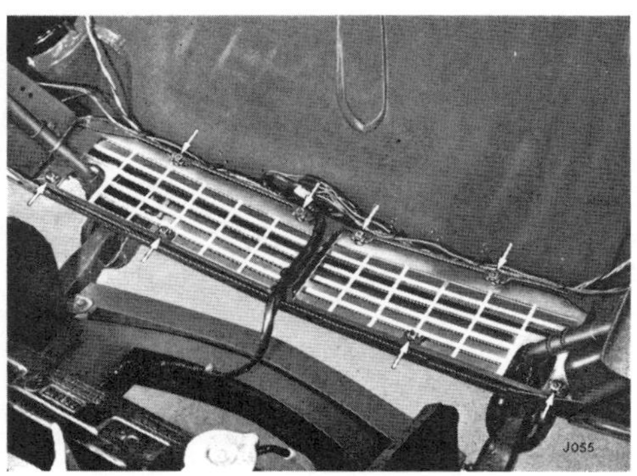
Fig. 16. Front grille attachment

Height Adjustment, Rear (Fig. 15)
Slacken the locknut (1) securing the cone-shaped buffer to the bonnet screw. Screw the buffer in or out to lower or raise the bonnet rear edge. Retighten the locknut. Re-adjust the bonnet fastener brackets (2).

FRONT GRILLE

SPITFIRE 4, MK. 2 AND MK. 3

To Remove
Remove eight screws (arrowed Fig. 16).

On Spitfire Mk. 3 only, collect four spacers from the four top fixing screws.

To Refit
Reverse the removal procedure.

FRONT VALANCE

SPITFIRE 4 AND MK. 2

To Remove
Remove front bumpers complete with mounting brackets see page 5·510. Take out bolts (1), (2) and (3) Fig. 17, from each side of the radiator.

Pull the valance forward and lower it clear of the body.

SPITFIRE MK. 3

To Remove
Take out bolts (1), (2) and (3) Fig. 18, from each side of the radiator.

Pull the valance forward and lower it clear of the body.

To Refit
Reverse the removal procedure.

ENGINE BAY VALANCES

SPITFIRE MODELS FROM COMMISSION No. FC.20753

To Remove (Fig. 19)
Remove four pan head screws, washers and nuts, (two each side) (1), valance to dash front panel and two bolts, washers and nyloc nuts (one each side) (2), valance to front suspension mounting bracket.

Take out four setscrews, washers and nuts, two each side (3), valance to radiator side brackets.

Pull engine bay valance clear of the engine compartment.

To Refit
Reverse the removal procedure.

OVERRIDERS

SPITFIRE 4 AND MK. 2

Front–To Remove (Fig. 20)
Take out bolts (16) and release the overrider.

To Refit
Reverse the removal procedure.

Rear–To Remove (Fig. 20)
Take out bolts (10) and (13) and release the overrider.

To Refit
Reverse the removal procedure.

SPITFIRE MK. 3

Front–To Remove (Fig. 21)
Remove bolts (2), (23) and (24), release the bumper, and take out the exposed screw retaining the overrider to the bumper.

To Refit
Reverse the removal procedure.
Rear – NOT FITTED to Spitfire Mk. 3.

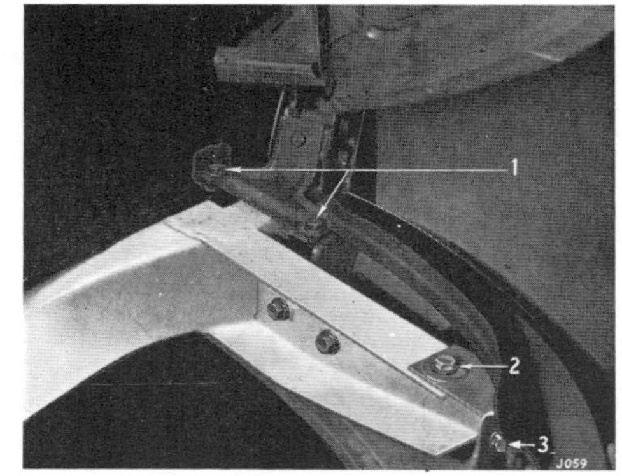
Fig. 17. Front valance attachment (Spitfire 4 and Mk. 2)

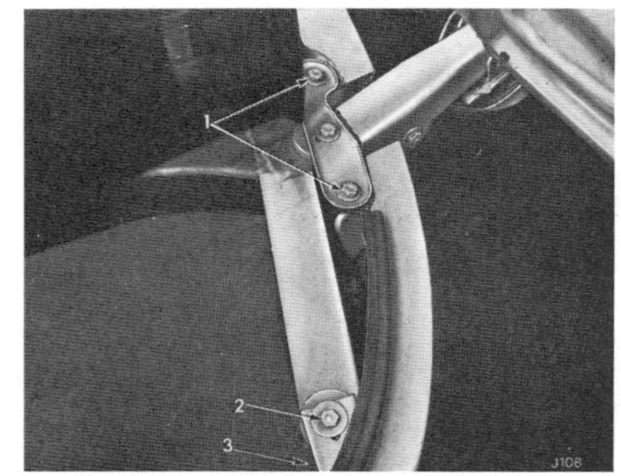
Fig. 18. Front valance attachment (Spitfire Mk. 3)

Fig. 19. Engine bay valance attachment

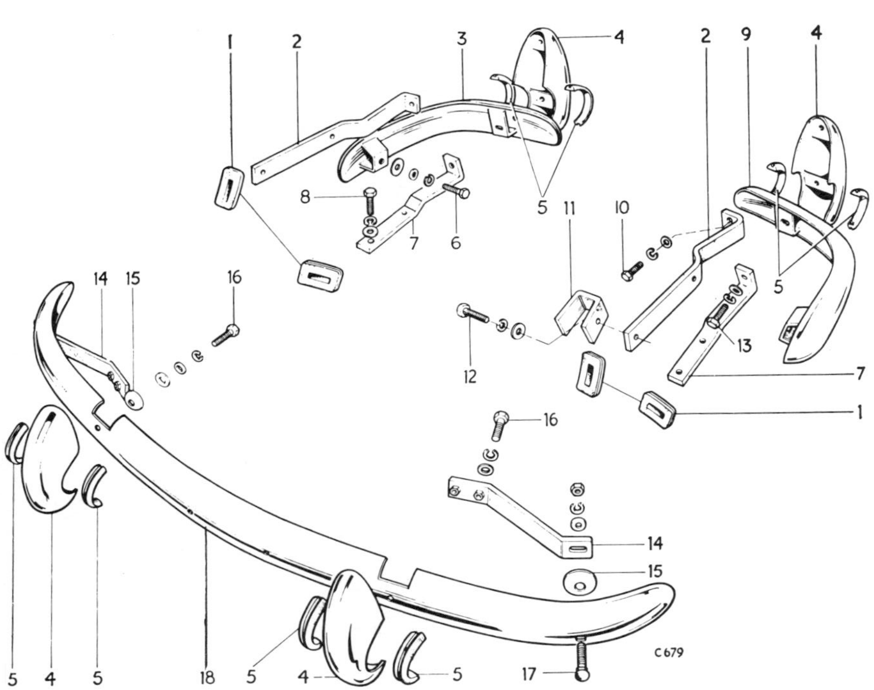

1	Grommet	10	Bolt — support bracket
2	Overrider support bracket	11	Jack stowage bracket
3	Rear bumper — R.H.	12	Bolt — support bracket
4	Overrider	13	Bolt — overrider mounting bracket
5	Moulding — P.V.C.	14	Front bumper support bracket
6	Bolt — side attachment	15	Distance washer
7	Bumper support bracket	16	Bolt — support bracket
8	Bolt — support bracket	17	Bolt — bumper to support bracket
9	Rear bumper — L.H.	18	Front bumper

Fig. 20. Bumper arrangement (Spitfire 4 and Mk. 2)

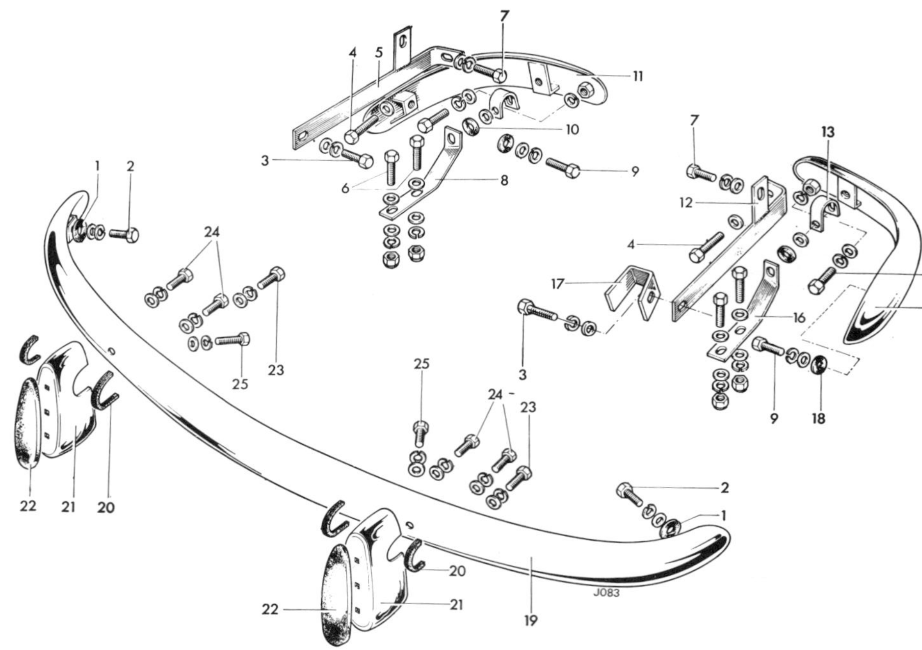

1	Rubber washer	14	Rear bumper — L.H.
2	Bolt — front bumpers to body	15	Bolt — support extension
3	Bolt -— support bracket	16	Rear bumper support
4	Bolt — spring bar	17	Jack stowage bracket
5	Spring bar — upper	18	Rubber washer
6	Bolt — support bar	19	Front bumper
7	Bolt — spring bar	20	Moulding — P.V.C.
8	Rear bumper support	21	Overrider assembly
9	Bolt — body side	22	Rubber buffer — overrider
10	Rubber washers	23	Bolt — lower overrider attachments
11	Rear bumper — R.H.	24	Bolt — front bumper to body
12	Spring bar upper	25	Bolt — overrider to front bumper
13	Support extension — rear bumper		

Fig. 21. Bumper arrangement (Spitfire Mk. 3)

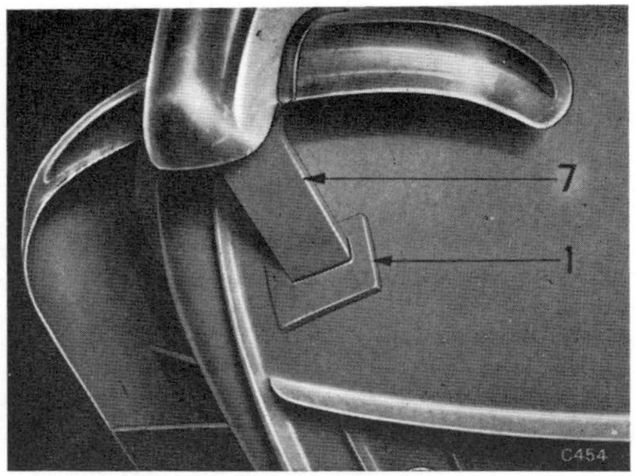

Fig. 22. Rear bumper underside attachment (Spitfire 4 and Mk. 2)

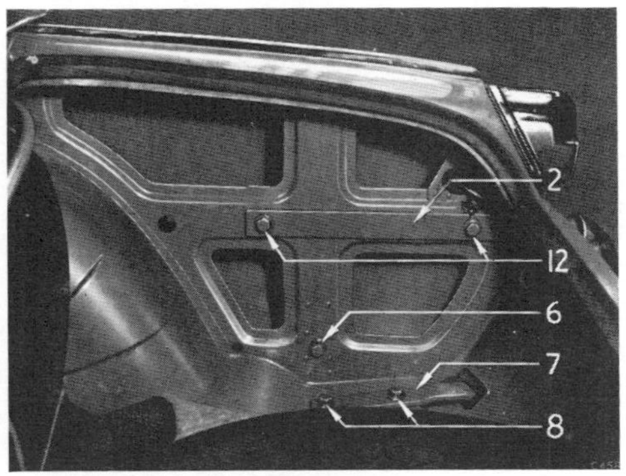

Fig. 23. Rear bumper attachment (Spitfire 4 and Mk. 2)

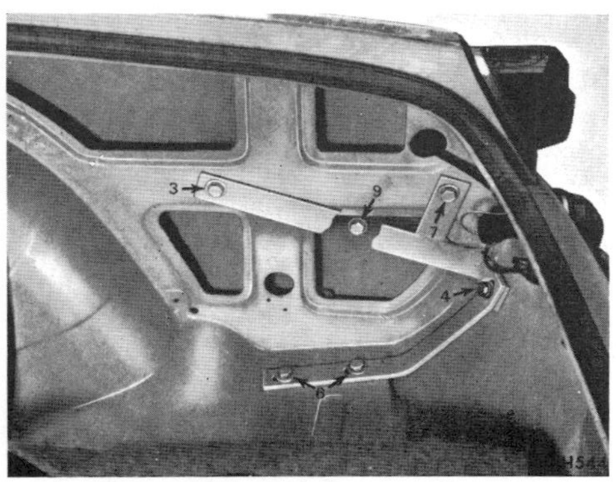

Fig. 24. Rear bumper attachment (Spitfire Mk. 3)

BUMPERS

SPITFIRE 4 AND MK. 2

Front–To Remove (Fig. 20)

Remove the overriders as previously described. Take out two bolts (17) and lift the bumper clear.

To Refit

Reverse the removal procedure and when refitting the washer (15) between the bumper and support bracket, ensure that its spherical face is adjacent to the bumper.

Rear–To Remove (Fig. 20 and 23)

Remove the overriders. Take out the bolt (6) from inside the luggage compartment to release the bumper. To remove the bumper and overrider support brackets, take out the bolts (8) and (12).

To Refit

Reverse the removal procedure.

SPITFIRE MK. 3

Front–To Remove (Fig. 21)

Take out the bolts (2), (23) and (24) and lift the bumper clear complete with overriders.

To Refit

Reverse the removal procedure, ensuring that the rubber packing washer (1) is fitted between the body and the bumper.

Rear–To Remove (Fig. 21 and 24)

Working inside the luggage compartment, take out the bolts (4) and (9) to release the bumpers. To remove the bumper support brackets, take out the bolts (3), (6) and (7).

To Refit

Reverse the removal procedure, ensuring that the rubber packing washer (1) is fitted between the body and the bumper.

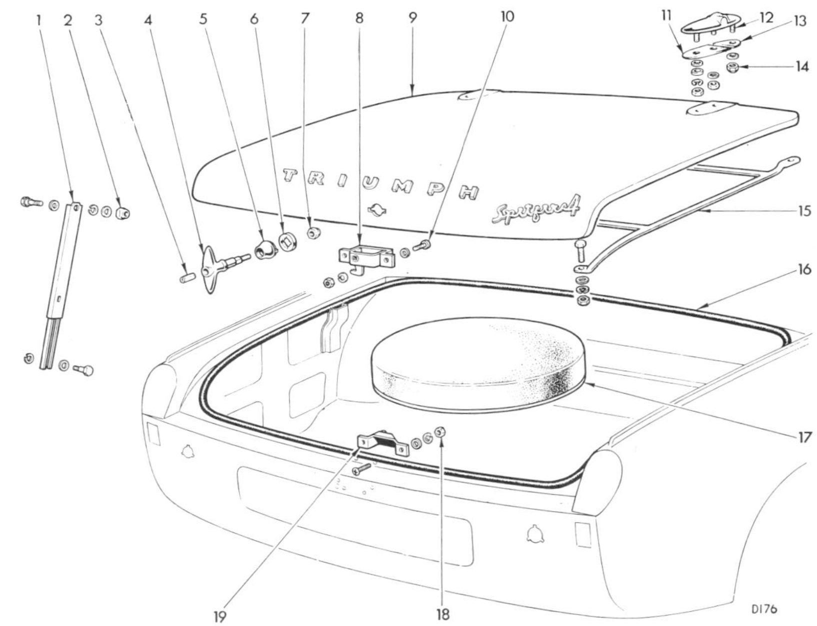

LUGGAGE COMPARTMENT LID

SPITFIRE 4, MK. 2 AND MK. 3

To Remove (Fig. 25)

Support the lid (9) in the open position and release the upper end of the stay (1) from the reinforcement tube (15). Remove the securing nut (14) from the forward stud of each hinge (12) located underneath the rear deck panel. Lift the lid, complete with hinges from the body.

If necessary, release the hinges (12) from the lid and note the position of the sealing washers (13).

To Refit

Reverse the removal procedure leaving the hinge nuts semi-tight. Oversize holes permit limited adjustment. Move the lid as required to effect a close fit and finally tighten the hinge nuts.

LOCK

To remove

Raise the lid, remove the nut (7) from the inner end of the handle (4) and withdraw the handle from the lock (8). Release the lock (8) by removing two securing screws (10).

To Refit

Reverse the removal procedure.

SEALING

Refer to "Dust and Water Sealing" Page 5·601.

Key to Fig. 25

1 Support stay
2 Nyloc nut — stay to lid
3 Lock device
4 Handle — compartment lid
5 Escutcheon
6 Seating washer — escutcheon
7 Nyloc nut — handle to lid
8 Budget lock
9 Luggage compartment lid
10 Screw — budget lock
11 Fibre washer
12 Hinge
13 Fibre washer
14 Nyloc nut — hinge attachment
15 Reinforcement tube
16 Trunk aperture weatherstrip
17 Spare wheel cover
18 Nut — catch plate attachment
19 Catch plate assembly

Fig. 25. Luggage compartment lid

DOOR DETAILS

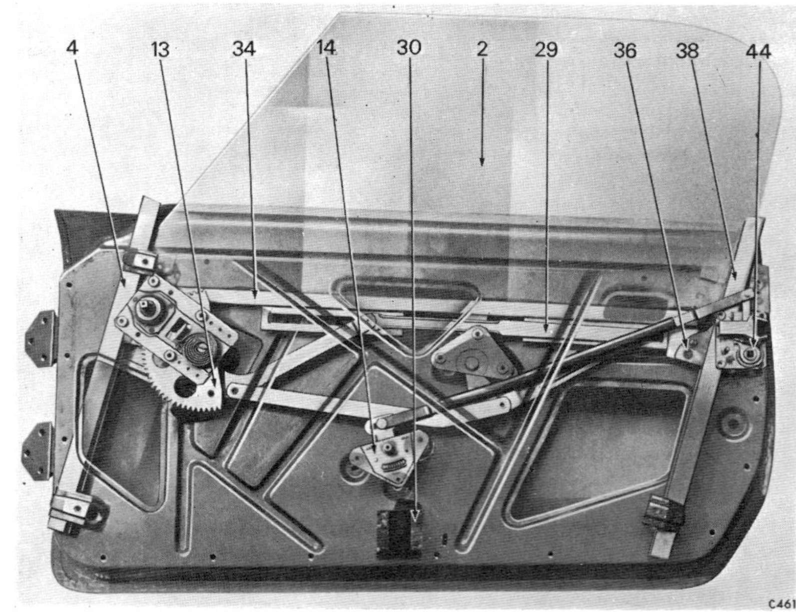

Fig. 27. Door components (Spitfire 4)

DOORS

Lubrication:

Before refitting the door casing and other items ensure that all moving parts are adequately greased. After assembly and once a month, introduce a few drops of thin machine oil into the outside key slots and on to the latch inside the lock case.

IMPORTANT: The private lock cylinders must not under any circumstances be lubricated with grease or graphite.

SPITFIRE 4

A TRIM PANEL

1. **To Remove** (Fig. 26)
   - (a) Remove two interior handles (20) and (22) by pressing the escutcheons (18) firmly against the trim panel and pushing out the retaining pins (19).
   - (b) Prise the trim panel from the door (Fig. 30).
   - (c) Remove the coil springs (17) from the spindles.
2. **To Refit**
   Reverse the removal procedure.

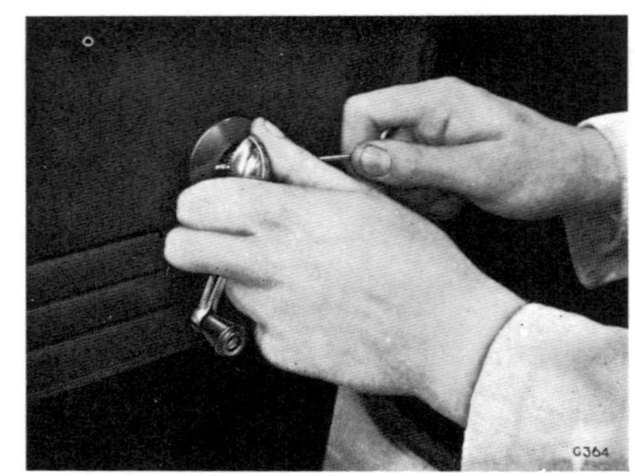

Fig. 28. Door handle removal

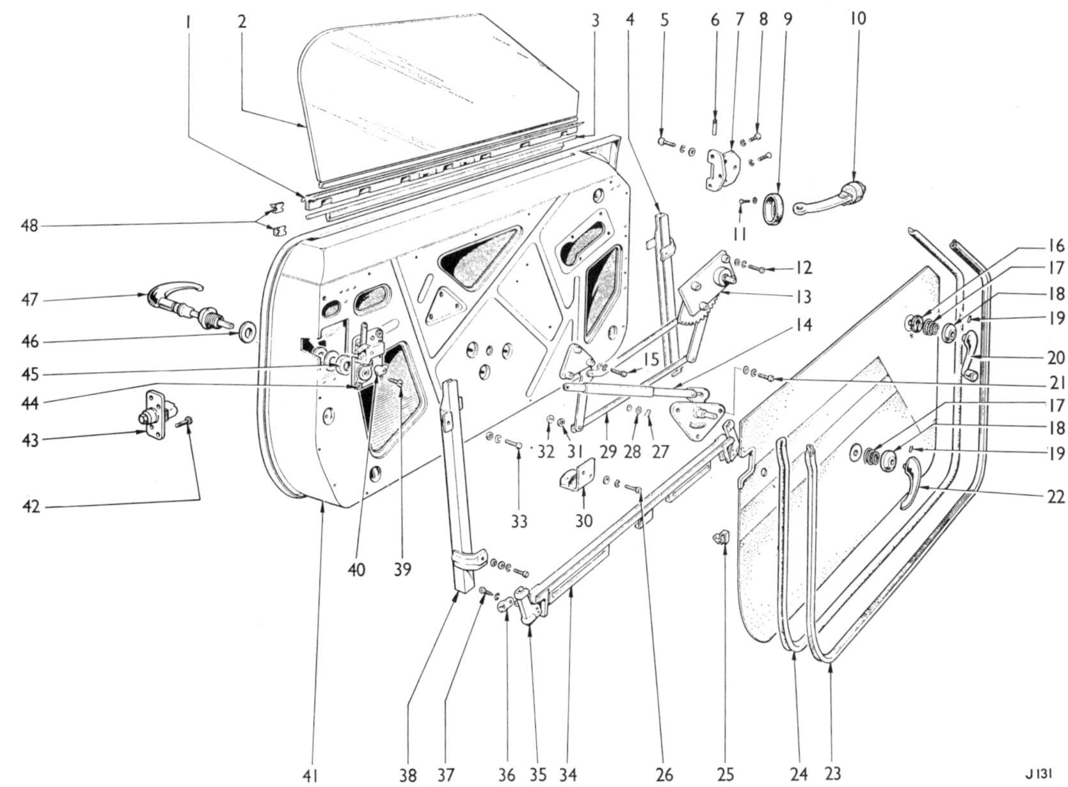

Fig. 26. Door details (Spitfire 4)

Key to fig. 26

1 Sealing strip — waist outer
2 Window glass
3 Weatherstrip
4 Glass channel assembly
5 Screw — hinge to 'A' post
6 Pin — door hinge
7 Door hinge
8 Screw — hinge to door
9 Seal — check arm
10 Check arm
11 Screw — check arm
12 Screw — regulator to door
13 Window regulator assembly
14 Remote control assembly
15 Screw — regulator plate to door inner panel
16 Sealing washer
17 Escutcheon spring
18 Escutcheon
19 Pin — handle attachment
20 Window regulator handle
21 Screw — remote control attachment
22 Remote control handle
23 Draught excluder
24 Door seal
25 Trim clip
26 Screw — door glass stop
27 Clip — remote control to lock
28 Waved washer
29 Window regulator link
30 Glass stop bracket
31 Washer } Regulator to channel
32 Stud retainer } Regulator to channel
33 Screw — glass channel to door inner panel
34 Channel assembly — window regulator
35 Channel guide block
36 Guide packing piece
37 Stop bolt — guide block
38 Glass channel assembly
39 Setscrew — lock to door inner panel
40 Safety catch knob
41 Door assembly
42 Screw — striker to 'B' post
43 Striker plate
44 Door lock
45 Locking ring — outside door handle
46 Packing washer
47 Outside door handle
48 Clip
49 Screw — securing outside handle — Refer to Fig. 32

50–65 Refer to Fig. 35:

50 Setscrew — door handle attachment
51 Seating washer
52 Locknut
53 Adjustment screw
54 Lock contactor
55 Screw — lock attachment
56 Anti-burst strap
57 Screw — striker plate
58 Anti-burst striker plate
59 Locking lever
60 Lock operating lever
61 Lever
62 Spring
63 Remote control unit
64 Spring collar
65 Seating washer

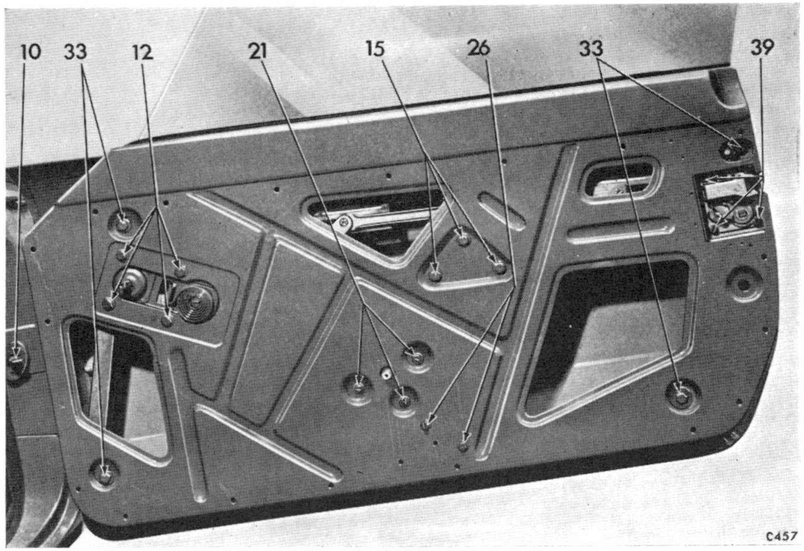

Fig. 29. Door component fixings (Spitfire 4)

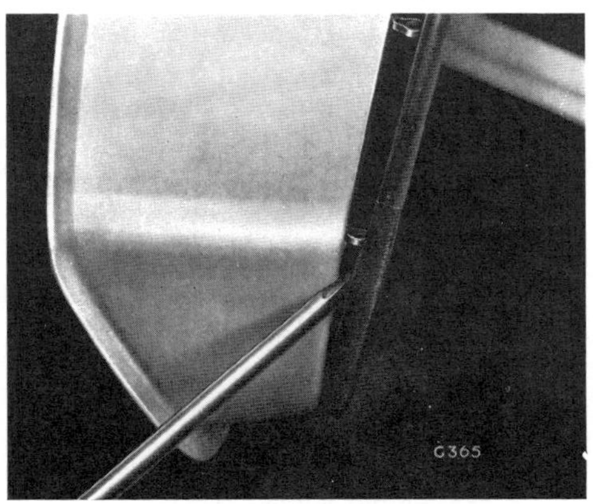

Fig. 30. Prising off door trim panel

B REMOTE CONTROL

1. **To Remove** (Fig. 26)
   (a) Perform operation A1.
   (b) Remove the spring clip (27) and waved washer (28) and release the link arm from the lock assembly.
   (c) Take out three screws (21) and remove the remote control mechanism (14) from the door (Fig. 31).

2. No adjustment is required.

3. **To Refit**
   Reverse the removal procedure.

C GLASS RUN CHANNEL

1. **To Remove** (Fig. 29)
   (a) Perform operation A1.
   (b) Perform operation G1.
   (c) Take out four bolts (33) securing the glass-run channel.
   (d) Lower the channel into the bottom of the door and manoeuvre it through the large aperture in the door inner panel.

2. **To Refit**
   Reverse the removal procedure.

D DOOR LOCK

1. **To Remove** (Fig. 32)
   (a) Perform operation B1 (a) and (b).
   (b) Take out the screws (39) and (49) securing the lock to the door panel.
   (c) Lift the lock away.

2. No adjustment is required.

3. **To Refit**
   (a) Reverse the removal procedure.

E EXTERIOR DOOR HANDLE

1. **To Remove**
   (a) Fully raise the glass and perform operation A1.
   (b) (For drivers door only). Take out the screw (49) (Fig. 32) from the centre of the spindle.
   (c) (For passengers door only). Unscrew the large nut (45) Fig. 33, which is accessible from inside the door.
   (d) Withdraw the handle, noting the rubber sealing ring between the escutcheon and the door outer panel.

2. **To Refit**
   Reverse the removal procedure.

F WINDOW REGULATOR MECHANISM

1. **To Remove** (Fig. 26 and 29)
   (a) Perform operation A1.
   (b) Disconnect the regulating arms from the channel at the base of the glass and remove the inter-connecting link (29).
   (c) Loosely refit the regulating handle and raise the glass to its highest position and, retain it with a small rubber wedge.
   (d) Take out four screws (12) and three screws (21) securing the regulation mechanism to the door inner panel and pass the assembly through the large aperture.

2. **To Refit**
   (a) Assemble the regulating mechanism to the door and loosely refit the securing screws (12) and (21).
   (b) Refit the link (29), attach both regulator arms to the glass channel, and secure them with leather washers and spring clips.
   (c) Remove the rubber wedge and fully tighten the securing screws.
   (d) Perform operation A2.

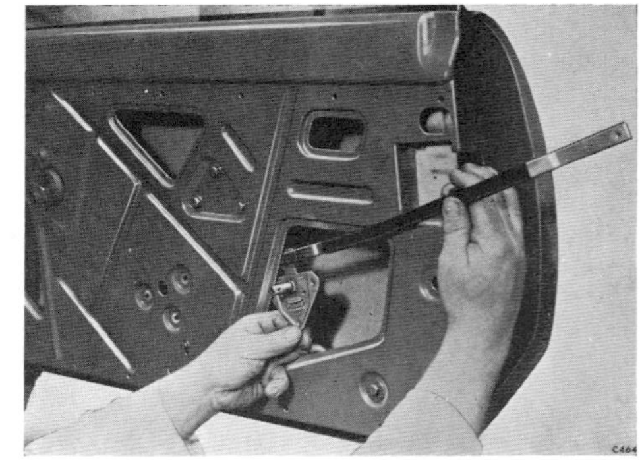

Fig. 31. Removing remote control from door

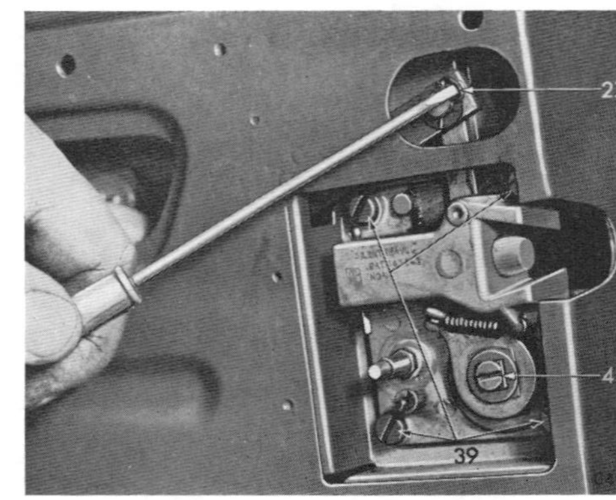

Fig. 32. Remote control link attachment to lock

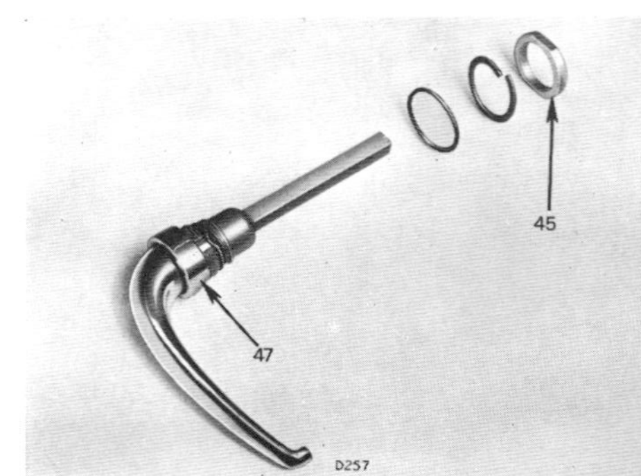

Fig. 33. Door locking handle (Spitfire 4)

Fig. 34. Door component fixings (Spitfire Mk. 2 and 3)

G DOOR GLASS

1. To Remove (Fig. 26 and 36)

(a) Perform operation A1.

(b) Loosely refit the regulating handle and lower the glass.

(c) Perform operation H1 (b).

(d) Take out the guide packing piece (36) from the lower end of the glass frame (one bolt) and partially raise the glass.

(e) Perform operation F1 (b).

(f) Lift the glass from the door.

2. To Refit

Reverse the removal procedure.

H DOOR INNER WEATHERSTRIP

1. To Remove (Fig. 26)

(a) Perform operation A1

(b) Remove the inner weatherstrip by pushing it downward into the door.

2. To Refit

(a) Refit the weatherstrip using an easily made tool shown on (Fig. 37).

(b) Perform operation A2.

J DOOR ASSEMBLY

1. To Remove (Fig. 26 and 38)

(a) Drill out the rivet securing the check arm (6).

(b) Take out three bolts (5) securing each hinge to the "A" post and lift the door from the vehicle.
Each hinge is secured to the door by three bolts (8).

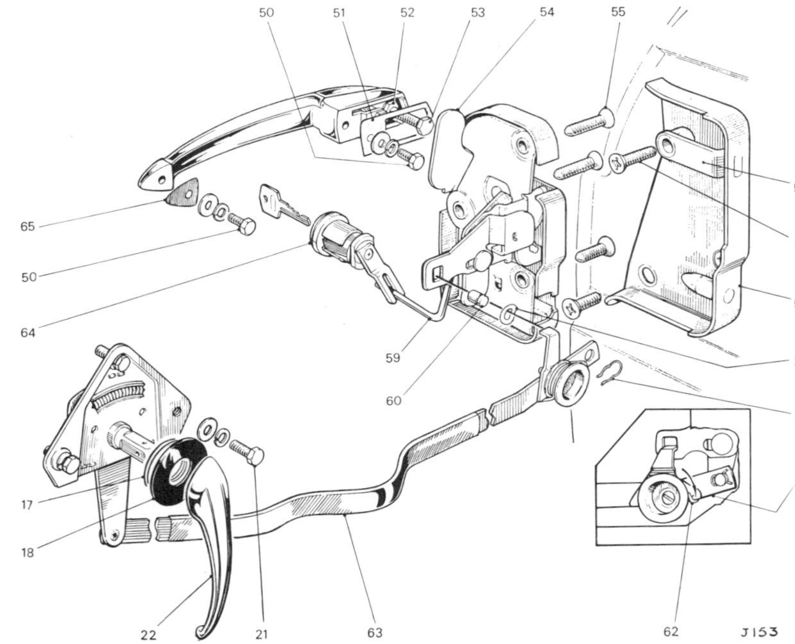

Fig. 35. Anti-burst door lock details (Spitfire Mk. 2 and 3)

2. Adjustments

(a) Tapped plates in the "A" post permit limited vertical fore and aft adjustment of the door. The door may be moved in or out by slackening the hinge to door bolts.

3. To Refit

Reverse the removal procedure.

SPITFIRE Mk. 2 and 3

A TRIM PANEL

1 & 2 To Remove and Refit – procedure as for Spitfire 4.

B REMOTE CONTROL

1 & 2 To Remove and Refit (Fig. 35) – procedure as for Spitfire 4.

C GLASS RUN CHANNEL

1 & 2 To Remove and Refit (Fig. 34) – procedure as for Spitfire 4.

D ANTI BURST DOOR LOCK

In the event of a collision causing severe distortion of the door aperture, this feature resists the separation of the latching elements and the consequent risk of the door flying open. The standard of the anti-burst meets the American Society of Automotive Engineers recommendation as follows:

*Longitudinal separation: (under an opening force of 200lb.)	Full latch 1500lb.
Transversely opening:	Full latch 1250lb. 1st safety 500lb.

**Applicable to cars built prior to Commission No. FD.20,000*

†Longitudinal separation: (under an opening force of 200lb.)	Full latch 2500lb. 1st safety 1000lb.
Transversely opening:	Full latch 2000lb. 1st safety 1000lb.

†*Applicable to cars built from Commission No. FD.20,000*

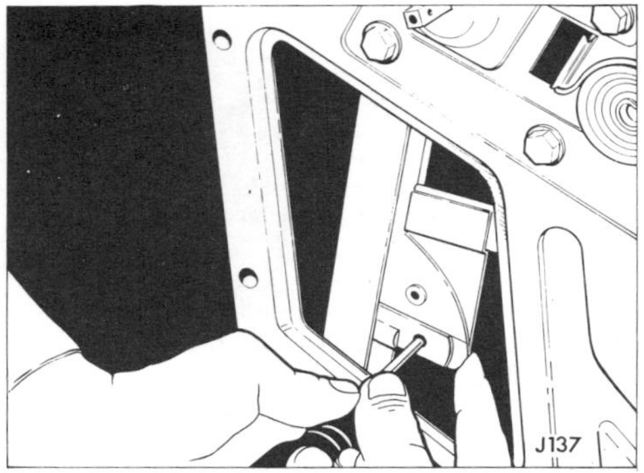

Fig. 36. Removing glass guide

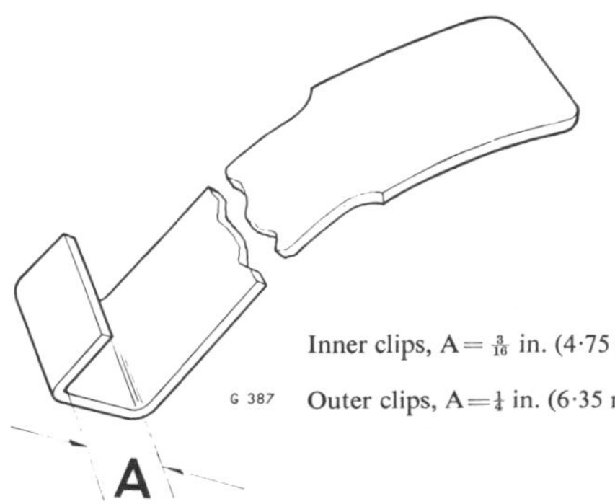

Inner clips, A = 3/16 in. (4·75 mm.)

Outer clips, A = 1/4 in. (6·35 mm.)

Fig. 37 Weatherstrip clip tool

Fig. 38. Door to body attachment

Inertia Loading: Components comprising the latch system must collectively withstand 30G in any direction without releasing.

1. **To Remove** (Fig. 35)
   (a) Raise the glass to the fully closed position and perform operation A1.
   (b) Perform operation B1 (b).
   (c) Take out three countersunk screws (55) retaining the lock unit to the door end panel.
   (d) Lift the lock operating lever (60) sufficiently to allow the lock unit to be withdrawn through its aperture in the door end panel.
   (e) No adjustment of the lock unit is required.

2. **To Refit**
   (a) Reverse the removal procedure and ensure that the door lock engages with the private lock (Fig. 39).

E EXTERIOR DOOR HANDLE

1. **To Remove** (Fig. 40)
   (a) Perform operation A1.
   (b) Loosely refit the regulator handle and raise the glass to the fully closed position. Release the handle by unscrewing two screws (50) and washers located on the inside of the door panel.

2. **To adjust push button**
   (a) Perform operation E1 (a).
   (b) Release the lock nut (52) and screw the bolt (53) in or out as required; finally retighten the lock nut.

3. **To Refit**
   Reverse the removal procedure.

F WINDOW REGULATOR MECHANISM

1 & 2 To Remove and Refit (Fig. 34) – procedure as for Spitfire 4.

G DOOR GLASS

1 & 2 To Remove and Refit – procedure as for Spitfire 4.

H DOOR INNER WEATHERSTRIP

1 & 2 To Remove and Refit – procedure as for Spitfire 4.

J DOOR ASSEMBLY

1, 2 & 3 To Remove, Adjust and Refit – procedure as for Spitfire 4.

K ANTI BURST STRIKER PLATE

1. **To Remove** (Figs. 35 and 41)
   (a) Remove three countersunk screws (57) and release the striker plate (58) from the 'B' post.

2. **To Adjust**
   (a) The striker plate (58) should not normally require attention, but when adjustment is required, it must be carried out by a process of trial and error proved by checking the door closing action and its position when closed. Ensure that the striker plate is in the horizontal plane relative to the axis of the door movement and that the securing screws are finally tightened.
   NOTE: Never slam a door when adjusting the striker plate as any misalignment may damage the components.

3. **To Refit**
   Reverse the removal procedure

L PRIVATE LOCK

The key operated locking barrel is retained by a twin-legged spring collar (64) inside the door.

1. **To Remove** (Fig. 35)
   (a) Loosely refit the regulating handle and raise the glass to the fully closed position.
   (b) Using a suitable tool compress the collar legs sufficiently to allow the barrel to be withdrawn from the outside of the door.

2. **To Refit**
   (a) Ensure that the collar (64) is in place, then insert the key operated locking barrel in the aperture of the door panel with its operating fork inclined towards the shut face (Fig. 39) and press firmly in position.
   (b) Perform operation A2.

M DOOR EXTERIOR MIRROR

1. **To Remove**
   (a) Perform operation A1.
   (b) Loosely refit the regulating handle and raise the glass to the fully closed position.
   (c) Release the nut retaining the mirror to the door, using a bent shafted ring spanner.
   (d) Withdraw the mirror from the door.

2. **To Refit**
   Reverse the removal procedure.

Fig. 39. Refitting anti-burst door lock (Spitfire Mk. 2 and 3)

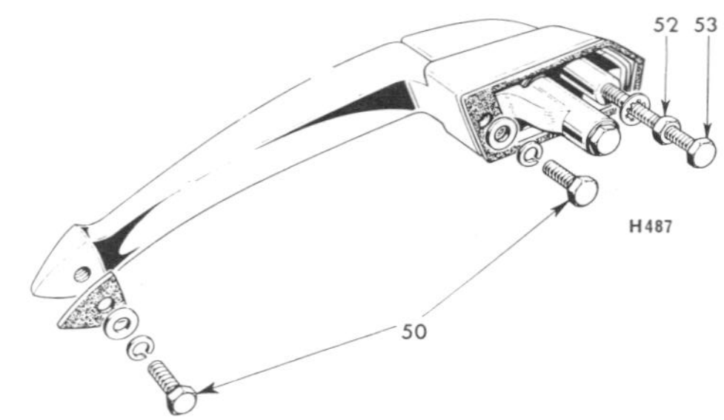

Fig. 40. Push button adjustment (Spitfire Mk. 2 and 3)

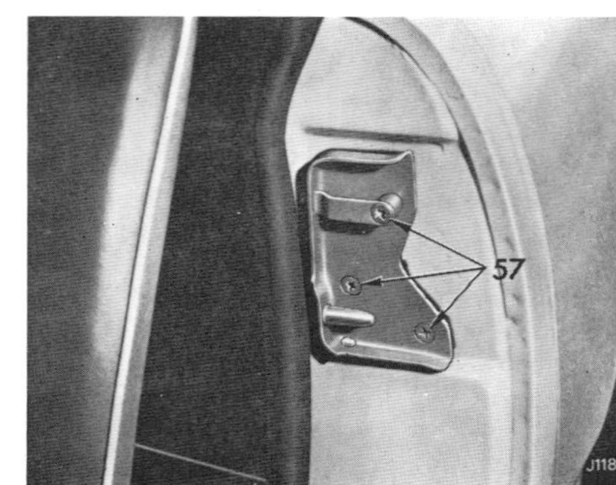

Fig. 41. Anti-burst striker plate (Spitfire Mk. 2 and 3)

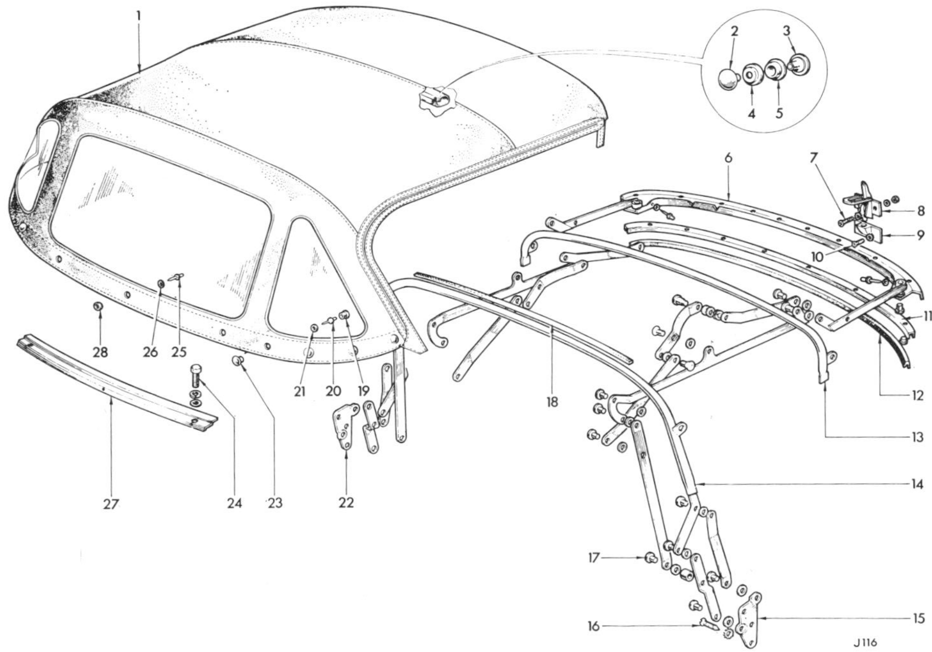

1 Hood sewn assembly	15 Mounting plate — hood frame to body
2 Button } Hood to intermediate hoodstick	16 Setscrew — mounting plate
3 Stud	17 Rivet — securing links
4 Socket	18 Strip — main hoodstick
5 Eyelet	19 Stud } Hood to rear deck
6 Header rail	20 Rivet
7 Setscrew — catch to header rail	21 Socket
8 Head catch assembly — hoodsticks	22 Mounting plate — hood frame to body
9 Head catch assembly — windscreen	23 Button
10 Setscrew catch to windscreen	24 Domed bolt — mounting angle to rear deck
11 Header rail — sealing rubber retainer	25 Imex rivet
12 Sealing rubber — header rail	26 Washer — stud and hood to retaining angle
13 Intermediate hoodstick assembly	27 Retaining angle
14 Main hoodstick assembly	28 Stud

Fig. 42. Soft top arrangement (Spitfire Mk. 3)

SOFT TOP

SPITFIRE 4 AND MK. 2

To Remove

1. Release the wire loop (1) from the hook (2) which is exposed by pushing the "A" post rubber forward, pull each corner edge away from the snap fastener (3) (Fig. 44).
2. Release the reinforced front edge of the fabric (4) away from the leading edge of the windscreen cappings (5) (Fig. 45).
3. Unhook the reinforced rear edge (6) from the lip of the bracket (7) at each side, and release each corner edge from the snap fasteners (Fig. 46).
4. With the aid of a second operator, withdraw the frame complete with fabric by turning each locking sleeve (8) (Fig. 47).

To Refit

Reverse the removal procedure.

SPITFIRE MK. 3

To Remove (Fig. 42)

1. Release the fasteners securing the fabric to the second hood stick and the toggles or catch levers retaining the hood to the windscreen header rail.
2. Release the fasteners (four each side) securing the edges of the hood to the body.
3. Remove two domed-head bolts and washers securing the soft top retaining plate to the rear deck.
4. With the aid of a second operator, remove four hex-headed screws and two counter-sunk screws and shakeproof washers securing the mounting plates (15) and (22) on the hoodsticks to the retaining plates in the "B" post. Lift off the soft top complete assembly.

To Refit

Reverse the removal procedure.

There is provision for limited adjustment between the hood stick mounting brackets and the retaining plates in the "B" post.

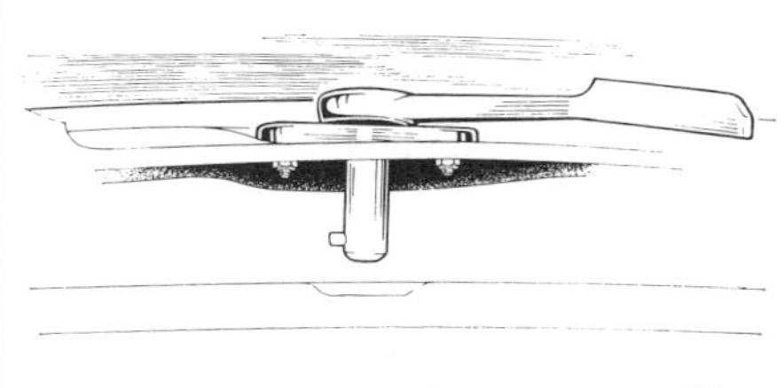

Fig. 43. Hood catch lever (From Commission No. FD 20001 L.H.S. and FD 15701 R.H.S.)

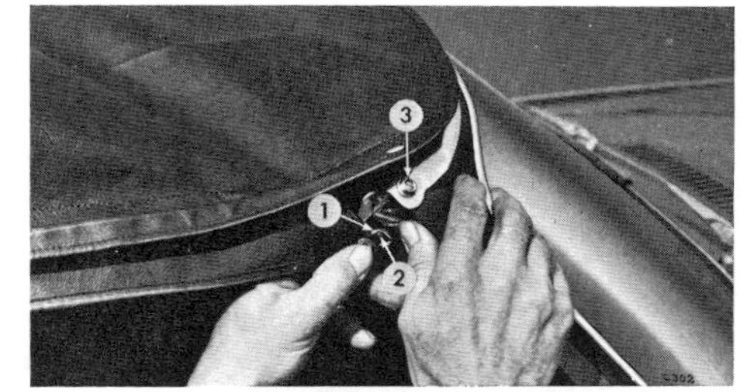

Fig. 44. Releasing the wire loop

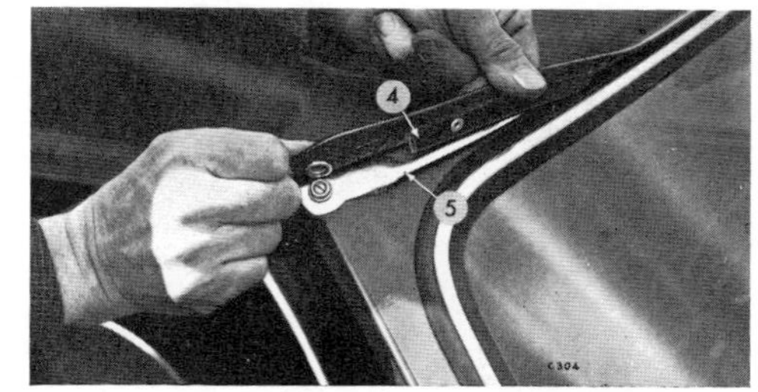

Fig. 45. Releasing the reinforced front edge

Fig. 46. Releasing the reinforced rear edge

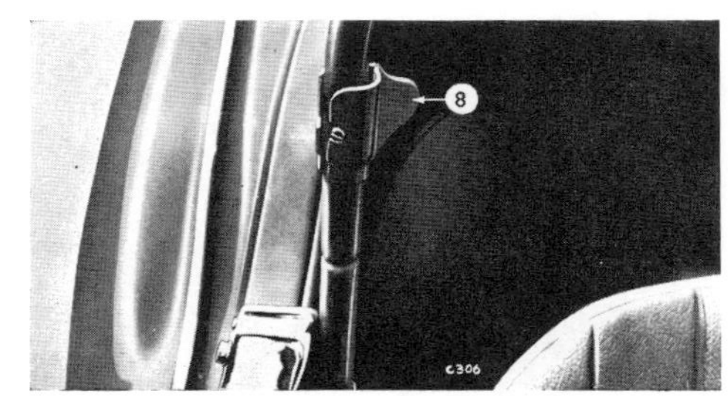

Fig. 47. Centre frame location

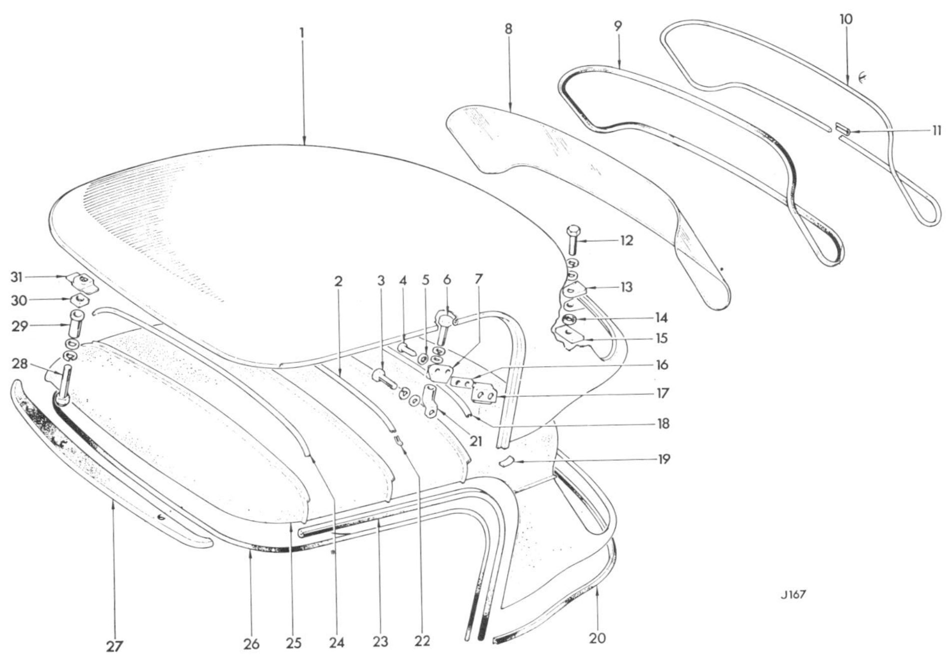

1 Hard top assembly
2 Centre listing rod
3 Domed bolt — tie bar to body
4 Bolt — bracket to roof
5 Shakeproof washer
6 Domed bolt — tie-bar to bracket
7 Fixing bracket — roof to body side
8 Backlight glass
9 Backlight glazing rubber
10 Glazing rubber insert
11 Clip — insert
12 Domed bolt — roof to rear deck
13 Finisher
14 Rubber washer
15 Tapped plate
16 Tapped plate
17 Tapped plate retainer
18 Rear listing rod
19 'B' post sealing pad
20 Weatherseal — roof to deck panel
21 Tie-bar — hard top to body side
22 Locating clip — listing rod
23 Sealing rubber — cantrail
24 Front listing rod
25 Headlining assembly
26 Snap-on finisher — headlining
27 Sealing rubber — hard top to windscreen
28 Domed bolt — hard top to windscreen
29 Distance tube
30 Square nut
31 Nut retainer

Fig. 48. Hardtop arrangement (Spitfire Mk. 3)

HARD TOP (OPTIONAL)

SPITFIRE 4 MK. 2 AND MK. 3

To Remove (Fig. 48)

1. Remove the domed-head bolts and washers securing the hard top header rail to the windscreen panel (Fig. 50).
2. Unscrew the domed-head bolts securing the hard top side brackets to the door pillar brackets (Figs. 51 and 52)
3. Remove the domed-head bolts, washers and finishers securing the rear of the hard top to the rear deck panel (Fig. 49).
4. With the aid of a second operator, lift off the hard top assembly and collect the rubber washers from the rear deck panel.

To Refit

Reverse the removal procedure.

HARD TOP – ROOF LINING

The instructions for maintenance, removing and refitting the roof lining, are basically similar to those given for the saloon and coupe models, see page 5.219. Additional to the roof lining, the hard top backlight lower strip is to be removed and refitted.

The colour coding of the listing rails is as follows:

(Viewed from the front of the vehicle).

Front	—	Green
Centre	—	White
Rear	—	Brown

Fig. 49. Rear deck attachment

Fig. 50. Top header rail attachment

Fig. 51. Side bracket attachment (Spitfire Mk. 3)

Fig. 52. Side bracket attachment (Spitfire 4 and Mk. 2)

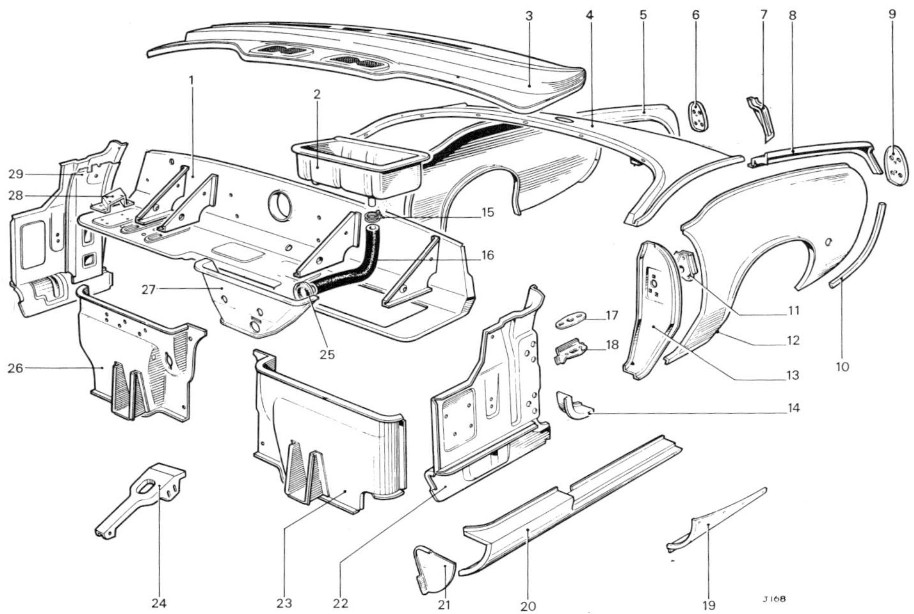

1 Dash shelf panel
2 Battery box assembly
3 Front deck panel
4 Rear deck panel
5 Rear wing — inner panel
6 Rear side lamp — filler plate
7 Support assembly
8 Rear wing — inner panel
9 Rear side lamp — filler plate
10 Rear wing joint finisher
11 Lock striker retainer
12 Rear wing outer panel
13 'B' post outer panel
14 'A' post outer lower panel
15 Clip — drain tube
16 Drain tube
17 Bonnet locating plate
18 Bonnect location bracket
19 Outer sill stone guard
20 Outer sill panel
21 Filler panel — sill
22 'A' post panel
23 Dash front panel — L.H.
24 Channel assembly — steering column
25 Drain tube grommet
26 Dash front panel — R.H.
27 Air box assembly
28 Wiper motor mounting bracket
29 'A' post panel

Fig. 53. Body side details

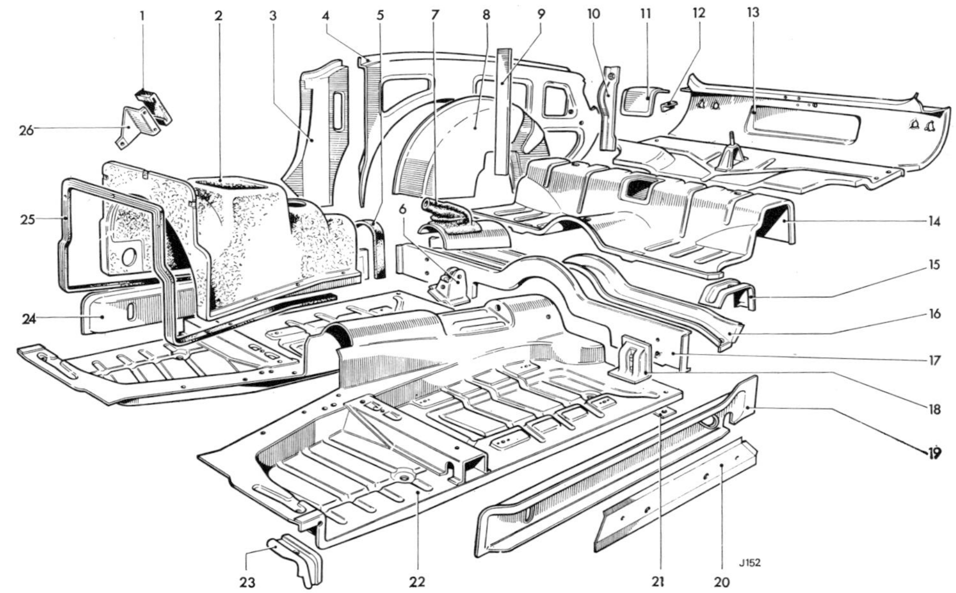

1 Foot rest rubber pad
2 Gearbox cover assembly
3 Front outer — rear wheelarch panel
4 Wheelarch outer panel
5 Gearbox cover — rear seal
6 Handbrake pivot bracket
7 Grommet and millboard assembly
8 Wheelarch inner panel assembly
9 Wheelarch to rear deck — support
10 Fuel tank — support bracket
11 Rear spring access cover
12 Rear valance to wheelarch — angle
13 Rear valance panel assembly
14 Rear seat pan assembly
15 Body mounting — reinforcement
16 Heelboard crossmember assembly
17 Heelboard panel
18 Radius arm mounting bracket assembly
19 Inner sill panel assembly
20 Sill reinforcement panel
21 Safety harness fixing — reinforcement plate
22 Main floor assembly
23 Dash front — outer mounting bracket
24 Sill inner panel
25 Gearbox cover seal — top and sides
26 Gearbox footrest

Fig. 54. Floor panel details

WINDSCREEN DETAILS

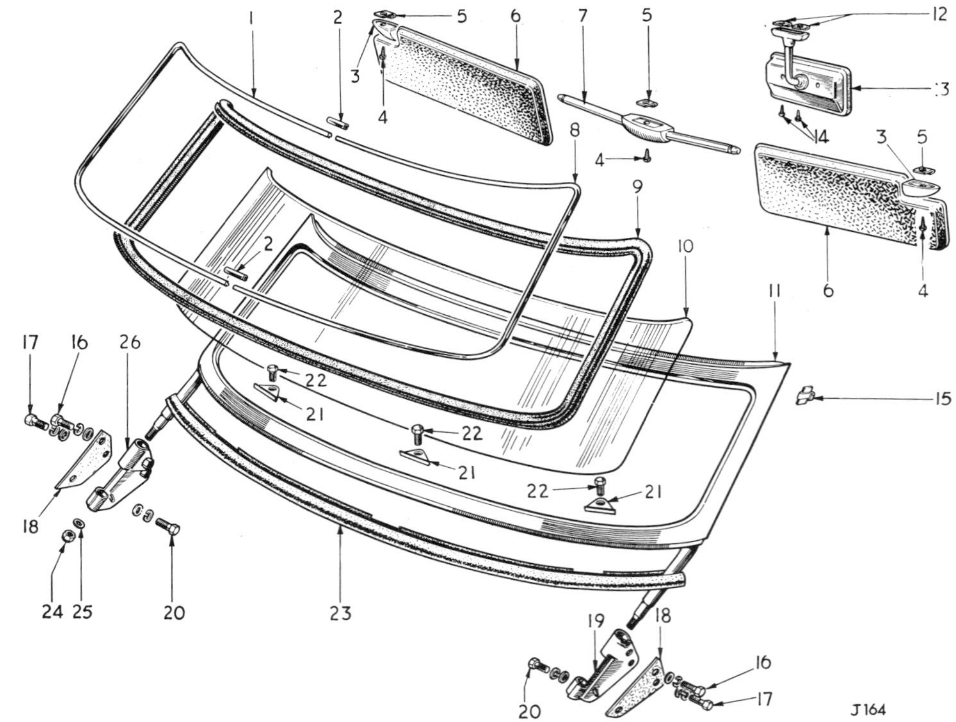

1 Moulding
2 Cover plate
3 Visor mounting
4 Screw } Visor attachment
5 Spirefix } Visor attachment
6 Sun visor
7 Visor support
8 Moulding
9 Rubber weatherstrip
10 Windscreen glass
11 Windscreen frame
12 Mirror stem packing piece
13 Interior mirror
14 Screws — mirror attachment
15 Bracket — windscreen to soft top
16 Bolt — mounting bracket
17 Bolt — mounting bracket
18 Packing piece
19 Mounting bracket
20 Bolt — mounting bracket
21 Cover plate
22 Bolt — windscreen to body
23 Sealing rubber
24 Nyloc nut
25 Washer
26 Mounting bracket

Fig. 55. Windscreen details (Spitfire 4 and Mk. 2)

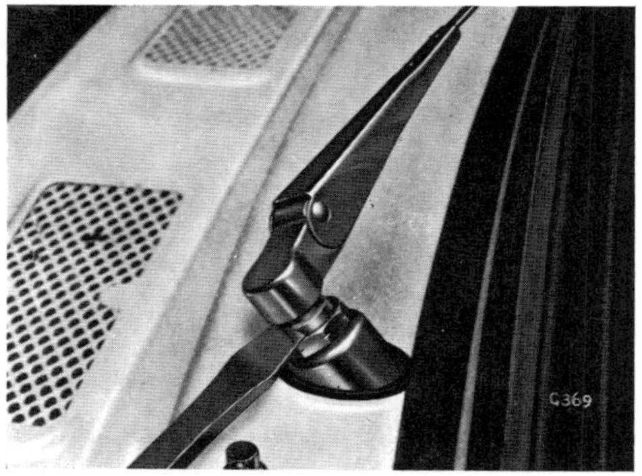

Fig. 56. Removing wiper arms

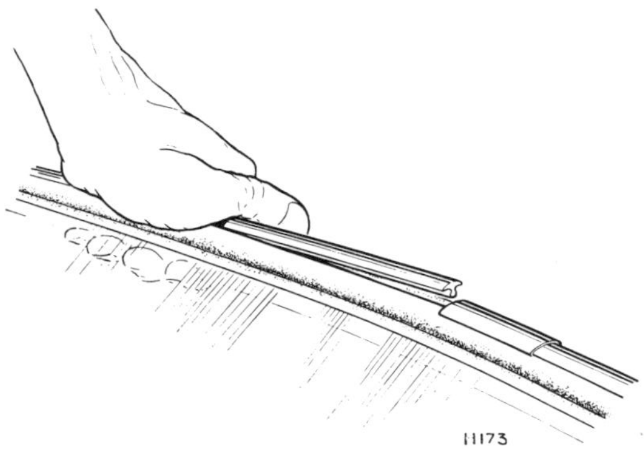

Fig. 57. Fitting windscreen moulding

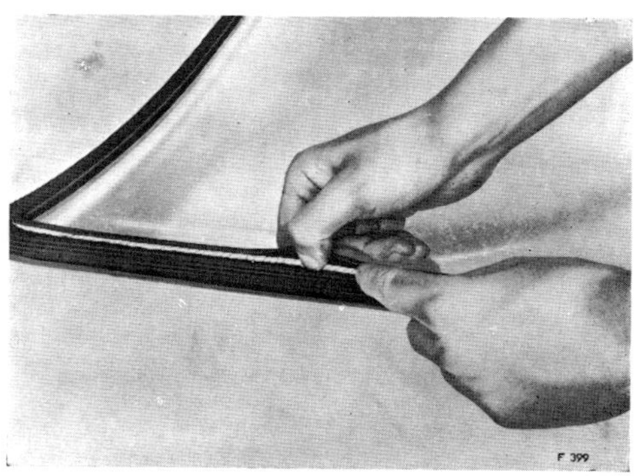

Fig. 58. Inserting cord in weatherstrip

WINDSCREEN

SPITFIRE 4, MK. 2 AND MK. 3

To Remove

Using a thin wedge of hardwood, with the point inserted under the rubber, break the Seelastik seal round the outer edge of the windscreen sealing rubber.

Prise off the windscreen wiper arms (Fig. 56). With a second operator steadying the glass from the outside, sit in the passenger's seat, place one foot against the glass and push out. Use a soft foot pad to avoid scratching the glass.

Examine the weatherstrip for evidence of deterioration and renew if necessary. Should the finisher strip need replacing, pull it out of the weatherstrip and push a new finisher strip, with the joint at the top, into the groove in the weatherstrip (Fig. 57).

To Refit

1. Use petrol or white spirit to remove the old sealing compound from the windscreen aperture edge.
2. Fit the weatherstrip to the windscreen with its joint at the bottom. Seal the rubber to the glass.
3. Insert a thick cord, of greater length than the periphery of the glass, into the inner channel of the rubber strip and permit the ends to protrude from the bottom edge of the weatherstrip (Fig. 58).
4. Apply a soapy water solution to the flange of the windscreen aperture. Position the windscreen centrally in the aperture after passing the ends of the cord through into the vehicle. With a second operator maintaining steady pressure on the outside of the glass pull the ends of the cord to bring the lip of the rubber over the body flange. It may be necessary to strike the outside of the weatherstrip with a rubber faced hammer to seat the windscreen properly.
5. Withdraw the cord completely and seal the weatherstrip to the body, pressing it firmly into contact. Remove surplus sealing compound using a cloth moistened with petrol or white spirit. Do not allow any excess liquid to seep into the joint and destroy the bond. Refer to Dust and Water Sealing, page 5·601.

WINDSCREEN FRAME

SPITFIRE 4, MK. 2 AND MK. 3

To Remove (Fig. 55)

1. Remove the sun visors and pull off the draught welting from the screen pillars.
2. Take out three bolts (22) and cover plates (21) securing the windscreen frame to the front deck panel.
3. Release the parcel tray outer fixing, pull back the corner of the tray and remove one nut (24) and washer (25) from the bottom of each screen pillar (11) (Fig. 59).
4. Slacken the bolts (16) and (17) which are accessible when the door is opened (Fig. 60).
5. With the aid of a second operator, lift out the windscreen frame assembly (11).
   Remove the rubber weatherstrip (23) from the back of the windscreen assembly.

To Refit

Remove the old sealing compound from the contacting surfaces of the windscreen weatherstrip and the front deck panel. Apply a fresh piece of seal-a-strip along the underside of the rubber and refit the windscreen frame assembly.

There is provision for limited adjustment between the windscreen frame and the door glass.

If adjustment is required, slacken the bolts (16), (17) and (20) on both sides of the car, raise both door glasses, and move the top of the windscreen to provide a uniform clearance between the glass and the windscreen. Re-tighten the bolts.

Seal the windscreen frame to the rubber with Seelastik. Refer to Dust and Water Sealing Section page 5·601.

Finally refit the draught welting to the screen pillars.

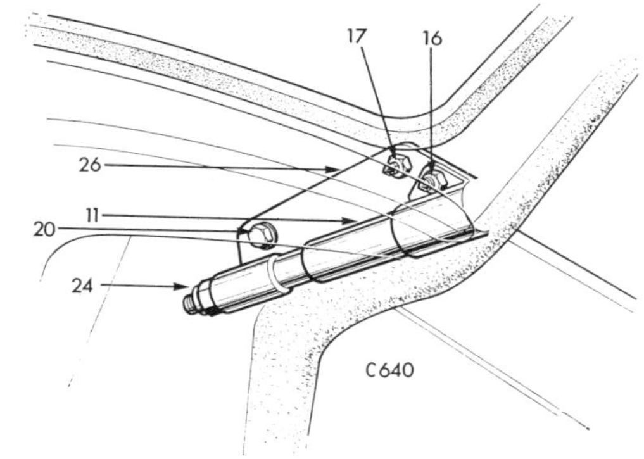

Fig. 59. Screen pillar fixing

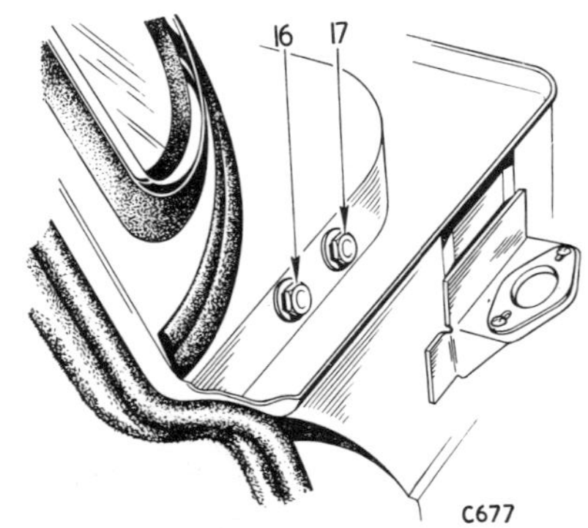

Fig. 60. Screen pillar upper fixing

Fig. 61. Removing the windscreen

FACIA DETAILS

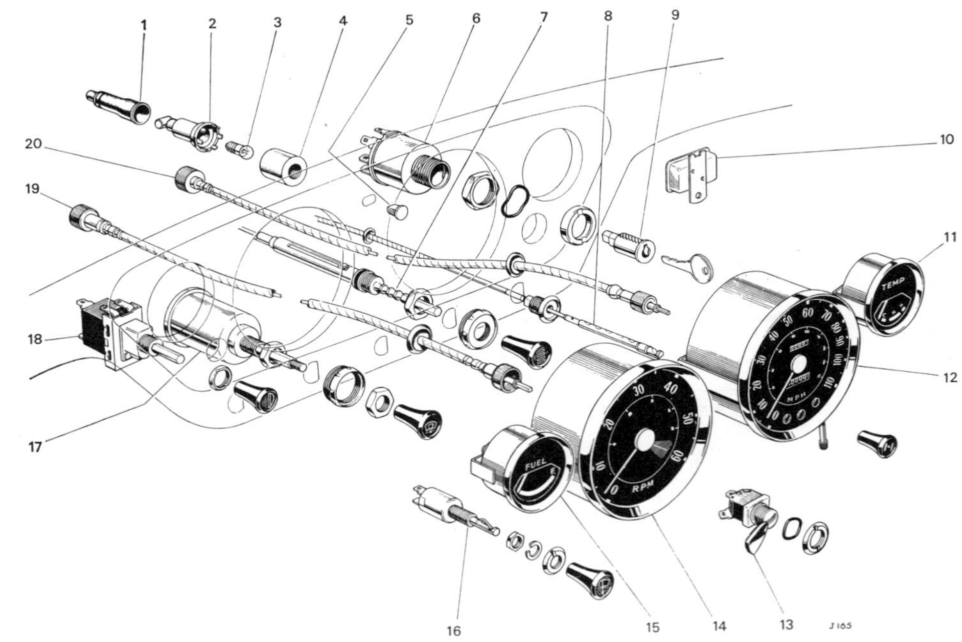

1	Sleeve	11	Temperature gauge
2	Bulb holder	12	Speedometer
3	Bulb	13	Blower switch
4	Lamp body	14	Tachometer
5	Lens	15	Fuel gauge
6	Starter/ignition switch	16	Wiper switch
7	Heat control cable	17	Windscreen washer pump
8	Choke cable	18	Lighting switch
9	Ignition barrel	19	Tachometer drive cable
10	Speedo voltage stabilizer	20	Speedometer drive cable

Fig. 62. Instruments, switches and controls (Spitfire Mk. 3)

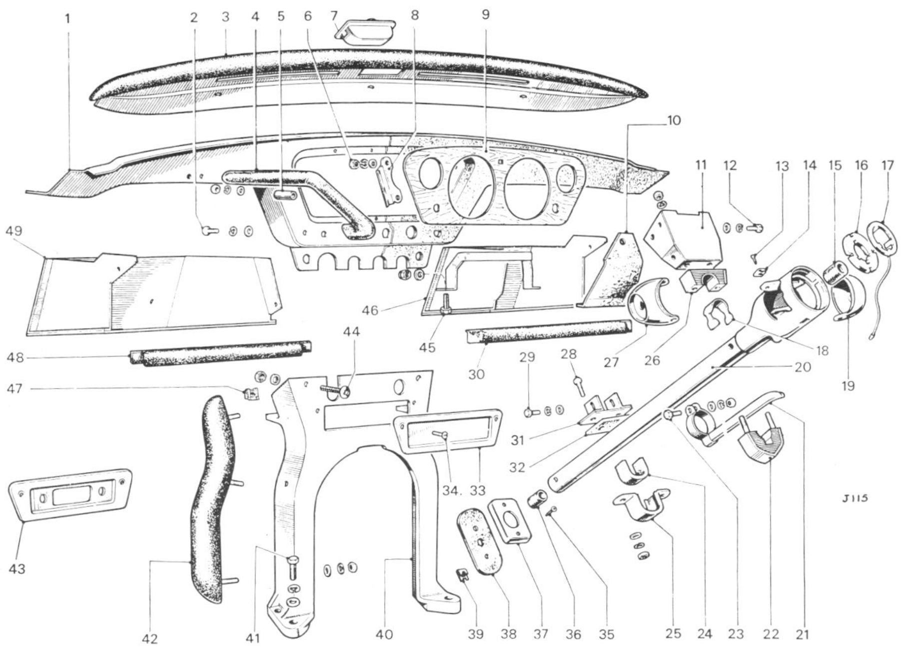

1	Panel assembly	18	Clasp ring	34	Screw — cover attachment
2	Bolt	19	Escutcheon	35	Screw
3	Crash pad	20	Steering column cowl	36	Bush — lower column
4	Grab handle	21	Harness cover	37	Retainer
5	Distance piece	22	Upper column clamp	38	Sealing rubber
6	Nut — veneer attachment	23	Bolt	39	Fix nut
7	Ash tray	24	Felt packing	40	Gearbox support bracket
8	Veneer clamp bracket	25	Lower clamp	41	Bolt
9	Veneer instrument panel	26	Clamp	42	Trim roll
10	Filler panel	27	Escutcheon	43	Cover plate
11	Support bracket	28	Bolt	44	Screw
12	Bolt	29	Bolt	45	Bolt
13	Screw	30	Trim roll	46	Parcel tray
14	Fix nut	31	Support bracket	47	Fix nut
15	Steering column bush	32	Felt packing	48	Trim roll
16	Slip ring	33	Cover plate	49	Parcel tray
17	Cable assembly				

Fig. 63. Facia arrangement (Spitfire Mk. 3)

FACIA COMPONENTS

SPITFIRE 4, MK. 2 AND MK. 3

PARCEL TRAY PASSENGERS SIDE

To Remove (Fig. 64)

1. Remove four cross/recess screws (1) and two hex/headed screws (2) washers and nuts.
2. Pull the parcel tray away from the dash.

To Refit

Reverse the removal procedure.

PARCEL TRAY DRIVER'S SIDE

To Remove (Fig. 65)

1. Remove four cross/recess screws (1) and three hex/headed screws (2), washers and nuts.
2. Detach the speedometer trip cable and manoeuvre the parcel tray away from the dash.

To Refit

Reverse the removal procedure.

FACIA SUPPORT BRACKET

To Remove (Fig. 66)

1. Remove four bolts (41) and washers securing the bracket to the floor.
2. Remove two cross/recess screws (44) securing the bracket to the facia.
3. Lift the support bracket clear.

To Refit

Reverse the removal procedure.

INSTRUMENT PANEL

To allow access to the instruments, the veneered instrument panel can be removed clear of the facia.

To Remove (Fig. 63)

1. Isolate the battery.
2. Remove both parcel trays as previously described.
3. Working behind the instrument panel, remove two clamp plates (8) (one each side of the panel), these are retained by four nuts (6) and washers.
4. Lift out the panel.

To Refit

Reverse the removal procedure.

INSTRUMENTS, SWITCHES AND CONTROLS

The procedure for removal and refitting of the above, is similar to Herald and Vitesse, refer to page 5·239.

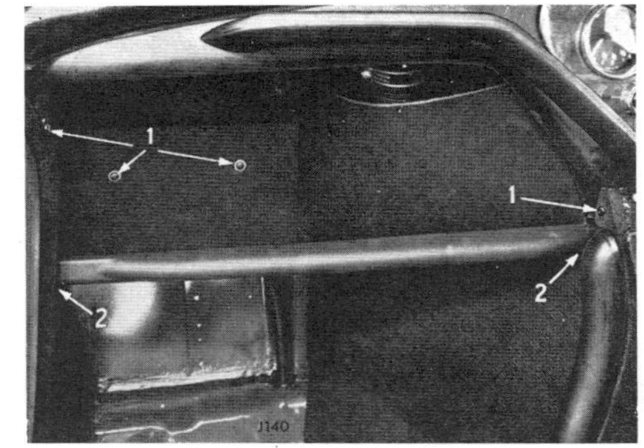

Fig. 64. Parcel tray passenger side

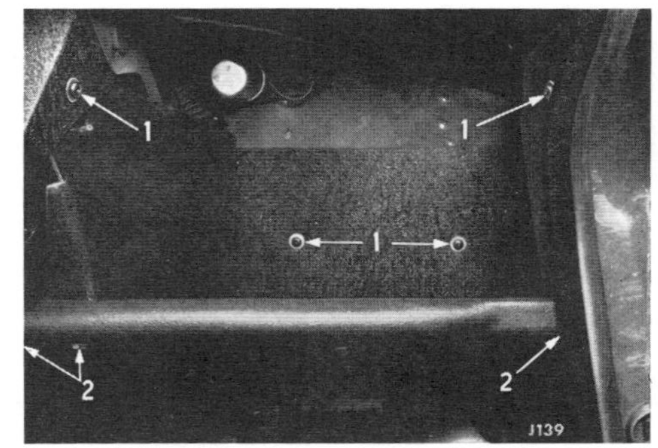

Fig. 65. Parcel tray driver's side

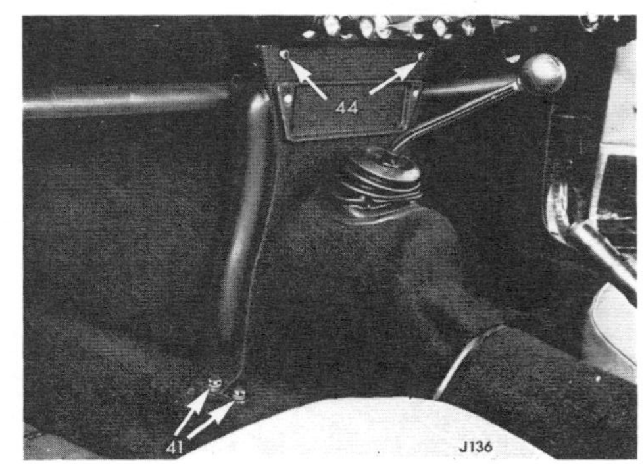

Fig. 66. Facia support bracket

HEATER AND VENTILATION SYSTEM

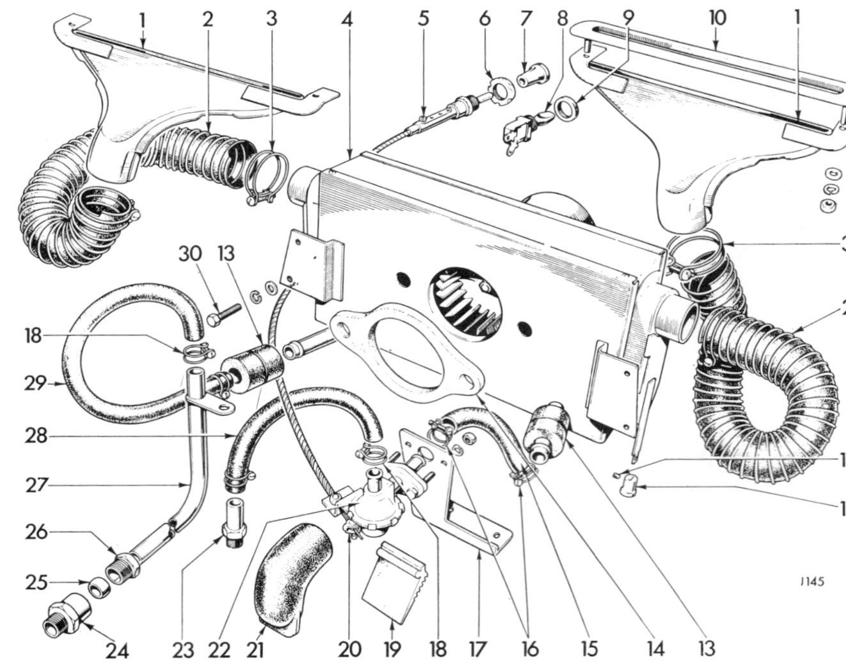

1	Demister nozzle	16	Hose clip
2	Air hose	17	Mounting bracket
3	Hose clip	18	Hose clip
4	Heater unit	19	Drain flap (fitted from April 1964)
5	Heat control assembly	20	Water valve lever
6	Bezel	21	Drain elbow (fitted up to April 1964)
7	Control knob	22	Water control valve
8	Blower switch	23	Adaptor — cylinder head
9	Bezel	24	Adaptor — water pump
10	Demister finisher	25	Olive
11	Screw	26	Nut
12	Flap knob	27	Water return pipe
13	Sponge packing	28	Water hose
14	Sealing ring	29	Water hose
15	Water hose	30	Bolt — heater attachment

Fig. 67. Heater unit arrangement (Spitfire 4 and Mk. 2)

Fig. 68. Heater pipe details (Spitfire Mk. 3)

Fig. 69. Water control valve

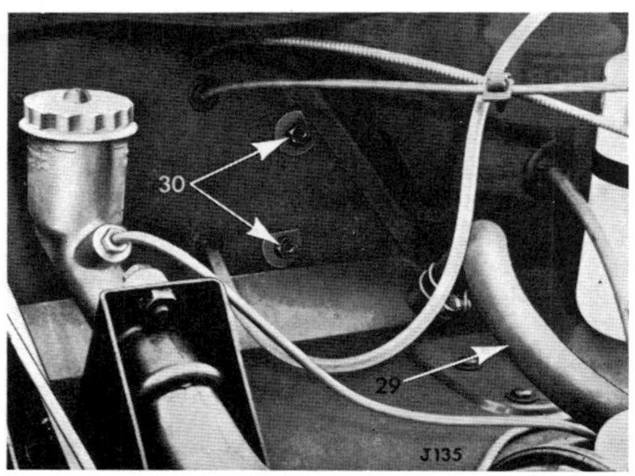

Fig. 70. Heater unit to body attachment

HEATER UNIT

SPITFIRE 4, MK. 2 AND MK. 3

To Remove (Fig. 67)

1. Isolate the battery and drain the cooling system.
2. Disconnect the heater hoses (15) and (29) from the heater box pipes (Fig. 69). Take out two screws securing the coil and water valve mounting bracket to the dash shelf, move the bracket (17) complete with valve away from the dash.
3. Working inside the car, release the facia support bracket by removing four hex/headed bolts (41) and two cross/recess screws (44) (Fig. 66). Lift the bracket clear.
4. Remove the passenger's and driver's parcel shelf, page 5·529.
5. Remove the small bracket clamping the choke and heater cable, located on the R.H. side of the heater box under the facia.
6. Disconnect the demister hoses (2) from the heater box and the cables to the heater blower motor.
7. Disconnect the speedometer and tachometer drive cables from the back of the instruments. Pull the cables through the heater box into the engine compartment, taking care not to damage the grommets during this operation.
8. Remove four bolts (30) retaining the heater box to the dash.
9. Plug the heater box pipes to ensure that any water left in the heater matrix is not spilled. Finally, manoeuvre the heater from behind the facia.

To Refit

Reverse the removal procedure. A second operation is required when refitting the four bolts (30) (Fig. 70). Refer to Dust and Water Sealing, page 5·601.

WATER CONTROL VALVE

To Remove (Figs. 67 and 69)

Drain the cooling system.

Disconnect the heater hoses (15) and (28) and temperature control cable (33) from the water valve (22). Remove the water valve by taking out two bolts (34) and washers.

To Refit

Reverse the removal procedure and reconnect the temperature control cable as follows:

Push the control cable (33) fully in and assemble it to the water valve. Turn the valve to the "OFF" position and retighten the trunnion nut.

NOTE: The water control valve is serviced only by replacement.

HEATER BLOWER MOTOR

To Remove (Fig. 72)

Remove the heater unit. Take out six screws arrowed (Fig. 71) securing the inner and outer heater box. Loosen the brass nut (4) in the centre of the impellor. Withdraw the impellor from the blow motor shaft. Unscrew the exposed nuts (2) and remove the blower motor (1) from the outer heater box.

To Refit

Reverse the removal procedure.

NOTE: The blower motor assembly is serviced only by replacement.

Fig. 71. Heater box attachment

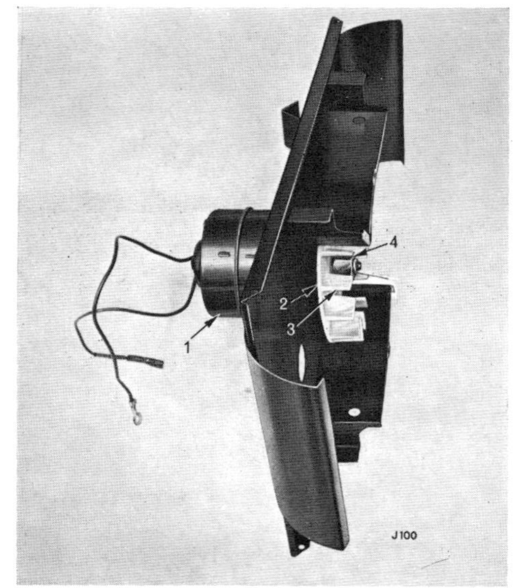

Fig. 72. Heater blower motor and impellor

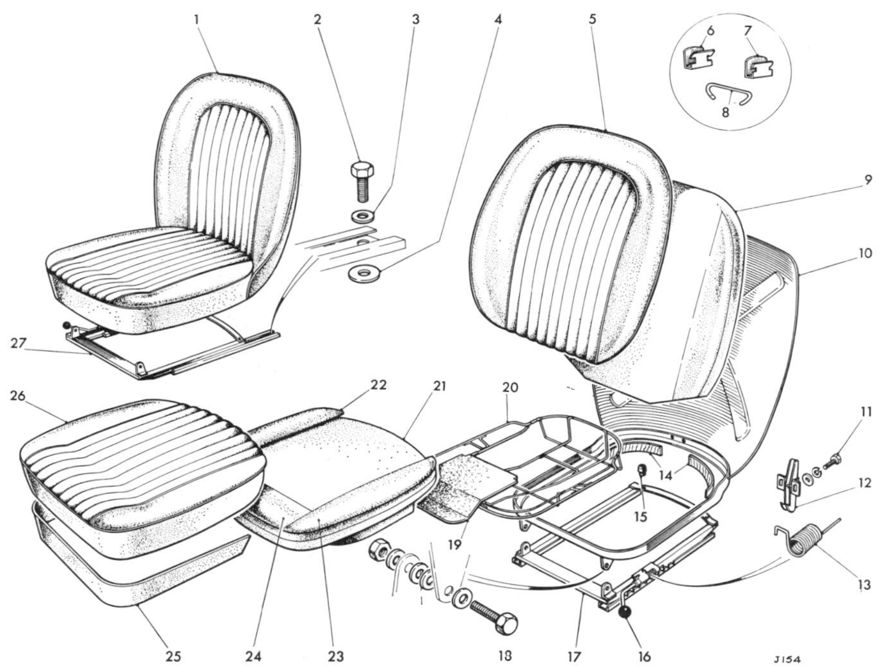

1 Front seat assembly	15 Rubber plug — seat slide to seat
2 Setscrew — seat slide to floor	16 Knob — seat slide
3 Plain washer	17 Seat slide assembly
4 Packing washer	18 Setscrew — seat slide to seat
5 Squab cover assembly	19 Cushion base
6 Trim clip	20 Cushion frame assembly
7 Trim clip	21 Cushion pad
8 Hog ring	22 Top cushion pad
9 Rubberised hair pad	23 Top cushion pad
10 Seat frame assembly	24 Front cushion pad
11 Setscrew — clip to seat	25 Cushion border foam
12 Seat clip	26 Cushion cover assembly
13 Catch rod spring	27 Seat slide assembly
14 Tacking piece — seat squab	

Fig. 73. Front seat details (Spitfire Mk. 3)

SEATS

SPITFIRE 4, MK. 2 AND MK. 3

To Remove (Fig. 73)

Move the seat fully forward and remove one bolt (2) from the rear of each channel. Push the seat fully rearwards and remove one bolt from the front of each channel. Lift the seat clear, complete with seat slide channel.

To Refit

Reverse the removal procedure.

Fore and Aft—Adjustment (Fig. 75)

The driver's and passenger's seats are adjustable for leg reach by lifting the lever at the outer side of each seat and sliding the seat to the desired position. Allow the lever to re-engage in the nearest adjustment notch.

On Spitfire Mk. 3 both seats will tilt forward to provide access to the rear compartment, when the clip (12) (Fig. 76) at the base of the seat back is released.

SAFETY HARNESS ANCHORAGES

Three-point fixing

SPITFIRE 4, MK. 2 AND MK. 3

To Remove

1. Release the latched hooks on the safety belt from the eye bolts (1) (Fig. 76).
2. Unscrew the pivot bolt and remove the waved washer and the pivot bolt spacer from the wheelarch (3) (Fig. 77).

To Refit

Pass the pivot bolt through the belt strap attachment plate, waved washer and spacer. Refit the assembly to the wheelarch.

NOTE: To convert a Spitfire 4 model from a two-point attachment to a three-point attachment refer to "Safety Harness Kit" fitting instructions part number 568496.

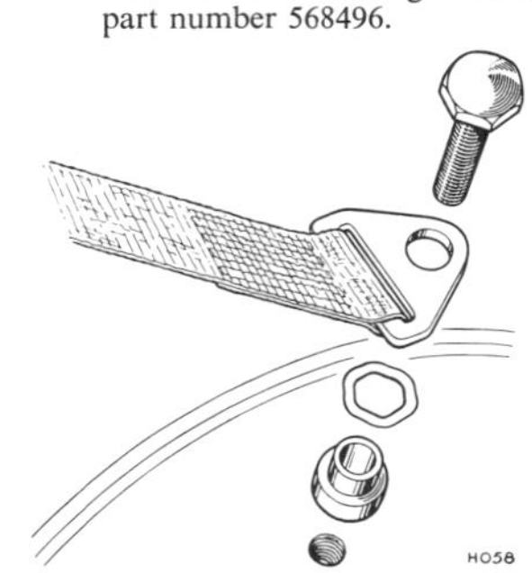

Fig. 74. Exploded view of wheelarch attachment

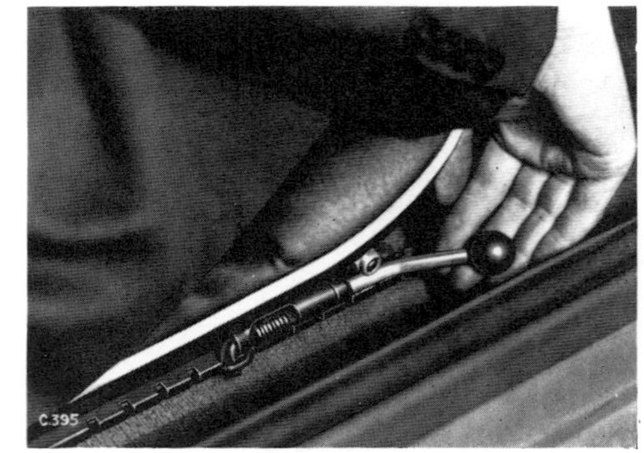

Fig. 75. Seat adjustment lever

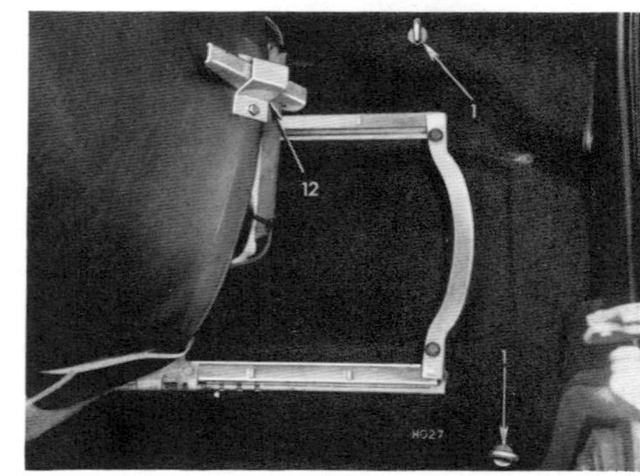

Fig. 76. Harness eye bolt attachment

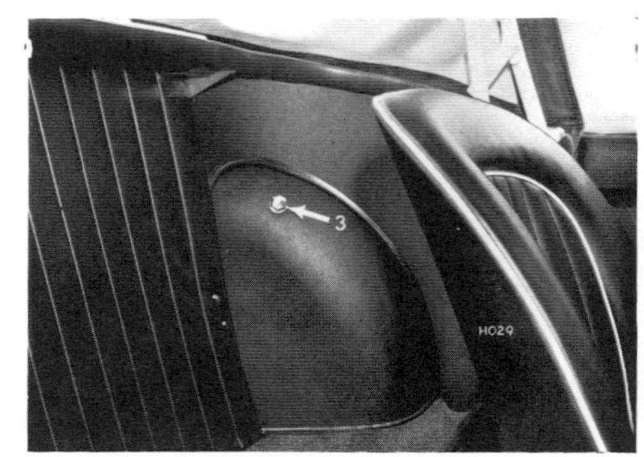

Fig. 77. Wheelarch harness attachment

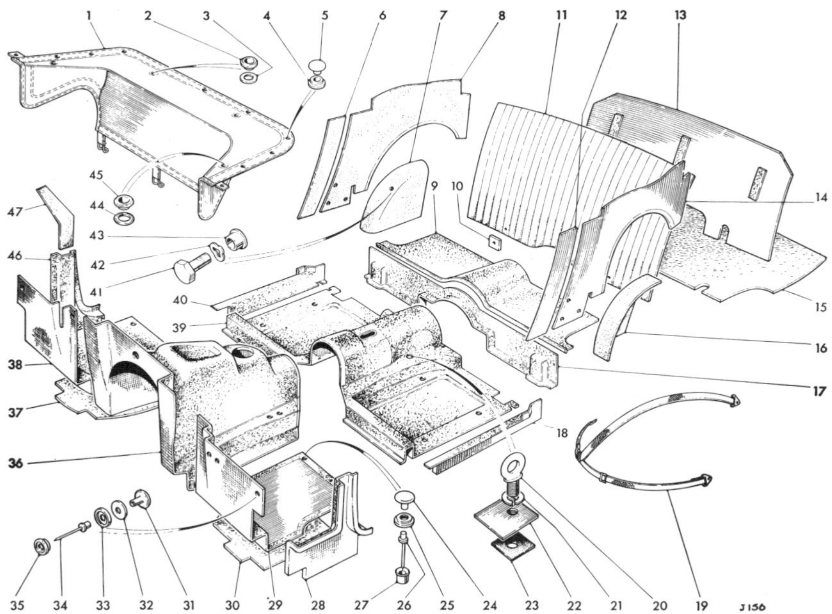

1 Hood stowage cover
2 Sail eyelet
3 'B' ring
4 Socket
5 Button
6 Trim finisher 'B' post
7 Wheelarch cover
8 Rear quarter — trim board
9 Rear seat pan carpet
10 Foam pad — squab board
11 Rear compartment — squab board
12 Trim finisher 'B' post
13 Fuel tank — casing board
14 Rear quarter — trim board
15 Luggage floor mat
16 Wheelarch — carpet
17 Heelboard — carpet
18 Sill carpet — L.H.
19 Safety harness
20 Safety harness — eyebolt
21 Lock washer
22 Reinforcement plate — safety harness
23 Mounting pad — safety harness
24 Button
25 Socket
26 Imex rivet
27 Stud
28 Dash side carpet
29 Front floor carpet
30 Front floor felt
31 Button
32 Plain washer
33 Socket
34 Imex rivet
35 Stud
36 Gearbox cover carpet
37 Front floor felt
38 Front floor carpet
39 Rear floor carpet
40 Sill carpet
41 Harness — bolt
42 Waved washer
43 Spacer
44 'B' ring
45 Sail eyelet
46 Dash side carpet
47 'A' post finisher trim

Fig. 78. Floor coverings and trim panels (Spitfire Mk. 3)

WING MOULDINGS

SPITFIRE 4, MK. 2 AND MK. 3

The wing mouldings are retained by small spring clips on the wing joints.

To Remove

Using a screwdriver from which all sharp edges have been removed, gently lever the mouldings off the clips.

To Refit (Fig. 79)

The clips are forced into position with light blows from a mallet and the mouldings sprung over the clips.

FUEL TANK

SPITFIRE 4, MK. 2 AND MK. 3

To Remove

Isolate the battery. Working inside the luggage compartment, remove the luggage mat and the spare wheel.

Remove the trim casing board (7 screws). Disconnect the cables from the tank unit, and remove the fuel filler pipe and hose from the top of the tank (2 clips).

Disconnect the fuel pipe from the base of the tank and drain the fuel.

Take out five screws (arrowed) (Fig. 80), and lift the tank from the luggage compartment.

To Refit

Reverse the removal procedure.

Fig. 79. Fitting wing mouldings

Fig. 80. Fuel tank attachment

DUST AND WATER SEALING

SPITFIRE RANGE

The following notes and diagrams indicate the locations of sealed joints and serve to familiarise dealers with the necessary materials and techniques employed to render the body shell dust and water proof.

The list of approved sealing compounds has been broken down into sections, appertaining to the progressive body build. The diagrams showing the location of sealed joints (heavy lines) show, in some cases, seams which are sealed with compounds which require curing in heated atmosphere. These compounds are listed under the general term "Plastisol" and are not suitable for application in service. In every case where Plastisol compounds have been used and the seal has failed, Hermetal "Double Bond" Metallic Cream, Docker's Compound or Hermetal Plastic Metal Filler should be used.

The scrap sections in the following pages correspond with the numbers on the diagram showing the complete car.

SEALING COMPOUNDS

COMPOUND	MANUFACTURER	COMPOUND	MANUFACTURER
Glasticon 303 Glasticord 305 and 400 Kelseal 3/315M. Kelseal 305.	Kelseal Ltd., Vogue House, Hanover Square, London, W.1.	Seelastik SR.51 Seelastrip LS.105	Expandite Ltd., Cunard Road Works, London, N.W.10.
Docker's Compound	Docker Bros. Ltd., Rotton Park Street, Birmingham, 16.	Boscoseal B.B. Plastisol Putty S.106.46	B.B. Chemicals, Ulverscroft Road, Leicester.
Supra Dedseal	Supra Chemical & Paint Ltd., Hainge Road, Tipton, Staffs.	Hermetal "Double Bond" Metallic Cream Hermetal Plastic Metal Filler	The Kenilworth Mfg. Co. Ltd., West Drayton, Middlesex.
3M's EC 1168 Mastic Sealer	Minnesota Mining and Manufacturing, 3M House, Wigmore Street, London, W.1.	Dunlop DS.5035/S Sealer	Dunlop Chemical Division, Chester Road, Erdington, Birmingham, 24.

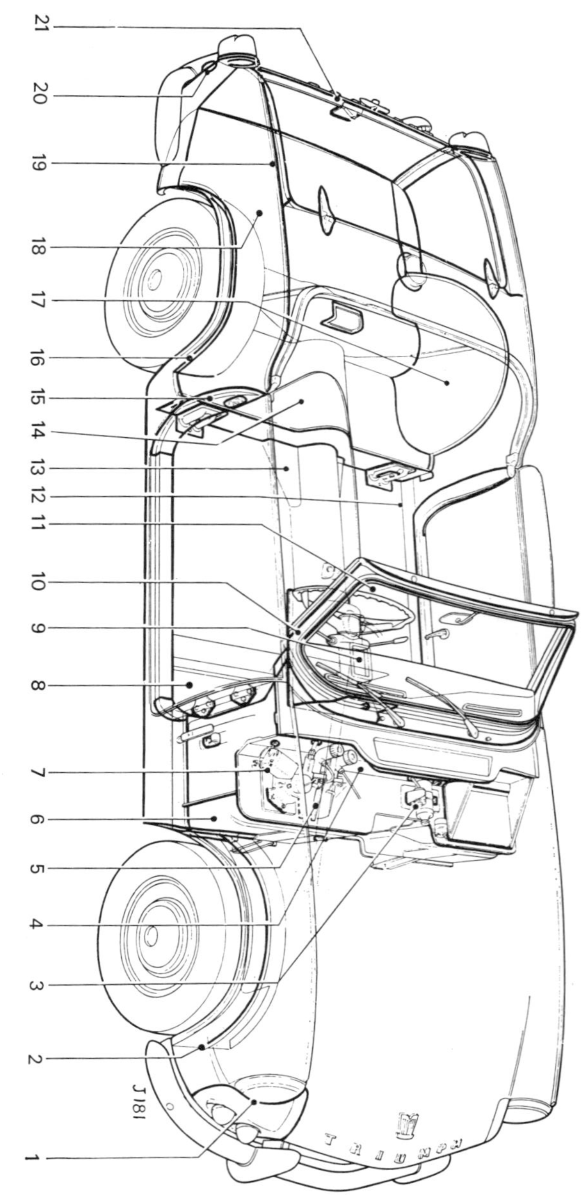

Fig. 1. Location of sealed joints (Spitfire)

Note. The locations given above relate to those numbered in the following pages.

APPROVED SEALING MATERIALS — BODY IN WHITE (UNPAINTED)

APPLICATION	MASTICS	STRIP SEALERS
Spotweld Sealers	553938 Expandite Seelastik (Natural) 559357 3 M's EC 1168	569630 Expandite Seelastrip LS.105 571214 Glasticord $\frac{1}{2} \times \frac{1}{2}$ 400 Strip Sealer
Plugging small holes		569630 Expandite Seelastrip LS.105 554422 Glasticon 303
Pre-Phosphate Sealer	566800-BB. Chemical S.23/206	

PAINT SHOP

APPLICATION	GUN APPLIED SEALERS	PUTTIES	PLASTISOL	REMARKS
Internal joints	514698–Plus Products PD 16/17 562959 Supraseal 574270 – Expandite – Heat Gel Sealer 607/1 574699 – Plus Products HG9 574700 – Dunlop Chemical Products DS5035/S			To be pumped with Graco equipment
External joints			560563 Kelseal 3/315 m. 574701 – Expandite Plastisol 869	Low temperature cure
Plugging small holes		554422 – Glasticon 303	564159 – B.B. Plastisol Putty S.106.46 564158 – Expandite Plastisol Putty	

APPROVED SEALING MATERIALS — TRIM AND FINISH

APPLICATION	MASTICS	STRIP SEALERS	PUTTIES	REMARKS
Windscreen sealers, rubber weatherstrips, plugs and grommets	566600 Seelastik SR.51			
Bolted metal to metal joints, metal mouldings, small holes, screw fixings, etc.	566600 Expandite Seelastik SR.51 554200 Expandite Seelastik M.I.	Prestik Expandite Seelastrip LS.105 Kelseal Strip 305 B.B. Chem. P.41.228	554422 Glasticon 303	Strip sealers have Part Nos. allocated according to section
Special Purpose i.e., paper to metal		Glasticord 400		

AFTER PAINT REPAIRS

APPLICATION	MISCELLANEOUS
External Joints	Docker's Compound Hermetal Double Bond

BODY UNDERSIDE PROTECTORS

APPLICATION	SOLVENT BASED
Sealing external joints and protection of vulnerable areas on underside of body	554419 SUPRA DEDSEAL 557167 BOSCOSEAL 9010 567815 BOSCOSEAL 9020 Plus Products LCHM 10

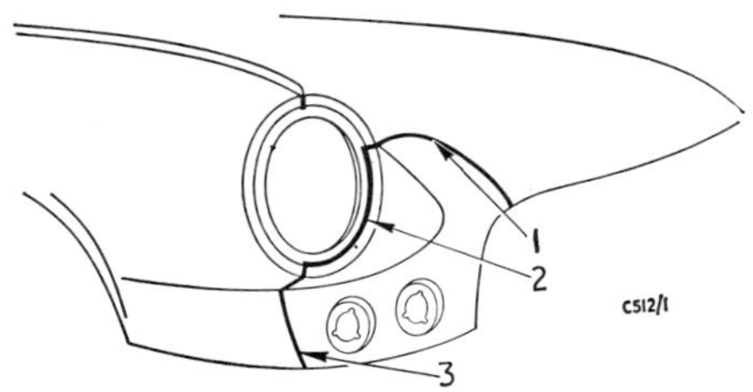

Location 1

1 Bonnet top and front panel (use approved Plastisol)
2 Front panel and lamp aperture (use approved Plastisol)
3 Front panel and wing (use approved Plastisol)

Location 2

1 Wheelarch and wing panel (use approved Plastisol)

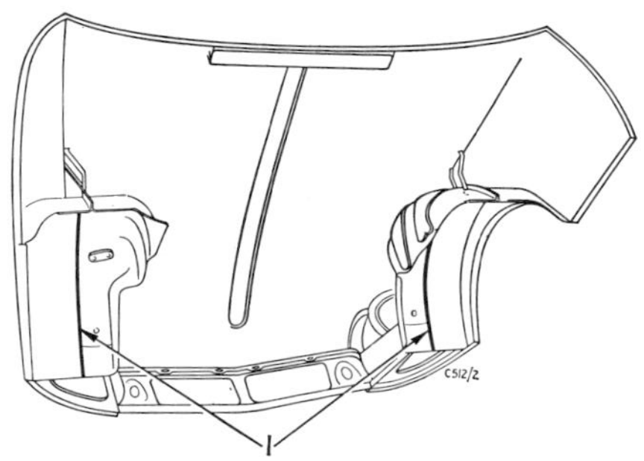

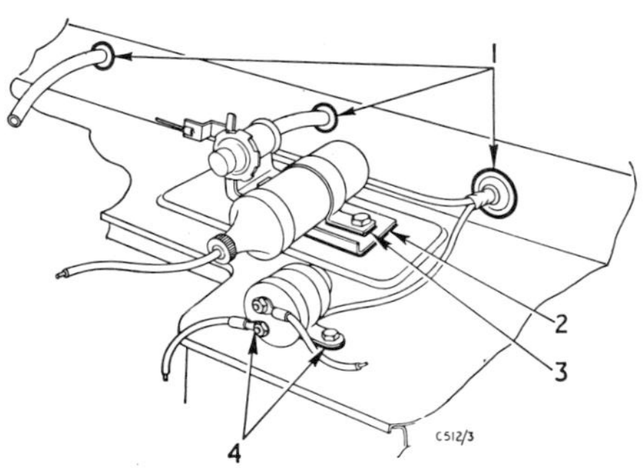

Location 3

1 Grommets and dash panel (use approved Mastics)
2 Heater water valve mounting bracket and dash panel (if fitted) (use approved Mastics)
3 Coil mounting and dash panel (if heater is not fitted) (use approved Mastics)
4 Starter solenoid and dash panel (use approved Mastics)

Location 4

1 Sealing rubber on heater unit or blanking plate and dash panel (use approved Mastics)
2 Sealing rubber on water pipes or rubber plugs and dash panel (use approved Mastics)

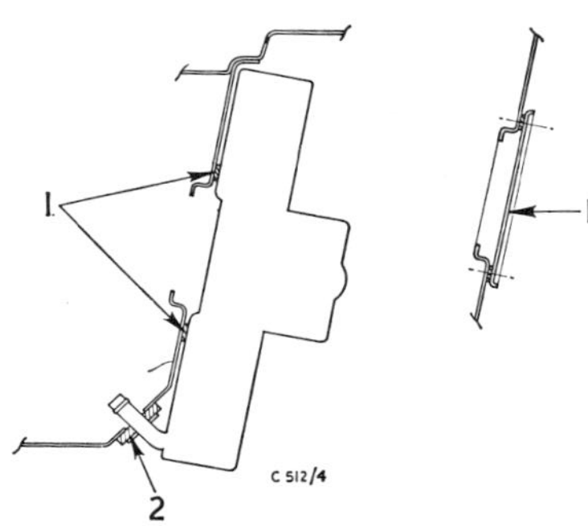

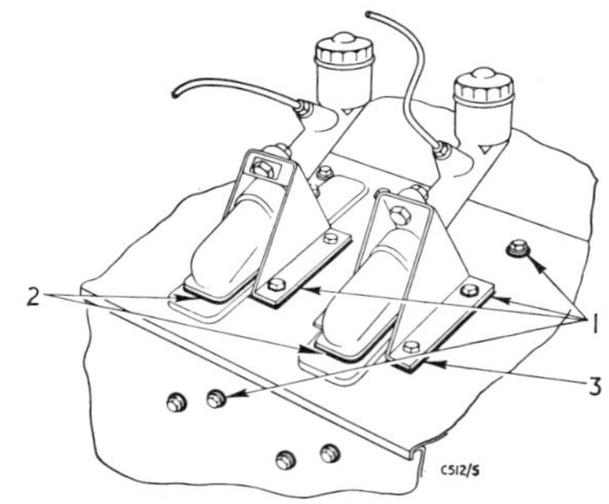

Location 5

1 Master cylinders and pedal fixing bolts (use approved Mastics)
2 Sealing rubbers and mounting bracket (use approved Mastics)
3 Mounting bracket and dash panel (use approved Mastics)

Location 6

1 Steering column grommet and lower dash panel (use approved Mastics)
2 Air box and upper dash panel (use approved Mastics)
3 Scuttle and upper dash panel (use approved Mastics)
4 Scuttle and side dash panel (use approved Mastics)
5 Battery box and upper dash panel (use approved Mastics)
6 Dash side and shelf (use approved Mastics)
7 Dash front and shelf panel (use approved Plastisol)
8 Dash front and side panel (use approved Plastisol)
9 Sill and dash panel (use approved Plastisol)
10 Sill closing panel and sill (use approved Plastisol)

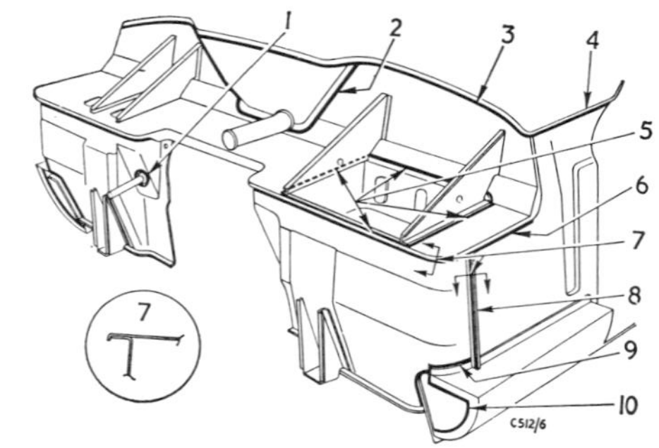

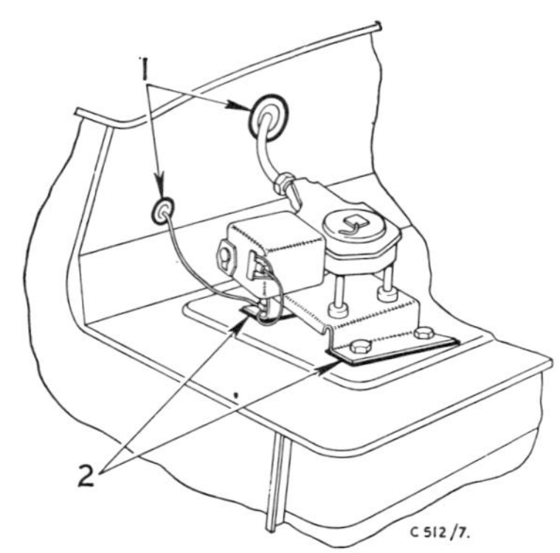

Location 7

1 All grommets and dash panel (use approved Mastics)
2 Wiper motor mounting bracket and dash panel (use approved Mastics)

Location 8

1 Floor and dash side panel (use approved Mastics)
2 Scuttle and dash side (use approved Mastics)
3 Dash side and dash lower panels (use approved Mastics)
4 Floor and dash lower panel (use approved Mastics)
5 Dash side and scuttle (use approved Plastisol)
6 Door seal retaining flange and 'A' post (use approved Mastics)
7 Door hinges and 'A' post (use approved Mastics)
8 Bonnet lock catch and dash side (use approved Mastics)
9 Sill and dash side panel (use approved Plastisol)
10 Sill and 'A' post (use approved Plastisol)

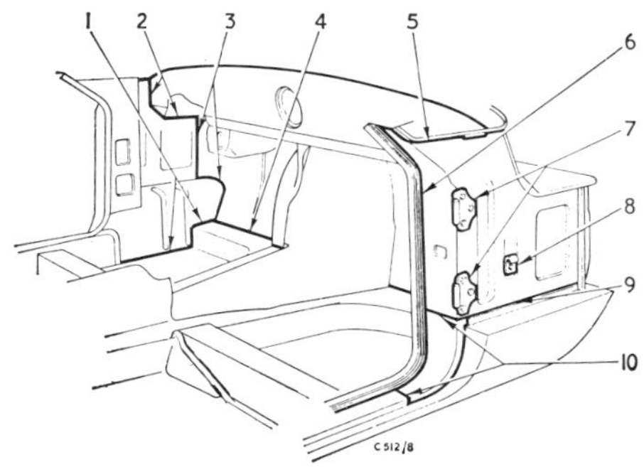

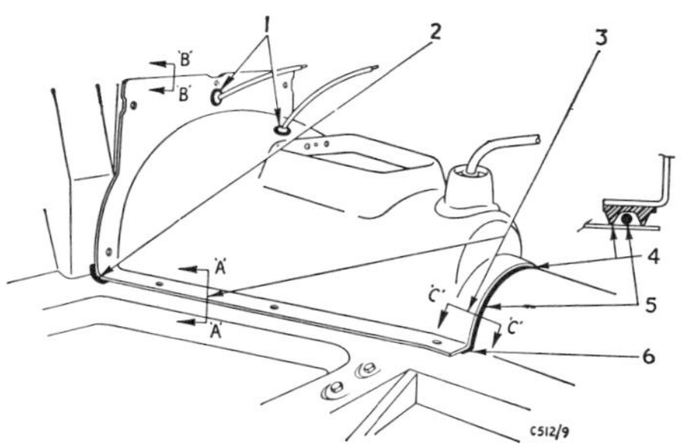

Location 9

1 Grommets and cover (use approved Mastics)
2 Plug corner (Glasticon)
3 Section through cover
4 Secure sealing rubber to cover (Bostik 8GC 122)
5 Apply approved Mastic in rubber channel
6 Double application of approved Mastic at corner and over tunnel

Location 10

1 Weatherstrip retainer and windscreen pillar (use approved Plastisol)

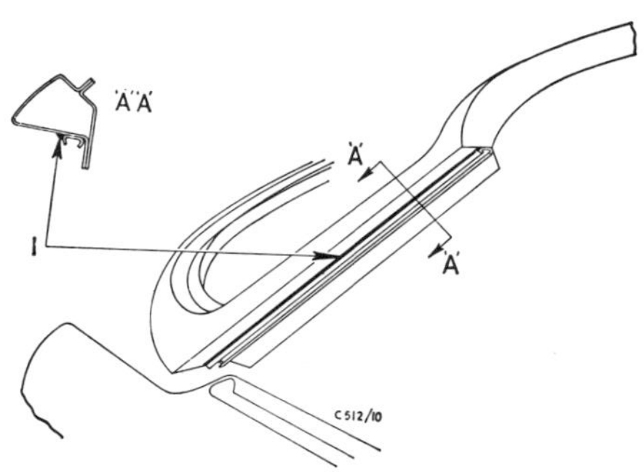

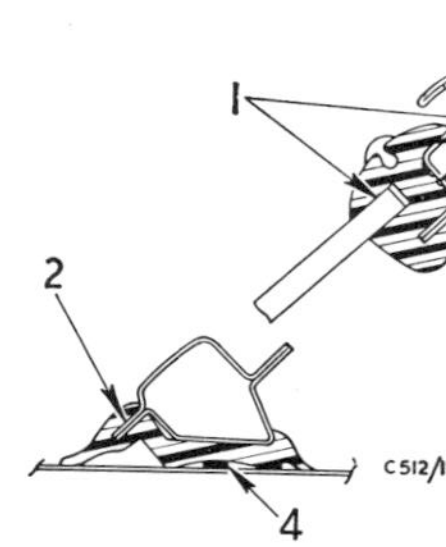

Location 11

1 Glass and rubber, and rubber frame (use approved Mastics)
2 Rubber and frame (use approved Mastics)
3 Header capping and frame (use approved Mastics)
4 Rubber and scuttle (Seelastik ⅛ in. dia.)

Location 12

1 Safety harness reinforcement plate (use approved Mastics)

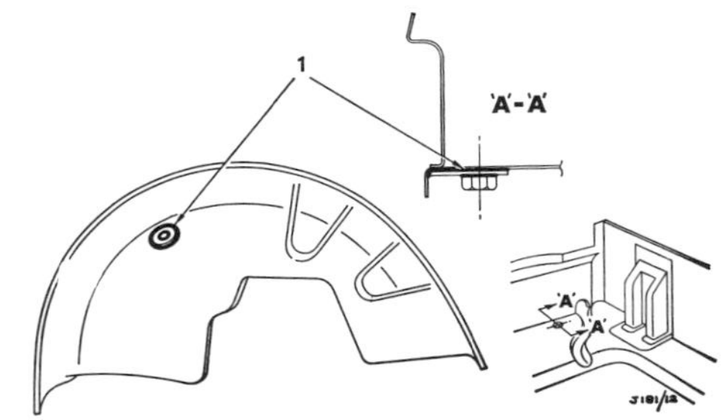

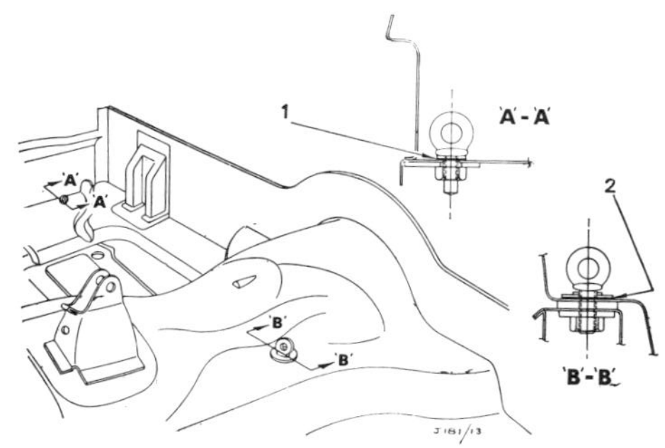

Location 13

1 Safety harness bolts and nuts to rear floor (use approved Mastics)
2 Seal safety harness bolts to floor tunnel (use approved Mastics)

Location 14

1 Wheelarch and seat panel (use approved Plastisol)
2 Wheelarch and body side panel (use approved Mastics)
3 Heelboard and 'B' post (use approved Mastics)
4 Radius arm fixings (use approved Mastics)
5 Reinforcement bracket and heelboard (use approved Mastics)
6 Heelboard and floor (use approved Mastics)
7 Heelboard and seat panel (use approved Mastics)
8 Spring access panel and seat panel (use approved Mastics)
9 Spring access fixing bolts (use approved Mastics)
10 Spring access panel and seat panel (Prestik, $\frac{1}{16}$ in. × ½ in.)

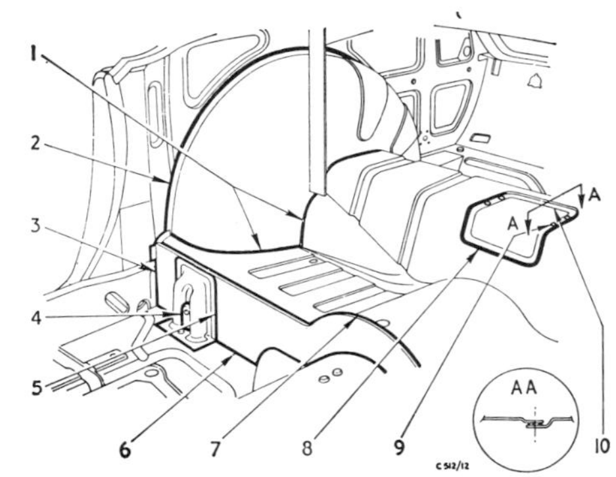

Location 15

1 Lock striker plate and 'B' post (use approved Mastics)
2 Rear wing and 'B' post (use approved Plastisol)
3 'B' post and inner panel (use approved Plastisol)
4 Sill and weatherstrip retainer (use approved Plastisol)

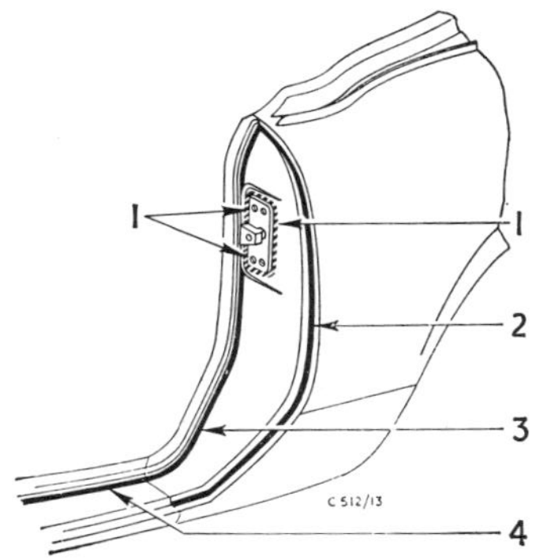

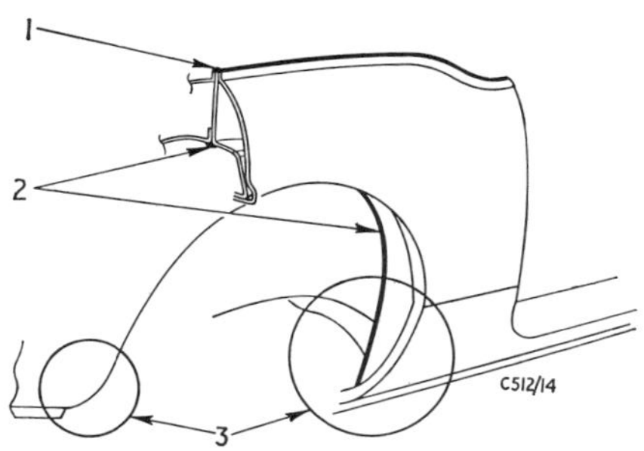

Location 16

1 Rear wing top joint (use approved Plastisol)
2 Inner and outer wheelarches (use approved Mastics)
3 All encircled joints (use approved Mastics)

Location 17

1 Under pivot bolt spacer (use approved Mastics)
2 Wheelarch safety harness fixing nut (use approved Mastics)

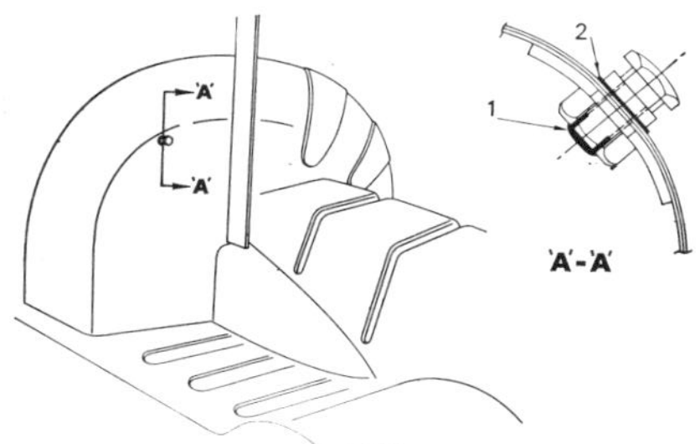

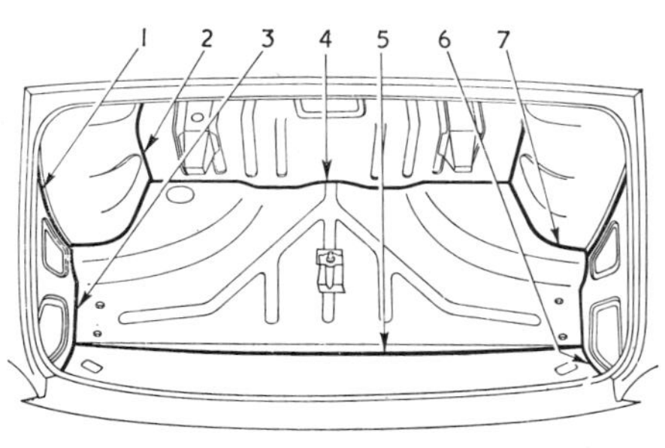

Location 18

1 Inner wheelarch and side panel (use approved Mastics)
2 Wheelarch and seat panel (use approved Mastics)
3 Spare wheel pan and side panel (use approved Mastics)
4 Spare wheel pan and seat panel (use approved Mastics)
5 Spare wheel and floor (use approved Mastics)
6 Floor and side panel (use approved Mastics)
7 Spare wheel pan and wheelarch (use approved Mastics)

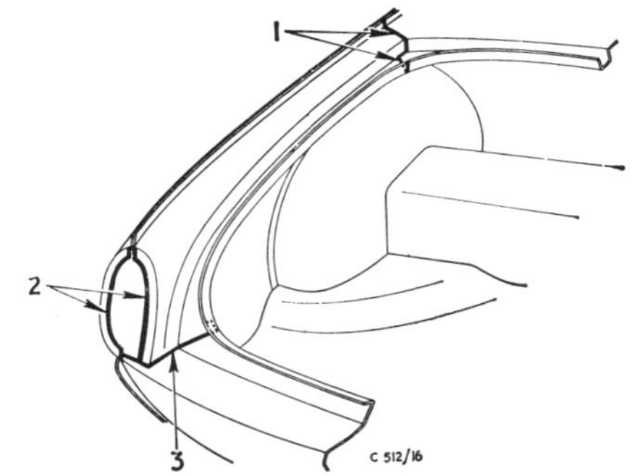

Location 19

1 Drain channel and rear deck (use approved Plastisol)
2 Tail lamp aperture and wing (use approved Plastisol)
3 Tonneau side and valance (use approved Plastisol)

Location 20

1 Wing finisher (use approved Plastisol)
2 Luggage locker weatherstrip (use approved Mastics)

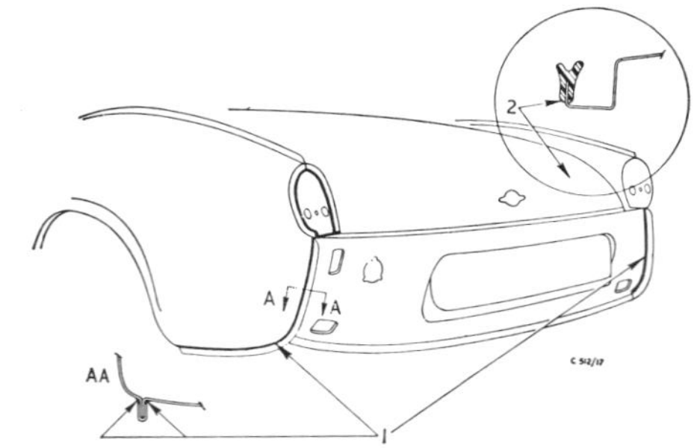

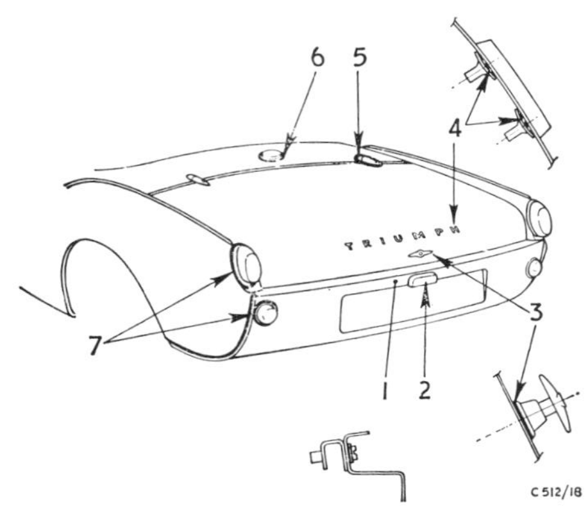

Location 21

1 Striker fixings (use approved Mastics under washer)
2 Lamp fixings and grommet (use approved Mastics)
3 Handle escutcheon and locker lid (use approved Mastics)
4 Locker lid and letters (Glasticon)
5 Hinges, locker lid and body (use approved Mastics)
6 Filler rubber and body (use approved Mastics)
7 Rubber of stop/tail and twin signal lamps and body (use approved Mastics)

TRIUMPH
HERALD, VITESSE 6
AND
SPITFIRE
WORKSHOP MANUAL

GROUP 6

Comprising :

Electrical Section

TRIUMPH
HERALD, VITESSE 6
and
SPITFIRE
WORKSHOP MANUAL

GROUP 6

CONTENTS

Information contained in this section details electrical equipment specific to the following vehicles that are all fitted with a negative earth electrical system.

Herald 1200 from approximately March 1968
Herald 13/60 introduced in October 1967
Spitfire Mark 3 introduced in March 1967

In all other respects the relevant information is contained in sections 1 and 2 of this group.

SPECIFICATIONS

Battery

Type BT.7A. (Home)	
Supplied dry and uncharged, or filled and charged	Lead acid.
Type BTZ.7A. (Export)	
Supplied dry but with plates charged	Lead acid.
Voltage	12.
Terminal earthed	Positive.
Capacity—at 10 hour rate	38 ampere hours.
—at 20 hour rate	43 ampere hours.
Plates per cell	7.
Electrolyte capacity (per cell)	1 pint imperial ; 1·2 pints U.S.A.; 570 c.c.
Specific gravity charged—Climates below 32°C.	1·270—1·290.
—Climates above 32°C.	1·130—1·150.
Initial charging current for BT.7A.	3·5 amperes.
Recharging current (both types)	5·0 amperes.

Generator

Model	C40—1.
Type	Two brush, two pole, compensated voltage control.
Rotation	Clockwise.
Field resistance	6 ohms. approximately.
Maximum output at 13·5 volts	22 amperes at 2,050—2,250 r.p.m. (connected to a load of 0·61 ohms.).
Brush tension	22—25 ozs. (0·62—0·71 Kgs.).
Minimum brush length	$\frac{11}{32}$" (9 mm.).

Generator (VITESSE ONLY) **C40L**

Type	Two brush, two pole, compensated current voltage control.
Rotation	Clockwise.
Field resistance	5·9 ohms approximately.
Maximum output at 13·5 volts	25 amperes at 2,275 r.p.m. (connected to a load of 0·54 ohm).
Brush tension	30 ozs. (0·85 Kg.) maximum.
Minimum brush length	$\frac{9}{32}$" (7 mm.).

Control Box (HERALD 1200 and COURIER VAN)

Type	RB.106/2.
Cut-in voltage	12·7—13·3.
Drop-off voltage	11—8·5.
Open circuit settings—*Ambient temperatures*	*Open circuit voltages.*
10°C. (50°F.)	16·1—16·7
20°C. (68°F.)	16·0—16·6
30°C. (86°F.)	15·9—16·5
40°C. (104°F.)	15·8—16·4

Control Box (VITESSE AND SPITFIRE)

Type	RB.340.
Cut-in voltage	12·6—13·4.
Drop-off voltage	9·3—11·2.
Contacts resistor	55—65 ohms.
Swamp resistor—measured on unit between centre and base	13·25—14·25 ohms.
Open circuit settings—*Ambient temperatures*	*Open circuit voltages.*
10°C. (50°F.)	14·9—15·5
20°C. (68°F.)	14·7—15·3
30°C. (86°F.)	14·5—15·1
40°C. (104°F.)	14·3—14.9

Electrical Settings of Current Regulator

The current regulator must be set to operate at a current value equal to the maximum rated output of the associated generator.

The nominal setting is stamped on the underside of the 'B-B' terminal plate or on the cover. The maximum rated output of generators is as follows : C40-1. 22 ± $1\frac{1}{2}$ amps.; C40L. 25 ± $1\frac{1}{2}$ amps.

SPECIFICATIONS

Starter Motor

Model	M.35G.
Type	Four pole, four brush, series wound.
Brush tension	32—40 ozs. (0·9—1·1 Kgs.).
Minimum brush length	$\frac{5}{16}$″ (8 mm.).

PERFORMANCE DATA

ARMATURE SPEED	TORQUE		CURRENT CONSUMPTION	
	lbs. ft.	Kgms.	Amperes	Volts
Locked	10	1·38	420—440	7·9—7·3
1,000 r.p.m.	5·4	0·75	250—270	9·3—8·9
7,400—8,500 r.p.m.	No load		45	12

IGNITION COIL

Lucas Part Number HA.125195 (Fluid Filled)

FITTED TO HERALD, VITESSE AND SPITFIRE

Primary Resistance (Cold at 20°C)	3·1 to 3·5 ohms.
Polarity of Earth for Test	Positive (+)
Maximum Test Voltage	12·5 volts.

IGNITION DISTRIBUTOR TEST DATA

HERALD 1200, 12/50 and COURIER VAN ENGINES

Distributor Type .. .. .. DM2 (Up to Engine No. GA67436 Low Comp. GA86619 High Comp.)
25.D4 (From Engine No. GA67437 Low Comp. GA86620 High Comp.)

Part Numbers

COMPRESSION RATIO	STANDARD-TRIUMPH PART No.	TYPE	LUCAS SERVICE No.
8 or 8·5 : 1	208968	25.D	40791
7 : 1	208967	25.D	40790
8 or 8·5 : 1	208362	DM2	40743
7 : 1	208460	DM2	40755

Design Data (all types)

Firing angles	0°, 90°, 180°, 270°, ± 1°.
Closed period (dwell angle)	60° ± 3°.
Open period	30° ± 3°.
Contact breaker gap	0·014″ to 0·016″ (0·36 to 0·41 mm.)
Rotation (viewed on rotor arm)	Counter clockwise.
Contact breaker spring pressure (measured at contacts)	18 to 24 oz.
Condenser capacity	0·18 to 0·25 mfd.

Distributor Test Data

The following r.p.m. figures relate to distributor speed and must be doubled for conversion to crankshaft speed. The angles, given in degrees, also relate to the distributor and must be doubled when converting to flywheel angles. For example: in the following table the distributor speed is quoted at 2,000 r.p.m. giving 8° to 10° distributor advance, this being equivalent to 4,000 crankshaft r.p.m., giving 16° to 20° advance measured around the flywheel or crankshaft pulley.

Centrifugal Timing Advance Tests

Part Nos. 208968 and 208362

8 or 8·5 : 1 Compression Ratio.

1. Set at 0° at a speed of less than 100 r.p.m.
2. Run distributor up to 2,500 r.p.m. advance to be 10° max.
3. Check at the following decelerating speeds:

Speed r.p.m.	Advance Degrees
2,000	8° to 10°
1,500	6° „ 8°
1,000	4° „ 6°
500	¾° „ 3°
450	½° „ 2½°

No advance below 120 r.p.m.

Part Nos. 208967 and 208460

7 : 1 Compression Ratio.

1. Set at 0° at a speed of less than 100 r.p.m.
2. Run distributor up to 2,000 r.p.m. advance to be 16° max.
3. Check at the following decelerating speeds:

Speed r.p.m.	Advance Degrees
1,600	14° to 16°
1,050	7° „ 9°
600	1° „ 3°
450	0° „ 1°

No advance below 370 r.p.m.

Vacuum Advance Tests

8 or 8·5 : 1 Compression Ratio.

1. Set at zero at a speed of 200 r.p.m.
2. Increase vacuum to 25″ mercury. Advance should be 6° to 8°.
3. Check at the following points with falling vacuum.

LUCAS VACUUM CURVE 3 / 18 / 7

Inches Hg.	Advance Degrees
15″	5½° to 7½°
10″	3½° „ 5½°
5½″	½° „ 2½°
2½″	0° „ ½°

No advance below 1½″ Mercury.

7 : 1 Compression Ratio

1. Set at zero at a speed of 200 r.p.m.
2. Increase vacuum to 18″ mercury. Advance should be 11° to 13°.
3. Check at the following points with falling vacuum.

LUCAS VACUUM CURVE 4 / 13 / 12

Inches Hg.	Advance Degrees
12″	10° to 12½°
8″	6° „ 8½°
5½″	½° „ 4°
3½″	0° „ ½°

No advance below 2″ Mercury.

IGNITION DISTRIBUTOR TEST DATA

VITESSE

Distributor Type .. .. Lucas 25D6 (Up to Engine No. HB15000)
Delco-Remy D200 (From Engine No. HB15001)
" " D202 (From Engine No. HB16302)

Part Numbers

COMPRESSION RATIO	TYPE	LUCAS	DELCO-REMY	STANDARD-TRIUMPH
8·75 : 1	25D6	40865	7953046	208914
8·75 : 1	D200		7953046	211407
8·75 : 1	D202		7953070	211414
7 : 1	25D6	40866		209050

Design Data (Lucas)

Firing angles	0°, 60°, 120°, 180°, 240°, 300°, ±1°
Closed Period (dwell angle)	35° ± 2°
Open period	25° ± 2°
Contact breaker gap	0·014″ to 0·016″ (0·36 to 0·41 mm.)
Rotation (viewed on rotor arm)	Counter clockwise
Contact breaker spring pressure (measured at contacts)	18 to 24 ozs.
Condenser capacity	0·18 to 0·25 mfd.

Design Data (Delco-Remy)

Firing angles	0°, 60°, 120°, 180°, 240°, 300°, ±1°
Closed period (dwell angle)	36° ± 1°
Open period	24° ± 1°
Contact breaker gap	0·020″ ± 0·001″ (0·508 mm.)
Rotation (viewed on rotor arm)	Counter clockwise
Contact breaker spring pressure (measured at contacts)	17 to 21 ozs.
Condenser capacity	0·18 to 0·25 mfd.

Distributor Test Data

The following r.p.m. figures relate to distributor speed and must be doubled for conversion to crankshaft speed. The angles, given in degrees, also relate to the distributor and must be doubled when converting to flywheel angles. For example: in the following table the distributor speed is quoted at 2,300 r.p.m. giving 13 to 15 degrees advance this being equivalent to 4,600 crankshaft r.p.m. giving 26 to 30 degrees advance measured around the flywheel or crankshaft pulley.

Centrifugal Timing Advance Tests (Lucas)

Lucas Part No. 40865 (8·75 : 1 Comp. Ratio)
1. Set at 0° at speed less than 200 r.p.m.
2. Run distributor up to 2,700 r.p.m. Advance to be 13° to 15°.
3. Check at the following decelerating speeds:

Speed r.p.m.	Advance Degrees
2300	13° to 15°
1800	11° " 13°
1200	9° " 11°
1000	6½° " 8½°
500	1° " 3°
300	0° " 1°

No advance below 200 r.p.m.

Lucas Part No. 40866 (7 : 1 Comp. Ratio)
1. Set at 0° at speed less than 225 r.p.m.
2. Run distributor up to 2,700 r.p.m. Advance to be 14° to 16°.
3. Check at the following decelerating speeds:

Speed r.p.m.	Advance Degrees
2000	14° to 16°
1150	12° " 14°
500	3° " 6°
300	0°

No advance below 225 r.p.m.

Vacuum Advance Tests (Lucas)

8·75 : 1 Compression Ratio
1. Set at zero at a speed of 200 r.p.m.
2. Increase vacuum to 12″ mercury. Advance should be 7° to 9°.
3. Check at the following points with falling vacuum.

LUCAS VACUUM CURVE 3 / 7 / 8

Inches Hg.	Advance Degrees
6″	6° to 9°
5″	3½° " 6½°
4″	1° " 4°
2½″	0° " 1°

No advance below 1½″ Mercury.

7 : 1 Compression Ratio
1. Set at zero at a speed of 200 r.p.m.
2. Increase vacuum to 18″ mercury. Advance should be 6° to 8°.
3. Check at the following points with falling vacuum.

LUCAS VACUUM CURVE 4 / 11 / 7

Inches Hg.	Advance Degrees
9½″	5° to 7°
4¾″	½° " 2½°
2″	0° " ½°

No advance below 1″ Mercury.

Centrifugal Advance Tests (Delco-Remy)

NOTE: At engine number HB.16302 a new cylinder head was introduced having re-shaped combustion chambers, giving quicker combustion. The D202 distributor was then fitted, having appropriately lowered centrifugal and vacuum advance values.

Delco-Remy D200 (8·75 : 1 C.R.)

1 Set at 0° at speed less than 200 r.p.m.
2 Run distributor up to 2,700 r.p.m. Advance to be 13° to 15°.
3 Check at the following decelerating speeds:

Speed r.p.m.	Advance Degrees
2,300	13° – 15°
1,800	11° – 13°
1,200	8½° – 11°
800	4¼° – 6½°
500	1° – 3¼°
400	0° – 2¼°

No advance below 200 r.p.m.

Delco-Remy D202 (8·75 : 1 C.R.)

1 Set at 0° at speed less than 200 r.p.m.
2 Run distributor up to 2,000 r.p.m. Advance to be 8½° to 10½°.
3 Check at the following decelerating speeds:

Speed r.p.m.	Advance Degrees
1,250	8½° – 10½°
1,150	7¼° – 9¼°
1,000	5½° – 7½°
900	4° – 6°
700	1½° – 3½°
550	0° – 2°

No advance below 400 r.p.m.

Vacuum Advance Tests (Delco-Remy)

Delco-Remy D200 (8·75 : 1 C.R.)

1 Set at Zero at a speed of 200 r.p.m.
2 Increase vacuum to 12″ mercury. Advance should be 7° to 9°.
3 Check at the following points with falling vacuum:

Inches Hg.	Advance Degrees
7″	7° – 9°
6″	5¾° – 8¼°
5″	3½° – 7°
4″	0° – 5½°

No advance below 2″ Mercury

Delco-Remy D202 (8·75 : 1 C.R.)

1 Set at Zero at a speed of 200 r.p.m.
2 Increase vacuum to 18″ mercury. Advance should be 5½° to 7½°.
3 Check at the following points with falling vacuum :

Inches Hg.	Advance Degrees
11″	5½° – 7½°
9″	3° – 7½°
8″	2° – 6°
6½″	0° – 4°

No advance below 4″ Mercury

DISTRIBUTOR

SPITFIRE 4

Part Numbers .. .. Delco Remy, 7952800. Standard-Triumph, 209697

Design Data

Moving contact spring tension	17—21 ozs.
Firing angle	0°, 90°, 180°, 270°.
Closed period	36° ± 1°.
Open period	54° ± 1°.
Contact breaker gap	0·020″ ± 0·001″.
Rotation (viewed on rotor arm)	Counter clockwise.

Centrifugal Timing Tests

1. Set 0° at distributor speed less than 400.
2. Run distributor up to 2,500 r.p.m.—advance to be 11°—13°.
3. Check at following decelerating speeds.

Speed r.p.m.	Advance Degrees
1,450	11 — 13
1,200	9·4 — 11·4
900	7·4 — 9·4
500	0 — 1·5

Vacuum Advance Tests	Check on Rising
Inches Hg	Advance Degrees
2	0
2½	1½
3	3
5	3 — 7
6	5¼ — 8
7	7 — 9
8	8 — 10
9	8½ — 10½
10	9 — 11 max.

SPITFIRE 4 Mk. 2

Part Numbers .. .. Delco Remy, 7953166, Standard-Triumph 212500

Speed r.p.m.	Advance Degrees	Inches Hg	Advance Degrees
400	0 to 1¾	5	0 to 1
600	3½ ,, 5½	6	¾ ,, 2½
700	6 ,, 8	7	2½ ,, 4¼
1200	7½ ,, 9½	8	4½ ,, 6
1600	9 ,, 11	9	5¾ ,, 7¾
1800	9½ ,, 11½	10	7½ ,, 9½
2000	10¼ ,, 12¼	11	9¼ ,, 10¼
2200	11 ,, 13¼	12	11 ,, 13
2300	11¼ ,, 13¼	16	11 ,, 13

WINDSCREEN WIPER MOTOR

Lucas Model DR.3A	Shunt wound single speed.
Light running speed	44 to 48 cycles per minute of wiper blades.
Stall current	13—15 amps.
Light running currents	2·7—3·4 amps. (Measured less cable and rack).
Resistance of field winding at 20°C. (68°F.) ..	8·0—9·5 ohms.
Resistance of armature winding at 20°C. (68°F.) ..	0·29—0·352 ohms. (Measured between adjacent commutation segments).
Brush tension	125—140 grammes.
Maximum permissible force to move rack in protective tubing with wiper motor disconnected and wiper arms removed	6 lbs. (2·7 kgs.).

BULBS — 12 VOLTS

HERALD 1200 AND COURIER VAN

	Stanpart No.	Watts.	Cap
Headlamps—Left-hand dip ..	508349	50/40	B.P.F.
—Right-hand dip	59469	36/36	B.F.F.
—Continental (Duplo) ..	501475	45/50	U.E.C.
—Vertical dip ..	60796	35/35	B.P.F.
Side (Parking)	59467	6	M.B.C.
Flashers	502379	21	S.B.C.
Stop/Tail	502387	21/6	S.B.C.
Plate Illumination	501436	6	S.B.C.
Panel Illumination and Warning Lamps	59492	2·2	M.E.S.
Interior Illumination—Amber	508997	6	Festoon
—Estate Car ..	59897	6	Festoon

VITESSE

	Stanpart No.	Watts.	Cap
Headlamps—Unit 1A (inner)—R.H.D.	305562	37½	3-lug
—Unit 2A (outer)—R.H.D.	305569	37½/50	3-lug
—Unit 1A (inner)—U.S.A.	305533	37½	3-lug
—Unit 2A (outer)—U.S.A.	305570	37½/50	3-lug
—Unit 1E—L.H.D.	305564	37½	3-lug
—Unit 2E—L.H.D.	305571	37½/50	3-lug
Side (Parking)	59467	6	S.C.C.
Flashers	502379	21	S.B.C.
Stop/Tail	502387	21/6	S.B.C.
Plate Illumination	59467	6	S.C.C.
Panel Illumination and Warning Lamps	59492	2·2	M.E.S.
Interior Illumination—Panel	59897	6	Festoon
—Roof	59897	6	Festoon

SPITFIRE 4

	Stanpart No.	Watts.	Cap
Headlamps—R.H.D.	500482	50/40	B.P.F.
—L.H.D.	59469	36/36	B.F.F.
—L.H.D.	501475	45/50	U.E.C.
—L.H.D.	510218	45/50	B.P.F.
—L.H.D.	510219	45/40	B.P.F.
—L.H.D.	60796	35/35	B.P.F.
Side (Parking)	57591	6	S.B.C.
Flashers	502379	21	S.B.C.
Stop/Tail	502287	21/6	S.B.C.
Plate Illumination	501436	4	S.C.C.
—U.S.A. only	59467	6	S.C.C.
Instrument Illumination and Warning Lamps	59492	2·2	M.E.S.
Sealed Beam Lamps—U.S.A.	508574		3-lug
—Continental	506373		3-lug

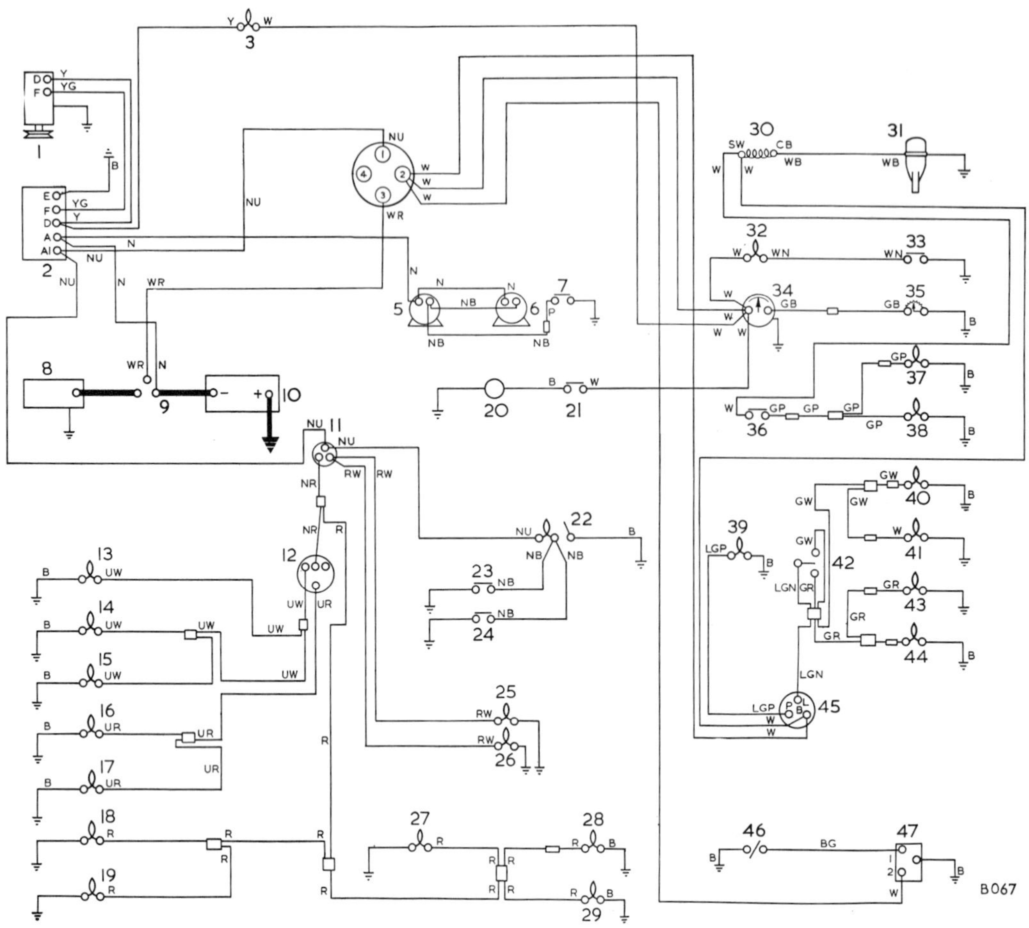

Fig. 1. Circuit diagram for Herald 1200 Saloon, Coupé and Convertible

Key to Fig. 1

1 Generator
2 Control box
3 Ignition warning light
4 Ignition/start switch
5 Horn
6 Horn
7 Horn push
8 Starter motor
9 Starter solenoid switch
10 Battery
11 Master lighting switch
12 Column switch
13 Main beam warning light
14 R.H. headlamp main beam
15 L.H. headlamp main beam
16 R.H. headlamp dip beam
17 L.H. headlamp dip beam
18 L.H. side lamp
19 R.H. side lamp
20 Heater motor
21 Heater switch
22 Interior light and switch
23 R.H. courtesy light switch
24 L.H. courtesy light switch
25 Panel illumination
26 Panel illumination
27 Number plate lamp
28 R.H. tail lamp
29 L.H. tail lamp
30 Ignition coil
31 Distributor
32 Oil pressure warning light
33 Oil pressure switch
34 Fuel gauge
35 Fuel tank unit
36 Stop lamp switch
37 R.H. stop lamp
38 L.H. stop lamp
39 Flasher warning light
40 R.H. rear flasher
41 R.H. front flasher
42 Flasher switch
43 L.H. front flasher
44 L.H. rear flasher
45 Flasher unit
46 Screen wiper switch
47 Screen wiper motor

Fig. 2. Circuit diagram for Herald 1200 Estate and Courier Van

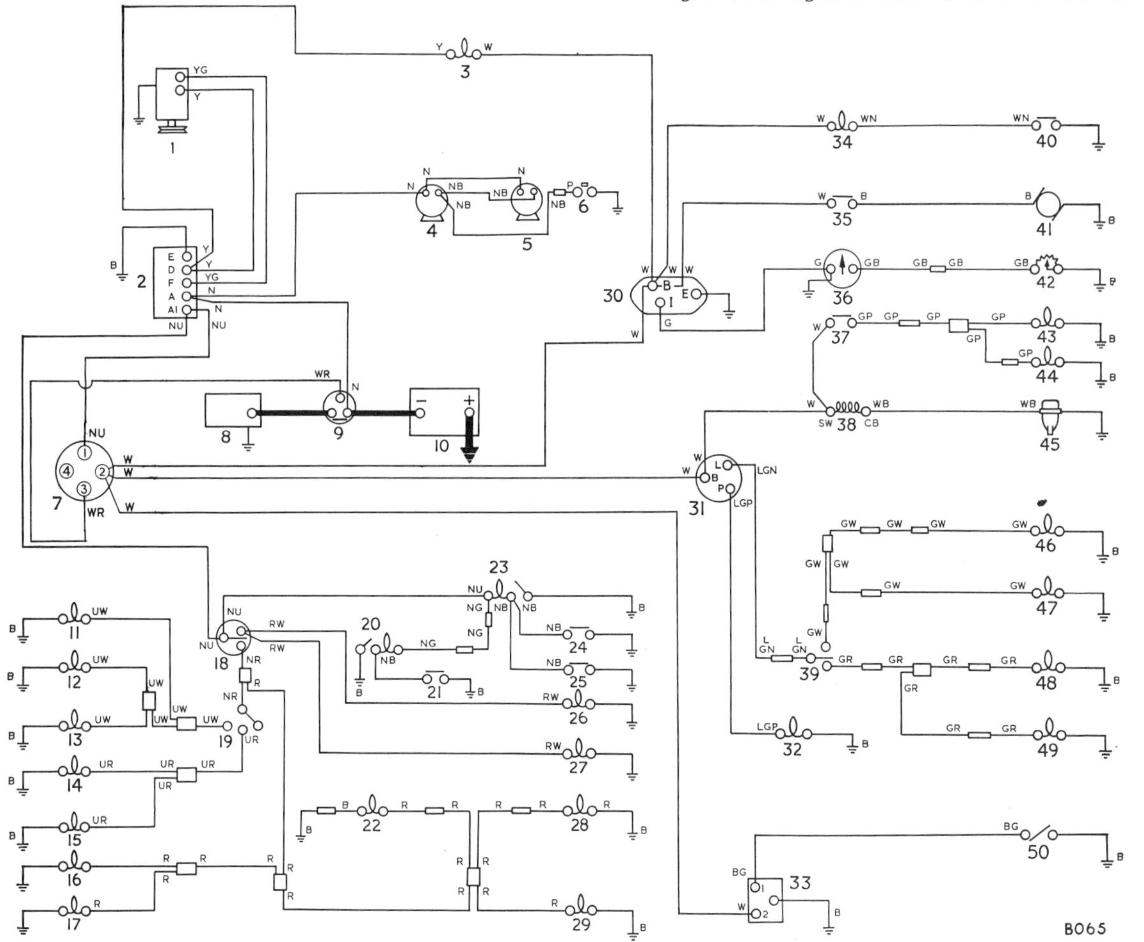

Key to Fig. 2

1 Generator
2 Control box
3 Ignition warning light
4 Horn
5 Horn
6 Horn push
7 Ignition/start switch
8 Starter motor
9 Starter solenoid
10 Battery
11 Main beam warning light
12 R.H. headlamp main beam
13 L.H. headlamp main beam
14 R.H. headlamp dip beam
15 L.H. headlamp dip beam
16 L.H. side lamp
17 R.H. side lamp
18 Master light switch
19 Column light switch
20 Tail gate light and switch
21 Tail gate switch
22 Number plate lamp
23 Interior light and switch
24 R.H. courtesy light switch
25 L.H. courtesy light switch
26 Panel illumination
27 Panel illumination
28 R.H. tail lamp
29 L.H. tail lamp
30 Voltage stabilizer
31 Flasher unit
32 Flasher warning light
33 Wiper motor
34 Oil pressure warning light
35 Heater switch
36 Fuel gauge
37 Stop lamp switch
38 Ignition coil
39 Flasher switch
40 Oil pressure switch
41 Heater motor
42 Tank unit
43 L.H. stop light
44 R.H. stop light
45 Distributor
46 R.H. rear flasher
47 R.H. front flasher
48 L.H. rear flasher
49 L.H. front flasher
50 Wiper switch

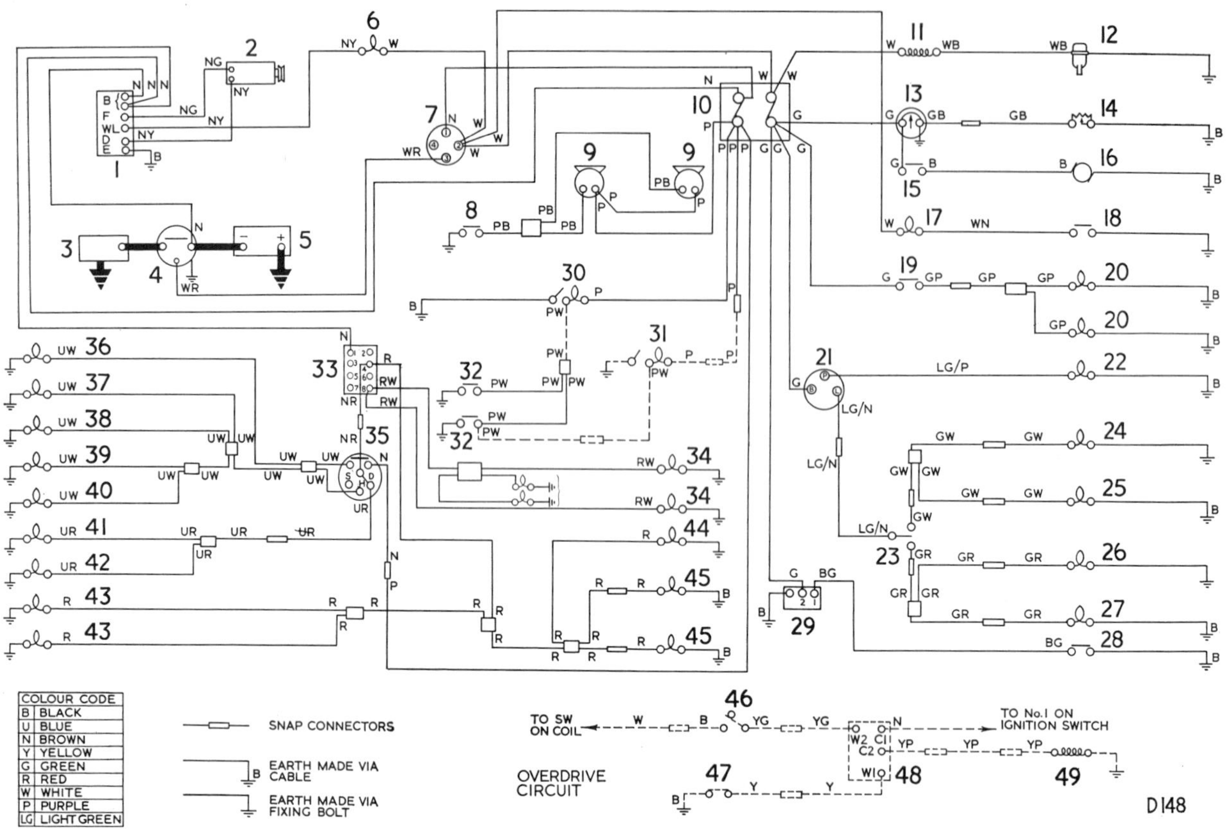

Fig. 3. Circuit diagram for Vitesse

The facia lamp (30) is operated from the courtesy switches (32), on Convertible models. On Saloon models, these switches operate the roof lamp (31) (which is not fitted to Convertible models) and the facia lamp is independently controlled.

Key to Fig. 3

1 Regulator
2 Generator
3 Starter motor
4 Starter solenoid
5 Battery
6 Ignition warning light
7 Ignition/start/accessory switch
8 Horn push
9 Twin horns
10 Fuse box
11 Coil
12 Distributor
13 Fuel gauge
14 Tank unit
15 Heater switch*
16 Heater motor*
17 Oil pressure warning light
18 Oil pressure switch
19 Stop lamp switch
20 Stop lamps
21 Flasher unit
22 Flasher warning lights
23 Flasher switch
24 R.H. front flasher
25 R.H. rear flasher
26 L.H. front flasher
27 L.H. rear flasher
28 Wiper switch
29 Wiper motor
30 Facia lamp
31 Roof lamp
32 Courtesy switch
33 Master lighting switch
34 Panel light
35 Column lighting and headlamp flasher switch
36 Main beam warning light
37 L.H. outer main beam
38 L.H. inner main beam
39 R.H. outer main beam
40 R.H. inner main beam
41 L.H. dip beam
42 R.H. dip beam
43 L.H. side lamp
R.H. side lamp
44 Number plate illumination lamp
45 R.H. tail lamp
L.H. tail lamp
46 Overdrive switch
47 Gearbox switch
48 Relay
49 Solenoid

* Special Order.

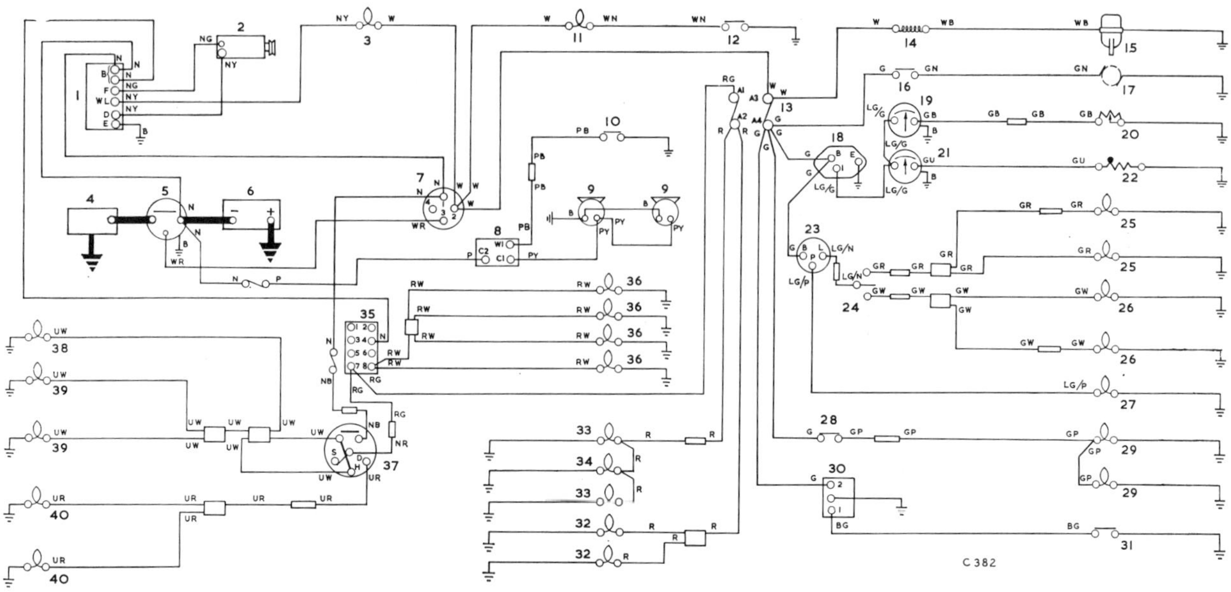

Fig. 4. Circuit diagram for Spitfire 4

Key to Fig. 4

1 Control box
2 Generator
3 Ignition warning lamp
4 Starter motor
5 Starter solenoid
6 Battery
7 Ignition/starter switch
8 Horn fuse
9 Horns
10 Horn push
11 Oil warning lamp
12 Oil pressure switch
13 Fuse unit
14 Ignition coil
15 Distributor
*16 Heater blower switch
*17 Heater blower motor
18 Voltage stabilizer
19 Fuel indicator
20 Fuel tank unit
21 Temperature indicator
22 Temperature transmitter
23 Flasher unit
24 Turn signal switch
25 Turn signal lamps, left-hand side
26 Turn signal lamps, right-hand side
27 Turn signal monitor
28 Brake/stop lamp switch
29 Brake/stop lamps
30 Windscreen wiper motor
31 Wiper motor switch
32 Front parking lamps
33 Tail lamps
34 Plate illumination lamps
35 Master lighting switch
36 Instrument illumination
37 Steering column light switch
38 Main beam warning lamp
39 Headlamp main beams
40 Headlamp dipped beams

* SPECIAL ACCESSORY

CABLE COLOUR CODE

B Black	**G Green**	**L Light**	**N Brown**	**R Red**	**U Blue**	**Y Yellow**
D Dark	**K Pink**	**M Medium**	**P Purple**	**S Slate**	**W White**	

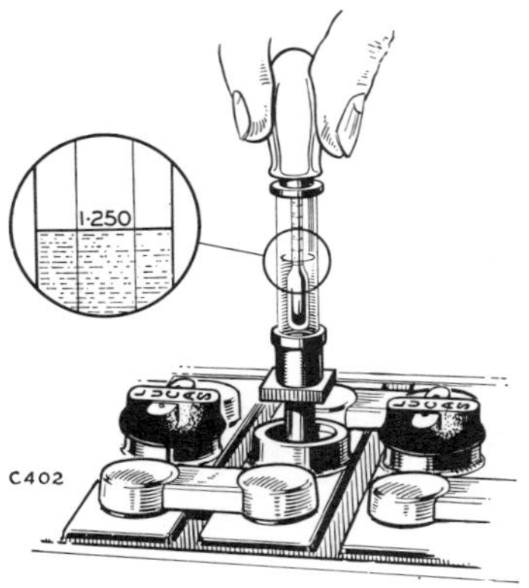

Fig. 5. Using a hydrometer to measure the specific gravity

TABLE 1. SPECIFIC GRAVITY OF ELECTROLYTE

Battery Condition	Climates below 90°F. (32°C.)	Climates over 90°F. (32°C.)
Fully charged	1·270 – 1·290	1·210 – 1·230
Half discharged . .	1·190 – 1·210	1·130 – 1·150
Completely discharged	1·110 – 1·130	1·050 – 1·070

TABLE 2.
SPECIFIC GRAVITY OF ACID REQUIRED FOR FILLING

Quantity to half-fill each 2-volt cell	Specific gravity of electrolyte corrected to 60°F. (15·5°C.)	
	Climates below 90°F. (32°C.)	Climates over 90°F. (32°C.)
½ Pint	1·270 (30·83° Baume)	1·210 (25·16° Baume)

TABLE 3. PROPORTIONS OF ACID AND WATER

To obtain specific gravity when cooled to 60°F. (15·5°C.)	Add one part by volume of Acid (1·835 S.G.) to distilled water by volume as below.
1·210	4·0 parts
1·215	3·9 ,,
1·260	3·1 ,,
1·270	2·9 ,,
1·275	2·8 ,,
1·290	2·7 ,,
1·320	2·3 ,,
1·340	2·0 ,,

BATTERY

If the battery is subjected to long periods of discharge without suitable opportunities for re-charging, a low state of charge can be expected. A defect in the charging system can also result in a discharged battery.

There are two reliable methods of assessing battery conditions. (1) Checking the specific gravity of the electrolyte, and (2) high rate discharge test.

1. Hydrometer Test

The specific gravity of the electrolyte varies with battery conditions (see table 1), and also with temperature, which should be corrected to the standard of 60°F. (15·6°C.) as outlined in table 4.

If it is necessary to top up the electrolyte, do not attempt to take a reading until the battery has been on charge for at least one hour. There should be little variation in the specific gravity readings between one cell and another of a battery in reasonably good condition.

A large variation, which is not the result of electrolyte loss, is probably an indication of an internal short circuit. If the electrolyte is very dirty, or contains small particles in suspension, it is possible that the plates are in bad condition.

2. Discharge Test

The high rate discharge test gives an indication of the condition and capacity of the battery. On test, the battery should maintain 100 amp. flow for 10 seconds with no appreciable fall in voltage.

Where a hand instrument (incorporating a low resistance device) is used for checking the individual cells of a battery, the actual reading obtained will depend upon the exact type of instrument used, but the cell voltage on a 5 to 6 seconds test should remain steady between 1·2 and 1·7 volts.

Variations in individual cell readings can indicate faults, but if all cells in any one battery fall below standard, recharge and again test before rejecting the battery.

Never make a high rate discharge test on a battery known to be low in charge.

Re-Charging from and external supply

If the above tests indicate that the battery is merely discharged and is otherwise in a good conditions, it should be re-charged until the specific gravity and voltage show no increase over three successive hourly readings.

Preparing New, Unfilled, Uncharged Batteries

Batteries should not be filled with electrolyte until required for initial charging. Approximately one pint (570 c.c.) of electrolyte is needed for each cell.

Electrolyte of the specific gravity is prepared by mixing distilled water and concentrated sulphuric acid, usually of 1·835 S.G. either in a lead-lined tank or in suitable glass or earthenware vessel. Slowly add the acid to the water, stirring with a glass rod. Never add the water to the acid, as the resulting chemical reaction causes violent and dangerous spurting of the concentrated acid.

The approximate proportions of acid and water are indicated in table 3.

Heat is produced by the mixture of acid and water. Allow the electrolyte to cool before taking hydrometer readings, or pouring it into the battery.

Filling the Cells

The temperature of the electrolyte, battery and filling room must not be below 32°F. (0°C.) freezing.

Break the seals in the filling holes or remove the moulded pegs from the vent plugs and half-fill each cell with electrolyte of the appropriate specific gravity. Allow the battery to stand for six hours and fill to the top of the separators. Allow to stand for a further two hours and then proceed with the initial charge.

Initial Charge

Charge at a constant 3·5 amperes for 40 to 80 hours until the voltage and specific gravity readings show no increase over five successive hourly readings.

If the temperature of any cell rises 20°F. (11·1°C.) above the ambient temperature, interrupt the charge until the temperature has fallen at least 10°F. (5·6°C.) below that figure. Keep the electrolyte level with the top of the separator guard by adding electrolyte of the same specific gravity as the original filling. Continue the charge until specific gravity and voltage readings remain constant for five successive hourly readings.

At the end of the charge, check and if necessary, adjust the specific gravity in each cell when corrected to 60°F. (15·6°C.). To adjust, siphon off some of the electrolyte and replace it either by distilled water or by electrolyte of the strength originally used for filling. Continue the charge for an hour or so to ensure adequate mixing of the electrolyte.

Preparing New, Dry-Charged Batteries

Break the seals in the filling holes and fill each cell with electrolyte of correct specific gravity to the top of the separators. The temperature of the filling room, battery and acid should be maintained at between 60°F. (15·6°C.) and 120°F. (48·8°C.). If the battery has been stored in a cool place, allow it to warm up to room temperature before filling.

Batteries filled in this way are up to 90 per cent. charged. When time permits, a freshening charge may be given at normal charging rate of 5 amps. for not more than 4 hours. Check the specific gravity of the electrolyte at the end of the charge; if 1·270 electrolyte was used, the specific gravity should now be between 1·270 and 1·290; if 1·210 electrolyte between 1·210 and 1·230.

TABLE 4.
SPECIFIC GRAVITY TEMPERATURE CORRECTION

Electrolyte Temperature		Correction required to obtain true specific gravity at 60°F. (15·5°C.).
Degrees F.	Degrees C.	
50	10·0	Deduct ·004 from observed reading
55	12·7	,, ·002 ,, ,, ,,
60	15·5	Normal
65	18·3	Add ·002 to ,, ,,
70	21·1	,, ·004 ,, ,, ,,
75	23·8	,, ·006 ,, ,, ,,
80	26·6	,, ·008 ,, ,, ,,
85	29·4	,, ·010 ,, ,, ,,
90	32·2	,, ·012 ,, ,, ,,
95	35·0	,, ·014 ,, ,, ,,
100	37·7	,, ·016 ,, ,, ,,
110	43·3	,, ·020 ,, ,, ,,
120	48·8	,, ·024 ,, ,, ,,

TABLE 5. MAXIMUM PERMISSIBLE ELECTROLYTE TEMPERATURE DURING CHARGING

Climates below 80°F. (26·6°C.)	Climates between 80–100°F. (26·6 – 37·7°C.)	Climates above 100°F. (37·7°C.)
100°F. (37·7°C.)	110°F. (43·3°C.)	120°F. (48·8°C.)

Fig. 6. Using a heavy discharge tester

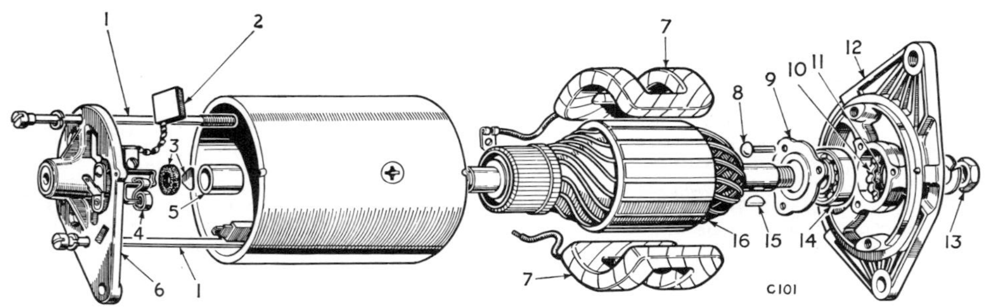

1 Bolts
2 Brush
3 Felt ring and aluminium sealing disc
4 Brush spring
5 Bearing bush
6 Commutator end bracket
7 Field coils
8 Rivet
9 Bearing retainer plate
10 Corrugated washer
11 Felt washer
12 Driving end bracket
13 Pulley retainer nut
14 Bearing
15 Woodruff key
16 Armature

Fig. 7. Dismantled generator

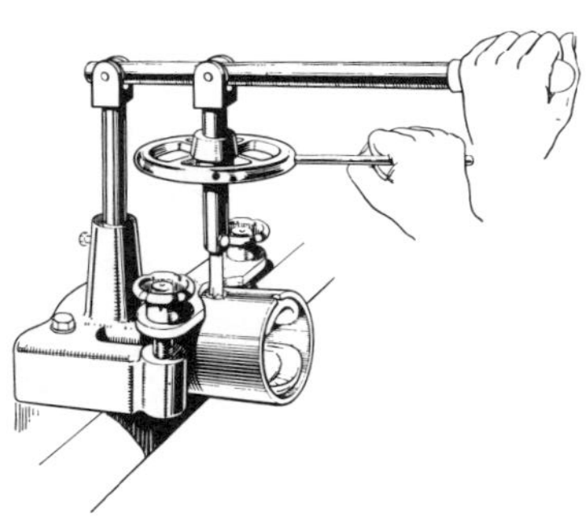

Fig. 8. Removing the pole pieces from the yoke

GENERATOR

To Dismantle

Remove the generator from the engine, extract the driving pulley and take out the woodruff key (15). Remove two bolts and withdraw the commutator end bracket (6) from the yoke. Note the fibre thrust washer adjacent to the commutator.

Withdraw the armature (16) and drive end bracket (12) complete with bearing. Support the bearing retaining plate (9) and press the shaft from the drive end bracket.

Field Coils

Renew as follows:—

1. Drill out the rivet securing the field terminal assembly to the yoke and unsolder the field coil connections.
2. Remove the insulation piece which prevents the junction of field coils from contacting the yoke.
3. Mark the yoke and pole shoes so that they can be refitted to their original positions.
4. Unscrew the pole shoe retaining screws, remove the pole shoes and lift off the coils.
5. Fit the new field coils over the pole shoes and re-position them inside the yoke.
6. Locate the pole shoes and field coils by lightly tightening the retaining screws; fully tighten them by using a wheel operated screwdriver. Lock the screws by caulking.
7. Replace the insulation piece between the field coil connections and the yoke.
8. Re-solder the field coil connections to the field coil terminal tags and rivet the assembly to the yoke.

Commutator

Burned commutator segments may be caused by an open-circuit in the armature windings. If armature testing facilities are not available, test the armature by substitution.

The commutator should be smooth and free from pits or burned spots. Slight burning may be rectified by careful polishing with a strip of fine glasspaper while rotating the armature. To remedy a badly worn commutator, mount the armature, with or without the drive end bracket, in a lathe. Rotate the armature at high speed and take a light cut with a very sharp tool, removing as little metal as is necessary to clean up the commutator. Polish the commutator with very fine glasspaper and undercut the insulators between segments to a depth of $\frac{1}{32}''$ (0·8 mm.), using a hacksaw blade ground to the thickness of the insulator (Fig. 9).

Brushes

Check that the brushes move freely in their holders, by holding back the tension springs and pulling gently on the flexible connectors. If a brush is inclined to stick, remove it from its holder and clean its sides with a petrol-moistened cloth.

Replace the brushes in their original position or renew those which are less than $\frac{11}{32}''$ (8·7 mm.) in length.

Test the brush spring tension using a spring scale. Fit new springs if the tension is below 15 ozs.

Bearings

Replace the bearing bush in a commutator end bracket as follows:—

Remove the old bearing bush from the end bracket by screwing a $\frac{5}{8}''$ tap squarely into the bush for a few turns and pulling out the bush with the tap.

Insert the felt ring and aluminium disc (3) in the bearing housing and using a shouldered mandrel press the new bearing bush into the end bracket until the bearing is flush with the inner face of the bracket.

Replace the ball bearing at the driving end as follows:—

1. Drill out the rivets (8) and remove the plate (9).
2. Press the bearing (14) from the end bracket (12) and remove the corrugated washer (10), felt washer (11) and oil retaining washer.
3. Clean and pack the replacement bearing with high melting point grease, such as Energrease RBB.3 or equivalent.
4. Place the oil retaining washer, felt washer and corrugated washer in the bearing housing and press in the bearing housing and press in the bearing.
5. Fit and rivet the retaining plate to the end bracket.

Re-assembly

1. Supporting the inner journal of the bearing to prevent damage, press the armature through the bearing assembled in the drive end bracket.
2. Assemble the armature and end bracket to the yoke.
3. Hold the brushes up by positioning each brush spring at the side of its brush.
4. Fit the commutator end bracket on the armature shaft until the brush boxes are partly over the commutator. Press each brush down on the commutator and move its spring to the operating position.
5. Fit the commutator end bracket to the yoke and refit the bolts (1).

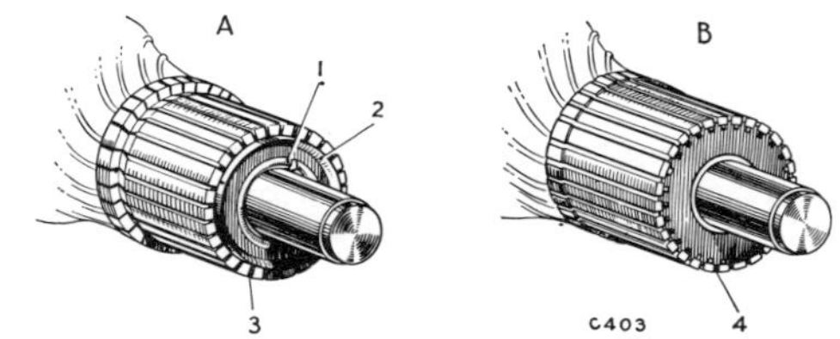

A. Fabricated commutator. B. Moulded commutator.
1 Metal roll-over
2 Insulating cone
3 Slot depth—0·032″ (0·81 mm.) maximum
4 Slot depth — 0·02″ to 0·035″ (0·508 to 0·89 mm.).

Fig. 9. Commutator details

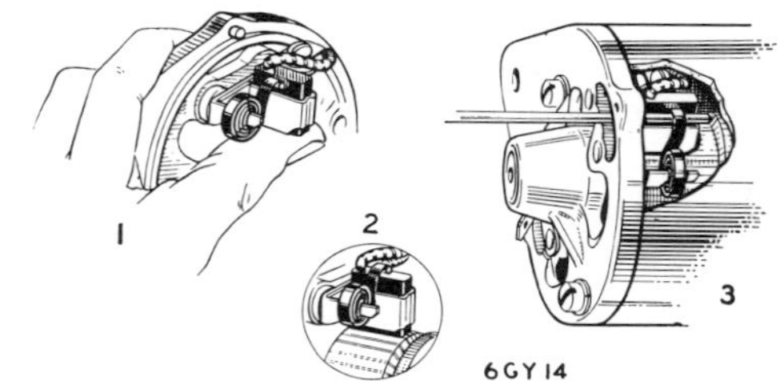

1 Method of trapping brush in raised position with spring
2 Normal working position
3 Method of releasing brush on to commutator

Fig. 10. Fitting commutator end bracket to "windowless" yoke generator

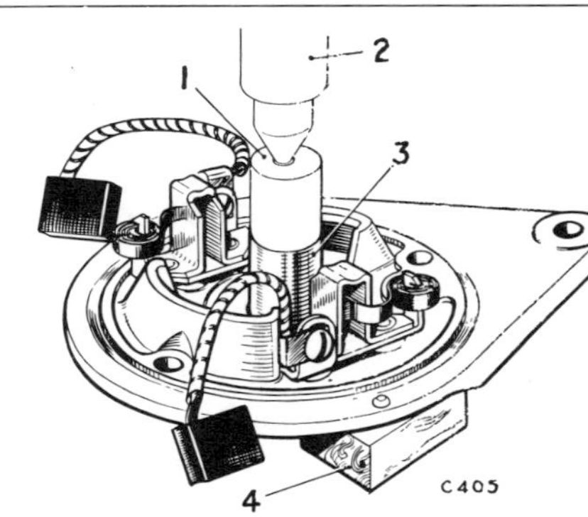

1 Mandrel
2 Press
3 Bush
4 Wood blocks

Fig. 11. Fitting a new bearing to the commutator end bracket

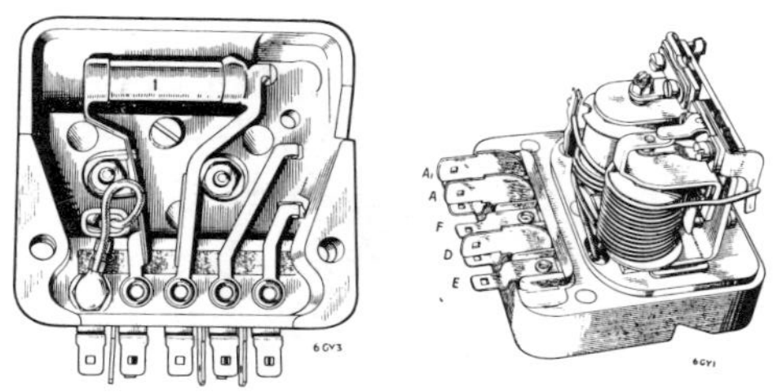

Fig. 12. The voltage regulator and cut-out

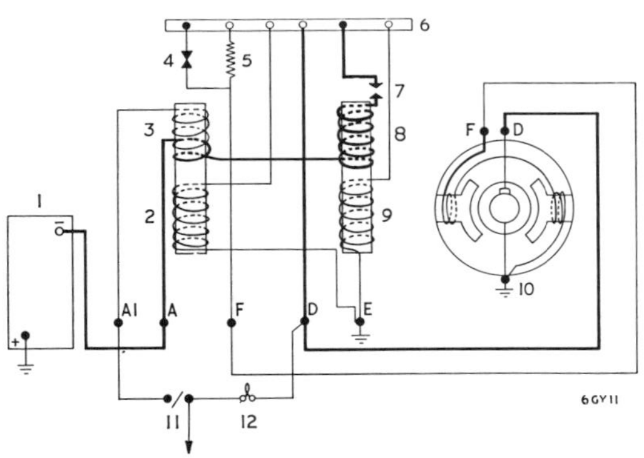

1 Battery
2 Voltage regulator relay coil
3 Split series coil
4 Voltage regulator contacts
5 Resistor
6 Main frame
7 Cut-out contacts
8 Series winding
9 Cut-out relay coil
10 Generator
11 Ignition switch
12 Ignition warning lamp

Nos. 2 to 9 are incorporated in the control box.

Fig. 13. Circuit diagram of generating system (Herald)

CONTROL BOX (HERALD 1200)

The control box shown in Fig. 12 contains two units — a voltage regulator and a cut-out. Although combined structurally, the regulator and cut-out are electrically separate.

The regulator is set to maintain the generator terminal voltage between close limits at all speeds above the regulating point, the field strength being controlled by the automatic insertion and withdrawal of a resistor in the generator field circuit.

Cleaning Contacts

(i) Regulator Contacts — use fine carborundum stone or silicon carbide paper.

(ii) Cut-out Relay Contacts — use a strip of fine glasspaper — never carborundum stone or emery cloth.

Voltage Regulator — Electrical Setting

It is important that only a good quality MOVING COIL VOLTMETER (0·20 volts) is used when checking the regulator.

Remove the cover and insert a thin piece of cardboard between the armature and the core face of the cut-out to prevent the contacts from closing.

Start the engine and slowly increase its speed until the generator reaches 3,000 r.p.m., when the open circuit voltage reading should be between the appropriate limits given on page 6·101, according to the ambient temperature.

If the voltage, at which the reading becomes steady, occurs outside these limits, adjust the regulator by turning the adjusting screw clockwise to raise the voltage or counter clockwise to lower.

Adjustment of regulator open-circuit voltage should be completed within 30 seconds otherwise heating of the shunt windings will cause false settings to be made.

Remove the cardboard.

Voltage Regulator — Mechanical Setting

A copper separator, in the form of a disc or square, is welded to the core face of the voltage regulator, and affects the gap setting between the core-face and the underside of the armature as follows:—

Where a round separator is used, the air gap should be 0·015″ (0·38 mm.).

Where a square separator is used, the air gap should be 0·021″ (0·53 mm.).

To adjust the air gap:—

Slacken the fixed contact locking nut and unscrew the contact screw until it is well clear of the armature moving contact.

Slacken the voltage adjustment spring-loaded screw until it is well clear of the armature tension spring.

Slacken the two armature assembly securing screws.

Insert a gauge of sufficient width to cover the core face, and of the appropriate thickness, between the armature and copper separator.

Press the armature squarely down against the gauge and re-tighten the two armature assembly securing screws. Without removing the gauge, screw in the fixed contact adjustment screw until it just touches the armature contact. Re-tighten the locking nut.

Re-check the electrical setting of the regulator.

CUT-OUT

Electrical Setting

If the regulator is correctly set but the battery is still not being charged, the cut-out may be out of adjustment. To check the voltage at which the cut-out operates, remove the control box cover and connect the voltmeter between the terminals D and E. Start the engine and slowly increase its speed until the cut-out contacts are seen to close, noting the voltage at which this occurs. This should be 12·7 – 13·3 volts.

If operation of the cut-out takes place outside these limits, it will be necessary to adjust. To do this, turn the adjusting screw in a clockwise direction to raise the voltage setting or in a counter clockwise direction to reduce the setting. Turn the screw only a fraction of a turn at a time and test after each adjustment by increasing the engine speed and noting the voltmeter readings at the instant of contact closure. Electrical settings of the cut-out, like the regulator, must be made as quickly as possible, because of temperature rise effects. Tighten the locknut after making the adjustment. If the cut-out does not operate, there may be an open circuit in the wiring of the cut-out and regulator unit, in which case the unit should be removed for examination or replacement.

Cut-out Relay

Slacken the adjustment screw until it is well clear of the armature tension spring.

Slacken the two armature securing screws.

Press the armature squarely down against the core face (copper sprayed in some units, fitted with a square of copper in others) and re-tighten the armature securing screws. No gauge is necessary.

With the armature still pressed against the core face, adjust the gap between the armature stop arm and the armature tongue to 0·032″ (0·81 mm.) by bending the stop arm.

Adjust the fixed contact blade so that it is deflected 0·015″ (0·38 mm.) by the armature moving contact when the armature is pressed against the core face.

Re-check the electrical setting of the cut-out.

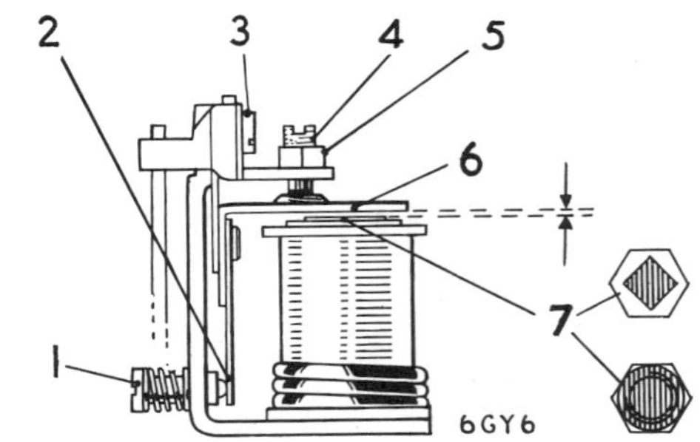

1 Voltage adjusting screw
2 Armature tension spring
3 Armature securing screws
4 Fixed contact adjustment screw
5 Locknut
6 Armature
7 Core face and shim

Fig. 14. Regulator air-gap settings

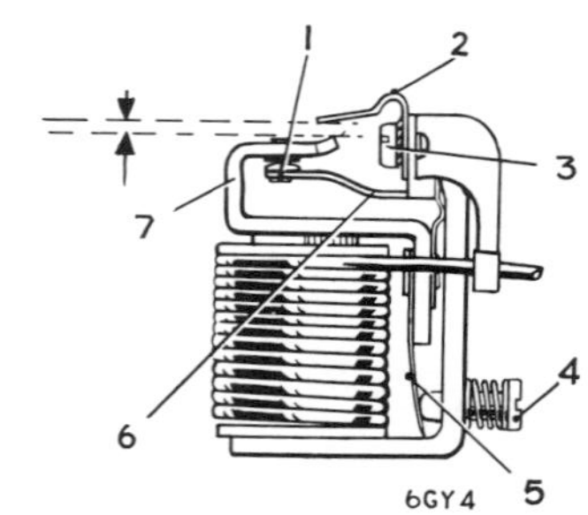

1 Follow through 0·010″ to 0·020″ (0·254 to 0·508 mm.)
2 Stop arm
3 Armature securing screws
4 Cut-out adjusting screw
5 Armature tension spring
6 Fixed contact blade
7 Armature tongue and moving contact

Fig. 15. Cut-out air gap settings

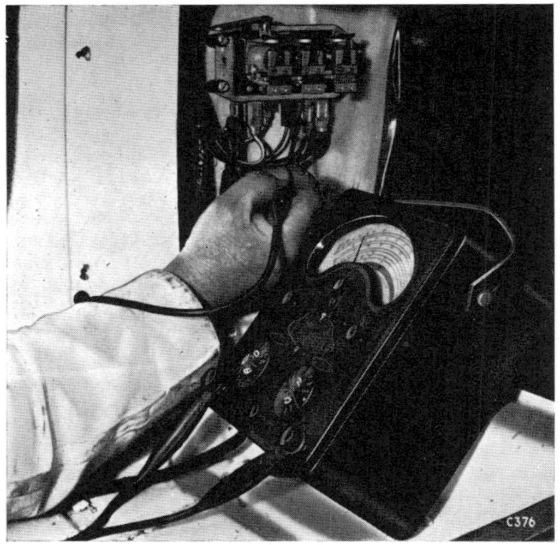

Fig. 16. Vitesse control box located behind left-hand side kick pad

Fig. 17. Spitfire control box on dash panel

CONTROL BOX

VITESSE AND SPITFIRE

Control box Model RB.340, is an electro-magnetically operated three-bobbin unit, operating on the current-voltage system of generator output regulation.

The control box comprises two separate vibrating armature type single contact regulators and a cut-out relay on a rubber mounted base plate. One regulator is responsive to changes in current and the other to voltage.

Electrical and Mechanical Settings

Except for adjustment of the cut-out relay drop-off voltage, which is effected by bending the fixed contact bracket, electrical settings are made by turning the toothed adjustment cam on the front of each frame. A special tool is available for this purpose. Rotation of the cam varies the spring tension acting on the associated armature.

The back air gaps are non-adjustable and the mechanical settings are restricted to the armature-to-bobbin core air gaps.

All bench settings in service must be made with the control box mounted as on the vehicle. Such settings should be made using a generator of the same model as that normally associated with the unit on the vehicle.

Temperature Compensation

The resistance of the coils in the cut-out and regulator rises and falls with temperature changes, and is caused by the ambient working conditions and the passage of the operating current through the coils.

The bi-metal strip on the cut-out suspension and voltage regulator springs, offsets the effect of temperature fluctuation on control box settings. This temperature effect is further minimised by the swamp resistors connected in series with the two shunt coils, which permit coils of lower resistance to be used.

The current regulator is not compensated, since the resistance of its coil is too low to vary significantly with temperature changes.

Figures for checking and setting of open circuit voltages are specified in Table 6.

Table 6

Ambient Temperature		Open Circuit Voltage SETTING
10°C. (50°F.)	..	14·9 — 15·5
20°C. (68°F.)	..	14·7 — 15·3
30°C. (86°F.)	..	14·5 — 15·1
40°C. (104°F.)	..	14·3 — 14·9

1 Swamp resistors
2 Cut-out relay coil
3 Cut-out relay current coil
4 Cut-out relay contacts
5 Current/control relay contacts
6 Current control relay coil
7 Contacts resistor
8 Voltage control relay contacts
9 Voltage control relay coil
10 Battery
11 Generator field coils
12 Generator armature

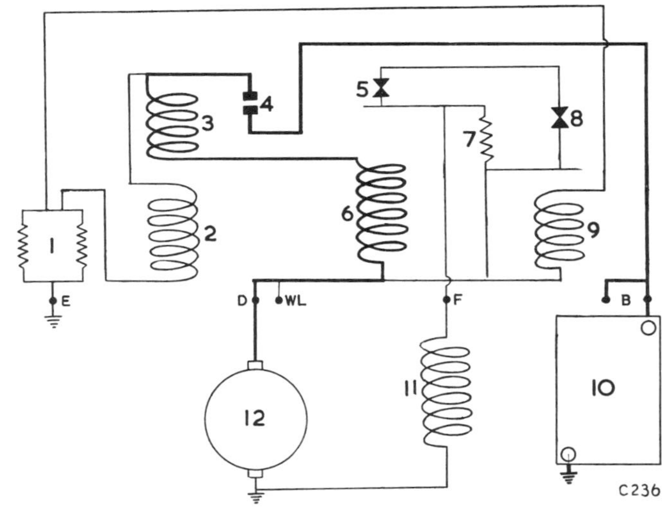

Fig. 18. Changing circuit diagram for Vitesse and Spitfire

Checking Charging Circuit

Before disturbing electrical or mechanical adjustments examine as described below to ensure that the fault does not lie outside the control box:—

In the event of reported undercharging, ascertain that this is not due to low mileage.

Check the battery by substitution or with an hydrometer and a heavy discharge tester.

Inspect the generator driving belt. This should be just taut enough to drive without slipping.

Inspect the wiring of the charging circuit and carry out continuity tests between the generator and control box.

Check earth connections, particularly that of the control box.

When making electrical and mechanical adjustments, always aim for the nominal setting.

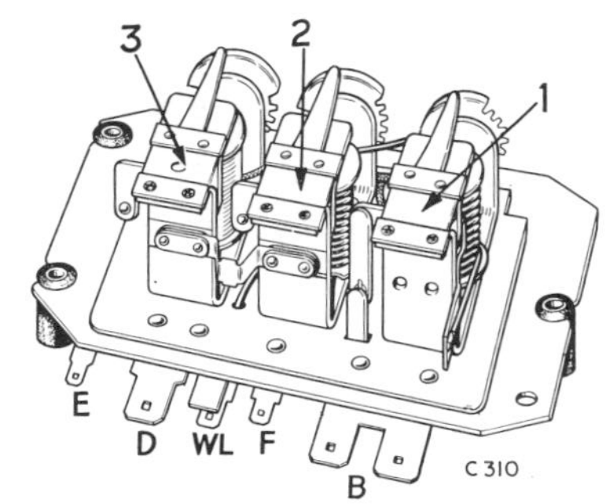

1 Cut out
2 Current regulator
3 Voltage regulator

Fig. 19. Top side view of RB340 control box

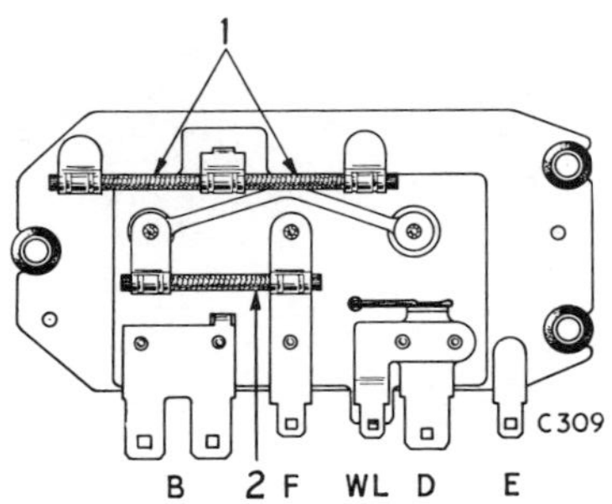

1 Ballast resistors 2 Field resistor

Fig. 20. Underside view of RB340 regulator

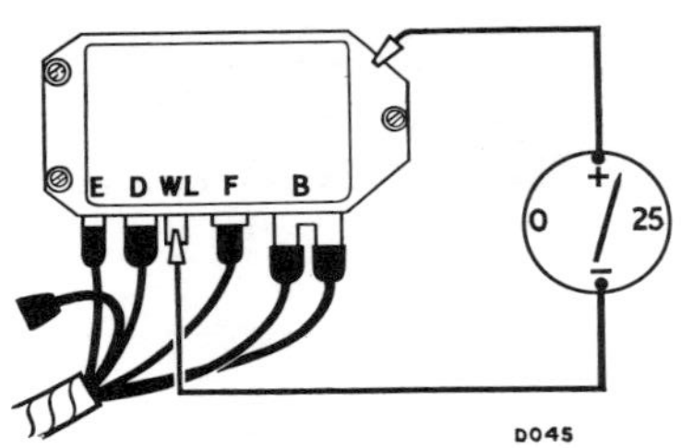

Fig. 21. Checking cut-in voltage

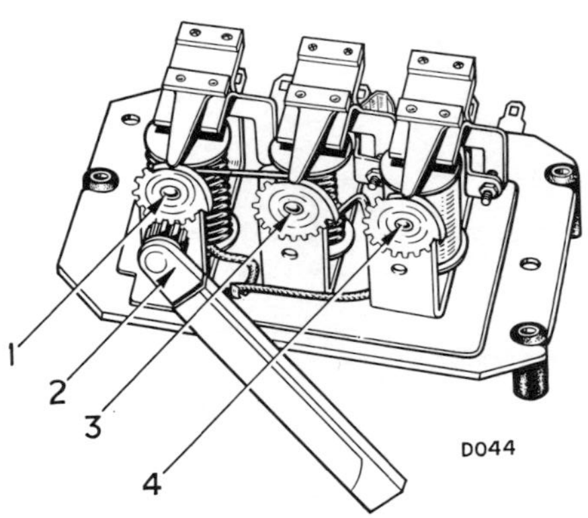

1 Cut-out
2 Special tool
3 Current regulator
4 Voltage regulator

Fig. 22. Adjusting cut-out

Voltage Regulator Open Circuit Setting

Complete the checks and adjustments as rapidly as possible to avoid errors arising from over-heating of the operating coil.

Remove the cover and insert a piece of cardboard between the armature and core of the cut-out to prevent the contacts closing.

Connect a first-grade 0-20 volt moving-coil voltmeter between control box terminal 'D' and a good earthing point.

NOTE: A convenient method of making this connection is to withdraw the ignition warning light cable from terminal 'WL' and clip the voltmeter negative cable to the exposed small terminal blade. This terminal is electrically common with terminal 'D'.

Start the engine and run the generator at 3,000 r.p.m.

Observe the voltmeter reading. This should be between the limits given in Table 6, according to the temperature.

An unsteady reading (*i.e.*, one fluctuating more than ± 0·3 volt) may be due to unclean contacts. If the reading is steady but occurs outside the appropriate limits, adjust as follows:—

Using the special tool, turn the voltage adjustment cam until the correct setting is obtained by turning the tool clockwise to raise the setting or counter clockwise to lower it.

Check the setting by stopping the engine and then again raising the generator speed to 3,000 r.p.m.

Restore the original connection and remove the cardboard.

Cut-out Relay Electrical Settings

Checking and Adjusting Cut-in Voltage

Complete the checks and adjustments as rapidly as possible to avoid errors arising from over-heating of the operating coil.

Connect a first-grade moving-coil voltmeter between control box terminal 'WL' and a good earthing point.

Switch on an electrical load, such as the head-lamps. Start the engine and slowly increasing its speed, observe the voltmeter reading.

The voltage should rise steadily and then drop slightly at the instant of contact closure. The cut-in voltage is that which is indicated immediately before the pointer drops back. It should occur between the limits given in table 6.

If the cut-in occurs outside these limits, reduce the engine speed to below the cut-in value and adjust as follows:—

Using the special tool, turn the cut-out relay adjustment cam clockwise to raise the setting or counter clockwise to lower it.

Switch off the engine, restore the original connections and refit the cover.

Checking and Adjusting Drop-off Voltage

Disconnect the cables from terminal 'B-B' and connect the 'S.W.' terminal on the coil to the battery. Connect a first-grade moving-coil voltmeter between control box terminal 'B-B' and earth.

Start the engine and run up to approximately 3,000 r.p.m. Slowly decelerate, and observe the voltmeter reading.

Opening of the contacts is indicated when the voltmeter pointer drops to zero. This should occur between the limits given in Table 6. If the drop-off occurs outside these limits, adjust as follows:—

Stop the engine and remove the control box cover.

Adjust the drop-off voltage by carefully bending the fixed contact bracket. Reducing the contact gap will raise the drop-off voltage; increasing the gap will lower the drop-off voltage.

NOTE: This should result in a contact "follow through" or blade deflection of 0·010" to 0·020" (0·25 to 0·51 mm.).

Restore the original connections and refit the cover.

Current Regulator Maximum Load Setting

The generator must be developing its maximum rated output at the time of setting.

Remove the control box cover.

Insert a piece of cardboard between the armature and core face of the voltage regulator to prevent the contacts of the regulator opening.

Withdraw the cables from the control box terminal blades 'B-B' and connect the cables from terminals 'B-B' to the load side of a first-grade 0 to 40 ampere moving-coil ammeter.
NOTE: Ensure that terminal 'B' carries only this one connection.

Switch on all lights and equipment. Run the engine at approximately 3,000 r.p.m. and observe the ammeter reading, which should be steady and indicate the maximum rated output of the generator.

An unsteady reading (*i.e.*, one fluctuating more than ± 1 ampere) may be due to unclean contacts. If the reading is too high or too low, adjust as follows:—

Using the special tool, turn the current adjustment cam clockwise to raise the setting and counter clockwise to lower it.

Switch off the engine and restore the original connections.

Remove the cardboard and refit the control box cover.

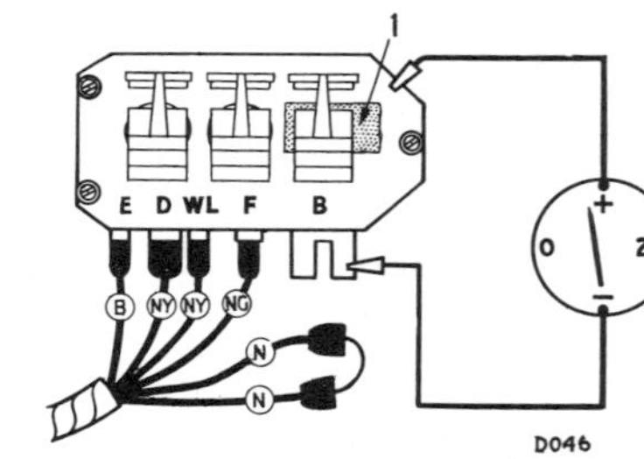

Fig. 23. Checking drop off voltage

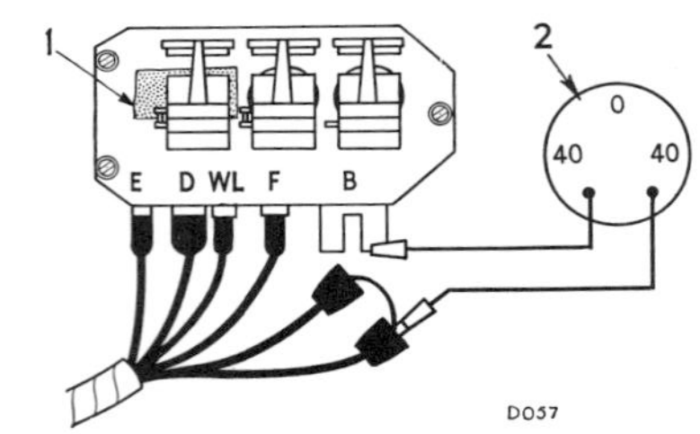

1 Cardboard under cut-out armature
2 0 - 40 ammeter

Fig. 24. Checking current setting

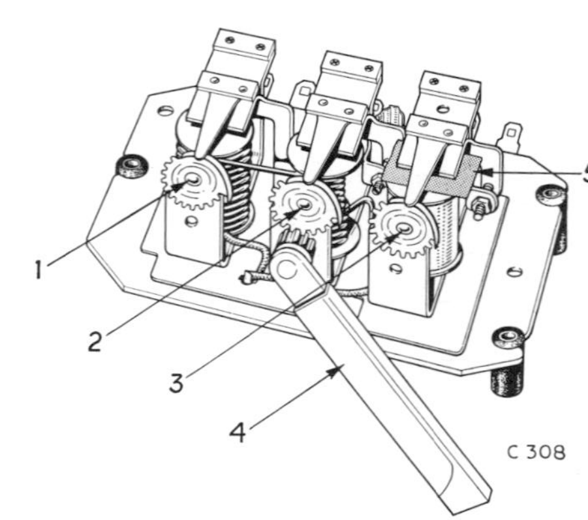

1 Cut-out cam
2 Current control cam
3 Voltage regulator cam
4 Special adjusting current control
5 Cardboard under voltage regulator

Fig. 25. Adjust current control cam

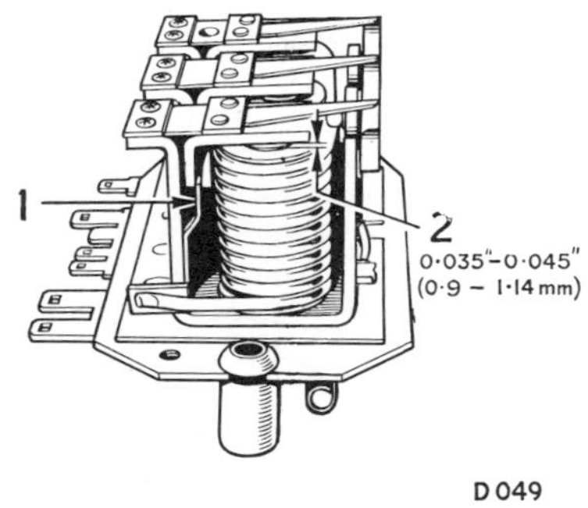

1 Voltage regulator contacts
2 Airgap setting

Fig. 26. Voltage regulator airgap setting

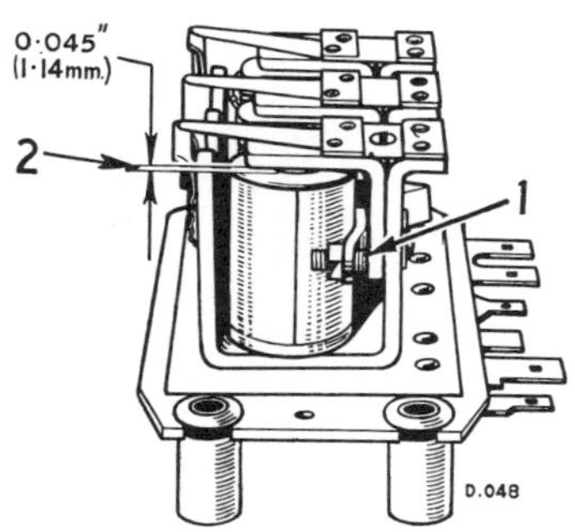

1 Backstop adjustment
2 Airgap settings

Fig. 27. Cut-out airgap settings

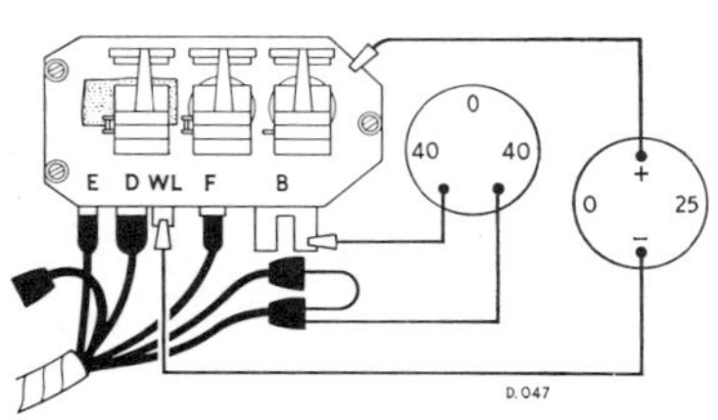

Fig. 28. Control box stability test

Adjustment of Air Gap Settings

Air gap settings on the control box may be reset as follows:—

Armature-to-Bobbin Core Gaps of Voltage and Current Regulators

Using the special tool, turn the adjustment cam counter clockwise for minimum lift of the armature tensioning spring.

Slacken the adjustable contact locking nut and screw back the adjustable contact. Insert a flat steel feeler gauge of 0·045″ (0·04 mm.) thickness between the armature and the copper separator on the core face, taking care not to turn up or damage the copper. The gauge should be inserted as far back as the two rivet heads on the underside of the armature.

Retaining the gauge in position, press squarely down on the armature and screw in the adjustable contact until it just touches the armature contact.

Readjust the electrical settings.

Contact "Follow-through" and Armature-to-Bobbin Core Gap of Cut-out Relay

Press the armature squarely down against the copper separation on the core face.

Adjust the fixed contact bracket to give 0·010″ to 0·020″ (0·25 to 0·51 mm.) "follow-through" or blade deflection of the moving contact.

Release the armature and adjust the armature back stop to give a core gap of 0·035″ to 0·045″ (0·9 to 1·04 mm.).

Check the cut-in and drop-off voltage settings.

Cleaning Contacts
Regulator Contacts

To clean the voltage or current regulator contacts use fine carborundum stone or silicon carbide paper followed by methylated spirits (denatured alcohol).

Cut-out Relay Contacts

To clean the cut-out relay contacts use a strip of fine glass paper—carborundum stone or emery cloth must not be used.

Control Box Stability Test

Connect a voltmeter as described in Voltage Regulator Open Circuit Setting and an ammeter as in Current Regulator maximum load setting.

Run the generator at 4,500 r.p.m.

Switch on and off a lamp load equivalent to 75 per cent. of the maximum output of the generator.

Assuming the generator and external circuits to be in good order, instability (*i.e.* violent fluctuations of the voltage and current reactions to the conditions imposed) could be due to:—

Air gap settings too narrow.
Foreign matter in air gaps.
Faulty internal connections causing intermittent open circuit.

TEMPERATURE INDICATOR

The temperature indicator, comprising a temperature transmitter and a gauge unit, operates on a 10 volts system which is controlled by a voltage stabilizer.

Temperature Transmitter

The temperature transmitter which is mounted in the right-hand side of the thermostat housing, consists of a temperature sensitive resistance element contained within a brass sleeve. The resistance element is a semi-conductor which has a high negative temperature co-efficient of resistance and its electrical resistance therefore decreases rapidly with an increase in temperature. As the temperature of the engine coolant increases, the decreasing resistance of the semi-conductor increases the flow of current through the indicator, similarly a decrease in coolant temperature will reverse the procedure.

Gauge unit

The gauge unit comprises a heater winding round a bi-metal strip which is linked to the pointer of the gauge unit. The flow of current through the heater winding is controlled by the temperature transmitter which reacts to any change in engine coolant temperature by varying the current drawn through the heater windings. This affects the bi-metal strip which in turn causes the pointer to indicate the temperature of the coolant. The slow movement of the pointer is caused by the time taken to heat or cool the bi-metal strip.

Voltage Stabilizer

The voltage stabilizer is a small sealed unit, located under the facia, and is used to provide a constant current of 10 volts for the operation of the fuel contents gauge and the Temperature Indicator.

The stabilizer is fitted adjacent to the ignition/starter switch on Herald Estate and Van models and adjacent to the fuse unit on Spitfire cars.

Since it is not possible to repair any of the units described above, a defective unit must, therefore, be renewed.

Testing

To establish which unit is defective, test for circuit continuity using an Ohmmeter or by substituting a known unit.

Do not connect any unit direct to the battery.

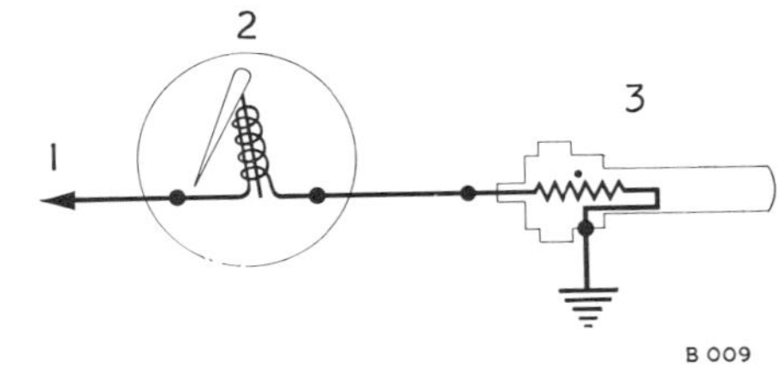

1 To "B" terminal on voltage stabilizer
2 Gauge unit
3 Transmitter

Fig. 29. Circuit diagram of temperature indicator

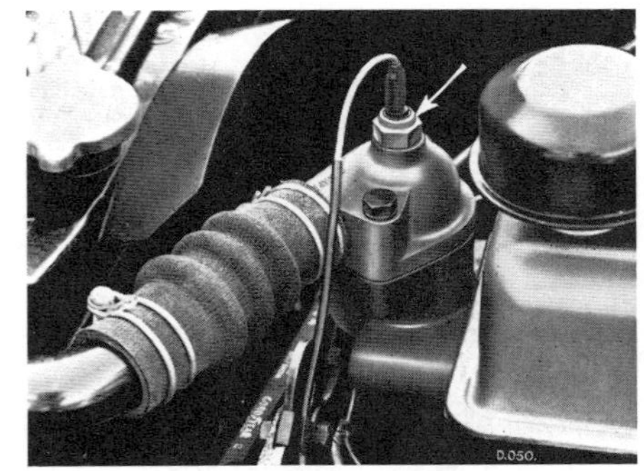

Fig. 30. Location of temperature transmitter

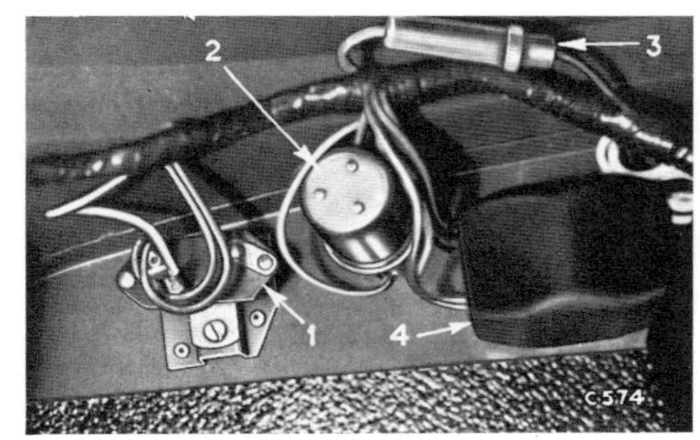

1 Voltage stabilizer (18)
2 Flasher unit (23)
3 Linefuse (8)
4 Fuse unit (13)

Fig. 31. Location on electrical components under the facia (Spitfire)

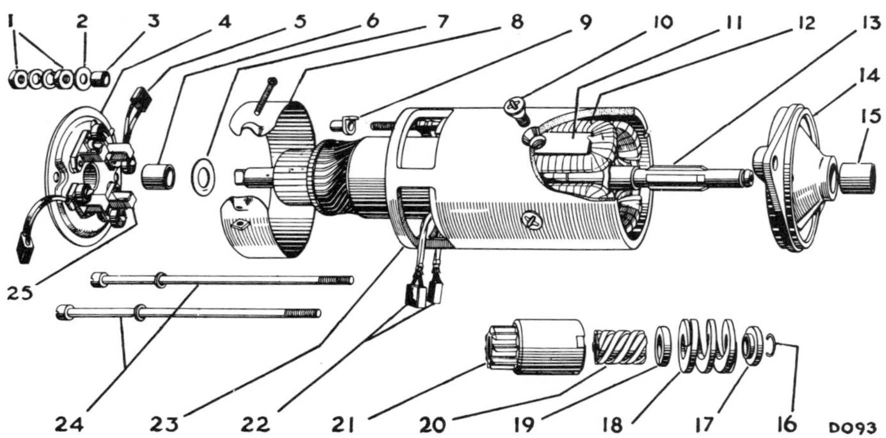

1 Terminal nuts and washers
2 Insulating washer
3 Insulating bush
4 End plate
5 Brush
6 Bush
7 Thrust washer
8 Cover band
9 Insulating bush
10 Pole securing screw
11 Pole piece
12 Field coil
13 Shaft
14 End bracket
15 Bush
16 Jump ring
17 Retainer
18 Main spring
19 Thrust washer
20 Sleeve
21 Pinion and barrel assembly
22 Brushes
23 Yoke
24 Through bolts
25 Brush box

Fig. 32. Dismantled starting motor

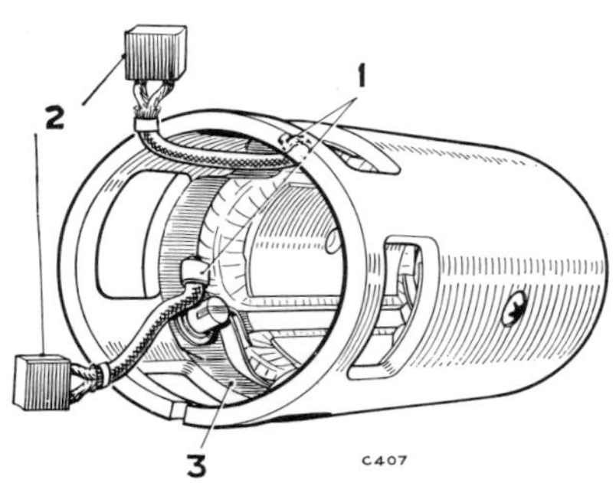

1 Field coil connections
2 Brushes
3 Yoke

Fig. 33. Brush connections

STARTER MOTOR

To Remove

Disconnect the cables from the battery and the starter motor terminals, remove the two starter securing bolts and withdraw the starter motor upwards.

To Refit

Measure the distance from the pinion side of the flywheel ring gear to the mounting face for the starter and measure the distance from the pinion end to the face of the starter.

Fit packing to obtain end clearance between the stationary starter pinion and the flywheel ring gear of $\frac{3}{32}$" to $\frac{5}{32}$"; this is usually called "out of mesh clearance".

Packing pieces and shims are available in 0·4", 0·5" and 0·016" thicknesses.

Re-connect the cables to the starter motor terminals and finally to the battery.

Dismantling

Remove the starter drive as follows:—

Using a hand press with suitable adaptors, support the end plate (4), and press down the retainer (17). Remove the jump ring (16) and lift off items 18 to 20. The pinion and barrel assembly (21) and screwed sleeve (20) should not be renewed independent of each other.

Loosen the brush cover screw and slide the cover (8) from the unit. Lift the brush springs (4) and withdraw the brushes (5) and (22) from their holders.

Unscrew the terminal nuts, the two bolts (24) and remove the end bracket (4). Withdraw the drive end bracket (14) and armature from the yoke (23).

Field Coils

To Renew:—

Unscrew the four pole-shoe retaining screws, using a wheel-operated screwdriver and pole expander tool for obstinate cases.

Mark the yoke and pole-shoes so that they can be refitted to their original positions.

Take out the pole-shoes, lift off the coils and unsolder the field coil tappings from the terminal post.

Fit new field coils by reversing the procedure, and replace the insulating pieces used to prevent the inter coil connectors from contacting the yoke.

To Re-assemble

Reverse the dismantling procedure.

Bearings

To Renew

Using a shouldered mandrel of the same diameter as the shaft, drive out the old bush and press the new bearing bush into the end bracket.

The bronze bushes are porous and must not be opened out after fitting, otherwise the porosity of the bush may be impaired.

Commutator

A commutator in good condition is clean, smooth and free from pits or burned spots. If cleaning with a petrol-moistened cloth is ineffective, carefully polish the commutator with very fine glasspaper while the armature is rotating. Do not use emery cloth.

To rectify a badly worn commutator, mount the armature in a lathe, rotate at a high speed and take a light cut with a sharp tool, removing the minimum of metal to obtain a clean finish. Finally, polish with very fine glasspaper.

NOTE : Do not undercut the mica insulators between segments.

Brushes

Check that the brushes move freely on their holders by holding back the brush springs and pulling gently on the flexible connectors. If a brush is inclined to stick, remove it from its holder and relieve its sides with a smooth file.

Replace the brushes in their original positions or renew excessively worn brushes as follows:—

Cut off the original brush flex $\frac{1}{8}$" (3 mm.) approximately from the aluminium and tin the brazed joint. Open out the loop, taking care not to allow solder to run towards the brush.

Place the original joint within the loop, squeeze up and solder. The brushes are preformed so that bedding to the commutator is unnecessary.

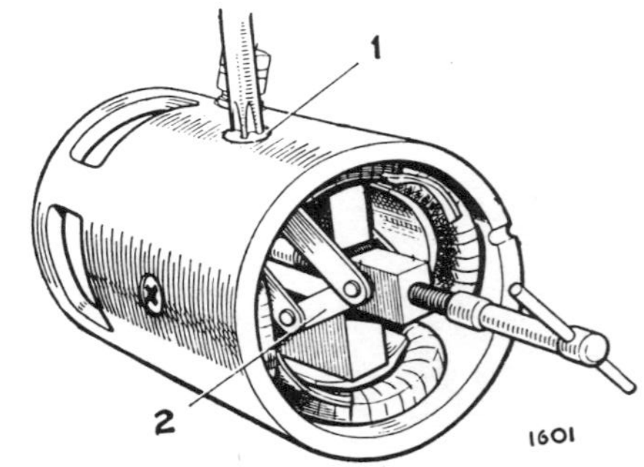

Fig. 34. Using a pole shoe expander to refit the field coils and retainer screws

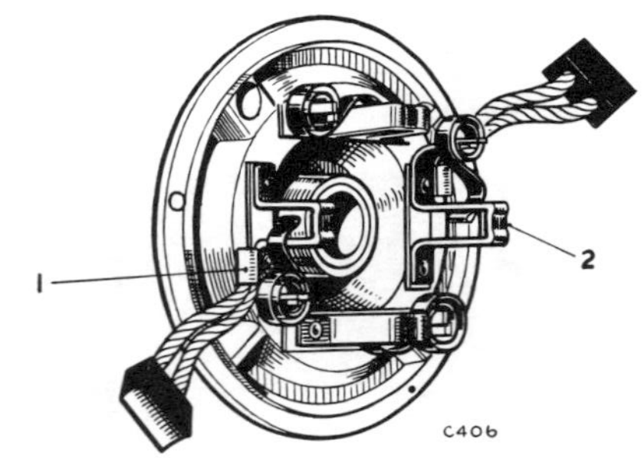

1 Brush connections 2 Brush boxes

Fig. 35. Commutator end bracket

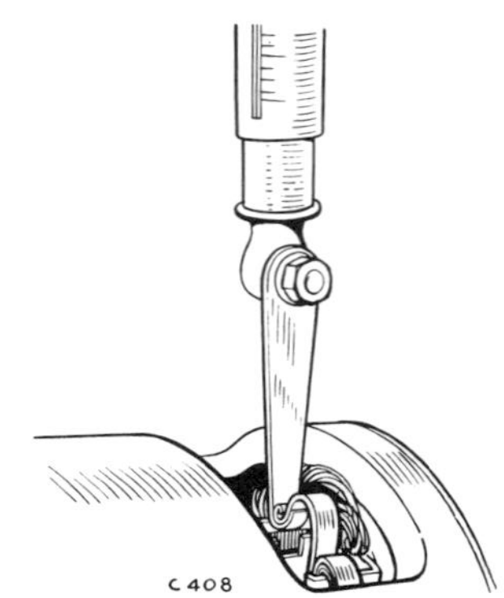

Fig. 36. Using a spring scale to test the brush spring tension

Fig. 37. Distributor contacts

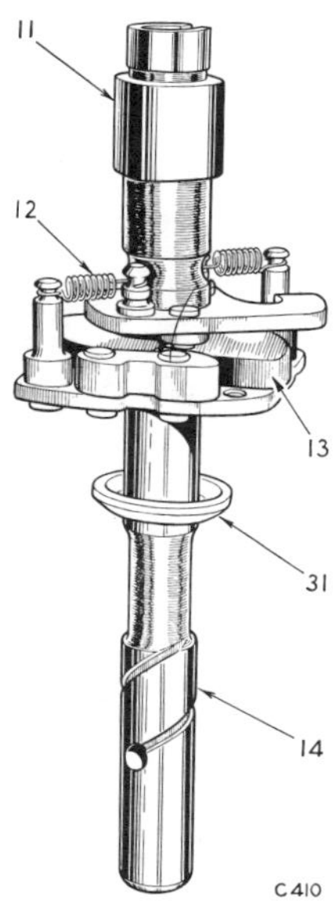

Fig. 38. Assembly of centrifugal weights and springs to the action plate

IGNITION DISTRIBUTOR

Contact Breaker Adjustment (Fig. 37)

Take off the distributor cap, remove the rotor arm and turn the engine until the contact breaker heel is on the highest point of the cam.

Slacken the screw (28), insert the blade of a screwdriver into the slots (31), and twist the screwdriver to adjust the gap between the contact breaker points, which should be 0·014″ – 0·016″ (0·356 – 0·406 mm.) measured with a feeler gauge.

Tighten the locking screw (28), re-check the gap and, if satisfactory, refit the rotor arm and cap.

Contact Breaker Renewal

Slight pitting or discolouration of the points may be rectified by use of a fine carborundum stone. Do not use emery cloth unless the points are removed first and thoroughly cleaned before re-assembly. Renew burned or deeply pitted contacts as follows:—

1. Remove the nut (3), insulating sleeve (2) and lift the black and green cables from the terminal pillar.
2. Lift the spring contact (1) from the pivot post and remove the fibre washers (29) and (30).
3. Take out the lock screw (28) and lift off the fixed contact (27).

To Refit

Reverse the above instructions and adjust the gap between the contact breaker points.

Distributor Capacitor

A short circuit, resulting from the breakdown of the dielectric between the electrodes of the capacitor, which is parallel connected across the contact breaker points, will prevent the interruption of the low tension circuit and cause ignition failure.

An open circuit in the capacitor may be suspected when the points are excessively burnt and difficult starting is experienced.

Renew the capacitor, as follows:—

1. Remove the distributor cap and rotor arm, unscrew the nut (3) from the spring contact terminal post, and lift off the capacitor lead.
2. Take out the capacitor retainer screw and remove the capacitor.
3. Secure the new capacitor in place, reconnect the lead to the terminal post and refit the nut (3). Refit the rotor arm and distributor cap.

Overhauling the Distributor

To Remove

Disconnect the high and low tension cables from the distributor and release the high tension cables from the spark plugs.

Uncouple the vacuum pipe from the distributor, unscrew two nuts at the base of the distributor and lift it from the engine.

To Dismantle

Remove the distributor cover and rotor arm. Disconnect the vacuum control (26) from the contact plate (7), take out two screws (8) and remove the contact breaker assembly.

Release the circlip (19) and remove the adjusting nut (18) and spring (17), taking care not to lose the ratchet spring (16). Withdraw the vacuum control unit (25) from the distributor body.

Release both springs (12) from the base of the cam (11) and the action plate (14). Take out the screw (10) and lift the cam (11) from the shaft (14).

At this stage, check the shaft (14) for end float which should not exceed $\frac{1}{32}$ (0·8 mm.). Drive out the pin (21), take off the driving dog (22) and the washer (23), and withdraw the shaft (14) from the distributor body.

Substituting a new shaft, or a test bar of 0·490″ (12·45 mm.) diameter, check the bearing sleeve (24) for wear, and renew the sleeve if required.

To reduce excessive end float, renew the nylon spacer beneath the action plate (14), and the washer (23) between the driving dog and distributor body.

To Re-assemble

Refit the nylon spacer under the action plate (14), reassemble the weights (13), spring (12) and cam (11) to the action plate (14) and secure the cam with the screw (10). Lubricate the shaft and insert the assembly into the distributor body.

Refit the washer (23) and, placing the offset driving dog (22) as shown on Fig. 39, secure the dog by inserting and swelling the ends of the pin (21).

Assemble the contact plate (7) to the fixed base plate (9) by springing the spring clip over the base plate slot edge, inserting the peg of the contact plate into a slot in the base plate and moving it slightly clockwise. Secure the assembly to the distributor body, using two screws (8).

Insert the vacuum unit (25) into the distributor body and assemble the ratchet spring (16), the coiled spring (17), adjusting nut (18) and the circlip (19). Hook the vacuum connecting spring (26) on to the pin attached to a cranked lug on the contact plate.

Assemble the capacitor and the contact breaker to the contact plate (7) and adjust the contact breaker points as described previously.

Refit the complete distributor to the engine, re-connect the vacuum pipe, the high and low tension cables, and re-adjust the ignition timing.

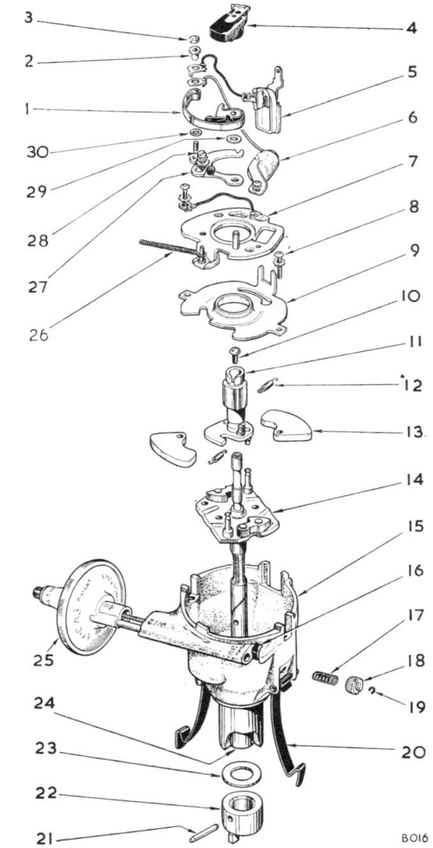

1	Spring contact	16	Ratchet spring
2	Insulating sleeve	17	Coiled spring
3	Nut	18	Adjusting nut
4	Rotor arm	19	Circlip
5	L.T. terminal	20	Cap retainer
6	Capacitor	21	Pin
7	Contact plate	22	Driving dog
8	Screw	23	Washer
9	Base plate	24	Bearing sleeve
10	Screw	25	Vacuum unit
11	Cam	26	Vacuum connecting spring
12	Centrifugal spring	27	Fixed contact
13	Centrifugal weights	28	Screw
14	Action plate and shaft assembly	29	Insulating washer
15	Distributor body	30	Insulating washer

Fig. 39. Dismantled ignition distributor

Fig. 40. Adjustments and lubrication

Fig. 41. Renewing contacts

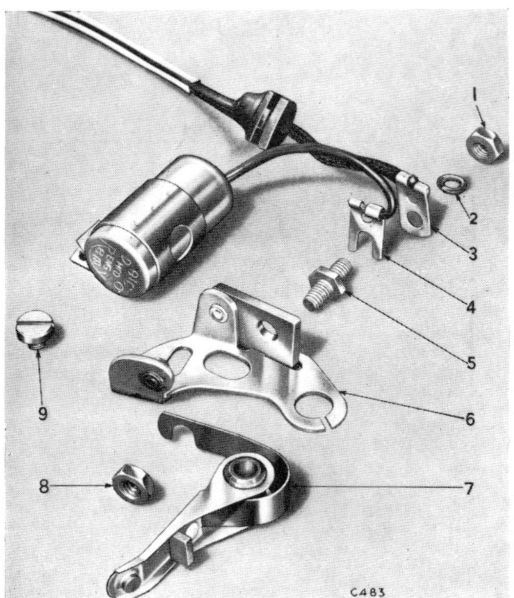

Fig. 42. Exploded arrangement of contact breaker

DISTRIBUTOR (A.C. Delco Type D200)

SPITFIRE

Lubrication (Fig. 40)

Release the clips and remove the distributor cap and rotor arm. Apply a few drops of thin oil to points (1), (2) and (3). Lightly grease the cam surface (4) and inject approximately 5 c.c. (one teaspoonful) of engine oil through the hole (5).

Contact Breaker Adjustment (Fig. 40)

Turn the engine until the moving contact is on the highest point of the cam lobe, *i.e.*, gap at its widest.

Having made sure that the contacts (8) are perfectly clean, slacken the fixed contact screw (7) and turn the eccentric screw (6) to obtain a gap of 0·015″ (0·04 mm.), measured with a feeler gauge, between the contact faces. Retighten the screw (7).

Contact Breaker Renewal (Figs. 41, 42 and 44)

Disconnect the L.T. cable from the CB terminal on the coil. Remove the distributor cap and rotor arm. Take out the fixed contact screw (9) and lift the contact breaker assembly sufficiently to gain access to the terminal nut (1). Remove the nut (1), washer (2) and take off the L.T. cable (3) and capacitor (4) from the terminal stud (5). Lift off the contacts (6) and (7). Remove the nut (8), the terminal stud (5) and discard the old contacts.

Fit new contacts by reversing the removal instructions.

Distributor—To Remove

Disconnect the L.T. cable from CB terminal on the coil; H.T. cables from the plugs and coil; tachometer drive cable from the distributor.

Remove the distributor cap and note the position of the rotor arm relative to the engine. Take out the bolt securing the clamp plate to the engine and withdraw the distributor assembly.

NOTE: Do not slacken the clamp bolt (22) as this will alter the ignition timing.

DISTRIBUTOR (A.C. Delco Type D200)

VITESSE (From Engine No. HB 15,001)

This is similar to the above Spitfire distributor except that the vacuum unit has no micro adjustment for static advance.

Type D202 (From Engine No. HB 16,302)

This is similar to D200 except that the vacuum advance unit is attached differently and the eccentric screw adjuster (6), Fig. 40, is not fitted.

To Dismantle

Take off the vacuum advance unit (13) and lift out the contact breaker base plate assembly (11).

Obtain a silver steel bar of $\frac{7}{32}$″ diameter and turn down one end to 0·15″ diameter × $\frac{1}{8}$″. Insert this spigot into the end of the tachometer gear and drive out the gear (24), thrust washer (23) and end cover (25).

Note that the teeth on the driving dog (20) are offset to the left when facing the slot which engages the rotor arm at the top of the shaft. Remove the rivet (21), driving dog (20) and spacer (19). Withdraw the shaft assembly (12) from the distributor body (17) and remove the spacer (14) from the shaft. Release the clip (16) and lift out the oil retaining felt (15).

To Re-assemble

Clean and dry all components. Soak the oil retaining felt (15) in clean engine oil and shake off the surplus oil. Refit the oil retaining felt and secure it with the spring clip (16).

Assemble the spacer washer (14) to the shaft (12) and the shaft to the body (17). Refit the spacer washer (19) and, with its teeth offset to the left when facing the rotor arm slot, rivet the driving dog (20) to the shaft.

Assemble the thrust washer (23) to the shaft of the tachometer drive gear (24). Lightly cover the entire drive gear and its shaft with petroleum jelly, and push the gear into position. Fit a new end cover (25) and peen over the body in four places to retain it in position.

Refit the contact breaker base plate assembly (11) and the vacuum advance unit (13). Check the contact breaker adjustment, fit the sealing ring (18), and install the distributor.

Key to Figs. 42 and 44

1	Nut	16	Felt retaining clip
2	Lockwasher	17	Distributor body
3	Low tension cable	18	Oil seal ring
4	Capacitor	19	Spacer
5	Terminal stud	20	Driving dog
6	Fixed contact	21	Rivet
7	Moving contact	22	Clamp plate & bolt.
8	Nut	23	Thrust washer
9	Screw (fixed contact)	24	Tacho. gear
10	Rotor arm	25	End cover
11	Contact base plate	26	Spring
12	Centrifugal action plate	27	Felt plug
13	Vacuum advance unit	28	Cap
14	Spacer	29	Screw
15	Oil retaining felt	30	Cap clip
		31	Setscrew

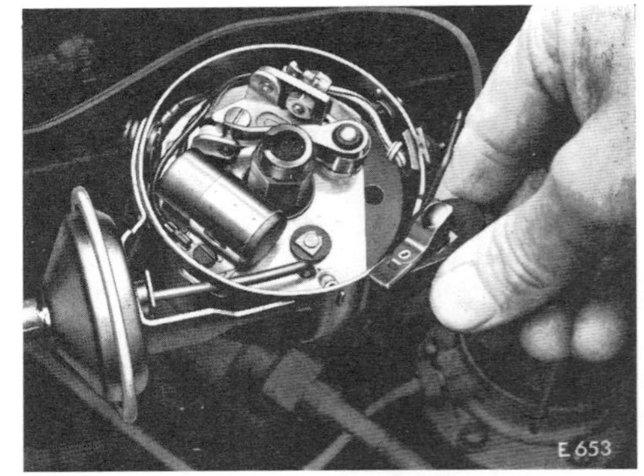

Fig. 43. Type D202 Delco distributor (Vitesse)

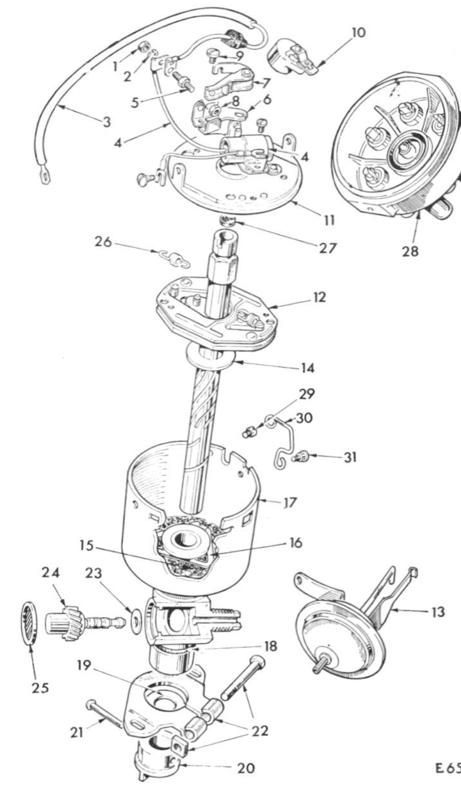

Fig. 44. Exploded arrangement of Vitesse distributor (A.C. Delco Type D202)

EXPLODED HEADLAMP ARRANGEMENT
HERALD, SPITFIRE AND VITESSE

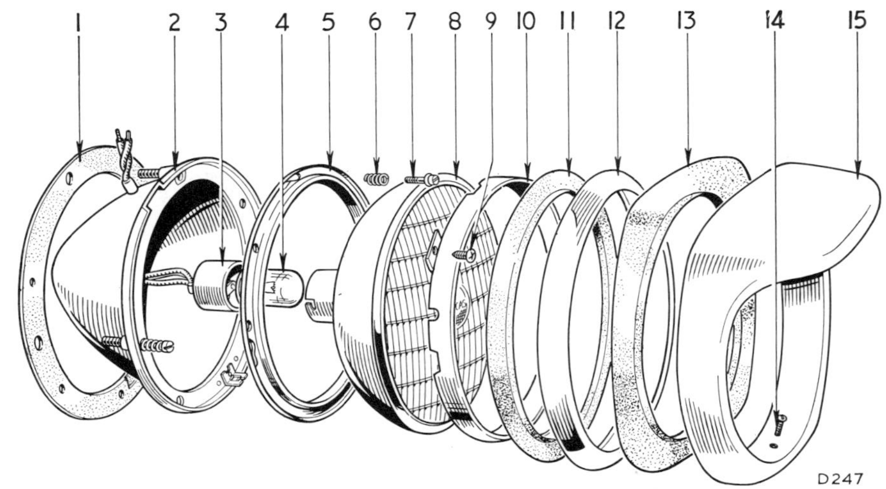

Fig. 45. Exploded arrangement of Herald 1200 and Spitfire headlamps

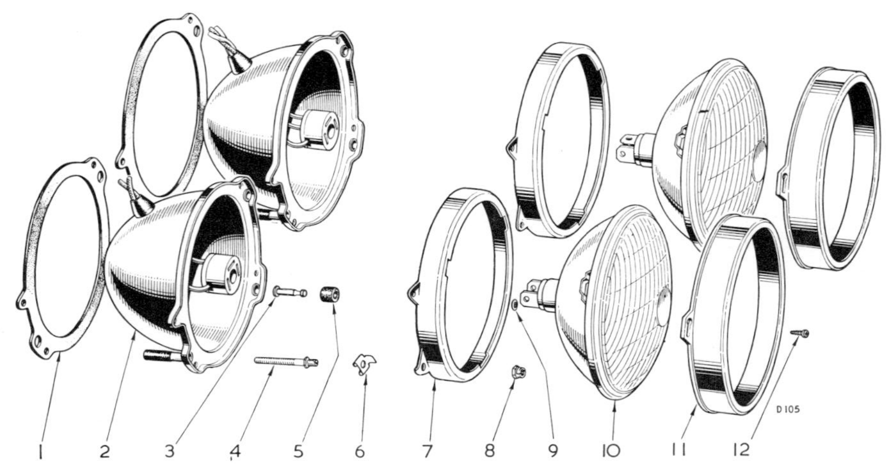

Fig. 46. Exploded arrangement of Vitesse headlamps

Key to Fig. 45

1	Rubber seal	9	Screw
2	Housing	10	Outer rim
3	Adaptor	*11	Sealing rubber
4	Bulb	*12	Snap-on rim
5	Inner rim	†13	Sealing rubber
6	Spring	†14	Screw
7	Screw	†15	Rim
8	Light unit		

*Spitfire only. †Herald only.

Key to Fig. 46

1	Seal	7	Adaptor
2	Housing	8	Locknut
3	Pivot	9	Clip
4	Adjuster	10	Light unit
5	Bush	11	Rim
6	Clip	12	Screws

Fig. 47. Adjusting main beam, Herald 1200 and Spitfire

Fig. 48. Renewing light unit, Vitesse

LAMPS

Headlamp Bulb Replacement (Spitfire)

Remove the Snap-on rim shown on Fig. 45 by inserting the end of the special tool (provided in the kit) behind the lower edge of the rim and levering sideways. Press in the lamp unit against the tension of the adjusting screw springs and turn in an anti-clockwise direction until the key-slot holes in the rim line up with the screw heads. The lamp unit can then be drawn off. Do not rotate any of the screws, as this will affect the alignment of the reflector when assembled.

Rotate the adaptor anti-clockwise and pull off, then the headlamp bulb can be removed. Care should be taken to see that the bulb does not drop out.

NOTE : Headlamp bulbs cannot be removed from the sealed beam units fitted to cars which are exported to the U.S.A. Bulb failure will necessitate unit replacement.

Headlamp Unit Replacement

Remove the lamp unit and bulb as described above. Unscrew three screws (9) and separate the inner and outer rims (5) and (10) from the light unit (8).

Fit a new unit by reversing the procedure and ensure that the locating clips at the edge of the light unit fit into corresponding slots in the rim.

Headlamp Alignment

The main beam is aligned in the vertical plane by turning the screw at the top of the lamp and in the horizontal plane by turning the screw on the side. Alignment of the beam on one lamp is best carried out with the other lamp covered.

Maximum illumination is obtained, and discomfort to other road users is prevented, by ensuring that the lamp beams do not project above the horizontal when the vehicle is fully laden.

Where adjustment is required, one of the following methods may be employed, subject to minor variations which may be necessary to meet varying conditions in different countries.

Method 1.

Lucas Beamsetter.

Remove the front rim and dust excluding rubber to gain access to the adjusting screws.

Roll the alignment bar into contact with the front wheels.

Wheel the beamsetter forward so that the two projecting arms butt against the alignment bar.

Adjust the height of the beamsetter unit to the level of the headlamp.

If the vehicle is not carrying its normal complement of passengers the height of the screen at the forward end of the setter may be adjusted to compensate for beam depression. The adjustment is calibrated in degrees and in inches per hundred feet and is effected by moving the lever to the appropriate angle of dip. This angle is dependent on the normal loading of the car. 0·5° = 2 ft. 7 ins. in 100 yards (0·787 metres in 91·44 metres).

Switch on the lamp under test and adjust the screws to bring the beam image between the marker lines on the screen with the highest meter reading.

Method 2.

Wall Chart.

Position the car on level ground with the front facing squarely the screen or wall at a distance of 12½ ft. (3·8 metres) from the screen.

Adjust the spheres (B) ⅞″ (22·2 mm.) below the centre line of the lamps and to an equal distance either side of the centre line of the car.

Where the screen is not available, a wall may be marked to correspond with the adjustments given with the screen.

With one lamp covered, adjust the screws on the other lamp to provide the pattern shown in Fig. 50.

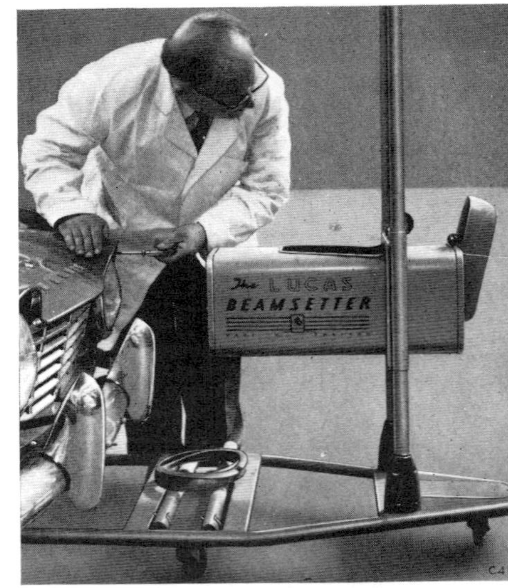

Fig. 49. Using Lucas beamsetters

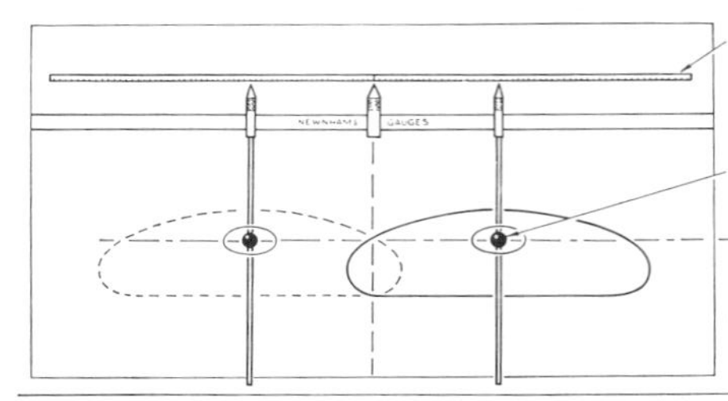

Fig. 50. Showing light pattern projected on new lamps gauge

Fig. 51. Checking floor level

Fig. 52. Setting floor level on Lev-L-Lite unit

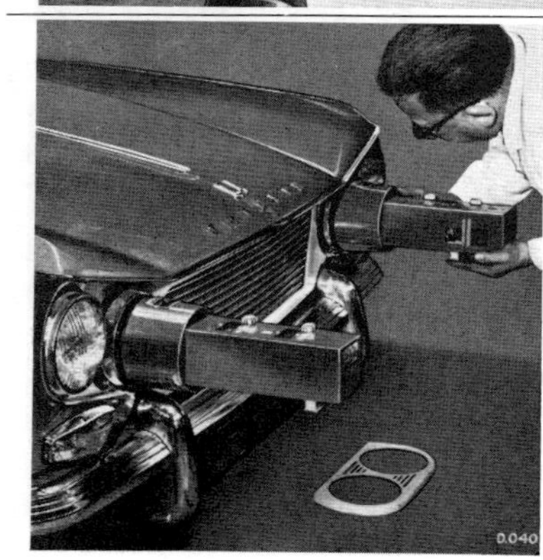

Fig. 53. Fitting Lev-L-Lite units to lamps

HEADLAMP SETTING

VITESSE

The use of a Lucas Lev-L-Lite mechanical aimer will ensure quick and accurate aiming of Vitesse sealed beam light units having aiming pads moulded to their lenses. Lamp aiming can therefore be accomplished by mechanically setting the plane of the pads in fixed relation to the direction of travel, thus dispensing with the need of having the headlamps switched on during adjustment.

Equipment

The complete kit consists of a right- and left-hand aimer, suitable for both 5¾″ and 7″ light units; a transit and target, for checking floor levels; two adaptor rings, for use with 7″ light units; and an instruction chart.

Transit and Target

Based on the split image principle and using a built-in spirit level as a reference, transit and target used together form a floor level indicator which is used as follows:—

The two units face one another on the same side of the vehicle, the target adjacent to the rear wheel and the transit adjacent to the front. After adjusting the transit until a single image is seen in the sights, a dial is turned to balance the spirit level. The reading obtained from here is used as a floor correction figure for both aimers.

The Mechanical Aimer

Here again the spirit level and split image principle is used in the design of the aimer. The complete assembly is held in position on the aiming pads, by a powerful rubber suction cup which engages with the headlamp lens.

When lateral aim is correct a single image should appear in the viewing port. After setting the aimer for the required angle of dip, vertical aim is correct when the spirit level is balanced.

Four Headlamp Adjustment

When aiming sealed beam headlamps with the Lev-L-Lite beam aimers, the following procedure should be adopted:—

Adjust the aimers for floor level as follows:—

Drive the car on to selected area, which need not be level but must be flat. Place the transit at front wheel and the target at the rear wheel, Fig. 51. Turn the transit until target is visible. Adjust screw on back of the transit until the split image is aligned. Turn dial on side of transit until bubble is centred in the level dial. Repeat for the other side of the car. Turn the floor level compensator on each aimer until adjoining dial reads the same as the plus or minus reading on the transit dial.

NOTE: Aimers may be used in additional locations after checking the floor level at each location with the transit and target and painting correction figures on the floor.

Check and, if required, adjust tyre pressures.

Rock the car sideways to equalize springs, and remove the lamp rims.

Clean the lens and attach the beam aimers to the lamps with the split image aperture facing the centre line of the car as follows:—

Place the front of the aimer over the locating pads spaced 120° apart on the lens. Hold the aimer firmly against the lens. Push the rubber cup against the glass using the white handle and then withdraw the handle until the retaining spring is heard to operate.

The aimer is now self-supporting.

Adjusting vertical aim:

Turn the knob at "Up-Down" dial until the pointer is at 2 down. This number indicates the number of inches the beam will drop in 25 ft.

Slacken the locknut and turn the headlamp vertical aim screw (1) counter-clockwise until bubble is off-centre. Then turn screw clockwise until bubble is centred for correct aim. Retighten the locknut.

Repeat the operation on other headlamp.

Adjusting horizontal aim:

Set "Right-Left" dial on zero. Check split image in viewing port. Rotate aimer slightly, if necessary, to locate target on opposite lamp. Slacken the locknut and turn the horizontal adjusting screw (2) on the lamp until the split image is aligned. Retighten the locknut.

Re-check and, if required, adjust vertical aim.

Repeat the above adjustments with opposite headlamp.

Hold the aimer, press the spring catch and push handle towards the headlamp to release aimer.

Repeat the above adjustments on other pair of headlamps.

Refit the rims.

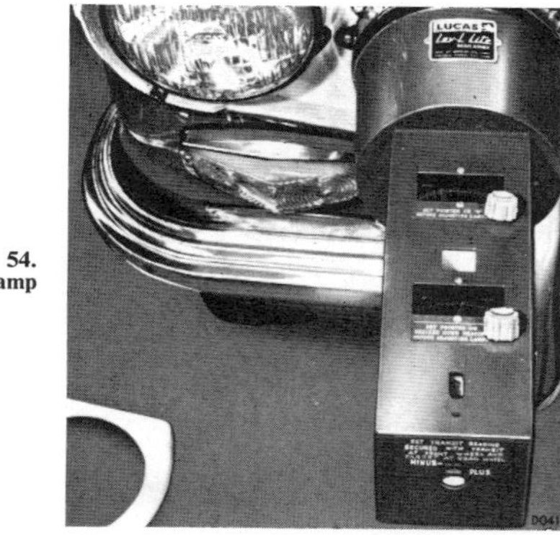

Fig. 54. Checking lamp

Fig. 55. Beam alignment adjustment screws

1 Vertical adjustment

2 Horizontal adjustment

Fig. 56. Refitting cowl

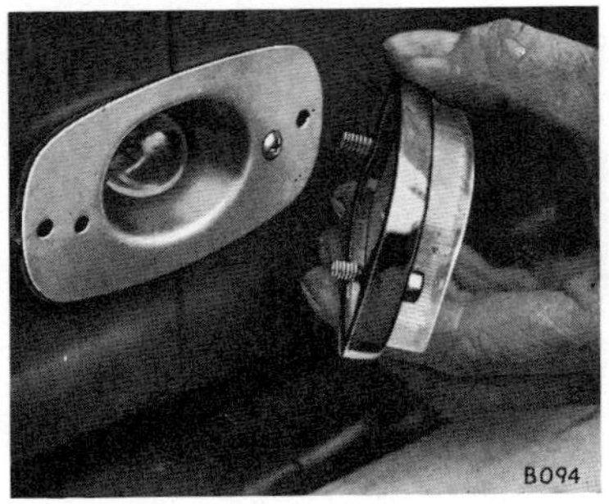

Fig. 57.
Front parking and flasher lamps (Herald)

Front parking and flasher lamps

HERALD 1200 (Fig. 57)

The side and flasher lamp has two filaments incorporated in the same bulb. The bulb is accessible after two screws have been removed from the rim, and the rim and lens lifted away.

Fig. 58.
Front parking and flasher lamps (Vitesse)

VITESSE (Fig. 58)

The side and flasher lamp has two bulbs incorporated in the same housing. The parking bulb is accessible after two screws have been removed from the rim, and the rim and lens lifted away. To gain access to the flasher bulb, withdraw the amber dome.

Fig. 59.
Front parking and flasher lamps (Spitfire)

SPITFIRE (Fig. 59)

With the aid of a thin screwdriver, turn back the rubber and remove the rim. This will permit the glass lens to be similarly removed to gain access to the bulb. When re-assembling the components, fit the glass lens first.

Fig. 60.
Tail/stop and flasher lamps (Herald and Vitesse)

Tail/stop and flasher lamps

HERALD 1200 AND VITESSE (Fig. 60)

The tail/stop and flasher lamp bulbs are incorporated in the same housing. To gain access to the bulbs, remove two screws and take off the lens. The flasher bulb, at the top, has a single filament. The lower bulb for "tail and stop" illumination incorporates twin filaments.

SPITFIRE (Fig. 61)

Take out two screws and remove the lens to gain access to the twin filament "tail and stop" bulb.

With the aid of a thin screwdriver, turn back the rubber and remove the rim. This permits the glass lens to be similarly removed to gain access to the single filament "flasher" bulb.

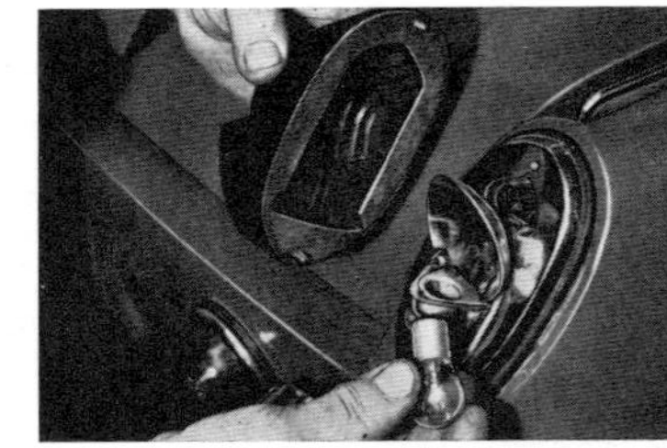

Fig. 61.
Tail/stop and flasher lamps (Spitfire)

Number plate illumination lamp

HERALD 1200

To gain access to the bulb, remove the cover securing screw and lift off the cover and the glass lens.

VITESSE (Fig. 62)

Raise the locker lid to gain access to the bulb.

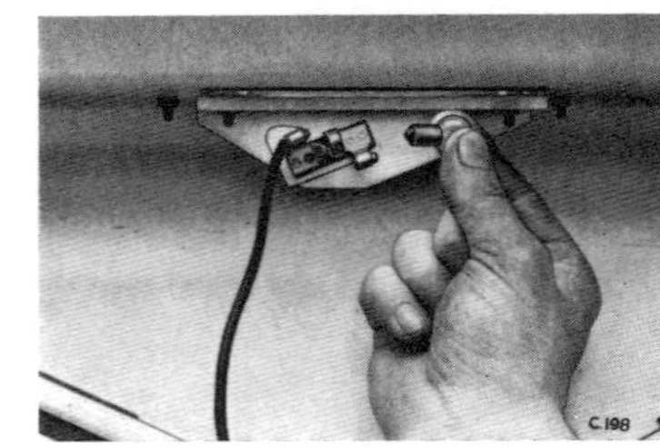

Fig. 62.
Number plate illumination lamp (Vitesse)

SPITFIRE (Fig. 63)

To gain access to the bulb, remove the cover securing screw and lift off the cover and the glass lens.

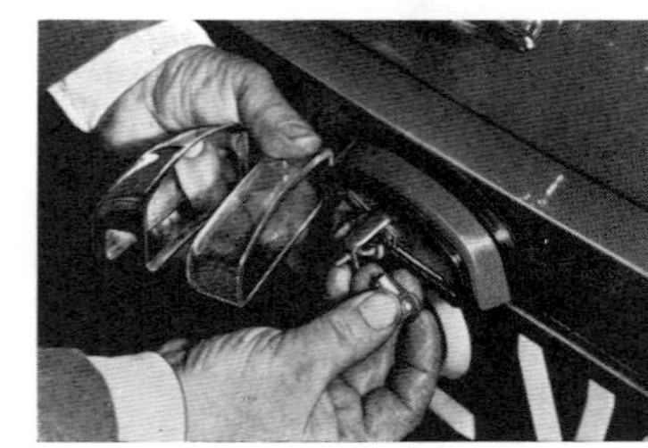

Fig. 63.
Number plate illumination lamp (Spitfire)

Instrument panel and warning lamps

HERALD 1200 AND VITESSE

Illumination bulbs are located in the rear of the instrument, which also houses the high beam, ignition and oil warning light bulbs.

The direction indicator monitor bulb is accessible from behind the facia.

Renewal of the facia illuminating bulb can be readily accomplished from the front of the facia.

SPITFIRE

Instrument illumination and warning light bulbs are accessible from behind the facia.

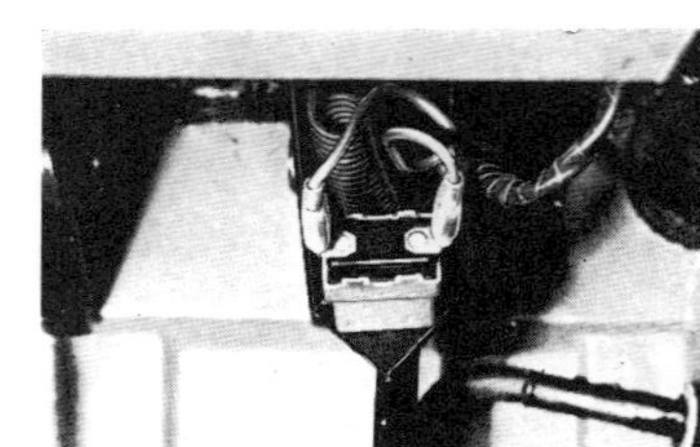

Fig. 64.
Stop lamp switch (Spitfire)

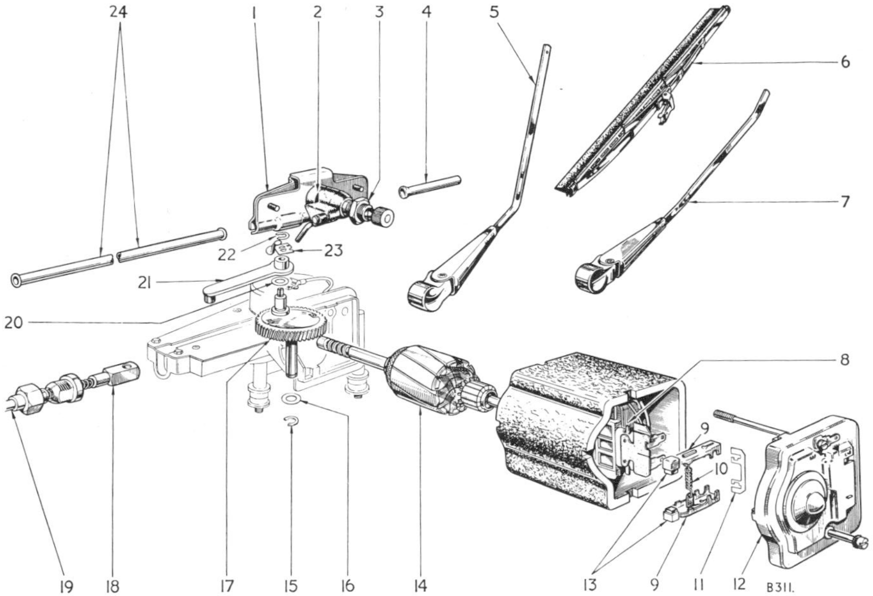

1	Wheel box	9	Brushgear	17	Final drive wheel
2	Jet and bush assembly	10	Tension spring and retainers	18	Cable rack
3	Nut	11	Brushgear retainer	19	Rigid tubing—left-hand side
4	Rigid tubing—right-hand side	12	End cover	20	Spacer
5	Wiper arm	13	Brushes	21	Connecting rod
6	Blade	14	Armature	22	Circlip
7	Wiper arm	15	Circlip	23	Parking switch contact
8	Field coil assembly	16	Washer	24	Rigid tubing—centre section

Fig. 65. Exploded arrangement of windscreen wiper mechanism

Fig. 66. Location of Herald 1200 windscreen wiper motor

WINDSCREEN WIPER

General

The motor and gearbox unit is mounted on three pillars cast integral with the unit body and is located on the right-hand side of the dash panel in the engine compartment. Rotary motion of the motor armature is converted to a reciprocating movement by a single stage worm and nylon gear to which a connecting rod is attached. This actuates the cable rack which consists of a flexible core of steel wire wound with a wire helix to engage with a gear in each wheelbox for transmitting the reciprocating motion to the wiper arm spindles.

A parking switch is incorporated in the domed cover of the gearbox. On switching off at the wiper control switch, the motor continues to run until the moving contact of the parking switch reaches the insulated sector portion and so interrupts the earth return circuit and stops the motor. The domed cover is adjustable to give the correct park position of the wiper blades.

Removal

Remove the wiper arms and blades.

Unscrew the large nut securing the outer tubing (19) to the gearbox.

Remove three bolts securing the motor mounting bracket to the dash panel and withdraw the motor complete with inner cable rack.

Dismantling

Mark the dome limit switch cover in relation to the gearbox lid, and remove the lid (four screws).

Release the circlip (22) and lift off the limit switch wiper (23).

Lift off the connecting rod (21) and cable rack (18). Note the spacer (20) between the connecting rod (21) and final drive wheel (17).

Remove two bolts and lift off the end cover (12).

Lift out the brushgear retainer (11) and remove the brushgear (9).

Remove the body complete with field coil; the red earth cable is long enough to permit the body to be lifted clear of the armature.

Remove the armature.

If further dismantling is required, remove the circlip (15) and washer (16). Use a fine file to remove any burrs from around the circlip groove and remove the final drive wheel (17).

Clean all parts and examine them for wear or damage.

Mark the yoke and field coil relative to each other. Remove two screws and withdraw the field coil pole piece and field coil.

Re-assembly

To re-assemble, reverse the dismantling procedure and note the following:—

Check brush tension. This should be between 125 and 140 grammes.

The adjusting screw in the side of the gearbox should be set and firmly locked to permit 0·008″ to 0·012″ (0·203 to 0·305 mm.) end play of the armature. Before re-connecting the inner rack, push the rack back into the tubing and wheelboxes and withdraw the rack from the tubing using a spring balance. The force required should not exceed 6 lbs.

Lubrication

The commutator and brush gear must be free of oil or grease. Apply Oilene, B.B.B. or engine oil to the bearings of the final drive wheel and armature.

If the gearbox has been washed clean, use 25 to 35 cubic centimetres of Ragosine Listate grease to refill.

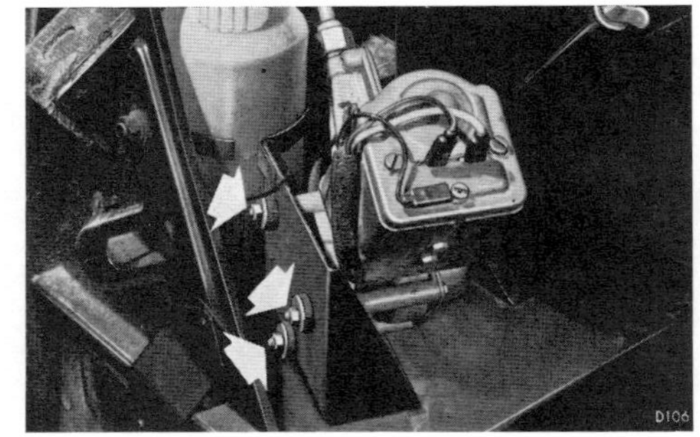

Fig. 67. Location of Vitesse windscreen-wiper motor

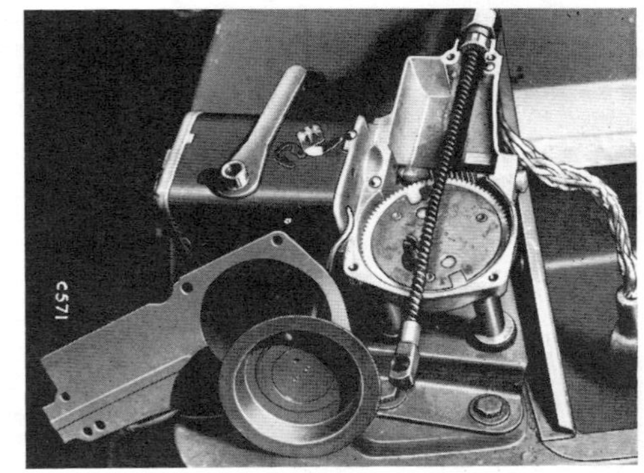

Fig. 68. Top cover removed

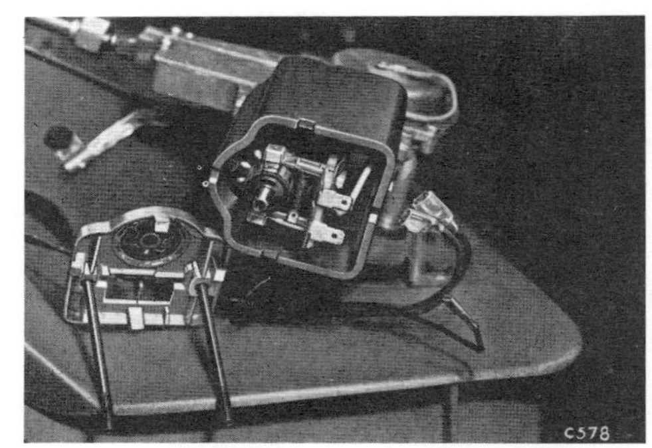

Fig. 69. End cover removed to show brush gear

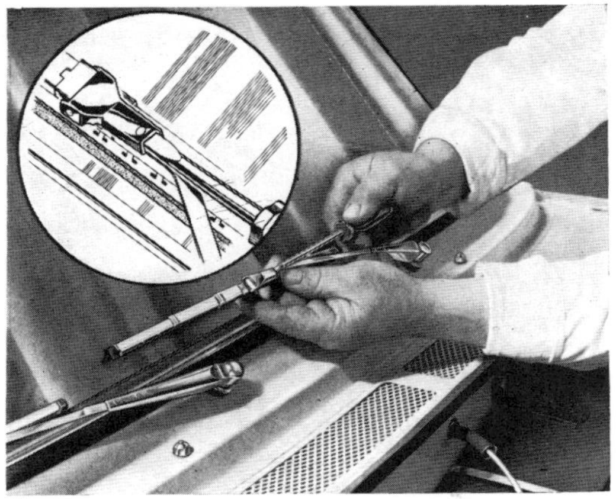

Fig. 70. Removing wiper blades

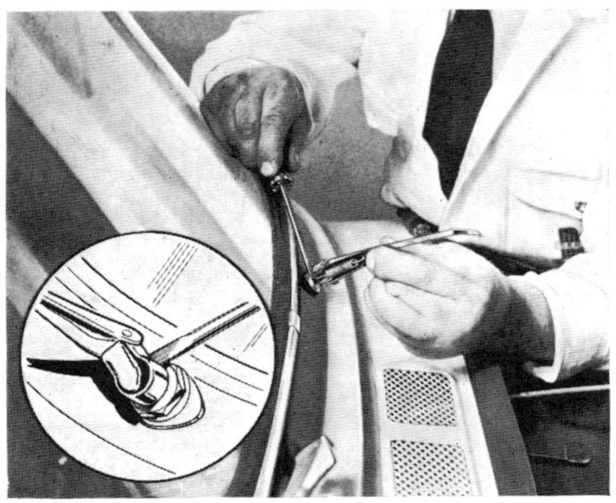

Fig. 71. Removing wiper arms

Fig. 72. Location of flasher unit (1) under the facia (Spitfire)

Wiper Wheel Boxes

To Remove

Disconnect the cables from the battery and wiper motor. Note the cable colours relative to the motor terminals.

Take off the wiper arms, complete with blades, and remove the wiper motor.

Remove the nut and rubber bush securing each wiper box to the lower windscreen rail and push the boxes into the car.

Working from inside the car, withdraw the boxes sufficiently to permit removal of the screws securing the tubing to the wheel box and withdraw the box.

To Refit

Reverse the above.

FLASHER UNIT DIRECTION-INDICATOR MODEL FL.5

Housed in a small cylindrical container, the FL.5 Flasher Unit incorporates an actuating wire which heats and cools alternately to operate the main armature and associated pair of contacts in the flasher lamp supply circuit. Simultaneously a secondary armature operates the pilot contacts which cause a warning light to flash when the system is functioning correctly.

Defective Flasher Units cannot be dismantled for subsequent reassembly and must therefore be renewed. Handle the Flasher Unit with care, otherwise the delicate setting may be disturbed and the unit rendered unserviceable.

Trace the cause of faulty operation as follows:—

(i) Check the bulbs for broken filaments.
(ii) Check all flasher circuit connections.
(iii) Switch on the ignition and check the voltage at terminal 'B' (12 volts).
(iv) Connect terminals 'B' and 'L' together and operate the direction-indicator switch. If the flasher lamps light, the Flasher Unit is defective. If the flasher lamps do not light, check the direction-indicator switch.

FUEL CONTENTS GAUGE

The fuel indicator gauge on Spitfire and Estate cars, operates on a stabilized 10 volts in conjunction with a Tank Unit and Stabilizer.

The Herald 1200 and Vitesse fuel indicator gauge operates on 12 volts in conjunction with a Tank Unit only. The indicator gauge, tank unit and stabilizer are sealed units which cannot be repaired but each may be renewed independently of each other.

Fault Finding

1. No reading on fuel indicator.
   (a) Check the fuse between A3 and A4.
   (b) Check the input and output voltages at the stabilizer. These should be at battery voltage and 10 volts respectively. If the input voltage is correct then the cable between the fuse unit and stabilizer is in order.
   If an incorrect or no-volts reading is obtained at the output terminal "T" on the stabilizer then the stabilizer is faulty and must be renewed.
   (c) Remove the tank unit and test by substituting it with a "known" unit.
2. High or low reading on fuel indicator.
   (a) Check the voltage stabilizer as described in 1 (b) above.
   (b) Check the instrument by substituting "known" components.
   (c) Check condition of insulation of interconnecting cables between the units for lead to earth.
3. Intermittent reading.
   (a) Check for loose connections.
   (b) Substitute voltage stabilizer.
   (c) Substitute indicator and tank unit in turn with similar type.

To Renew

Disconnect the cables from the battery and tank unit.

HERALD 1200 AND VITESSE

Take out six screws and remove the old unit from the tank, noting the position of the arm and float.

Remove the cork seal and all trace of the old sealing compound.

Liberally coat the contacting surfaces of the new cork seal and tank unit with sealing compound. Enter the float and arm of the new unit into the tank aperture and, taking care not to bend or distort the arm, secure the unit with six screws.

Reconnect the cables to the unit and battery.

SPITFIRE

Using a screwdriver, turn the retaining ring (see Fig. 75) to release the tank unit. Withdraw the unit from the tank and replace it with a new unit. No sealing compound is required.

Fig. 73. Location of tank unit (Herald and Vitesse)

Fig. 74. Removing tank unit (Herald and Vitesse)

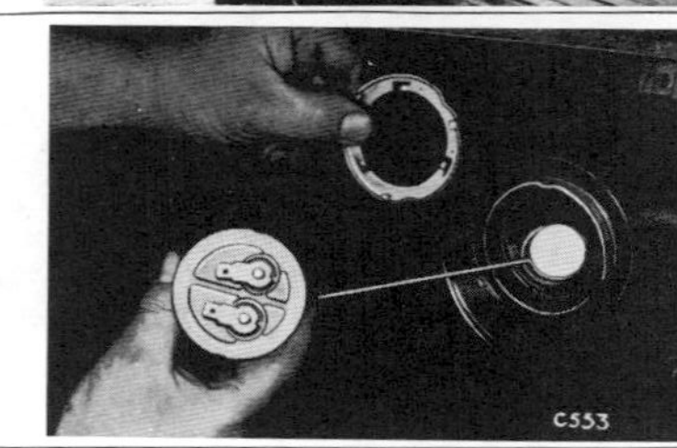

Fig. 75. Removing tank unit (Spitfire)

Fig. 76. Location of tank unit (Spitfire)

Fig. 77. Adjusting the horn

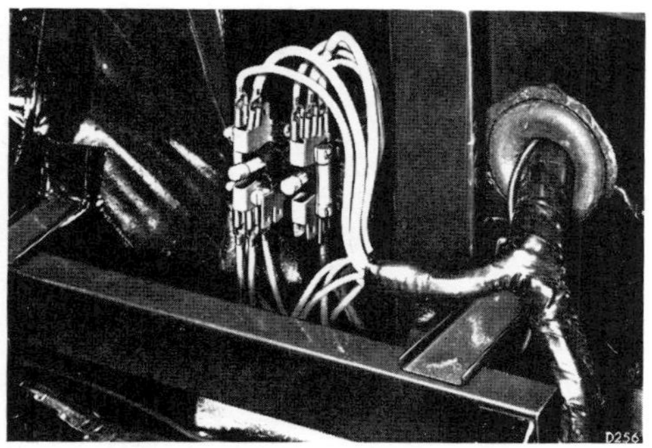

Fig. 78. Vitesse fuse unit (cover removed)

1. Voltage stabilizer
2. Flasher unit
3. Line Fuse
4. Fuse Unit

Fig. 79. Location of Spitfire fuses

WIND TONE HORNS MODEL 9H

Maintenance

If a horn fails to sound or its performance is unsatisfactory, check the following and rectify as necessary :—

1. Battery condition.
2. Loose or broken connection in the horn circuit.
3. Loose fixing bolts.

If the above points are in order, adjust the horn as follows :—

Adjustment

Adjustment does not alter the pitch of the note but merely takes up the wear of moving parts.

Disconnect one horn whilst adjusting the other, and take care to avoid earthing disconnected live wires. Connect a first grade moving-coil 0-10A ammeter in series with the horn and adjust the small serrated adjustment screw on the side of the horn at which the cables terminate.

Turn the adjusting screw clockwise to increase the current, or anti-clockwise to decrease it, until the best performance is obtained with the least current.

If adjustment is being made without an ammeter, turn the adjusting screws anti-clockwise until the horn just fails to sound; then turn it back one quarter of a turn.

WARNING

Do not disturb the central slotted stem and locking nut.

FUSES

A Lucas Type 4FJ fuse unit housing two 35 ampere fuses is fitted on Vitesse and Spitfire cars.

VITESSE

The fuse unit fitted to the Vitesse is located behind the battery or the clutch and brake master cylinders. One fuse, fed by a brown input cable, protects the horn, courtesy light and headlamp flasher circuits.

A second fuse, fed by a white cable from the ignition switch, protects the instruments and ancillary equipment.

SPITFIRE

The fuse unit fitted to the Spitfire is located adjacent to the flasher unit under the facia panel on the left-hand side of the car. One fuse, fed by a red/green cable from the master lighting switch, protects the front parking and tail lamp circuits.

A second fuse, fed by a white cable from the ignition switch, protects the instruments and ancillary equipment.

The horns and headlamp flasher circuits are protected by an "in line" fuse, located near the fuse unit.

HERALD

None of the circuits are protected by fuses.

CABLE CONNECTORS

Servicing

Connectors which are similar in design to those fitted in production are available as service replacements. The new connectors may be fitted as shown in Fig. 80.

1. Push the rubber sleeve clear of the end of the cable and strip the insulation from the conductor for approximately $\frac{5}{16}''$ (8 mm.) for 12 ampere connector or $\frac{7}{16}''$ (11 mm.) for 35 ampere connector.
2. Pass the conductor through the aperture and secure the cables with the tags.
3. Bend the conductors back over the connector and spread flat.
4. Solder the conductors neatly to the connector. Do not allow the solder to run freely through the aperture. Re-tighten the rubber insulating sleeve.

High Tension Cables

The 7 mm. neoprene covered H.T. cables are of the resistive type having resistance of approximately 420 ohms per inch (2·5 cm.).

Suppression of ignition interference to radio and television is effected by a conductor composed of carbon impregnated nylon or cotton cords.

A serviceable cable should measure between 3,000 and 12,000 ohms.

These resistive cables must not be replaced with cables having tinned copper conductors.

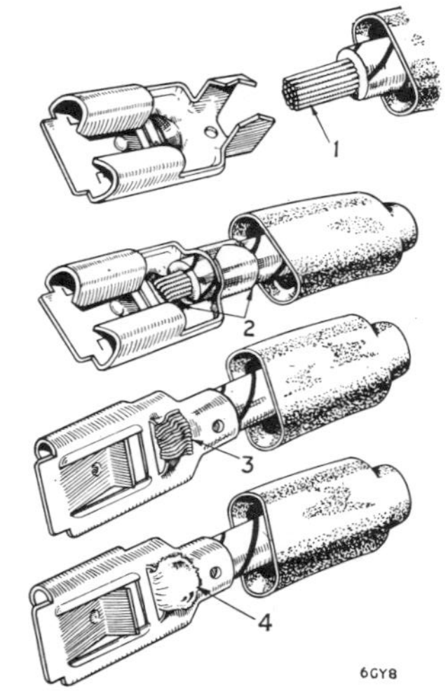

Fig. 80 Lucar connectors

SPITFIRE

The loom, which extends from the top centre of the grille to the rear lamps, is secured to left-hand side of the chassis frame with clips welded to the frame.

The front end of the loom terminates with the group of snap connectors for the front end lighting. Branches for the horns, generator, oil pressure switch and temperature gauge, leave the loom before it passes through the dash panel to the instrument panel where branches re-enter the engine compartment at two places. The first is adjacent to the coil with connections for the starter solenoid control box and coil. The second branch is on the right-hand side of car with connections for the wiper motor.

The loom passes from the instrument panel to the fuse unit, voltage stabilizer and flasher unit located under the left-hand side of the facia, with a branch for the brake stop lamp switch, along the floor to the rear of the car, to the tank unit and rear end lighting.

HERALD AND VITESSE

A two section harness loom joined by a group of snap connectors located under the left-hand side of the facia is employed.

The run of the loom which commences with a group of connectors for the front end lighting at the front end of the bonnet, is secured to the left-hand side of the chassis frame. Branches for the horns, generator, oil pressure switch, and brake stop lamps (and the fuse unit on Vitesse only) leave the harness before passing through the dash panel to the switches, facia and the snap connectors referred to above. The harness re-enters the engine compartment on the right-hand side of the car with connections for the wiper motor.

The loom passes along the left-hand side of the floor, to the rear of the door. At this point it passes behind the trim panel to the rear of the fuel tank and terminates with connectors for the rear end lighting.

DIAGNOSIS OF FAULTS, TEST EQUIPMENT AND SPECIFICATIONS

Diagnosis of Faults, Test Equipment and Specification.

To those familar with the use of test equipment the following section will require little explanation. The use of test equipment in a logical sequence has proved the most satisfactory method of detecting defects and mal-adjustments which affect the performance of the engine. For test purposes there are five main "areas".

1. The Starting System .. .. .. Battery, starter motor and circuit.
2. The Charging System .. .. .. Battery, generator, regulator and circuit.
3. The Ignition System .. .. .. Spark plugs, distributor, coil, condenser and circuit.
4. The Fuel System .. .. Fuel pump, carburettors, air cleaners, fuel filters and delivery pipes.
5. Compression and Induction .. .. Valves, pistons and rings, head gasket, inlet manifold and flanges.

This division is only made for convenience. Obviously the performance of the engine as a whole is dependent on the relation between all its working parts as well as their individual behaviour.

Equipment suitable for detailed testing of these areas or systems is commercially available, and the following are representative and suitable.

1. Battery-starter tester and slow/fast battery charger.
2. Volt amp. tester with generator field control and load control.

3, 4 and 5.
Console type tester including oscilloscope, voltmeter, ammeter, combustion analyser, fuel pump tester, vacuum tester, tachometer, timing stroboscope and various accessories.

Fig. 1. Crypton "Motorscope" analyser

The Ignition Oscilloscope

This is an adaptation of a laboratory instrument which has been used for many years in the electrical and electronic fields. It displays the operation of the ignition system **as a whole.** Its chief advantage is that it enables any departures from normal operation to be seen very quickly. It is not, however, a specific fault finder. It displays the ionisation or firing voltage developed by the coil before current flows across the spark plug electrodes and forms the spark, and the steady voltage at which the current flow occurs. Both these are valuable in determining spark plug condition, especially under "snap acceleration". However, the firing voltage is of extremely short duration and is, in fact, altered by the very process of measuring it. For this reason it is necessary to use the equipment manufacturers' manual when interpreting the results obtained, since different manufacturers use different methods of obtaining these measurements.

The graphical picture of the voltage changes occurring in the coil windings does enable the presence of ignition faults to be detected very quickly and the electrical nature of these faults can be seen. Specific test instruments such as the ohmeter, voltmeter, coil tester and condenser tester can then be used to "pin-point" the actual cause of the trouble.

NOTE: The manufacturers of the test equipment shown provide instruction and training in its use, and this is not part of the function of this manual.

The test procedures shown, form a sequence, and might be called a "Quality Control Quick Check", either to determine the exact service needs of the vehicle (which might include further testing), or as an inspection procedure to establish that the vehicle is correctly adjusted and has no defective components. The time normally taken by an experienced tester would be 10 minutes approximately.

It is essential that the test procedure is adhered to, and that the very minimum of adjustments are actually made until the whole picture has been obtained.

Fig. 2. Distributor tester

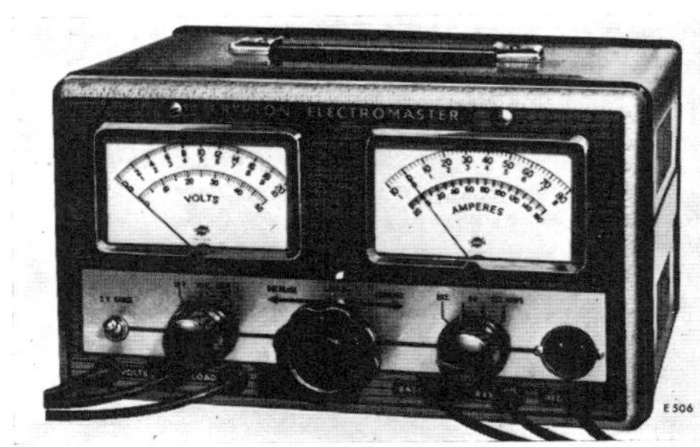

Fig. 3. Volt/Amp. tester

Fig. 4. Battery tester and charger

Startability

NOTE: Connect to the switch side of any ballast resistance on coil.

STATIC. With the ignition switch "ON" the current flows from the battery through the voltage regulator series winding, through the ammeter (if fitted), through the ignition switch to the auxiliary circuit and coil "SW" terminal. Note: "CB" terminal on coil must be connected to earth when making this test. The circuit and all connections are good if 11·5 volts or more are shown at the coil "SW" terminal.

Cranking

With the "CB" terminal still earthed. This test further confirms the STATIC test and also checks the following items—the battery under full starter load, the action of the starter switch, the starter motor, the flywheel ring gear, also the connections to the battery and chassis earths. The result is good if 10 volts or better are recorded when the engine is warm.

Charging

Remove "CB" earth. Start the engine and speed up to about 2,000 r.p.m. to make the generator charge the battery. Between 13 volts and 14 volts should be recorded at coil "SW" terminal. If reading is under 13 volts the fan belt may be slipping or the regulator set low. If more than 14 volts are recorded there is a risk of the light bulbs failing due to excessive voltage. Check for a high regulator setting.

Volt Drop Through Distributor

With the engine stationary, the ignition switched on and the distributor contact points closed, a reading at the coil "CB" terminal of 0·2 volt or less should be obtained on Lucas systems and 0·1 volt or less on other systems. This test proves that the circuit from the coil to the distributor, through the distributor internal connections, and the ignition points to earth is satisfactory.

Distributor Points Dwell

This test indicates any difference in timing between cylinders. It can be caused by slack in the chain or gears driving the camshaft, also the skew gears driving the oil pump and distributor, or the dog coupling to the distributor where this is used. It may be an indication of trouble in the distributor. The overlap should not exceed 3°. This represents 6° at the crankshaft and so could be the cause of an engine running rough, particularly on high compression sports type engines.

Spark Plug Minimum and Spark Plug Maximum

All cylinders should indicate within about 2 KV of each other. The actual value obtained depends on a number of factors, some of these being: the compression ratio, rich or weak carburettor setting, radio suppressors or suppressed leads, the distributor rotor gap or the type of H.T. cable harness used, *e.g.*, long bunched leads or short spaced leads. The behaviour of the oscilloscope on different types of vehicle is quickly learnt with practice. In general, the average plug voltage should not exceed half the available coil H.T. with engine running light or two thirds of the available coil H.T. when under load.

Rotor Gap

By shorting various spark plugs to earth in turn it is possible to see the KV required to bridge the rotor gap. This should not exceed 5 KV or be less than 2 KV. If too high a rotor gap KV is shown the engine may miss at high speed or under load, whilst low rotor gap KV can result in misfiring due to the lack of the spark intensifying action needed to fire sooted or oiled spark plugs.

Coil H.T. Output

The coil output is established by removing the H.T. lead from any convenient spark plug. When the rotor is opposite this distributor cap segment there will be no path for the H.T. current to earth; the oscilloscope will therefore indicate the voltage available at the coil. Voltages between 10 KV and 24 KV can be expected according to the type of coil and vehicles. Link this H.T. KV reading with the spark plug KV readings previously obtained—the reserve KV available is what matters.

NOTE: Always test at exactly 1,000 r.p.m. so that a standard coil input voltage is maintained. Also remember that if a "sports" or very high voltage coil which is not a standard unit is fitted, it is possible for the spark to jump to earth inside the distributor cap so limiting the coil KV shown. This can usually be heard.

Power Check r.p.m. Drop

In this test each spark plug in turn is prevented from firing. If the cylinder compressions are equal, the tappet adjustment correct, there is no air leak on the induction pipe and multi-carburettors (when fitted) are in synchronisation, there should be an equal drop of engine r.p.m. on each cylinder.

Set Idle to the r.p.m. figure shown in data.

Timing at Idle should be noted.

Some makers give a stroboscopic timing figure but where a static timing figure only is given it is usually in order to add 2° to this figure to make up for any backlash which exists in the distributor drive and any movement of the advance weights. It is important to establish that the timing marks indicate either Top Dead Centre or are Firing Marks, otherwise serious errors in ignition timing will result. Our published data gives this information.

Air/Fuel Ratio at Idle

Should be recorded and used as a guide if carburettor adjustment proves necessary.

Timing Without Vacuum Advance at 3,000 r.p.m.

This is beyond doubt the most important test in the entire sequence. A serious error of timing at this speed could destroy the engine. Our published data shows the advance which should be obtained. Where limits are given, the higher figure will usually give the best performance—these figures should never be exceeded. If it is not possible to obtain correct timing at idle and 3,000 r.p.m. remove and test the distributor. Where it is not possible to service the distributor as required, it may be better to set the ignition timing at 3,000 r.p.m. and let any error that exists occur at the idle speed. Poor idling may result from this action but there is less risk of the engine being damaged until proper servicing takes place.

Timing with Vacuum Advance

With the engine still running at 3,000 r.p.m., the vacuum pipe should be replaced on the distributor and the additional ignition advance observed with the timing light. Not all vehicles have a vacuum advance unit, for this is an economy device, very valuable on touring vehicles, but not always capable of the precise timing needed on very high performance engines. Faults which may exist include: vacuum take-off on the carburettor not drilled, or incorrectly located, drilling blocked by gum or carbon, pipe to the distributor may be blocked or leaking, the vacuum diaphragm may be punctured or the movement inside the distributor restricted mechanically.

Air/Fuel Ratio at 3,000 r.p.m. should be recorded.

It is at this speed that a dirty or otherwise restricted air filter on the carburettor intake will show up. Some engines will not run correctly with the air silencer unit removed or with the filter element left out. Locate cause of an unusual reading.

Final Idle Speed

Set to the maker's suggested speed. Modern engines cannot be expected to run as slowly as was once possible. It is better to have the engine turning over easily and without the risk of stalling.

NOTE : Most manufacturers of cars and test equipment quote air/fuel ratios when testing carburettors and exhaust gases. Where exceptions to this exist a percentage figure is given. Fig. 5 shows the relationship of one to another.

WORK STUDY ON SIX CYLINDER ENGINE

QUALITY CONTROL QUICK CHECK

(Average of three timed checks)

		Secs.
1. Startability		
Lift Bonnet, Connect Test Leads		41·7
Volts at coil switch terminal	a. Static	18·3
	b. Cranking	12·3
	c. Charging	17·0
Volt drop through distributor	d.	21·3
2. At 1000 r.p.m.		
Distributor points dwell	.... Degrees	49·3
Distributor dwell overlap	.... Degrees	
Spark plugs minimum	.... KV	13·3
Spark plugs maximum	.... KV	
Rotor gap	.... KV	28·3
Coil H.T. output	.... KV	
Power check r.p.m. drop	1.... 2.... 3.... 4.... 5.... 6.... 7.... 8....	93·7
3. At Engine Idle Speed		
Idle set to	.... r.p.m.	32·7
Timing at idle	.... ° B.T.D.C.	42·3
Air/fuel ratio	.... /1	
Engine at 3000 r.p.m.		
Timing without vacuum advance	.... ° B.T.D.C.	58·3
Timing with vacuum advance	.... ° B.T.D.C.	
Air/fuel ratio	.... /1	8
Final Idle Speed		
In neutral	.... R.P.M.	28·0
In drive	.... R.P.M.	16·7
Remove the test leads, close bonnet		36·7

Job No.......... Car No.......... Tested by.......... Date..........

Times include completing record card .. .. .. **Total 8 min. 38 secs.**

The Quality Control Quick Check report card reproduced above indicates the comprehensive nature of the engine testing this method makes possible.

STANDARD-TRIUMPH 1964/5 MODELS

QUALITY CONTROL QUICK CHECK — PASS READINGS (ENGINE WARM)

TEST	HERALD 1200	HERALD 12/50	SPITFIRE 4	SPITFIRE 4 MK. 2	VITESSE
Startability—volts at coil, "switch" ignition on: (C.B. earthed) Engine Static . . . . Starter Cranking . . Generator Charging . .	11·5 min. 10·0 min. 13 to 14 V	11·5 min. 10·0 min. 13 to 14 V.	11·5 min. 10·0 min. 13 to 14 V.	As Spitfire	11·5 min. 10·0 min. 13 to 14 V.
Volt-drop through distributor, ignition on, engine static, distributor points closed	0·2 max.	0·2 max.	0·1 max. Delco Distributor	As Spitfire	0·1 max. Delco Distributor
Engine running at 1000 r.p.m. Distributor points dwell Spark plugs, min. . . Spark plugs, max. . . Rotor gap KV . . . . Coil H.T. output . .	60° ± 3° 5 KV 7 KV 5 max. 14 to 15 KV	60° ± 3° 5 KV 7 KV 5 max. 14 to 15 KV	36° ± 1° 5 KV 10 KV 5 max. 18 to 20 KV	As Spitfire	36° ± 1° 5 KV 10 KV 5 max. 18 to 20 KV
Engine idle speed	600 r.p.m.	600 r.p.m.	700 r.p.m.	700 r.p.m.	600 r.p.m.
Stroboscopic timing at idle Air/fuel ratio at idle . .	17° B.T.D.C. 12·8/1 to 13·0/1	17° B.T.D.C. 12·8/1 to 13·0/1	15° B.T.D.C. 12·8/1 to 13·0/1	17° B.T.D.C. 12·4/1 to 12·8/1	12° B.T.D.C. 12·8/1 to 13·0/1
Stroboscopic timing without vacuum advance . . . . Stroboscopic timing with vacuum advance . . Engine running at 3000 r.p.m. Air/fuel ratio . .	35° ± 2° 50° ± 4° 13·2/1 to 13·4/1	35° ± 2° 50° ± 4° 13·2/1 to 13·4/1	39° ± 2° 59° ± 4° 13·5/1 to 13·7/1	42° ± 2° 53° ± 4° 12·6/1 to 13·0/1	30° ± 2° 43° ± 4° 13·5/1 to 13·7/1

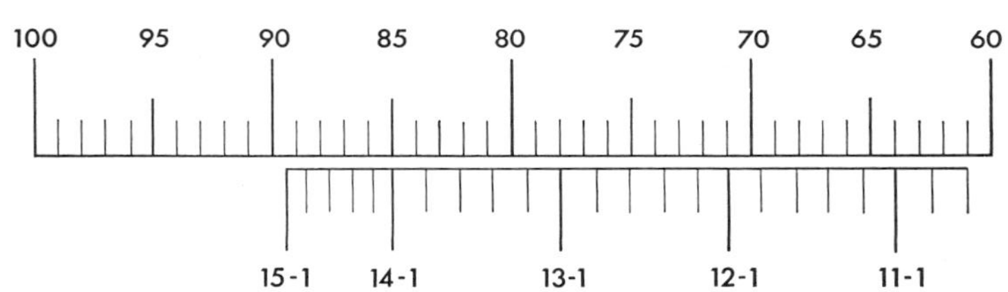

Fig. 5. Air/Fuel Ratio

INTRODUCTION TO SECTION 3

Information contained in this section details electrical equipment specific to the following vehicles that are all fitted with a negative earth electrical system.

Herald 1200 from approximately March 1968

Herald 13/60 introduced in October 1967

Spitfire Mark 3 introduced in March 1967

In all other respects the relevant information is contained in sections 1 and 2 of this group.

CAUTION: THE ABOVE MENTIONED VEHICLES ARE FITTED WITH A NEGATIVE EARTH ELECTRICAL SYSTEM. ENSURE THAT THE BATTERY EARTH LEAD IS ALWAYS CONNECTED TO THE BATTERY NEGATIVE TERMINAL.

EXERCISE CARE WHEN CONNECTING INTO CIRCUIT ANY ACCESSORY THAT MAY CONTAIN SILICON DIODES OR TRANSISTORS. IRREPARABLE DAMAGE MAY RESULT TO SUCH POLARITY SENSITIVE COMPONENTS IF INCORRECTLY FITTED.

NOTE: No polarity sensitive components are fitted to the vehicle during production. However, any of the following accessories — approved or unapproved by Leyland Triumph — may contain such components: alternator systems, automatic anti-dazzle mirrors, automatic dipping systems, automatic parking lamp systems, electronic ignition systems, electronic tachometers and radios.

WIRING DIAGRAM — HERALD 1200
WITH NEGATIVE EARTH

KEY TO WIRING DIAGRAM — HERALD 1200 WITH NEGATIVE EARTH

CAUTION: HERALD 1200 VEHICLES PRODUCED FROM APPROXIMATELY MARCH 1968 – COMMISSION NUMBERS GA 238107 AND GB 57263 – ARE FITTED WITH A NEGATIVE EARTH ELECTRICAL SYSTEM. ENSURE THAT THE BATTERY EARTH LEAD IS ALWAYS CONNECTED TO THE BATTERY NEGATIVE TERMINAL.

EXERCISE CARE WHEN CONNECTING INTO CIRCUIT ANY ACCESSORY THAT MAY CONTAIN SILICON DIODES OR TRANSISTORS. IRREPARABLE DAMAGE MAY RESULT TO SUCH POLARITY SENSITIVE COMPONENTS IF INCORRECTLY FITTED.

NOTE: No polarity sensitive components are fitted to the vehicle during production. However, any of the following accessories—approved or unapproved by Leyland Triumph—may contain such components: Alternator systems, Automatic anti-dazzle mirrors, Automatic dipping systems, Automatic parking lamp systems, Electronic ignition systems, Electronic tachometers and Radios.

1 Generator
2 Control box
3 Ignition warning light
4 Ignition/starter switch
4A Ignition/starter switch radio supply connector
5 Horn
6 Horn
7 Horn push
8 Battery
9 Starter solenoid
10 Starter motor
11 Master light switch
12 Column light switch
13 Main beam warning light
14 Main beam
15 Main beam
16 Dip beam
17 Dip beam
18 Front parking lamp
19 Front parking lamp
20 Heater switch
21 Heater motor
22 Facia lamp
23 Door switch
24 Door switch
25 Instrument illumination
26 Instrument illumination
27 Plate illumination lamp
28 Tail lamp
29 Tail lamp
30 Ignition coil
31 Ignition distributor
32 Oil pressure warning light
33 Oil pressure switch
34 Voltage stabilizer
35 Fuel indicator
36 Fuel tank unit
37 Stop lamp switch
38 Stop lamp
39 Flasher unit
40 Flasher switch
41 L.H. Flasher lamp
42 L.H. Flasher lamp
43 R.H. Flasher lamp
44 R.H. Flasher lamp
45 Flasher warning light
46 Windscreen wiper motor
47 Windscreen wiper switch

COLOUR CODE

N.	Brown	**LG**	Light Green
U.	Blue	**W.**	White
R.	Red	**Y.**	Yellow
P.	Purple	**S.**	Slate
G.	Green	**B.**	Black

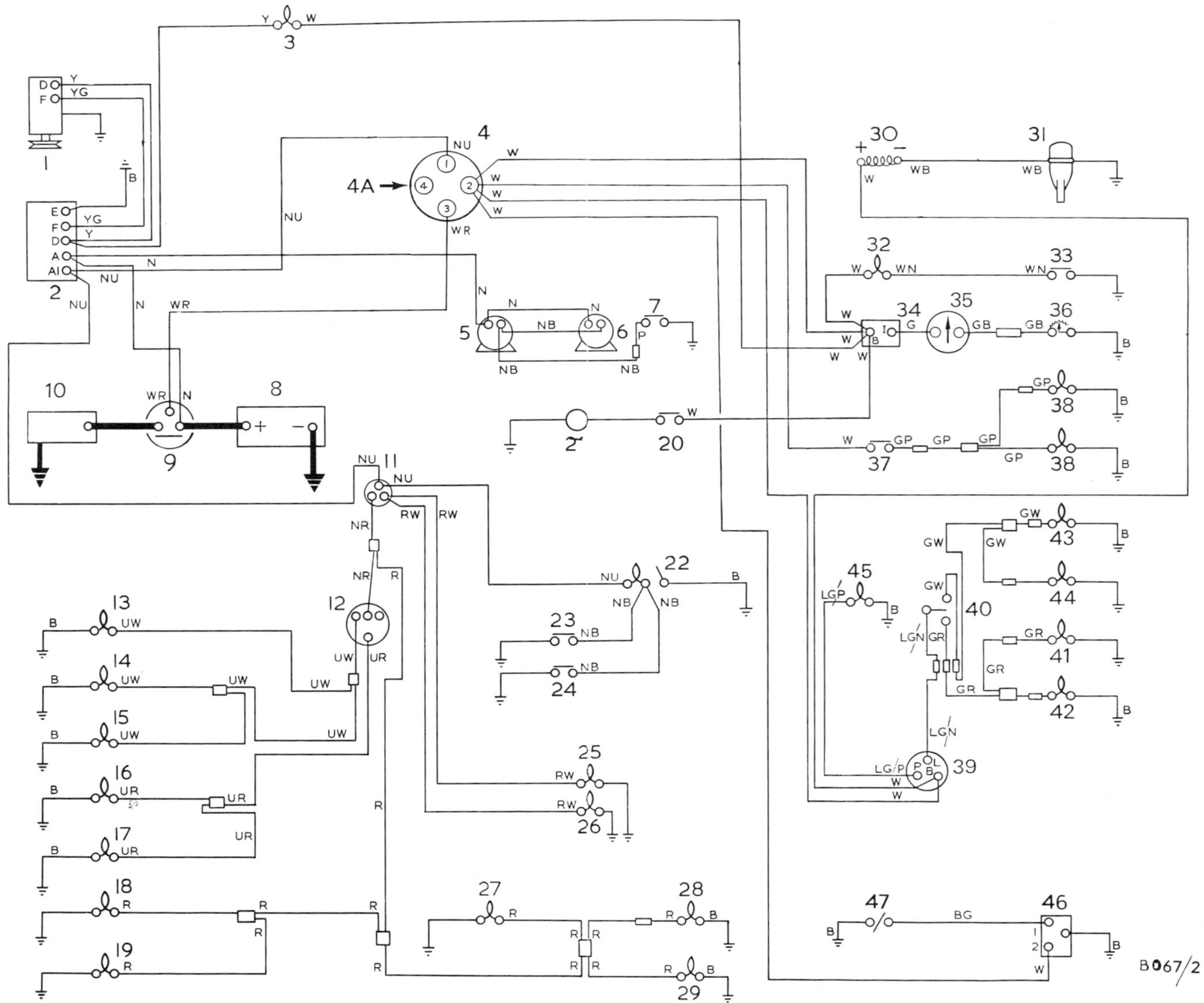

Fig. 1. Wiring diagram — Herald 1200 with negative earth

WIRING DIAGRAM — HERALD 13/60

KEY TO WIRING DIAGRAM — HERALD 13/60

CAUTION: THIS VEHICLE IS FITTED WITH A NEGATIVE EARTH ELECTRICAL SYSTEM. ENSURE THAT THE BATTERY EARTH LEAD IS ALWAYS CONNECTED TO THE BATTERY NEGATIVE TERMINAL.

EXERCISE CARE WHEN CONNECTING INTO CIRCUIT ANY ACCESSORY THAT MAY CONTAIN SILICON DIODES OR TRANSISTORS. IRREPARABLE DAMAGE MAY RESULT TO SUCH POLARITY SENSITIVE COMPONENTS IF INCORRECTLY FITTED.

NOTE: No polarity sensitive components are fitted to the vehicle during production. However, any of the following accessories—approved or unapproved by Leyland Triumph—may contain such components: Alternator systems, Automatic anti-dazzle mirrors, Automatic dipping systems, Automatic parking lamp systems, Electronic ignition systems, Electronic tachometers and Radios.

1 Generator
2 Control box
3 Ignition warning light
4 Battery
5 Ignition/starter switch
5A Ignition/starter switch – radio supply connector
6 Starter solenoid
7 Starter motor
8 Ignition coil
9 Ignition distributor
10 Master light switch
11 Line fuse
12 Column light switch
13 Main beam warning light
14 Main beam
15 Dip beam
16 Front parking lamp
17 Tail lamp
18 Plate illumination lamp
19 Instrument illumination
20 Facia lamp
21 Door switch
22 Voltage stabilizer
23 Fuel indicator
24 Fuel tank unit
25 Temperature indicator
26 Temperature transmitter
27 Oil pressure warning light
28 Oil pressure switch
29 Heater switch
30 Heater motor
31 Flasher unit
32 Flasher switch
33 L.H. Flasher lamp
34 R.H. Flasher lamp
35 Flasher warning light
36 Windscreen wiper motor
37 Windscreen wiper switch
38 Stop lamp switch
39 Stop lamp
40 Horn
41 Horn push
42 Tailgate lamp (Estate only)
43 Tailgate lamp tailgate switch (Estate only)

COLOUR CODE

N.	Brown	**LG**	Light Green
U.	Blue	**W.**	White
R.	Red	**Y.**	Yellow
P.	Purple	**S.**	Slate
G.	Green	**B.**	Black

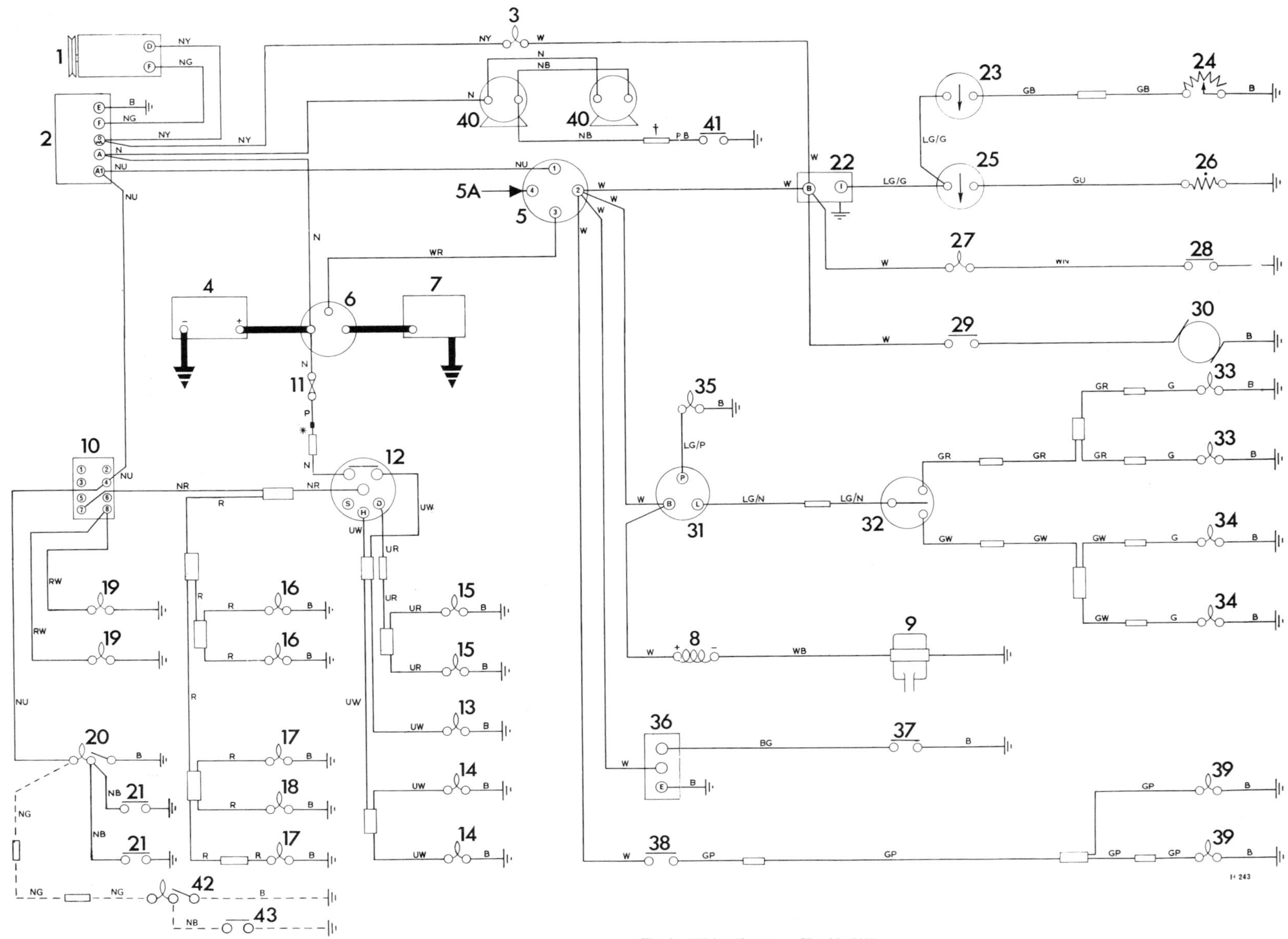

Fig. 2. Wiring diagram — Herald 13/60

WIRING DIAGRAM — SPITFIRE MARK 3 — RIGHT-HAND STEER

KEY TO WIRING DIAGRAM — SPITFIRE MARK 3 — RIGHT HAND STEER

CAUTION: THIS VEHICLE IS FITTED WITH A NEGATIVE EARTH ELECTRICAL SYSTEM. ENSURE THAT THE BATTERY EARTH LEAD IS ALWAYS CONNECTED TO THE BATTERY NEGATIVE TERMINAL.

EXERCISE CARE WHEN CONNECTING INTO CIRCUIT ANY ACCESSORY THAT MAY CONTAIN SILICON DIODES OR TRANSISTORS. IRREPARABLE DAMAGE MAY RESULT TO SUCH POLARITY SENSITIVE COMPONENTS IF INCORRECTLY FITTED.

NOTE: No polarity sensitive components are fitted to the vehicle during production. However, any of the following accessories—approved or unapproved by Leyland Triumph—may contain such components: Alternator systems, Automatic anti-dazzle mirrors, Automatic dipping systems, Automatic parking lamp systems, Electronic ignition systems, Electronic tachometers and Radios.

1 Generator
2 Control box
3 Ignition warning light
4 Battery
5 Ignition/starter switch
5A Ignition/starter switch radio supply connector
6 Starter solenoid
7 Starter motor
8 Ignition coil
9 Ignition distributor
10 Master light switch
11 Instrument illumination
12 Column light switch
13 Main beam warning light
14 Main beam
15 Dip beam
16 Fuse assembly
17 Horn relay
18 Horn push
19 Horn
20 Tail lamp
21 Plate illumination lamp
22 Front parking lamp
23 Reverse lamp switch
24 Reverse lamp
25 Voltage stabilizer
26 Fuel indicator
27 Fuel tank unit
28 Temperature indicator
29 Temperature transmitter
30 Heater switch (optional extra)
31 Heater motor (optional extra)
32 Flasher unit
33 Flasher switch
34 L.H. Flasher lamp
35 R.H. Flasher lamp
36 Flasher warning light
37 Stop lamp switch
38 Stop lamp
39 Windscreen wiper motor
40 Windscreen wiper switch
41 Oil pressure warning light
42 Oil pressure switch

A **Overdrive (optional extra)**
43 Overdrive relay
44 Overdrive column switch
45 Overdrive gearbox switch
46 Overdrive solenoid

a From ignition/starter switch – connector 2
b From ignition/starter switch – connector 1

COLOUR CODE

N.	Brown	**LG**	Light Green
U.	Blue	**W.**	White
R.	Red	**Y.**	Yellow
P.	Purple	**S.**	Slate
G.	Green	**B.**	Black

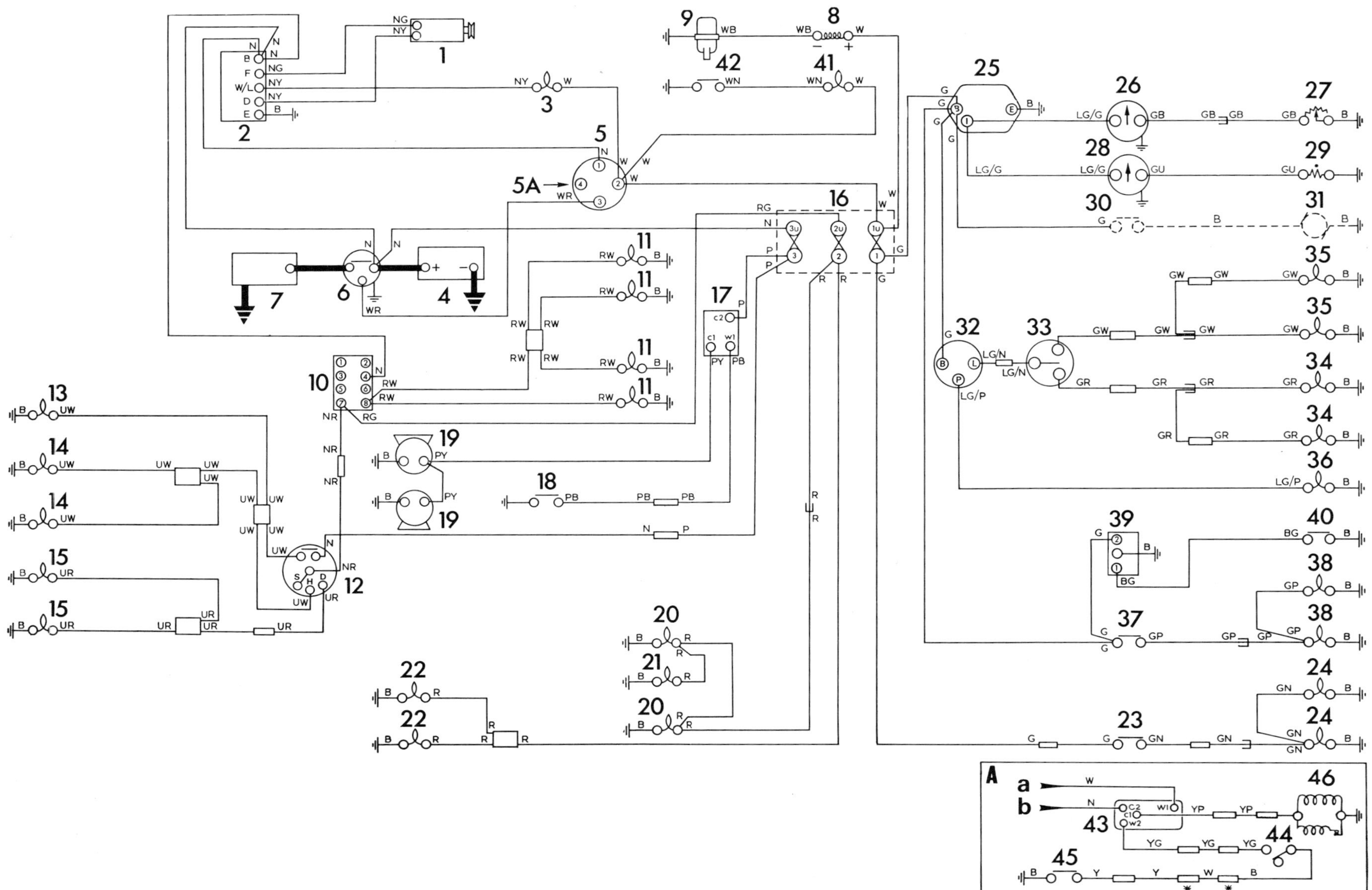

Fig. 3. Wiring diagram — Spitfire Mark 3 — right-hand steer

WIRING DIAGRAM — SPITFIRE MARK 3 — LEFT-HAND STEER

KEY TO WIRING DIAGRAM — SPITFIRE MARK 3 — LEFT HAND STEER

CAUTION: THIS VEHICLE IS FITTED WITH A NEGATIVE EARTH ELECTRICAL SYSTEM. ENSURE THAT THE BATTERY EARTH LEAD IS ALWAYS CONNECTED TO THE BATTERY NEGATIVE TERMINAL.

EXERCISE CARE WHEN CONNECTING INTO CIRCUIT ANY ACCESSORY THAT MAY CONTAIN SILICON DIODES OR TRANSISTORS. IRREPARABLE DAMAGE MAY RESULT TO SUCH POLARITY SENSITIVE COMPONENTS IF INCORRECTLY FITTED.

NOTE: No polarity sensitive components are fitted to the vehicle during production. However, any of the following accessories—approved or unapproved by Leyland Triumph—may contain such components: Alternator systems, Automatic anti-dazzle mirrors, Automatic dipping systems, Automatic parking lamp systems, Electronic ignition systems, Electronic tachometers and Radios.

1 Generator
2 Control box
3 Ignition warning light
4 Battery
5 Ignition/starter switch
5A Ignition/starter switch radio supply connector
6 Starter solenoid
7 Starter motor
8 Ignition coil
9 Ignition distributor
10 Master light switch
11 Instrument illumination
12 Column light switch
13 Main beam warning light
14 Main beam
15 Dip beam
16 Fuse assembly
17 Horn relay
18 Horn push
19 Horn
20 Tail lamp
21 Plate illumination lamp
22 Front parking lamp
23 Reverse lamp switch
24 Reverse lamp
25 Voltage stabilizer
26 Fuel indicator
27 Fuel tank unit
28 Temperature indicator
29 Temperature transmitter
30 Heater switch (optional extra)
31 Heater motor (optional extra)
32 Flasher unit
33 Flasher switch
34 L.H. Flasher lamp
35 R.H. Flasher lamp
36 Flasher warning light
37 Stop lamp switch
38 Stop lamp
39 Windscreen wiper motor
40 Windscreen wiper switch
41 Oil pressure warning light
42 Oil pressure switch

A **Overdrive (optional extra)**
43 Overdrive relay
44 Overdrive column switch
45 Overdrive gearbox switch
46 Overdrive solenoid
a From ignition/starter switch – connector 2
b From ignition/starter switch – connector 1

B Dip beam flasher (Italy only)
12 Column light switch
a From fuse assembly
b From master light switch
c To main beam circuit
d To dip beam circuit

C **Modifications to comply with U.S. Federal standards**
41 Oil pressure warning light
42 Oil pressure switch
47 Brake line failure warning light
48 Brake line failure switch

COLOUR CODE

N.	Brown	**LG**	Light Green
U.	Blue	**W.**	White
R.	Red	**Y.**	Yellow
P.	Purple	**S.**	Slate
G.	Green	**B.**	Black

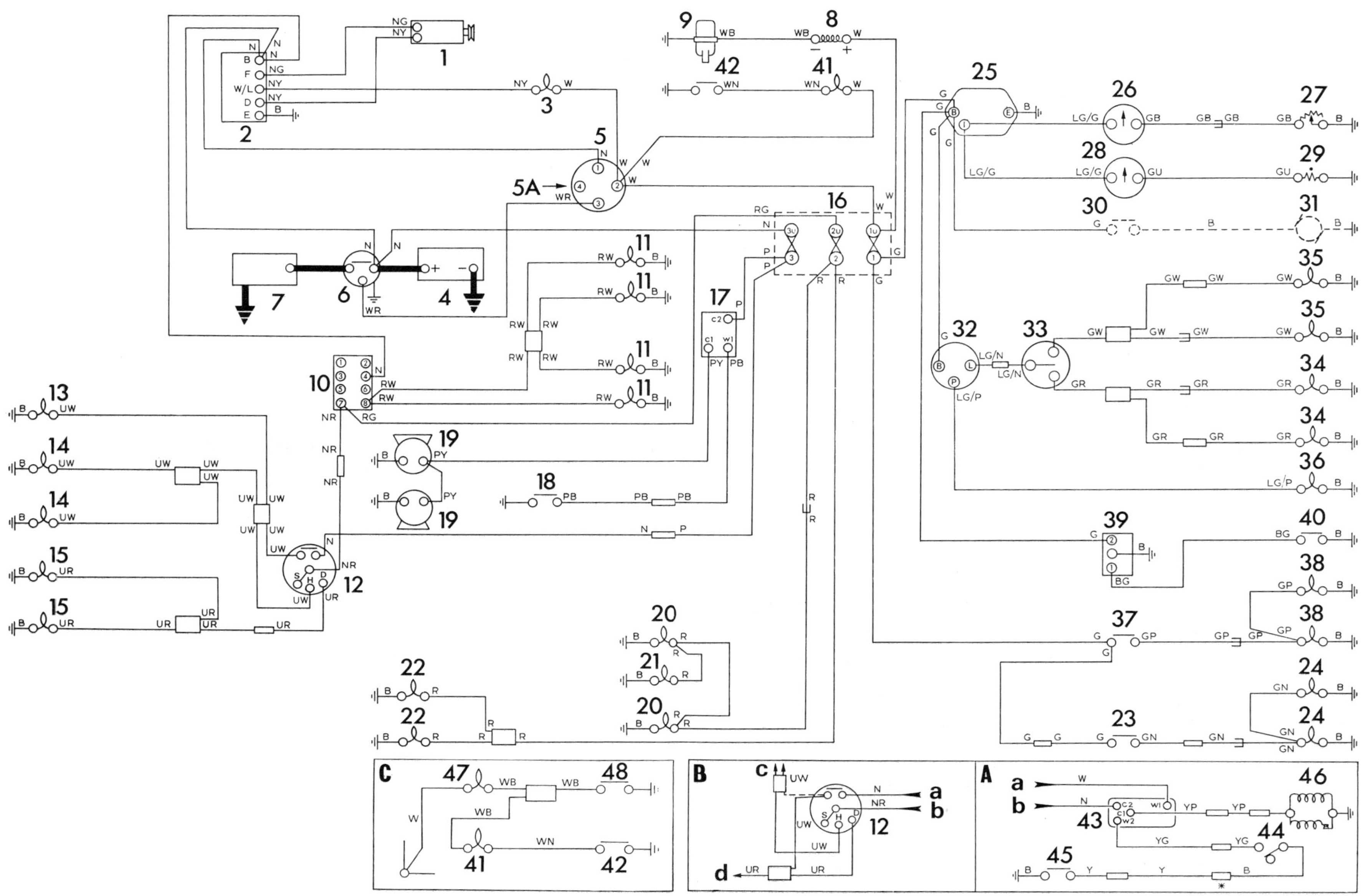

Fig. 4. Wiring diagram — Spitfire Mark 3 — left-hand steer

FACIA CONNECTIONS — HERALD 1200 WITH NEGATIVE EARTH

KEY TO FACIA CONNECTIONS — HERALD 1200 WITH NEGATIVE EARTH

NO.	COLOUR	CONNECTION	COMPONENT
1	LG/P and B	Bulb holder	Flasher warning light
2	W	Lucar	Heater switch
3	NW	Lucar	Heater switch
4	W and Y	Bulb holder	Instrument – ignition warning light
5	RW	Bulb holder	Instrument illumination
6	W and WN	Bulb holder	Instrument – oil pressure warning light
7	RW	Bulb holder	Instrument illumination
8	UW	Bulb holder	Instrument – main beam warning light
9	B	Eyelet – 2 wire	Instrument
10	G	Lucar	Fuel indicator
11	GB	Lucar	Fuel indicator
12	W	Lucar – 2 wire	Voltage stabilizer
13	W	Lucar – 2 wire	Voltage stabilizer
14	G	Lucar	Voltage stabilizer
15	NR and R	Double snap connector – 2 wire	Column light switch
16	UW	Double snap connector – 2 wire	Column light switch
17	UR	Snap connector	Column light switch
18	LG/N	3 way snap connector – 3 wire	Flasher switch
19	GR	3 way snap connector – 3 wire	Flasher switch
20	GW	3 way snap connector – 3 wire	Flasher switch
21	NB	Snap connector	Horn push
22	NU	Lucar	Ignition/starter switch
23	W	Lucar – 2 wire	Ignition/starter switch
24	W	Lucar – 2 wire	Ignition/starter switch
25	WR	Lucar	Ignition/starter switch
26	NU	Terminal end	Facia lamp
27	NB	Terminal end – 2 wire	Facia lamp
28	B	Terminal end	Facia lamp
29	NU	Screw terminal – 2 wire	Master light switch
30	NR	Screw terminal	Master light switch
31	RW	Screw terminal – 2 wire	Master light switch
32	BG	Screw terminal	Windscreen wiper switch
33	B	Screw terminal – 3 wire	Windscreen wiper switch

a. NW — to heater motor

b. W and GP — to stop lamp switch

c. NB — to R.H. door switch

d. W BG B and B — to windscreen wiper motor

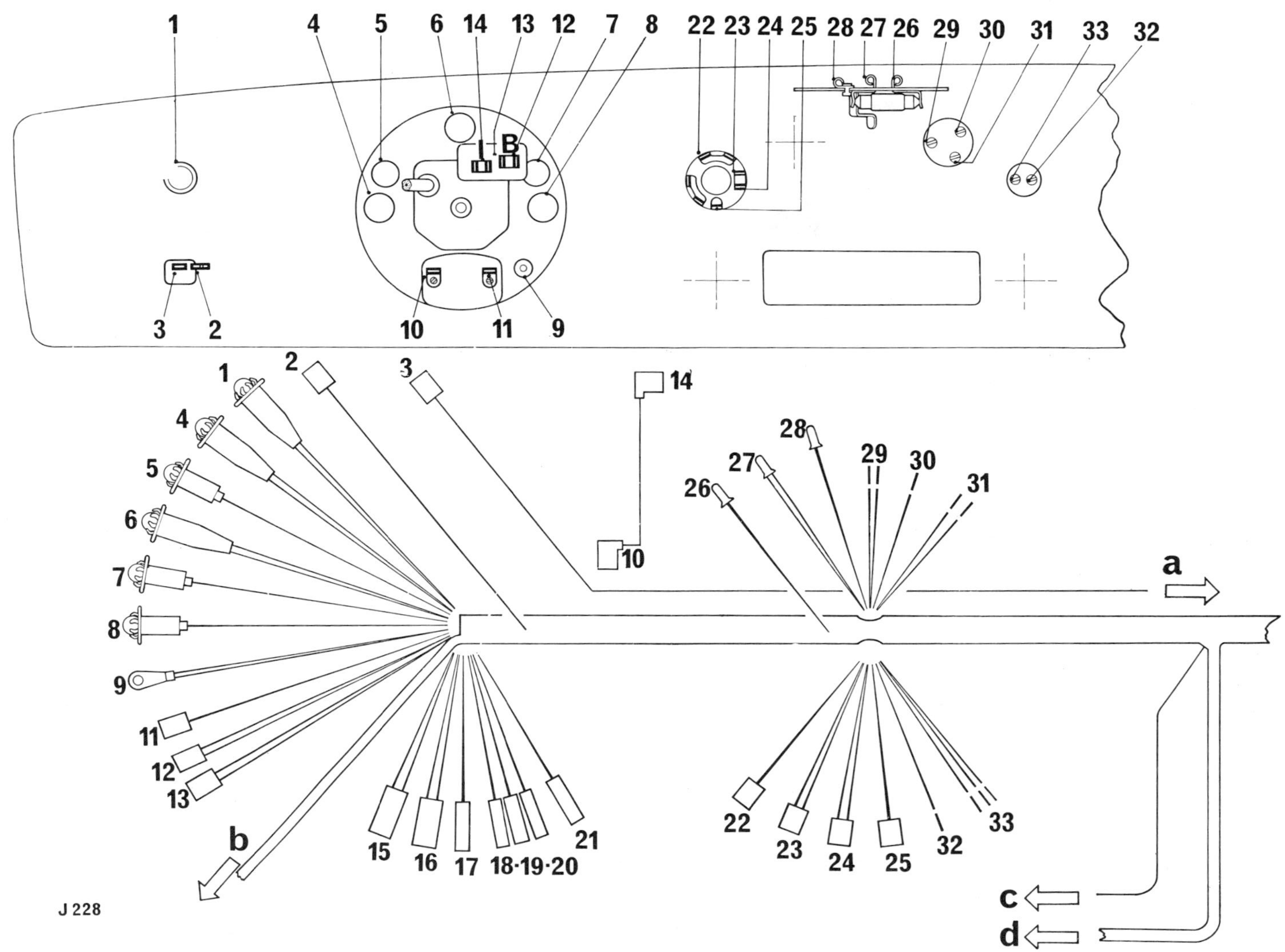

Fig. 5. Facia connections — Herald 1200 with negative earth

FACIA CONNECTIONS — HERALD 13/60

KEY TO FACIA CONNECTIONS — HERALD 13/60

NO.	COLOUR	CONNECTION	COMPONENT
1	B	Lucar	Windscreen wiper switch
2	BG	Lucar	Windscreen wiper switch
3	GU	Lucar	Temperature indicator
4	LG/G	Lucar	Temperature indicator
5	GB	Lucar	Fuel indicator
6	LG/G	Lucar – 2 wire	Fuel indicator
7	LG/P	Bulb holder	Fuel/temperature instrument – flasher warning light
8	RW	Bulb holder	Fuel/temperature instrument – instrument illumination
9	UW	Bulb holder	Fuel/temperature instrument – main beam warning light
10	B	Eyelet – 2 wire	Fuel/temperature instrument
11	RW	Bulb holder	Speedometer – instrument illumination
12	W and WN	Bulb holder	Speedometer – oil pressure warning light
13	W and NY	Bulb holder	Speedometer – ignition warning light
14	B	Eyelet – 3 wire	Speedometer
15	LG/G	Lucar blade	Voltage stabilizer
16	W	Lucar – 2 wire	Voltage stabilizer
17	W	Lucar – 2 wire	Voltage stabilizer
18	NR and R	Double snap connector – 2 wire	Column light switch
19	UW	Double snap connector – 2 wire	Column light switch
20	UR	Snap connector	Column light switch
21	P with brown ident.	Snap connector	Column light switch
22	LG/N	3 way snap connector – 3 wire	Flasher switch
23	GR	(3 way snap connector – 3 wire)	Flasher switch
24	GW	(3 way snap connector – 3 wire)	Flasher switch
25	NB	Snap connector	Horn push
26	NU	Lucar	Ignition/starter switch
27	W	Lucar – 2 wire	Ignition/starter switch
28	W	Lucar – 2 wire	Ignition/starter switch
29	WR	Lucar	Ignition/starter switch
30	NU	Lucar – 2 wire	Master light switch
31	NR	Lucar	Master light switch
32	RW	Lucar – 2 wire	Master light switch
33	W	Lucar	Heater switch
34	GY	Lucar	Heater switch
35	NU	Terminal end	Facia lamp
36	PW	Terminal end	Facia lamp
37	B	Terminal end	Facia lamp

a. GY — to heater motor

b. W BG B and B — to windscreen wiper motor

c. PW — to R.H. door switch

d. W and GP — to stop lamp switch

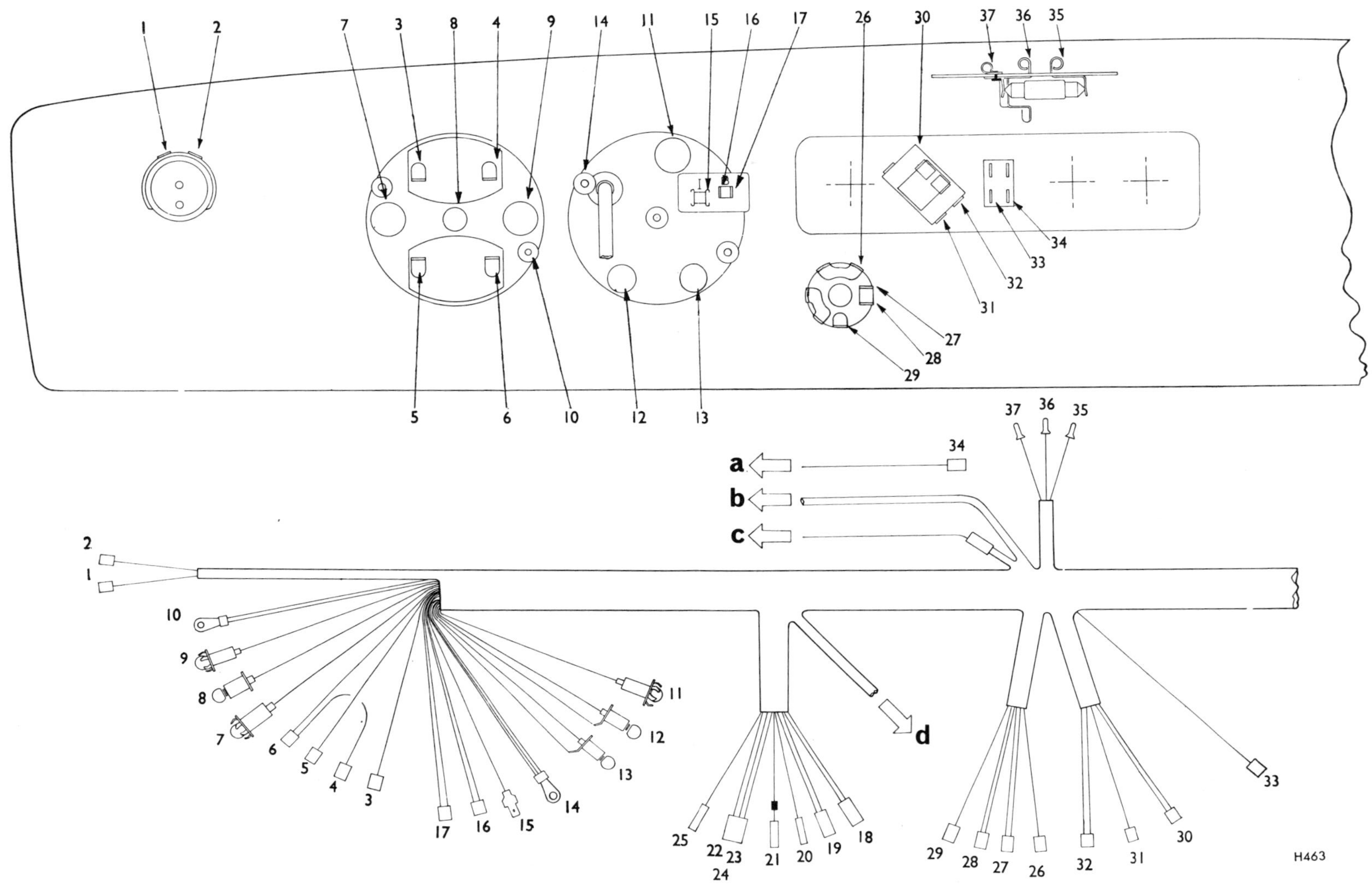

Fig. 6. Facia connections — Herald 13/60

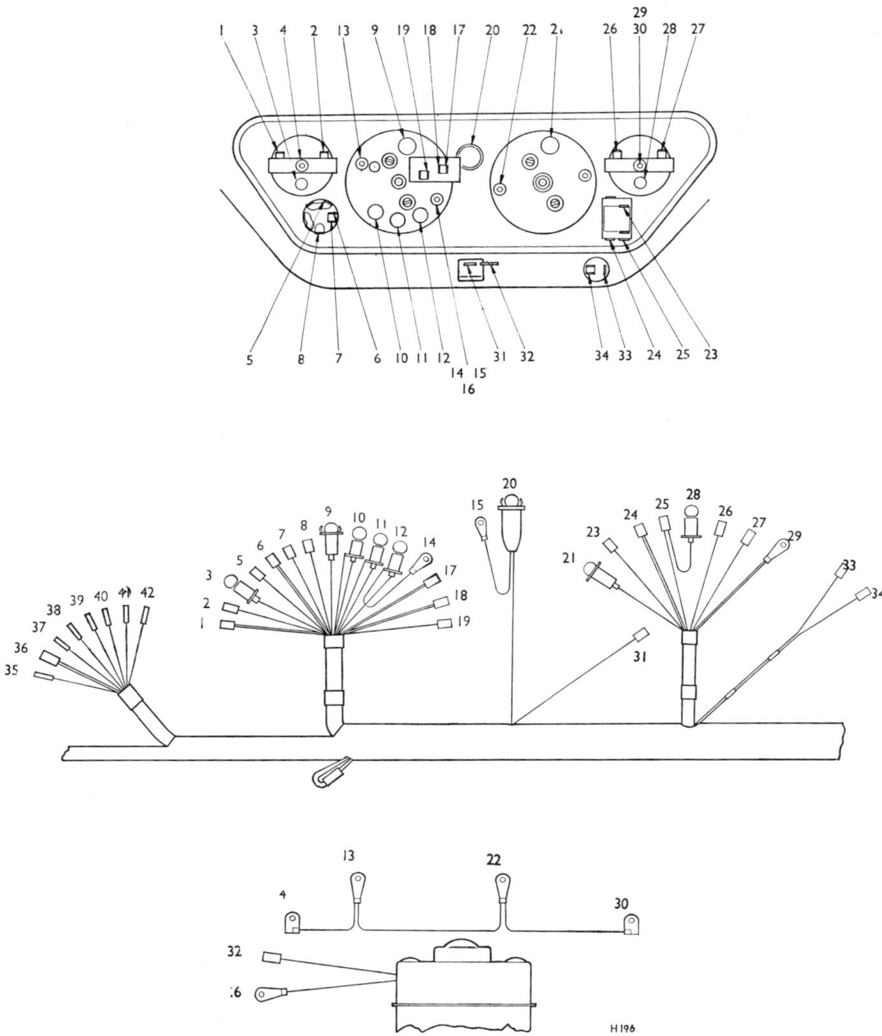

Fig. 7. Facia connections — Spitfire Mark 3

KEY TO FACIA CONNECTIONS — SPITFIRE MARK 3

NO.	COLOUR	CONNECTION	COMPONENT
1	LG/G	Lucar – 2 wire	Temperature indicator
2	GU	Lucar	Temperature indicator
3	RW	Bulb holder	Temperature indicator
4	B	Flag eyelet	Temperature indicator
5	N	Lucar	Ignition/starter switch
6	W	Lucar – 2 wire	Ignition/starter switch
7	W	Lucar	Ignition/starter switch
8	WR	Lucar	Ignition/starter switch
9	RW	Bulb holder	Speedometer
10	W and NY	Bulb holder	Speedometer – ignition warning light
11	W and WN	Bulb holder	Speedometer – oil pressure warning light
12	UW and B	Bulb holder	Speedometer – main beam warning light
13	B	Eyelet – 2 wire	Speedometer
14	B	Eyelet	Speedometer
15	B	Eyelet	Speedometer
16	B	Eyelet	Speedometer
17	G	Lucar – 2 wire	Voltage stabilizer
18	G	Lucar – 2 wire	Voltage stabilizer
19	LG/G	Lucar	Voltage stabilizer
20	LG/P and B	Bulb holder	Flasher warning light
21	RW	Bulb holder	Tachometer
22	B	Eyelet – 2 wire	Tachometer
23	N	Lucar	Master light switch
24	NR and RG	Lucar – 2 wire	Master light switch
25	RW	Lucar – 2 wire	Master light switch
26	GB	Lucar	Fuel indicator
27	LG/G	Lucar	Fuel indicator
28	RW	Bulb holder	Fuel indicator
29	B	Eyelet – 2 wire	Fuel indicator
30	B	Flag eyelet	Fuel indicator
31	G	Lucar	Heater switch
32	B	Lucar	Heater switch
33	BG	Lucar	Windscreen wiper switch
34	B	Lucar	Windscreen wiper switch
35	NR	Snap connector	Column light switch
36	UW	Double snap connector – 2 wire	Column light switch
37	UR	Snap connector	Column light switch
38	P	Snap connector	Column light switch
39	LG/N	Snap connector	Flasher switch
40	GR	Snap connector	Flasher switch
41	GW	Snap connector	Flasher switch
42	PB	Snap connector	Horn push

FUSE SYSTEM — HERALD 13/60

Data

Fuse

Manufacturer	Lucas
Rating	25 amp.
Lucas part No.	188216
Stanpart No.	503488
Lucas colour code	Pink
Current capacity	12·5 amp.
Fusing current—Prolonged	25 amp.
Instantaneous	30 amp.

Description

One line fuse is fitted to protect the headlamp flasher circuit.

The line fuse is a component of the main harness. It is positioned at the bulkhead adjacent to the ignition coil. The unit contains one operational fuse. The two parts of the fuse holder are retained together by a bayonet fitting.

Failure of the fuse is indicated when the circuit protected by it becomes inoperative. If a new fuse fails establish the cause and rectify the fault before fitting a second replacement.

Fig. 8. Line fuse

FUSE SYSTEM — SPITFIRE MARK 3

Data

Fuse

Manufacturer	Lucas
Rating	35 amp.
Lucas part No.	188218
Stanpart No.	58465
Lucas colour code	White
Current capacity	17·5 amp.
Fusing current—Prolonged	35 amp.
Instantaneous	40 amp.

CIRCUITS

The top fuse fed by a white cable from the ignition/starter switch protects the following circuits:

Reverse lamp circuit
Fuel indication circuit
Temperature indication circuit
Heater motor circuit (optional extra)
Flasher lamp circuit
Stop lamp circuit
Windscreen wiper motor circuit

The centre fuse fed by a red/green cable from the master light switch protects the following circuits:

Tail lamp circuit
Plate illumination lamp circuit
Front parking lamp circuit

The bottom fuse fed by a brown cable from the battery protects the following circuits:

Horn circuit
Headlamp flasher circuit

Description

The fuse assembly is a component of the main harness. It is secured to an aperture provided on the bulkhead by integral plastic clips. The unit contains three operational fuses and has provision to house two spares. The fuses are protected by a pull off transparent plastic cover.

Failure of a particular fuse is indicated when all the circuits protected by it become inoperative. If a new fuse fails establish the cause and rectify the fault before fitting a second replacement.

Fig. 9. Fuse assembly installed

STARTER SOLENOID

Data

Manufacturer	Lucas
Type	4ST
Lucas part No.	76766
Stanpart No.	121269
Plunger pull in voltage	4 – 9 volts
Plunger release voltage	0 – 2·5 volts
Winding resistance	2·3 – 2·8 ohms.

Fig. 10. Starter solenoid

Description

The starter solenoid is normally solenoid operated by remote control from the ignition/starter switch. It may also be actuated manually from the engine compartment by depressing the rubber cap shown arrowed on figure 10.

Service – No maintenance is required.

Repair – Repair is by replacement.

1 Supply from ignition/starter switch
2 Shunt winding
3 Plunger contact
4 Battery terminal – with battery to harness connectors
5 Starter motor terminal

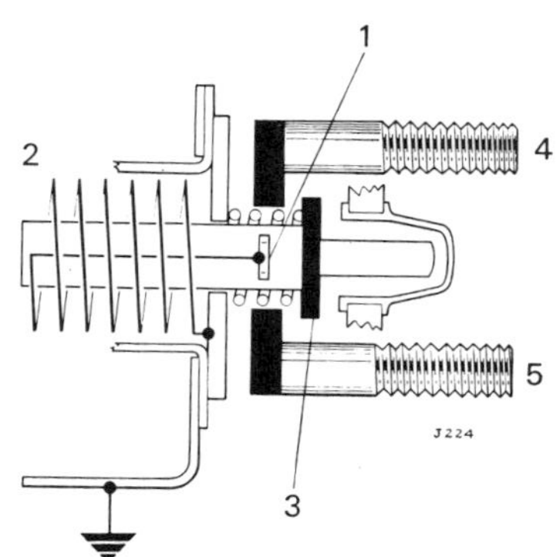

Fig. 11. Component wiring diagram

IGNITION DISTRIBUTOR — HERALD 1200 WITH NEGATIVE EARTH

Data – normal compression ratio engine 8·5 : 1

Manufacturer	Lucas
Type	25D4
Lucas part No.	41230
Stanpart No.	215046
Contact gap	0·014 – 0·016 in.
Rotation – viewed on rotor	Anticlockwise
Firing angles	90 ± 1 degs.
Dwell angle	60 ± 3 degs.
Open angle	30 ± 3 degs.
Moving contact spring tension	18 – 24 ozs.
Capacitor capacity	0·20 mfd.
Engine firing order	1 – 3 – 4 – 2

Centrifugal advance

Check at decelerating speeds

Distributor r.p.m.	Degs. distributor advance		Crankshaft r.p.m.	Degs. crankshaft advance	
	Minimum	Maximum		Minimum	Maximum
Below 120	No advance to occur		Below 240	No advance to occur	
450	0·5	2·5	900	1	5
750	3·0	5·0	1500	6	10
1250	5·0	7·0	2500	10	14
2000	8·0	10·0	4000	16	20
2500	—	10·0	5000	—	20

Vacuum advance

Ins. of mercury vacuum	Degs. distributor advance		Degs. crankshaft advance	
	Minimum	Maximum	Minimum	Maximum
Below 1·5	No advance to occur			
2·5	0	0·5	0	1
5·5	0·5	2·5	1	5
10·0	3·5	5·5	7	11
15·0	5·5	7·5	11	15
25·0	6·0	8·0	12	16

IGNITION DISTRIBUTOR — HERALD 13/60

Data – normal compression ratio engine 8·5 : 1

Manufacturer	Lucas
Type	25D4
Lucas part No.	41127
Stanpart No.	212292
Contact gap	0·014 – 0·016 in.
Rotation – viewed on rotor	Anticlockwise
Firing angles	90±1 degs.
Dwell angle	60±3 degs.
Open angle	30±3 degs.
Moving contact spring tension	18 – 24 ozs.
Capacitor capacity	0·20 mfd.
Engine firing order	1 – 3 – 4 – 2

Centrifugal advance

Check at decelerating speeds

Distributor r.p.m.	Degs. distributor advance		Crankshaft r.p.m.	Degs. crankshaft advance	
	Minimum	Maximum		Minimum	Maximum
Below 300	No advance to occur		Below 600	No advance to occur	
400	0	1·0	800	0	2
550	0·5	2·5	1100	1	5
850	3·5	5·5	1700	7	11
1100	6·0	8·0	2200	12	16
1500	6·0	8·0	3000	12	16

Vacuum advance

Ins. of mercury vacuum	Degs. distributor advance		Degs. crankshaft advance	
	Minimum	Maximum	Minimum	Maximum
Below 3·5	No advance to occur			
5	0	0·5	0	1
8	0·5	2·5	1	5
16	5·0	7·0	10	14
25	6·0	8·0	12	16

IGNITION DISTRIBUTOR — SPITFIRE MARK 3

Normal component

Data – normal compression ratio engine 9·0 : 1

Manufacturer	Delco Remy
Series	D200
Delco Remy part No.	7953460
Stanpart No.	214088
Contact gap	0·015 in.
Rotation – viewed on rotor	Anticlockwise
Firing angles	90 degs.
Dwell angle	40 – 42 degs.
Open angle	48 – 50 degs.
Moving contact spring tension	22 – 26 ozs.
Condenser capacity	0·18 – 0·23 mfd.
Engine firing order	1 – 3 – 4 – 2

Centrifugal advance

Distributor r.p.m.	Degs. distributor advance		Crankshaft r.p.m.	Degs. crankshaft advance	
	Minimum	Maximum		Minimum	Maximum
300	No advance to occur		600	No advance to occur	
400	0	1·90	800	0	3·8
725	6·00	8·00	1450	12·0	16·0
1100	7·50	9·50	2200	15·0	19·0
1500	9·00	11·00	3000	18·0	22·0
2500	—	13·25	5000	—	26·5

Vacuum advance

Ins. of mercury vacuum	Advance
4·0 – 6·2	Distributor must start to advance
7·7 – 10·7	5·5 degs. distributor advance – 11 degs. crankshaft advance – must occur
20	7·5 degs. distributor advance – 15 degs. crankshaft advance – must not be exceeded

IGNITION DISTRIBUTOR — SPITFIRE MARK 3

Emission control component

Data

Manufacturer	Delco Remy
Series	D200
Delco Remy part No.	7953557
Stanpart No.	214799
Contact gap	0·015 in.
Rotation – viewed on rotor	Anticlockwise
Firing angles	90 degs.
Dwell angle	40 – 42 degs.
Open angle	48 – 50 degs.
Moving contact spring tension	17 – 21 ozs.
Condenser capacity	0·18 – 0·23 mfd.
Engine firing order	1 – 3 – 4 – 2

Centrifugal advance

Distributor r.p.m.	Degs. distributor advance		Crankshaft r.p.m.	Degs. crankshaft advance	
	Minimum	Maximum		Minimum	Maximum
258	No advance to occur		516	No advance to occur	
300	0	1·00	600	0	2·00
750	9·80	11·80	1500	19·60	23·60
1000	10·58	12·58	2000	21·16	25·16
1600	12·44	14·44	3200	24·88	28·88
2000	14·00	16·00	4000	28·00	32·00
2500	—	16·00	5000	—	32·00

Vacuum advance

Run distributor at 500 RPM maximum in the appropriate direction of rotation.

Ins. of mercury vacuum	Advance
0 – 4·0	No advance to occur
4·0 – 6·2	Distributor must start to advance
7·7 – 10·7	5·5 degs. distributor advance – 11 degs. crankshaft advance – must occur
20	7·5 degs. distributor advance – 15 degs. crankshaft advance – must not be exceeded

BULB CHART — HERALD 1200 WITH NEGATIVE EARTH AND HERALD 13/60

Lamp	Watts	Lucas Part No.	Stanpart No.	
Headlamps—L.H. Dip	60/45	54521872	512231	*
R.H. Dip—Normal	45/40	410	510218	
France	45/40	411	510219	
U.S.A.	50/40	54522231	—	*
Front parking lamps	6	989	59467	
Front flasher lamps	21	382	502379	
Rear flasher lamps	21	382	502379	
Tail/stop lamps	6/21	380	502287	
Plate illumination lamp	6	989	59467	
Facia lamp	6	254	59897	
Tailgate lamp (Estate only)	6	254	59897	
Instrument illumination	2·2	987	59492	
Warning lights	2·2	987	59492	

BULB CHART — SPITFIRE MARK 3

Lamp	Watts	Lucas Part No.	Stanpart No.	
Headlamps—L.H. Dip	60/45	54521872	512231	*
R.H. Dip—Normal	45/40	410	510218	
France	45/40	411	510219	
U.S.A.	50/40	54522231	—	*
Front parking lamps	6	207	57591	
Front flasher lamps	21	382	502379	
Tail/stop lamps	6/21	380	502287	
Rear flasher lamps	21	382	502379	
Reverse lamps	21	382	502379	
Plate illumination lamp—Normal	6	939	59467	
U.S.A.	4	222	501436	
Instrument illumination	2·2	987	59492	
Warning lights	2·2	987	59492	

*Sealed beam light unit

BRAKE LINE FAILURE AND OIL PRESSURE INDICATION
— SPITFIRE MARK 3 — U.S.A. ONLY

Data

Brake line failure switch –

Manufacturer	Girling
Stanpart No. – early unit with single pin	148159
later unit with twin pins	149971
Pressure differential required to actuate switch	Approx. 200 PSI
Plunger load – with plunger contact surface 0·522 in. below seat flange	5·2 – 6·4 lb.
Thread	$\frac{3}{8}$ in. – 24 UNF – 2A
Torque load – fitting switch to pressure differential warning actuator body	2·0 – 2·5 lb. ft.

Oil pressure switch –

Manufacturer	A.C. or Smiths
Stanpart No.	121398
Operating pressure	3 – 5 PSI
Thread	$\frac{1}{8}$ in. – 27 NPTF

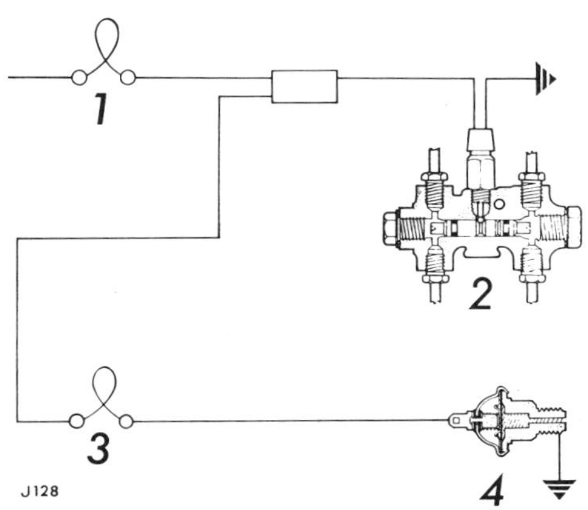

1 Brake line failure warning light
2 Brake line failure switch
3 Oil pressure warning light
4 Oil pressure switch

Fig. 12. System wiring diagram

Description

The brake line failure indication system consists of a warning light mounted on the steering column clamp mounting bracket and a switch which is a component part of the pressure differential warning actuator detailed in Group 3.

The oil pressure indication system consists of a warning light housed in the speedometer and a switch fitted to the cylinder block. The switch is in communication with the main oil gallery.

The brake line failure indication circuit is amalgamated with the oil pressure indication circuit so that when the ignition circuits are energised both warning lights will illuminate faintly to indicate no bulb filament failure.

When the engine is started the oil pressure will rise causing the oil pressure switch diaphragm to be actuated outwards. The contact plate is isolated from earth. Both warning lights will extinguish.

Should pressure loss occur in either front or rear brake lines the brake line failure switch will actuate as detailed in Group 3. The "BRAKE" warning light will illuminate brightly.

Should the oil pressure fall below the safe operating pressure while the engine is running the oil pressure switch will actuate. Both the "OIL" and the "BRAKE" warning lights will illuminate faintly.

Service – No maintenance is required.

Repair – Repair of all units is by replacement.

Fig. 13. Brake line failure warning light

Fig. 14. Brake line failure switch

Fig. 15. Oil pressure warning light

Fig. 16. Oil pressure switch

Brake and oil warning light summary

Condition	"BRAKE" warning light	"OIL" warning light
Ignition on—Engine not running	ON FAINT	ON FAINT
Engine running	OFF	OFF
Engine running—Brake line pressure low	ON BRIGHT	OFF
Engine running—Oil pressure low	ON FAINT	ON FAINT

ENGINE — DIMENSIONS AND TOLERANCES

PARTS & DESCRIPTION	HERALD 1200, 12/50 & SPITFIRE 4				HERALD 13/60, SPITFIRE 4 & Mk. 3				VITESSE 1600 c.c.			
	DIMENSIONS		CLEARANCES		DIMENSIONS		CLEARANCES		DIMENSIONS		CLEARANCES	
	ins.	mm.	ins.	mm.	ins.	mm.	ins.	mm.	ins.	mm.	ins.	mm.
Oil Pressure Relief Valve Spring												
Free length	1·54	39·11			1·54	39·11			1·54	39·11		
Fitted length	1·25	31·75			1·25	31·75			1·25	31·75		
Load at fitted length	14·5 lbs.	6·58 kg.			14·5 lbs.	6·58 kg.			14·5 lbs.	6·58 kg.		
Rocker Shaft diameter	0·5612 0·5607	14·26 14·24	0·0023 to 0·0008	0·06 to 0·02	0·5612 0·5607	14·26 14·24	0·0023 to 0·0008	0·06 to 0·02	0·5612 0·5607	14·26 14·24	0·0023 to 0·0008	0·06 to 0·02
Bore of rockers	0·562 0·563	14·27 14·30			0·562 0·563	14·27 14·30			0·562 0·563	14·27 14·30		
Valves	HERALD 1200, 12/50											
Inlet valve head diameter	1·308 1·304	33·22 33·12			1·308 1·304	33·22 33·12			1·301 1·305	33·045 33·15		
	SPITFIRE 1·245 1·241	 31·62 31·52										
Inlet valve stem diameter	0·311 0·310	7·89 7·87	0·001 0·003	0·025 0·075	0·3112 0·310	7·90 7·87	0·0008 0·0023	0·02 0·06	0·311 0·310	7·89 7·87	0·001 0·003	0·025 0·075
Exhaust valve head diameter	1·182 1·148	29·26 29·16			1·172 1·168	29·76 29·66			1·176 1·180	29·87 29·97		
Exhaust valve stem diameter	0·309 0·308	7·85 7·82	0·003 0·005	0·075 0·13	0·310- 0·3105	7·874 7·887	0·0015 0·003	0·0261 0·075	0·309 0·308	7·85 7·82	0·003 0·005	0·075 0·13
Flywheel Run-out at 3·0″ (76·2 mm.) radius from spigot centre	0·002	0·051			0·002	0·051			0·007	0·051		
Concentricity (mounted on crankshaft)	0·004	0·100			0·004	0·100			0·004	0·100		

DIMENSIONS AND TOLERANCES

PARTS & DESCRIPTION	HERALD 1200, 12/50 & SPITFIRE 4				HERALD 13/60 SPITFIRE 4, & Mk. 3				VITESSE 1600 c.c.			
	DIMENSIONS		CLEARANCES		DIMENSIONS		CLEARANCES		DIMENSIONS		CLEARANCES	
	ins.	mm.	ins.	mm.	ins.	mm.	ins.	mm.	ins.	mm.	ins.	mm.
Valve Guides												
Length	2·25	57·15			2·0625	52·387			2·72	69·088		
Bore	0·313 0·312	7·95 7·92			0·313 0·312	7·95 7·92						
Outside diameter	0·502 0·501	12·75 12·72			0·502 0·501	12·75 12·72			0·502 0·501	12·75 12·72		
Amount valve guides protrude above cylinder head top face	0·749 0·751	19·025 19·075			0·749 0·751	19·025 19·075			0·749 0·751	19·025 19·075		

VALVE SPRINGS

	HERALD 1200 AND 13/60		HERALD 12/50 AND SPITFIRE 4, Mk. 2 and 3		VITESSE 1600 c.c.	
Fitted length	ins. 1·36	mm. 34·54	ins. 1·38	mm. 35·03	ins. 1·36	mm. 34·54
Fitted load	lbs. 27 - 30	kgs. 12·25 - 13·61	lbs. 32 - 42	kgs. 14·51 - 19·05	lbs. 27 - 30	kgs. 12·25 - 13·61
Total No. of coils	7¼		6		7¼	

ENGINE — DIMENSIONS AND TOLERANCES